American Usage and Style
THE CONSENSUS

American Usage and Style THE CONSENSUS

Roy H. Copperud

 VAN NOSTRAND REINHOLD COMPANY
NEW YORK   CINCINNATI   TORONTO   LONDON   MELBOURNE

Copyright © 1980 by Van Nostrand Reinhold Company Inc.

Library of Congress Catalog Card Number: 79-11055
ISBN: 0-442-21630-0
ISBN: 0-442-24906-3 pbk.

Manufactured in the United States of America

Published by Van Nostrand Reinhold Company Inc.
135 West 50th Street, New York, N.Y. 10020

Van Nostrand Reinhold Publishing
1410 Birchmount Road
Scarborough, Ontario MIP 2E7, Canada

Van Nostrand Reinhold
480 Latrobe Street
Melbourne, Victoria 3000, Australia

Van Nostrand Reinhold Company Limited
Molly Millars Lane
Wokingham, Berkshire, England

15 14 13 12 11 10 9 8 7 6 5 4 3 2

Library of Congress Cataloging in Publication Data

Copperud, Roy H 1915-
    American usage and style, the consensus.

    "This book revises, brings up to date, and
consolidates [the author's] two earlier ones: A
dictionary of usage and style and American usage:
The consensus."

    1. English language—Idioms, corrections,
errors.   2. English language—Rhetoric.
3. English language in the United States.
4. English language—Dictionaries.   I. Title.
PE1460.C648 428 79-11055
ISBN 0-442-21630-0
ISBN 0-442-24906-3 pbk.

Preface

This book revises, brings up to date, and consolidates two earlier ones: *A Dictionary of Usage and Style* and *American Usage: the Consensus*. The first represented my own views on disputed points. The second compared the judgments of the then seven current dictionaries of usage and gave the consensus. The present book also takes this approach, and in addition gives my own views concerning points that have not been taken up elsewhere.

The authorities that were compared for *American Usage: the Consensus* were *The Careful Writer*, by Theodore M. Bernstein; *Current American Usage*, by Margaret M. Bryant; my own *Dictionary of Usage and Style; A Dictionary of Contemporary American Usage*, by Bergen and Cornelia Evans; *The ABC of Style*, by Rudolf Flesch; *Modern American Usage*, by Wilson Follett and others; and *A Dictionary of Modern English Usage*, by H. W. Fowler, Second Edition, revised by Sir Ernest Gowers. To these I have added, for the present work, the two substantial books that have been published on the subject in the meantime: *Encyclopedic Dictionary of English Usage*, by Mager and Mager; and the *Harper Dictionary of Contemporary Usage*, by William and Mary Morris.

Because the editors of general dictionaries have access to voluminous files on current practice, far transcending anything available to authors of dictionaries of usage, and also take a more impersonal attitude toward disputed points, careful attention has been paid to their views as well. I have consulted the two so-called unabridged American works, *Webster's New International Dictionary*, Third Edition, and the *Random House Dictionary of the English Language; The American Heritage Dictionary of the English Language;* the *Standard College Dictionary;* the *American College Dictionary; Webster's New World Dictionary;* and the *Oxford English Dictionary*, together with its recent abridgments, such as the *Concise Oxford Dictionary*, particulary for differences between British and American usage. Other dictionaries, both general and specialized, and works on grammar have also been compared.

If a single opinion is given in an entry, it is that of all the authorities that took up the point at hand. Dissents are carefully recorded. When it appears to serve a useful purpose, authorities are cited by name. This is particularly true of Fowler. Though that work, the pioneer in this field, is held in deservedly high regard, it should be kept in mind that its views represent British practice, which often diverges from American practice, a fact that the revised edition sometimes explicitly acknowledges. Citations of "Fowler" refer to the revised edition; references to the first edition are specified. Citations of "Webster" refer to the Third

Edition of *Webster's New International; Webster's New World* is so identified. "OED" refers to the *Oxford English Dictionary*.

Dictionaries of usage often disagree, but they have one quality in common: presumption. It could not be otherwise, for the authors are saying to the reader, "I know best." Yet correct usage, whatever that may be, is not a matter of revealed truth, but oftener than not reflects taste or opinion. Such books cast a wide net. Their judgments cover common errors in grammar, misapprehensions of the meanings of words, and the acceptability of changed meanings, to name their principal concerns. The implication is that the critic is reflecting the preponderance of educated practice. But this is not necessarily so, or there would be more agreement among the authorities.

Great indignation was aroused by the publication of the Third Edition of Webster's New International Dictionary in 1961. It admitted as standard many usages that had been and continue to be widely criticized. The American Heritage Dictionary, published in 1969, was clearly intended as an antidote to Webster. The editors appointed a panel of more than 100 presumed experts—writers, editors, teachers, and officials—to give judgments on disputed points. But the experts divided all the way from 50–5 to 98–2 per cent. In making hundreds of judgments, they were unanimous only once, irrefutably illustrating the principle that even experts cannot agree on usage.

After having written about usage for many years, and having made innumerable comparisons of authorities, I reached the conclusion given earlier: that dictionaries of usage, including my own, reflect presumption above all. I decided that a more useful purpose would be served by comparing the views of these books, and indicating where the weight of opinion lay. But since authorities on usage (all self-appointed, and regarded as authorities only because they have found publishers and audiences for their views) differ, like panelists, it is a fair question whether a consensus of their opinions may not also be suspect. At least they have had the experience of considering thousands of disputed points, and the time to form their own judgments coolly.

By indicating the spread of opinion and the consensus of authorities on disputed points, it is hoped that this book will help the user to make intelligent choices of his own. As in the past, I want to express my appreciation to Jerome H. Walker, now retired as executive editor of the magazine *Editor & Publisher,* who encouraged my early efforts as a word-watcher. I am also indebted to my wife, Mary, who typed the manuscript of this book.

ROY H. COPPERUD

American Usage and Style
THE CONSENSUS

A

a, an. Seven authorities agree that *a*, rather than an, should be used before certain words beginning with *h* (notably *hilarious, history, hotel, humble, hysterical, habitual, hallucination*). The test is whether the initial *h* is sounded in pronouncing the word: *a* (not *an*) *historian, hotel, humble,* etc. Similarly, *a* is required with *unique, utopia, eulogy,* etc., which begin with a consonant sound. The persistence of usages like *an hotel, an humble, an historical,* and their appearance in old books, reflect the fact that the initial *h*s formerly were not sounded, or were sounded lightly.

Some exceptions remain in which the *h* is not (and perhaps never was) sounded: *heir, honest, honor, hour.* These of course take *an.* The pronunciation, then, is the key. Not *a $800 salary,* but *an $800 salary;* not *a RCA contract,* but *an RCA contract.* The principle governing the choice between *a* and *an* is that *a* precedes consonant sounds and *an* precedes vowel sounds.

Phrases like *a 100 miles* and *a 1,000 tankloads,* sometimes seen in print, overlook the fact that the numbers are read *one hundred, one thousand,* not simply *hundred* and *thousand.*

Two critics discourage misplacement of *a, an* in such a sentence as "Can anyone suggest more valuable a book?" *a more valuable.* This error seems rare. One critic and American Heritage say the article is superfluous in such constructions as *no more striking a triumph* and *no brighter an hour.* See also *the; of a.*

a-. Solid as a prefix: *amoral, achromatic, atonal,* etc.

Abbreviations. It is not good form to abbreviate the month without the date (*last Dec. we went . . .*) or the state without the city (*The factory is in Ala.*). Proper names should not be abbreviated by any but their owners (*Robt., Wm.*). Clipped forms like *Ed* do not take periods. See also *Acronyms; Alphabetical Designations; lb., lbs.; State Descriptives and Abbreviations.*

British usage is practical in omitting the periods after Mr., Mrs., Dr., conforming with Fowler's dictum that abbreviations that begin and end with the same letters as the forms they stand for should be written without periods. This practice, though a labor-saving device, is unknown in the U.S. The Postal Service has adopted a new set of two-letter capitalized abbreviations for states (*CA* for *California,* for example); it remains to be seen whether they will drive out the old forms (*Calif.*) in general printed matter. New stylebooks published since by *The New York Times* and the large press associations rejected them in favor of the traditional forms.

Coining alphabetical abbreviations for unfamiliar names (IOELB for International Organizations Employees Loyalty Board) is a bad habit of newspaper writers that only impedes readability. In cases like this, subsequent references should be in the form *the board,* or whatever noun is appropriate. Some critics counsel avoidance of abbreviations entirely for the sake of readability, and there is no doubt that their use is overdone in much published matter.

abdomen. See *belly.*

able. Improper in passive constructions: *able to be melted, able to be deciphered.* Preferably *can be melted, can be deciphered.*

ability, capacity. Two critics say capacity is innate, ability is acquired. But dictionaries say ability may be either.

abjure, adjure. Sometimes confused; the first means *forswear,* the second *admonish.*

ablutions. Two authorities call the term facetious, and there seems good reason for this. It is indisputably quaint, except in religious connections (i.e., ceremonial washing).

abode. Two critics consider it facetious or pretentious in modern use.

abolishment, abolition. Three authorities prefer the second as the more usual form.

about. Redundant with indications of approximation, as in "The victims were described as about 45 to 50 years old" (omit *about*); "The number of beans in the jar was estimated to be about 6,000"; *estimated at 6,000.* Three authorities, in reference, for example, to blows, approve such expressions as *about the head;* one dissents. The criticism seems captious; the suggested substitute, *on,* does not convey the meaning of "on all sides" or "here and there upon" as *about* does. The consensus is that *about* is standard in such contexts.

about to. See *not about to.*

above. Approved by six authorities in the sense *previously mentioned* or *cited;* disapproved by two. These forms, then, are acceptable: *the statement above, the above statement, repeating the above.* Those who find this usage objectionable for whatever reason can always resort to *previously mentioned.* Some objectors say that what is referred to as *above* must be on the same page, but this seems captious.

abrasions. See *Technical Terms.*

absent. Strange as it looks, *absent* has become a preposition meaning *in the absence of;* a company president forecast the best year in history for his firm "absent unforeseen events." A *Newsweek* columnist wrote, "But absent a revolution or a towering figure like DeGaulle . . ." And still another *Newsweek* columnist: "A place to ponder Israel's situation, absent peace, is . . ." (The fact that the last two citations came from the same publication illustrates an interesting fact about usage: writers encountering new usages imitate each other. This probably accounts for the use of *on line,* originally a Briticism, in New York and along the Eastern seaboard, displacing *in line,* in reference to a queue: "They were standing on line.") Whether *absent* as a preposition will win any wide acceptance only time will tell. It *has* found its way into Webster.

Absolute Comparatives. Such comparatives as "the better stores," "older automobiles," are primarily peculiarities of advertising prose; Bryant describes them as "informal standard." They hardly contribute to precise expression; better or older than what? Than stores that are worse or automobiles that are newer, presumably. *Older* is often used as a euphemism in reference to people in avoidance of *old,* which to some sounds too harsh. But of course this is an age of excessive squeamishness and of unmerited preferment, as in referring to janitors as sanitation engineers and to cow colleges as universities. See *Ad Lingo; older; better; Universities.*

Absolute Constructions. Fowler warns against the first comma in such constructions as "The day, having dawned brightly, the weather soon grew dull and cloudy." (The second comma is correct, however.) Flesch makes a blanket criticism of such locutions, and recommends avoiding them entirely by recasting.

Absolutes. For comparison of absolutes, such as *more unique, most unique, etc.,* see *Comparison 3.*

abysmal, abyssal. Formerly synonyms, but in modern use the first means *deep* in a figurative sense (*abysmal ignorance*) and the second has become a technical term of oceanography.

Academe. Criticized by two authorities as variously pompous or wrong in reference to a school (except for *The Grove of Academe*). But dictionaries validate its wide use in references to the world of higher education. Sometimes used facetiously or scornfully. *Academia* is, for practical purposes, a synonym.

accelerate, exhilarate. Described by two critics as sometimes confused, but such ignorance seems beyond the reach of correction.

accent, accentuate. Two critics agree that *accentuate* now predominates in figurative senses (emphasize, draw attention to: "accentuate the positive") and *accent* in literal senses (stress in speaking or writing: "accent the second syllable") but say this usage is chiefly British. Evans says that Americans who observe this distinction should reserve *accentuate* for small matters. Dictionaries do not recognize any distinction, treating the words as synonyms.

Accent Marks. Their use has all but disappeared in American English except for newly imported foreign words and some others that have retained them: *passé.* Anyone sophisticated enough to use such terms is unlikely to need advice about them. *Fiance, fiancee, protege* and others are often seen without the accents they possess in French, though the accents are generally retained in dictionaries. Careful writers are referred to a dictionary when in doubt. The tendency is to drop the accents from words that have found wide use in English. The German umlaut is often indicated by adding *e* to the umlauted letter: *Götterdämmerung* becomes *Goetterdaemmerung,* but often any indication of the umlaut will simply be omitted. The dieresis (as in *coöperate*), about the only remaining native diacritical mark, has nearly disappeared. Flesch and some other critics counsel avoidance of foreign terms entirely in favor of their English equivalents, when possible. See also *Diacritical Marks.*

accept. Confusion reigns over the choice of prepositions to go with *accept.* The admissions office of an otherwise reputable university sent out thousands of letters to applicants over a period of years informing them that they had been accepted *to* the school. *Accept* takes *by,* not *to,* and one may wonder what effect this error may have had on linguistically sensitive parents of applicants, who may well have decided to send their offspring elsewhere. Evidently the composer of this letter confused *accept* with *admit,* which does take *to* (and also *by,* in appropriate contexts); "We were admitted by the doorman"; "She was admitted to the university."

acceptable. Sometimes misused for *receptive.* "The natives of the island are acceptable to Christianity" does not say what the writer intended. He meant to describe them as ready to sign up, but instead gave the impression they had passed some kind of entrance examination.

acceptance, acceptation. The first is the act of accepting, the second now the interpretation or usual meaning of something; for example, a concept, word, or doctrine, though there is some overlapping.

access, accession. The first means an opening or opportunity, the second ascent or attainment, two critics hold. The correct term for assumption of monarchial status is *accession* (to the throne), not *access. Access* has newly become a verb in computer technology ("Any one of 235 cards can be randomly accessed"). This sense is still too new for most dictionaries, but its triumph seems undeniable. *Accession* is an old verb, but lives mostly in the vocabulary of librarians, in reference to acquiring books.

accessorize. See *-ize, -ise*.

accident, mishap. Two critics agree that chance is the primary attribute of an accident, and that *mishap* implies undesirability or misfortune. One of them restricts *mishap* to what is unimportant. Dictionaries do not associate the idea of unimportance with *mishap*, however. The Standard College Dictionary makes the comment, "*Mishap* and *mischance* suggest a single unforeseen occurrence: a *mishap* on the road interrupted our trip." Webster cites *a great mishap,* such as a landslide.

   Mishap is a favorite with newspaper headline writers because of its convenient length, and they tend to use it indiscriminately.

accidentally, accidently. The second form is recognized only by Webster, and users of it take the chance of being considered poor spellers. The same is true of *incidentally* vs. *incidently*.

accommodate. In the form *accomodate,* one of the most misspelled words.

accompanist, accompanyist. The first form is now overwhelmingly predominant. Fowler, the strict etymologist, regrets that *-nier* or *-nyist* did not win popular favor.

according to, accordingly. *According to* is preferably avoided in attribution because it may cast a shadow on the credibility of the speaker. Flesch criticizes *accordingly* and *in accordance with* as clumsy.

accrue. Two critics recommend restricting the word to fiscal contexts. Most dictionary definitions concern money and the like, but an extended sense (*benefits accruing to society*) is usually included.

accumulative, cumulative. The second is preferable to and has nearly displaced the first as smoother.

accuse, accused. Take *of,* not *with: accused of a crime.* Designations like *the accused thief,* in reference to one who has been charged but not convicted, are widely criticized because they imply guilt before it has been established. The same is true of *suspected*.

accustom. Takes *to,* not *with: accustomed to luxury.*

acid test. A cliché.

acquaintanceship. Superfluous beside *acquaintance*.

acquiesce. Takes *in,* not *to: acquiesce in the arrangement.* Authorities are unanimous on this point; *acquiesce to* is now considered old-fashioned.

Acronyms. Refers to abbreviations that form pronounceable words, not merely to alphabetical abbreviations (like FHA, CIO). *Radar* (for *radio detecting and ranging*) is an acronym that has become a full-fledged word. Three authorities warn against the indiscriminate use of such devices when they may not be familiar to the reader, a favorite practice among newspaper writers in their headlong urge to compress. See also *Alphabetical Designations*.

act, action. Though one will do where the other will not, the vagaries of idiom affecting the choice make it impossible to formulate any useful rule. It is agreed, however, that only *action* has a collective sense; that is, more than one act may make up an action. *Act* in modern usage also generally indicates the thing done, and *action* the doing of it. A sentence about children who had emptied their piggy bank to pay their father's fine said, "The judge dug into his pocket and reimbursed them after learning of their action." **act.** The slangy phrases "where the action is" and "a piece of the action" where *action* displaces *activity* or *proceeds* (generally of a questionable kind) are disparaged by Harper.

activate, actuate. Two critics hold that the first means to make active, the second to cause to move. But dictionaries do not recognize any hard and fast distinction.

actual, actually. Often used for a meaningless emphasis, especially in conversation. "No sooner had the Reds appeared than they were actually pelted with tomatoes"; "The stocks were sold above actual market prices." Omission of *actually* and *actual* from these sentences has no effect on meaning or emphasis. Pointless intensives like this play the writer false by detracting, instead of adding, emphasis.

ad. Standard for *advertisement,* six of seven authorities agree; American Heritage calls it informal. This is a clipped form, not an abbreviation, and thus takes no period.

A.D. In a letter to the *Los Angeles Times* after the landing of Apollo 11 on the moon, Rockwell Schnable wrote, "Notwithstanding the phenomenal precision of the scientists concerned with the moon shot, a little mistake was overlooked. The inscription engraved on the plaque left on the moon reads, 'Here Man From the Planet Earth First Set Foot Upon the Moon, July 1969 A.D.' B.C. follows the year, whereas A.D. precedes it. How odd that in spite of man's superhuman achievements, this error—a grammatical one—has occurred in the first printed words in outer space."

While A.D. (for *anno domini,* the year of our Lord) logically and thus usually precedes the year, this usage is not invariable. Webster approves placement after the year, and American Heritage calls this sequence informal. The application of A.D. to centuries is also sometimes criticized ("the twelfth century A.D.") as illogical. Once again, Webster approves and American Heritage considers it informal. Apparently the tendency to counterpoise A.D. to B.C. is often too strong to resist.

adapted. Inappropriate as a synonym for *suitable* because it implies *changed* (to meet a requirement, for example).

add an additional. A common and careless redundancy.

added fillip. In such constructions as "He gave the project an added fillip," *added* is redundant unless there was a previous fillip.

addicted. Two critics and Random House agree that the term should be reserved for what is harmful, and criticize its facetious use for what is not (*addicted to grapes*). Webster, however, quotes Galsworthy: "addicted to pleasure." *Addicted* takes *to* and is not followed by an infinitive: not *addicted to smoke* but *addicted to smoking.*

addition. See *in addition to; Number in Addition.*

additionally. A clumsy synonym for *also:* "Additionally, he had acquired three houses and two cars." *He had also acquired . . .*

address. Pompous where *speech* will do.

adequate. A euphemistic counter word of the reviewing profession, employed in praising faintly, two authorities say. When the critic reports that a performance was adequate he generally believes it was something less than equal to the occasion, and should realize the reader senses this. See also *impeccable; consummate.*

adequate enough. Redundant; one or the other.

adhere. Five authorities approve it in such contexts as *adhere to a plan;* one dissents, on the ground that the suggestion of glue is ludicrous. The expression *give adhesion* (to a political party) is common in Britain but not used in the U.S.

adjacent. Means *near,* not necessarily *touching.* Two critics prefer simpler words such as *next to, near,* or *close to.* Takes *to,* not *of:* "The store is adjacent of the Lincoln Avenue School." *to.*

adjectivally, adjectively. The first is preferable.

Adjectives. See *Absolute Comparatives; Comparison; Modifiers.*

adjure. See *abjure, adjure.*

adjust, readjust. Often euphemistic, particularly in reference to cuts in pay and sometimes even to raises. See *Euphemisms.*

Ad Lingo. Admen gain their sometimes bizarre, sometimes amusing effects by making the old college try. Effort in writing is preferable, even if it misfires, to the automatic repetition of stereotypes.

The slogan has been abandoned, but perhaps none in advertising history caused such a commotion among purists as "Winstons taste good, like a cigarette should." The fact was—and is—that the rule against *like* as a conjunction had seen its best days, and so the advertiser was doing nothing very heinous.

It is intriguing the way *better* and *older,* which began as comparatives, have become positives in advertising. Certain products, we are told, are to be found in the *better* stores. Not *good* stores, mind you, nor the *best,* but the *better* ones. We must admit that the adwriters have invested *better* with a mysterious toniness that even *best* now lacks in these contexts. Old Hospice Beer, the admen proclaim, is so much *more* refreshing. But more refreshing than what?

Automobiles, homes, and people are never *old* in the ads; they are merely *older,* though cars generally take a specialized descriptive: *older-* (or *early*) *model.* Pre-owned has come over the horizon and is gaining favor; *second-hand* is all but a dirty word. Who would buy a house baldly conceded to be old? Thus *older* fills the adman's bill, even if it does not meet the requirements of logical expression.

It is perhaps antisocial these days to speak of people as old; in the ads and elsewhere they are *older people,* or better yet, *mature.* The magazine of the American Association of Retired Persons, whose members must be at least 55, is entitled *Modern Maturity.* Such euphemisms have been taken up by many journalists, who have nothing to sell but writing, but whose imitation of poor models is nevertheless notorious. If *old* is too harsh an adjective to apply to people, how about *Time's* favorite noun, *oldsters?* The euphemism *senior citizens* is distasteful to many.

We read of bread that is as many as *eight ways better.* If Elizabeth Barrett Browning had been a huckster, she might have written:

How do I love that soap?

Let me count the ways . . .

administer, administrate. Synonyms, though *administrate* is an Americanism and may be considered unnecessary beside *administer.*

admission, admittance. *Admission* predominates. *Admittance* denotes physical entry, *admission* the allowance of certain rights and privileges, a view held by five authorities. Four others consider the words synonymous and one describes the distinction as disappearing.

admit, admit to. *Admit to* is criticized by four authorities in the sense *confess* ("He admitted to having stolen the money"). Evans says the addition of *to* has a deliberately weakening effect, a view that seems quixotic. *Admit* is unsuitable in attribution unless there is reason to suggest what is undesirable or previously concealed, or to indicate a response to a challenge: "Clark admitted he had been working on the plan to restore the neighborhood." In using *admitted* as a random variant of *said,* the writer made it sound as if the neighborhood restorer were owning up to a misdeed, for the context did not justify *admitted.*

admonishment, admonition. Two critics recommend the second as the more usual form. This advice seems unarguable.

ad nauseam. (To the point of nausea.) Often misspelled *ad nauseum*.

Adolescent *they*. The use of a singular verb with the plural pronouns *they* or *their* is one of the most prevalent faults of the age. An example: "The church welcomes all students to participate in the varied programs they offer." Since *the church* is singular, *they offer* should have been *it offers*, further, *church* has already properly been the subject of a singular verb, *welcomes*. Sentences like this prompted Theodore M. Bernstein, who critiqued *The New York Times*, to ask: "They does?" "The street will be blocked at night to prevent anyone from parking their cars there." *his car*. Sometimes the use of *their* instead of *his* is advocated to avoid the purported sexism of the masculine pronoun. It is a delusion, however, that the impersonal *he, his, him* is necessarily masculine. It is considered neuter in such contexts in both grammar and law. "When a non-English-speaking person calls the operator using Spanish, they are immediately connected with a Spanish-speaking operator." *he is;* or *When non-English-speaking people.* An alternative that avoids *his* in the second example: ". . . to prevent drivers from parking their cars." Golfers are instructed to keep their eyes on the ball, and writers should likewise keep their eyes on verbs and pronouns to see that they correspond in number. "The judge said that because the administration finances the program, they are free to suspend it." *it is free.*

Most collective nouns, like *administration*, are regarded as singular in America, though there are exceptions depending on what the writer wants to emphasize. In Britain, things are different, many collectives Americans consider singular are construed as plurals, the most notable, perhaps, being *government* ("the government are"). But whether the noun is regarded as singular or plural, the verb and pronouns referring to the subject should be of the same number.

Indefinite pronouns (now referred to by some linguists as indefinite nouns), such as *anybody, anyone, everybody, everyone, somebody, someone, each,* are allowed plural verbs by some authorities. The reader is referred to the entries for these words.

The term "adolescent they" to describe the fault discussed here is admittedly a coined one. It was suggested by the fact that this misuse reflects an immature style.

Adolf (Hitler). One of the most misspelled names in recent history; often given *Adolph*.

adopt. Three authorities warn against confusion with *adapt;* see *adapted*. To adopt is to accept, to adapt is to change.

adopt a wait-and-see attitude. A windy cliché of journalism, displacing *wait and see. Adopt a hands-off policy,* for *keep hands off, let alone,* is another.

adopted, adoptive. While the common American use is *adopted* in reference to parents, the British *adoptive* is preferable; Fowler and American Heritage favor this form. One critic warns that *adoptive* may be regarded as overcorrect; Random House and Webster consider the forms interchangeable.

adult. The current euphemism for *pornographic,* as applied to books, movies, etc.

adumbrate. Means *foreshadow,* and is derogated by three critics as formal, literary, and unsuitable for ordinary contexts.

advance, advancement, advanced. The first is preferable for the general idea of progress, the second for promotion. *Advance* is redundant with *warning, planning, preparations,* and the like. Sometimes it erroneously displaces *advanced,* as in *advance writing classes* or *advance degree.*

Adverbial Genitive. The term describes such expressions as *days* in "He worked days" and *afternoons* in "They slept afternoons." Bryant reports the form well established in informal standard expression (as against such alternatives as *during the day, every day, in the afternoon*). Evans calls such forms standard usage in the U.S. but obsolete in Britain.

Adverbs. An erroneous idea that compound verbs (like *have seen, will go*) should not be separated by adverbs (*have* easily *seen, will* soon *go*) has become widespread, and is perhaps most firmly established among newspaper journalists. Most commentators agree that it is apparently an offshoot of the prohibition against splitting an infinitive, which in its absolute and arbitrary form is also a superstition. (See *Infinitives 1.*) Some examples in which the verb is split by an adverb (italicized): "The budget was *tentatively* approved"; "The decision was *automatically* delayed"; "Experts are *now* pinning their hopes on the House." In many sentences, the adverb falls naturally between the parts of the verb, and in negative sentences it is impossible to place the adverb (*not*) anywhere else: "He would not concede the election"; "The decision will not block action." Five authorities, including Fowler, who says that placing the adverb anywhere else than between the parts of the verb requires special justification, agree on the foregoing. Newspaper editors are assiduous in plucking *also* from compound verbs. Thus "He was also singled out for commendation," which says that among other things the subject was singled out, is likely to be changed to "He also was singled out . . ." which may alter the sense to "He in addition to others . . ."

An adverb should not intervene between a verb and its object: "He said every chance would be given to complete satisfactorily the negotiations." *to complete the negotiations satisfactorily.* "An applicant for a federal job should have a chance to explain informally derogatory information." *to explain derogatory information informally.* The examples cited sound like clumsy translations from German. See *Modifiers;* for wrongly hyphened adverbs, see *Hyphens 7.*

adverse, averse (to). The expression is *averse to* ("She was not averse to a drink before dinner"); not *adverse*. Evans says *averse to* is preferable but allows *averse from*. Fowler allows either *to* or *from* with *averse*. Random House and Webster give *averse to;* this is the consensus. American Heritage says usually *to*, less often *from*.

advert to. Two critics consider it obsolete for *refer to*.

advertize. Acceptable, but *advertise* greatly predominates. See *-ize, -ise*.

advise. Criticized when it displaces *say, tell, write, inform*, especially in business correspondence ("beg to advise," which itself is a Victorianism) and in journalism, three authorities agree. Some critics of the journalistic use say "Save *advise* for giving advice." But American Heritage and Webster approve *advised* for *said* or *told*.

adviser, advisor. Insistence on *-er* is one of the peculiarities of journalism; a former editor says *-er* is preferred but neglects to explain on what grounds. Perrin calls *-or* now probably predominant. All dictionaries give both forms as synonyms and as standard.

ae, e; oe, e. The digraphs, once often given as joined characters, that is, ligatures, have been almost entirely abandoned in favor of *e* alone in such words as *archeology* (*archaeology*), *esthetic* (*aesthetic*), *encyclopedia* (*encyclopaedia*), *esophagus* (*oesophagus*), *fetus* (*foetus*). Fowler's examples show that British usage is somewhat more traditional.

aegis. A favorite of journalists, who often misuse it in the sense of *jurisdiction, surveillance*, without the connotation of *protection*. Dictionary definitions generally corroborate this view.

aero-, air-. *Aeroplane* and similar forms have disappeared from the U.S., and Fowler reports despairingly that American influence is doing them in even in Britain.

affect, effect. Although the confusion of *affect* with *effect* is perhaps the commonest error of them all, noted unanimously by authorities, it seems almost superfluous to explain that *affect* means influence ("The moon affects lovers") and *effect* means accomplish ("A merger was effected"). *Affect* is always a verb except in a specialized sense as a noun, peculiar to psychology, which never appears in nontechnical contexts. *Effect* may be either verb (as illustrated) or noun ("The effect was satisfactory").

affiliated (associated, identified) with. Hifalutin ways of saying *belongs to, works for*.

affirmative, negative. Pretentious and perhaps ridiculous displacements of *yes, no* ("He answered in the affirmative" for "He said yes" or "He agreed"). These are notably military mannerisms. A newsmagazine reported that civilian secretaries at the Manned Space Center in Houston had taken to saying *negative* over the telephone when most people would say *no*.

afflict, inflict. See *inflict, afflict*.

afford. Does not take *with* (*afford some protection;* not *afford with*).

affray. A favorite of newspaper journalists, though the term is seldom seen in other writing, for *fight, contest, game,* etc. In its technical legal sense, an affray is a fight that constitutes an offense by disturbing the peace.

affrontery. The now defunct *National Observer,* a meticulously edited paper in its early years, slipped as time passed and once said, "America's brutality to its creatures is an affrontery to our nation." Regrettably, there is no such word. Even *affront,* meaning *insult,* would not have fit this context as well as *reproach.* Then there is *effrontery* (*boldness, insolence*).

aforementioned, aforesaid. Legalese; unsuitable for ordinary contexts, in the opinion of two critics. See also *said* as used in this sense. Usually any of these is superfluous, because the definite article (*the*) suffices to specify whatever is being referred to.

Africander, Afrikander; Africaner, Afrikaner. Some commentators restrict the first pair to a breed of sheep or of cattle, and the second to South Africans of Boer descent, but dictionaries now treat the forms as interchangeable. The context, presumably, must be relied upon to determine whether the subject is people or cattle.

after. In Irish dialect, it does not mean *about to,* as is often assumed, but *have just done.* "I am after taking a walk." *have just taken,* not *intend to take.*

aftermath. Should be reserved for what is disagreeable, and not used for what merely follows upon something else. The distinction is supported by American Heritage, the Standard College Dictionary, and Random House, but Webster cites *The New York Times* in "a gratifying aftermath." The consensus favors the distinction.

afterward, afterwards. Interchangeable in the U.S.; only *afterwards* is used in Britain.

age, aged. Expressions like *at age 65* and *children aged 9 to 12* sound actuarial and old-fashioned, respectively. The numbers indicating age can be used without the descriptive words: *at 65, children 9 to 12.*

agenda. Unanimously described as a standard English singular ("the agenda includes . . .") though it is technically a Latin plural, which sometimes causes pedants to attempt to revive *agendum* as the singular. The established English plural is now *agendas*.

aggravate. Eight authorities agree that the word now may be used in the sense *annoy, irritate;* one alone holds to the traditional view that it can mean only *make worse.* The overwhelming consensus, then, is that both meanings are standard: "We were aggravated by the swarms of buzzing flies"; "His tight shoes aggravated the sore on his foot." Among dictionaries, both Random House and Webster regard the new sense as standard; American Heritage calls it informal.

ago. Redundant with *since:* "It is only 20 years ago since the treaty was signed." *years since* (or *ago* that).

agree. The revised Fowler points out and sanctions a British curiosity unknown in America, namely, *agree* as a transitive verb not followed by a preposition (*to, on*): "The council has the authority to agree its own minutes." What howls would be raised by traditionalists if such a usage sprang up in this country—until, perhaps, they discovered it had been imported from England.

Agreement. See *Subject-Verb Agreement.*

ah, aw. One critic holds that *ah* should be reserved to express delight, pleasure, and *aw* to express regret, contempt, incredulity: "Ah, this is a splendid wine"; "Aw, we have lost the title." Random House and Webster concur in this on *aw* but assign both meanings to *ah,* as does American Heritage, which gives only this form.

ahold. Not standard for *hold* with *get* or *take:* "I'd like to get ahold of that information." *get hold.*

aid, aide. Loosely interchangeable in the sense *assistant. Aide* is preferred in military connections, however, and more or less also in diplomacy and nursing. Newspaper headlines would be less ambiguous if *aide* were used invariably as the noun (*the general's aide*).

aim to. One critic calls this standard in the sense *intend,* but concedes some consider it dialectal. Random House calls it chiefly dialectal; Webster and American Heritage consider it standard. Fowler says that the usage originated in America and somewhat surprisingly adds that it has established itself as acceptable in Britain. Evans evidently considers it standard, since it is cited without qualification. This is the consensus.

ain't. One critic calls *ain't* illiterate and another nonstandard. Three critics regret that it is not acceptable for *am not,* since there is no other contraction for this form; one critic and American Heritage deplore *aren't I* but Fowler calls it "colloquially respectable,'' reflecting a difference between British and American usage that is corroborated by Evans. Bryant says *aren't I* is relatively rare and that cultivated speakers prefer *am I not*. Some critics regard *aren't I* as schoolgirlish. Flesch says *ain't* is on its way to full acceptance. All his examples, however, are either quoted speech or jocular.

The fact is that *ain't* is sometimes boldly used in writing by those who are sure of themselves, though most readers are likely to consider it the hallmark of the uneducated. *Ain't* for *am not* is considered nonstandard by Random House and American Heritage, but accepted in speech by Webster; all consider it nonstandard for *have not*. The consensus is that it is best avoided in writing.

air. Unexceptionable for *broadcast*. May be ambiguous in newspaper headlines, however, where the word is also used to mean *expose, discuss, explore*.

a la. Not *ala; à la* (in the style or manner of) *Hollywood*. As noted under *Accents,* the French *grave* accent over *a* is often disregarded, as is true of many naturalized foreign words. The reason may be that much American typesetting equipment does not include letters with foreign accents. Book publishers are generally prepared not only for accents but also for Cyrillic, Greek, Hebrew, and other Western alphabets, though not always for Chinese, Japanese, or Arabic characters.

alas, poor Yorick. See *Misquotation*.

albeit. Considered archaic a generation ago; now evidently making a comeback, to judge by its acceptance as standard by Fowler and two unabridged American dictionaries.

Alger, Horatio. The name is often used to characterize a successful man (''The Horatio Alger of the insurance business, a millionaire who once supported himself as a busboy''). In fact, Horatio Alger was the name of the author, not of any of the heroes, of the rags-to-riches tales.

alibi. The technical meaning in law is a defense against a criminal charge by a plea of having been elsewhere (the meaning of *alibi* in Latin is *elsewhere*). The term is in common use in the sense *excuse;* Evans points out that one of Ring Lardner's best-known characters was Alibi Ike, who earned the sobriquet by perpetually having ready some extenuation of his shortcomings. *Alibi* in this sense is sometimes bitterly criticized, particularly by lawyers who consider the extended sense a corruption, and Fowler stands with them. This must be regarded as a British view, however; three American critics approve the popular sense, and it is admitted, sometimes with the qualification ''informal'' or ''colloquial'' as standard by all current American dictionaries. American Heritage admits it as informal, though only 41 percent of its usage panel approved. Sir Ernest Gowers, Fowler's reviser, might be dismayed to discover that even the Oxford Universal Dictionary, an abridgment of the great OED, approves the popular sense.

align, aline. Both versions are given as standard by dictionaries, but the first is far more common and Fowler calls it the correct one.

alive. See *live.*

alive and well. It has grown tiresome to say of a person that he is alive and well.

all. Often used redundantly, apparently for meaningless emphasis: "All airport users were asked to allow extra time to get there."

all-. Hyphenated as a prefix: *all-round, all-out, all-seeing,* etc.

All-America, all-American. The latter is the form given in dictionaries for the sense "representing the best in any field of U.S. sport." The press associations and other organizations, however, have their own choices for this accolade, and designate them *All-America.*

all-around, all-round. One critic favors *all-round* as more logical in such phrases as *all-round athlete.* But both forms are in common use and the distinction is footless. The Standard College Dictionary cites *all-around athlete,* and other current American dictionaries unanimously equate *all-round* and *all-around.* American Heritage, however, adds that *all-round* is preferable. The consensus is that the forms are interchangeable. See also *round, around.*

allege, alleged, allegedly. One critic says that while *alleged* strictly applies to a deed and not a person, journalistic necessity makes it acceptable in the sense *supposed (alleged forger).* It is a delusion that the use of the term confers immunity from suit for libel. Some commentators point out that it may have a mitigating effect. *Alleged* has a nice legal ring, however, and this would probably keep it in use even if everyone were aware it does not offer the protection now often assumed.

Alleged is often used redundantly: "The suspect was indicted for alleged perjury." An indictment is an accusation, and consequently would be *for perjury,* not *alleged perjury.* This is true of any charge; people are charged with offenses, not alleged offenses. The charge itself is an allegation.

Alleged is the adjective, *allegedly* the adverb: "This book lets us look through the eyes of an alleged unbiased lawyer." *allegedly,* unless it is intended to say that he was an alleged lawyer. *Allege* is sometimes misspelled *alledge.* See also *accused.*

allergic. Disapproved by three critics in the nonmedical, often facetious sense (*allergic to television*); Fowler approves of this sense as useful; the Standard College Dictionary calls it informal (as does American Heritage) and cites *allergic to work.* Random House and Webster admit it without qualification; this is the consensus.

all is (are) not. See *not . . . all, all . . . not.*

Alliteration. The repetition of sounds at the beginnings of words or in accented syllables: *after life's fitful fever.* Young people who discover in themselves a bent for writing go through a phase in which they overdo alliteration, but usually recover. The consensus is that this literary device should be employed sparingly and with care; too much of it (and very little is too much) becomes tiresome. Often flaunted in journalistic and advertising prose. Flesch calls it silly in ordinary writing. Spiro Agnew, while vice president, attracted great attention with his rhetorical denunciations of the press, television, crime, whatever. He was fond of alliteration; one of his famous phrases was "nattering nabobs of negativism," which by itself should have been enough to destroy alliteration.

all of. Two critics object to *all* with *of* where it is unnecessary, as in *all (of) the papers, all (of) the money.* Bryant says *all* is much more frequent than *all of* where *of* is optional, as in the examples cited. Two critics approve *all of* in such examples by analogy with *none of,* though one concedes *of* may well be omitted as superfluous when it is optional. Another critic says a good writer or editor automatically changes *all of* to *all* (presumably he means only when *of* is optional, for there are instances, as with personal pronouns [*all of them*] when it is essential). Random House and Webster accept both forms; American Heritage gives a slight preference to *all* where *of* is dispensable. This is obviously a morass of conflicting opinion. The point is hardly an important one, since the choice has no effect on meaning and is unlikely to be noticed by the reader.

allow of. Admitted by two critics in specified senses; a third says *of* is superfluous, but American Heritage, Random House, and Webster accept it for *permit:* "The agreement allows of two interpretations." Still, *of* is unnecessary.

all-points bulletin. What the police are forever issuing in newspaper stories. Surely some substitute for this threadbare phrase could be found.

all power corrupts . . . See *Misquotation.*

all ready, already. The first means *completely prepared,* the second *by this time, before, previously.* "Your car is all ready to go." "What, already?"

all right, alright. Although often seen in print, *alright* is regarded as nonstandard by four authorities, American Heritage, and Random House. Flesch expresses confidence it will establish itself, and Webster says it is in reputable use, though not so common as *all right,* which is favored by the consensus. *Alright* probably evolved in imitation of *already.*

all-round. See *all-around, all-round.*

all that. As in "If things were all that bad he would have heard about it" or, more commonly, in the negative, as "The speech wasn't all that bad," criticized by three authorities and American Heritage. Bernstein says *all* used in this way is unnecessary and inappropriate in writing. The phrase is a Briticism that sounds affected in the U.S. As for its native habitat, Fowler calls the use of *all* as an adverb, of which *all that* and *not all that* are examples, a colloquialism that is approaching literary acceptance. The consensus is against it. *Not that* ("He's not that rich"), when no basis for a comparison has been stated, is similar.

Not all that bad, for example, is a comparison that hangs in the air, lacking a basis, and displacing *not bad.* The crystal ball reveals no clear indication of its prospects, but in America it may well be a fad that will disappear. Yet it appears to reflect the trend toward euphemism and the softening of direct statements and positive judgments. So Fowler may be right.

all the (easier, etc.). *All* with a comparative is confirmed as standard English by Bryant and Evans, a judgment that may surprise many to whom it would never have occurred that such confirmation was necessary. American Heritage and Random House give the usage as standard, but Webster, oddly enough, calls it chiefly dialectal. The consensus is that it is standard.

all the farther. Two critics prefer *as far as* ("This is as far as I can go").

all-time record. Redundant for *record* alone.

all together, altogether. Often confused, authorities agree; *all together* means *in a group; altogether* means *entirely:* "We will go all together"; "The idea is altogether ridiculous." See also *in the altogether.*

all told. One critic would restrict the phrase to counting, as "All told, there were 50 crows in the tree," and considers its use as a general summation wrong. Webster, however, cites "All told, it had been one of the most frustrating experiences imaginable." American Heritage also gives the general sense.

allude, refer. To allude to is to suggest without naming the thing; to refer to is to name it. *Allude* is often misused for *refer.* Authorities unanimously concur in this view.

allusion, elusion, illusion. Two critics warn against confusion of the terms. (*Allusion* is *suggestion* or *unspecific reference; elusion*—a rarity—is *avoidance* or *escape; illusion* is *deception.*) The adjectival forms *allusive, elusive,* and *illusive* are sometimes confused. Flesch is critical of the literary device of allusion; that is, incorporating in one's writing fragments of well-known quotations with the aim of dressing it up. Two critics say literary allusions are useful but that the writer should be wary of making them too esoteric.

almost. As an adjective modifying a noun, as in *an almost* accident, sanctioned as standard and well established by Evans, Fowler, and Webster. Despite this, however, the construction is likely to be regarded as an error in America. Neither American Heritage nor Random House recognizes it. Perhaps it may be best classified as literary and British. *Almost* is described by Evans as designating a shorter space than *nearly,* a distinction that no other authority suggests, much less corroborates. *Almost* is often unnecessarily hyphenated, like adverbs ending in *-ly; an almost-open break.* This applies also to *less, more, most, much, nearly, once,* and *sometimes* as adverbs. See also *most.*

   Boswell quoted Johnson as saying, "The chaplain . . . could tell me scarcely anything" and then commented in a footnote, "It has been mentioned to me by an accurate English friend, that Dr. Johnson could never have used the phrase *almost nothing,* as not being English; and therefore I have put another in its place. At the same time, I am not quite convinced it is not good English. For the best writers use the phrase 'little or nothing,' i.e., almost so little as to be nothing." The vote here, backed by Harper, goes with Boswell's speculation as soundly based. See also *times less.*

almost more, less (better, worse, etc.). The phrases are examples of muddy writing and fuzzy thinking. They are flat contradictions in terms and thus nonsense. A condition is either almost, equal to, or more than another; it cannot be two at once. *Almost* and *more* taken together, if they mean anything, cancel each other out precisely on the line of equality. "The whole orchestra is used with almost more than the composer's usual adroitness." What did the writer mean? More adroitness? No, not quite. Less? No, more than that. The composer's usual adroitness? We can only guess. "Direct intervention, if successful, would have been almost less harmful than failure." *Perhaps less harmful* would have made the sense the writer aimed at and missed. Fowler, concurring with the foregoing by analogy, cites *almost quite* as incompatible. For a similar incongruity, see *times less, times more.*

alongside of. *Of* is unnecessary.

along with. See *with.*

Alphabetical Designations. Two authorities criticize the largely journalistic trick of following an unfamiliar designation (e.g., *International Monetary Fund*) with its alphabetical abbreviation (*IMF*) and thereafter referring to it by the abbreviation alone, as confusing to the reader, especially when more than one such abbreviation figures in the same piece of writing. Readers then must fumble back to the beginning for the key every now and then, meanwhile cursing the abecedarian who encoded the names. In such instances reference by the generic term is preferable, calling the International Monetary Fund *the fund,* the Board of Governors the *board,* rather than the BOG. The abecedarians know no shame. They may start out with the translation of a foreign name, for example General Federation of Labor, and in continuing will use an abbreviation based on the original (CGT for *Confédération Générale du Travail*). All this is not to discourage the use of abbreviations everyone recognizes, such as FBI, CIA, UN). It is aimed instead at discouraging the abbreviation of the unfamiliar, thereby diminishing readability.

already. Not joined to an adjective with a hyphen: "an already confused (not *already-confused*) labor dispute."

alright. See *all right, alright.*

also. Disapproved by five authorities as a conjunction: "A typical picnic menu includes wieners, buns, beer, also potato salad." *and;* or possibly *and also.* "The automobile needs repair, also it must be repainted." Such lapses can usually be corrected by adding *and,* substituting *moreover, in addition, besides,* or by shifting the position of *also.* Random House and Webster, however, admit *also* as a conjunction. Two of the authorities alluded to add that *also* at the beginning of a sentence or clause is wrong: "Also on the agenda are . . ." in which *also* is used as an adverb but has been taken out of its normal position: "are also on the agenda." Starting with *also* is a journalistic mannerism, related to *Inversion,* which see.

altar, alter. Sometimes confused; the first is the church structure; *alter* is a verb meaning *to change.*

alternate(ly), alternative(ly). The noun and adjective forms *alternate* and *alternative* are often confused. *Alternate* as an adjective means *by turns; first one and then the other.* "Alternate (not *alternative*) gain and loss." An alternative is another choice: "There was an alternative course of action." The idea that *alternative* may apply to a choice between two and no more is a pedantry discountenanced by no fewer than nine authorities: "There were several alternatives to the decision." Flesch urges *choice* as simpler, and of course it avoids the danger of using the wrong word.

altho. Although simplified spellings have much to commend them, they have not found favor in print, and in fact are universally unacceptable. See *Spelling.*

although, though. See *though, although.*

altogether. See *all together.*

aluminum, aluminium. The second is the British preference.

alumnus, etc. The correct forms are *alumna,* feminine singular; *alumnae,* feminine plural; *alumnus,* masculine singular; *alumni,* both masculine and mixed plural. These are among the few Latin terms that have not acquired English plurals. *Alumni* is substandard as a singular: "He is an alumni of the state university," four authorities agree, although Evans curiously allows *alumnus* in reference to a woman. Random House and Webster give asexual definitions of *alumnus,* though Webster adds that the reference is usually masculine and American Heritage gives only the masculine. Use of *alumnus* for other than the masculine is nevertheless so rare it is likely to be thought an ignorant error, especially by those who are themselves alumni.

amass. Best used in reference to a great quantity; in the sense *accumulate* or *score* (points) it is beloved by sportswriters.

a.m., p.m. Such phrases as *6 a.m. in the morning* and *9 p.m. tonight* are redundant, since the letters designate the half of the day. Whether *a.m.* and *p.m.* are capitalized is an arbitrary matter that publications settle in their stylebooks. The lower case seems predominant.

ambiance, ambience. Equally acceptable variants.

Ambiguity. For examples, see *Pronouns; Modifiers; Dangling Modifiers; False Comparison; Meaning; Restrictive and Nonrestrictive Clauses.*

ambiguous, equivocal. Roughly synonymous, but two critics say the second suggests deception, the first merely an inadvertent double meaning. Dictionaries do not positively define *equivocal* in this way, but give *deceptive* as one meaning, as well as *ambiguous.*

ambivalence, ambivalent. Two authorities criticize use of the terms to indicate duality in general, rather than a conflicting or contradictory attraction and repulsion; Fowler calls the words too technical for ordinary contexts. The connotation of conflict is supported by dictionaries.

ameliorate. Criticized by two authorities as pretentious for *improve.* Some writers use it without knowing what it means. "The diplomat set himself the job of ameliorating the singleminded fascination that the Soviet problem holds for Americans." Mrs. Malaprop rides again. What the writer really had in mind is a good question: *mitigating* or *counteracting,* perhaps.

amend, emend. See *emend(ation).*

American. Despite occasional complaints, the application of the term primarily to the U.S. and its inhabitants is so well established and so well understood as to be beyond reasonable criticism, four authorities agree; dictionaries concur. The objection is usually based on the geographical fact that the North American continent includes Canada, Mexico, and Central America, as well as the U.S. Some objections have come from Canadians, who have said inhabitants of the U.S. had no right to monopolize the term. The American Newspaper Guild, however, changed its name to the Newspaper Guild in response to protests by *Canadian* members that *American* is interpreted as referring to the U.S., as it usually is.

What counts is what people generally understand by the term. It stretches more easily over Canadians than over other inhabitants of the continent. Unfortunately, there is no other convenient expression to describe inhabitants of the U.S.; if there is any room for doubt, *American* will not be exact enough but in this case the writer will avoid it anyway, by saying, for example, *U.S. residents.* Only the unreasonable and hypersensitive will complain that the term is unduly restrictive, for this did not happen by design any more than the confusing dual application of *Indian,* which has persisted for five centuries.

The United States is more exact than *America* but the distinction is not absolute here either, for *America* has been enshrined in paeans (*America; America, the*

Beautiful; God Save America) that are unmistakably understood to refer to the United States.

Americanisms. Describes terms that originated or are in use in America in contrast to differing British versions: *tire* for *tyre*, *elevator* for *lift*, etc. What with modern means of instantaneous communication and the heavy traffic in words across the Atlantic, such differences are growing fewer and probably will disappear entirely one day. But there are diehards in Britain, particularly, who feel the purity of the language is degraded by Americanisms. By contrast, some Americans regard British versions (both different words and different spellings of the same word) as elegant and to be emulated. This, however, is a glaring affectation.

amid, amidst. Criticized by four authorities as bookish or quaint.

amok. See *amuck*, etc.

among, amongst, amid. *Among* is generally used with three or more countable things: *among my friends, among the audience, among the trees.* With singular nouns that are not collectives, *amid* is preferable: *amid the wreckage, amid the confusion.* This is the consensus of five authorities, except that Harper also accepts *among* with a singular. Two critics call *amongst* quaint or overrefined, though it is standard in Britain. Bernstein disapproves of *among the news* ("Among the news was a small item about the abdication") though *amid the news* sounds strange.

among them. In constructions like "He has accompanied numerous artists, among them Beverly Sills," not followed by a comma.

amoral. See *immoral, amoral*.

amount. Not good usage, four authorities agree, in reference to what is countable: *a large amount of people.* Preferably, *number.* Flesch calls *in the amount of* usually unnecessary for *of* or *for:* "A check in the amount of $10." *for.*

Ampersand (&). Should be used only in the names of businesses that use it themselves: Wellington & Co. It was one of H. W. Fowler's engaging idiosyncrasies that he used it abundantly in place of *and* in ordinary text, and also in the form &c. (for *et cetera*), presumably to save space, but more likely to assert his spiky individuality. In his revision of *Modern English Usage*, Sir Ernest Gowers swept away the ampersands and substituted *ands* without a word of explanation, nor did he even include *ampersand* as an entry. This was curious considering his great deference to Fowler's views; the revision often retains judgments that obviously needed bringing up to date. Margaret Nicholson, in *her* revision of Fowler (*A Dictionary of American-English Usage*) was not so venturesome. She not only reverently left the ampersands bespangling such of the original text as she retained, but used ampersands in her own additions. It is hardly necessary to say that ampersands are not considered acceptable outside firm names, formulas, and other abridged or tabular matter.

amphibian. The journalese variant for *frog*.

ample, enough. *Enough* is enough, but *ample* is more than enough; *ample* should not be used where *enough* will do, one critic holds. Two others, however, allow the terms to be used interchangeably, and so do Random House and Webster. The weight of opinion is that *ample* may mean either *enough* or *more than enough;* presumably the context will indicate which.

am to, are to, is to. See *Infinitives*.

amuck, berserk. *Amuck* is the preferred spelling, rather than *amok*, three authorities agree, though dictionaries give both. *Amuck* is stronger than *berserk;* it connotes murderousness; *berserk* merely means enraged.

an. See *a, an*.

Anachronism. A misplacement in time, as, for example, describing Victorians as having watched television. Often misused for *contradiction, anomaly, paradox*, authorities agree. "The cell warder is played by an actor with a British accent. But since the action takes place in Hungary, this casting seems a bit anachronistic." *inconsistent* or *inappropriate*.

analysis. *In the final* (or *last*) *analysis* is criticized as pretentious by two authorities.

and. There is no reason why sentences should not begin with *and,* six authorities agree. And when this is done, *and* should not be followed by a comma unless it is the first of a pair of commas setting off a parenthetical phrase following. Nor should a comma follow the conjunction that begins a clause: "They have found it pays, and, we have too." Omit the second comma. But the comma is correct, once again, after the conjunction to set off a parenthetical element (italicized): "They have found it pays, and, *I must admit,* we have too." These principles apply to *but, or, so,* and other conjunctions as well. See also *Comma*.

and also. Generally redundant for *and*.

and I quote. A superfluous pomposity; quotation marks suffice.

and/or. Denounced as a legalism with varying degrees of vehemence by seven authorities. Most of them point out that usually *or* would suffice when *and/or* is used.

and (but) which, and (but) who. In general, *and which* is either wrong or undesirable unless it comes after a parallel *which:* "Most Italians believe that the booty, *which* is known as the Dongo Treasure, and *which* has been valued at $32 million . . .'' The comments on this subject apply equally to *but which, and who, but who. And who, but who* must, of course, be preceded by *who.* Fowler devotes five pages to modifying the rule cited above. The reasoning is involved, however, and his general conclusion corresponds with the principle stated here. Partridge agrees with this principle, and it is observable that careful writing follows it. Often *and which* and *and who* are used where *which* or *who* or *and* alone would be smoother, as will be illustrated in examples to follow.

In revising *Modern English Usage,* Sir Ernest Gowers retained Fowler's discussion almost verbatim. *And (but) who* presents the same problem as *and (but) which.* In summary, nearly all Fowler's examples are disagreeably involved or quaint to the modern ear, and would likely be stated today in ways that would not cause the *and which* problem to arise.

Flesch's prescription is to cross out *and* in *and which,* and if this does not work, cross out *which.* He deals with *and who,* recommending that *and* be deleted.

The examples that follow are intended to present as simply as possible the problems likely to arise and the easiest means of solving them. Usually insertion of the first *who* or *which* and deletion of the second suffices.

"Life has two strikes on children deserted by their parents, and who never experience the love and home life adoptive parents can give them." Either *who have been deserted by their parents and never experience* or *who have been deserted . . . and who . . .*

"Production of European-type grapes, which are grown almost exclusively in California and Arizona, and which account for most of this year's crop . . .'' This conforms with the rule but *and account for* would be simpler.

"Most men entering their eighty-ninth year and who have won wealth and fame might be content to sit back at ease." *who are entering . . . and have.*

"Fritz Weaver, who played Hamlet last summer, and who is one of the most versatile actors in the American theater, is shockingly believable as the haunted weakling." *summer and is one.*

"The Copts are a forgotten people but who made interesting contributions to art." *people, who made* or *people, although they made.*

anent. Denounced variously as quaint, pretentious, or heavily humorous by six authorities. Sometimes, compounding the felony, misspelled *annent.* Random House and Webster recognize it as standard for *concerning.*

anesthesiologist, anesthetist. The distinction is that the first is a physician trained in the specialty of administering anesthetics.

angle. Mildly criticized by Evans and Flesch when used as a noun in the sense *approach, point of view, position* ("He had a peculiar angle on the situation"), Evans saying it is overworked in journalism, and Flesch that it sounds slangy but has no entirely satisfactory substitute. Sir Ernest Gowers, however, in *The Complete Plain Words,* criticizes this usage for imprecision. Random House, Webster, and most desk dictionaries give *viewpoint, standpoint, point of view* as standard senses of *angle*. The conclusion may be drawn that this sense of *angle* is under a faint shadow that is fast disappearing.

annual. While swallowing camels, editors often strain at the gnat of referring to some function as "the first annual," on the ground that to be so designated it must have been held twice. But this is just another journalistic superstition; there is nothing in dictionaries to validate it. If an event is planned to be held annually, the first one is the first annual occurrence of it.

anoint. Sometimes misspelled *annoint*.

another. "Eighteen persons were summoned as witnesses, and another six were interrogated." This use of *another* is a favorite journalistic construction, some-times criticized, as by Bernstein and Harper, on the ground that *another* means *one more of the same kind,* and that thus the sentence could not be correct unless the second number were the same as the first. Current dictionaries, however, all give one sense of *another* as *different, distinct,* or *not the same,* which invalidates the criticism. In many sentences of this kind, however, *another* is simply super-fluous. See *other.*

ante-. Solid as a prefix: *antedate, anteroom, antemarital,* etc. But *ante-Norman* (followed by a capital).

antedate. There was a time when *antedate* was familiar and *predate* was rarely seen. Now *antedate* has all but disappeared. *Predate* is not a neologism, however; it goes back more than a century. "The pyramids of Egypt predate [antedate] those of the Maya ruins in Mexico."

anti-. Generally solid as a prefix; *antiwar, antitrust,* etc. But *anti-American* (fol-lowed by a capital) and *anti-intellectual* (to avoid doubling the *i*). The hyphen may be desirable to avoid creating a word with a strange and possibly confusing look, such as *antibias, antilabor.*

anticipate. Criticized by four authorities when it displaces *expect,* as in "Agricul-tural officials anticipate production will be about the same as last year" and "The principal anticipated normal attendance." *Anticipate,* in the strict view, has the sense of seizing time by the forelock, of preparing or being prepared in some way for what is to come. "We anticipated the storm by taking our umbrella." Nevertheless, the word has an irresistible lure, and for many has entirely dis-placed *expect.* Perhaps they consider it more elegant. This cause appears to be lost, however, since all current dictionaries give *expect* as a synonym of *antici-pate.* Curiously enough, in the light of their usual traditionalism, both Follett and American Heritage accept *anticipate* for *look forward.* Discriminating writing, nevertheless, continues to observe the distinction. Nearly always the word wanted is *expect,* and if it fits, it should be used. *Anticipate* is seldom required, and when *expect* will do, *anticipate* sounds pretentious.

The addiction to *anticipate* sometimes produces amusement for those who have a feel for its pristine sense: "The woman said she was pregnant and anticipating a child within two months." Madam, leave those calculations to your doctor. The ad that ballyhooed a film as "The most anticipated motion picture of our time" was an unintentional example of truth—the awful truth—in advertising. "An anticipating audience was treated to a delightful program." *eager, expectant.*

anxious, eager. Four authorities agree that *anxious* connotes foreboding, and should not be used for *eager* in such sentences as "We are anxious to see the play." Evans and Fowler say *anxious* for *eager* is fully established, and Webster and Random House call it standard. Opinion is thus divided.

any. For *of any, than any (other)* see *Comparison 1;* see also *than any, than anyone.*

any and all. A redundant pomposity: "Any and all efforts to remove the statue will be resisted." Either *any* or *all* or neither will do.

anybody, everybody. One word as pronouns; not *any body, every body.* References to *anybody, anyone, each, either, everybody, everyone, either, nobody, no one, somebody,* and *someone,* all of which are technically singular, are nevertheless often in the plural (*they, them, their*): "Everybody shouldered their pack and moved on"; "Anyone who fails the examination can lose their license." Four authorities approve the plural reference outright; four others are indulgent of it in talk but disapprove of it in writing; Random House calls it nonstandard and Harper rejects it. Thus opinion is mixed on this usage. See also *anyone, of any, of anyone; than any, than anyone; Plural and Singular; Adolescent they.* See *else, else's* for *anyone's else, anyone else's.*

any more. Misused in positive statements, like "They certainly have good television programs any more" and "One can get terribly discouraged by reading the newspapers any more." *Any more* properly requires a negative context or implication, four authorities agree: "We hardly see her any more"; "They don't go there any more." Bryant and other authorities say *any more* in a positive sense is standard in some parts of the country, however. Preferably two words, though *anymore* is given by both American Heritage and Webster.

anyone. One word as a pronoun: "Any one of the group will help" (adjective plus pronoun) vs. "Anyone may apply" (pronoun). Four authorities agree. With *they, their, them,* see *anybody, anyone;* for *anyone's else,* etc., see *else.*

any other. See *Comparison 1.*

anyplace. Described by Bernstein and Bryant as colloquial for *anywhere,* accepted by Fowler as a U.S. usage, and considered standard by two authorities, Evans and Flesch. Webster and American Heritage consider it standard, but

Random House calls it informal. Here, as in other instances when the authorities fall out, the writer may safely make his own decision.

anyway, any way, anyways. *Anyway* is the word in the sense *regardless:* "We'll go anyway." Otherwise, four authorities agree, in the sense *in any manner,* two words: "We did not understand him in any way." American Heritage adds that the forms are interchangeable in this sense: "The books were scattered anyway [or *any way*] on the floor." *Anyways* for *anyway* is substandard.

anywheres. Substandard for *anywhere.*

A-OK. Taken up, during the expeditions to the moon, from the astronauts' way of saying everything was in order. It quickly grew tiresome in common parlance, and fortunately now seems all but forgotten.

a period of. Usually verbiage before designation of an interval: "He resided in Japan for a period of five years." *for five years.*

apologize, apologise. The second is the British preference.

a poor thing. See *Misquotation.*

Apostrophe. See *Contractions; Plural and Singular; Possessives.*

apparent. Often criticized in contexts like "The man died of an apparent heart attack," a usage common in newspapers. Critics say sentences like this are ambiguous, though no one misunderstands that the intention is "A heart attack apparently was the cause of death." Even so, exact statement is a good thing to practice.

appear. Often ambiguous with an infinitive, and to be avoided in sentences like "The budget was approved after no one appeared to protest," which can be taken to mean either that no protesters appeared or that statements made about the budget apparently were not protests.

appendix, appendices, appendixes. Either *appendices* (the Latin form) or *appendixes* is correct; in nontechnical contexts, *-ixes* probably predominates, three critics conclude. Random House and Webster recognize both forms as standard.

appoint. See *as.*

Appositives. The distinction between restrictive (or close) appositives, which are not set off by commas, and nonrestrictive appositives, which are, is often neglected. An example: "He had been married to his wife Ethel for twenty-six years. Their daughter, Eve, is married to a Harvard man." Since Ethel was the only wife, the name should have been set off by commas. Setting off *Eve* indicates she was the only daughter; "their daughter Eve is married . . ." would have indicated the existence of other daughters. See also *Dangling Modifiers; Modifiers 1; False Titles; Restrictive and Nonrestrictive Clauses.*

appraise, apprise. Often confused, especially *appraise* with *apprise. Appraise* means *set a value on,* as "appraise a property"; *apprise* (usually with *of*) means *inform, tell,* or *notify,* as "apprise him of danger" and "apprise us of developments." "I don't care to comment," the lawyer said, "until I have been appraised of the circumstances." *apprised.* Dictionary definitions corroborate the distinction.

appreciate. Approved by five authorities in the sense *be grateful for* ("We appreciated the favor"). Evans inexplicably considers it grudging and dishonest, and Flesch calls it overworked. Traditionalists regard this use as an illegitimate extension of the sense *notice:* "He appreciated her charms." Fowler criticizes as overdone the use of the word in the sense *understood:* "It is appreciated that . . ." especially in business correspondence.

apprise. See *appraise, apprise.*

apropos. Takes *of,* or no preposition at all, not *to:* "This comment is apropos to the controversy." *of.* Fowler warns against confusion of the term with *appropriate; apropos* means *pertinent, with reference to; appropriate* means *suitable, fitting.*

approximately. Criticized by Flesch as pretentious and by Follett as inappropriate for *about;* Fowler calls it the formal displacement of *about,* and adds that it connotes more precision. Webster gives *about* as a synonym. The consensus is that when *about* will do, it is preferable.

apt, liable, likely. *Apt* and *likely* are often used interchangeably in the sense *tend to:* "It's apt to be cold on the pier." Two critics recommend *apt* for the senses *fit* or *suited:* "His reply was sarcastic, but it was apt." Current dictionaries, however, equate *apt* with *likely,* the consensus is that they are interchangeable. *Liable* is often loosely used for *likely:* "At this rate, we are liable to win the award." But discriminating use generally applies *liable* only to what is undesirable: "An overheated radiator is liable to explode." Current dictionaries generally concur in this distinction, calling *likely* in such contexts colloquial or informal. *Liable* is also used in the sense *exposed to legal action:* "If a stair is broken, the landlord may be liable." Bernstein, Evans, and Harper concur in these general distinctions. See *liable, likely.*

Arab, Arabian, Arabic. *Arab* pertains to Arabs (*an Arab custom*), *Arabian* to Arabia, and *Arabic* to matters of language and writing (*Arabic numerals*). *Gum arabic* is an exception.

arbiter, arbitrator. Fowler says the arbiter has absolute power, whereas the arbitrator is answerable for his decision, but this is a British distinction. The terms are interchangeable in the U.S., dictionaries agree. *Arbitrator* is the usual term in labor disputes, and *arbiter* in other connections, e.g., fashions, philosophy, literature. See also *arbitrate, mediate*.

arbitrate, mediate. An arbitrator's decision is binding; the mediator merely attempts to help disputants come to an agreement, and has no authority over them. Evans discusses *arbitrator* as if it meant *mediator*.

arc, arch. Something needs to be done about the verb forms *arced* and *arcing*, but it's hard to say what. The verb *arc*, from which they come ("The power will arc across the lines"; "The demented assassin tried to arc his grenade close to the ministers' bench") is pronounced *ark*, but the *c* would ordinarily be soft in *arced* and *arcing*. This makes it seem as if the pronunciation should be *arsed* and *arsing*, which, of course, is not merely wrong but unseemly. Dictionaries give *arcking*, which solves the problem, as a variant spelling, but it is not used. By attempting to discourage the use of *arc* as a verb in this technological age, one would only be making an *arce* of himself. The answer in some contexts may be *arch*.

Archaisms. Should be avoided in ordinary contexts, especially by unpracticed writers. Some examples: *anent, aught, yclept, derring-do, howbeit, parlous, perchance, betwixt, quoth, spake, betimes, illume, forsooth*.

area. Criticized by three authorities as a vague fad word displacing *field, problem, issue, question*. "But the whole area has been clouded with misunderstanding." *issue, field. Area* in this and similar general senses where a more specific term is called for is pompous or careless and has become tiresome.

aren't I. See *ain't*.

are to, am to. See *Infinitives*.

argot, jargon. Argot is the language peculiar to a group, for example thieves' cant; jargon was originally unintelligible speech, but now the term is applied to a special vocabulary, for example of a profession, art, etc.

arithmetical, geometrical. Often inaccurately used with *progression* and *ratio*. An arithmetical progression is a sequence that grows by addition of the same quantity: 2, 4, 6, 8, for example, in which the added quantity is 2. A geometrical progression grows by multiplication by the same quantity; for example, 2, 4, 8, 16, in which the multiplier is 2.

armed with. Its figurative use, especially in newspaper journalism, has become a cliché. Literally, one who is armed has a weapon—a gun, club, perhaps only a pop bottle. *Armed with* has become an automatic substitute for *possessing, prepared with, carrying,* and other more appropriate expressions. Considering the bellicose connotation of *armed with,* it is surely objectionable to speak of a man winning new friends by being armed with a wide smile, or of a father going to his children armed with boxes of toys.

aroma. Properly applied only to a scent that is pleasant, and should not displace *odor* or *smell* unless the writer intends to be facetious.

around, about. *Around* is informal for *about* (*around three o'clock*), four authorities agree. On the other hand, three authorities give *around* for *about* as standard. The consensus is narrowly that the usage is informal. See also *all-around, all-round; round, around.*

arrant, errant. See *errant*.

arrest. It is sometimes assumed that an arrest consists in the mere act of being halted by a police officer. This assumption apparently arises from confusing different senses of *arrest*. One of them is simply *to stop:* "The hurtling boulder was arrested by a crevasse." The legal sense is something else; it is "to take or keep in custody."

When the issuance of a traffic ticket is described as an arrest the recipient suffers an undeserved indignity. In such instances it is more accurate and not unjustly derogatory to say that the suspect was given a summons or a ticket, or was cited.

art, state of. See *state of the art*.

artful, artistic. *Artful* is a synonym for *artistic,* and in another sense means devious or crafty, like Dickens' Artful Dodger. *Artistic* means only *possessing the quality of art: an artistic arrangement of flowers; artistic ability.* Dictionaries give both senses for *artful,* but the tendency is to avoid it in the sense *artistic.*

article. Often loosely, sometimes misleadingly, applied to short pieces, particularly editorials, signed columns, and letters to the editor. An article is a piece of nonfictional prose that does not fall into some more specific category like those named, especially with respect to newspaper journalism. See also *piece.*

Articles. See *a, an; Appositives; the.*

artisan, artist. "These works are without malice or hatred despite the virtually insufferable bigotry that surrounded their artisans." The context showed unmistakably that the writer thought *artisan* is a synonym for *artist,* but this is not so, though it once was. *Artisan* for *artist* is now obsolete; *artisan* denotes a lower order of creator, usually what we might otherwise refer to as a craftsman. Webster gives us, for *artisan,* "one trained to manual dexterity or skill in a trade."

as. Unnecessary and unidiomatic as a preposition after such verbs as *named, appointed, elected:* "He was appointed as vicar." *appointed vicar. As* should be used with care in attribution; it identifies the writer with the statement attributed, and thus is a form of editorializing. "As he explained, the technique of flying had been the big thing for too long." The effect of this is that the writer or the publication agrees. See also *as . . . as, so . . . as; as* vs. *because, since; as* (prep.); *as (so) far as; as follows; as how; as if, as though; as is, as are; as is well known; as* vs. *like; as long (far) as, so long (far) as; as of; as regards; as such; as though; as to; as well as; as with; Attribution 8.*

as . . . as, so . . . as, not so . . . as. The second *as* of the pair *as . . . as* is sometimes carelessly omitted. "The critic said the play was as good or better than last season's hits." *as good as.* "He likes to be known as a philosopher as much as a theologian" lacks an essential *as.* Filling out the construction would give "He likes to be known as a philosopher as much as as a theologian." The third *as* is required to complete the comparison, and the fourth is the preposition that is needed with *theologian.* As revised, of course, this sentence is impossible; it might be called half-*as*'d despite its abundance of *ases.* The only cure here is recasting: "He likes to be known equally as a philosopher and as a theologian." *So* is not necessarily required in a negative statement: "The moon is not so large as it was last night." *not as large* is equally acceptable, although this point was a shibboleth among English teachers a generation or two ago, like the myths that a sentence may not end in a preposition and that an infinitive may not be split. Six authorities agree that in a positive statement, *as . . . as* is preferable to *so . . . as*: "This leader is likely to run the show as (not *so*) long as he lives." Bernstein and American Heritage hold that locutions like "His word was good as his bond" require *as good;* Evans considers it acceptable to drop the first *as.*

as, because, since (causal *as*). *As* for *since* or *because* is avoided in careful writing; partly, perhaps, because sometimes it may be confused with *while* or *during the time that,* but mostly because it grates on the well-tuned ear as unidiomatic. "As the door was locked, he turned and walked away" is ambiguous, for *as* may be understood as conveying either "while the door was being locked" or "because the door was locked." "Porter's design is called the Revised Springfield, as he made it while living in Springfield, Mass." *because* or *since.* Fowler accepts *as* if it comes early in the sentence, apparently a British usage. Five critics object, but Bryant, Evans, and Webster consider the causal *as* standard. The consensus is that it is unidiomatic and objectionable.

as everyone knows. See *of course.*

as (so) far as . . . is concerned. It has become a journalistic mannerism, or perhaps inadvertency, to omit *is* (or *are*) *concerned* from this construction: "Many of the nation's gridiron experts have nothing to say as far as candidates for the All-America squad." Add *are concerned.* Flesch and Fowler discourage the whole expression as an unnecessary inflation in such sentences as "The increase in price does not seem to have had any effect as far as the customers are concerned." *on the customers.* Those who have trouble filling out the *as far as* construction might consider *as for* or *as to* instead. Often *about* or *concerning* suffices.

as follows. Always in the singular, authorities agree; never *as follow*. The idiom is inflexible no matter how many items follow: "The tools used by the mason are as follows: the trowel, the plumb line, the level, and the groover."

as for. See *as to*.

as good (as) or better. See *as . . . as,* etc.

as how. Substandard for *that* ("He explained as how the pump was broken"). Bernstein includes *being as how* and *seeing as how* (for *since* or *considering that*) in the same category. The expressions have a quaint, possibly rural, flavor.

Asian, Asiatic. *Asiatic* has a derogatory connotation, four authorities agree. American editors settled on *Asian flu* in preference to *Asiatic flu* when this doubtful import arrived some years ago, perhaps with the commendable purpose of not affronting the exporters for something they could not help.

as if, as though. Interchangeable and must be followed by the conditional form of the verb in a statement contrary to fact: "The liquor tastes as if it were (not *was*) watered," two critics agree. Flesch flatly dissents and cites a long list of examples, apparently from newspapers, using the indicative. It is hardly arguable that *was* is driving *were* out of such sentences even in well-edited, educated expression. See also *Subjunctive; like, as 2* for the substitution of *like* for *as if, as though*.

as is, as are (than is, than are), etc. Making a comparison by putting *as* or *than* in front of a misplaced verb is both artificial and unnecessary: "The defendant (as did everyone in the courtroom) knew the verdict was coming." Clumsy and unnatural, though often found in the press. *The defendant, like everyone else . . .* "The president is probably as popular as was his predecessor after his first month in office." *as his predecessor was after . . . .* "Obviously the people of the United States are as anxious as are the people of Russia for peace and friendship." Drop the second *are*.

as, like. See *like, as*.

as is well known. See *of course*.

as long (far) as, so long as. Bryant finds the forms used with about equal frequency: "I have no objection as (so) long as it's a step forward"; "As (so) far as he knew, the matter was closed." Evans considers *as long as* unacceptable for *since* in formal writing: "As long as it's raining, we may as well stay home." Bryant, however, cites reputable examples of its use, as well as of *so long as,* which she reports occurs less often. Both Random House and Webster give *as long as* as standard; Webster also gives *so long as,* quoting Bertrand Russell in an example.

as of. Sometimes criticized as a pomposity or a legalism in constructions like *as of the first of the month.* Three authorities say it can easily be omitted or avoided by using other prepositions; in the example, *on.* All criticize *as of now,* variously suggesting *now, right now, at present* instead.

as regards. See *regard.*

assaulted. See *attacked.*

assay, essay. Sometimes confused as verbs. To assay is to analyze or evaluate; to essay is to attempt.

assess. The word means *evaluate,* or *impose a levy upon,* and thus is misused in the simple sense *impose,* as "A jail sentence was assessed"; dictionaries corroborate this view.

assist, assistance. Should not displace the plainer *help,* two critics hold.

associated with. See *affiliated with.*

as such. Sometimes used meaninglessly: "The horse, as such, played an important role in the development of civilization." In such instances, there is no possibility that what is modified by *as such* is being considered in any other role than its own. The test of its utility is to leave it out and decide whether anything has been lost.

as, such as. See *such as.*

assume, presume; assumption, presumption. The first are tentative, the second more positive, two critics hold.

assure. Takes an object, dictionaries agree: "The United States, the president assured, will always be willing to discuss the situation." *assured the gathering,* or whatever. See also *ensure, assure.*

Asterisk (*). Used to indicate a footnote; placed at the end of what is footnoted and at the beginning of the footnote, though it is sometimes mistakenly supposed that it should come at the beginning of the footnoted sentence. Sometimes asterisks ("little stars") are used to indicate omission of material (that is, ellipsis) but three spaced periods are now universally used for this purpose. *Asterisk* is sometimes mispronounced *asterik,* and consequently thus misspelled. The correct version will be remembered by those who have heard the following slightly vulgar verse:

Mary bought an aeroplane
　Among the clouds to frisk
Now wasn't she a plucky girl
　Her little * ?

as vs. that. "I don't know as I can come." *whether, that, if.* American Heritage calls this displacement improper except in deliberately informal contexts. It appears, however, to be a regionalism.

as the crow flies. A cliché and an archaism, two critics hold.

as though. See *as if, as though.*

as to, as for. Useful to focus attention at the beginning of a sentence on some element that would otherwise have to be postponed: "As to Jones, his conduct was unexceptionable," three critics agree. *As to* is often superfluous: "There is some question as to who came in next," five authorities agree. *As to whether* is perhaps the most frequent offender: "There was some question as to whether he had eaten dinner." *whether. As to* is also criticized for fuzzily displacing other prepositions, including *about* or *concerning* ("There was some doubt as to the proper pitch" *of;* "peculiar ideas as to conduct" *about;* "The children were lectured as to behavior" *on*). Bryant concludes that *as to, as to whether,* and similar expressions are standard even though they add nothing. Bernstein says it is a superstition that *as to* is preferable to *as for; as for,* in fact, seems to predominate. American Heritage equates them. All this seems like much ado about (or as to) very little.

astronomical. Overused and inappropriate to convey the idea of a large number, three authorities agree. "The odds against detection in the act are astronomical." Dictionaries, however, give this usage as standard.

as was (we) discussed. This is a common infelicity ("The budget is inadequate, as was discussed at the last meeting"). The objection to it lies in the fact that *discuss* is treated as an intransitive verb. And common usage, following the lead of all dictionaries (or vice versa), gives *discuss* as transitive (that is, requiring an object: "We discussed the problem").

as well as. This connective does not change the number of the verb: "John as well as Jane was (not *were*) late for dinner." See *with.*

as with. See *like 3.*

at about. Criticized by three authorities as redundant for *about* ("At about 6 p.m."). Evans defends the phrase on the ground that *at* is often followed by *almost, nearly, exactly,* and so why not *about?* Follett points out that *at about* is sometimes inescapable: "The meat was sold at about $2 a pound." Bryant concludes that *at about* is normal in informal contexts, even when *at* may be omitted without changing the sense, and, like Evans, compares it with *at almost, at around, at approximately,* and *at exactly.* The consensus appears to be that it is most open to criticism in reference to time of day.

athletic, -ics. See *-ic, -ics.*

at vs. in. Three critics agree that there is no workable rule to govern the choice in such expressions as *in* (*at*) San Francisco, *at* (*in*) *the Municipal Auditorium.* Often the prepositions are interchangeable, and when they are not, idiom rather than any definable principle controls the choice. One critic warns that such constructions as "Where is the ball at?" are ungrammatical because *at* requires an object and *where,* as an adverb, cannot serve. American Heritage points out that *where . . . from* is acceptable but says that *where . . . at* and *where . . . to* are not. See also *where . . . at.*

at present, at the present time. The second is excessive for the first and both are excessive for *now,* unless a contrast with some other time is being pointed. Any indication of time is often unnecessary in a sentence whose verb is in the present tense. See *presently.*

attacked. Before greater candor in language invaded the printed page, *attacked* was a euphemism for *raped, sexually assaulted,* sometimes leading to absurd results: "The woman's arm was broken, her ear cut off, and her cheek slashed, but she had not been attacked." Fowler has a similar example (under *Euphemism*) in which the word is *assaulted.* But in these blunt days such glossing over is seldom encountered. The British, John Moore relates in *You English Words,* have their own peculiarities in this connection: "I read, let us say, that the body of a 'partially clad' young woman has been found in a lonely quarry, and that she has 'apparently died from strangulation' after having been 'interfered with' (one of the most horrible euphemisms in the English language today)."

at that. In the sense *nevertheless, even so, notwithstanding* ("The car cost $12,000 and did not run well at that"), approved by Fowler and Webster. Sometimes confused with *with that* (*at that point, as a consequence, then*): "They told him he was not qualified for the job. With that [not *at that*] he jammed on his hat and left."

at the rear of. Clumsy for *behind.*

at this point, etc. One of the newest of the pomposities is *at this point* (sometimes *moment*) *in time,* which inexplicably displaces *now.* It expresses the bureaucrat's yearning to complicate and fatten up the simple, in an attempt to suggest profundity and importance. It is as if "at this particular point of the earth's surface" were to displace *here,* and no one would be surprised if it did in government prose. John Dean, one of the witnesses at the Watergate hearings, is often given credit (or castigated) for having popularized *at this point in time* among millions of unthinking but admiring television watchers. Of course, he also aroused a storm of protest, but it had the usual effect in such instances—none that could be detected.

atop. Use of the word as a preposition is called journalese by Evans (*atop the mountain*), and other criticisms of this construction are occasionally heard. The disapproval apparently arises from the fact that this was once an American usage, not ordinarily heard in Britain. But no current dictionary questions *atop* as a preposition, not even the British Concise Oxford Dictionary.

attorney, lawyer. An attorney is not necessarily a lawyer, but merely one who has been authorized to act for another; that is, one who has been given power of attorney. In the U.S. *attorney* is the genteel word for *lawyer*, the workaday term for one who is licensed to practice law. Most lawyers thus prefer to be referred to as attorneys, and newspapers, often sedulously deferential in these matters, cater to them. There are lawyers who unpretentiously announce themselves as such on their shingles, and there are also newspapers that shun on principle any word intended to confer a specious dignity. See also *council,* etc.

attorney general. See *general.*

attractive. Criticized by two authorities as the journalistic catchall for *beautiful, comely, lovely, handsome, good-looking* in reference to women. Yet a woman described as attractive may not be pretty but may attract by her charm alone. *Attractive,* in fact, is a tame substitute for *pretty, beautiful,* etc. Women, who seem fondest of using it, may be choosing the word subsconsciously as a means of giving credit where it is due with one hand and watering it down with the other. *Handsome* may properly be applied to a woman as well as to a man, contrary to some ideas, but it suggests elegance more than beauty. *Comely* and *fair* are now quaint. See also *beauteous.*

Attribution. 1. Inversion in attribution. Such forms as *said he, declared she, asserted Smith* are a tiresome device for gaining variety in structure. Fowler said the writer who employs it makes a damning admission that he is afraid of boring his readers. His reviser, Gowers, has decided that inversion with *said, replied,* or any other inconspicuous word is now all right as long as the attribution comes at the end of the sentence. Evans considers the normal order (*he said*) preferable. *Said he* has a faintly poetic or literary flavor that makes it unsuitable for ordinary prose, and in any event attracts attention to itself, which is ordinarily considered undesirable.

2. Misleading attribution. Some ill-advised forms of attribution have the effect of associating the writer or the publication in which they appear with the statement being made. *Pointed out* implies that the statement is factual: "The senator has an ugly record of broken promises, his opponent pointed out." So do *as he said, admitted, noted, conceded, explained,* and *cited the fact that,* which should be used only in reference to verifiable statements, not accusations or derogatory comments. "A young TV comedian admitted in New York that all funnymen are sick and desperately in need of psychoanalysis." The effect here is not so much that the writer agrees as that the speaker is stating a generally accepted fact. There was no occasion for *admitted,* because the point of view was a novel one. Possessives carelessly used may have the same effect: "The couple were indicted as spies by a grand jury but have denied their guilt." *Their* convicts them; *denied guilt. According to* (like *said he believes*) may suggest doubt of credibility; apart from this, it is a clumsy and overworked displacement of *reported, announced, said. Disclose* and *reveal* are appropriate only in reference to what has been concealed. It is obviously stupid to speak of some commonplace event, such as a weekly Rotary club luncheon, as *revealed; announced.* See also *as.*

3. Excessive attribution. In giving the substance of reports it seems superfluous to obtrude *the report said* or something of the kind in every statement unless it is questionable or damaging. An occasional reminder that the reader is getting the substance of a report should suffice.

4. Utterance by proxy. The purported utterance of words by smiling, grimacing, frowning, laughing, and otherwise than speaking is criticized by three authorities: " 'Romance seems to be out of fashion these days,' he grimaced"; " 'I'd rather work from the neck up,' the actress smiled"; " 'This equipment is not included in the budget,' the auditor frowned." Fowler traced this idiosyncrasy back to Meredith, and cited examples including *husked, fluted, defended,* and *surrendered.* This appears to be a variation of what Ruskin described as the pathetic fallacy—ascribing lifelike acts to inanimate things, such as having the sun smile. Fowler also criticized some words that come closer to indicating utterance, such as *scorned* and *denied.* Flesch cites *blushed, needled, dimpled, tch-tched, shrugged.* The ultimate may have been reached by an example quoted in *The New Yorker:* "He shrugged over the phone." Writers who employ this mannerism should be aware that it is conspicuous and regarded by many as tiresome. It has been taken up by the press, which, as Fowler said in another connection, has not yet ceased to find it beautiful. The alternative is *he said, grimacing; she said, smiling.* Those who use this device must be prepared to defend themselves against the logical, though perhaps hairsplitting and pedantic, complaint that words cannot be formed by smiling, frowning, etc. In any event, it is harmless, since no one is misled.

5. Speech tags. The term is a journalistic expression for phrases that attribute: *he said,* etc. Quotations should not be broken into awkwardly with them: "I," the producer said, "will not accept this responsibility." This not only interrupts at an undesirable place but also lays meaningless stress on *I.* But unpracticed writers consider this device clever. "We have never," the curator of birds said, "had any previous complaint about our pelicans biting people." The writer fancied, perhaps, that his awkward insertion of the speech tag afforded some humor. The attribution of an extensive quotation should come early, however; no later than the end of the first sentence.

Insertion of speech tags in every paragraph of a continuing direct quotation is excessive and annoying: " 'The toughest place to cross is the Southwest,' a leader of the expedition said. 'Towering mountains and the distances between communities pose particular problems,' he said." The last attribution should be omitted. One attribution in a continuing quotation is enough; if it is extremely long, an occasional reminder is acceptable.

6. Needless attribution. Troubles with attribution among journalists often have their root in police and court stories, where there is particular danger of libel. The young reporter quickly learns that damaging statements must be ascribed to the authorities, or to privileged documents. The danger, both moral and legal, of aspersing someone on the writer's say-so is impressed on the reporter so unforgettably that he comes to think of attribution as a great virtue, to be practiced whenever possible. In fact, it can be irksome, and like other rules blindly followed, it often carries writers overboard: "Highway patrolmen said the car skidded 80 feet before striking the truck, which, they said, was parked on the shoulder." Can anyone reasonably hold that the first *said* will not easily carry the weight of all that follows? It sounds absurd to attribute bits of general information, but one school of thought insists on attributing *everything* in police stories: " 'The lake is about 20 miles from Hilltown and about 12 miles in circumference,' the officers said." This suggests to the reader that the publication has no confidence in any part of the information. Such supercaution might easily result in "The sun rose on schedule, according to the investigator."

Accounts of crimes in which no arrest has been made hardly need more than one citation of the source, for an unnamed burglar or whatever cannot be libeled. Similarly, the fact of an arrest is a matter of public record, and needs no qualification. Consider "Officers George Hamilton and Walter Schroeder said the dancer was arrested on a charge of indecent exposure." The names of the officers in such contexts is often superfluous unless the publication is currying favor with them.

7. Doubled attribution. "The secretary and his associates were criticized for what the committee said were 'political and other considerations.' " Either *what the committee said* or the quotation marks suffice. "Truman told reporters that his memoirs will explain what he said was the part Eisenhower played in the incident." *what he said was* is superfluous.

8. Unsuitable attributives. *Advise, contend,* and *claim* are sadly overworked and at the same time inexactly used in attribution. *Advise,* as in "The meeting will be postponed, he advised," is journalese. *Contend* is suitable only where there is contention or disagreement, and *insist* only where there is insistence. *Claim* may excusably be used in headlines for *say* or *assert,* but in text, where there is no space problem, it is questionable. (See *claim.*) "The informant claimed he did not know the name of his source." *Stress* and *emphasize* are suitable only where there is indeed stress or emphasis, not as random displacements of *said.*

Much hinges on the choice between *as* and *for* in certain attributive constructions. To say that one was criticized *for committing perjury* is to say the perjury was committed; *as committing perjury,* on the other hand, places the burden of proof on the accuser.

9. *Said* and its variants. Not many years ago it was the journalistic custom to use *said* in the first of a series of quoted statements, after which it was discarded as used up. Next came *asserted,* then perhaps *averred, asseverated* (seldom called into play because nobody was quite sure what it meant), *declared,* and of course that old standby, *stated.* These and a few others, perhaps *opined* (now quaint) were enough to see a reporter though most interviews. If not, it was considered legal to start over again with *said,* the theory being that the reader would not realize by that time that he was getting a warmed-over word. The point was not to use *said* or any of the others twice, or at least twice in succession. The variants were dropped in automatically, as if they all meant the same thing. No consideration was given the possibility that one or another might be the most appropriate with a given quotation.

A distinguished editor, citing an example of a substitute that produced a misleading, not to say damaging, statement, said (or perhaps declared), "There never was a better word than *said.*" This enthusiasm, while understandable under the circumstances, may have been excessive.

The best word is probably different for every quotation, although it must be conceded that *said* is no doubt the most useful for ordinary, conversational statements. Sometimes the best word may be *roared* or it may be *mumbled. Stated,* for reasons unknown, is a great favorite among young writers. The more experienced eschew it as having too formal a tone for most purposes. *Said,* in fact, even when repeated, is common coin that the reader does not notice, and thus the writer's exertion to find variants is wasted.

Here are some words that can stand duty for *said* when they fit: *admitted, admonished, affirmed, agreed, avowed, barked, begged, bellowed, called, chided, contended, cried, croaked, declaimed, demanded, disclosed, drawled, emphasized, entreated, exclaimed, hinted, implored, insisted, maintained, mumbled, murmured, muttered, pleaded, proclaimed, proposed, rejoined, retorted, roared, scolded, shouted, shrieked, yelled, wailed.*

Some variants are uncomplimentary to the speaker, but they may be called for in an accurate account: *grumbled, insinuated, prated, ranted, spouted, stammered, whined, whimpered.* Then there are a number of neutral substitutes for *said: added, announced, answered, asserted, commented, continued, declared, observed, remarked, replied, retorted, responded, returned.*

According to is often considered objectionable because it can be understood as implying doubt of the speaker when no such doubt is intended.

audience. By derivation, an audience would be listeners only (*a radio audience*); Bernstein would limit the term to those who are both listeners and spectators, e.g., a circus audience. Two other critics allow it to be applied to spectators alone. But the word is approved for listeners, spectators, and even readers of a book by four authorities and most dictionaries. The consensus overwhelmingly approves the broader application: watchers, hearers, readers.

audit. Criticized by one authority when it displaces *listen* or *hear.* No dictionary recognizes this sense, though undeniably it appears in print. American Heritage gives "an audience or hearing," but this is not the same thing. *Audit* as a verb for *hear* has a journalistic twang.

aught. Archaic in modern contexts and thus, perhaps, pretentious.

augment (supplement). Augmentation is addition of more of the same thing; thus rain may augment a stream but, in contradiction to Random House, commissions may not augment a salary, but rather supplement it, since the salary itself is not increased. A hairsplitting distinction.

au naturel. Oftenest used as a synonym, or perhaps a euphemism, for *naked,* and sometimes misspelled *au natural.* The writer who resorts to foreign expressions is often showing off, or suspected of doing so, and must take special care at least to get them right.

auspices. "Under the auspices of," commonly used to describe simple sponsorship of an event by an organization, is pompous. *Auspices* has to do with "protection, patronage, and care" and derives from the superstition of omens seen in the flight of birds. Instead of "The bazaar will be under the auspices of the Young

People's League," it is preferable to say "The Young People's League will sponsor [give, hold] the bazaar."

authentic, genuine. Two critics concede that they are often synonyms, but also offer examples of distinctive uses. No attempt will be made to strain the reader's powers of discrimination by giving examples here; the distinctions are too finely drawn. The most useful conclusion seems to spring from Fowler's comment that the difference is artificial and is far from universally observed (he means, of course, by discriminating writers). When a distinction is necessary, the right word will probably come by instinct. No one would call a novel genuine, rather than authentic, for example, in describing its fidelity to historical background. The words are given as synonyms in dictionaries.

author. Disapproved as a verb ("He authored several books") by five authorities but considered standard by Random House and Webster. The consensus is that books are written, not authored.

authoress. See *Feminine Forms*.

authoritative. Sometimes misspelled *authoritive* or *authorative*.

automation, mechanization. Automation does not mean simply the substitution of hand labor by machinery; it refers, rather, to the automatic control of machines. A thermostatically controlled heating system is an example of automation; a mechanical coal stoker that does the work of a man is not. Dictionary definitions bear this out. Fowler complains that both *automate* and *automation* are barbarisms (that is, words improperly formed) but concedes it's too late now to do anything about it

avenge, revenge, vengeance. In general, *avenge* and *vengeance* have to do with justice and legal process; *revenge* with getting even, four authorities agree.

aver. Objectionable as a variant of *say*. American Heritage gives "to declare in a dogmatic or positive manner."

average, median, mean. Sometimes loosely interchanged. The average of a group of quantities is their sum divided by the number in the group; the average of 6, 10, 14, and 2 (which add up to 32) is 8 (32 divided by 4). The median of a set of quantities is the one above which and below which an equal number of quantities occur; if the median pay rate is $4.30, there are as many rates higher than $4.30 as lower. The mean, in ordinary use, is the midpoint; the mean temperature on a day when the maximum was 90 and the minimum 60 would be 75. In nonstatistical use, Evans says, *average* should not be used as a synonym for *common, ordinary, typical,* or *mean,* and adds that *common* or *ordinary man* should be used instead of *average man.* Two other critics say, however, that *average* is commonly used to mean *ordinary* or *typical,* a judgment concurred in by dictionaries.

averse. See *adverse.*

avert, avoid, prevent. *Avoid* sometimes usurps the place of *avert* or *prevent,* when *keep from happening* is the sense wanted. "The firemen fought to avoid flying sparks setting fire to neighboring roofs." *to prevent . . . from.* "No expedient could have avoided the flood after the dam broke." *averted, prevented. Avoid* has the sense of *sidestep.* This view is borne out by dictionaries.

aviatrix. Now rare; the last aviatrix, perhaps, was the unfortunate Amelia Earhart. See *Feminine Forms.*

avoid. See *avert,* etc.

aw. See *ah, aw.*

away back. See *way back.*

away, way. See *way, away.*

aweigh. See *under way.*

awful(ly). Through the frequent use of *awful* to describe what is merely unpleasant or disagreeable, and of *awfully* for *very,* the words have been devalued from their original sense of awe-inspiring ("The weather is awful"; "We were awfully cold") authorities agree. American Heritage does not even give the original sense. It may yet be necessary to spell the word *aweful* to restore its original sense, as one writer did in referring to "The aweful powers of the presidency." Thus does the wheel of corruption come full circle. Other words have suffered a like fate, such as *dreadful(ly),* *terrible (-bly).* The looser sense of these terms was given at the end of a long list of the original ones in the Century Dictionary (1889), a massive work that is as close as America has come to the formidable OED. The looser senses were labeled "colloquial and vulgar."

awhile, a while. Often confused. *Awhile* is an adverb—"We loafed awhile"—and *a while* are article and noun—"We loafed for a while." This makes *a while* wrong in the first example and *awhile* wrong in the second. Flesch concludes that *awhile* for *a while* is establishing itself, and Evans admits that the confusion is widely reprobated but is indulgent toward it. Webster regards the interchange as standard but the consensus favors the distinction.

awoke, etc. *Awoke, awakened, awaked, wakened,* and *woke* are equivalent and standard.

ax, axe. *Axe* is the British preference.

B

baby boy, girl. Sometimes objected to in references to births on the ground that *baby* is redundant.

Back-Formation. This term, which appears occasionally in this book, describes the formation of a word from what is mistakenly assumed to be its derivative. Generally it applies to verbs formed from nouns: *donate* from *donation, sculpt* from *sculptor, drowse* from *drowsy*. Such terms are objectionable only when new and recognizable as back-formations; many, like the examples, have long since graduated to standard usage. The process is continuous, and usefulness is what wins back-formations acceptance.

background. Criticized by two authorities as pretentious for *origin, cause, reason, qualifications, history,* or some other more precise term. The popularity and usefulness of *background*, however, is such that few are likely to be influenced by such criticism.

backlash. In its new sense of an antagonistic reaction, for example to aspects of the civil rights or women's movements, considered informal by one critic but standard by American Heritage, by the most recent abridgment of Webster III, and by Webster's New World. The citations in Barnhart also indicate it is standard.

back of, in back of. Generally discouraged in the sense *behind;* Bryant says both forms have moved from colloquial to informal standing, but that *behind* is still preferred in formal prose. Random House calls both informal. Webster considers *back of* colloquial and *in back of* standard; Evans considers both standard.

back yard, backyard. American Heritage is the only dictionary that notes the odd fact that this term has frequently become one word in recent years, although the conventions of pronunciation then require it to be pronounced *back'yard*. It is not actually pronounced that way, however, but rather as two words with equal stress. American Heritage gives both forms but enters the two-word version first, indicating that it predominates; this is now questionable. The defense of *backyard* would justify *frontyard*, but this form is unknown. The same reasoning applies to *home town* vs. *hometown*. A case can be made out, however, for both *backyard* and *hometown* when they are used as modifiers (*a backyard incinerator, a hometown hero*) because then the stress shifts to *back* and *home*.

bad, badly. *Bad* as an adverb for *seriously, severely* ("He was beaten up bad"; "Her head ached bad") is disapproved by three authorities; Random House labels it informal. Four authorities approve *badly* for *very much* (*badly in need of repair*). *Badly* (and *painfully*) are sometimes criticized in such phrases as *badly injured*, on the ground that an injury cannot be anything but bad (i.e., undesirable) and thus the phrases are ·redundant. But this is pedantry; *badly* in this context equals *severely*. See also *feel bad, badly*.

bad off. Considered standard, surprisingly, together with *badly off,* by Random House and Webster in such contexts as "The town isn't as bad off as many of us like to think."

bail, bale. *Bail* means to *dip water out of* or *post a bond; bale* means to tie in a bundle. Boats and prisoners are bailed; hay is baled. Fowler says British usage prefers *bale* for dipping water and for jumping from an airplane; the American form for the latter is *bail* (*out*).

balance. Discouraged in the sense *rest* or *remainder* in nonfiscal contexts: "The balance (to concoct a ludicrous example) is silence." This is one of the usages that the editors of American Heritage approved in the face of rejections (53 percent) by its own Usage Panel; Harper also approves. Webster gives *remainder* as a standard sense; Random House concludes there is still a shadow over it in the general sense. Five critics disapprove; the consensus is heavily against it.

balding (growing bald). A neologism, said to have been coined by *Time,* and denounced by one critic as needless. Six authorities, however, accept it without cavil.

baleful, baneful. American Heritage calls attention to the distinction that *baleful* means *malevolent, hateful: a baleful expression. Baneful* applies usually to poison, or what is otherwise destructive or ominous. It is not easy to differentiate the definitions in Webster, but the words are not given as synonyms. *Baneful,* in any event, is a rarity.

band, orchestra. See *orchestra, band.*

bank, banker. Improperly applied to savings and loan institutions (whose loans are restricted by law to real property) and their officials. Savings and loan institutions are very sensitive to the distinction, and in some states it is illegal to refer to them as banks. With respect to another sense of *bank,* the left and right banks of a river are determined by imagining oneself as facing in the direction the water flows.

banquet. The term seems to be growing quaint, facing the same fate as *repast* and *collation;* at any rate, it is considered pretentious by three authorities for most large dinners.

baptismal name. Evans and Fowler make the point that this expression (as well as *Christian name*) is unsuitable for general use because of its religious basis. *First name* or *given name* sidesteps this difficulty. Fowler recommends *forename,* but this is a Briticism.

bar, saloon. The changes in American drinking habits and attitudes have been accompanied by changes in the words associated with them. Before Prohibition, which took effect in October, 1919, the place for public drinking was a saloon and nothing else. Its chief characteristics were swinging doors, a free lunch, and a clientele that was exclusively male (though some saloons had "family rooms" in the rear, where mixed groups could drink more or less privately, or at least out of sight of the bar). Those were the days when a boy could be sent out with a bucket to fetch some beer.

Saloon, just a neutral designation at one time, was successfully associated by the dry, or Prohibition, interests with disreputability, low-lifes, "Father, dear Father, come home with me now" and that sort of thing. Perhaps because of this propaganda, *saloon* became undignified, if not derogatory, and in some states its use to designate a place of business is forbidden by law. On the other hand, its revival by the legal gambling resorts of Nevada, prompted perhaps by its Old West flavor, has had a refreshing effect, at least to those who prefer calling a spade a spade.

In spite of its more or less low estate, *saloon* has a more or less distinguished ancestry. It developed from the French *salon,* meaning a reception room or hall, especially in a palace or great house. Later the term was extended to the gatherings of literati and other intellectuals that were conducted by French ladies of fashion in such rooms.

Saloon at one time had other applications than to a drinking place. People once spoke of the dining saloon aboard a ship, for example (it is now a *salon*). By the time Prohibition was repealed in 1933 *saloon,* in reference to a bar, was in such bad odor that its general revival was out of the question, especially from the standpoint of businessmen who opened bars. A great effort was made to popularize the word *tavern* for this purpose, but it never really caught on except in the names of establishments, and these were mostly what were (and still are) referred to in the vernacular as *beer joints.*

Cocktail lounge is rather specialized, calling to mind a somewhat tony place, more likely to be frequented also by women. But the word-of-all-work for a drinking establishment today seems to have become *bar,* which is equally and neutrally applicable up and down the scale of respectability.

Barbarism. A term sometimes applied by critics of usage to expressions that seem to them uncultivated. Fowler commented, "That barbarisms should exist is a pity. To expend much energy on denouncing those that do exist is a waste." To Fowler, a barbarism was a word improperly formed on its Latin or Greek roots, a consideration that most people would regard as laughable today. American Heritage finds confusion with *barbarity,* which means cruel behavior. Oddly, in using *waste* as he did, Fowler was anticipating by about a half-century what became a fad in America. An American would have said *waste of time,* or *of effort.*

barbecue, barbeque. Both are standard but the first predominates and is also closer to the generally assumed derivation (from the American-Spanish *barbacoa*).

barbiturate. Often misspelled *barbituate.*

barely. See *hardly.*

bar sinister. The correct form of the heraldic term to denote illegitimate birth is *band* or *baton sinister,* not *bar.* But considering the widespread use of the corruption, Fowler regards correction of it as pedantry; Evans recommends *bastard* instead, advice not likely to be widely followed, but more likely now than when it was given, in 1957. Random House calls *bar sinister* erroneous in this sense; Webster describes the popular interpretation as suppositious; American Heritage accepts it. Fowler's advice is sensible.

basal, basic. The original edition of Fowler (1926) pointed out that both words were relatively newly coined technical terms relating to botany, chemistry, and architecture, and recommended *fundamental* in other connections. The revised Fowler, however, together with three other authorities, concedes that *basic* is here to stay and is preferable in most contexts to the ponderous *fundamental.* One critic restricts *basal* to technical contexts (most commonly, *basal metabolism*); Random House agrees but Webster gives *basic* as a synonym of *basal.* See *on the basis of.*

base, bass. Sometimes confused; perhaps because *bass (deep-toned)* is pronounced *base.* "The adventure had the nation all but wired to its communication systems, listening for the next base-toned announcement." *bass,* unless the voice was ignoble. It's always *bass* in musical connections: *basses, bass viol, bass clarinet, bass clef.*

based on. See *Dangling Modifiers; on the basis of.*

basically. The correct form; *basicly,* though sometimes seen in print (like *incidently* and *accidently*) is unrecognized. The other two have found their way as variants into Webster but not into American Heritage or Random House.

basis. See *on the basis of.*

bastion. One critic says the term must be limited to a projection from a fortification, or a fortified outpost. Current dictionaries unanimously recognize a second general sense of *strong point* or *stronghold* or *fortified place* as exemplified by the common and figurative *bastion of democracy.*

bathroom. Often used in avoidance of *toilet,* which needs no euphemism. "Black children who are bused to schools in white neighborhoods are not allowed to eat lunch or go to the bathroom with white students." *toilet;* schools do not have bathrooms.

Battle of Waterloo. See *Misquotation.*

be advised. As used in business correspondence, a Victorian pomposity ("Be advised that nothing of the sort is contemplated"). It recalls "Yours of the 16th inst. received and contents noted."

B.C. See A.D.

beauteous. Decried by Flesch as an ugly, barbaric, unnecessary synonym for *beautiful.* Fowler in the original, on the other hand, described it as a poetic form suitable only for exalted contexts, and so does Harper. Webster defines it as stressing the sensual aspects of beauty; Random House considers it literary; American Heritage defines it as *visually beautiful.* The word has also been regarded as having a derogatory tinge. Perhaps no greater variety of connotations can be found for any word. When encountering it, the reader may suspect that *beautiful* has been sidestepped, and may assume that this has been done for a reason, perhaps to dilute the tribute.

beauty. The term has become popular in such constructions as "The beauty of the arrangement was that it was cheap," and one authority criticizes this use. Current dictionaries, however, give as standard senses of *beauty* "any very attractive feature," "a pleasing excellence," "the quality that pleases and gratifies." Webster cites "the beauty of this mathematical demonstration" and Random House has a corresponding example. The overriding consensus is that the extended sense, going beyond esthetics, is standard.

because. See *as vs. because; reason is because.*

become. See *get.*

behalf. Four authorities agree that in strict usage *on behalf* means *representing* or *as the agent of; in behalf* means *for the benefit* (or *advantage*) *of.* But the distinction has been blurred beyond recovery by indiscriminate use. It is preserved by Webster's New World and the American College Dictionary; the Standard College Dictionary says it tends to disappear in modern usage; Random House and Webster ignore the distinction, and so does British usage. It may be worth noting that the American Heritage panel's decision was one of its numerous photo-finishes; 58 percent voted for the traditional usage, the rest accepted the variants as having either of the senses given above. Partridge bemoaned disregard of the distinction. The consensus is that it has been done in, and the forms are now interchangeable.

being as how, being that. See *as how.*

belabor, labor (a point, question, etc.). Dictionaries agree that the forms are interchangeable.

believe. See *feel.*

bells. Landlubbers sometimes assume, in an effort to give a salty flavor to a piece of writing, that bells as the term is used on shipboard are the equivalent of hours; i.e., that six bells would be six o'clock. Bells formerly were sounded to divide four-hour watches into half-hour intervals, so that six bells would be eleven o'clock, three o'clock, etc.

belly. As applied to people, the word is unexceptionable but shunned as vulgar, somehow, four authorities agree. One critic holds that *stomach,* as an internal organ, is an inexact substitute, but Random House, Webster, and all current desk dictionaries give *stomach* as a synonym (though Webster's New World calls this application loose). Two critics admit *stomach* in this sense. *Abdomen* in place of *belly* is somewhat technical or clinical. *Tummy,* used by others than children, is deplored by three critics.

belong to. See *affiliated with.*

belt out (a song). A cliché.

benedict. The journalistic variant for *newly married man* or *bridegroom,* probably less used now than formerly, considering the diminished preoccupation of society pages with social events of limited interest except to the participants. Strictly, it should be *benedick,* from the character in *Much Ado About Nothing.* But *benedict* is well established.

benefit of clergy. The expression has two distinct senses: sanction of the church, generally by means of the marriage ceremony (as referred to in the title of Kipling's story); and the ancient privilege of the clergy to be tried in ecclesiastical courts.

berserk. See *amuck, berserk.*

beseeched, besought. One critic prescribes *beseeched* as the newer form, but this contradicts two others and observable usage, which is all but invariably *besought.* Random House does not give *beseeched* at all; American Heritage and Webster give *besought* as predominant.

beside, besides. *Beside* means *at the side of:* "We stood beside the river"; *besides* means *in addition to.* "Besides the lecture there was a concert."

bet, betted. Both forms are standard as the past tense for the word meaning *wager,* though *bet* tends to be preferred in the U.S., according to two critics and Random House. Webster equates them; one critic insists on *betted.*

bête noire. (From the French, *black beast;* something or someone to be feared or avoided.) Three authorities call *bete noir* an error, but that did not prevent Webster from accepting it as a variant spelling.

betted. See *bet, betted.*

better. Frequently criticized in the sense *more,* as *better than a week, better than fifty dollars.* This sense is recognized as standard, however, by all current dictionaries, including the Concise Oxford. American Heritage, while recording this sense, reports that 69 percent of its usage panel disapproved, as does Harper. *Better* for *had better* or *had best* ("You better take your umbrella") is described by two critics as informal, by another as unacceptable in writing, and by a third as an incipient idiom. The consensus is that it is not open to serious criticism. For *best* vs. *better* in comparison see *Comparison 3.* For *the better stores* see *Ad Lingo; Absolute Comparatives.*

between. 1. vs. *among.* No one would use *among* with only two objects ("among you and me") but there is a misguided though prevalent idea that *between* cannot be used with more than two: "Agreements were reached between six nations." The proper use of *between* does not depend on the number of objects but on whether they are being considered in pairs. Even this is open to question as an absolute rule; Follett insists on it. The OED specifies that *between* may be used of relations between two or more things: "It is still the only word available to express the relation of a thing to many surrounding things generally and individually; *among* expresses a relation to them collectively and vaguely." The preceding is a summarization of six views.

2. *Between you and I.* Considered questionable by one critic and wrong by four others and American Heritage; most of them concede that there are many (bad) examples of the expression in literary classics. By the standards of conventional grammar, of course, it *is* inescapably a blunder; the preposition *between* calls for an object in the accusative: *me.* But the recent acceptance of "It's me" for the strictly correct "It is I" no doubt has encouraged such deviations.

3. *Between each, every.* Considered unacceptable by five authorities and acceptable by one. Here, too, many classical authors are cited as having used the construction. The point, of course, is that *between* implies, if not demands, two objects; it is logically impossible to be between one. "Between each act there was an intermission." *between acts.*

4. *Between . . . and, to, or. And,* not *to* or *or,* follows *between* in such constructions as "Reporters on Florida newspapers were receiving between $150 to $200 weekly."

bi-. In such expressions as *biennially* and especially *bimonthly* and *biweekly, bi-* has become ambiguous; the reader cannot be sure whether it means *every two* or *twice a,* five authorities agree. It is safer to say *every two years* (*months, weeks,* etc.) or *twice a year,* or *semiannual(ly), semimonthly, semiweekly,* as appropriate.

American Heritage unassailably holds that *bi-* means *every two,* but since 16 percent of the panelists did not concur, the warning given here gains validity.

Bible, bible. Capitalized in reference to the Scriptures; lower-cased in the figurative sense of a fundamental reference work ("This book is the bible of woodworking.")

bid. The word has a number of senses; the one usually criticized is its use as a verb to mean *try* or *attempt,* often used in newspaper headlines: "Navy flight bids to save Russian." Unfortunately, headlinese tends to seep into text. Three authorities discourage *bid* in the sense *attempt;* Evans considers it standard. In the cited headline the exact sense would be given by *tries; bid* in the sense *try* or *attempt* would never be used in text. Note also "Scientist predicts next bid in 4 weeks." *Predicts next try* would have been better. *Bid* as a noun for *a try* or *an attempt* is ambiguous; we do not know whether the scientist is predicting an experimental attempt or a bid on a contract. Here too the idea would never have been expressed this way in text. The gist of it all is that *bid* cannot be used for *try* or *attempt* as either noun or verb without danger of ambiguity. Current dictionaries, including American Heritage, all recognize *bid* as a noun (as distinguished from a verb) for *attempt* without restriction ("A bid to succeed"); only American Heritage accepts it as a verb. The consensus is that *bid* for *attempt* as a verb is nonstandard.

In the sense of an offer or proposal, the form of the past and the participles is *bid;* (*has bid, had bid*); in other senses (*direct, command, tell*) the forms are *bade* and *bidden,* by analogy with *forbade* and *forbidden:* "We bade them farewell"; "The visitors were bidden to come in."

bid in. A technical term that means topping a bid on behalf of the owner of the property; sometimes mistakenly used as a synonym for *bid.*

billion. All the more regrettably these days when the term has come into such common use, it means different things in the United States, France, and Germany on the one hand, and Britain and its imitators in linguistic matters on the other. The American billion is a thousand million; the British, a million million. The American billion is the British milliard. The disparity persists throughout the names of other large numbers ending in -illion: trillion, quadrillion, quintillion. Both systems are detailed with the definition of *number* in Webster III.

birthday anniversary. Some stylebooks insist that one can have only one birthday—the day of his birth—and that recurrences of this date must be his *birthday anniversary.* The idea is pedantry, unsupported by either dictionaries or usage.

bit. As used in expressions like *the whole bit, the liberal bit,* meaning an instance of behavior, rejected as slang by four authorities. This expression comes from the world of the theater, where a piece of business is referred to as a bit; also, *bit part* (*a small role*). See *Theatrical Cant.*

bit, bitten. *Bit* is disapproved by American Heritage for the passive: "She was bit by mosquitoes." This judgment, however, does not appear to accord with cultivated expression, which is as likely to use *bit* as *bitten*.

bitch. A great injustice is done in using *bitch, bitchy, bitchiness* to denote ill nature. Any dog owner, and for that matter, any dog observer, knows that the qualities described by these terms as applied to women are unknown among dogs. True, a dog may be mad, or vicious, but who has ever seen or heard of one that showed the peculiar inherent meanness that we have in mind when we call a woman a bitch? It is undeniable that, on the whole, this would be a better world if people were more like dogs. When kindly treated, and often even when not, they show a devotion and loyalty that the human race might well emulate. The misapplication of *bitch* and its analogues to people can only be ascribed to the immoral principle of "give a dog a bad name and hang him." All of which calls to mind the haughty lady who was shopping for a pet. When the proprietor called her attention to "the bitch in the window," she stiffened. Sensing something amiss, he said, "Surely, madam, you are familiar with the term *bitch?*" "Certainly," she snapped, "but I've never heard it applied to dogs."

bivalve. Considered obligatory by some journalists as the second reference to *clam* or *oyster,* to avoid repetition of the word. But as Fowler observed, conspicuous variation to avoid repeating a term is worse than repetition. It attracts the reader's attention to the different form of reference, and may make him wonder why it was used.

black. An old term for *Negro,* in the past considered more or less derogatory. That connotation seems to have come from its use by whites, dating from the colonial era in Africa, to refer to native bearers and other servitors; at best, it was patronizing. Inexplicably, it was seized upon during the civil rights confrontations of the 1960s by many Negroes as the designation they preferred. At first, this preference was expressed mainly by militants, but Negroes later came to apply *black* more and generally to themselves. Some of them demanded that the term be used by others, and decided to see something derogatory in *Negro,* even though *Negro* means *black*. Before long, the term became a neutral variant of *Negro* and is now in general use in the press and otherwise, having all but put *Negro* out of business; at any rate, there is a noticeable tendency to shun *Negro*. *Negro* remained the preferred form among members of that race, according to a poll published by *Newsweek* in 1969. Thirty-eight percent of the sampling preferred *Negro,* 20 percent preferred *colored people,* and 19 percent preferred *blacks*. The terms liked least were *colored people* (31 percent) and *blacks* (25 percent). A poll taken today no doubt would show strikingly different results. The user, white or black, of *Negro* may well feel called upon to explain his choice. Whether *black,* which is now nearly universal, should be capitalized is a matter usually decided in the stylebooks of publications. Some black spokesmen have insisted it should, but the tendency is to lower-case it. This no doubt comes from the established practice of lower-casing words denoting color in connection with race: *white, yellow, red* The term *white* is probably in wider use than ever, for evident reasons; *yellow* and *red* are seldom seen. At any rate, capitalizing *white, yellow,* and *red* is virtually unheard-of. *Colored* for *Negro* or *black* is now also avoided, though it survives in the name *National Association of Colored People.* Special racial applications in other countries are not used in the U.S. See also *Negro.*

black, blacken. American Heritage holds that *black* is proper in the sense of applying color (*black one's shoes*) and *blacken* to derogate or defame, as a reputation. Webster agrees in general, although *blacken* is given as a synonym for *black;* that is, one could *blacken* (as well as *black*) one's eye. This interchange seems well accepted on cultivated levels.

blacken acres. The journalistic stereotype is reference to forest and brush fires; almost invariably used in place of *burn, burn over, char, consume,* etc.

black humor. The term easily lends itself to ambiguity. A new expression, it is listed in the Barnhart Dictionary of New English since 1963 and in the 1971 Addenda Section to Webster III. It came along about when *black* began to displace *Negro.*

But *black humor* does not mean what some writers seem to think it does, that is, humor concerning or characteristic of blacks. American Heritage gives us "The humor of the morbid and the absurd, especially in its development as a literary genre." Barnhart says, "A form of humor in literature based on absurd, grotesque, or morbid situations." Webster's version is "Humor marked by the use of usually morbid, ironic, grotesquely comic episodes that ridicule human folly."

Black humor appears to be a modern displacement or modification of *gallows humor,* which, oddly enough, only Random House lists: "ghoulish or macabre humor." Thus the film *The Godfather* might be cited as containing examples of black humor, such as the popular *mot,* "Make him an offer he can't refuse" (i.e., an offer whose refusal would have fatal consequences for the refuser). But we would not cite *Porgy and Bess* or *Green Pastures* as examples of black humor without confusing matters, since their humor concerns blacks but is not macabre or ghoulish. In a word, *black humor* does not necessarily have anything to do with blacks. It is, perhaps, a synonym of *sick humor.*

blame for, on. *Blame on* ("Don't blame it on him") is denounced by two critics but defended as standard by five. The expression is extremely common in well-edited writing and few are aware that any question arises concerning it. Every current American dictionary cites *blame on* without qualification, and so the criticism may be dismissed as pedantry.

blatant, flagrant. *Blatant* is often used where *flagrant, offensive, rank, gross, glaring* or other terms would be more exact. Bernstein appears to conclude that *blatant* should be limited to connections involving noise, because of its derivation (the Latin *blaterare,* to *shatter, bleat, croak*), but all current dictionaries recognize such extended senses as *disagreeably conspicuous, notorious, shocking;* American Heritage adds that it connotes wrong or evil. Harper regards *flagrant* as stronger than *blatant,* and connoting outrage. Consider the following examples: "It was a blatant display of pleasure for pleasure's sake" (*conspicuous?*); "And far too frequently they are blatantly corrupt" (*flagrantly?*); "In fact, many cities have bent over backwards to avoid blatant ethnic imbalances" (*gross?*); "His writing was characterized by blatant contradictions" (*glaring?*). There seems little doubt that *blatant* has become a counter word.

blaze, blazon. Bernstein and Evans hold that a trail is blazed; *blazon* means *make public, proclaim, display prominently.* But Random House and Webster also give *exhibit vividly,* or the equivalent, for *blaze.*

blink (at). "Democratic politicians aren't blinking the fact that his popularity gives them a slight chance of recapturing the legislature." The idiom is *blink the fact,* not *blink at.* One blinks at a strong light; *not to blink* something undesirable (the usual form of the expression) means to take it into account, six authorities agree.

bloc, block. The first is preferred for the political alignment.

blond, blonde. *Blonde* should be reserved for women; *blond* may be used of either sex. Fowler in the original recommended that *blond* should displace *blonde;* his reviser concludes that *blonde* is usual in reference to a woman. Six works on usage and current dictionaries concur. These comments apply to *blond(e)* as a noun ("The shapely blonde in the front row of the chorus"; "Like most Swedes, he was a blond"). As an adjective (*a blond girl; blond veneer*) *blond* is preferable in all instances. American Heritage, Random House, and Webster call *blond* predominant as the adjective, though the first two acknowledge that *blonde* (adj.) is often used of women. Harper prescribes it (*the blonde waitress*).

blood, sweat, and tears. See *Misquotation.*

blows my mind. A peculiarly obnoxious slang phrase meaning *amazes, astounds me,* that emanated from the hippie subculture and fortunately seems to be fading away. One critic said users of it had no minds to blow.

boast. Some critics (including 45 percent of the American Heritage Usage Panel) disapprove the use of the word to mean *take pride in possession of:* "Such clubs now number more than a thousand and boast assets in the millions." The imputation of boasting, which many consider discreditable, is often made undeservedly, for there may be no intent to boast. Dictionaries and Harper, however, recognize it as standard.

boat. Strictly speaking, the term applies to a small craft, as distinguished, generally, from a seagoing vessel. But restricting it to this sense is a nautical technicality; it is established in reference to ocean liners. Both Random House and Webster equate *boat* with *ship,* recognizing general usage.

bogey, bogie. The first is the preferred form for the golfing term (one stroke over par on a hole).

bona fide, bona fides ("in good faith"). The first is the adjective (*a bona fide friend*), the second the noun, and it is singular, not plural: "Our bona fides was (not *were*) under suspicion."

boost. The journalese stereotype for *increase, raise: a boost in pay.* This sense is considered standard by Random House, American Heritage, and Webster, however.

born, borne. *Born* is sometimes used where *borne* is called for as the participle of the verb *bear* that means *carry* (*the burdens were borne patiently*). "Helicopter-born troops were landed." *borne.* References to birth are always *born* except in such constructions as "She had borne four sons," where the basic verbs are *bear, bore.*

bosom(s). *Bosoms* is a euphemism for or an evasion of *breasts,* three critics hold. *Bosom* is asexual; in reference to a woman, it includes the breasts. It was a sad thing to see the nice-Nellyism *bosoms* employed by a nationally known theater critic, whose prose was usually notable for unflinching directness. He reported a scene in which the "false bosoms" were torn from the dress of an actress. *False bosoms,* besides, is surely the long way around for *falsies. Bosom* for *breast,* in the asexual sense ("pressed them to his bosom") has become literary, if not poetic. *Busts* was once popular as a euphemism for *breasts,* but was never reputable. Perhaps it is only to be expected that the tendency to cover up the thing itself should extend to the language chosen to name it. Avoidance of vulgarisms, or what may once have been imagined to be vulgarisms, is getting to be a thing of the past, however.

boss. Derogated as colloquial in the sense *employer, supervisor, political leader* by one critic. Desk dictionaries generally concur, but two other critics, Random House, American Heritage, and Webster accept it as standard.

both. 1. Redundantly used. Since *both* indicates duality, it is redundant with such words as *equal, alike, agree, together:* "Both are equally deadly." *They are . . .* "Both appeared together." *They appeared . . .* "Both looked alike." *They looked . . .* "Both agreed." *They agreed. Both* is also redundant with *as well as;* in this instance, *both* should usually be omitted or *as well as* should be changed to *and;* "Both John as well as his wife left" *Both John and . . . Both* can be omitted from the corrected version unless its emphasis is desired.

2. *Both* for *each.* "Both seemed to have blamed his martyrdom on the other." *Each.*

3. Placement with prepositions. *Both* is often misplaced before, instead of after, prepositions governing the elements it modifies: "Foreign policy, both under the present and preceding administrations . . ." *under both.* However, *both under the present and under preceding administrations* (repeating the preposition *under*) is correct.

bottleneck. As Gowers points out in his revision of Fowler, the word seems never to have been used in its literal sense—that is, the neck of a bottle. It came into currency in the U.S. and Britain during World War II to describe narrow streets that choked traffic. Gowers had some fun with mixed metaphors in his book, *The Complete Plain Words:* "Bottlenecks must be ironed out." But short of such examples, he concedes the utility of the word, which is recognized as standard in current dictionaries.

bottom line. One of the newer slang expressions, graphic enough in its indication of *final outcome, conclusion, upshot, culmination,* but overwork has made it tiresome.

bound. Solid as a suffix: *earthbound, heavenbound;* but hyphened with proper names: *Europe-bound, Chicago-bound.* It can be ambiguous, for it may mean either *headed for* or *restricted by* (e.g., *snowbound*).

boundary. Often misspelled *boundry.*

bovine. The journalese variant for *cow.*

boy. Blacks of all ages were formerly often addressed in this way; its patronizing, if not derogatory, effect is now almost universally sensed.

brackets [ ]. Often confused with parentheses, especially in conversational references. Brackets present a different appearance, as should be evident, and their principal uses are to set off words inserted, usually into quoted matter, by someone other than the writer, and to indicate parenthetical material within parentheses. Brackets can be fabricated on typewriters that do not have them by use of the slant and the underline.

brag, brag on. *Brag* is acceptable as a noun (*his brag and bluster*), but it is nonstandard when used in reference to a specific statement rather than in a general sense: "We resented his brag that he was the son of a general." *boast. Brag on* is dialectal: "He liked to brag on his ancestors." *brag about.* These views are the consensus of dictionaries.

Brahms. In the possessive the name of the composer sometimes emerges as Brahm's; correctly, Brahms'.

brand. One authority is sharply critical of the term in a noncommercial sense, such as *kind, variety* ("His peculiar brand of humor"); another is equivocal. Among current dictionaries, only Webster recognizes this sense.

breach, breech. Like *affect* and *effect,* often confused. In their commonest senses as nouns, a breach is a place that has been broken open (*a breach in the dike*) and a breech is the back end of a gun. As a verb, *breach* means *break open* (*breach a cask*). *Breech* as a noun has no current sense.

break, broke. It has been seriously argued, usually by newspaper style arbiters, that "Mrs. Jones broke her arm" is improper and absurd unless she did it intentionally. This is a good illustration of the perception that often enters into the composition of newspaper stylebooks. The sentence is good, unmistakable idiom, and recognized as standard by both Random House and Webster, both of which explicitly cite "He broke his leg." See *sustain*.

breakdown. One critic objects to the term in the sense *analysis* or *itemization* ("a breakdown of the supplies on hand"), a view possibly adopted from that captious and misinformed critic of American English, Lord Conesford. Three critics warn that the term may sound ludicrous when used in the analytical sense concerning something that can be physically broken down (*the buildings were broken down by age and use*). One adds, however, that when this danger is avoided, the term is unexceptionable in the analytical sense. American Heritage, Random House, and Webster recognize it as standard.

breakthrough. Criticized by two critics as overworked. Sometimes erroneously hyphened or given as two words, which is the proper form for the verb (*break through the barrier*) but not for the noun (*a scientific breakthrough*).

break up. In the sense *to be* (or *cause to be*) *overcome by laughter* ("His witticisms broke up the speaker") considered slang by one critic and American Heritage and standard by Random House and Webster's Collegiate. This is evidently *Theatrical Cant* (see), like *catch the show*, that has percolated into general use.

breast. See *bosom, breast*.

brickbat. Sometimes the press takes on the function of a museum of obsolescent words. That seems to be the explanation for the continued use of *brickbat,* as in "threw brickbats" or "dodged brickbats." The reader senses that a brickbat is a missile of some kind, probably, but does not know exactly what it is since the term has gone out of general use. A brickbat is a fragment of a brick. Of course, the term can be used figuratively, and often is, to indicate abuse. Then it often becomes *verbal brickbats,* although the context usually makes the phrase redundant. *Brickbats* was once in general use among literary writers, at a time when its meaning was familiar to readers. But that time seems to be past.

bridelet. A curiosity found on the society pages of some newspapers to denote a recent and presumably young bride. The expression has no standing and fills no need, since *bride* itself ceases to be used once the bloom is off the nuptials.

bring, take. *Bring* indicates motion toward the speaker or agent, and *take* motion away from him. Webster's Dictionary of Synonyms cites as an illustration of their correct use: "A mother asks a boy setting out for school to *take* a note to the teacher and to *bring* home a reply." Often confused.

Britain, British. See *Great Britain*.

Briticism. In an entry retained intact from the original edition of 1926, Gowers' revision of Fowler (1965) complains that this term, which is often used in this book, is a barbarism and that only the forms *Britannicism* or *Britishism* are acceptable. *Briticism* is considered primary and standard, however, by all dictionaries, including the British Concise Oxford Dictionary (1964). The term is, moreover, given as primary and standard in the OED, which also gives the variant *Britticism*. It appears that the lordly Fowler was hoist by his own countrymen.

Britisher, Briton. *Britisher* has a hint of derision or at least chaffing that *Briton* does not; Harper equates the terms; Evans considers *Britisher* an obsolescent Americanism. The revised Fowler, however, says "No Englishman, or perhaps no Scotsman even, hears himself referred to as a *Britisher* without squirming" and for general use, at least in Britain, he prefers *England, English* to Britain, British. History, sentiment, and patriotism are all implicit in *England* for the Englishman, he holds.

broadcast, broadcasted. Both forms are standard, but four authorities prefer the first for the past tense, and indeed it greatly predominates. See *forecast, telecast*.

brother, sister. Fraternal cant in reference to members of an organization, particularly a labor union. Two critics comment that it is sometimes regarded as a simpleminded and hypocritical mannerism. It seems especially inappropriate among members of groups whose members pretend to some sophistication and professionalism.

browse. Sometimes misspelled *brouse*. Which is reminiscent of the gymnasium that had a sign in the window reading, "Come in and bruise around."

brunet, brunette. As with *blond, blonde*, the first was formerly the masculine form exclusively. But *brunet* is sometimes now applied to women. (Random House says the term is usually applied to a male, but Webster no longer recognizes this distinction. American Heritage maintains it only for the nouns.) *Brunette*, the usual feminine form, continues in wider use than *blonde*.

bug. In connection with electronic eavesdropping, considered standard as a noun ("They found a bug behind the picture") and also as a verb ("The agents bugged the hotel room") by American Heritage and slang by Harper, Random House and Webster. But in the years that have elapsed since the latter judgment was made, it is safe to say that the word has become standard in both forms considering how prominently the practice has figured in the news. In the sense *irritate, annoy*

("Stop bugging me with those petty details"), considered slang by four authorities.

bugger. Widely enough known in the sense *sodomite* to be offensive in its alternative sense as a term of affection ("a cute little bugger") or even in its neutral sense *fellow*. *Bugger* as a verb ("Bugger—or bugger up—the works"), meaning to confuse or frustrate, suffers from the unsavory associations of *bugger* in the sexual sense.

bulk. See *largely*.

bulk of. *Most of* is generally preferable to *bulk of*. Bernstein defends *bulk of* as preferable to *majority* when indefiniteness is indicated. In the press, *bulk of* has all but displaced the more natural *most of*.

bullet, cartridge, shell, round. *Bullet* is often regarded as loosely used for *cartridge*. Technically the bullet is the projectile that leaves the gun; the cartridge comprises both the shell containing the explosive charge and the bullet although some projectiles also contain explosive charges. *Cartridge* and *round* are interchangeable. Random House, American Heritage, and Webster, however, recognize *bullet* as the equivalent of *cartridge*. It may be concluded that this is general usage.

bureaucrat. As American Heritage points out, the term is "almost invariably derogatory unless the context establishes otherwise." Webster conveys the same idea by implication.

burgeon. Two critics hold that the word can only mean *put forth buds;* Random House and Webster, however, also recognize the senses *flourish, expand, grow,* which, it must be confessed, are now predominant though probably newer. These usages were popularized by *Time* magazine. Flesch accepts *grow* but discourages *burgeon* as fancy in any sense. The American Heritage panelists narrowly (51 percent) rejected *grow* but approved figurative applications of *put forth buds: his burgeoning talent.*

burglarize. Criticized by Evans as journalese and defended by Bernstein as economical and thus justified. Grudgingly accepted by Flesch. Considered standard by American Heritage, Random House, and Webster. Objections to the term are thus pedantry. See also *-ize, -ise.*

burglary. Means *breaking and entering,* and should be distinguished from *robbery,* taking away by force or threat; *theft,* taking what belongs to another; and *holdup,* which is essentially the same as robbery but involves the use of a weapon to enforce the threat. Under the common law, burglary is defined as forcible entry into a dwelling at night with intent to commit a felony. Thus the nouns *robber, burglar, thief* are not interchangeable.

burst, bust. The past tense of *burst* is predominantly *burst;* "The water main burst last night," although Webster also accepts *bursted.* Five authorities consider *bust* as a verb nonstandard: "They busted the door down" (*broke*) though Webster accepts it as standard. *Bust* as a noun meaning *failure* ("The corporation was a bust") is standard. Expressions like *bronco busting* and *trust busting* must be regarded as having won their way to respectability.

bus. As a verb in the sense *transport by bus* ("The children are being bussed across town"), narrowly rejected for writing by American Heritage but considered standard by Random House and Webster. From time to time when this procedure was new bitter complaints were raised against *bussing, bussed,* in favor of *busing, bused,* on the ground that *bussing* is a quaint term for *kissing.* It would seem, however, that the context would make any confusion impossible, and that the objectors were merely exhibiting pride of knowledge, described by Fowler as a most unamiable characteristic. Dictionaries now accept either form in the sense at hand. *Bus* has also become a verb in an even newer sense: to clear away dishes. It derives, obviously, from *busboy.* Thus, in school cafeterias signs often exhort the eaters to bus their own trays. This usage, like most new ones, may offend traditionalists, but its utility seems certain to win it an unassailable place.

Business English. There is really no such thing, although books have been published with the term in their titles. Insofar as the language of business differs from standard, current expression (e.g., "Yours of the 12th inst. received and contents noted," "Be advised that . . . ," "We are in receipt of your letter . . ." and similar survivals from the Victorian age) it is non-English. Vigorous efforts have been made by businesses in recent years to clear up their communications and thus improve efficiency. An essential part of such efforts should be discarding the idea that business expression should exhibit peculiarities. *Pidgin English* derived from *business English*—something to think about.

bust, busts. See *bosom, breast; burst, bust.*

but. 1. *But what, but that.* Bernstein and Harper disapprove of *but what* for *but that* ("I do not doubt but what society feels threatened by the homosexual"); Bryant finds *but what* standard usage for *but that,* and it is also accepted by Webster. In fact, *but* is excessive in *but that.* American Heritage rejects both *but that* and *but what* for *that* alone, a good principle. The question concerning these expressions is sometimes directed at the fact that they occur in sentences already containing negatives, and thus create a double negative. Evans calls this doubling established literary idiom. See also *cannot (help) but; not . . . but.*

2. *But however, but nevertheless.* Both are redundant; use either *but, however,* or *nevertheless* alone.

3. *But as conjunction or preposition. But* may be regarded as either preposition or conjunction; the question arises when the word is followed by a pronoun in such constructions as "They were all educated but (me, I)," "All but (us, we) received tickets." Two critics agree that either form of the pronoun may be considered technically correct. Two others consider *but* a preposition in such

examples, calling uniformly for *but me, but us.* Bernstein, Webster and American Heritage prescribe regarding *but* as a preposition when the pronoun following it comes at the end of the sentence, and putting the pronoun in the same case as the word that precedes *but* when the phrase comes early in the sentence. Examples: "Everyone but I contributed to the confusions" (early occurrence); "Dissent came from all but him" (late occurrence; *but* is here construed as a preposition; in the early occurrence it is construed as a conjunction). The distinctions seem hairsplitting; instinct will probably lead most of us to the more agreeable choice. The most famous occurrence of this expression undoubtedly is in Felicia Dorothea Hemans' poem *Casabianca,* in reference to the boy standing on the burning deck "whence all but he had fled." Early editions of Bartlett's *Familiar Quotations* carried a footnote saying, "The first American edition of Mrs. Hemans' *Poems* (1826) gave this line 'Whence all but him had fled.' English editions and subsequent American editions seem evenly divided between 'but him' and 'but he.' The last edition published while Mrs. Hemans was still living and presumably approved the contents gives 'but he.' "

   4. *But* followed by comma. As a conjunction, *but* (like other conjunctions, notably *and, so,* and *or*) is often wrongly followed by a comma: "The wood was dry, but, the fire wouldn't light." The rule also applies when *but* begins the sentence: "But, there were some objections." Omit the commas. There is no reason, incidentally, why *but* (or any other conjunction) should not begin a sentence.

   5. *But which.* See *and (but) which, and (but) who.*

   6. *Buts* in succession. As Fowler comments, *but* cannot do its work of indicating a contrast in constructions like "But the storm continued through the night, but the river did not rise dangerously" ("The storm continued . . . but . . ."). *But* should not be used unless there is a contrast: "The snake was not venomous, but its bite did no serious harm." *venomous; its bite . . .*

buy. As a noun in the sense *a bargain* ("It was a good buy"), described as informal by one critic and not standard by two others; five authorities consider it standard; Random House and the Standard College Dictionary call it informal. Webster's New World and the American College Dictionary designate it colloquial. The consensus appears to be that the term is well on the way to formal acceptance, if it has not already arrived. *Buy* for *a purchase (it was a sensible buy)* is regarded as nonstandard only by Evans. *Buy* for *accept* or *believe* ("I won't buy that idea") is slang.

by-. Usually solid as a prefix: *byplay, bylaw, bypath.* Usage is inconsistent, however; the best advice is to consult your favorite dictionary.

by means of. Usually redundant for *by* or some other preposition alone: "The fish are caught by means of a net." *by, in,* or *with.*

by the same token. Now quaint and wordy. Usually *similarly* will do as well and more economically.

by way of being. A fancy phrase of indeterminate and perhaps no meaning: "European industry is by way of being as sophisticated technologically as our own." European industry is or is not as sophisticated; the writer should not confuse the reader with *by way of being,* which may suggest *becoming, ostensibly, apparently,* and other things.

byzantine. The word was in wide use in a figurative sense before that meaning was to be found in any dictionary. But finally it appeared in the 1971 Addenda Section to Webster III, which gave "of, relating to, or characterized by a devious manner of operation (the government, with its own Byzantine sources of intelligence— Wesly Pruden)." The Eighth Edition of Webster's Collegiate gave "labyrinthine" ("searching in the Byzantine complexity of the record"). But no dictionary yet explains what there was about ancient Byzantium (the modern Istanbul) that gives rise to the figure, although associations with art, architecture, and literature are listed. The context usually makes the intended meaning clear. When used figuratively, *byzantine* should not be capitalized.

C

cablegram. Criticized by Bernstein as applied to messages sent from ships, which are necessarily radiograms (Random House and Webster concur); and by Fowler when used as a verb displacing *cable*.

caesarian. See *cesarean, caesarean, etc.*

calculate. Five authorities describe it as dialectal for *suppose, assume:* "I calculate it will rain"; Random House, American Heritage and Webster identify it as a regionalism.

caliber, calibre. Designations of the caliber of pistols and rifles should be preceded by decimal points since they indicate hundredths of an inch (.22 caliber, .45 caliber). *Caliber* is the preferred spelling in the U.S., *calibre* in Britain.

callous, callus. The adjective is *callous,* the noun *callus: a callous attitude; callus on the finger. Calloused* and *callused* as adjectives are interchangeable, according to Webster, the only authority that deals with this point, though here too the general distinction that the *-ous* form indicates emotional insensitivity applies.

Calvary, cavalry. Sometimes ignorantly or carelessly confused. Calvary was the place of the crucifixion; cavalry are troops mounted on horses, a vanishing breed except for ceremonials.

came the . . . Criticized by Flesch and Fowler as an affectation in such constructions as *came the war, came the dawn.*

campus. Formerly applied only to colleges; now often applied to high schools, especially in the West.

can, may. Bernstein says that except in informal English *can* in the sense *be able* should be used to indicate possibility. American Heritage holds to the strict traditional use of *can* for possibility, *may* for permission except in negative or interrogative statements, where it inconsistently prefers *can't* to *mayn't.* (Examples of the traditional distinction, of which much was made by English teachers a generation or two ago: "You can [are able to] succeed"; "You may [have permission to] leave the room"). Bryant finds *can* is used on all levels to express permission, but that *may* is used in formal written English. Three authorities say *can* is interchangeable with *may*. Harper and The Standard College Dictionary and Webster's New World call this use colloquial; and Random House and Webster recognize it as standard though Random House says *may* is preferred for asking permission. The consensus favors *can* as standard for *may;* the authorities are unanimous that this use is informally acceptable.

can but, cannot but, cannot help but. *Cannot but* and the more usual *cannot help but* have been widely criticized on the ground that they contain a double negative (*but* plus *not*). Grammar books once were unanimous that *cannot* (*help*) *but* was objectionable. Yet Bernstein calls it the usual and acceptable form; Bryant, citing a number of studies, says it has been used by cultivated writers for more than fifty years; Evans says it is preferred and irreproachable in the U.S., adding that a double negative is not actually formed. (One scholar reached the conclusion that in general a double negative is not formed unless the reader misinterprets.) Flesch sees no reason why the expression should not be used, and American Heritage approves both *cannot but* and *cannot help but.* Follett, however, disapproves of *cannot help but* as "a grammarless mixture" and Fowler calls it indefensible; Harper also rejects it. But if *cannot help but* is such bad grammar what is it doing in the *Kenyon Review* and the writings of John Ciardi and Stephen Vincent Benet, Hugh Walpole, and Lord Alfred Douglas, Oscar Wilde's literate companion? The weight of authority overwhelmingly favors the legitimacy of *cannot help but.* Curme cites a number of quotations from literary classics where it occurs. Webster recognizes it as standard; Random House warns it is common but frowned on. *Can but* (*can only*) and *cannot but* (*cannot help*) sound literary and are unlikely to be used except by the affected. Follett approves *cannot help* (*doing,* or whatever, omitting *but*), *cannot but,* and *can but.* The writer who wants neither arguments nor criticism can make it *cannot help* (*feeling,* etc.) a form about which no one yet has said a hard word. Bryant finds it more frequent in formal writing, and it has Fowler's approval, too. See *help*.

candelabra. Technically the plural of *candelabrum.* Two authorities approve its use as a singular but Fowler disapproves. *Candelabra* as a singular (with the Englished plural *candelabras,* sure to outrage Latinists) is given by all current dictionaries, including the British Concise Oxford.

candor and frankness. This redundant pair occurs often: "We appreciate the candor and frankness with which you have expressed your views." One or the other, not both at once.

canine. The journalese variant for *dog;* discouraged by three authorities.

cannibalize. In the sense *use as a source of spare parts,* the term was derided by Conesford. But Fowler regards it as felicitous, as indeed it is (the expression originated in the Army, where, for example, parts from a damaged airplane might be used to repair other planes). It is given without qualification in all current dictionaries, including the Concise Oxford.

cannot, can not. The predominant form now is one word, although both are standard.

can't hardly. A substandard double negative. See *hardly*.

can't help but. See *can but,* etc.

can't seem. Often criticized as illogical, but it is considered idiomatic and acceptable by six authorities.

canvas, canvass. Often confused. The heavy cloth is canvas; solicitation from door to door and the verb for doing so are *canvass*. Certain forms of the verb are especially liable to error: *canvasses* (not *canvases*) *the neighborhood; canvassing the town.*

capacity. A pomposity in such contexts as "What is his capacity?" Translation: "What is his job?" "What is his capacity?" is sometimes replied to with some such comment as "One quart at a time," and deserves to be. This usage resembles the displacement of *belongs to, is a member of* by *affiliated with*.

capital, capitol. The capital is the city, the capitol the building.

Capitalization. Apart from such nearly universally observed rules as those prescribing that sentences and proper names begin with capitals, practice shows a wild diversity. Capitalization beyond the basic rules noted is a matter of style or preference—sometimes deference—not of right or wrong. Most publications solve the problem by specific prescription in their stylebooks. American dictionaries (but not the British Oxford dictionaries) indicate preferred, or predominant, capitalization. The writer who is uncertain of his own preference and not governed by a stylebook is advised to use a dictionary as a guide. Even publications having their own stylebooks, after laying down general and special rules, are well advised to refer their staffs to a specified dictionary for instances not already covered. The important thing is consistency; inconsistency in this and other mechanical matters distracts and perhaps annoys the reader. It may leave him with the impression that the writers and editors are careless or confused, and thus may create a general mistrust of the factual content.

Just as written expression has grown strikingly more informal in this century, the trend has been toward less ceremonious capitalization. A recent development in the writing of newspaper headlines is that increasingly they are capitalized like sentences (which, essentially, is what they are) instead of like titles, in which all important words have traditionally been capitalized.

Ceremonious capitalization is a personal matter of showing respect. A Catholic publication, for example, would invariably capitalize Pope, and perhaps the designations of other positions in the hierarchy (cardinal, archbishop, bishop, etc.). Public relations operatives invariably make it *the Company* in reference to their employer. No British paper would consider anything but *the Queen*. Such kow-towing is sometimes regarded with mild amusement, but it is harmless after all.

Ceremonious capitalization has been less widespread in publications aimed at general audiences in the U.S.; even so, until recently it was *de rigeur* for newspapers to make it *the President* in reference to the president of the United States. In recent years, however, there has been a noticeable trend toward the lower case, perhaps reflecting diminished respect for the presidency. New and comprehensive stylebooks published in 1977 by the Associated Press and United Press International, from which most newspapers take their stylistic cues, prescribe lower case for *president* (of the U.S.). *The New York Times*, however, known for its traditionalism, holds to *the President* in its newest stylebook (as well as *the Senator*, etc.). Some American newspapers persist in oddities like *the Flag* (in reference to the U.S. flag), *Federal*, and *Nation*. It hardly needs saying that the Canadian Press capitalizes *the Queen*, as well as other royal and noble titles standing alone in reference to a previously named person.

Newspapers differentiate what they call the "up style" (capitalizing generic terms: *Mississippi River, Rocky Mountains*) and the "down style" (lower-casing generic terms: *Lincoln school; First ward*). The down style was once widely followed, evidently on the assumption that its informality made for a breezy style. But in recent years, countering in this instance the trend toward increasing informality, the press associations and many leading newspapers have gone to the up style, perhaps recognizing that it was almost invariable in other publications, and that it was what children were taught in school, when they were taught anything at all about writing, which was seldom.

The ignorant approach to capitalization is to capitalize terms that are unfamiliar. For example, an article about antelopes identified the Chamois as a goatlike Antelope. But the wolf was denied the dignity of upper case (not exotic enough, apparently). Yet the accolade of capitalization was accorded to the Beagle. In fact, chamois, antelope, wolf, and beagle are all common nouns. As noted, most questions of capitalization, disregarding arbitrary stylistic prescriptions, may be resolved by consulting a dictionary, although these works are not all as forthright on the subject as we might wish. Most desk dictionaries, including the Webster Collegiate, Webster's New World, the Standard College, American Heritage, and American College, indicate prescribed capitalization by capitalizing entries. The OED evades the issue by capitalizing *all* entries, and thus is of no help. Webster III lower-cases them all, but does specify *cap* or *usu cap*, a practice less convenient for the user than capitalizing the entries themselves.

caption. Fowler (in the original) objected to the term for *title* or *heading*. Other critics have said it should apply only to the heading that stands above a picture, and not to the legend beneath. (Typographical studies have shown, however, that the desirable position is beneath, and few such headings appear above the picture any longer.) Usage even on publications, including newspapers (which, incidentally, are notoriously inexact and inconsistent in their own technical terminology) applies *caption* indifferently to headings and explanatory matter, regardless of position, although precise usage calls for *cutlines* for the explanatory matter. Dictionaries, as well as two authorities, recognize as standard the use of *caption* for either heading or legend. The insistence that a caption should be a heading arises, apparently, from a mistaken idea that the word derives from the Latin *caput* (head).

capture. In connection with sports events, particularly, a wornout variant of *win*.

car. The criticism is still occasionally heard that *car* is improper, or at least undesirable, for *automobile*. This notion may have arisen from a fear of confusion with streetcars, but these are now almost extinct. *Car* is the predominant word for *automobile* and will be so understood unless the context indicates otherwise. *Auto* is fully acceptable but little used.

carat, caret. The first is the unit of weight (200 mg) for precious stones and metals, and the second the mark (∧) used to indicate an insertion in written or printed material. *Carat* is sometimes spelled *karat*.

cardiac. See *heart attack*.

careen, career. To careen is to heel over, lean, or sway; a sailboat careens. To career is to move at high speed; the word may also connote erratic movement. Fowler notes that Webster allows "lurch or toss from side to side" for *careen*. When *careen* is applied to automobiles it is difficult to establish the writer's intention; a wildly driven automobile may sway. American Heritage approves *careen* for fast and erratic movement regardless of swaying. Perhaps the best that can be said is that *career* does not suggest swaying. Two critics regard *careen* as having displaced *career* in American usage, which appears to be a sound conclusion.

care less. See *couldn't care less*.

care of. The abbreviation is c/o, not the percent symbol (%).

cartridge. See *bullet*.

case. Its use in various phrases was unforgettably ridiculed in the lecture "Interlude: on Jargon" by Sir Arthur Quiller-Couch, as published in his *On the Art of Writing*. Somehow, these expressions seem immune to attack, which has come from all directions. We have *in case*, which displaces *if; in most cases* (*usually*); *if that were the case* (*if so*); *not the case* (*not so*); *in the case of*, which often may be omitted entirely, and if not, replaced by *concerning;* and *as in the case of* (*like*). "It is possible that this material may become mixed with clouds in some cases and produce rain sooner than otherwise would have been the case." Stripped of its excrescences: "This material may mix with clouds and bring rain sooner." Follett concurs generally in these criticisms, but argues plausibly that *case* for *instance, the event of,* for example *in case of fire,* is idiomatic and beyond cavil.

casket. Originally a euphemism for *coffin,* and its use in that sense is still criticized by those who have neglected to notice that the word is no longer used in any other sense. A euphemism ceases to be one when people are not conscious of it.

cast, caste. The spelling is *cast (moral cast, cast of temperament)* in all senses except that of the social stratification in India, or something analogous, which is *caste.*

casualty. Although the term originally meant only *accident,* the sense *victim* (of fighting, for example) is standard. Harper comments that it has been misused for *death count,* perhaps deliberately to reduce the figure (which otherwise would be higher, including both fatalities and injuries) in wartime.

catastrophe, -phes. Often erroneously *-phy, -phies.*

catch fire. The form of the idiom; not *catch on fire.*

catch the show. See *Theatrical Cant.*

catchup, catsup, ketchup. Fowler calls *ketchup* the established spelling, and Evans says it predominates in the U.S., a conclusion that seems doubtful, since *catsup* is also common, and dictionaries are not unanimous. *Catchup* is unusual, but all forms are recognized as correct.

category. Use of the term in other than scientific or philosophical connections, when *class* will do, is discouraged as pretentious by four authorities.

Catholic. The term does not belong exclusively to Roman Catholics although spokesmen for their church have been known to insist that it does. However, Roman Catholics have also been known to object to the designation *Roman,* mainly on the ground that it dates back to an era when it was used derogatorily in England. No such connotation can be said to exist today. There are several varieties of Catholics, including the Eastern Orthodox, Anglican, and Old Catholic, and *Roman Catholic* should be used when it is desirable to make a distinction.

Caucasian. Evans (writing before the civil rights movements that began in the 1960s) says the term is vulgar and offensive as a euphemism for *white.* Such a judgment is meaningless today, although *Caucasian* is now seldom used. For a time early in the civil rights ferment, newspapers, often enthusiastic devotees of the long or technical term in spite of an avowed preference for simplicity, seized upon *Caucasian,* though probably not as a euphemism. What could have been euphemistic about it, anyway, at any time? It may well have been pretentious. At any rate, the overwhelmingly predominant word now has become *white* (not capitalized).

caused from. The wrong preposition; *caused by*.

cause is due to. Redundant: "The cause of the flood was due to heavy rain in the foothills." *cause was,* or *the flood was due to.* See *due to.*

cavalry. See *Calvary, cavalry.*

ceiling. Evans and Fowler complain that the term in its relatively new use meaning *the upper limit* (*price ceilings*) as well as *floor* for *lower limit* tends to be overworked and sometimes figures in mixed metaphors. Regardless, usefulness has solidly established both terms.

celebrant, celebrator. Bernstein and Evans hold that the original distinction should be maintained: that a celebrant is one who takes part in a religious rite, and a celebrator one who celebrates in the sense of having a good time. But regrettably the difference is being done in by careless interchange, a view that is noted by Harper and supported by dictionary definitions. The Standard College Dictionary gives as the first sense of *celebrant* "one who participates in a celebration." Similar definitions are given by Webster, Random House, and American College; American Heritage approves *celebrant* for *celebrator* by a narrow margin. Webster's New World, however, holds to the distinction. The consensus overwhelmingly accepts the interchanged usage.

cello, 'cello. The apostrophe has long since been dispensed with; it indicated the abridgment of *violoncello* that is universal.

Celsius, centigrade. Some confusion may be caused by the use of these designations for temperature under the metric system. They are two names for the same thing: a scale divided into 100 degrees, with the freezing point at zero and the boiling point at 100. *Celsius* commemorates Anders Celsius (1701–1744), the inventor of this scale, just as *Fahrenheit* commemorates the inventor of the scale more familiar in America. The American Heritage Dictionary tells us that *Celsius* has been the official designation since 1948, although *centigrade* remains in use, but neglects to explain how official standing is conferred in such matters. At any rate, the question of choice is more or less academic, since for the most part the abbreviation C. is used anyway.

cement, concrete. Technically, cement is the powder that is one of the ingredients of concrete (the others usually being sand, gravel, and water). Some critics make much of the common use of *cement* where they believe *concrete* is called for (*cement sidewalks*). *Cement* has lost its distinctiveness, like many technical terms that have come into common use; the context always shows, anyway, which sense is meant. *Cement* is thus interchangeable with *concrete* for the finished product, two critics hold. Dictionaries generally are not explicit on this point, except for Webster, which equates the terms.

cemetery. Often misspelled *cemetary*.

censor, censure. Often confused. To censor is to prohibit or suppress; to censure is to disapprove or criticize sharply. People may be censured but not censored; writings, speeches, and other forms of expression may be either censored (prohibited in whole or in part, or examined with a view to possible prohibition) or censured (condemned). Ours is a waspish age, unhappily, that grows increasingly full of both.

center about, around. These expressions, rather than *center on, in, at* are declared wrong by five authorities; two critics concede that they are illogical but regard them as established idiom. Webster cites "a hamlet that was centered around a church" and "centered around the political development" among several examples of the denounced use, and goes further to specify that *center* is used with *in, at, upon, about,* or *around*. Random House calls the questioned versions informal. The Concise Oxford defines *center* as "be concentrated in, on, at, round, about." The opinions are evenly divided.

centigrade. See *Celsius, centigrade*.

Centuries. Confusingly designated by a number one higher than seems right at first glance; 1863 was in the nineteenth century, 1963 in the twentieth, etc.

ceremonial, ceremonious. What is ceremonial pertains to a ceremony; what is ceremonious is marked by pomp or ostentation (a ceremonious manner, tone of voice, gesture). Random House and Webster generally bear this out but also give the words as synonyms.

certain. Sometimes ambiguously used. "If there were a fixed agenda this system could not work. Instead the conference would be bound to negotiate one certain proposal." *Assured?* No, *particular* or *specific*. Another kind of lapse: "This little town has a certain, awkward fame." Not *assured* or *definite* but *unspecified; a certain* (whatever) is an idiom, and the comma in this sense was wrong.

cesarean, caesarean, etc. The operation known as cesarean section, which effects delivery by cutting through the walls of the abdomen and uterus, is commonly supposed to have taken its name from the legend that Julius Caesar, like Macduff, "was from his mother's womb Untimely ripp'd," but this has been disputed. It has also been held that the term comes from the Latin *caedere*, to cut. At any rate, the preferred spelling now, and the one used in medical circles, is *cesarean*. The terminations *-ean* and *-ian* are both acceptable, but *-ean* tends to be favored for the operation, and *-ian* for the adjective meaning *pertaining to Caesar* (*Caesarian ambition*). It has been the practice for some time not to capitalize the name of the

operation however spelled, though Random House gives *Caesarean* as the preferred form in both senses.

chafe, chaff. Sometimes confused. To chaff is to tease good-naturedly; to chafe is
to irritate, literally or figuratively. A man's wrists might be chafed by handcuffs, or
he might be irked by chaffing. "The mayor was chaffing at his confinement in the
hospital." *chafing;* expressing impatience. "They were chaffing him about his
long hair" illustrates a correct use: *teasing.*

chain reaction. A technical term often misused. Webster defines it as "a series of
events so related to each other that each one initiates the succeeding one." Thus a
flood of telephone calls to the police, prompted by the sound of an explosion, is
not a chain reaction, as so often described in the press, but simply a case of cause
and effect.

chair. As a verb ("Mrs. Adams chaired the meeting") disapproved by Bernstein
and Evans, although Harper, American Heritage, Random House, and Webster
give it as standard. *Chairman* as a verb ("Smith chairmanned the conference")
seems even more disagreeable, but once again the dictionaries approve. In the
current vogue, however, it would likely be *chairpersonned,* which, if it has not
yet actually appeared, seems inevitable. See *Feminism.*

chairperson. See *Feminism.*

chaise longue. *Chaise lounge* is the corrupted form of this originally French term
(for *long chair*). The effect may not be as outrageous to precisians as it could be,
since usually the term is clipped to *chaise* alone. Three critics accept the new
form; three reject it.

chalk up. A chiché of journalism, as in *chalk up points.*

chaperon, chaperone. Both spellings are correct and recognized by dictionaries,
but the first predominates; Fowler, reflecting British usage, calls *chaperone*
wrong.

character. Often used in a way that has a woolly effect; *the delicate character of
the music (delicacy); activities of a public-spirited character (public-spirited activities); concentration of an intermittent character (intermittent concentration).*
"It is regrettable that an incident of this character has occurred" (*an incident like
this, of this kind*). Five authorities concur. In general, *character* is best applied to
people; its use concerning things, in the sense *quality, kind, sort* and the like is a
species of personification. A company advertised itself as "maker of watches of
the highest character." In such contexts, *character* is usually the equivalent of
personality, a quality possessed only by people, or of *reputation,* a sense of
character now obsolescent.

charge. Takes *with,* not *of; charged with a crime.* See *in charge of.*

charges. See *Plural* and *Singular.*

chastise. Often misspelled *chastize.*

chat. A journalese stereotype. It is especially prevalent in identifications beneath pictures, where people no longer talk, converse, palaver, speak, consult, confer, discuss, say, tell, or declare. They *chat. Chat* denotes casual, inconsequential talk. Similarly, in the press, people do not eat food, they *munch* it; nor to they drink beverages, they *sip* them.

cheap. Means low in value, strictly speaking. Goods may be cheap but prices are low, if the consumer is lucky. *Cheap* also means *inexpensive,* but the word has a derogatory connotation.

cheap shot. A new expression, widely popular, meaning an unfair thrust or advantage. Evidently it derives from football or hockey, referring to the deliberate commission of a foul by one player against another out of sight of the referee. Obviously slang.

check into, up on. Legitimate and useful expressions. A critic cited as examples "He is kept busy checking into developments" and "She had asked someone to check into such rumors," saying *into* was unnecessary. But *check* without *into* would have been ambiguous, for it might have been understood as *curb.* Another critic regards *check up on* as excessive for *check,* and a third says *into, on, out, over,* and *up* are all excessive. The writer who follows this advice must test to see whether omitting the preposition causes ambiguity. There is no question of general acceptability; the combinations with *check* are considered standard by Random House, Webster, and American Heritage.

chicano. Like *black* and *gay,* the term came to be self-applied in the last decade or so by Mexican-Americans. The Barnhart Dictionary of New English Since 1963 says the word comes from the Mexican Spanish *chicano,* which comes in turn from the Chihuahua dialectal pronunciation of *Mejicano.* Whether *chicano* should be capitalized is a moot question; the tendency now is to lower-case it, as is true of *black* in the racial sense. Although on occasion *chicano* has been ignorantly described as disparaging, the term is actually preferred by Mexican-Americans. In Los Angeles, for example, a city with the largest population of Mexican descent of any city in the world except Mexico City, numerous organizations use the term in their names. It is a standard term of reference in newspapers. So far, only American Heritage lists it.

chief justice. The correct federal title is *chief justice of the United States,* not *of the Supreme Court.*

childish, childlike. As applied to adults, the first denotes the disagreeable, the second the appealing, qualities of childhood (*a childlike trust*). *Childish* is not invariably disparaging, however: *a childish treble*.

chile, chili. Either form is correct, though American dictionaries prefer *chili*. At the same time, two of them give *chile* (rather than *chili*) *con carne* (a dish of Mexican origin); the translation is chili (a hot pepper) with meat. It has become widely popular in the Southwest, and is available in cans anywhere in the country.

Chinaman. Considered derogatory; neutrally, *Chinese,* which as a noun is both singular and plural: *A Chinese operated the laundry; numerous Chinese.* Evans says *Chinaman* is accepted in Britain, but Fowler says no.

chinchy, chintzy. For *cheap, unfashionable, miserly, gaudy, chintzy* overwhelmingly predominates. *Chinchy* is not listed in Wentworth and Flexner's Dictionary of American Slang; Random House and Webster give it as a Southern and Midwestern regionalism for *miserly, stingy;* in this sense, *chintzy* is regarded as a variant of *chinchy.* American Heritage and Random House give *chintzy* as standard.

Chinese Names. The part of a Chinese name that follows the hyphen is lowercased, not capitalized: Chou En-lai, Chiang Kai-shek.

choice, pick. See *pick, choice.*

chord, cord. Although they have the same ancestor and both can mean *string, chord* in its commonest sense means a group of tones sounded together in a pattern. The folds in the throat that produce the sound of the voice are vocal *cords,* not *chords;* also spinal *cord* (not *chord*).

chore. A routine task, especially a tedious or disagreeable one. A few generations ago the term applied most commonly to duties assigned to the boy of the household, such as fetching water, splitting firewood, shoveling snow from the sidewalks, and whitewashing the fence. The word is questionably appropriate to describe what is merely a customary act, or what is even likely to excite pleasure or interest. "One of his first chores on getting up in the morning is reading the paper." This would not be a chore except for someone for whom it was part of his job and perhaps, the editor would hope, not even then. *Chore* is often misused, especially in newspaper writing, of what is neither routine, obligatory, nor unpleasant.

Christian name. Evans and Fowler point out that the expression is not properly applicable except to those of the Christian faith. Evans recommends instead *first name;* Fowler advocates *forename,* a rare form in the U.S. *Given name* is perhaps at least as frequent as *first name* and disposes of the objection to *Christian name.*

Christmas tree. It is a stereotype to say that a police telephone switchboard lighted up like a Christmas tree in some emergency or other.

chronic. Means *long-continued, habitual;* misused in the sense *severe,* four authorities agree.

circum-. Solid as a prefix: *circumnavigate, circumambient, circumlocution, circumscribe,* etc.

circumstances (*under* vs. *in the c.*). Both versions are standard and established beyond quibble. Fowler called the objection to *under* puerile; four authorities concur. Fowler refines matters by limiting *in* to statements of condition (*in reduced circumstances*) and *under* to situations affecting action (*under the circumstances, he fled*) and Bernstein agrees.

cite. "The suspect's record of Communist associations was cited" is improper unless such a record exists; it is not the same thing as "The suspect *was said to have* (or *was accused of having*) a record of Communist associations," which was the intended meaning. *Cited the fact that* is often misused in reference to what has not been established as a fact at all, but is merely an allegation. See also *attribution.*

citizen. Since the word has the meaning, among others, of one who owes allegiance to a state and is entitled to protection by it, it should be used with care to prevent the ambiguity that often arises when *inhabitant* or *resident* would be a better choice. People were citizens (like Paul) of cities in the days when cities were states; it may be better now to speak of them as inhabitants, or residents, of their cities. "A citizen met the bus that delivers the papers." Since this was merely a resident, and not a citizen as distinguished from an alien, *resident* would have been more suitable. "The county now has 221,900 citizens, a record." This sentence, from a population report, referred to inhabitants, and could be misleading as distinguishing between citizens and aliens. It is not wrong, however, to speak of "a citizen of Chicago" or "a citizen of Utah" for *resident.* The British have their own word for it; they have not citizens but *subjects.*

civilian. Among dictionaries, only Webster defines the terms as distinguishing those not on military duty, and extends it to those who are not members of police or fire-fighting forces. But the use of *civilian* to distinguish those not in any kind of uniform, for example policemen, seems questionable. Bernstein allows the extension to distinguish nonpolice and nonfiremen, but protests further stretching. The consensus appears to be that any extension beyond a contrast with the military is dubious usage.

clad. Criticized by Evans, Flesch, and Fowler as bookish and archaic for *clothed.* A favorite mannerism of journalism. Flesch also objects to *unclad* as a euphemism for *nude,* which in turn has been objected to as a euphemism for *naked.*

claim. Three authorities object to the term in the sense *say* or *assert* ("He claims the weather is too cold"); Fowler allows it in demanding belief for the improbable: "She claims to have heard a ghost." All three trace the loose use of *claim* for *say, assert, declare,* etc., to the press. Flesch is willing to allow *claim* in any of these senses, saying common usage does not recognize any distinction. Current dictionaries do not go much beyond Fowler. Although some, like American Heritage, allow *claim* for *assert* (especially in a context indicating insistence or disagreement), none can be understood as loosely permitting it for *say* or its synonyms. See *Attribution*.

clamp. Journalese in such contexts as *clamp a lid of secrecy on, place security clamps on.*

clarify. Means *clear* or *clear up,* and is wrong in the sense *answer:* "He spoke to clarify questions farmers may have about tractors." Only the asker, if a question is obscure, can ordinarily clarify it; this speaker's intention was to *answer* the farmers' questions. Apart from this, *clarify* is overused in official prose, where things are always supposedly being clarified. Sad to say, they are rarely *cleared up* in such contexts.

classic, classical. Five authorities agree that the choice (when the reference is to the literature of Greece and Rome and analogous senses) is a matter of idiom. *Classical* is usual though *classic* is acceptable in "Classical works of ancient Rome," "a classical statue"; but *classical* is necessary with *education, allusions.* The term for *outstandingly important* is *classic: a classic game of chess.*

clean, cleanse. *Clean* is literal, whereas *cleanse* is generally literary and ceremonious; it is used, for example, in religious connections.

Clerical Titles. See *Reverend.*

clever. Not quite the compliment that many suppose; it does not measure up to *ingenious, inventive, creative, witty.* The word connotes skill in small matters.

clew, clue. *Clue* is preferred in the sense (*piece of evidence*) for which the forms are interchangeable.

Clichés. A dictionary definition of cliché is "a trite phrase; a hackneyed expression." This leaves wide open the question, trite or hackneyed to whom? Language is full of stock phrases, many of which are indispensable, or at least not replaceable without going the long way around. The expressions that draw scorn as clichés, however, are generally those that attempt a special effect—usually drama or humor. Whether a particular expression is regarded as a cliché depends on the discrimination of the regarder, and sometimes on the context. A good way to acquire an extensive and acute awareness of clichés is to read Frank Sullivan's reports from his cliché expert, Magnus Arbuthnot, as set down in such books as *A*

Pearl in Every Oyster, A Rock in Every Snowball, and *The Night the Old Nostalgia Burned Down.* Every book on usage has an entry on the subject, some of which point out that the use of clichés is by no means the worst literary fault that can be committed, and that the conspicuous avoidance of a cliché can be worse than the cliché itself.

Since there is no limit to the number of clichés, and since what constitutes a cliché is to some extent a matter of opinion, no space has been wasted on collecting and exhibiting them in this book. Hundreds of them may be found as entries in Evans, and the subject is also explored in Fowler under the headings *Cliché, Battered Ornaments,* and *Hackneyed Phrases;* and in Follett under *Set Phrases.*

Ill-read and dull-witted writers will always be proud of having picked up expressions that the finer-grained despise. Even on the upper levels of ability, opinions will differ whether a particular expression is overworked. George Orwell once fiercely proposed that a writer should rigorously excise from his work every turn of phrase he did not invent himself. This may be going too far. Writing that contained nothing familiar or at least recognizable in this respect might leave the reader ill at ease. In any event, no writing exists that does not contain clichés by one standard or another. This state of affairs was once described in verse:

> If you scorn what is trite
> I warn you, go slow
> For one man's cliché
> Is another's *bon mot.*

Cliché is often redundantly qualified by *old, usual (the usual parting clichés).* Conceivably there are old and new clichés, but *old* is superfluous unless clichés are being differentiated on the basis of age. See also *Journalese,* etc.

client. Best reserved for the customers of professionals, particularly lawyers, but not doctors, who have *patients.* In other connections, where the *quid pro quo* is goods or something more tangible than professional service, *client* may sound highfalutin.

climactic, climatic. The first refers to a climax, the second to climate. "That is the climactic scene in the play"; "Climatic conditions are agreeable in California."

climate (of opinion, etc.). The figurative extension of *climate* is considered acceptable by Evans but criticized by Fowler as a cliché and by Flesch as a fad. Random House, American Heritage, and Webster all consider it standard; this is the consensus.

climax. Bernstein insists, on the basis of the derivation from the Greek, that the term can properly mean only an ascending gradation, not the apex, acme, or culmination. This is a technical sense applicable to rhetoric. Two other critics acknowledge that in general use climax means *culmination,* a sense recognized by every dictionary, including the Concise Oxford.

climb down. Defended by two authorities as standard despite criticism that it is illogical; recognized as standard also by every American dictionary and by the Concise Oxford Dictionary.

close (closed) corporation. Either form is correct in reference either to the original term, denoting a corporation whose shares are held by a few persons and rarely traded on the open market, or in the extended sense of any group or organization whose membership is exclusive.

(in) close proximity. Redundant for *close, near,* etc.

close to. A gaucherie for *nearly* or *almost:* "Close to 750 delegates are expected to attend the convention." *almost.* The set phrase *close to home* (meaning affecting personal interest) is an exception.

clôture. Bernstein holds that the form is an affectation beside *closure,* the only form that Fowler approves. Whatever the merits of this, journalists are addicted to *clôture,* which has the advantage of being distinctive and unmistakable in the parliamentary sense; dictionaries all give it as the primary form for closing off debate. Both forms are correct, however.

cloud no bigger . . . See *Misquotation.*

clue. See *clew, clue.*

co-. Usually solid as a prefix: coauthor, coequal, coeducation, etc. *Co-operate, co-ordinate* are sometimes hyphened, but the tide is running strongly toward one word (and also toward dropping the *Dieresis,* which see). *Co-* in the sense *associate, partner* is sometimes distinguished by the use of the hyphen. This leads to *co-producer, co-signer.* The distinction seems useless, however, as long as there is no ambiguity. Some deem the hyphen necessary to distinguish correspondent from *corespondent* (a man or woman charged with adultery in a divorce suit) but Webster does not.

coal oil. See *kerosene.*

cockamamie. A new term, said to derive from a corruption of *decalcomania,* and defined by most dictionaries as meaning *foolish, absurd, nonsensical,* by some as of *poor quality, inferior,* and by still others in both senses. The term is slang.

coed. Just as *campus* (which see) is now applied to high schools, *coed* is applied to high-school girls. This sense has made its way into some dictionaries, though the extension of *campus* is not well established.

cohort. Criticized in the sense *colleague, associate, companion.* In the Roman Army a cohort was one of the ten divisions of a legion, and in fastidious current usage the word means a band of people. Follett says it is appropriate only for members of a large group engaged in a contest of some kind. Yet all but the American College Dictionary now accept the criticized usage, which indicates that popular acceptance (the final arbiter in all such questions, no matter how critics complain) has carried the field. Flesch considers the term contemptuous but there is no evidence for this. Those who have studied Latin are likely to be most critical of the new sense. But for the modern use, or misuse, the word would have sunk into history.

Coined Titles. See *False Titles*.

collation. Now quaint for *banquet* (itself growing quaint) or *dinner*.

collective. Pretentious and meaningless in such contexts as the following: "The industry has its collective eye on Washington"; "Local experts merely cocked their collective eyebrow at the prediction"; "The committee seemed to have its tongue in its collective cheek." The last example is even more absurd than the others; how a collective cheek without a collective tongue? *Collective* correctly means *shared by a group* ("The collective opinion of the faculty"). The misuse almost invariably applies to parts of the body, which it is preposterous to think of as being shared, and makes for a ridiculous figure of speech. No dictionary definition gives any warrant for the usage criticized here. The American Heritage Panel was asked its opinion, but for some reason it was not reported in the dictionary. The misusers of *collective* are apparently eager to flaunt their learning, for they are dimly aware that *collective* is a technicality of grammar, applied to words that denote a group: *assemblage, group, crowd*. From there they leap to a mannerism they hope is cute. The usage is likelier to be found in the press, which is forever straining for effect, however meretricious, than elsewhere.

Collective Nouns. Terms like *couple, group, team, crowd, committee, class, jury*, take singular or plural verbs depending on how the writer regards them (as a unit, or as a collection of individuals) and on logic: "A score were injured in the wreck"; "The crowd was dispersed"; "The audience were waving their programs." Consistency should be observed: not "The team is proud of their season" but "The team is proud of its season." See also *Adolescent they*. Bryant and Evans concur in the basic principle of consistency. Ordinarily, nouns for organizations regarded as an entity, like *company*, are referred to by *it*, not *they*. "The company redefined its (not *their*) policy on retirement." Sums of money, distances, and the like are logically considered singular, not plural: "The delinquency was $55 million, of which $44 million was (not *were*) owed by the Communist bloc." "Twelve miles was (not *were*) covered the first day." British usage tends much more than American to use plural verbs with collective nouns: *the government are* (envisioning the government, presumably, as composed severally of the members of the cabinet); but even *Rolls-Royce are designing a smaller model; the committee were in disagreement*. Evidently the British regard collectives as distinctly composed of their constituent parts, while Americans tend to consolidate and regard them as units. It is written, in the apocrypha of journalism, that a certain editor deemed the word *news* to be plural. This was a curse and abomination to his staff, but being wage-earners and dependent on him, they held their peace. And it came to pass that one day he sent forth a scribe to a far city, where great tidings were awaited. But many hours passed, and there was no word, and this same editor chafed in his impatience. At length he dispatched a message to the scribe asking, "Are there any news?" And lo, the scribe was strained beyond endurance, and gnashing his teeth, he answered straightway, "Not a single new." *Number* has its own rule of thumb: preceded by *a,* it is plural; preceded by *the,* it is singular. "A number of us are going on a picnic"; "The number was too large for the vehicle." *Couple* and *pair,* in reference to a man and woman, always take a plural verb. "The couple will spend its honeymoon in the Bahamas" is preposterous; *their.*

collide, collision. A *collision* must involve two moving objects; therefore, objects described as colliding must both be in motion. A moving object, however, may be said to collide with a stationary one: *the waves collide with the shore;* but not *the waves and the shore collide,* nor *there is a collision of waves and shore.*

Colloquialisms. *Colloquial* means *characteristic of spoken* (rather than written) *expression.* Webster was at pains to explain (in the introduction to the Second Edition) that *colloquial* is not a derogatory descriptive, and that terms so described are standard and acceptable. Nevertheless, there is no overcoming the stigma that has attached itself to the term. When it was in widest use, *colloquial* was counterpoised to *formal,* and though *formal* was not susceptible of precise definition as applied to writing, the inescapable implication was that what was colloquial was loose if not worse. As the result of this stigma, writers on language now tend to avoid *colloquial* as misleadingly pejorative. Webster III does not use the label *colloq.* nor any equivalent; the editors hold that what is colloquial is standard. Other dictionaries and works on usage have adopted such substitutes for *colloquial* as *informal, familiar, conversational, casual,* none of them entirely satisfactory. The confusion has been heightened by the fact that in the last generation written expression for all purposes has veered sharply toward the informal; it is difficult today to identify a category of writing that would invariably fit the description *formal,* apart, perhaps, from legal documents and proclamations, both of which preserve the archaic, and neither of which is likely to be a satisfactory model for the writer of anything else. It may be useful to give here the definitions of *informal* as presented in the two principal dictionaries that use it as a status label. American Heritage says: "The label must not be taken to imply ignorant or inferior usage. It describes what has been called the 'cultivated colloquial,' that is, the speech of educated persons when they are more interested in what they are saying than in how they are saying it. Informal terms may, of course, appear also in writing when the flavor of speech is being sought." The foregoing appears in the introduction. The applicable definition in the lexicon runs, "Belonging to the usage of natural spoken language but considered inappropriate in certain cultural contexts, as in the standard written prose of ceremonial and official communications." (Presumably, once again, proclamations, legal documents, and government and academic prose.) Random House says of *informal,* "Suitable to or characteristic of casual, familiar, but educated speech or writing." The inescapable conclusion here is that what is informal is standard and acceptable in any context that is not deliberately stiff. The interpretation of *colloquial* is further confused by the fact that no well-defined line can be drawn between colloquialisms and slang. *Colloquial* can no longer be contrasted with *literary;* contemporary literature is nothing if not colloquial. See also *standard.*

collusion. Not to be confused with *cooperation, collaboration, concert,* all of which refer neutrally to joint action; *collusion* connotes a fraudulent or dishonest purpose.

Colon. The main uncertainty is whether a complete sentence following a colon should begin with a capital letter. Two critics say no, one says yes, and a third says the writer may decide. This, then is one of those points on which an arbitrary decision may best be made in a publication's stylebook, or by the writer. The colon is mistakenly used to introduce a series that immediately follows the verb: "Members of the committee are: Jane Doe, Richard Roe, William Rose, Perry Moore, and Lucinda Knight." Omit the colon. The series that is properly introduced by a colon forms an appositive: "Members of the committee are all students: Jane Doe, Richard Roe, etc." A comma or dash would be possible in place of the colon here.

colored (in the racial sense). See *black.*

colossal. Facetious use of the word for *entertaining, delightful, terrible,* or as an intensive to indicate qualities other than great size, is sharply criticized. This was for a time a vogue, now waning. It probably was an adaptation of the German *kolossal.*

combine. As a noun for a combination of people, may have a derogatory connotation and should be used with care. Bryant considers the term standard and neutral in this sense, but concedes that it sometimes connotes intrigue. *Combine together* is a common redundancy.

come of age. The form of the idiom; not *become of age.*

comic, comical. Two authorities say the basic distinction is that what is comic is intentionally amusing, and that what is comical is amusing whether or not that is the intention. Consequently, *comical* may be derisive. Both concede, however, that the distinction is obscured by interchangeable use, and no sign of any such differentiation is to be found in any current dictionary. The terms are, in effect, synonyms; rhythm or idiom may govern the choice.

comity. Three critics point out that though the word means *courtesy,* it is often misused in the sense *company, association, league, federation.* The comity of nations is a code of civilized conduct, not an association.

Comma. 1. Adverbs and commas. The modern tendency is to use fewer commas, and it is encouraged by four authorities. It is especially noticeable in the trend away from setting off adverbial modifiers: "We know that, in the individual man, consciousness grows" (Huxley). The tendency today would be not to set off *in the individual man*. The commas setting off the adverbs are also unnecessary and somewhat old-fashioned in these examples: "There [,] he ogles pretty girls"; "Finally [,] the president took action"; "In the machine shop [,] alone, 26 windows have been broken." Opinion is divided on setting off such adverbial elements as *of course* and *therefore,* and *however* as a conjunction.

2. Adjectives and commas. Commas are often also superfluously used to separate adjectives that apply cumulatively rather than separately: *a hard* [,] *second look; a balky* [,] *old sultan; two* [,] *short, gloomy acts.* The test is whether *and* can be substituted for the comma; if not, the comma is excessive. There is a tendency, however, to omit all commas from a series of adjectives; *a short exciting chase; a hot dusty road.* Commas are better omitted from such constructions entirely than used where they don't belong. See also 6 and 12 below.

3. One-legged comma. Elements that must be set off require two commas (unless they occur at the beginning or the end of the sentence). Often the comma is placed at one end of such an element but left off the other: "All New Orleans schools were closed as a precaution but the storm, bringing winds of 64 miles per hour [,] passed the city without causing much damage"; "Dr. Manlio Brosio, Italian ambassador to Britain [,] flew to Rome yesterday." The first is a participial phrase, the second an appositive; both must be set off. Some appositive constructions are ambiguous because they are faultily punctuated: "The publication will be edited by Dr. William Ney, conference secretary, and a member of the faculty. This implies that two men will do the editing. One man: *Dr. William Ney, conference secretary and a member of the faculty* (omitting the second comma). "Severe storms [,] accompanied by hailstones up to three-quarters of an inch in diameter, pounded western Texas"; "A 47-year-old man [,] who had just been released from jail for drunkenness, was found burned to death beside a fire." These examples require two commas or none, depending on whether the writer regards the modifying clauses as nonrestrictive or restrictive.

"This, obviously [,] was a planned diversionary movement." Once again, two commas or none, depending on whether it is desired to set *obviously* off. As explained under 1, the modern tendency is away from setting off single adverbs.

4. Comma with reflexives. Commas setting off reflexives are excessive: "A few lawgivers, themselves, call it the biggest boondoggle in Washington history." *A few lawgivers themselves . . .*

5. False linkage. The comma is desirable between coordinate clauses unless they are very short, and even then clarity of sense should govern: "He was a man of action [,] and words interested him less than deeds." The comma is necessry for ease of comprehension.

6. Serial comma. Opinion is divided on whether the comma should be used before *and* in a series; the parade, led by newspapers, is turning away from it. Meticulous writing and editing preserves this comma; care in this matter is advocated by three critics. Two others consider the serial comma optional. Usually its absence does not affect meaning, but sometimes it does: "They had brown, green, gray and blue eyes." *Gray eyes and blue eyes* is meant, but *gray-and-blue eyes* may be understood without the comma.

7. Comma with nouns of address. The comma is necessary but is sometimes neglected: "Johnny says, 'I'd like to take photography Mr. Counselor.'" *photography, Mr. Counselor.*

8. Comma after conjunctions. Often used, but superfluous, whether the conjunction starts a sentence or a clause: "So [,] I took him up on it"; "They have found it pays, and [,] we have too." But the comma is required after the conjunction to set off a parenthetical element (italicized): "They have found it pays, and, *I must admit*, we have too." Commas are oftenest unnecessarily used after *and, but, so, or.*

9. Commas with suspensive modifiers. These are desirable: "Ancient Ostia is near, but not on [,] the sea."

10. Qualifiers with *but.* Need not be set off: "Notables from neighboring [,] but friendly [,] provinces."

11. Comma with dash. This combination is old-fashioned: "They jar the ear of some,—the soul of others." Either mark alone should be used. If a dash is used to set off one end of a phrase, a dash (not a comma) should be used at the other end: "Hoses were played on the structure—a wooden frame building of three stories, from all angles, but smoke rose stubbornly." *stories—from.* Occasions for combining the comma with the question mark and the exclamation point seldom occur: *The senior author has argued this point in a magazine article, "Are Professional Societies too Powerful?," published in* True; *The crowd cried "Vive le Roi!," but demanded that the queen show herself.* Since the succession of ?," and !," seems cluttered and excessive, it is recommended that the comma be omitted from such constructions, since it serves little if any purpose of separation.

12. Separation of subject and verb. One of the commonest of errors: "A barefoot, tattered boy [,] leads two pet black goats down a concrete street"; "On July 5, she and eight other American students [,] set sail for Southampton." A similar error separates modifiers from modified: *white, ragged, fluffy* [,] *clouds.*

13. Comma for period or semicolon. This fault is sometimes described as the comma splice: "German land investments have sent values rocketing in some areas, good farms of 200 acres now cost twice as much." *areas. Good . . .* or *areas; good . . .* Sometimes *and* is displaced by the comma: "Here visitors can get information about roads, weather conditions, sightseeing." *and sightseeing.* This may be either an oversight or a stylistic mannerism, endemic in some newsmagazines; it is generally considered objectionable.

14. Comma with place-names. Constructions like "George Smith of Poughkeepsie said . . ." and "John Jones of New York arrived . . ." often cause uncertainty whether the *of*-phrase should not be set off by commas: "George Smith, of Poughkeepsie, said . . ." and "John Jones, of New York, arrived . . ." The *of*-phrases should be set off because they are what grammarians call free or nonrestrictive modifiers. Omission of the commas makes the *of*-phrases close or restrictive modifiers, and implies, when we say "George Smith of Poughkeepsie said . . ." that we are differentiating between a George Smith who lives in

Poughkeepsie and someone of the same name who lives elsewhere. Consider such analogous designations as *William of Normandy* and *Lawrence of Arabia*. These *of-*phrases are close modifiers, serving to identify the person, and thus are not set off.

15. Word as a word. Quotation marks or italics rather than commas are called for to set off a word referred to as such: "Sometimes he used the term, ecliptic, incorrectly." *the term "ecliptic"* or "the term *ecliptic*."

Commandments. Confusion and accusations of ignorance repeatedly arise from the fact that there are two ways of dividing Exodus 20:2–17 (and Deuteronomy 5:6–21) into sets of ten commandments. To Catholics and Lutherans, the sixth prohibits adultery and the seventh theft, while to most other denominations the seventh deals with adultery and the eighth with theft. The moral is that reference to a commandment by number alone is likely to be ambiguous and to generate arguments.

A towel-company ad that appeared in a number of national magazines read: "Friend of ours in the hotel business received a conscience note enclosing a five-dollar bill the other day. 'I am an old lady with a Christian upbringing . . . don't know what possessed me, but when I left your nice hotel last week I broke the Seventh Commandment. Now I can't sleep nights. Please forgive me . . . '"

A critic commented, "O.K., lady, far be it from me to cast the first stone." The conscientious lady had made off with a towel, and was sending in the money to pay for it, but no doubt some readers assumed she was confessing adultery.

The assignment of the Seventh Commandment to adultery and the Eighth to theft corresponds to the sequence in the King James Version of the Bible. Those who essay to quote Scripture for their own purposes are warned that reference to a commandment by number alone may not be enough, and may indeed be the broad road to perdition. There is no doctrinal difference between the two ways of dividing the Biblical verses that contain the commandments; it's a matter of combining the material differently, which will not be gone into here.

commence. Considered old-fashioned and inappropriate when it displaces *begin* or *start*.

commentate. "Mrs. Jones will commentate [on] the fashions being shown." This does not mean *comment,* but *function as a commentator. Commentate* is a revival, rather than a neologism; the Oxford Universal Dictionary traces it back to 1859. American Heritage and Harper roundly reject it. Among other current dictionaries, only Webster gives it.

common. See *mutual.*

common sense, commonsense. Two words as adjective and noun (full of common sense); solid as a modifier (*a commonsense decision*).

communicate, communication. *Communicate* is a new pomposity for *tell,* and *communication* is an old one for *letter.* A. J. Liebling commented interestingly on the spread of these terms in connection with journalism: "Communication means simply getting any idea across and has no relation to truth. It is neutral . . . *Journalism* has a reference to what happens day by day, but communication can deal just as well with what has not happened, what the communicator wants to happen." The use of *communication* to describe what schools of journalism teach has coincided revealingly with their introduction of courses in advertising and public relations.

Communist, Socialist. *Communist, Socialist,* and derivative terms give rise to confusion in the matter of capitalization. Analogies with *Democratic* and *Republican* may be helpful. There is no disagreement that *Democrat(ic)* and *Republican* should be capitalized in reference to the parties. Nor is there any indecision about lower-casing *democratic* and *republican* in their general, nonpartisan senses (*a democratic system; the republican form of government*).

But the analogy does not carry us all the way. Although a Republican is democratic, and a Democrat is a republican, in general, there is a sharp distinction between the partisan and the philosophic senses. But a Communist (party member) and a communist (theoretical) are hard to distinguish with the naked eye, and this is equally true of a Socialist as against a socialist.

The question usually raised is this: Should *Communist* and *Socialist* be reserved for party members, and *communist* and *socialist* be applied to nonparty members who are nevertheless believers in the principles? Some think so, and it is impossible to refute their reasoning. But it is also difficult to make such a distinction in a practical way. Often it is not possible to determine party membership; as a practical matter, the descriptives are seldom called into play except in reference to those whose affiliation has been established.

One rule of thumb that is widely used calls for uniformly capitalizing the forms *Communist* and *Socialist* and for lower-casing *communism* and *socialism*, arbitrarily and consistently, *a notorious Communist; the Communist Party; a Fabian Socialist; a Socialist mayor; the communism of Marx; creeping socialism.*

This generally works out to preserve the distinction we have noted as between party membership and philosophy. Exceptions may occasionally be desirable, however, as in *communist philosophy* when the reference is to general theory rather than the party line.

Communistic is an alternative form of *Communist* as an adjective, just as *Socialistic* is an alternative form of *Socialist*. The shorter forms are tending to displace the longer.

A word of warning: If you call someone a Communist, you had better be prepared to prove it, because the term is libelous when misapplied. The designations *Republican* and *Democrat* are derogatory only in such places as Atlanta, Ga., with respect to the first, or San Marino, Calif., and Scarsdale, N.Y., with respect to the second.

Comparative (Absolute). See *Absolute Comparatives*.

comparatively, relatively. Use of these expressions in the senses *somewhat* or *fairly*, when no basis of comparison has been stated or implied (*It was a compara-*

tively trivial matter; comparative to what?), is criticized. *A comparatively few* is criticized as not standard; *a comparative few, comparatively few.*

compare to, with. *Compare to* means to state similarities; *compare with* to examine with a view to noting differences or similarities. Perrin notes, however, that in the common construction with the past tense, *with* and *to* are used indiscriminately. Current desk dictionaries note the distinction, but Random House and Webster do not. The consensus is that it still holds good. Nevertheless, the distinction is widely disregarded, even by careful writers, and perhaps has lost its practical usefulness; *compare to* and *compare with* will generally be taken to mean *note differences or similarities or both.*

Comparison. 1. Illogical comparison. Expressions like "the longest bill of any bird"; "the worst storm of any last year"; "the smartest lawyer of any one I know" are often criticized as illogical on the ground that *any* includes the thing compared in the group it is being compared with. American Heritage rejects them. Bryant, however, says that such forms date back to Chaucer and have been used by writers of such standing that they defy criticism and must be regarded as standard; Bernstein also approves of *any* here. Bryant finds that illogical comparison with the comparative, rather than the superlative, as in "He is more popular than any [other] financial writer in New York," is rare; American Heritage recommends *any other.* See also *False Comparison.*
    2. Comparison of adjectives. Strictly, forms like *better, richer, smarter* (comparative adjectives) are used for comparing two things, and *best, richest, smartest* (the superlative forms) are used for comparing three or more. This nicety tends to be disregarded, however, and the superlatives are used indifferently in both circumstances: *the best (smartest, richest) of the two.* This gives the purist apoplexy; he insists it should be *the better (richer, smarter). Of the two* is then unnecessary, he reasons, because the comparative forms themselves imply two. The distinguished authority C. C. Fries says, in *American English Grammar*, "The use of the superlative rather than the comparative for two, thus ignoring a dual as distinct from a plural, is a fact of standard English usage and not a characteristic of vulgar English." Two critics defend this practice as standard; two others say that while it should normally be avoided there are admissible exceptions. Bryant finds it frequent in speech and in informal English, but rare in formal written English. Fowler permitted himself to say (of *dinghy* vs. *dinghey*), "The first is best"—not *better,* as Fowler's self-appointed betters, such as Harper, would insist. Fowler's reviser, however, omitted this entry, whether because of its triviality or because he could not bring himself to correct his mentor's English, we can only speculate.
    What may be called the suspended comparative, that is, one lacking a specified or clearly implied positive, is oftenest found in advertising: *the better stores, a more refreshing beer.* Sometimes it is a euphemism: *older homes* (instead of *old*). This usage is a curiosity; Bryant calls it informal standard, and Harper disapproves. See also *all that.*
    3. Absolutes. *Perfect* and *unique* are often cited as terms incapable of comparison, and three critics so cite them. The expressions usually criticized are *more*

unique and *most unique,* on the ground that what is unique is *sui generis.* One critic finds such comparisons acceptable as informal English, while two other critics defend them as standard. Fowler and American Heritage will not allow *more, most,* or *less* with *unique,* but will allow *quite, almost, nearly, really, surely, perhaps, absolutely.* Webster accepts *more unique* and *most unique,* but Random House will not admit any comparison. The current desk dictionaries are divided on whether *rare, unusual* (which admit of comparison) are standard or informal senses of *unique.* The consensus is that *unique* is now comparable, at least in informal expression.

Fowler says, of the doctrine that *perfect* cannot be compared, that logic is an unsure guide to usage, and cites with approval *a more perfect character,* which seems flatly inconsistent with his judgment on *unique.* Bryant cites *a more perfect union* in the Constitution. Bernstein cites and flouts it.

Complete is also sometimes described as uncomparable, but two critics and American Heritage permit comparison. American Heritage also approves comparison of *certain* and *equal,* which are sometimes considered absolutes.

4. Forms of comparatives. Most monosyllables (like *loud, soon*) are compared by adding *-er, -est; loud, louder, loudest; soon, sooner, soonest. More loud* is not wrong; the form *louder* is preferable and predominant. Many disyllables are compared by adding *-er, -est,* but here there is more of a choice: *nobler, holiest, narrower; more noble, most holy, more narrow.* Longer words are seldom compared other than with *more, most. Beautifuler* is something a child still getting a grip on the language might say, but it would not ordinarily be written except by the unpracticed or the affected. Fowler cites such forms as examples of disagreeable stylistic tricks when they are used intentionally (*delicater, admirablest,* etc.).

These comments reduce the principles of comparison to their simplest form. Detailed analyses that have been made by some critics, however, put one in mind of the rules governing English spelling: it is easier to learn to spell than to learn the rules. In general, the ear is the best guide to the formation of comparatives. When in doubt, use the form that sounds more agreeable, or agreeabler. Comparative forms are given in dictionaries. See also *false comparison; absolute comparatives.*

compatible, -ibility. Sometimes misspelled *-able, -ability.*

compendious, compendium. Not all-embracing, as is commonly assumed; a compendium, or what is compendious, is a brief compilation, list, summary, or outline; dictionary definitions concur.

compensate. In the sense *make up for* ("His tactlessness was compensated by his kindness"), approved as standard by dictionaries.

competence, -cy. Interchangeable in the U.S. in the sense *ability,* though the first predominates. In Britain, according to Fowler, *competence* is favored for ability and *competency* for modest means; American dictionaries equate them in the first sense.

competent. As used in criticism of performances, the equivalent of *adequate* (which see).

compile. Not the equivalent of *write* or *compose*. To compile is simply to gather together or assemble; compiling is what the anthologist does. To say of a man who has written a book that he compiled it is to insult him.

complacent, complaisant. Sometimes confused; the first means *self-satisfied*, the second *eager to please*.

complected. An error for *complexioned*, as in *a dark-complected* woman. Webster reports it is not often in formal use; Random House does not label the term but, like American Heritage and Webster, regards it as irregularly formed.

complement, compliment. To complement is to complete or fill out; to compliment is to praise. "The jacket complements her ensemble"; "She was often complimented on her taste in clothes."

complete. For *more complete*, etc., see *Comparison 3*.

completely destroyed. Often criticized as redundant for *destroyed*. Harper narrowly rejects it but accepts *partially*.

complex. For *fixed idea* or *obsession*, criticized as a misapplied technical term: *a complex about racing*. But Random House and Webster recognize this sense as standard.

compose, comprise. See *comprise*.

Compound Modifiers. See *Hyphens*.

Compound Nouns. See *Hyphens*.

Compound Verbs (separation of). See *Adverbs*.

comprise. The whole comprises the parts; thus *is comprised of* is wrong. "The district comprises three counties, and part of a fourth," not "Three counties and part of a fourth comprise . . . ," five critics hold. By this reasoning *comprised of* should be *composed of* and parts that are said to *comprise* the whole in fact *compose* it. Random House and Webster, however, allow the parts to comprise the whole—"Three counties comprise the district"—and Random House also allows *comprised of*. The consensus favors the principles first stated in this entry.

concede. See *Attribution*.

concept. Criticized as a fad for *idea, rule, plan, design, program*, etc. The basic sense is more or less technical, belonging to philosophy and science, and is that of an abstract idea generalized for particular instances. Current dictionaries, however, also recognize as standard one or more of the senses *thought, general notion, idea.* It is the fate of technical terms, if they catch the public fancy, to be enthusiastically taken up and distorted from their original meanings, and then finally to be recognized as standard in the distorted senses. The process often generates indignation and sometimes outrage. See also *nth.*

concert, recital. *Concert,* by derivation, implies a performance by a group, whereas a recital is a performance by a soloist. The distinction is generally observed, although *concert* is sometimes applied to what are technically recitals without arousing public indignation. A performance by an orchestra, however, is never referred to as a recital.

concertize. Sometimes aspersed by being classed with verbs unnecessarily created by affixing *-ize. Concertize* is entirely reputable, however, like many another established word in *-ize.*

conciseness, concision. Synonyms; *concision* is newer. Evans accepts them on equal terms; Fowler considers *concision* something of an affectation, and he and Follett reason that *concision* connotes the process of cutting down, *conciseness* the quality of being concise. Dictionaries equate the terms in the literary sense, and regard the meaning *cutting up* or *off* or *down* as obsolete.

conclave. The term applies to a secret or private meeting, specifically that of the cardinals to elect a pope. Newspapers use *conclave* as a random variant for *convention* or *conference.* Webster and Random House accept this sense but American Heritage does not.

conclude. Unidiomatic followed by an infinitive: "The citizens' committee concluded to file a separate report." *decided to* or *concluded that it would.*

concrete. See *cement, concrete.*

concretize. Standard in the sense *make specific.* Users of the term should be aware that it bears some of the same opprobrium as *finalize* (which see) and other new verbs in *-ize,* and will be disdained by many as gobbledygook.

condemn, contemn. *Contemn* is not a fancy synonym for *condemn,* as is sometimes assumed; it means treat with scorn or contempt. *Condemn* is close enough to *damn* so that the association should be kept in mind. The usual error is to use it as a synonym for *criticize* or *blame.* The writer of a letter of recommendation said, for example, that he did not believe the subject should be condemned for having changed jobs, and made his beneficiary wince.

condition. Criticized as used in *heart condition, lung condition,* as a faceless euphemism for *ailment, disease*. American Heritage, acknowledging the criticism, sanctions this usage as standard, and so does Webster; Random House does not recognize it.

confess to. Clumsy and excessive for *confess:* "He confessed to an interest in the occult." But dictionaries consider it standard. See also *admit, admit to*.

confidant, confidante. Fowler says *confidant* is masculine; in the U.S., however, though *confidante* is feminine, *confidant* is bisexual.

conform. Takes either *to* or *with*.

congestion. Sometimes misspelled *conjestion*.

congratulate, congratulations. Almost always mispronounced *conGRADulate, conGRADulations* over the air and often elsewhere. The dictionaries unanimously give conGRACHulate, conGRACHulations, and this is the version used by educated talkers. Whatever the origin of the mispronunciation, it is comparatively new, dating perhaps from no later than the late 1950s. The error is so prevalent it might be expected to have given rise to the corresponding misspelling, but there is no sign of this.

(the) Congress. See *the*.

Congressional Medal of Honor. A misnomer oftener applied than the correct designation, Medal of Honor, to the nation's highest military award.

congressman. There is every reason why the word should mean either *senator* or *representative*, and some insist that it does. A senator is so rarely referred to thus, however, that it may as well be conceded that usage has attached *congressman* exclusively to representatives.

Conjunctions. See the entry for the specific word (*and, but,* etc.); *Comma*.

connection, connexion. The latter is British spelling, and it would be sensible if such forms were adopted in the U.S. See also *in connection with*.

connive. Often misused to mean *conspire*, rather than *shut one's eyes to* (usually, an evil). Three desk dictionaries concur, though American Heritage, Random House, and Webster also give *conspire, intrigue*.

connote, denote. What a word denotes is what it specifically means; what it connotes is what it suggests.

conscience'(s) sake. See *sake*.

consensus of opinion. Redundant for *consensus,* which, incidentally, is often misspelled *concensus.*

consequential. Rejected by American Heritage in the sense *important, significant,* rather than *following upon* (*consequential findings by the grand jury*) but considered standard by Random House and Webster.

conservative. It may be misleading to capitalize this term as a political descriptive in the U.S., since it suggests a nonexistent national Conservative Party. Such parties have been organized within states, and when reference is made to a member of them, it should be explicit: *a member of New York's Conservative Party,* not *a Conservative.* See also *liberal.* After earlier indignation, Fowler now admits *conservative* in the sense *moderate* with such words as *estimate;* Evans defends it and Flesch derides it. This sense, however, is specifically sanctioned by dictionaries.

consider. In the sense *regard,* not idiomatically followed by *as:* "He was considered [as] a coward." This applies also to *term:* "They were termed [as] infidels by the natives." The error probably arises from a mistaken analogy with *regard,* which does take *as:* "He was regarded as an interloper." *To be* is also superfluous after *consider:* "He was considered to be a rogue." *Consider* is often carelessly used in place of *deem, believe, think, conclude:* "The office of public information does not consider that bias has been shown." *believe, conclude,* etc. Nor does *consider* idiomatically have a clause as its object: "The general considers the art work is obscure." Omit *is.* "My mother's family was opposed to her marriage with my father, considering that he was not good enough for her." *Considering that* may easily be understood in the sense *because,* but the writer intended *regarding him as not good enough.* "Naturally, if they can get it at that price, the Soviets will consider that they have a bargain." *Decide, conclude,* or *consider it a bargain.*

considerable, considerably. *Considerable* is not standard for *considerably:* "He was considerable put out by the criticism." Seven authorities recognize *considerable* as a noun ("He has done considerable for the university"), though American Heritage and Random House consider this informal.

consist in, of. To *consist in* is to inhere or reside in: "The value of the advice consists in its honesty"; to *consist of* is to be made up, or composed, of: "The cake consists of flour, milk, eggs, and other ingredients."

consistency is the hobgoblin . . . See *Misquotation.*

consistent, -ly. Sometimes misspelled *consistant, ly.*

consummate. Often misused as an adjective by music critics and as a verb by society writers. The more ecstatic kind of critic links *consummate* with *artistry.*

Consummate in this context means *perfect;* it is the kind of praise that should be too seldom bestowed to create the cliché that *consummate artistry* unquestionably is.

Since Nice Nellyness is the ruling spirit of the society page, it comes as a thunderbolt to read there, in an otherwise prim account of a wedding, that the marriage was *consummated.* Disaster perhaps justly lies in wait for the writer who picks up a phrase that sounds impressive and takes it for her own without making certain what it means. *Consummate* in this connection has to do with sexual intercourse; the consummation of a marriage is a legal consideration, hardly a fit subject for society-page reportage. Sometimes these felonies are compounded by spelling *consummate* with one *m.*

contact. The objections to *contact* as both verb ("I'll contact him") and noun ("George has some good contacts in that town") no longer have much validity. In the past, *contact* as a verb was not only objected to as such but complained of as hopelessly overworked. It is a nice question whether this use has now subsided or whether we are so used to seeing it we no longer particularly notice. As the shortest distance between two points, *contact* will hardly be pushed aside. It conveys an inclusive meaning that none of the substitutes sometimes proposed can offer. "In this event, the family physician is contacted." *Called?* This is ambiguous for *telephoned* or *summoned,* and neither may fit. *Consulted* is possible, but unlikely. "Eleanor said her mother has not tried to contact her since her arrest." *Call?* This does not include *visit. Get in touch with* is always possible; it is what *contact* means. *Contact* as a verb *can* be avoided, and it is up to the writer to decide whether it is worthwhile. In deciding, he may as well keep in mind that *contact* as a verb has not fully emerged into the sunshine of full acceptance. Six authorities now consider it fully acceptable; Bernstein remains doubtful of it and American Heritage rejects it. Random House and Webster both recognize it as standard; this is the overwhelming consensus. *Contact* as a noun ("He made a number of useful contacts on the trip") is no longer open to aspersion.

contagious, infectious. Diseases that are contagious are transmissible by contact; those that are infectious are transmissible by organisms, and may or may not also be contagious. In popular use the terms are interchangeable, but all dictionaries maintain the distinction and the Standard College Dictionary explains it.

contemporary. Two critics say that the word can mean only existing at the same time, and thus a thing must be said to be contemporary with something else. This rules out applying the term to one thing alone (*a contemporary fashion*) in the sense *current, modern, of today.* This use, however, is widespread and clearly understood. Evans explicitly accepts it, and so do American Heritage, Random House, and Webster. American Heritage warns of possible ambiguity in reference to the past, when the reader may be uncertain whether *contemporary* means relating to the past time under consideration or to the present.

contemptible, contemptuous. These deserve to be told apart, as much as *infer* and *imply*. What is contemptible is deserving of contempt: *a contemptible evasion*. What is contemptuous expresses contempt: *a contemptuous smile*.

contend. An unexplainable variant for *say, assert,* and the like when used, as it often is, of statements with which no disagreement is indicated. "When the average man takes his daily shave, he removes almost as much skin as hair, a dermatologist contends." *reports, explains, says.*

contiguous. Although *contiguous* is sometimes admitted in a looser sense, it is best restricted to what touches: "California and Nevada are *contiguous*." *Adjacent* and *adjoining* are suitable in the senses *near to one another* or *side by side*.

continual, continuous. In traditional usage *continual* means recurring at intervals and *continuous* means going on without interruption; the distinction is set forth by five authorities. Follett believes that careless interchange is destroying its usefulness, and it seems likely that this process is now complete. There is no point in attempting to maintain distinctions that are lost on most educated readers. Most current dictionaries, including Webster, give the words as synonyms, but American Heritage and Random House maintain the distinction. Bryant, writing in *Word Study*, has cited statistics to show that even literary writers now use the terms interchangeably.

The writer who wants to be sure of conveying his intended meaning would do better to use *intermittent* rather than *continual* and *incessant* or *uninterrupted* rather than *continuous*. For the benefit of those who are intent on preserving the distinction, Bernstein has invented a mnemonic device: the *ous* of *continuous* may be regarded as standing for *one uninterrupted sequence*. But perhaps the mere need for such a device is the final proof of hopeless confusion of the terms. Curiously, instinct leads us to the right choice in tangible connections: we naturally say *a continuous rope, a continuous electrical conductor*.

continue on. Redundant for *continue*.

Contractions. Contractions (*I'll, we've, he'd, it's*) are sometimes aspersed, but their use in informal contexts is described as standard and an aid to readability by three authorities. Flesch made a strong case for their use in *The Art of Readable Writing,* concluding, "If you want to write informal English, the use of contractions is certainly essential." In his book on usage, he says words not contracted in speech should not be contracted in print, but gives no examples. He adds that an impression of stiffness may be given by writing *is he not* rather than the more natural *isn't he*. See *Poesy*. Fowler (under the entry *elision*) takes a skeptical view of contractions, saying that while on the one hand they follow the pattern by which *-es* became *'s* to form possessives, "the printing of these elided forms in serious prose will no doubt continue to grate on some old-fashioned ears." The tone of the context governs the decision whether contractions are suitable; if it is exceedingly formal, contractions are out of place. They are usually appropriate in direct quotations and in journalism.

contractual. Sometimes misspelled *contractural.*

controversial. ". . . we have changed the meaning of the word *controversial.* It now means something (or someone) about which we cannot afford to engage in controversy—virtually the opposite of the former meaning. Even for lawyers controversy is made to sound like a disreputable thing, as this description suggests: 'His background has not prevented him from building a lucrative practice, mainly with respectable trade unions but with some controversial ones as clients.' "—Jacques Barzun, *The House of Intellect.* In a similar vein, Follett deplores the wide use of *controversial* to mean not, in its original sense, *engaging in controversy,* but rather *disapproved of* or *causing criticism.* Thus *a controversial figure* might now be used to mean merely one who arouses controversy or debate, not necessarily one who engages in controversy. Random House, however, gives *subject to controversy; debatable,* and Webster defines the term similarly. Considering this, and the fact that the word in the criticized sense is in such wide use, Follett's distinction seems useless and hairsplitting. See also *noncontroversial issue.*

contusions. See *Technical Terms.*

convince. The displacement of *persuade* by *convince* flouts idiom, four critics hold. One is convinced *of* a fact, or *that* it is so. This is the customary usage, and the meaning of *convince* is *create belief in. Persuade,* on the other hand, means *talk into* or *induce.* Idiomatically, *convince* is not followed by an infinitive: "The director of the museum had convinced Brancusi to part with the sculptures for a while"; "The decree of nationalization has all but convinced Western capitalists to zip shut their billfolds"; "We can only hope Congress can be convinced to finance the dam and the canal at the same time." In each instance, the word should be *persuade,* or the sentence must be recast to read *convinced that he should part with, that they should zip shut, that Congress can be induced.* Flesch says *convince* with *to* is a new idiom, and Harper surprisingly accepts it, but neither Webster, American Heritage, nor Random House does. The consensus overwhelmingly disapproves of *convince* with *to.*

cool, cooly, coolly. As an adjective applied to large sums of money (*a cool million*) *cool* has been under fire as hackneyed for many years. *Coolly* is predominant and preferable to *cooly.*

cooperate, co-operate, coöperate. *Cooperate* is now the preferred version, dictionaries agree. But the clipped version of *cooperative* as a noun is *co-op.*

coordinate, co-ordinate, coördinate. *Coordinate* is recommended.

cop. Many a stricture has been placed against the use of this word by newspapers, on the ground that it does not indicate respect for officers of the law. Whether it is actually derogatory, as Harper concludes, is doubtful. Many are likely to boggle at the idea of paying any special deference to police, to the extent of banning a useful and generally accepted word. Language, in any event, can only reflect respect; it cannot create it. Though *cop* may be objected to as not showing respect, it does not show any particular disrespect either. It does suggest familiarity, perhaps of a kind that many policemen like to think of as existing between themselves and the public. *Cop,* still generally regarded as slang, is prevalent enough so that it is recognized in some dictionaries as standard. The term is traced by Simeon Potter in *Our Language* to "copper, one who *cops* or *caps* (Latin capere, 'to take')."

The late John Lardner, writing in *The New Yorker,* drew a distinction between *cop* and *copper.* The latter, he said, is invariably disparaging, and he speculated that objectors to *cop* are confusing it with *copper. Copper,* it is true, is favored by fugitives from justice, though it may now have been superseded. Some critics of *cop* hold that the term is the equivalent of *shyster* as applied to a lawyer, or of *quack* as applied to a doctor. This view has no real basis, however, for no question of competence or integrity is implied in its use. Hal Boyle of the Associated Press wrote in part: "Cops don't like the average citizen to call them cops. But what do they call themselves when talking to other members of their profession? Cops! . . . What man in the long blue line doesn't take pride in being called 'a good cop'? What policeman can resent a big-eyed kid who looks up at him and says, 'When I grow up I want to be a cop just like you'? . . . People can be policed, but nobody can police a language."

The *Police Review,* a police force magazine in London, reported the British bobby prefers to be called a cop. *Bobby* was described as sounding a bit prissy.

cope. Until recently, *cope* was always used with *with* and an object in the sense *contend with:* "He did his best to cope with the situation." Frequently, however, it now stands alone: "He was unable to cope," a usage that is recognized as standard by one critic, called casual by another, and given as standard by Webster. Random House and three desk dictionaries give only *cope with;* American Heritage and Harper reject the new usage. This is the consensus.

cord. See *chord, cord.*

corespondent, correspondent. A corespondent is one charged with adultery in a divorce case—the man or woman at the outer point of the triangle. A correspondent is one who sends information in writing—letters, dispatches, whatever. Hyphenating *co-respondent* is now old-fashioned.

corn. The difference between British and American usage sometimes causes confusion. In the U.S. corn is Indian corn (or maize); in Britain it is wheat, oats, or barley.

corporal, corporeal. The term is *corporal* (i.e., bodily) *punishment; corporeal* usually relates to the body in contradistinction to the spirit.

corps. Pronounced *core;* singular and plural are identical in form. Sometimes ignorantly given *corp* in such designations as *Corps of Army Engineers* and *corps of cadets*.

corpus delicti. Often used in reference to the body of a victim of murder, but it does not mean that at all. It is the evidence necessary to establish that a crime—not necessarily murder—has been committed.

cost out. Governmentese for *cost* as a verb meaning to determine the cost of: "I costed the program out, and it came to two billion." Commenting on this expression, Paul Neely of the Riverside (Calif.) *Press-Enterprise* said it is common among economists, especially in relation to government programs. "Costing out involves estimating the costs of a program over whatever time span it might have," he explained. "The cost of a conventionally powered ship may be less than that of a nuclear-powered ship. But 'costing it out' to include fuel, maintenance, foreign bases for refueling, etc., may show that the nuclear-powered ship is cheaper in the long run. Costing out is a relatively new concept. Secretary of Defense Robert McNamara's whiz kids were responsible for popularizing it." Webster's Collegiate gives this new usage; other dictionaries give *cost* alone as a transitive verb: "Some colleges try to cost menus before they use them."

couch. For *say, express* ("The offer was couched in extravagant terms"), criticized as pretentious in ordinary contexts.

couldn't care less. A vogue expression that has not only grown tiresome but also has apparently fatigued some of its users to the extent that they cannot get it all out, and end by reversing its sense. The distinguished chancellor of one of the country's leading universities said, for example, in a speech: "They use the word *obscene* to describe rat-bitten children in Chicago. They could care less about the striptease joints in the same city." *couldn't care less*.

council, -sel, -cilor, -selor, consul. A council is a governing or consultative body (*city council; council of elders*). *Counsel* is a noun meaning advice (*good counsel is often ignored*), the designation of one who advises (*the defendant was represented by counsel*—in this case, a lawyer), or a verb meaning *to advise* (*we were counseled to change our plans*). "He preached a council of moderation" is wrong; *counsel.* A modern consul is a government official who looks after commercial interests in a foreign country.
   Councilor and *counselor* may both be spelled with two *l*'s. A councilor is a member of a council, although sometimes the term is used as the title of an office without reference to a council. A counselor is one who counsels or gives advice; there are, among other varieties, investment counselors, camp counselors, and student counselors. *Counselor* is also a term of address directed, usually by judges in a courtroom, to a lawyer serving as counsel. Applied to a lawyer in other circumstances, it is usually jocular. A county council is a governing body; a county counsel is a legal adviser.

count noses. A journalistic stereotype, supposedly whimsical, used in reporting the size of audiences, etc.

counter-. Solid as a prefix: *counteraction, counterattack, counterproposal,* etc.

Counter Word. Used in this book to describe certain expressions. American Heritage defines it as "a word commonly used without regard for its precise meaning, as *nice* or *awful.*"

Counting, (meaningless). See *Numbers 6.*

couple, couple of. In reference to people, *couple* (like *pair*) takes a plural verb: *The couple are* (not *is*) *honeymooning.* Bryant says either singular or plural is acceptable. See also *Collective Nouns.* Two critics say the omission of *of* after *couple* (*a couple halfbucks, a couple rounds*) is not standard.

course (*in, during the course of*). Redundant for *during,* etc.: "During the course of the questioning." *During the questioning.* See also *of course.*

court litigation. Redundant. Litigation is inevitably associated with a court.

court-martial. Here the adjective stands in the unusual position after the noun, rather than before; a court-martial is a martial court. All authorities except Fowler agree that the term is hyphenated as both noun and verb; they are inconsistent on formation of the plural. Two critics, American Heritage, and Random House prescribe *courts-martial* for the plural form, but *court-martials* is approved by two others and Webster. Thus either form is acceptable. See also *general* for titles formed with it.

Court of St. James's. The strictly correct form for the British royal court; knowledge of this and of the spelling *restaurateur* (rather than *restauranteur*) was for many years what marked the difference between cubs and more experienced reporters on American newspapers. Evans and Random House say that now, however, *Court of St. James* is acceptable; American Heritage gives only *James's.*

covered. Preferably takes *with* or *by,* not *in:* "Covered *with* (not *in*) grease."

coveted. A journalistic stereotype in reference to awards, prizes, etc.

cowardly. Two authorities criticize the term as applied to acts where fear is not present, and where *bullying, arrogant, overbearing, cruel, mean, unsportsmanlike,* etc., would be more appropriate.

crack. Wornout and journalese as applied to trains, regiments, divisions, etc., one critic holds, but Fowler notes the term without aspersion. As a clipped form of *wisecrack,* see *quip.*

crack down on. A journalistic stereotype in reference to law enforcement and the like.

cracked. See *quip, quipped.*

craft. As a verb for *make, design, produce,* etc. ("We proudly craft every cabinet"; "Two plays were crafted by Mr. Halley"), considered superfluous by two critics but may be regarded as established beyond cavil, because this is a revival, not a neologism. Dictionaries recognize it as standard. *Craft* is both singular and plural as a noun in reference to a plane or a boat, though *crafts* is also acceptable; in reference to a skill, the plural is *crafts.*

crass. Often misused for *cheap, mercenary, greedy.* There is no warrant for this; dictionaries agree that the meaning is *stupid, coarse, thick, obtuse.*

credit. Two critics hold that *credit* is improperly used in the sense of *attribute* in connection with unfavorable or discreditable things. Current dictionaries corroborate this opinion. A newsmagazine, for example, referred to a band of terrorists "that is credited with dozens of robberies and killings." *Credited* is surely out of place here; what about *blamed for?* (The same reasoning applies to *thanks to:* "Thanks to sit-ins by workers, factory production was dropping." Unless the writer was being sardonic, which seemed unlikely in the context, the straightforward and neutral *because of* would have been preferable.)

credulous, credible, creditable. Both *credulous* and *credible* have to do with belief; *credulous* applies always to people, and means *willing to believe.* It generally connotes simplemindedness. *Credible* means *believable, worthy of belief,* and applies usually to statements and the like, though it may apply to people: *The explanation was credible; a credible witness.*

criminalize, decriminalize. These are new words; the most frequently used is *decriminalize,* and it was engendered by the efforts, to some extent successful, to reduce the penalties associated with the possession of marijuana, which were regarded in some quarters as excessively severe. Neither is to be found in any conventional dictionary; the Barnhart Dictionary of New English since 1963 gives *criminalization* and *criminalize* ("to cause to become criminal; to declare a person or activity to be criminal") but not its antonym. The words seem useful additions and are instantly understandable, but whether they will endure will probably depend on the persistence of the issues that spawned them.

criterion, criterions, criteria. *Criterions* is acceptable as the plural; so is the original Latin form, *criteria. Criteria* should not be used as a singular: "This is the criteria that has been set up." *criterion.*

critical. As used concerning one who is ill, the word means not simply *in serious condition* but *at a crisis* or *turning-point.*

criticism, criticize. The terms have taken on a generally adverse coloration, and it is no use to argue, as some do, that they are properly used only in the neutral senses *assess, appraise, judge.* The context shows what is intended; music criticism, for example, may be favorable, fault-finding, or, in the usual case, both at once. Although this is generally understood, it does not prevent *criticism* from having a connotation of disfavor. At best, it produces an image of the critic as one who is hard to please. *Criticise* is the British spelling.

critique. Criticized by Evans, Flesch, and Fowler as pretentious for *criticism, review, notice.* This view seems dated and pedantic. Dictionaries give it as standard as a noun, but only Webster lists it also as a verb (*critique the performance*). This use is widespread, however, and will probably gain recognition.

crochet, crotchet, crotchety. *Crochet* (cro-SHAY) is needlework; a *crotchet* (CROT-chet) is a quirk. *Crotchety* (cranky) is often misspelled *crochety.*

crumby, crummy. The slang term meaning *shoddy* is *crummy;* inconsistently, a fellow held in low esteem is a *crumb;* American Heritage and Webster give both forms but indicate *crummy* predominates.

crystal. Sometimes misspelled *chrystal.*

culture, cultured. Everyone knows what is meant by culture in the general sense under consideration here—appreciation and cultivation of the arts. But the word has fallen under a certain amount of suspicion as implying a self-conscious and perhaps ostentatious effort. This connotation may have been encouraged by the heavy-handed dedication to culture that has characterized many Communist countries. Their idea of culture corresponds roughly with ours, but it has as a central feature the prescription by the upper levels of bureaucracy of what is acceptable as culture, and the repression of artists whose productions do not fit the state's mold. We reject and even scorn the management of artistic expression in any field, knowing that what is worthwhile springs from inspiration, and that the surest way to mediocrity is by laying down mandatory guidelines for the artist.

Cultured as applied to a person has acquired an unfavorable connotation that reflects not so much on the described as on the describer, for the term is never used except with the intention of paying a compliment. *Refined* was once commonly used to convey the idea of education and breeding, but it is now quasi-humorous. *Cultured* may also suggest an essential crudity overlaid by a veneer of interest in artistic and intellectual matters—an interest maintained, that is, mainly for effect. Fowler speculates that *cultured* has been tainted by association with *kultur* as it connotes militarism, race, arrogance, and imperialism.

What then? It is observable that to put across the idea that would once have been given by *cultured,* people who choose their words carefully now tend to use *cultivated,* to which no shadow clings.

cum. The persistence of this Latin preposition, which means *with,* in phrases like "the vagaries of want-cum-debt creation" and "education-cum-football" is intellectual ostentation; indeed, such phrases have taken on a facetious overtone. Those who know no Latin may be confused by *cum,* and the rest enjoy no advantage from its use. Even by those who know what *cum* means, "the vagaries of want *accompanied by* debt creation" and "education *with* football" are worth consideration. The use of such foreign snippets in writing aimed at a wide audience is dubiously justifiable when they have exact English equivalents.

cumulative. See *accumulative.*

cupfuls, cupsful. See *-ful.*

currently. See *presently.*

custom, custom-built. Once meant "built to the specifications of the buyer," and dictionaries still give this definition, but it has been debased by the advertising gentry. When these expressions are encountered in advertisements, everyone now realizes they mean "mass-produced, but having some pretensions, not necessarily justified, to quality." The terms are generally misapplied to houses and automobiles.

cut, halftone. There is nothing wrong with using the terms within the publishing fields for *engraving,* but there is small excuse for their appearance in print aimed at a general audience, displacing *illustration, picture, photograph, drawing,* etc., as suits the occasion.

cut in half. There have been bitter protests against *cut in half* (and its analogues, *saw, break,* etc., *in half*). The objectors argue that *cut in half* is illogical; make it *cut in halves,* they say, or state it otherwise, as *cut in two.* Logic, unfortunately, will not unsnarl tangled language, especially where idiom is entrenched. (Idiom, in a nutshell, is established, natural expression that defies logical or grammatical analysis.) *Half* lends itself to a number of other forms where any other fraction will not do: *half an apple* (but never *quarter an apple*). He who can swallow *half an apple* but chokes on *cut in half* is inconsistent; both are idioms. *Cut in half* is one of those cases in which the writer is free to avoid the expression if it offends him, but is on uncertain ground in criticizing its use by others. Two critics and two dictionaries agree; none demurs.

czar, tsar. *Czar* now predominates.

D

Dame. The British title is equivalent to *Sir* and may not properly be used with the last name alone (*Dame Sybil Reagan* or *Dame Sybil;* never *Dame Reagan*).

damn it, damnit. With the greatly increased use of profanity, blasphemy, and vulgarity in print, it may not be amiss to point out that the form *damnit* is unsuitable as appearing to confuse the pronunciation. Either *damn it* or *dammit.* The analogy with *damnable* and *damnation,* in which the *n* is sounded, is too strong to permit *damnit.* If this be nit- (or damn-nit) picking, make the most of it. Webster and Random House both give *dammit.* They also give *damfool* and *damfoolish.* "The damnest social town" should, of course, have been *damnedest; damndest* is also acceptable.

dampen. The word too often inappropriately describes the effects of rain in newspapers, displacing the more accurate *wet.*

Dangling Modifiers. "Dear Sir: We enclose herewith a statement of your account. Desiring to clear our books, will you kindly send us a check in settlement?" The reply to this letter ran: "Sirs: You have been misinformed. I have no desire to clear your books." This exchange, adapted from an example in Fowler, neatly illustrates the dangling participle. But to start at the beginning, it may be advisable to answer the question, What is a participle? It is a verb form ending in *ing* or *ed,* like *desiring* or *settled,* and often used as a modifier. Past participles (those usually ending in *ed*) take auxiliaries: *having settled, being seen.* Participial phrases occurring at the beginning of a sentence usually modify the subject of the clause that follows. The fellow being dunned in Fowler's example knew enough grammar to be able to take his creditors literally.

Dangling participles rarely confuse the meaning. They may well bring the reader up short and cause him a moment of confusion while he matches up the modifier with the modified, a job the writer should have done. Sometimes, however, they create a ludicrous effect, as will be further illustrated, and reflect on the writer as lacking in command of sentence structure. "Applying the brakes, the car skidded off the road." But the car did not apply its own brakes, as this appears to say. "Born of a poor but proud Catholic family, few would have predicted greatness for young Konrad." But it was Konrad, not few, who was born of that family.

"Turning the corner, a church steeple appeared." The steeple did not turn the corner.

D. C. Claypoole, the journalist to whom George Washington confided his decision not to run again, reported, "He received me kindly and after paying my respects to him desired me to take a seat near him." This example is cited to show that the hopelessly muddled dangler reaches far back into American history, for how could Washington have paid Claypoole's respects to himself?

Seven authorities are critical of the dangling participle when there is actual ambiguity. But Bryant finds that the construction has been used for centuries in cultivated English, and adds that *when the meaning is unambiguous* (emphasis added) it is informal standard usage. Evans favors the rule against it, but gives ambiguous examples.

Six authorities agree that certain participles in this position have become prepositions or conjunctions and are not open to criticism. Some examples: "*Considering* the polls, voters are likely to turn out in force"; "*Speaking* of lions, this beast was a bad-tempered specimen"; "*Barring* objections, the measure should pass"; "*Granting* good faith, a contract will be signed." Some others: *failing, allowing for, generally speaking, provided, owing to, assuming.* It would be impossible to make up a complete list. The essential point is that the participial constructions based on these words are felt as applying to the whole clause that follows, and not just to its subject. Whether the writer senses this depends on his discrimination.

Dangling participles are less obvious and less objectionable when the subject of the clause that follows is indefinite (like *there* or *it*): "Reading recent speeches of Albanian officials, it is clear they embrace the full Communist line." Nonetheless such sentences can be improved. Two critics make allowances for them, however.

Appositives are also often danglers: "Until recently a resident of San Carlos, Peaches' real name is Mrs. Ralph Willson" (it is not her name that was the resident); "A devout, old-fashioned Moslem, his concubines are numbered by the hundreds" (it is not the concubines who are intended to be described as a devout, old-fashioned Moslem).

Adjectives may be similarly misplaced: "Tiny and slender, Yuomi's straight hair is clipped close in the trademark of a nurse" (her hair is not tiny and slender); "Now forty-four years old, his assignments have taken him around the world" (his assignments are not, it is to be hoped, forty-four years old). Gay and Skillin, in *Words Into Type,* offer a helpful test for a dangling modifier, namely, placing it after the subject, which makes its inappropriateness instantly evident: "His assignments, now forty-four years old, have . . ."

Dangling Participle. See *Dangling Modifiers.*

Dash. Dashes serve usually to mark a sharp break in the train of thought in a sentence, or to set off a parenthetical element. Bernstein and Flesch cite examples of excessive use of dashes, or of dashes where commas would be preferable. These objections may be most simply summarized by advising that no more than a pair of related dashes (setting off either end of a phrase) be used in a single sentence, and that commas be considered before dashes are used. See also *Hyphen.*

dash to safety. A cliché.

dastardly. Three critics and American Heritage hold that the word means *cowardly* (which see), and is often misused to describe acts that require courage though they may be mean or vicious. Nevertheless, Random House gives "meanly base" and Webster gives "insidiously or despicably mean." Flesch considers the term, even though correctly used, old-fashioned for *cowardly,* and the comment seems valid.

data, datum. *Data* with singular verb ("The data is unreliable") is disapproved by four critics and considered acceptable by four. The American Heritage panel divided equally on this point. (Technically, *data* is a Latin plural of which *datum,* a rarely used term, is the singular.) Fowler recognizes that *data* is often considered a singular in the U.S. Three of four current desk dictionaries, as well as Random House and Webster, explicitly recognize *data* as a singular, and so the consensus is heavily on this side. *Data,* of course, is still also correct as a plural ("These data are unreliable").

daylight-saving, savings (time). The first is correct; see *saving, savings.*

de-. Solid as a prefix: *decentralize, defoliate, deoxidize, desegregate, desalt,* etc. The hyphen is usual, however, to keep from doubling the *e: de-emphasize, de-energize.*

de, du, la, le, van, von, zu, etc. It is common practice to lowercase such particles when they occur within a name (*Charles de Gaulle*) but to capitalize them when they stand first (*De Gaulle, Von Hohenzollern*). This is a matter of mechanical style, however, in which consistency is what counts.

dead body. Redundant for *body.*

dear. Campaigns have been mounted against the use of *dear* in the salutations of letters, especially those addressed to people with whom the writer is not on familiar terms or may dislike. *Dear* in a salutation, however, is simply an impersonal formality. *My dear* (with a name) is more formal than *dear.*

debut. Regarded by some as slangy as a verb, but considered standard by both Random House and Webster. "The automobile industry debuts its new models in the fall"; "Prohibition debuted last week south of the border." The American Heritage panel almost unanimously rejected it; so does Harper.

Decimals. The form *.24 of an inch* (of rain, for example) is preferable to *.24 inches* as less liable to both misinterpretation and typographical error. The form *24 hundredths of an inch* is even less so. See also *Fractions.*

decimate. Although the term originally meant (in Latin) to strike down every tenth man by lot as a punishment for mutiny, it is used today in the sense *destroy a large part of,* and is accepted as standard in that sense. All the commentators warn, however, of such uses as combining *decimate* with a fraction or a percentage (*decimated a third of the rats*), which is illogical, or of such contexts as "Some classrooms were nearly decimated by the student strike," when some other word (in this case *emptied*) is called for.

declare. Often used as a random variant for *say,* but it is more emphatic.

decline (or refuse) comment. A journalistic telescoping of *decline* or *refuse to comment. Decline* or *refuse* when not followed by an infinitive indicate rejection of something that has been offered. "The spokesman declined use of his name" should be *refused* (or *declined*) *to allow his name to be used.* A reader commented: "Very rarely does a newspaper story say 'The sheriff refused to give out information.' And when you ask a man if he beat hell out of a prisoner or stole the money from the state treasury, I don't think he *declines* to answer, I think he *refuses*. It's invariably *declined,* and for some reason this has always struck me as being a pink-tea expression."

decriminalize. See *criminalize, decriminalize.*

deduction. See *induction, deduction.*

deem. Criticized as pretentious for *think.*

defend to the death. See *Misquotation.*

defense, defence. The first is the American, the second the British, preference in spelling.

defi. The work once peppered the front pages (it means *defiance, challenge*); defis were always being hurled. But now it has sunk, for some mysterious reason, into oblivion.

deficit. A stereotype of sports reporters in referring to the number of points by which a team is behind; the word seems more at home on the financial page.

Defining and Nondefining Clauses. See *Restrictive, Nonrestrictive Clauses;* for a parallel problem, see *Appositives.*

definite, definitely. Three critics say *definite* and *definitely* are overused for an often meaningless emphasis; *definitely* also displaces *certainly, decidedly,* etc.:

"This car is definitely the best on the market." Something of a fad. But American Heritage approves. For *yes* or *of course, definitely* and *but definitely* are unquestionably fads, now more or less outworn. Sometimes misspelled *definate, -ately.*

defy. An absurd and misleading effect is created when *defy* is inadvertently followed by an infinitive, a construction common in journalism: "Blacks defied National Guard troops to stage a demonstration." It was not that the National Guard was defied (i.e., *challenged*) to demonstrate; rather *Blacks defied National Guard Troops by staging.* See also *Infinitives 2.*

degree. Fowler says the phrase *to a degree,* though illogical, is established beyond attack. Bernstein says *degree* and *extent* are often used verbosely, as in *to a serious degree* for *seriously.*

degreed. As a verb in the sense *awarded a degree* ("He was degreed by Harvard") disapproved by Harper but accepted by Webster; Rarely seen; likely to be encountered only in the nether world of academia.

Degrees (honorary and earned). See *Dr.*

delectable. Fowler says the word now is chiefly ironic, but this is not so in the U.S. Flesch discourages it as arch for *charming, delightful,* etc.

deli. It was inevitable that *delicatessen* would be clipped to *deli.* The consensus is that *deli* is informal.

delusion, illusion. A delusion is a mistaken belief; an illusion is a misleading appearance, or an idea based on one. An illusion is tentative, while a delusion is firmly fixed in the mind. The terms are sometimes interchangeable. A superstition is a delusion; the impression of reality created by a stage performance is an illusion, as is the effect of a mirage.

delve. Means *search* or *dig* (archaic): thus "The mine delves 560 feet into the ground" was wrong. The writer evidently was groping for a graphic verb, but erred. *sinks, descends.*

demean. Three critics point out that this is two different words: *to behave, conduct,* or *comport oneself;* and *to debase* or *disparage.* This latter is an incorrect formation by confusion with the adjective *mean.* Two critics are leery of it; two defend it as standard. The main point here is that *demean* in the first sense is obsolescent, while in the second it is in wide use. Dictionaries recognize both senses as standard.

demise. Pretentious for *death* in ordinary contexts.

Democrat, -ic. In recent years, some leaders of the Republican Party drummed up a national crusade to encourage the use of *Democrat* as an adjective, rather than *Democratic:* for example, *Democrat senators.* The object, as might be assumed, was political rather than linguistic. The sponsors of the crusade explained they feared that *Democratic* suggested Democrats have a monopoly on or are somehow the anointed custodians of the concept of democracy. The usage was first noticeably employed by the late Senator Joseph L. McCarthy, whose handling of language exhibited other peculiarities.

Evans comments, "In the 1956 presidential campaign the Republicans, insisting on calling their opponents the Democrat Party, to avoid the favorable implication of *Democratic,* managed to make even *democrat* sound unpleasant." This foible was delicately pinpointed in a *New Yorker* piece by Richard H. Rovere, who described how the writer of a letter being read before a congressional committee, "employing a well-known mannerism, had written of *Democrat senators.*" The man reading the letter, Mr. Rovere recorded, "paused after *Democrat,* coughed a polite little cough, and said 'ick senators.' " It is interesting to observe that the more conservative the politician, the more likely he is to use *Democrat* as an adjective. The leading sponsor of this practice at this writing is Ronald Reagan. But most Republicans themselves evidently consider this a disagreeable usage and say *Democratic* like everyone else. This is the kind of petard most likely to behave like Hamlet's, and make a fool of the user. No dictionary recognizes *Democrat* as an adjective. Harper calls this usage "the idiotic creation of some of the least responsible members of the Republican Party."

The capitalized forms (Democrat, -ic) refer to the party, the lowercase forms to democracy as a philosophy of government.

denote, connote. See *connote, denote.*

depart. A question is occasionally raised about its use as a transitive, as in "The plane departed New York on time." This is well-established idiom; consider the familiar, if now somewhat quaint, phrase, *depart this life.* Milton wrote "depart the Land" in his *History of England,* and Samuel Purchas, in the 16th century, wrote "depart their houses." These citations may sound as if the usage is archaic, but not so; it is found on every hand today, and is unexceptionable.

depend(s). Two critics and American Heritage criticize *depends* as an intransitive verb not followed by *on* or *upon* in such constructions as "Whether the picnic will be held depends whether it rains" and "It all depends whether . . ." Random House and Webster bear out this judgment.

dependant, -ent. Both forms are acceptable as the noun: "There is a tax deduction for dependents (dependants)." As an adjective, however, only *dependent* is acceptable: "Our plans are *dependent* on the weather."

deprecate, depreciate. *To deprecate* is *to disapprove of* ("Dropping out of school is deprecated"); *to depreciate* is to *belittle, devalue, disparage* ("He depreciated his opponent's arguments"). *Deprecate* for *depreciate* (*a self-deprecating man-*

ner) is given as standard by Random House and narrowly approved by American Heritage; the confusion is not recognized by Random House. Harper says the distinction has been blurred.

derisive, derisory. Fowler holds that *derisive* means *showing derision* and that *derisory* means *prompting derision* (*a derisory offer*). No such distinction is recognized in the U.S., however; the terms are given in dictionaries as synonyms, often in both senses, though the sense of *prompting derision* must be considered rare for either form.

desalinate, desalt. *Desalting* is the simple word for taking the salt out of sea water, and the one everyone would understand instantly. But usually *desalination* or *desalinization* is used. Even this was not good enough for a press association, however, which came out with its own invention, *desalinification*. It shows originality but no regard for either the reader or existing terms, which seem sufficient. *Desalinification* was just a wild jump off the end of the dock, deep into the undesalinified briny.

description. Criticized in fuzzy formulas like "automobiles of this description," where *kind* or *sort* would do. See also *character; nature*.

desegregation, integration. By and large, the terms are used interchangeably. Efforts have been made, notably by the Southern Education Reporting Service, to establish a distinction to the effect that *desegregation* would apply to the abandonment of racial separation, for example in schools and the use of other public facilities, and *integration* to the disappearance of all discrimination based on race, in social contacts and otherwise. Webster recognizes both the broad sense of *integrate* and the narrow one, in which it is equated with *desegregate*. Bernstein regrets that the newer sense of *integration*, having to do with race, as distinguished from that having to do with unifying in general, has made the word ambiguous. But the context, as he concedes, always indicates which sense is meant. Fowler and Evans criticize *integrate* as a vogue word in its basic sense, but do not deal with its racial application.

desert, dessert. Sometimes nonfused. The first is dry, barren land, the second the sweet that ends the meal. *Deserts* are also what one deserves; the common phrase, *just deserts*, is thus redundant. The error may be encouraged by the fact that these deserts are pronounced like the sweet, with the accent on the second syllable.

-designate. Hyphenated as a suffix: *chairman-designate, secretary-designate*, etc.

designed. Overworked, especially in the press, for *intended* or *planned:* "The rose bushes are designed to act as a net to catch cars hurtling off the road"; "The new fire engine is designed for protection of the entire county." Sometimes used superfluously: "Theater officials announced a new program [designed] to appeal to service clubs."

desire, be desirous of. Pretentious for *want to.*

despatch. See *dispatch.*

despite (in spite of) the fact that. The long way around for *although.*

dessert. See *desert, dessert.*

destined to. Criticized as wornout as used in looking backward ("He was destined to succeed").

destroyed. See *completely destroyed.*

develop. Criticized by Flesch in the sense *become known, come to light,* but this meaning is described by Evans as standard, a judgment concurred in by dictionaries ("It developed that the venture was underfinanced"). In the sense *contract* in reference to disease ("The girl developed eczema"), approved by American Heritage and Webster.

device, devise. The first is the noun meaning a contrivance or mechanism, and the second ordinarily a verb meaning to contrive; *an ingenious device; devise a solution.*

devil's advocate. Fowler says the phrase is often misused in the sense of a tempter, or of one who espouses the cause of evil, whereas in fact the devil's advocate is the blackener of the good, not the whitewasher of the evil. This comes from the sense of the term in its native habitat, the proceedings for canonization. Dictionaries recognize the extended sense of a person who upholds the wrong side, or argues perversely, and Evans too regards such senses as standard. This is one of numerous instances of popularization (and, inevitably, distortion) of a technical term.

dexterous, dextrous. Both forms are correct; the shorter is preferred.

Diacritical Marks. When most type was set in metal, the typesetting equipment of many publications, especially newspapers, did not ordinarily include such marks as the German umlaut, French accents, the cedilla, the tilde, and others. This meant that such marks were usually ignored. The new printing technology makes them much more accessible. All that is required is the knowledge when they should be used, which may be an even bigger obstacle. When the umlaut is not available, it is sometimes indicated by spelling (*Luebeck* for *Lübeck,* for example). Words that have been taken over from French into English, such as *fiance, protege,* and *cliche,* are tending to lose their accents. About the only English diacritical mark is the dieresis, which appears over the second *o* in *coöperate*, indicating a separate sound. The usual forms now, however, are *cooperate, coordinate*, dispensing with both diereses and hyphens. Dictionaries retain the accents on *fiancé, cliché, protegé*, among others. In doubtful cases, recourse to a dictionary is recommended. For fabrication of some diacritical and other marks on typewriters that lack them, see *Typewriter Tricks*.

diagnose. It is the ailment that is diagnosed, not the person, and thus it is wrong to say of someone that he was diagnosed as suffering from something. Dictionaries bear out this criticism.

dichotomy. Criticized as an often pretentious displacement of *division, split, difference, cleavage*, etc. It properly means division into two usually contradictory parts or branches.

diction. Once used only concerning choice of language, *diction* is now also applied in the sense *enunciation:* "His diction was polished." This added meaning is universally accepted despite earlier criticism.

Dictionaries. A lack of esteem for them prevails in some supercilious quarters on the ground that they are not infallible. They are indeed fallible, like all human endeavors. Webster III, published in 1960, did more than anything else to encourage a lack of confidence, although its predecessor, the Second Edition, enjoyed a standing second only, perhaps, to Holy Writ. The new Webster stirred up a great fuss because it accepted as standard many expressions and usages formerly, and even now, regarded by some as suspect. This acceptance was not a whim, but rather was based on millions of citations culled by professional readers, on which the definitions were based. The editors found these expressions in surroundings reputable enough to conclude that they had become standard. But prejudices about usage die hard; the dictionary was accused of permissiveness, corruption of the language, and other crimes.

The editors of the Third Edition could have spared themselves much obloquy by describing disputed expressions as "Often (or *sometimes*) criticized in this sense," or something to this effect, acknowledging well-known differences in acceptance.

For some years, the august *New York Times*, which is traditional in its prescribed approach to language, retained the old Second Edition, published in 1926, as its final authority. Its present stylebook, published in 1976, cites as its primary authority Webster's New World Dictionary of the American Language (not to be confused with the Merriam-Webster series), and for words not to be found there, the Third Edition of Webster. The Third Edition is relied upon particularly for new words, and not for usage. Webster's New World has also been adopted as the primary arbiter by the press associations and the *Los Angeles Times*, a fact that may gall the publishers of American Heritage, who took unprecedented pains, for a general dictionary, to deal with problems of usage.

There is no such thing as an unabridged dictionary; such a work would, by definition (or definitions) contain all words in the language. Webster is the most comprehensive American dictionary; it contains about 450,000 words, but this is less than half the number scholars have determined to be in use. Still, it is the rare user of the dictionary who will miss any of the omissions, most of which are technical and obsolete terms. The Random House Dictionary of the English Language (1966) is perhaps the best-known of the other American "unabridged" dictionaries; its content is even smaller. But it includes proper names (as of characters in literature) and other nonlexical material that Webster omitted, but that people had grown accustomed to finding in a dictionary. So does American Heritage.

The closest thing to a genuinely unabridged dictionary is the massive Oxford English Dictionary, recently issued in a two-volume microtype edition, complete with magnifying glass. But no book, however massive or scholarly, can keep up with the constant changes in language.

The *American Heritage Dictionary,* which was not an attempt at an unabridged version but falls somewhere between an unabridged version and the so-called desk or collegiate size, was published in 1969 as an antidote to Webster. Its distinctiveness lies in the fact that it formed a Usage Panel, composed of 100 writers, editors, and other presumed experts, to give judgments on disputed usages. Their opinions are recorded in the form of percentages following the definitions. But the editors themselves do not always agree with the panel, and the percentages are often too close to be assuring. And the panelists agreed unanimously only once in making something like 500 decisions.

Among the desk dictionaries, apart from American Heritage, Webster's New World (no relation to the Merriam-Webster series to which the castigated Webster III belongs) is the most attentive to points of usage. It is for this reason, perhaps, that *The New York Times,* the Associated Press and United Press International have adopted it as their dictionary of first resort.

In recent years the study of language, under the name linguistics, has become a scientific though esoteric discipline. One of the few things on which linguists agree is that the business of a dictionary is to describe the way words are actually used and to frame definitions accordingly, and not to attempt to impose individual preferences on the user. But there's the rub; what writings are to be accepted as models? Formerly the models were literary; the practice now is to reflect general educated usage. Dictionaries of usage attempt to fill the gap, but not very successfully because on many points they disagree wildly. This book bases its judgments on the consensus of leading usage works, supplemented by leading dictionaries, which is perhaps as close to Revealed Truth as one can get in this field.

It is not true that preferred meanings are indicated in general dictionaries by the order in which they are listed. No current dictionary follows any such plan. All meanings, unless explicitly labeled (for example, as slang or substandard) are to be regarded as of equal standing. Some dictionaries (Webster, for example) list meanings in the order of historical development, while Random House and American Heritage place central or common meanings first and obsolete, archaic, and rare ones later.

If more than one spelling is given for a word (*adviser, advisor*) the one given first is the more common, but both are correct. Dictionaries have many uses; they give us not only meanings, but spellings, pronunciations, origins, and correct syllabication. Syllables, incidentally, are separated in dictionary entries by heavy dots, not to be confused with hyphens. Hyphenation is indicated by bold or double hyphens.

As explained in the preface, references to "current dictionaries" in this book mean Random House, Webster III, the Webster Collegiate, the Standard College, Webster's New World, American Heritage, and the American College Dictionaries. Occasional references are made to dictionaries of the Oxford series, primarily for purposes of comparison of British and American usage, and also for derivations.

die, dice. Evans says that *dice* (rather than *die*) is acceptable as the singular but only Webster's New World Dictionary recognizes this usage. The consensus thus is against it.

die from. Disapproved in favor of *die of,* the traditional usage, by two critics and American Heritage. *Die from* appears to be gaining ground, however, and may easily become standard. There is no denying it is widespread in carefully edited writing, and possibly more often used than *die of.*

Dieresis. See *Diacritical Marks.*

diesel. Although the name of a man, this descriptive, as applied to the engine he invented, has passed into general use and is seldom capitalized.

dietitian. Often misspelled *dietician.*

different. Often used unnecessarily: "We called on twelve different people." If *unlike* cannot be substituted for *different,* it is better omitted, though *different* is sometimes used simply as an intensive. *Various* is preferable to *different* to indicate diversity without emphasizing unlikeness: "Various (not *different*) actors have performed the role." Random House and Webster give *various* for *different,* but the consensus is with the objectors to this usage. Fowler adds disapproval of the term as used in advertising, particularly (but it is also common in conversation in the U.S.), when no indication is given of what is being compared; that is, describing something simply as "different" without saying different from what. Random House and Webster recognize this sense (*unusual, not ordinary*), however.

different from, than. Two critics hold that *different than* (rather than *different from*) is acceptable only in special circumstances, such as when it is part of an elliptical construction. Evans quotes Walter Page's "See that you use no word in a different sense than it was used in a hundred years ago" as an example, in which some such phrase as *that in which* has been omitted after *than.* (Page's exhortation, incidentally, is puristic nonsense.) Another example is Cardinal Newman's

"It has possessed me in a different way than ever before" (*than that in which it had ever possessed me*). Fowler agrees that *different than* is better than the long way around in such constructions, but Random House reports the form is generally frowned upon. Two critics and Webster accept *different than* as a standard variant of *different from* in any context.

Different than, which Follett declares suspect and American Heritage rejects, though widespread, is most objectionable in simple comparisons: "Frogs are different than toads." Bryant finds that *different from* is usual in such constructions, but adds that *different than* is standard, which is the consensus.

Different to is all but unknown in the U.S., but is common in Britain. Fowler defends it vigorously.

differ from, with. The first indicates dissimilarity: "Oranges differ from apples." *Differ with* indicates disagreement ("They differed with me") though *differ from* is acceptable in this sense.

dilapidated. It is sometimes objected that the term properly applies only to what is made of stone, but like many another, it has parted from its Latin derivation. All dictionaries give the general sense of *decayed, in disrepair, deteriorated*. Sometimes misspelled *de-*.

dilemma. Strictly speaking, the term describes a situation presenting a choice between *undesirable* things; not merely a choice, or a choice between good and bad. The retention of this sense, as against using the word as a loose synonym for *difficulty, predicament, problem*, etc., when no choice is present, is advocated by six critics and American Heritage. This view is illustrated by the phrase *horns of a dilemma*. Thus, in traditional usage, the problem of a choice between the love of two beautiful women would not be a true dilemma, for neither alternative is distasteful; nor is a choice between what is desirable and what is undesirable a dilemma. Both Random House and Webster accept the extended sense, however. Flesch discourages *dilemma* as a pretentious displacement of the other terms.

diminution. Often misspelled *dimunition;* it should be remembered that the word comes from *diminish*.

diphtheria, diphthong. Often misspelled *diptheria, dipthong*.

dis-. Solid as a prefix: *disassociate, disadvantageous, disfranchise*, etc.

disadvantaged. See *underprivileged*.

disapprove of what you say. See *Misquotation*.

disassemble. See *dissemble*.

disassociate. See *dissociate*.

disastrous. Sometimes misspelled *disasterous*.

disburse, disperse. Often confused, especially *disburse* with *disperse*. To disburse is to pay out; to disperse is to scatter. "Police used tear gas to disburse some 800 youths." *disperse*.

disc, disk. Harper and Mager say the first is preferred for the phonograph, the second for other uses (e.g., *disk wheels*). An esoteric distinction recognized by no other reference, and also a useless one, for the context will be decisive.

disclose. See *Attribution 2*.

discomfit. Three critics point out that the primary meaning is *rout, overwhelm,* and that it tends to be used in too weak a sense, *make uneasy*. This is indisputable, but the weaker use is widely prevalent. Dictionaries, including American Heritage, agree that the weaker sense has established itself, for all give as synonyms such words as *disconcert, embarrass, confuse, make uneasy*.

discover, invent. Often confused. To discover is to find what already exists; to invent is to devise or create. Natural laws (like that of gravity) are discovered; machines are invented.

discreet, discrete. The difficulty here generally arises out of the intention to use *discreet,* which means *circumspect. Discrete* means *separate.* "The information was discretely distributed to more than a thousand publishers." Separately? Unlikely. *Circumspectly,* i.e., *discreetly*.

discuss. Often used in a clumsy construction: *as we discussed, as was discussed last night.* The difficulty is that *discuss,* a transitive verb (meaning that it must take an object: *discuss the proposal*) is being used intransitively.

disfranchise. Preferable to *disenfranchise*.

disinterested, uninterested. Six critics and American Heritage criticize the use of *disinterested* (strictly, *impartial*) for *uninterested* (*lacking interest*). The umpire, ideally, should be *disinterested;* one who did not care about the game would be *uninterested.* A useful distinction is being blurred. Flesch concludes the battle is already lost, and Fowler wistfully wonders whether rescue is still possible. Some desk dictionaries regard *disinterested* for *indifferent* as loose or colloquial, but Random House and Webster accept *disinterested* for *uninterested* as standard, though Random House points out the difference. Despite the criticisms, the battle does seem lost, and the writer who wants to be certain of being understood had better use *impartial* rather than *disinterested*.

dismiss against. When the defendant is in luck, it is often reported that "The charge was dismissed against him." This is a clumsy arrangement, and would be better put "The charge against him was dismissed."

dispatch, despatch. Fowler says that *dispatch* is preferable, but that *des-* occurs often. This may be true in Britain, but *des-* has disappeared from view in the U.S.

dispel. Sometimes misspelled *dispell.*

disposal, disposition. In general, *disposal* relates to getting rid of, *disposition* to arrangement (among other meanings). "The disposition of the papers (i.e., *arrangement*) was confused." This use is uncommon. *Disposition* is often used of the final resolution of court cases: "The disposition of the case is expected Monday."

dissatisfied. Sometimes misspelled *disatisfied.*

dissemble, disassemble. The first means to *pretend* or *misrepresent,* the second to *take apart.* Emotions may be dissembled, automobiles disassembled. Fowler considers *disassemble* unnecessary beside *take apart.*

dissension. Sometimes misspelled *dissention,* probably under the influence of *dissent.*

dissociate, disassociate. Both are correct, but the first is encouraged on the principle that what is simpler is preferable.

distaff. Another obsolescent word, like *brickbat,* that the press has created a museum for. Newspaper readers know that it means *pertaining to women,* but few know its literal meaning. A distaff is a device used in hand spinning of yarn. Variously discouraged as journalese and pretentious for *female, women's.*

Distances. See *Collective Nouns.*

distinctive, distinguished. Sometimes confused; the first means *different, characteristic,* and the second *eminent* or *outstanding.*

dived. See *dove.*

Division of Words. See *Word Division.*

divulge. Criticized by three authorities as a random variant for *say, tell, announce. Divulge,* like *disclose* and *reveal,* connotes previous concealment.

dock. Bernstein and Follett hold that only in loose, casual usage does *dock* mean *pier* or *wharf;* they would restrict the term to a waterway between or beside piers or wharves. This, however, is nautical cant, like restricting *boat* to nonseagoing craft. Evans agrees that *dock* is interchangeable with *pier* and *wharf.* This view is borne out by all current dictionaries. *Dock workers,* for example, almost invariably refers to longshoremen, although of course it can mean those working in drydocks (which, for that matter, are not waterways).

doctor. See *Dr.*

doff, don. Regarded as affected by Evans and Flesch.

dogs. Few things are more tiresome than the habit, in newspaper pieces about dogs, of having recourse to expressions such as *a dog's life, going to the dogs,* and *doggoned*—except, perhaps, referring to dogs as canines.

dollars. Often used redundantly in such forms as *$780 million dollars;* the denomination has already been established by the dollar sign.

dollar-value. The term has jumped the chasm (or is it just a crevice?) from advertising to editorial text ("The dollar-value was quoted as $6,000"). Redundant; *value.* Or it may be that the writer wants to reassure us that he is not dealing with rubles, drachmas, or zlotys.

Dolley Madison. The usual form is *Dolly,* and this is how it is to be found in some reference works. *Dolley,* however, is the form Mrs. Madison used herself; the fact is amply documented.

don. See *doff, don.*

donate. Once often criticized as a back-formation, which of course it is, but it is recognized as standard. It is formal or possibly pretentious for *give,* which is ordinarily preferable. Writers should keep in mind that it connotes charity or philanthropy. Random House and Webster consider the term standard.

done. For *finished, completed* ("The book is nearly done"), narrowly approved by American Heritage, considered standard by Random House and Webster.

don't let's. Not good usage ("Don't let's count on it"). Suitable for a folksy or jocular effect; common in conversation. Otherwise, "Let's not count on it."

donut. This simplified spelling, like most others (*nite, thru, tho*) is generally rejected by publications of all kinds.

dope. Recognized as standard for *narcotic.*

double entendre. Not French, as many assume, but English, established since the seventeenth century. The French phrase, which has a wider range of meanings, not limited to the sexual suggestion of the English, is *double entente.*

Double Genitive (Double Possessives). See *Possessives 3.*

double in brass. Probably open to criticism as a cliché when used as a figure of speech, but apart from this its point is often blunted. A photographer for a newspaper, for example, was described as doubling in brass because he also took pictures for a magazine. *Double in brass* is applied in the world of music to a player whose primary instrument is a string or one of the woodwinds, but who is capable of playing a brass instrument, such as a trumpet or trombone, when necessary. The term has also been used in vaudeville and circuses concerning performers who doubled as musicians. A reporter who was also a photographer might be described figuratively as *doubling in brass,* but the expression is no more suitably applicable to one who does the same thing in different places than to a musician who plays the violin in two orchestras.

Double Negative. The consensus on this subject is that the ordinary double negative is conspicuous and avoided by all except the unlettered ("It didn't do me no good"). The construction is more noticeable in short sentences than in longer ones, where the more sophisticated are often unwittingly guilty of it. The idea that the negatives cancel each other out and make the statement positive is a superstition fostered by old-fashioned grammar school teachers, except that such expressions as *not uncomfortable* do make a positive, albeit a weak one, and are standard (see *not un-*). Double negatives ordinarily reinforce each other, and this is clearly felt by the reader. Double negatives with words other than *no* or *not* may be ambiguous, however, and some doubling slips by unnoticed: "Few will deny that the high temperatures of the last few days weren't pretty uncomfortable." The negatives are *deny* and *weren't;* strictly, *were pretty uncomfortable.* Few, however, would mistake the sense intended here.

  Double negatives, even when consciously and correctly used, are to be avoided because they place on the reader the burden of sorting out the meaning: "I would not be annoyed if they did not agree with me." Clearer: "I would not be annoyed if they disagreed with me." See also *can but,* etc.; *hardly; minimize; underestimate; undue; fail.*

Double Passives. Bernstein and Fowler warn against clumsy constructions like "The speaker was attempted to be contradicted," which any writer of sensitivity would avoid by instinct: "An attempt was made to contradict the speaker."

Double Possessives. See *Possessives 3.*

Double Punctuation. No longer considered meaningful, as in "Here, indeed, may be the real purpose of this bill,—to dull our awareness of taxation." Either the comma or the dash should be used. Here the dash is called for. See also *Dash.*

doubt(ful). Fowler says *that* should be used after these words only in negative statements. By this reasoning, *I do not doubt that* is right and *I doubt that* is wrong. Bernstein, Follett, Harper, and American Heritage say *that* may be used in a positive sense when unbelief rather than uncertainty is indicated. All prescribe *whether* or *if* to express uncertainty. Fowler's view on *doubt that* may describe British usage, but Bernstein's and Follett's surely describe American usage.

doubtlessly. Cumbrous for *doubtless.*

dove. Bernstein, apparently following British practice, objects to *dove* as the past tense of *dive;* the American Heritage panel narrowly rejected it (51 percent), but as in other instances when the editors seemingly did not agree with the panel, they chose to state the minority acceptance. Four authorities consider it standard. Two of the current desk dictionaries consider it informal, two of them consider it standard; both Random House and Webster accept it. The consensus favors full acceptability for *dove.*

down-, -down. Solid as both prefix and suffix: *downgrade, downhaul, downstream, downtrend,* etc; *breakdown, comedown, rundown,* etc.

downplay. Journalese, evidently fashioned from *play down:* "Exports of food from Communist China are downplayed or not mentioned." *played down.*

downward revision. See *Euphemisms.*

Dr. No question ordinarily arises over whether to bestow the title in print upon doctors of medicine and dentists. With respect to doctors of philosophy, veterinarians, optometrists, chiropractors, and osteopaths, it is another story. Ukases denying the title to some or all of these have appeared in the stylebooks of the mightiest newspapers in the land, though the present trend is to use the title for all these professions. The decision with respect to doctors of philosophy and other academic doctors generally follows the preference of the holder. Around great universities, where such doctors abound, it may be considered sophomoric for the holder of the title to use it, though it is often applied by others as an honorific to the heads of departments and the like.

Those who use the title on the strength of an honorary degree are usually scorned if the fact becomes known. The commonest offenders in this respect are clergymen (usually D.D.'s).

If an academic doctor is identified as Dr., it is well to identify him further as an economist, or whatever, since the reader is likely to assume that he is a medical doctor in the absence of further information.

The commonest honorary degrees are D.C.L. (civil law), D.D. (divinity), D.Sc. (science), D.Litt., D.Lit., Litt.D. (literature), L.H.D. (humanities), LL.D. (laws). The commonest earned doctorates outside the medical fields are Ph.D. (technically philosophy, though awarded in many specialties of the humanities), S.T.D. and Th.D. (theology), and Ed.D. (education).

Curiously, to an American, physicians in Britain do not all hold the doctorate, but out of courtesy are addressed as *Dr.* regardless; surgeons, especially those who have made a reputation, are addressed as *Mr.*

Indications of the title *Dr.* should not be repeated: *Dr. George Anderson, M.D.,* should be either *Dr. George Anderson* or *George Anderson, M.D.*

drama critic, dramatic critic. See *-ic, -ical.*

dramatic, -ics. See *-ic, -ics.*

dropout. Overwhelmingly sanctioned by the American Heritage panel in the educational sense; considered standard by Random House and Webster.

drouth, drought. Equally correct although *drouth* is in greater favor, perhaps for the same reason that *draft* has supplanted *draught* in some senses.

droves. What, as usually reported in the press, people stay away from entertainments and other public events in. The expression is seldom seen in any other modern context than *stayed away in droves.* Reviewers seem responsible for perpetuating this cliché. Somehow, people never *attend* anything in droves. For *drove,* American Heritage gives "A large mass of people moving or acting in a body." Oddly enough, when people stay away from something, they do not do so in a body, and so the expression is not only tiresome but wrong.

drowned, was drowned. *Drowned* is preferable to describe an accident: "He drowned last year in the channel." "He *was* drowned" implies murder, although this form is often used and understood as intended when there is no such suggestion.

drug. Although narcotics are generally drugs, and commonly thus referred to, many drugs are not narcotics, and for the sake of precision *narcotic(s)* is preferable when it applies. American Heritage on *narcotic:* "Any drug that dulls the senses, induces sleep, and with prolonged use becomes addictive." On *drug:* "A substance used in medicine in treatment of disease."

drunk, drunken. The question is whether *drunk* is permissible as an attributive adjective, that is, standing before the noun: *drunk (drunken) driver.* Two critics will not have it; another says *drunken* is preferable but that *drunk* is winning acceptance: Evans that *drunken* sounds quaint; Fowler that *drunk* is increasingly used colloquially, as both attributive adjective and noun (*a common drunk*); Bernstein will have neither.

Fowler makes the perceptive point that *drunken* is always called for in the sense *given to drink* (*a drunken bum*) as against the sense *intoxicated,* and that it is idiomatic in some other contexts (*a drunken brawl*). Random House gives only examples showing *drunk* used predicatively ("The porter was drunk"), and Webster comments explicitly that the word is usually used in this way, though it quotes Truman Capote in an attributive use. Both dictionaries accept *drunk* as a noun meaning both *a drunken person* and *a spree* (*a week's drunk*).

The consensus, in which the American Heritage panel concurs, favors the adjective *drunk* in the predicate position; *drunk* as a noun is standard.

ducat. Journalese for *ticket.*

due to. The point of dispute is whether *due to* can be used in the sense of, and interchangeably with, *because of* or *owing to,* in such contexts as "Due to Asian flu, he missed school" as well as (unassailably) "Asian flu is due to a virus." In the latter, *due to* may be smoothly replaced by *attributable;* this is the test of the difference in use. *Due to* has been objected to in the first construction because it modifies a verb (*missed*); or, to put it another way, because the phrase is used as a preposition. The distinction is hairsplitting, and cannot be defended on grammatical grounds. *Due to* is extremely popular in the criticized construction. Five critics consider it standard; three others concede that the fight against it is being lost. The only adamant holdout is the American Heritage panel (83 percent against); the editors imply lack of sympathy with the panel, saying the usage is widely employed informally. The consensus thus favors the criticized usage, which Webster too recognizes as standard. Random House gives only *attributable;* that is, the traditional usage.

It has been demonstrated that *owing to* and *due to* are identical in origin, and if *owing to* can become a preposition, why should the way be barred to *due to?*

For those who insist on the traditional usage, there is an easy test. If *because of* can be substituted for *due to, due to* is wrong—according to the old rule. "Asian flu is *because of* a virus" is clearly impossible, and thus *due to* is called for. But "Because of Asian flu, he missed school" is unexceptionable, and thus *due to* is wrong. All this, once again, is balderdash in the view of most authorities.

due to the fact that. Wordy for *because*

dumbfound, dumfound. Both are correct, and about equally prevalent.

dump. The press is spellbound by *dumped* in reporting the fall of rain or snow ("The storm dumped two inches of rain on the city"). Although this expression began as a figure of speech, it is used so often that many journalists have evidently come to regard it as literal and perhaps inevitable. But it has become a hopeless stereotype. It is a pleasant surprise now to read a weather story (or hear a news broadcast) that says rain simply *fell* instead of being dumped, or that a storm *brought* a certain amount of precipitation.

duo. See *trio.*

during the course of. Redundant for *during.*

during the time that. Redundant for *while.*

dwell. Unsuitable for *live* in everyday contexts, two critics hold.

dyeing, dying. The confusion is in using *dying* (expiring) for *dyeing* (coloring).

E

each. When *each* stands as subject, it takes a singular verb: "Each *takes his* ration and *moves* along." Strictly, this is true also when *each* is followed by an *of*-phrase: "Each of the prisoners *takes his* ration and *moves* along." Four critics hold to this strict construction. Two others recognize that the second example here would often be given "*Each* of the prisoners *take their* ration(s) and move along." Evans adds that when *each* refers to both men and women, it may be referred to in the plural: "Each carried their own pack." Two critics regard such usage as standard; American Heritage calls it informal. Bryant regards plural verbs and references with *each* as standard, but finds the singular twice as frequent. Random House says that careful speakers make certain that *each* is used with a singular verb; Webster allows the plural. Opinion is thus evenly divided. What is unquestionable is that plural verbs and references with *each* are extremely common in carefully edited material, and growing commoner. A similar problem occurs with other technically singular pronouns like *anyone* (which see).

When *each* is not the subject but modifies it, the number of the verb is governed by the subject: "We each are . . ."; "The messengers each receive two assignments"; "John and Mary each are entitled to commendations" (not *is,* though American Heritage accepts it).

Two critics agree that the number of a later noun or pronoun when a plural subject is followed by *each* depends on whether *each* comes before or after the verb. If it comes before, the reference to the subject is plural: "We each are accountable for our own families" (not *his own family*). If *each* comes after the verb, the reference will be singular: "We are each responsible for his own family" (not *our own families*). See *Adolescent they; anybody, anyone; between 3.*

each and every. Criticized as a pomposity, characteristic of officialese, and redundant.

each other. The possessive is *each other's,* and is followed by a plural, not a singular; *each other's hats* (not *hat*). *Each others'* is an error.

Five critics and American Heritage agree that *each other* and *one another* are interchangeable, and that there is no point in the efforts to restrict the first to two and the second to three or more. "All three hated each other" (or *one another*); "Mary and Sally admired one another" (or *each other*).

eager. See *anxious, eager.*

early on. A Briticism for *at an early stage,* or simply *early* or *soon,* that is likely to sound affected in America. The expression has spread in the East, particularly New York. Too new to be in general dictionaries; Harper finds it "charming."

earth, moon, sun. The age's preoccupation with space and the frequent references to planets and stars seem to have given rise to an uneasy feeling that the most important planet of all (to us) is not getting its due, and as a result efforts are made to right matters by writing *Earth* and, less often, *Moon* and *Sun.* The lower-case usages are so well established, however, that the capitalized versions look stilted. Dropping the article with these nouns is unidiomatic and may be ambiguous: *earth* without *the* means *soil.* "A report on the discovery of a new planet 500 times as large as earth was made . . ." *the earth.*

East. As a part of the United States, by common consent (like North, South, West, Southwest, etc.) usually capitalized. Often capitalized in reference to the orient (which, however, itself is usually lower-cased). *West* is also usually capitalized in reference to the nations of the non-Communist world.

Easter Sunday. Technically redundant, but so well established that criticism of it is quibbling.

easy, easily. *Easy* may not be used as an adverb except in such set phrases as *take it easy, go easy:* "We accomplished it easily," not *easy.*

echelon. One critic deprecates the term in the sense *rank (the upper echelons of the civil service)* as a fad, and another as a distortion of the primary term, a military expression meaning a staggered formation. A third calls it pretentious. Random House and Webster, however, both recognize the sense *rank* or *level of command.* In any event, it is now so popular that uprooting it would be a fearsome task.

eclectic. Means *selected from various sources,* not necessarily *the best;* thus it is not a synonym for *fastidious* or *discriminating.* The dictionaries concur.

ecology. It was in the late 1960s, when concern for our surroundings and life systems approached full flower, that the word suddenly became popular. By that time more than 50 newspapers had an environmental editor. But as usual when a technical term is pressed into wide service, it was misused. Its meaning always had been "the relationship between organisms and their environment." In popular use it became, instead, simply an unnecessary synonym for *environment.* No dictionary at this writing recognizes the new sense, which merely diffuses the previously precise technical meaning. Barnhart, however, in listing new words since 1963, recognizes the extension, giving "*any* balanced or harmonious system" (emphasis added) and offers a figurative example in which the term, enclosed in quotation marks, is applied to the workings of a business.

As noted, there is a strong tendency for the layman to seize with glee an interesting-looking technical term and warp it to his own purposes. It happened also to *viable*. Specialists in the fields the terms come from are indignant at this, but that makes no difference. And no doubt headline-writers were glad to have a shorter and more manageable synonym for *environment,* thus encouraging the misuse. Sometimes *ecology,* as a result, becomes ambiguous: "The waste heat that will be given off by the power plants will damage the ecology." Probably *environment* was meant. Consider, however, "Many scientists are worried about the adverse effects the great dam may bring to the ecology of plant, marine, and human life in Egypt." The writer not only did not know the meaning of *ecology,* but expressed himself redundantly, for *ecology of* could well have been omitted. One critic commented that *ecology,* in its extended sense, ironically enough had become a form of verbal pollution.

economic, -ical. Although *economic* may mean either *pertaining to the science of economics* or *money-saving,* usage favors *economical* for *thrifty, money-saving:* "Economic, as well as social, factors were considered"; "The use of dried milk is economical." "The present system is an economical waste" is an absurd contradiction; *economic.* See also *-ic, -ical.*

economics, economies. Economics is the science; dismal, they once called it. *Economies* is the plural of *economy,* in one ordinary sense a business and industrial system; in another, a saving. "The Common Market has boosted to unprecedented heights the economics of its members" is therefore wrong; *economies.* See also the preceding entry.

ecstasy. Sometimes given *ecstacy,* likely to be regarded as a misspelling; only Webster gives it as a variant.

edifice. Regarded as pompous in ordinary contexts when *building* will do.

editorial. Often confused in relation to journalism. *Editorial,* the noun, is the name of the article in which the newspaper sets forth its own views and policy; readers often apply it to news articles or to contributed matter, such as columns, in which the writer's views are set forth. The confusion is encouraged by the fact that within the newspaper field, the adjective *editorial* relates to all the nonadvertising content of the paper, and *editorial department* to the department which produces and edits that content, without specific reference to editorials as such.

Editorial (and Royal) we. The use of *we* for *I* is out of place except in editorials, it is agreed by five authorities; and this applies also to such expressions as *this writer, the present writer, this correspondent,* and the like as used in false modesty. By analogy with the royal *we,* the form used by kings and queens and popes, writers are led to such forms as *we ourself,* which sound absurd. The editorial *we,* as used by individuals, is likely to be associated by many readers with the royal *we,* and thus to suggest not so much modesty as hauteur and presumptions to power and status. A columnist addicted to the editorial *we* repeatedly referred to *our wife,* which seemed to suggest polyandry.

The editorial *we* is particularly inappropriate under a by-line, which has already announced the writer's single identity. Editorialists, who have a legitimate reason to use the editorial *we* as expressing the views of a group or organization, do not always guard against distinguishing between the editorial and the national *we* (referring to the people of the United States or its government). Naming the newspaper ("The *Times* believes . . .") is more explicit. Fowler cautions that *our* and *I* may be similarly ambiguous, though conceding that this confusion is rare. See also *one.*

editress. See *Feminine Forms.*

Educationese. See *Pedagese.*

educationist, educator. *Educator* is regarded with some suspicion among those to whom it is applied; three critics agree that it is pompous. *Teacher* is better where it fits. *Educationist* is often derisory.

-ee. For the most part the suffix *-ee* denotes the person to whom something is done, rather than the doer: *lessee, draftee, trainee, addressee, appointee.* Three critics discourage the tendency to coin such designations, particularly when they designate the doer rather than the—well, doee. Some exceptions are recognized as standard: *refugee, escapee, absentee, standee,* and many others. For the standing of other terms (*quizzee, examinee,* etc.) the reader is referred to his favorite dictionary. Fowler will not admit *escapee,* preferring *escaper,* as does Follett, but *-ee* is well established in the U.S., while *escaper* is rarely used. Both Random House and Webster recognize *escapee* as standard. A surprising number of *-ee* terms have found their way into Webster, among others *civilizee, counselee, interviewee, permittee, quizzee. Honoree* is widely used on society pages (meaning a woman who is guest of honor at a party) but has found its way into no dictionary.

effect. See *affect.*

effete. Two critics point out that the term means *exhausted, spent,* or *unable to reproduce,* and protest that it is often misused in such senses as *effeminate, decadent,* or *weak.* Random House and Webster recognize *decadent,* and the Standard College Dictionary gives also "having lost strength or virility." Bernstein is surely right when he says the word is used a hundred times in the criticized sense for every time it is used in the primary one. The sense objected to may soon establish itself with the benefit of such towering odds of popularity. American Heritage, the newest of the desk dictionaries, gives *decadent* as one sense. Harper also approves extended senses.

efficacy, efficiency. Sometimes confused. *Efficacy* means *effectiveness: efficiency* has to do with economy of effort and productivity. "The panel disagreed on the relative efficacy of alcoholics and reformed alcoholics." *efficiency:* the reference was to the way they did their jobs.

e.g., i.e. Often carelessly interchanged. *E.g.* stands for *exempli gratia: for example*. *I.e.* stands for *id est: that is*. Thus *e.g.* should be reserved for the citing of an example, *i.e.* for the citing of an equivalent, five authorities agree. In ordinary contexts, the abbreviations should be avoided in favor of words spelled out in English.

egghead. At worst, a disparaging, and, at best, a patronizing, term for *intellectual,* though why intellectuals should be either disparaged or patronized is a depressing question. *Egghead* was said to have been first applied to the followers of Adlai Stevenson by a Connecticut Republican, John Alsop, whose brother, Stewart, used it in a nationally syndicated newspaper column on Sept. 26, 1952, *Newsweek* reported. Warwick Deeping, however, wrote of "a little eggheaded pedant" in *Second Youth* in 1920. Those who enjoy demeaning intellectuals as eggheads might ponder these words of Ken Purdy as they appeared in the *Democratic Digest:*
"Whatever illusions to the contrary they are currently entertaining in Washington, the fact of the matter is that the world, when it is a place worth living in, is run by eggheads. It was an egghead, not a practical man, who found fire, an egghead cut the first wheel and wrote the first law. The bow and arrow was invented by an egghead, and the atomic bomb was made possible by an egghead—a long-haired egghead at that—who sat for a long time staring at some funny symbols on a blackboard. The practical men—characters with the talents of bricklayers who wear signs on their chests saying 'I am a Production Genius'—are apt to forget that they owe their very reasons for existence, always and in every case, to an intellectual."

egoist, egotist. The distinction generally observed, five critics agree, is that the egoist places his own interest first as a principle of conduct; the egotist is a braggart. There is some blurring of the sense owing to careless interchange. Random House equates the terms; Webster acknowledges that *egotism* is sometimes used for *egoism* but in general differentiates the terms; the differentiation between *egoist* and *egotist* is unqualified, which indicates they are interchangeable.

egregious. Evans and Fowler agree that the sense of the word has been narrowed so that it is now only derogatory; Flesch discourages it as likely not to be understood. Oddly enough, its sense has been reversed. It once meant remarkable for good quality, distinguished, striking; now it means, as the critics point out, conspicuous for bad quality or taste. This is the only sense given in American Heritage and other desk dictionaries; the older meaning is labeled archaic by Webster.

either. 1. In the sense *each of two* or *both* ("There are slums on either side of town"), *either* is considered formal or archaic by one critic, standard in America but not in Britain by another, and standard by two other critics and by Random House, American Heritage, and Webster.

2. *Either* with more than two ("Either of the three versions is acceptable," displacing *any*) is considered abnormal usage by one critic, rare but standard by two others, questionable by American Heritage and loose by another critic.

3. *Either*, strictly speaking, is singular when denoting one of two, and thus takes a singular verb: "Either of them is satisfactory." Two critics and Webster hold that the plural verb ("Either of them are . . .") is acceptable in the U.S. Three critics, American Heritage, and Random House say the plural verb is wrong.

4. A singular verb is generally used with *either . . . or* (or *neither . . . nor*) but if one of the nouns joined is singular and the other plural, the verb agrees with the nearer: "Either food or materials are required."

5. *Either* is often misplaced, as in "No date has been set either for the election or independence." *for either the election.* "The fire either has burned out or it has been put out." *Either the fire has burned . . .* The point here is that *either . . . or*, as correlative conjunctions, must be placed in grammatically parallel positions. In the first example, *for* has as objects both *election* and *independence*, and *either* stands in the same relation to *election* that *or* does to *independence*. This means that *either* must be placed after *for* and before *election*.

6. *Either* as an intensive. ("I don't, either, water the beer") is often unnecessarily set off by commas as in the example.

7. For *either* with *they, their, them*, see *anybody, anyone*.

eke out. Three critics insist that *eke out* can mean only *add to* and thus that *eke out one's income* is correct but *eke out a living* is impermissible. Five current dictionaries, however, cite this expression specifically with the meaning *make a living with difficulty*, and so the objection to it may be dismissed as pedantry.

elapse. Now archaic or rare as a noun; thus *the elapse of time* is objectionable for *lapse*, two critics hold. Random House and Webster still give it as standard, but it is rarely if ever seen.

elder, eldest, older, oldest. Two critics and American Heritage say that *elder, eldest* may be used only concerning people, whereas *older, oldest* may be used concerning either people or things. Neither Random House nor Webster recognizes this distinction, however.

elderly. Efforts by editors to fix a starting point, say at sixty or seventy years of age, for the application of the term constitute one of their more harmless follies. No dictionary attempts this. It is noticeable that, as the editors themselves grow older, their starting points tend to rise. Elderliness, like some other qualities, often resides in the eye of the beholder. Unless applied conspicuously too soon (to, say, middle age) *elderly* is a gentler term than *aged* or *old*, and as such has its uses. See also *senior citizen*.

-elect. Hyphenated as a suffix: *president-elect, secretary-elect,* etc.

electric, electrical. See *-ic, -ical.*

electro-. Solid as a prefix: *electrodynamics, electroplate, electromagnet,* etc.

electronic, -ics. See *-ic, -ics.*

Elegant Variation. This is Fowler's term for the unskillful and inadvisable use of synonyms to avoid repetition of a word, as in "About 76 percent of Russia's doctors are women, while in the United States only 6 percent are female." The change from *women* to *female* may make the reader wonder whether there is a reason for it. The analysis of this problem by Fowler has nowhere been equaled; it is treated in various aspects in his *Modern English Usage* under the headings *Elegant Variation, Repetition of Words or Sounds,* and *Sobriquets.* These discussions are commended to the reader. A treatment of the problem, including some aspects of it that appear to be peculiar to America, will be found in this book under the heading *Variation.* "Elegant variation," incidentally, is one of two of Fowler's invented names that have become more or less standard terms; the other is "fused participle."

elemental, elementary. Three critics agree that *elemental* relates to the elements (i.e., the forces of nature) and *elementary* to what is simple, basic, or introductory. The distinction is borne out by Random House but Webster gives *elementary* in the sense of *elemental* (elementary powers).

elevated. Pretentious as a substitute for *high* ("Elevated temperatures are a symptom of disease"). This is true also to some extent of its use in place of *promoted:* "He was elevated to his present position last January."

eliminate. Often misused for *prevent;* what can be eliminated must already be present. "Use of this material will eliminate possible failure caused by brittleness." *prevent.* "The surface eliminates rings caused by dishes." *prevents.* Flesch says that *eliminate, elimination* too often displace simpler terms like *get rid of, do away with, cut out,* etc. See also *avert.*

Ellipsis. This is the grammarian's word for omission of what the reader will readily understand or supply. It also describes abridgment of quoted material.

   1. In some instances ellipsis would improve a sentence, making for both smoothness and economy: "McDonald said 189,344 members are on leave and 257,026 (members are) on part-time schedules"; "The plant is capable of handling 650 tons per hour, but is handling only 500 (tons per hour)"; "Jones was cited for driving without due caution, and Smith (was cited) for driving without a license." The dispensable elements are in parentheses. The principle here is that an element may well be omitted from the second of parallel constructions in which it would be repeated in the same position.
   2. The first part of a compound verb may be omitted, two critics hold, even if its

form changes on second occurrence: "One person was killed and seven injured in the accident" (for *were injured*). This principle is limited to forms of *be* and *have*. Two critics express doubt about the propriety of such omission.

3. However, the *second* part of a compound verb may not be omitted if there is a change in number or form: "The spokesman said another firm has or is about to file for a franchise." *has filed.* "The county is now or will develop a nature-study center on the tract." *is now developing.*

4. An improved style results from canceling the pronoun (*which, who, that*) plus companion forms of *to be* (*is, are, was, were*) in relative clauses: "Work is under way on an ice rink (*that is*) scheduled to open next month"; "The bridge would give access to an island (*which is*) now served by a ferry." Sometimes only the pronoun may be omitted: "Sibelius was stricken with a brain hemorrhage at the villa (*that*) he built near Helsinki fifty-three years before"; "Local issues were responsible for the clobbering (*which*) the Republicans took in the Maine election." Here again the dispensable words are in parentheses.

5. For the omission of *that*, see that entry; for ellipsis after *than*, see *False Comparison.*

6. Extensive ellipsis, used usually to shorten quoted matter, is indicated by spaced periods, usually three: "The speaker said the book was 'ill-conceived, hastily written . . . and obviously the work of an ignoramus.' " The use of asterisks (***) for this purpose is old-fashioned and seldom seen. The use of three periods, with the addition of a fourth indicating the ending of a sentence within the ellipsis, may be considered standard practice, as indicated by Summey's *American Punctuation* and Perrin's *Writer's Guide and Index to English.* But this is not universal. The University of Chicago Press specifies four plus a fifth as appropriate, and Random House says either three or four. But it seems unlikely that anyone will count the periods.

7. In such constructions as "Adjectives become nouns and nouns, verbs" the comma may be used between *nouns* and *verbs* to mark the place where *become* is understood, but it is not necessary: "A sentence should contain no unnecessary words, a paragraph no unnecessary sentences." The comma is optional after *paragraph.* Sometimes a negative is wrongly carried over from one part of a sentence to another. An example of this fault, which can take various forms: "Then the conference would not be held at all and the students disappointed." Omission of part of the verb from the second clause suggests to the reader that he should carry over *would not be,* making *would not be disappointed* and reversing the intended sense. The correction is to supply the positive *would be.* As with *Double Negatives* (which see), the reader is seldom actually misled by such constructions, but he may be momentarily put off, and they are what Fowler would have called slovenly.

elope. One critic says that elopement means running off and does not necessarily involve marriage, but this latter sense is specifically recognized by both Random House and Webster and, indeed, is the one in almost invariable use.

else, else's. The question is whether one should say *everyone's else* or *everyone else's.* The second is now the idiomatic form. The first, which was once prescribed, remains correct, but is unusual and now sounds stilted. The principle holds for all combinations with *else: someone, nobody, who,* etc.

elusive, illusive. See *allusion, elusion, illusion.*

emend(ation). Now restricted to the correction of printed matter; *amend* means to improve or alter in general.

emigrate, immigrate. The choice is a matter of viewpoint. One who leaves a country emigrates from it; one who comes in immigrates. Thus someone in the U.S. may speak of a person emigrating from another country, or immigrating into this one. The same principle holds for *emigrant* and *immigrant. Out-migration* and *in-migration* were born, evidently, of inability to distinguish between *emigration* and *immigration.*

eminent(ly), imminent(ly). *Eminently* means *notably* or *conspicuously: "The settlement was considered eminently fair." Imminently* means *in a short time* or *very soon,* and is usually said of something that threatens: "The attack was expected imminently." Then there is *immanent,* which means *existing within:* "The god was believed to be immanent in the stone image." Only sheer ignorance accounts for the confusion of these terms.

emissary. Once had a predominantly unfavorable sense, suggesting spying or similarly underhanded activity. All dictionaries now give the neutral sense of *one sent on a mission,* as well as the other. The widespread use of the term in newspapers in the neutral sense probably hastened its acceptance.

emote. A back-formation from *emotion;* it has a distinctly jocose connotation. It has been generally associated with acting, and thus suggests pretense or insincerity, two critics hold. Random House and Webster also give the neutral sense, however, of *show emotion.*

employ. Pretentious where *use* will do: "Force was employed to gain their point."

employe, employee. The difference is a matter of preference in spelling. Newspapers at one time tended to insist on *employe* (and on *cigaret*), but *employee* now predominates and most of them have reverted to it. The forms once made a distinction by sex (as in French) but this is no longer so.

enamored. Preferably takes *of,* not *with: enamored of the chambermaid.*

endeavor. Pretentious where *attempt* or *try* will do.

ended, ending. *Ended* is preferable for what is past, *ending* for what is to come: "The report covers the decade ended in 1950"; "He is enrolled in a course ending next year." *Ending* is permissible, however, for what is past.

endemic, epidemic. A disease is endemic that continuously prevails in a locality; one that breaks out and then subsides is epidemic. But one critic, invoking derivation, an unreliable guide to usage, insists that *epidemic* may apply only to people, and that the term for a disease of animals is *epizootic*. Fowler calls this distinction pedantry, and Webster designates it technical. Only specialists are aware of its existence.

endorse, indorse. Fowler holds to the old (in the U.S., at least) view that *endorse* can only mean to sign or to support an argument. This rules out such uses as endorsing products, but he acknowledges that this is American practice. The terms are interchangeable in the U.S., but *endorse* predominates in all senses.

end result. *End result* is redundant, unless there is occasion to differentiate between final and intermediate results. *End product* is criticized on the same basis.

engine, motor. The occasional efforts to pretend there is a distinction that can be consistently applied are wasted. Machines run by steam are engines; those run by gasoline are indifferently engines or motors; those run by electricity are nearly always motors. Derivation is no help; a motor is that which imparts motion, and an engine is the product of ingenuity. *Engine* is sometimes applied to machines run by electricity but having a reciprocal action. In rocketry, *engine* is applied to rockets that use liquid fuels and *motor* to those that use solid fuels.

engineer, scientist. The general distinction is that a scientist is concerned with the creation of knowledge, an engineer with its application. Others who apply technical knowledge but do not originate it may be referred to as technicians. *Scientist* is so general, even when properly used, that it is often unsatisfactory these days. Some more explicit designation, such as biologist, astronomer, or physicist, is desirable. *Engineer* is often devalued, sometimes facetiously and sometimes seriously, by such terms as *sanitation engineer* for *garbage man*.

England, English. See *Great Britain*.

enhance. Fowler gives as an example of error a sentence in which Spain is said to be enhanced by neutrality, and adds that the term cannot apply to a person or people, but must apply to a quality or condition such as value, attractiveness, prosperity. Bernstein and Flesch concur in this; Bernstein adds that while *enhance* ordinarily connotes what is favorable, it is also correctly used in the sense *augment* concerning what is unfavorable ("His bad reputation was enhanced by the disclosure"). These views are borne out by Random House and Webster.

enigmatic. Means *puzzling* or *mysterious*, but often misused in the senses *dubious* or *questionable:* "The success of the new system was enigmatic" was intended to mean not that the success was inscrutable but that it was in doubt.

enjoin. The legal and the ordinary senses are opposites. To enjoin (with *from*) in a legal context is to forbid; to enjoin (with *upon* or followed by an infinitive) in ordinary contexts is to command or urge.

enormity. Four critics and American Heritage hold that the word may be properly used only in the sense *outrage* or *wickedness* or *crime*. Two others note that it is now commonly used to mean *enormousness, hugeness, vastness: The enormity of the Merchandise Mart.* The difficulty is that a noun derived from *enormous* is felt to be needed and, as Fowler concedes, *enormousness* is clumsy. Both Random House and Webster recognize the divergent sense *immensity;* 93 percent of the American Heritage panel rejects it. The OED defines *enormity* in the new sense as an incorrect use, and notes that the error dates from 1846. The consensus rejects it.

enough. See *sufficient.*

en route. Correctly, two words, though *enroute* is commonly used and may yet conquer.

ensure, insure. Interchangeable in the sense *make certain*—"Hard work will ensure success"; "Careful workmanship insures quality"—but *insure* has a noticeable edge. *Insure* is the only form for *guarantee against loss.* Flesch says *ensure* means only *make certain,* and *insure* only *guarantee against loss,* but this is an imaginary distinction recognized nowhere else, including the major dictionaries. See also *assure.*

entangling alliances. See *Misquotation.*

enthuse. A back-formation from *enthusiasm* that is disapproved for one reason or another by four critics and American Heritage. It is noticeably shunned in careful writing. *Enthuse* is accepted as standard by Random House, which points out, however, that it is widely criticized, and by Webster.

entitled, named, called. A name or title following any of these words (and others conveying the same thing) is not set off by a comma: *a book entitled "The Naked and the Dead"; "A Streetcar Named Desire"; a man called Peter.* Not *entitled, named, called, (Peter).* Among the numerous superstitions to be found in newspaper stylebooks (and nowhere else) is the idea that *entitled* may not be used in the sense *given a name or title* ("a magazine entitled *Collier's*") but must be reserved for the meaning "possessing a right to have or do" something: "entitled to honors"; "entitled to a reward." The newspaper critics hold that a book (or whatever) may only be titled, not *entitled.* The sense they reserve *entitled* for is a legitimate but separate one, and the restriction is nonsense.

entomology, etymology. Entomology is the study of insects, etymology the study of the derivations of words. The nouns for the practitioners are *entomologist, etymologist.*

enure. See *inure*.

envelop, envelope. The verb for *cover* or *surround* is almost always *envelop*, though *envelope* is a variant; the noun for what encloses a letter is usually *envelope*, though *envelop* is acceptable.

envisage, envision. Evans makes the distinction that in the usual sense of *imagine, call up an image, envision* is more poetic and connotes less immediacy than *envisage*, which is considered closer to reality. All the current dictionaries but Webster corroborate this. Fowler protests that *envisage* is often pretentiously substituted for plainer words like *imagine, visualize*. The first meaning sometimes given for *envisage* is *confront*, but this sense appears to have grown rare.

epic. Evans and Fowler protest that the word has been debased by loose application to movies (*an epic of the Panhandle*), in sports writing (*an epic home run*) and in gossip columns displacing *fabulous*. The original meaning is a narrative poem celebrating the exploits of a hero.

epidemic. See *endemic, epidemic*.

epithet. Four critics all recognize that to many the connotation is derogatory; an epithet is a term of abuse. In its primary sense, however, *epithet* is neutral, and means simply a descriptive term, like William *the Conquerer*. American Heritage, Webster's New World, Random House, and Webster recognize the derogatory sense; the Standard College Dictionary terms it loose; Fowler calls it a corruption. In the U.S., the neutral sense is generally found in literary contexts, particularly works on literature. The derogatory sense is in far more common use, and the writer should be careful to use the term in a context that will not make it ambiguous.

epitome. A summary, condensation, abstract, or an ideal representation; not an acme, apex, high point, or climax. "His attire was the epitome [ideal representation] of fashion" is correct but "That triumph was the epitome of his career" is not; *high point, climax*.

epoch, epoch-making. An epoch is the beginning of an era, but this distinction is little noted. Fowler complains that *epoch-making* is loosely used of circumstances that are far from marking a turning point. Random House and Webster concur generally in the limited sense; American Heritage gives broader definitions, equating *epoch* with *era*.

equal. As an absolute, see *Comparison 3*.

equally as. Criticized as redundant: "He remained equally as uncompromising on the other issues." *equally uncompromising*. When a comparison is expressed rather than implied, *as* alone should be used: "He remained as uncompromising on the issue as his colleagues." Evans adds, however, that *equally as* is often used by people who are not lacking in education. Bryant finds that *equally* is far more prevalent than *equally as*, which she traces to confusion with *just as*.

equine. An objectionable variant for *horse;* often journalese. See also *Variation.*

equivalent. As a noun, takes *of:* "the equivalent of [not *to*] Boston's Massachusetts Institute of Technology." The adjective takes *to:* "It was equivalent to Boston's . . ."

equivocal. See *ambiguous, equivocal.*

-er and -est, more and most. See *Comparison 4.*

era. See *epoch.*

ere. See *Poesy.*

errant, arrant. Sometimes confused. *Errant* means *wandering* or *straying; arrant* means *thoroughgoing* or *outstandingly bad.* "This is errant nonsense." *arrant.*

errata. American Heritage rejects *errata* (strictly, the plural of *erratum*) with a singular verb (*the errata is on the first page*) as well as the bastardized plural *erratas;* Random House concurs, but Webster accepts both.

erstwhile. Criticized as archaic for *former* and unsuitable for ordinary contexts.

escalate. Criticized by Fowler as an unnecessary back-formation. He concedes, however, that it is likely to become established. It is often inappropriately used and overworked. American Heritage and Random House recognize the new and widely popular sense of *increase in intensity, magnitude,* etc.: *to escalate a war.* Webster does not give this sense, probably because it came into vogue after publication of the Third Edition in 1961.

escape. Two critics and American Heritage reject *escape* without *from* in connection with confinement: "They escaped from the stockade" (not *escaped the stockade*).

escapee. See *-ee.*

especial, special; especially, specially. *Special* is driving *especial* to the wall. *Especially* means *to an outstanding extent; specially, for a particular purpose.* Thus "I like soft drinks, specially cream soda" should be *especially* (*outstandingly, particularly*). An example of the correct use of *specially:* "The troops were specially selected for the assignment" (that is, *specifically*). *Special* is overused in journalism; it exemplifies the occupational disease of straining for effect. "A special invitation was extended to wives''; ''The supervisor made a special presentation of an award.'' Usually the term is superfluously used to describe what is self-evidently out of the ordinary, as in these examples. See also *Journalese*.

espresso. The correct term; not, as often given, *expresso*.

-ess. See *Feminine Forms*.

-esque. Solid as a suffix: *Kiplingesque, Junoesque*.

essay. See *assay, essay*.

-est, -eth. See *-eth*.

estate. The term has had a damaging comedown, at least in real-estate promotion. No one is surprised or even amused any more to find ordinary subdivisions ballyhooed as ''estates''; the term has even been applied to trailer parks. It's almost enough to make a man wish he weren't rich.

establishment. The faddist use of the term to denote the ruling or influential members of any organization, particularly in government or politics, is decried by Fowler, who sees in it a sinister connotation, although this does not necessarily hold true in the U.S. The newly popular use is recognized as standard by American Heritage and Random House but is not given in Webster, probably because it had not yet become widespread when the Third Edition was published in 1961. Later abridgments give it, however.

estimate, estimation. *Estimate* is the judgment, *estimation* the process of forming it. Thus usually the phrase *in my estimation* is wrong, when an opinion fully formed is given without reference to forming it. Evans concedes, however, that the interchange of the terms is so frequent as to be nevertheless standard; Random House, American Heritage, and Webster recognize it as such.

et al. *Et al.* is an abbreviation of the Latin *et alii* (*and others*); *others* refers here to people, not things. ''He was interested in the discussion of bills having to do with education *et al.*'' is an error, for the writer meant *and other* (presumably related) *subjects*. *Etc.* (which see), meaning *and other things, and so forth,* would have been preferable from the standpoint of exactness, but the use of such catchalls is slipshod at best, and they should be avoided unless the reader can be expected to have a clear idea what they are intended to suggest. In *et al., et,* as a complete word, does not take a period, but *al.,* for *alii,* does. This nicety is sometimes disregarded. Sometimes, too, the parts are erroneously run together: *etal.* The natural habitat of *et al.* is legal documents, where it is used to indicate persons whose names may not be known: *John Jones, Edward Thomas, George Swift, et al.* Perhaps the expression had best be left to such contexts. *Et al.* may also mean *et alibi* (*and elsewhere*).

etc. The common mistake is to misspell it *ect.* and thus advertise one's ignorance that it is the abbreviation for *et cetera* (Latin, *and so forth*). Partridge called it insulting when applied to people; Fowler says it is needless purism to restrict its sense to *and other things* as opposed to *and other persons.* A comma before *etc.* is unnecessary unless more than one term precedes it. *Etc.* is often lazily used as a bushel basket, as in "They form their own opinions about economics, etc." The reader should easily see what *etc.* is intended to suggest. Like *et al.* (which see), however, *etc.* is suited to technical contexts and not to ordinary prose. *And etc.* is redundant.

-eth. The unavoidable demand on the writer who shows off is that he know what he is doing. He makes a fool of himself, for example, by using foreign words or phrases in the wrong sense, or by misspelling them. After having gone out of his way to exhibit his erudition, he is surely in a ridiculous position when he shows that his grip on it is shaky.

The writer who finds it desirable to revert to archaisms for special effect should keep in mind that the termination *-eth* indicates the third person singular (*he, she, it*): *He thinketh, she smileth, The Iceman Cometh, from whence cometh my help.* It invites derision to write things like *I cometh, you smileth.* The second-person ending is *-st,* and calls for *thou* as subject (*Thou doest*). (Quaker usage is specialized, and calls invariably for *thee*). Flesch discourages use of the *-eth* ending as a phony device. See also *thee, thou.*

-ette. See *Feminine Forms.*

eulogy. Takes *a,* not *an.* See *a, an.*

Euphemisms. Life is a hard business, as someone has said, and we often seek to soften its blows by giving them agreeable names. This device—for example, saying *passed away* instead of *died*—is known technically as *euphemism,* or pleasing talk. Euphemism is not something that can or should be done away with. In many instances, the bluntest names for things are intolerable in polite society and censurable in print. The so-called four-letter words are an example although they are now often seen. On the rare occasions when they appear in print the effect on the reader may be one of shock, refreshment, amusement, or a mixture of all three, although this reaction too is changing as printed matter becomes more earthy.

We should at least be aware when we are using terms that are at one or more removes from the most explicit versions. Euphemisms are distasteful when they indicate unnecessary squeamishness. The trend of our ordinary expression for many years has been away from the complex, the pretentious, the coy, and the flowery, and toward the simple, the unassuming, the frank, and the unadorned. There was a time in this century when *social disease* was as close as anyone but a doctor would come to saying *syphilis* or *gonorrhea*—and even the euphemism was used with reluctance. In fact, the medical campaign to curb syphilis was seriously impeded by the refusal, at first, of mass publications to even name the disease.

Here are some typical euphemisms. A cut or increase in wages or prices is often glossed over as a *downward revision* or an *upward revision* (or *adjustment*). In the jargon of business, especially, prices are unlikely to be raised, but more likely to be delicately *adjusted upward.* This may be all right for the public relations man, whose vocation is to gloss, but certainly such genteelisms should not be adopted by others with the idea that they possess some desirable elegance.

Realistic is a key euphemism in collective bargaining. *Realistic,* in this connection, is what the user's proposals are, in contrast to those of the other side, which are *unrealistic.* During World War II the public became familiar with *planned withdrawal,* the military's euphemism for *retreat* (usually *to prepared positions*). General Jonathan Wainwright was so outraged by this kind of mush that he described one reverse in these unequivocal terms: "We took a hell of a beating."

The name "Women's Christian Temperance Union," as nearly everyone must be aware, is a misnomer, for its members advocate abstinence, not temperance. *Belly* is all but indecent; the genteel speak of the *abdomen* or *stomach. Bathroom* and *restroom* are favored euphemisms for the more exact *toilet,* which surely is not indecent.

evacuate. Standard in the sense of removing people from a place, as well as in the sense of emptying the place itself, although the former has been criticized. The matter is settled by the presence of *evacuate* in this sense as well as *evacuee* (for the person removed) in all current dictionaries. See also *-ee.*

even. Problems of the placement of *even* in a sentence correspond to those of the placement of *only,* which see. The matter warrants careful attention.

event. See *in the event that.*

eventuate, eventuality. Criticized as pompous for *occur(rence), develop(ment)* or *happen(ing)*
ever. As an intensive, see *however, how ever; whatever, what ever.* Often unnecessarily joined to an adjective with a hyphen: *ever-increasing size.* In the sense *in history* or *on record* ("She was the youngest ever") the word has an adolescent ring.

ever so often, every so often. The first means *very frequently,* the second *now and then.*

every. Evans says it is used only as an adjective, a judgment in which the dictionaries concur. Yet Bryant points out that it occurs sometimes as an adverb in such phrases as *every so often, every now and then, every significantly new philosophy.* Whether *every* in these constructions, of which the dictionaries list the first two and analogous ones, is indeed an adverb may be a matter of opinion, American Heritage calls it an intensifier with idioms. At any rate, the phrases are idioms. For the number of the pronoun following *every* in such constructions as "Every one of the boys has (his, their) own canoe," see *each.*

everybody, everyone, every one. 1. Two critics say that though these pronouns take singular verbs, it is standard to refer to them by *they,* rather than *he.* Another critic and American Heritage say that, strictly speaking, the singular reference should be used—"Everybody shouldered his pack and moved on" (rather than *their packs*)—and adds that the plural reference (*they, their*) is permissible in conversation. Fowler tends to be equivocal on this question but on the whole recommends the singular reference. The question is discussed also under *Adolescent they; anybody, anyone;* and *each*. Evans points out that a singular pronoun in reference to *everybody, everyone* is impossible in a coordinate clause: "Everyone has gone home and it is about time he did." *they*.

2. The pronoun *everyone* must be distinguished from the adjective and pronoun *every one*: "He had something cheerful to say to everyone of his admirers." *every one*. Fowler adds that the test of the acceptability of *everyone* is whether *everybody* can be substituted.

3. *Everyone* and *everybody* are equally acceptable and interchangeable. See also *else's*.

everybody talks about the weather . . . See *Misquotation*.

everyday, every day. The adjective *everyday* (*an everyday occurrence*) and the adverbial phrase *every day* (*It happens every day*) should be distinguished. "Everyday the papers are full of his exploits." *Every day*.

everyone. See *everybody, everyone*.

everyone knows. See *of course*.

everyplace. Recognized as standard by three critics and Webster as a synonym for the adverb *everywhere*. American Heritage and Random House label it informal. *Every place* is a variant. See also *anyplace*.

every time. No dictionary recognizes *everytime*.

evidence. Criticized as inexact or pretentious as a verb where *show* or *exhibit* will do. "The equipment evidenced misuse." *showed*.

evidently, evidentally, evidentially. *Evidently* means *perceptibly*, obviously. *Evidentially*, sometimes misused for it (probably as a misspelling) means *related to evidence*. *Evidentally* is a misspelling and nothing more.

evince. Criticized as pretentiously displacing *show;* Fowler says it is misused for *evoke*.

ex-. The question is whether the prefix must be attached to a noun (*ex-headwaiter*) or whether it may be attached to an adjective (*ex-Waldorf headwaiter*). Fowler will not permit attachment to the adjective. But two other critics say this is permissible and, in fact, usually unavoidable: compare *ex-bathing beauty* with *bathing ex-beauty*. The deciding point seems to be that readers (in the U.S., at least) are well accustomed to interpreting *ex*-phrases in the senses intended, and Fowler's objection that a phrase like *ex-bathing beauty* would be understood as meaning the subject was formerly bathing but still a beauty sounds captious. The problem occurs mainly in composing newspaper headlines; when there is any danger of ambiguity it can easily be sidestepped in text by using *former*.

The stylebook of *The Washington Post*, expressing a preference for *former* for this reason, goes on to say, "Nevertheless, there are times when *ex-* is a perfectly suitable prefix. It prevents such howlers as the story that called the Export-Import Bank (familiarly known as the Ex-Im Bank) 'the former Im Bank.' "

Ex- is hyphenated as a prefix meaning *former: ex-convict, ex-president, ex-queen,* etc. Otherwise, in the sense *out of,* it is solid: *excommunicate, expropriate, exterritorial,* etc.

exact, exactly. *Exact* may not be used as an adverb, as in this common construction: *the exact same policy. exactly the same policy.* Neither Random House nor Webster admits *exact* as an adverb. The problem of the placement of *exactly* is analogous to that of the placement of *only,* which see.

exaggerate. See *underestimate*.

exceedingly, excessively. The first means *to a great extent*, the second means *too much*. Sometimes confused.

except, excepting. Regardless of some differences among grammarians, *except* is a preposition and thus takes the objective case: *except me*. As prepositions, *excepted, excepting* are undesirable except in a negative statement: "Everything about the new cars is easier to handle excepting the payments." *except*. An example of correct use: "The movies were exciting, not excepting the American entry."

exception proves the rule. The commonly accepted meaning of this is that the rule is strengthened or its validity is enhanced or certified by exceptions. Fowler devotes nearly two pages to the expression, setting forth five interpretations of it, all of them esoteric, and terming the generally understood one wrong. Evans makes essentially the same point in less space. It seems reasonable to suppose, however, that logical or not, an expression means what the overwhelming number of its users understand it to mean, regardless of its technical origins or the distortions it has undergone in arriving at its present popular sense. Webster's New World Dictionary says of the phrase, "the exception tests the rule; often used to mean 'the exception establishes the rule.' " This illustrates the argument over the strict and the popular interpretations. (Evans recognizes the *tests* interpretation as the most generally accepted explanation of the phrase: Fowler does not mention it.) Evans comments, "There are few phrases in the language concerning whose exact meaning there is so much dispute." But it must in truth be added that it is the rare educated reader who is not confident he knows the meaning (the wrong one, i.e., *establishes,* according to traditionalists like Fowler).

excess verbiage. Redundant; *verbiage* alone denotes excess.

excessively. See *exceedingly*.

Exclamation Point. Overused. But this is not the vice it once was, to judge from the criticisms that appeared in style manuals of a generation or two ago. Columnists (and others writing in a colloquial tone) often use the exclamation mark to call attention to a japery; perhaps they would be better advised to append (joke). At any rate, this punctuation adds no humor, and may, by reason of its obtrusiveness, subtract some.

Interjections in a single word (Ouch! Indeed!) generally take the exclamation mark. Fowler complains that it is often needlessly used with such statements as *You surprise me. How dare you?* and *Don't tell such lies,* which are described as mere statement, question, and command. This seems, however, to overlook the fact that emphasis is conveyed by the exclamation mark. *You surprise me* (period) is cool and tame; *You surprise me!* conveys excitement, if not indignation. *How dare you?* is much less indignant than *How dare you! Don't tell such lies* (period) is contemptuous; *Don't tell such lies!* is outraged. Whether such statements should be followed by exclamation points must be left to the judgment and intention of the writer. He is not open to critical quibbling over the suitability of his punctuation if he conveys what he intends, and does not falsify or misrepresent the tone. It should be noted that all these examples are conversational. The end of Fowler's discussion of this subject seems to open a window that was earlier closed; that is, he says the mark may be used to convey a special tone. Flesch apparently would outlaw the mark altogether, a view that seems quixotic.

Exclamation points used after ordinary statements with the hope of giving them a transfusion are gushy; fortunately, this kind of thing is seldom found in print except for letters to the editor; more often it occurs in schoolgirls' letters. All this goes double for doubled (or otherwise multiplied) exclamation points ("I appeal to you for advice!!"; "Some of us are in a minority all the time!! Must we be content with perpetual inconsideration? I think not!!!").

F. Scott Fitzgerald, confronted with an example of such overexcited style, advised: "Cut out all those exclamation points. An exclamation point is like laughing at your own joke" (*Beloved Infidel*).

The exclamation point may be formed on the typewriter that does not have one by striking the apostrophe and period while holding the space bar down, or by striking the apostrophe, back-spacing, and striking the period. This latter method, while more trouble, brings the mark more neatly up against the word preceding.

Some newspaper editors of a couple of generations ago had the habit of referring to the exclamation point as an *astonisher,* but the term did not find its way into dictionaries and now appears to be extinct.

execution. Complaints have been expressed against the use of this term to describe killings carried out by terrorists, for example. Dictionary definitions bear them out, for they define *execution* as the taking of life by due process of law. Often the way out is to describe such killings as *execution-style;* they are politically motivated, and in this sense resemble a true execution more than other murders do.

ex-felon. An absurdity often encountered in the press. Once a felon, always a felon. Users probably have in mind *ex-convict*.

exhaust. As applied to people, a transitive verb, which means it must take an object. "She exhausted easily" thus should be put "She became exhausted easily" or "Things easily exhausted her."

exhibit. One critic says an exhibit is an item or a collection of items in an exhibition, and thus such an expression as *art exhibit* is wrong. No such limitation is recognized by any current dictionary, however.

exhilarate. Often misspelled *exhilirate*. See also *accelerate*.

exist. The superstition was at one time fairly widespread that only what is alive can exist. It means *be* as well as *live*, and is properly applied to inanimate things and even insubstantial ones, such as ideas. This view is borne out by definitions in American Heritage, Random House, and Webster.

existence. Sometimes misspelled *existance*.

exorbitant. Sometimes misspelled *exhorbitant*.

exotic. The word originally meant only *of foreign origin*, but two critics point out that it now is almost invariably understood in the senses *strange, glamorous, unusual, strikingly out of the ordinary*. The American College Dictionary calls this more common use colloquial; the three other desk dictionaries recognize it as standard, as do American Heritage, Random House, and Webster.

expatriot. An occasional error for *expatriate;* occurrences of it in a headline and story in *The New York Times* were complained of in the Winter 1966 edition of the *Columbia Journalism Review. Expatriot*, to be found in no dictionary, could only mean a former patriot. An expatriate is one who lives more or less permanently in some other country than his own.

expect. In the sense *suppose* or *believe* ("I expect it will rain"; "I expect the chickens have been fed"), described by Evans as standard in the U.S., but denounced in Britain. Fowler, however, defends it as firmly established in colloquial use. Two American authorities criticize this sense as affected, local, or dialectal. Among the dictionaries, Random House and Webster recognize the sense *suppose* as standard, the Standard College and American Heritage call it informal, and the American College and Webster's New World call it colloquial. The consensus is that this use is not entirely out of the shadow of criticism. See also *anticipate*.

expectorate. Discouraged as a euphemism for *spit*.

expel. Often misspelled *expell*, perhaps on the model of its past tense, *expelled*.

expensive. Means *high-priced*. Thus "The average man found the prices expensive" would better be *found the prices high*. Goods may be expensive, prices high.

expertise, expertize. The first is a noun meaning *expertness;* it is in high fashion with pundits and those who aspire to being thought wise. *Expertize,* a comparatively odd fish, is a verb meaning *give expert judgment on.* They are unlikely to be confused in talking unless mispronounced, for *expertise* ends in *eez*. But writing is another matter: "He named a committee of conservative businessmen to expertise the foreign aid program." *expertize*. The confusion may arise from the assumption set forth by Random House, that in British usage *expertize* is spelled *expertise*. This seems to be a rarity, however; neither the Oxford Universal Dictionary nor the Concise Oxford Dictionary gives it. The OED gives only "act as an expert" for *expertize* and gives *expertise* (as of French origin) in the supplement, indicating that it is a comparatively new word. Flesch criticizes *expertise* as a fad for *knowledge*.

explain. See *Attribution 2*.

explicit, express. While both terms (as adjectives) describe what is lucidly and completely set forth, *express* goes farther, indicating a commitment or particular intention: *his express purpose*.

explore every avenue. A cliché.

expose. Often used in a mushmouthed way: "Entering freshmen are now so deficient they must be exposed to a remedial reading course before they can proceed." This would better be expressed exactly: *must take a remedial reading course. Exposure* suggests what is undesirable, ephemeral, or both; neither sense is appropriate to the example. "Children are being exposed to new exhibits in art, music, and science at the preschool level." *are being shown, are seeing*.

exposé. Criticized as a French word that is unnecessary beside the English *exposure* and *exposition*. Exposé, however, has become so popular in the sense of revealing what is blameworthy that it is unlikely to be dislodged. Dictionaries list it without disparagement.

express. Fowler criticizes the omission of *as* after *express,* as in "She expressed herself somewhat surprised" (*expressed herself as*). This is obviously unidiomatic though it is seen fairly often in the U.S. See also *explicit*.

extended. Unnecessary, inexact, and pretentious as a variant of *long,* as in *an extended illness*. What is extended is that which has been given greater extent, and thus an extended illness is not simply a long one, but one that has gained a new grip on its victim after signs of remitting.

extension. Sometimes, oddly enough, misspelled *extention,* perhaps by mistaken extension from *extent.*

extol. Often misspelled *extoll,* perhaps because the *l* doubles in the past and participial forms (*extolled, extolling*).

extra-. Usually solid as a suffix: *extracurricular, extralegal, extramarital,* etc.

exuberant. Often misspelled *exhuberant.*

eye of the storm. Sometimes misused in reference to storms that have eyes (typhoons, hurricanes), especially in figurative senses. The eye, as the center around which the wind is spinning, is a dead calm, not the height of the disturbance.

F

fabulous. Criticized as a vogue word for *incredible, astounding, astonishing,* and the like. The original sense was *mythical, legendary;* that is to say, relating to a fable. The faddish use of the word is found mostly in advertisements, where it may be applied to anything from girls to typewriters. This new sense is recognized, however, by dictionaries without cavil.

Facetiousness. Care should be exercised, particularly in journalism, where this lapse of judgment oftenest occurs, not to treat a tragic event with levity, even though it may have its humorous aspects to those not the victims of it. If we can assume that the typical reader possesses at least average human sensibilities, many more readers will be put off than amused by such callousness—or, more likely, desperate attempts to be amusing.

A picture in a generally well-edited newspaper showed a helicopter at work removing a body from the side of a cliff into which a plane had crashed. The legend began: CLIFF HANGER—a deplorable choice of language, for the expression is facetious. Once more common, perhaps, than it is today, it describes a segment of a movie or television serial that ends with the characters in a precarious fix and direly in need of rescue. The object, of course, is to hold the reader's interest for the next episode. The expression is often used facetiously, as it was in the example.

face up to. Two critics spiritedly defend the phrase as meaning something more than *face* and as serving a useful purpose. It means not merely to confront but to stand one's ground. The expression was among Americanisms criticized at one time by Lord Conesford, who found little good in the language he encountered on a visit to the U.S. Fowler too concedes that *face up to* is not the same as *face.* Harper and dictionaries also explicitly recognize the expression as standard.

facile. Has a derogatory connotation; what is described as facile is understood to be not merely easy but too easy, and thus somehow lacking in virtue.

facilitate. One critic holds that acts may be facilitated, but not the doer of them; thus one may not say "The teacher was facilitated in his lecture by a complete set

138

of notes." The *lecture* was facilitated. But both Random House and Webster say a person may be facilitated in the sense *aided, helped.* Flesch criticizes the word when it displaces the simpler *ease, help.*

facility, facilities. Criticized as displacing more precise terms such as *factory, center, establishment;* for example, *scientific facilities* for *laboratory.*

fact, facts. *The fact that* is often superfluous, as in "We admit the fact that an injustice has been done." *We admit that.* The phrase is sometimes used to describe what is not fact but supposition or assertion: "This could be just an expression of the fact that the Russians are unconcerned and content to play a waiting game." The context, however, made clear that this was merely speculation, and gave alternative explanations. *True facts* is redundant, for what is true must be fact by definition. Flesch defends *true* (and *real*) facts as offering a distinction from false facts or lies. No current desk dictionary defines *fact* in a way that allows *true facts;* reality and truth, or the assumption of them, are essential to facts in these definitions. Random House and Webster, however, allow *facts* for what may be open to question, which seems to permit *true facts.* The consensus, nevertheless, is that *true facts* is redundant.

factious, factitious, fictitious. Two critics warn against confusion, pointing out that *factious* pertains to politics, *factitious* means *artificial,* and *fictitious* means *fictional* or *invented. Fictitious* is often misspelled *ficticious,* and the term is often misapplied to checks written with intent to defraud. *Fraudulent* seems a better choice, for, as Webster notes, "fictitious applies to fabrication or contrivance, often artful, without necessary intent to deceive."

factor. Properly used for a cause contributing to a result, and thus such phrases as *personal safety factor* (for *personal safety*) and *contributing factor* (for *factor*) are objectionable. *Factor* is often also used superfluously, and in any event is regarded as a counter word too often replacing more precise expressions such as *element, ingredient, component, constituent.*

faculty. Two critics disapprove the use of the term for *faculty members,* a popular locution around colleges: "Eight of the objectors were students and six were faculty." *faculty members, from the faculty.* The error is in treating *faculty* as other than a collective.

Fad Words. The term applies to words that have become too popular and thus tiresome. Many entries are so described in this dictionary. *Image, status symbol, task force, charismatic, know-how, viable, crash program, rationale, angry young men, long hot summer,* should be enough to show what the critics have in mind.

faerie, faery, fairy. One critic says that *fairy* as a slang term for *homosexual* is so widespread in the U.S. that it is almost impossible to use it in any other sense in public. This seems rather too sweeping; the context determines the sense. At any rate, *fairy* now seems less frequent for *homosexual* than *fag* (also derogatory) or the adjective and noun *gay,* a neutral term, self-applied by homosexuals and in wide general use. Fowler (quoting the Oxford English Dictionary) had perhaps the same thing in mind in saying that *faerie* (of which *faery* is a variant) might be used "to exclude various unpoetical or undignified associations connected with the current form *fairy.*" But *faerie, faery,* are rarely seen in the U.S. except in connection with Spenser, the inventor of *faerie* (*The Faerie Queen*).

fail. Carries a strong implication of falling short in an attempt, but it is often misused, especially by newspapers, when there is no question of an attempt: "Buckingham Palace failed to confirm the story"; "The burning bed failed to disturb the sleeper." If there is any virtue in precise statement, *did not confirm* and *did not disturb* are preferable. *Failure* is often misused in the same way. *Fail* often figures in unconscious reversal of sense, as in "The decision can hardly fail to pass unnoticed," when the intention is *can hardly fail to be noticed.*

fail to dampen. A journalese stereotype used to describe rain, usually, that does not affect enthusiasm.

fair-trade laws, agreements. Political and commercial euphemisms. Such laws or agreements have nothing to do with fair trade from the consumer's viewpoint; their purpose is to force retailers to maintain a price structure fixed by the manufacturer, a stratagem that the bargain-hunter, at least, considers highly unfair, as does the cut-rate merchant. But it is called free enterprise. Some publications, unwilling to fall into the trap of misrepresentation set by this term, preface it by *so-called.*

fairy. See *faerie,* etc.

fall. This term for *autumn* is an Americanism and exceptionable in Britain. In the U.S., *autumn,* while still in service, is perhaps taking on a faintly literary tinge; the ordinary word is *fall.*

fallacy, fallacious. In logic, a fallacy is an error in reasoning, and in the more common sense it denotes what is misleading, not merely wrong. Thus to describe a mistaken report as fallacious is objectionable; the word should be *false, mistaken, erroneous.* Dictionary definitions bear out this view.

false bomb threats. We read of them often these uneasy days, but at least they are preferable to genuine bomb threats. The result of such threats is that buildings are emptied and exhaustive, fruitless searches are conducted. Yet the expression, when reflected upon, makes it sound as if the threat is false, though it is as genuine as can be. A threat is as much a threat whether it is acted on or not; fortunately, most threats, of whatever kind, are not acted on. No one is actually misled by the expression *false bomb threats,* but the fact remains that it is misbegotten and imprecise. *Baseless bomb threat,* or *bombless threat,* might describe the circumstances better. These expedients, however, are somewhat artificial. How about *bomb scare?*

False Comparison. Careless writers, apparently by carrying ellipsis too far, often stumble into false comparison. They write "Older houses are still selling here, unlike many cities" or "Like many patient folk, Russian violence can be brutal." The need is for "unlike *those in* many cities" and "like *that of* many patient folk." In the examples, *older houses* are actually though unintentionally compared with *many cities,* and *patient folk* with *Russian violence.* A variation of the same error: "Receipts from livestock sales were 7 percent less than the corresponding period last year." *less than in.* Fowler generally prescribes recasting *(than they were in the corresponding period).* See also *Comparison 1.*

false illusions. A common redundancy; falsity (i.e., unreality) is the essence of illusion.

False Linkage. See *Comma 5.*

False Possessive. See *Possessives 4.*

False Titles. "*Griffelkin* is an opera for children by distinguished young California composer Lukas Foss." Piling up descriptives in this fashion is an idiosyncrasy of journalism, brought on by the urge to compress. The result, however, is hard to digest. For some reason, journalists are hostile to the appositive construction, which the false title displaces. Instead of *Renata Tebaldi, an Italian soprano,* they write *Italian soprano Renata Tebaldi;* instead of *Eddie Crews, a carnival concessionaire,* they write *carnival concessionaire Eddie Crews;* instead of *Angelo Litrico, a Rome tailor,* they write *Rome tailor Angelo Litrico.* (Of course, the description could as well stand before the name and still be in the appositive form: *a Rome tailor, Angelo Litrico.*) Sometimes journalists compound the error by using the comma but omitting the article: *Rome tailor, Angelo Litrico.* This mannerism is repeatedly deplored in newspaper stylebooks and critiques of journalistic writing. One critic calls this stylistic device offensive; two others identify it as one of the affectations invented by *Time* magazine. It is criticized also by Flesch. Perrin says, "Rhetorically, piling up nouns in front of nouns results in a rather awkward and heavy style: The progress report committee chairman fund is low = The chairman of the committee on the progress report doesn't have enough money. While a string of prepositional phrases is not very graceful, a string of nouns is less so."

False titles, as noted, generally are occupational descriptives that do not have the standing of formal titles; (e.g., *athlete, author, janitor, clergyman,* as compared with *Dr., Professor, Senator, Councilman*) but are placed before a name as if they were formal titles. The disease has spread beyond occupational designations: "This one was defined the other day by astute observer Philip Geyelin"; "friend George Gasset said . . ."; "The art was produced by precocious fourth-grader and grandson of renowned Mexican muralist Jose Clemente Orozco . . .'' The cure, of course, is easy: "This one was defined the other day by (the, an) astute observer, Philip Geyelin . . .''; "(his, a) friend, George Gasset, said . . .''; "The art was produced by a precocious fourth-grader and grandson of the renowned Mexican muralist Jose Clemente Orozco . . .''

Obviously a small difficulty may arise in using the appositive, as illustrated, instead of the false title. Should the article be *a, (an),* or *the?* Solving the difficulty requires a decision whether the person described is well-known enough so that the reader can be expected to recognize his name. Obviously, "He quoted from a playwright, William Shakespeare" would be absurd in most contexts; *the playwright.* Borderline cases, or those in which there is uncertainty about the fame of the person, can be handled as appositives with the descriptive following the name, omitting the article: "William Anderson, author, wrote . . .''

Newswriters often seem oblivious to the disagreeable constructions that grow out of the use of false titles: "Jones comes from Pontiac, Mich., and a family of distinguished musicians that includes older brother pianist Hank and trumpeter Thad.'' No one with the smallest feeling for stylistic felicity could be guilty of anything like this, which was culled from *Newsweek.* Translated into English, "his older brother, Hank, a pianist, and Thad, a trumpeter.''

An Associated Press report once referred to "Glass jar manufacturing heir John A. Kerr's divorce decree.'' When the chief of the bureau that produced this story was criticized for it, he replied, "All I can say is that it's a good thing for Associated Press subscribers that Kerr's old man didn't invent the International Harvester Company's two-row cotton-picking machine.''

It is a good idea to shun false titles entirely as tending to make writing sound like the text of a telegram. By omitting what is desirable for clarity, or by distorting natural forms, these devices, however cute, demand unnecessary effort from the reader. Sometimes there is an attempt to have it both ways, including mixed capitalization, in the same sentence: "Art Dealer Joseph Duveen was once trying to sell a painting to millionaire collector, Samuel H. Kress, whose interest was only lukewarm.'' Those who like it that way can have it. Others will prefer "Joseph Duveen, the art dealer, was once trying to sell a painting to a millionaire collector, Samuel H. Kress, whose interest was only lukewarm.''

The false title is so entrenched in journalism that there is no hope of uprooting it. But this advice at least may be offered: do not capitalize ordinary occupational designations; do not follow them with commas when they precede a name; and, most important for readability, avoid descriptives that are made up of more than one word.

If *Time* magazine did not indeed invent the false title in its early attempts to jazz up newswriting, it certainly popularized this mannerism. Some of its early creations, like *cinemactress,* were diverting. But *Time* has grown somewhat staid in its old age, and eschews the tortuous prose of its youth. No longer could it be accurately said of *Time*'s style, as Wolcott Gibbs once did, that it had crystallized into gibberish, and that "backward ran sentences until reeled the mind.''

Nonetheless, *Time* clings to its falsies, and in what surely must be the most freakish stylistic quirk extant, it *capitalizes* them: " 'He sure as hell wasn't for the subway trade,' remembers Fellow Columnist William S. White" (in a reference to the late Arthur Krock); and even more incredible, "It was only in April that Watergate Burglar James McCord confirmed much of Woodward and Bernstein's reporting."

In new, voluminous stylebooks published in 1977, from which many newspapers take their stylistic leads, the press associations only half-heartedly and none too specifically discouraged the false title. Yet in countless memoranda and analyses of their writing the wire services themselves have criticized this device.

Obviously, the natural habitat of the false title is the press and its imitators. It is never heard in speech, which often is a good model for clarity in writing. The objection to the false title is that it defies English idiom, often compelling the reader to keep suspended in his mind too many descriptives before he arrives at the name of the person described.

Newscasters are sedulous imitators of the bad stylistic habits of newspapers, but in this instance, books on broadcast journalism discourage the false title because it tends to baffle the listener. And so it may be concluded that the use of the false title degrades any writing. The presence of false titles is an important criterion by which insensitivity to style may be judged. See also *Titles*.

famed. Criticized variously as journalese and as a peculiarity displacing *famous* ("an internationally famed physicist"). *Famed* is more palatable as a predicate modifier than as an attributive (standing before the noun): "His deeds were famed in song and story" vs. "The world's most famed beer garden." Dictonaries recognize it as standard; the example in Random House gives it in the predicate position and that in Webster in the attributive.

fanatic, fanatical. See -ic, -ical.

fantasy, phantasy. Equivalent variants; the first is the predominant form, a judgment concurred in by dictionaries.

far be it from me. Criticized as a cliché and often deceptive, and as stilted and old-fashioned. The latter descriptive seems curious considering the popularity of the expression.

farcical. Sometimes given *farcial,* but there is no such word.

far from the maddening . . . See *Misquotation.*

farther, further. The purist holds that *farther* applies to physical distance and *further* to anything else, e.g., *a farther journey, a further consideration.* This is the position of the American Heritage panel and Harper. Bernstein predicts that the distinction will be lost fifty years hence; four other critics say that it is already gone. *Farther* is never used in the abstract or figurative sense; no one says *a farther consideration, farther effort.* The nondistinctive *further* is accepted by both unabridged dictionaries. Fowler speculated that *further* would drive out *farther*, and the prediction is repeated in the revised edition, but there is no sign of this in the U.S., at least.

fartherest, furtherest. Not standard forms.

fatal, fateful. *Fatal* means death-dealing, *fateful* productive of great consequences, for either good or evil.

fault. As a verb meaning *find fault with* or *blame* ("It's pretty hard to fault the tactics of Ralph Nader in his war with General Motors") the term is criticized as a fad, and defended as a useful revival to which exception should not be taken. Two current desk dictionaries recognize the sense as standard and two designate it "rare" showing that they are not as well up with the times as they might be. American Heritage (narrowly), Webster, and Random House also admit *fault* as a verb; the consensus is that it is standard.

faze, phase. *Faze* means *disconcert* or *daunt*, and is usually used with a negative: "We were not fazed by the setback." *Phase*, often wrongly used in that sense, is a noun meaning *aspect:* "The lecturer described the phases of the moon." Webster gives *phase* as a variant of *faze*, but neither Random House nor any desk dictionary recognizes this usage. The consensus favors the distinction. American Heritage gives *fease, feaze,* as variants of *faze,* but these versions are rare.

   With *in* or *out, phase* is a verb, usually found in military contexts, meaning *place in* (or *take out of*) *operation by stages:* "The program will be phased out by Christmas." Bernstein derogates this sense as a fad, but *phase in* and *phase out* are recognized as standard by American Heritage, Random House and Webster. Dictionaries, except for Webster, call *faze* colloquial or informal.

feasible, possible. *Feasible* means *capable of being done*, and *possible* means *capable of happening*. Critics warn against misuse of *feasible* in such senses as "a storm seems feasible," where *possible* or *probable* is called for.

feature. Overworked, especially in advertising and journalism, in the sense *exhibit prominently:* "Yankee Stadium usually features bases 90 feet apart"; "Detergents are featured in this week's sale." Two critics defend the term against criticisms of it as an objectionable novelty that were made a generation ago; one such appeared in the original Fowler. Gowers, in the revised edition, speculates that the term is now worn out, at least in the world of entertainment. Journalists are addicted to referring to "the featured speaker" when there is only one.

feel. Use of the term in the sense *think, believe* has been widely criticized. The argument usually runs that *feel* should not be used in this sense except to indicate emotion; one critic says strong emotion or groping. Another dissents from this idea, and cites Shakespeare, Trollope, Thomas Hardy, and Abraham Lincoln as having used *feel* in contexts where it was interchangeable with *think* or *believe*. The Oxford English Dictionary gives one sense as "to apprehend or recognize the truth of something on grounds not distinctly perceived," and gives as an example

"The proposed legislation was felt to be expedient." Fowler criticizes *feel* only as too weak for the announcement of official decisions, for which apparently it is often used in Britain. Current dictionaries unanimously give senses of *feel* that equate it with *think, believe, perceive, have a conviction of*. The consensus is overwhelmingly that *feel* is standard in these senses, divorced from either emotion or groping, a conclusion that is easily corroborated by observation of current educated usage.

feel bad, badly. The traditional view is that only *feel bad* is acceptable to describe either physical condition ("I have a cold; I feel bad") or emotional state ("We feel bad about the defeat"). *Feel badly*, then, could be correctly used only in the rare instance of impaired sense of touch; one whose fingers were numb could be said to feel badly. Two critics prescribe the traditional usage. Webster, however, accepts *badly* as an adjective in this locution, and Random House describes it as informal, which means that *feel badly* is considered acceptable to describe one's general physical state. The Standard College Dictionary says *feel badly* in this sense is in such common use it can no longer be considered substandard. Another critic says the forms are now standard and interchangeable; yet another says *feel badly* is established colloquially but that *feel bad* is strictly correct. American Heritage rejects *feel badly* in writing but accepts it for *be regretful* in speech. Flesch draws the distinction that *feel bad* should be used to describe physical discomfort or illness and *feel badly* to describe regret. Bryant finds usage almost evenly divided between the two forms. The consensus is that *feel bad* and *feel badly* are standard and are interchangeable with respect to both emotional state and physical condition. Evans holds that with other than linking verbs like *feel*, *badly* is preferable: *It ached badly*. See *bad, badly*.

feline. Journalese as a variant of *cat*.

female, feminine. One critic says *female* is unsuitable or forcedly facetious in place of *girl, woman, lady*. Two others, in essential agreement, say it is suitable for stressing the distinction of sex, and thus technical or scientific; another would restrict its application to animals, a curious conclusion. The consensus is that the term is inappropriate, as either noun or adjective, when applied casually to girls or women, and particularly as an adjective to describe qualities of the human female, for which the preferable word is *feminine*. *Female* is too clinical for use in ordinary contexts. Two critics disapprove *feminine* as a substitute for *woman:* "The problems of being Irish and feminine." *a woman*. "The accused said the suspect sometimes bought feminine clothes in London's West End." *women's clothes*. The reason *feminine* rings false in this example is that it applies properly to women as such, or suggests human female qualities, and does not suitably describe anything else, such as clothes. In the sentence about the Irishwoman, the word lays an unintended stress on the possession of feminine qualities.

Feminine Forms. Many of these, such as *ancestress, aviatrix, authoress, poetess*, have fallen into disuse, perhaps proving that equality of the sexes is finally here.

Postmistress is not recognized by the federal government, which designates all postmasters *postmasters*. This is an old practice, but since the upsurge of the women's movement federal agencies have gone to great lengths to prescribe or devise asexual descriptions for jobs whose titles formerly implied that the holders were males. Some feminine forms remain in common and undisputed use, however, such as *abbess, actress, governess, hostess, seamstress, stewardess, adventuress, waitress, usherette*. Fowler disparages *drum majorette*, but it has become indispensable in the U.S. Such designations as "woman lawyer" and "lady physicist" are often considered objectionable; indeed, to many women they are intolerable. Fowler in the original, whose crystal ball may have been clouded, urged not only the retention but the multiplication of feminine designations as "a special need of the future," proposing *doctress, teacheress, singeress,* and *danceress*. But the trend was rapidly in the opposite direction even before the women's movement. A woman who signs a letter with first initials, however, or whose first name may also be that of a man (*Leslie, Lee, Jean*) may leave her respondent in a quandary how to address her in reply.

Feminism. Feminists appear to be getting more and more worked up over the tendency to apply apparently masculine designations (such as *chairman, chairmen*) to women or mixed groups. In an article entitled "Language and Sexism: a Note" (in the *Modern Language Association Newsletter*), Deborah Rosenfelt and Florence Howe argued earnestly that applying masculine nouns and pronouns to women or mixed groups unconsciously reinforces sexism (a new word, by the way).

They object, for example, that a sentence like "The employee can appeal to the state if he feels that he is being exploited" implies that employees are necessarily male, or at any rate that women, though intended to be included, are beneath specific notice as such. These critics would make it "The employee can appeal to the state if he or she feels that he or she is being exploited." But, as they admit, it has long been felt that such constructions are clumsy, and thus the masculine forms have been used for references to both sexes. The plural, however, usually offers a way out, they agree: "Employees can appeal to the state if they feel that they are being exploited."

It has long been well established that in general references as well as in legal documents, the masculine pronoun *he* is understood as referring to both sexes. Webster says, under *he*, "that one whose sex is unknown or immaterial (find out who is ringing the doorbell and what he wants) . . . used as a nominative case form in general statements (as in statutes) to include females, fictitious persons (as corporations), and several persons collectively (if a customer is dissatisfied he may return the goods)." American Heritage says of *he*, "Used to represent any person whose sex is not specified: *Everyone knows he is mortal.*" It is doubtful that readers, apart from feminists searching for suggestions of discrimination, think in masculine terms in reading statements like this. The argument that the suffix *-man* is necessarily masculine is also without basis. Webster defines the noun *man* first of all as "a member of the human race; a human being: PERSON—now used of males *except* [emphasis supplied] in general or indefinite applications with collective adjectives or in the plural (every man must do his duty) . . ." This seems to include *chairman* as an asexual designation.

It is interesting to note that *salesperson* (usually applied to clerks in stores) appears to have antedated the new feminism. This is an instance where it was indeed incongruous to apply *salesman* to a woman. *Chairperson*, used in reference to a specific individual, seems to be defeating its own purpose; we know now that when it is used the chair is occupied by a *chairwoman*.

The variations that have been played on -*person* vs. -*man* are endless, and have been justly scorned. It seems inevitable that some pretentious ass will suggest displacing *mankind* with *personkind*, or that *countryperson* replace *countryman*. Perhaps the most obnoxious of these toadying expressions is *newsperson* for *reporter*. Once again, a foolish fad has been followed out the window, for *reporter* is as asexual as it can be. Perhaps the most preposterous changes that have been suggested are *waitperson* for *waitress* and *personhole cover* for *manhole cover*.

Newspapers generally have been very responsive to the exhortations of the new feminists. Many papers adopted *Ms.*, only to discover, when they polled their readers, that most women prefer *Miss* or *Mrs.* The tendency now is to use *Ms.* only with the names of women who express a preference for it.

We are on dangerous ground, for William Congreve recorded truly three centuries ago that hell has no fury like a woman scorned, and as is well known this is no less true if she only *thinks* she has been scorned or even slighted. *He or she* may be asking too much, but the sexless plural ("All who haven't registered should sign their names" instead of "Anyone who hasn't registered should sign his name") is the way of discretion when possible. Meantime let us brace ourselves against the inevitable complaint that there is no such thing as a grandmother clock.

fever. See *temperature*.

few (fewer) in number. Belongs to a family of redundancies: *small* (or *large*) in size; *rectangular* (or whatever) in shape. Omit *in number, in size, in shape.*

fewer, less. The general rule is that *fewer* applies to readily distinguishable units (*fewer people, ships, houses*) and *less* in other circumstances (*less sugar, time*). Two critics and American Heritage point out that *less* is used with plurals regarded as indicating a unit, such as distances (less than 150 miles), periods of time (less than 20 minutes), and sums of money (less than $200). Porter G. Perrin (*Writer's Guide and Index to English*) observes, "*Fewer* seems to be declining in use and *less* commonly takes its place," and cites *less hands* and *three less seats*. Bryant finds that although the preference follows the rule as stated, *less* is often found with plurals even in formal contexts, and two other critics consider this usage acceptable. Webster and Webster's New World give *fewer* as a synonym of *less*; Harper, American Heritage, Random House, and the American College and Standard College dictionaries follow the rule. The consensus favors the rule, though strong forces are working against it.

fiancé, fiancée. Among the few French imports that have retained distinctive forms; the first is the man, the second the woman. Generally, too, the acute accent is retained over the first *e* in both words.

Fiberglas, fiber glass. The first is a trademark, and in deference to its owners should be capitalized, though there is no way such deference can be compelled. The generic term, which may be preferable for ordinary use, is *fiber glass* (sometimes *fibrous glass* or *spun glass*).

fictitious. See *factious, factitious, fictitious*.

fiddle, violin. Except as applied to what country performers play, *fiddle* is considered derogatory by the layman, who respectfully says *violin*. *Fiddle* is the common expression among musicians; nevertheless, they may resent its use by others.

field. In such constructions as *the field of telemetry, the field of* can often be omitted; Follett disparages the term, in reference to branches of learning, as belonging to the jargon of education. *Area* (which see) is similarly used.

fight with, against. *Fight with* is ambiguous: "He fought with the Spaniards" fairly prompts the question "Which side was he on?" The context usually explains. Nevertheless, *fight against* or recasting is worth consideration.

figuratively. See *literally*.

figure. Disparaged by two critics for *suppose* or *think:* "I figure things will all work out." This usage is considered informal by Random House and standard by Webster. *Figure* is standard, however, in the sense *calculate* or *compute*. *Figure* is the term for the numerical symbol (1, 2, 3) and *number* can refer either to the symbol or the word expressing it (one, two, three). See also *Numbers*.

figurehead. Often misapplied to people. "The teacher is one of the figureheads if not the most important member of our community." A figurehead is a symbol, one with no real authority or responsibility, a leader in name only. Calling a person a figurehead thus is derogatory; the meaning intended in the example was *leading citizens*. "Bach is now recognized as the figurehead to whom all musical innovators have turned for inspiration in the twentieth century." Unintentionally demeaning. *trail blazer,* perhaps.

Figures. See *Numbers*.

filet, fillet. Though these are variants of the same term, *filet* now is reserved for *filet mignon* and the name of a kind of lace; in other senses (a slice of boneless meat or fish, a headband, and many others) usually *fillet*.

final culmination. "This club is the final culmination of the kind of intimate feeling we have been searching for." Redundant; *culmination.*

finalize. Criticized variously as gobbledygook or as an unnecessary neologism for *complete, finish, end.* The word has been widely derided, though on one occasion it was pointed out that President John F. Kennedy used it in a speech. American Heritage rejects it. The Standard College Dictionary points out that although frowned upon, the term has been in standard use for more than twenty years. The New World Dictionary calls it a neologism, Webster considers it standard, and the American College does not list it. Random House extends the span of its standard use from twenty years to the last forty, and says it usually occurs in formal contexts. The weight of opinion, however, is against it, although it seems that, like *normalcy,* it has to some extent been unjustly aspersed. This may be the penalty for having been found so often in bad company, that is, the prose of bureaucracy.

financial. Criticized as often used pretentiously concerning small sums or in place of *money; financial matters* for *money matters.*

fine. It is a superstition that the term may not be used as an adjective to denote superior quality, as in *a fine man, a fine day,* but must be reserved for the idea of physical fineness (*fine-grained*). The broader view is supported by all current dictionaries. Bryant points out that it has become a counter word and is overused in place of more specific descriptives. Four critics say it is colloquial as an adverb ("He is doing fine") and all dictionaries except Webster, which considers it standard, agree.

finical, finicky. The second is the commoner form, as is easily observable.

finishing touch. Sentences employing this and similar phrases including *touch* are often subjected to some painful twists. A finishing touch sounds like something that would be *given* a building, plan, or whatever. But frequently we see that finishing touches are being *made to, made on,* or *put to.* "He put a personal touch to his story"—surely a gaucherie for "He gave his story a personal touch." *Put the touch on* is obsolete slang for *seek a loan:* "He put the touch on me for five dollars."

fire. Slang for *dismiss, discharge,* three critics say. Random House and Webster consider it standard; American Heritage labels it informal. Among sportswriters, *fire* is the stereotype describing how golfers score; the simple, natural *hit* has been outlawed.

fire off. Another journalistic stereotype, used to describe the sending of a letter. In *Newsweek,* particularly, letters are always *fired off,* never mailed.

firm. The technical meaning is a partnership of two or more persons not recognized as a legal person distinct from the members composing it. Thus it is unacceptable as a synonym for *corporation,* a distinction that all current dictionaries but Webster concur in.

first and foremost. Criticized as bombast.

first come, first served. The form of the expression. It is often heedlessly bobtailed to *first come, first serve,* which changes its sense, and thus it is the victim of the same kind of inattention that affects *As (so) far as . . .* and *Couldn't care less,* which see.

firstly, secondly, etc. Two critics say the long-continued arguments over these forms vs. *first, second,* and especially the criticism of *firstly,* etc., are pedantry; three critics recommend *first, second,* which are adverbs as much as *firstly,* etc. To this it may be added that at least the user should be consistent: either *first, second,* etc., or *firstly, secondly,* etc., not *firstly, second,* etc. All current dictionaries recognize *firstly* without qualification.

first name. See *Christian name.*

fish, fishes. Both forms are standard as the plural.

fission. Used as a verb, the word may make the reader uneasy ("The element will fission under the proper conditions"). Only Webster recognizes it. As a noun, it is the act of splitting into parts. *Fission* is usually encountered in the expression *nuclear fission,* a technical term of physics, and if it is used in writing aimed at a general audience should be briefly explained or avoided by the use of more familiar words.

fit, fitted. Two critics say *fit* is preferable for the past tense when the verb is used intransitively, as in reference to clothing: "The suit fit perfectly." Evans adds that *fitted* is invariable when the verb takes an object ("The key fitted the lock"; "The work fitted his temperament"). Two critics insist on *fitted* without distinction, and the examples in Random House use *fitted* with an object and *fit* without one. Webster gives examples with both *fit* and *fitted* used transitively (*fitted his job, fit him to perfection*). Thus the distinctions given by the critics of usage are ignored, and the forms are used interchangeably. There is no consensus, only a diversity of opinion.

fix. The word has many senses as both noun and verb in the U.S.; four critics disapprove of it as a word-of-all-work, especially in the sense *repair,* that often would better be replaced by something more specific.

flack, flak. The difference between them is threatened, if it has not already been done in. *Flak* emanated from World War II; at that time, everyone knew what it meant: antiaircraft artillery, and particularly the fragments of shells fired by it. The word is an acronym on the German *Fliegerabwehrkanone* (antiaircraft gun).

It survived the war in a figurative sense for *criticism:* "We got a lot of flak from the public after that decision." But in this sense the word was so often misspelled *flack* that Webster and Random House both now recognize it as a variant. Still, as everyone in the media fields knows, *flack* has long been a not entirely admiring term for *press agent* or *public relations writer.* You can speak of antiaircraft fire, or criticism, as either *flack* or *flak* and stay more or less within the law (though the distinction is still widely honored in the observance), but a press agent can only be a *flack.* More recently, *flack* has become a verb: "She was fired for flacking for her employer's competitor." *Flack* is slang.

flagrant. See *blatant, flagrant.*

flagship. "The *President Jackson* was the first American flagship to enter the canal." Unhappy compression is at the root of the trouble here, which is recurrent. The writer meant "the first ship flying an American flag." The sentence is confusing and erroneous, for a flagship is a naval vessel carrying the commander of a force, or, occasionally, a merchantman designated as foremost in a fleet.

flair, flare. *Flair* in the primary sense means *a keen scent;* one critic approves the extension to *discernment, instinctive feeling for,* but disapproves the senses *flourish, talent, aptitude;* in a somewhat cryptic entry, Fowler apparently would allow none except the figurative extension *keen scent for,* and cites an example where *flaire* (sic) is used for *eagerness* or *enthusiasm.* One critic allows *talent, aptitude, perception,* and in some contexts *fondness.* Two critics warn against confusion with *flare* (usually a flame, but sometimes a widening, a sense in which *flair* may also be used). Dictionaries give such meanings as *natural aptitude, bent* for *flair,* and the American College also gives *fondness.* The consensus is that *aptitude, bent, knack* are acceptable senses of *flair; fondness* is questionable.

flamboyant. Fowler says the term should be held to its original sense of *flamelike;* Evans approves *showy,* and so do dictionaries. This, in fact, is the most popular sense of the term, and it is doubtful that the general user is even conscious of the sense *flamelike* or of the technical architectural applications of the term.

flaming inferno. Redundant; both terms denote fire.

flammable, inflammable. Fire underwriters and others interested in safety have promoted the use of *flammable* in preference to *inflammable* on the assumption that *inflammable* may be misunderstood to mean *noncombustible.* The terms are synonyms for *combustible* and equally reputable. Fowler objects to *flammable* and calls it rare. This may be so in Britain but not in the U.S. There is no sign that *flammable* is displacing *inflammable.*

flaunt, flout. *Flaunt* is incessantly confused with *flout. Flaunt* means display in an ostentatious or boastful manner: "The faction flaunted its superior strength." *Flout* means *mock* or *scoff at:* "A speeding motorist flouts the law."

flautist, flutist. Three critics point out that the second term is the older and regard it as preferable, though *flautist* looks like a charming antique. Fowler says *flautist* has displaced *flutist,* but in the U.S. it is in fact something of an affectation, only occasionally met. *Flutist* greatly predominates.

flay. Few perhaps are now aware that the original sense was *strip the skin off.* It is now primarily a headline word meaning *criticize harshly, excoriate.* One critic considers it misused in any but the primary sense; two others discourage it as overwrought for *criticize.* The secondary (and commoner) meaning is recognized as standard by dictionaries, though it is true that it is probably unsuitable for ordinary contexts. Owing to the advantage of its shortness, however, no discouragement is likely to drive it from headlines, but there readers have come to understand it as usually used in a much weakened sense, ranging from mild reproof to stern criticism.

flier, flyer. *Flier* predominates for *aviator, flyer* for *handbill.*

floor. See *ceiling.*

flotsam, jetsam. Since these terms are often paired, they are assumed to be the same or similar things. Flotsam is goods lost by shipwreck and found floating in the water; jetsam is what is thrown overboard during a storm or other emergency to lighten a vessel. The relation to *float* and *jettison* can serve as a reminder of the difference.

flounder, founder. Often confused. To flounder is to struggle or thrash about; a fish out of water flounders. To founder is to go down, in the case of a ship to fill with water and sink. Ships are sometimes described as floundering, as well they may in a stormy sea, but the intended meaning usually is *founder.* "This attitude misses the whole point on which the policy of the United States has floundered." Conceivably; but more likely *foundered* (failed). "In public favor, the governor is foundering even worse." *floundering.*

flout. See *flaunt, flout.*

flu. Except by Webster, the term is regarded by dictionaries as informal or colloquial for *influenza,* though the long form is so seldom seen that the clipped version seems certain to become standard, if it has not already done so. There is no occasion for *'flu.*

flunkey, flunky. The sentence "If I had thought he was going to turn the government over to two flunkies, I would have thought twice about it," was scathingly criticized by a reader who thought it should have been *flunkeys.* Only *flunkey, flunkeys* are admitted by British dictionaries; *flunky, flunkies* as well as *flunkey, flunkeys* have been used in America for at least a century. The version complained of, in fact, usually appears first in American dictionaries, meaning that it predominates.

fluorine, fluorescent, etc. Often misspelled *flourine, flourescent.* Fluorine is one of the elements; it has nothing to do with flour.

flush, flushed. *Flush* is the term for *fully supplied, well filled;* one who had just received a pay check might describe himself as flush. *Flushed* is the term for *excited, thrilled,* as in *flushed with victory.*

fob, foist. The idiomatic forms of the phrases are *fob off on* and *foist on; foist off* is wrong.

Fogg, Phileas. Among literary and historical references, this name, that of the hero of Jules Verne's *Around the World in Eighty Days,* is often misspelled *Phineas.* The reason may be that another man, who looms large in American folklore, was named Phineas T. Barnum.

-fold. Solid as a suffix: *twofold, fourfold,* etc.

folks. *Folks* for *people* or *relatives* is considered colloquial or informal—"You folks are all right." Fowler recognizes the locution without disparagement; it is described as primarily American. Random House considers only the application to members of one's family informal; Webster gives both applications as standard.

follow(s). See *as follows.*

following. Criticized where it displaces a simple *after* ("Following the movie, we had some ice cream"). Fowler considers it permissible as a preposition when the idea of consequence or result is present: "Following the war, terms of occupation were agreed on."

for. The word must be used with care in connection with criticisms or accusations: to say that a man was criticized for committing perjury is to assume that the perjury was committed. Recasting to attribute the criticism to whoever made it is required so that the writer does not unintentionally leave the impression he concurs in it: criticized *as.* Starting sentences with *for* and *thus* is an affectation of some writers, particularly columnists. This is warranted only when the sentence draws a conclusion based on what has gone before; the words in such constructions are the equivalent of *consequently.* "But will the prisoners again read into the president's words a promise such as they thought they had in April 1961? For they risked their lives then." The second sentence does not draw a conclusion from the first; it merely carries the argument forward: "They risked their lives then."

force, forced. Often used inappropriately, conveying a stronger sense of compulsion than is warranted. "Pupils through the third grade at the Roosevelt School will be forced to attend half-day sessions this term." This conjures up an image of the wretched kids manacled together and marching to their half-day sessions in lockstep. It would be more in key with the circumstances to say "Half-day sessions will be necessary" or that the pupils *will have to attend* half-day sessions. "Some of the sixteen squad cars were forced to go bouncing over bumpy roads to catch the elusive hotrods." *had to go. Force* seems the wrong word in these examples because it connotes overcoming resistance, which in these instances is not evident. This view corresponds with definitions and examples in Random House and Webster.

forceful, forcible. Both words mean possessing, or using, force, but *forcible* is generally preferred for physical contexts: *a forcible entry* (the police broke down the door). Instinct serves us here; we would be unlikely to describe these circumstances as *a forceful entry. Forceful* is generally the word for abstract contexts: "It brought a forceful reminder of another truth." Fowler says the distinction turns on the amount of force and regards *forceful* as the stronger. He considers *forcible* the ordinary word, which may be true in Britain, but not in the United States. Fowler's examples, however, bear out the distinction set forth. To recapitulate, *forceful* is preferable except to denote physical or exceptional force. *Forceful* often also has a favorable connotation, relating to force used admirably; *forcible* is either neutral or pejorative.

fore-. Solid as a prefix: *forebrain, foredeck, foredoom, foregoing,* etc.

forecast, forecasted. Both forms are acceptable as the past tense, but forecast is preferable, four critics agree. The same principle holds for other words ending in *-cast: broadcast, telecast.*

Foreign Terms. Five critics warn against the dangers of misspelling and misusing foreign terms; the consensus is that such terms are best avoided if there is an English equivalent. The danger of misapprehending them is one reason. There is also the likelihood of confusing the reader, or of giving the impression of showing off. A good test of the suitability of a foreign term in ordinary contexts is its presence in an English dictionary of at least the desk or collegiate size.

foremost. American Heritage and Harper allow the term to apply to more than one: *one of the foremost musicians.* Neither Random House nor Webster is explicit on this point.

foreseeable future. The phrase is sometimes criticized as foolish on the ground that not even the next second is foreseeable. See also *future.*

foreword, introduction, preface. In reference to the front matter of a book, the words are now synonyms. Two critics, Random House and Webster say *preface* applies more properly, however, to a statement by the author, and other current dictionaries except Webster's New World confirm this distinction. *Introduction* is the term usually applied to a statement contributed by someone other than the author. *Foreword* is often misspelled *foreward,* under the influence, perhaps of *forward.*

Fowler denounced *foreword* as an interloper that had displaced *preface,* and wistfully expressed the hope that *foreword* would be unhorsed. The words have survived, however, side by side, a monument among many others to the feebleness of the influence of those who would influence the course of the language, however slightly, in accordance with their own preferences.

for free. Objectionable for *free* or *free of charge:* "The pennants will be distributed for free." The reason is that *free* is not a noun and thus cannot be the object of a preposition. Nevertheless, Webster recognizes the expression as standard and quotes four reputable writers in its use.

Formal. The term is avoided as a status label in this book, unless it is attributed, for reasons given under *Colloquialisms.*

formally, formerly. Sometimes confused. *Formally* relates to *formal; formerly* means *previously.*

former, latter. Three critics, American Heritage, and Random House say both terms should be used to refer only to one of two things, not to one of three or more. "He spotted a man and a woman and two children, all obviously hurt, the former more seriously." This is a misuse, they hold; the right words here would be *the first* or *the man.* This view represents the consensus. Evans, however, approves of *the latter three;* another critic and Webster allow *latter* to refer to the last of more than two. Fowler adds that *former* and *latter* may not be used to refer to pairs of dissimilar things, such as people and objects. Three critics point out that *former* and *latter* are objectionable in that they often make the reader look back and figure out which is which. Another critic says that *latter* should refer to a noun (*Jones; the dog*); not a pronoun (*he; it*). Boswell said of Dr. Johnson: "He never used the phrases the former and the latter, having observed, that they often occasioned obscurity; he therefore contrived to construct his sentences so as not to have occasion for them, and would even rather repeat the same words, in order to avoid them." See also *was a former; latter.*

formulate. Criticized as pretentious for *form,* as in *formulate an opinion.*

forthcoming. Being used, especially in the East, to displace *forthright.* "The president's statement was forthcoming," was a television commentator's verdict. No dictionary gives any such meaning for *forthcoming.* Its standard senses are *about to appear* ("the forthcoming holidays") and *readily available* ("new funds will be forthcoming after the election"). The displacement of *forthright* (*direct, straightforward*) or, sometimes, *outgoing* (*friendly, responsive*) by *forthcoming* is regrettable and should be discouraged. It can cause ambiguity, because its standard meanings usually fit the contexts in which it supersedes *forthright.* For example, "The president's statement was forthcoming" could be understood to mean that it was about to be made, not that it was forthright.

for the purpose of. Verbiage in place of an infinitive construction. *For the purpose of circumventing* equals *to circumvent.*

for the (simple) reason that. Excessive for *because;* beyond this, *simple* may insult the reader's intelligence.

for . . . to. Such locutions as "I want for him to be elected," in which the *for*-phrase is the object of a verb (in this case *want*) are objectionable, three critics say. Another holds that their acceptability depends on whether the infinitive is replacing a *that*-clause, as in "The lawyer said for him to file suit immediately," which is described as standard on the ground that it replaces *that he should file. For* before the infinitive "He hoped for to sell the farm" is substandard. This is the consensus.

fortuitous. Means simply *chance* or *accidental,* as in *a fortuitous encounter.* It is often incorrectly used in the sense *fortunate,* as in *a fortuitous deal.* "A time of transition may be fortuitous after all, went the argument." *favorable, advantageous.* Random House, oddly enough, considering its generally conservative bent, allows *lucky, fortunate;* Webster does not. Random House's example, however, is ambiguous: *a series of fortuitous circumstances that advanced her career; fortuitous* here could just as easily mean *accidental.*

forward. Criticized when it displaces *send,* rather than *send on.* Webster, however, gives *transmit.*

for whom the bell . . . See *Misquotation.*

founder. See *flounder, founder.*

fraction. Criticized by one authority in the sense *a small part* (rather than simply *a part,* large or small). Another reports, however, that this usage is more than three hundred years old, and Fowler concludes that the sense has established itself. Random House regards it as standard, but Webster does not give this sense. The consensus narrowly favors it.

Fractions. It is well to defer to consistency by shunning such mixtures as *one and ½ feet, two and ¼ miles,* in favor of *1 ½ feet, 2 ¼ miles,* or *one and one-half feet, two and one-quarter miles.* And *.13 of an acre* is preferable to *.13* acres as less likely to lend itself to error. Technical publications often place a zero in front of a decimal point: *0.13 of an acre.* When fractions must be constructed on the typewriter, it is better to separate the numerator and the denominator with the virgule than with the hyphen: 6 7/8 (not 6 7-8).

The hypen is used as indicated in writing fractions out: *one-fourth, six thirty-seconds.*

Frankenstein. Often as not applied to a monster. The eponym was not the monster, however, but the scientist who created it, as set forth in the novel of that name by Mary Shelley. Two critics regard the shift in sense as an error, though admitting it is prevalent. It is recognized by all current dictionaries except Random House; Evans regards it as established and derides Fowler's description of it as "almost but not quite sanctioned by custom" (which appeared in the original of 1926 and was retained in the revision of 1965; Follett defends it as following a natural process). The consensus overwhelmingly favors *Frankenstein* as either a monster or anything that destroys its creator.

frankness. See *candor and frankness.*

free for nothing, free gratis. Wornout humor.

free, freely. *Freely* means *liberally, without stint,* and may be ambiguous for *free of charge.* The person who wrote of *a freely distributed paper* did not mean it was distributed widely or without restraint, but rather that it was a throwaway, distributed at no cost to the recipients. *Distributed free of charge* would have been unambiguous. "They charge for the groceries, but Della distributes freely her cures for what ails you." *free, free of charge.* The confusion probably arises out of a feeling that *free* is an adjective, not an adverb, and needs -*ly* to make it an adverb; in fact, *free* is both adjective and adverb in the sense *without cost.* This view is corroborated by dictionary definitions. See also *for free, free for nothing.* In the trade, incidentally, newspapers that are distributed free of charge (often known as *shoppers*) are genteelly referred to as "controlled circulation" publications. After all, *throwaway* is hardly a laudatory term, and it may put ideas in the mind of the householder.

free gift, pass. Redundant; passes and gifts are free by definition.

free rein. The expression comes from the horsy world; often mistakenly given *free reign. Free* (sometimes *full*) *rein* gives the horse his head, allowing him to choose the pace, and the expression is a useful metaphor, although possibly also a cliché. The misapprehension is illustrated by "Now, with sexual permissiveness in full reign on college campuses . . ." and "He turned over the reigns of the program to his successor." *Reign* means *rule* (*the reign of Henry VIII*); reins are the straps by which a horse is controlled.

freezing, subfreezing. Freezing weather requires subfreezing temperatures; thus *subfreezing* is unnecessary.

frenetic, phrenetic. Variants, equally acceptable; the meaning is *frantic.* The first version predominates.

friendlily, friendly. *Friendlily* is standard but seldom used because it is awkward. *Friendly,* however, may also be used as an adverb: "A few were not very friendly disposed toward him." This too, however, is likely to jar most writers and readers; recasting is recommended.

frightened of. Should not be used in place of *afraid of,* two critics say. Random House and Webster specifically sanction *frightened of,* however.

from. Redundant in sentences like "The only other source of money is from the general fund." *is the general fund.*

from . . . to. A redundant construction in such contexts as "The Chinese still hold from 12,000 to 14,000 square miles of Indian territory." *hold 12,000 to 14,000.* See also *of between, of from, etc.*

from hence, from whence, where. *From* is redundant with *whence,* which means *from which.* In addition, two critics consider *whence* bookish; another flatly calls it obsolete (though dictionaries give it as standard), recommending *from where.* Evans allows *from whence,* disagreeing with four other authorities. *Hence* is also somewhat stilted; *from hence* is considered archaic. *From where* is questionable even though *where* can be considered a pronoun and thus the object of a preposition. The feeling for *where* as an adverb is so strong that *from where* is likely to be avoided by instinct. *From where* is easily acceptable, however, when the word-order is inverted: "Where did the cake come from?" (though Fowler considers this clumsy and recommends *whence*). *From here* and *from there* are well established, and it seems likely that from *where* will establish itself. The Bible says, "I will lift up mine eyes to the hills, from whence cometh my help." (Psalms CXXI:1), though Fowler disparages this as an archaic and thus inapplicable example. See also *see where.*

front runner. Originally meant only an entrant in a race who does best when ahead, but now the sense nearly always intended is simply *leader* (as in a race). Criticism of the change, which was prevalent until recently, is probably futile, since the general sense is recognized by both Random House and Webster. The idea that it meant a fast starter who soon falls behind is a misconception long prescribed in newspaper stylebooks.

fruition. Three critics insist that the term can mean only *enjoyment,* not *bearing fruit.* The fact is, however, that the sense *enjoyment* is all but unknown in ordinary discourse. All current dictionaries give without qualification such meanings as *attainment of anything desired, a state of bearing fruit, realization.* The insistence on the rare sense of the word, flying as it does in the face of overwhelming usage, can only be regarded as pedantry.

-ful. Plurals of words ending in *-ful* are normally formed by adding *s: handfuls, teaspoonfuls, cupfuls;* not *handsful, teaspoonsful, cupsful.*

full-fashioned. In reference to hosiery and meaning *knit to fit the leg,* this is the correct form; not *fully fashioned.*

fulsome. Means *excessive* or *disgusting,* not *ample* or *abundant.* "There are fulsome and informative chapters on what to pack, what to buy." *Fulsome praise* is objectionable, not lavish, praise; the word connotes insincerity and baseness of motive. "He has had a very nice, fulsome public career," Spiro Agnew said of Averell Harriman, at a time when Mr. Agnew himself was better known for his own fulsome rhetoric than other things that came to light later.

fun. As an adjective (*a fun party*), deplored by one critic, considered informal by two others, American Heritage, and Random House, and standard by Webster. As a conversational expression, its chances of survival seem good. Not included in Barnhart, which indicates it probably sprang into existence since 1963.

function. As a noun in one sense, *function* means a ceremony or meeting of some importance, and is misapplied to lesser events, such as tea parties. As a verb, it is pretentious for more specific words such as *work, operate, act*—"The machine is functioning properly." Saying that something is a *function* of something else, as in mathematics, is often pretentious for *depends on*.

fund. A highly popular revival as a verb in the sense *finance*. "The money will be used to fund a scholarship." Random House and Webster give only technical definitions from the world of finance; only Webster's New World gives "to provide for by a fund," which appears to validate the popular usage. Harper approves.

fundamental. See *basal, basic*.

funds, funding. Criticized as pretentious when *money* or *raising money* will do ("I was completely out of funds").

funny. It is naive to label what one is setting down as funny; if the reader does not perceive the fun unassisted, no amount of labeling will convince him it is there. See also *interesting; quip, quipped*. Two critics consider the word under a shadow in the sense *strange* or *peculiar* ("That's funny; it was here a minute ago." "He gave them a funny look"). Another calls the usage "widespread and not without charm." All the current dictionaries but Webster and American Heritage, which give it as standard, consider the usage informal or colloquial.

furlough. No longer current in military connections; all branches of the armed services now use the term *leave*.

furnish, furnishings. *Furnish* is sometimes criticized as a verb in the sense *supply* (*furnish refreshments*), but this sense is recognized by all current dictionaries without qualification. Similarly, it is sometimes said that furniture is what one puts in a house, and furnishings are what a haberdasher sells. *Furnishings* is correct in both senses.

furor, furore. Some dictionaries make a distinction, to the effect that *furor* means *rage, angry* or *maniacal fit, enraged behavior*, and *furore* means *contagious excitement, general commotion, stir, public disturbance, controversy, uproar*. An example: "The furore over corruption in government . . ." Webster, however, gives *furore* as a variant of *furor*, but not the converse. Random House and American Heritage give only *furor* for all senses, and call *furore*, with the distinctive meaning *fad*, a Briticism. The difference is lost in the U.S., if it ever was observed here, and in any event the context is likely to indicate which sense is meant.

further. See *farther, further.*

fuse, fuze. The common term for the device used to ignite explosives and also for the electrical circuit breaker is *fuse. Fuze* is generally preferred in connection with ordnance, especially in technical contexts.

Fused Participle. This is the name Fowler invented for a gerund with a subject that is in the objective rather than the possessive case. "I object to him being appointed" is an example, and the correct form would be "I object to *his* being appointed." The reasoning is that *him* cannot modify *being appointed,* and so the adjective *his* is necessary. The principle applies to nouns as well: "She resented John('s) ringing the doorbell." The possessive is far from invariable in this construction, however. Curme, who went into the subject more exhaustively than Fowler, cites numerous examples from good writers to show that the possessive is most likely to be used when the subject of the gerund is a pronoun. But he then adds: "We regularly use the accusative [that is, objective] when the subject is emphatic: 'She was proud of *him* doing it.' The emphasis often comes from contrasting the subjects: 'We seem to think nothing of *a boy smoking,* but resent *a girl smoking.*' "

All other current authorities but American Heritage, which stands with him, take exception to Fowler's flat prohibition of anything but the possessive (or genitive) in this construction. Gowers, in revising *Modern English Usage,* was constrained to qualify Fowler's dictum with a long addendum. Gowers points out that Jespersen challenged Fowler on this point, and that it continues to be a subject of controversy. Gowers concludes that the fused participle is objectionable only with a proper name or personal pronoun: "We approved of John going" (*John's*): "Nobody noticed us arguing" (*our*). Five critics concur in this qualification of Fowler's original view, with some special variations.

In his reply, Fowler replied with what some might consider arrogance, but what his admirers are likely to consider just one more display of his endearing, if spiky, independence: "I confess to attaching more importance to my instinctive repugnance for *without you being* than to Professor Jespersen's demonstration that it has been said by more respectable authors than I had supposed." Supreme self-confidence in the expression of one's prejudices against all odds has been the hallmark of books on usage, and explains why they so often disagree. Such self-confidence was all right, perhaps, in the quarter-century when Fowler's was the only such book, but since dictionaries of usage have multiplied, it seems increasingly foolish to take such a stance. At any rate, an effort has been made in this book to abstain from it and to give the reader information, whether or not opinions conflict, instead.

Follett follows Curme in allowing the fused participle for emphasis on the subject of the gerund, and points out that some words are incapable of possessive forms, for example *that* ("I doubt the likelihood of that [hardly *that's*] happening"). He also exempts phrases that form cumbersome possessives ("Constitution of the United States") and abstractions, on which possessives cannot logically be formed ("philosophy becoming a major issue"). One critic recommends the possessive form whenever it is possible, and recasting when it is not. Another says the possessive is used now only with personal pronouns, and sounds stiff with nouns. Still another allows a free choice between the possessive and other forms with either nouns or pronouns. Gowers' conclusion is perhaps the closest to a consensus on this problem, together with the advice to use the possessive when possible (and, it might be added, when it makes for a smooth and idiomatic construction).

Fowler expressed the hope that his discussion would leave the reader sick to death of the fused participle, but the sad truth is that most of the examples he cited to bring on this mortal illness do not even make us queasy today. But his interminable discussion of it, to which Gowers unabashedly added instead of subtracting, might well bring on the result Fowler hoped for.

futilely. Sometimes misspelled *futiley.*

future. The key word in two fuzzy expressions: *in the near future,* which means *soon,* and *in the not-too-distant future,* which may mean *before long, eventually, finally, next year, sometime,* or *sooner or later.* See also *foreseeable future.*

future plans. Redundant, as is *advance plans,* since plans, unless otherwise qualified, are inevitably for the future. See also *Redundancy.*

G

gabardine, gaberdine. Technically interchangeable, but the first is so predominant for the fabric that *gaberdine* is likely to be taken for an error. *Gaberdine,* furthermore, has a distinct sense as the name of a medieval garment or, by extension, any cloak.

gag, gagged. See *quip, quipped.*

gag it up. A tiresome descriptive in the legends beneath pictures showing people, usually from show business, engaged in horseplay.

gainsay. Considered old-fashioned by Flesch and literary by Fowler for *deny.*

gambit. The basic sense, which comes from chess, is an opening move made at a deliberate sacrifice of some piece. Thus three critics object to the extended use of the term to mean simply any opening, for example of a conversation, without the idea of an attendant sacrifice. Fowler cites the use of *gambit* for *opportunity,* but this is not observable in the U.S. Dictionaries recognize as standard the general sense of *opening;* Random House gives the precise extended sense; American College and Webster's New World recognize only the application to chess. The consensus is that the extension should preserve the idea of sacrifice for an advantage.

Gandhi. Often misspelled *Ghandi.*

gantlet. See *gauntlet, gantlet.*

garb. Regarded by two critics as an affectation for clothing.

gas. Unexceptionable for *gasoline.* Ambiguity and possible confusion with cooking gas should be guarded against in some contexts.

gauge, gage. The first gives so much difficulty, often being misspelled *guage,* that the simpler version might have been expected to displace it. *Gage* is preferred in technical writing, perhaps for this reason.

gauntlet, gantlet. The first was originally a glove, the second a form of military punishment in which the victim ran along a lane formed by men who struck him (hence, *run the gantlet*, which is often used figuratively). Two critics say *gauntlet* is preferred for the glove and *gantlet* for what is run or endured. The usual form, however, is *run the gauntlet;* dictionaries give *gauntlet* as predominant for both senses, with *gantlet* as a variant. Thus opinion is divided.

gay. As used to mean *homosexual,* the term shares with *black* and *chicano* the distinction of having been self-applied by the segment of society it describes, and of having also been generally adopted, although the usual fate of such inventions is to be ignored. Previously, synonyms for *homosexual* tended to be disparaging or contemptuous (*fag, fruit, queer*) but *gay* is neutral. A number of recent dictionaries contain it, and all label it slang, although the indications are that it will quickly become standard, if it has not already done so. One commentator speculated that the self-application of *gay* was a kind of whistling in the dark if it is regarded as a transference of the original meaning of the word (lighthearted). The meaning of *gay* in the new sense is so widely known that the word must now be used with care in the original sense.

geared to. Journalese: "The product is geared to mass acceptance." *suited.*

gendarme. A gendarme is not the counterpart of an American policeman, but rather corresponds to a sheriff's officer or state policeman. French cities have policemen; smaller communities have what we would call constables. *Gendarme,* then, in indiscriminate reference to any French police officer is inaccurate, and in reference to an American policeman is wornout humor, two critics hold. Both Random House and Webster, however, give *a French policeman* as a general sense.

gender. *Gender* for *sex* is felt to be a facetious extension; the term usually applies to grammatical classifications, which do not correspond with sex. "Two performers of the feminine gender" would better be "Two women performers."

general. When the term forms part of a title like *attorney general* it is an adjective in the unusual predicate position; the meaning is *general attorney,* and the parts are not hyphenated. This applies to similar terms like *secretary general.* Dictionaries (except American Heritage) sanction both *attorney generals* and *attorneys general* for the plural. The consensus is that forming the plural of this and similar titles on *general* rather than on the noun is predominant, though either form is acceptable. See also *court martial.*

general consensus. Redundant, since *consensus* implies generality. See also *consensus of opinion.*

general public. Says nothing that *public* alone does not, when there is no contrast with some segment of the public.

Genitive. See *Possessives 3.*

gentle art. The *gentle art* of whatever the writer names is ridiculed by Fowler as a battered ornament.

gentleman. For ordinary use, or when there is a choice, *man* is preferable. The relation of *gentleman* to *man* is analogous to that of *lady* to *woman*. A gentleman was once defined as a man who never insults anyone unintentionally. And a lady has been defined as a woman who always remembers others and never forgets herself.

genuine. See *authentic, genuine.*

Geographical Descriptives. See *National Descriptives.*

geometrical. Often used in contexts where it conveys no precise meaning: "a geometrically shaped plot of land." The plot could have been circular, rectangular, polygonal. A geometrical shape can be bounded by any combination of lines and curves. Probably readers would have taken the description to mean an irregular plot bounded by straight lines, but this would have been only speculation.

geometrical (progression). See *arithmetical, geometrical.*

Gerunds. A maladroit construction results from putting a gerund (a verbal form that can be used as a noun, like "the *singing*") between *the* and *of,* on the model of *The Taming of the Shrew* and *The Shooting of Dan McGrew*. In these instances, of course, it accomplishes what is intended, namely, setting the gerunds (*taming* and *shooting*) in the forefront. But consider "Stevens repeated that the responsibility for the filing of the charges was his." It is recommended here that *the* and *of* be omitted, making the succeeding element the object of the gerund: *the responsibility for filing the charges.* As Perrin notes in *Writer's Guide and Index to English,* "This emphasizes the verbal phase of the word and makes for economy and force." Other examples: "Improvement in (the) gathering (of) and reporting (of) such data is needed"; "The proposals call for (the) setting up (of) a joint staff."

Fowler points out that a possessive pronoun modifying a gerund, as in "He was disappointed at his missing the show," is superfluous when the pronoun refers to the subject of the sentence: "He was disappointed at missing the show" (omitting *his*). See also *Fused Participle.* The worst has been saved for the last: "The kids made their own caps out of box-tops, and cheesecloth served for the holding on of the hats." Hard to believe, but it appeared in print. *used cheesecloth to hold them on.*

gesticulation, gesture. A gesture is the motion (in the literal sense) of head, hand, etc.; gesticulation is the act of making a gesture or gestures.

get. Two authorities criticize the substitution of *become* for *get* in attempts at elegance in such idiomatic phrases as *get sick, get lost,* though one of them describes this usage as more characteristic of speech than of writing. Another considers *get* weak for *obtain*. The substitution of *obtain* for *get*, when *get* comes naturally, is an affectation. Evans says *get* implies coming into possession of by any means, while *obtain* implies effort, and cites *get* (vs. *obtain*) *the measles*. See *got, gotten; obtain; secure*.

get under way. See *under way*.

Ghanaian, Ghanian. Though Random House and Webster give both forms, *Ghanaian* is the preference of the government of Ghana, and on the principle that their owners are the final judges of the spelling of names, it is correct.

GI. The term is applied to enlisted men, not to officers. The letters stand for "government issue," as originally used to describe supplies and equipment.

gibe, jibe. *Gibe* means *taunt, jeer at:* "The hazing went no farther than gibing at the freshmen." *Jibe,* in its commonest sense, means *match* or *correspond* with: "His performance did not jibe with his campaign promises." Confusion is encouraged by the fact that the words are pronounced identically. The foregoing represents the views of two critics and Random House; American Heritage and Webster give *jibe* as a synonym of *gibe*.

gift. Disapproved by three critics as a verb in the sense *give* or *make a gift of* ("He was gifted with a book for Christmas") though it is recognized without qualification by all current dictionaries except Webster's New World, which does not list it, and American Heritage, which roundly rejects it.

gild the lily. See *Misquotation*.

gimmick. Flesch reports that the term is listed in the dictionaries as slang (which is true, except for Webster) and protests that it has long since graduated into standard English. Fowler identifies the word as an Americanism that came to Britain after World War II and "passed in record time through the slang and colloquial stages to the dignity of use without inverted commas in leading articles and reviews in *The Times*." This judgment is followed by a long list of examples. Despite Flesch and Fowler, in the U.S., at least, *gimmick* retains a slangy tone, for all its usefulness and prevalence.

give(s) (furiously) to think. Disparaged whether used facetiously or seriously.

given. See *was given*.

given name. See *Christian name*.

give way. The idiom (not *give away*) for *yield to* or *be displaced by*. "Radio gave way [not *away*] to network television."

glamour, glamorous. Three critics protest that *glamour* is applied indiscriminately. One of them says the tendency is to forget its basic suggestion of magic and to use it for any kind of attraction or impressiveness. Another singles out its use as a synonym for beauty in reference to women as a misapplication. Somehow, the word seems to have gone out of fashion in the last few years, with the advent of freakish attire and a general air of deshabille among the generations most likely to have used it. If we had to stop applying *glamour* and *glamorous* to women we might as well throw the words away.

   Both Random House and Webster give a combination of beauty and charm as constituting a sense applicable to a person. The spelling *glamour* is given as preferable to *glamor*, and the adjective is preferably *glamorous*, not *glamourous*.

glance, glimpse. A glance is a quick look, a glimpse what is seen by it.

glean. Means to gather laboriously, little by little (the term comes, of course, from the work of those who follow the harvesters in a field of grain and gather what has been left on the ground). One authority particularly criticizes its figurative use in the sense of *learn, understand, discover,* etc., though both Random House and Webster give such meanings as standard.

glittering. A journalese counter word, too often automatically applied to anything that is new, elegant, or impressive in any way: "a glittering new shopping center"; "John Steinbeck accepted the Nobel Prize for Literature at glittering ceremonies"; "the appointee has a glittering name." Literally, that which glitters shines or sparkles. Some dictionaries give the sense *showy,* which would fit some of these examples but not all. Even so, overwork has made *glittering* a tiresome descriptive. Moreover, Webster gives as one sense of *glitter* "to be brilliantly attractive in a superficial way," which means that careless users of *glittering* risk being thought derogatory when they intend to be complimentary.

Gobbledygook. The use of the term in its present sense (the turgid language characteristic of bureaucracy) was popularized by Maury Maverick in an article that appeared May 21, 1944, in *The New York Times Magazine. Governmentese, federalese, officialese,* and in England, *pudder, barnacular,* and *gargantuan* are sometimes used in this sense, but *gobbledygook* predominates in the United States. Some hold that Representative Maverick did not originate the term, but there is no question that his article, protesting the diction used in reports of the Smaller War Plants Corporation, of which he was then chairman, popularized it. "Be short and say what you are talking about," Maverick exhorted. "Stop 'pointing up' programs, 'finalizing' contracts that 'stem from' the district, regional, or Washington levels. No more 'effectuating' or 'dynamics.' Anyone using the words 'activation' or 'implementation' will be shot." But alas, nearly 40 years have gone by and Washington prose is worse than ever. Not only that, but many of the expressions Maverick denounced have gone into common use.

   The word is sometimes spelled *gobbledegook;* this is the way it appears in

Evans and Random House, and Webster recognizes this form as a variant. The version with *y* is much commoner, however, and in any event is the one Representative Maverick used. *Gobble-de-gook* and *gobbledygook* are errors. A good illustration of gobbledygook and its cure developed in a wartime press conference at which President Franklin D. Roosevelt read an order concerning blackouts that had been prepared by the director of civilian defense:

"Such preparations shall be made as will completely obscure all federal buildings and nonfederal buildings occupied by the federal government during an air raid for any period of time from visibility by reason of internal or external illumination. Such obscuration may be obtained either by blackout construction or by terminating the illumination. This will of course require that in building areas in which production must continue during a blackout, construction must be provided so that internal illumination may continue. Other areas, whether or not occupied by personnel, may be obscured by terminating the illumination." After the reading of this order had been interrupted several times by laughter, President Roosevelt directed that it be reworded.

"Tell them that in buildings that will have to keep their work going, put something across the windows. In buildings that can afford it, so that work can be stopped for a while, turn out the lights."

The difference between gobbledygook and plain English is the difference between *terminate the illumination* and *turn out the lights*.

Another splendid example of gobbledygook appeared in the Federal Register in Washington as an attempt to define the term *ultimate consumer* in connection with eggs:

"Ultimate consumer means a person or group of persons, generally constituting a domestic household, who purchase eggs generally at the stores of retailers or purchase and receive deliveries of eggs at the place of abode of the individual or domestic household from producers or retail route sellers and who use such eggs for consumption as food."

This was indignantly translated as "Ultimate consumers are people who buy eggs to eat them."

A related problem is dealt with under the heading *Pomposity*.

Other fields than government have become notorious for the pomposity and unintelligibility of their prose, which has been christened with such names as *educationese, officialese, Pentagonese, pedagese, sociologese* (one of the worst of all).

God bless. One of the most asinine expressions that have gained some currency in recent years is the truncated *God bless*, uttered, of course, as a benediction. The comedian Red Skelton may not be to blame for having invented it; at any rate, it was his customary valedictory for his television show, delivered in an unimagina bly mawkish tone. "May God bless you" is an ancient invocation that makes sense; why leave out *you?* It is as if instead of saying "Thank you" we were to curtail it to "Thank." Dear Abby, an adviser on all sorts of problems, many of them troubling idiots, picked up "God bless," presumably addressing it to those of her correspondents whose problems required divine intervention. This meant only that it was exposed to additional millions, among whom there were inevitably many who could not wait to imitate some new mannerism of expression.

God rest ye merry. See *Misquotation.*

-goer. Solid as a suffix: *concertgoer, playgoer, moviegoer, theatergoer,* etc.

goes without saying. The critic may object that if it goes without saying, why not leave it unsaid? Flesch says that *naturally, of course,* or omission is preferable. Fowler points out that the expression is a translation from the French, but describes it as nearly naturalized and unobjectionable; he does not challenge it on logical grounds. See also *needless to say; of course.*

Goldwynisms. The more contemporary term for what were once referred to as Irish bulls, a species of malapropism. Some examples: "Anyone who would go to a psychiatrist ought to have his head examined"; "The next time I take you anywhere you'll stay home"; and this one, from a *New York Times* book review: "If Harold Ross were alive today, he'd be turning over in his grave." Webster gives for *Goldwynism* "a phrase or expression (as 'include me out') involving a grotesque use of a word." For *Irish bull* it gives "an expression containing apparently congruity but actually incongruity of ideas ('it was hereditary in his family to have no children')." There is reason to suspect that both *Irish bull* and *Goldwynism* are libels on their eponyms. *Irish bull,* perhaps, arose from the tendency of the British to ridicule the people they could not keep down, or perhaps from the ignorance and consequent mistakes of uneducated Irish immigrants to America. But who is to say the Irish were any more ignorant, or any more prone to errors in diction, than any other uneducated immigrants, including the English?

As for *Goldwynism,* there seems to be good evidence that most such expressions (the most famous of which is "include me out") were delightedly fabricated by MGM flacks and attributed to Sam Goldwyn, the famous motion picture producer, with his permission. Perhaps Goldwyn had uttered one or two on occasions when he was off guard and his comments were subject to quotation, and this may have got the thing started. But who has never made such errors in casual speech?

At any rate, true Irish bulls and Goldwynisms are unconscious. The example quoted from the *New York Times* was deliberate humor. A proposal was made a few years ago in Altadena, Calif., to develop some wild land into a cemetery, a project that aroused environmentalists, who wanted the land left as it was. Groucho Marx was reported to be one of the prospective investors, but quickly sensed that discretion was the better part of valor when questioned about it by a reporter. "I don't know anything about any cemetery," he replied. "I wouldn't be caught dead in one." A fitting rejoinder from the man who said he wouldn't join a club that would have him as a member.

good. Two critics call *good* as an adverb ("He doesn't see good") an error, a judgment so obvious that other commentators have not even troubled to make it.

Yet Bryant somewhat surprisingly concludes that *good* is becoming increasingly common in standard usage in reference to inanimate things. She cites as an example, "The car runs good." Otherwise, Bryant says, except after *feel* ("He doesn't feel good") the usage is substandard. Webster's New World and the American College dictionaries say *good* for *well* is variously regarded as substandard, dialectal, or colloquial; Webster III says "not often in formal use." Random House describes this usage as uncommon in educated expression and disagrees with Bryant by saying *well,* rather than *good,* is proper after *feel.* American Heritage rejects the adverbial *good* out of hand. There is little question that *good* for *well* is to be avoided.

good and sufficient reason. An overblown phrase, like *rules and* regulations; one of the adjectives is enough.

(a) good few. Considered an old fashioned expression by Evans; sometimes criticized as a regionalism.

goodwill, good will. These forms seem preferable as both noun and modifier to *good-will;* this is the consensus of dictionaries. Fowler, while concurring in general, recommends *good-will* as an attributive modifier: *a good-will offering.* American usage, however, holds predominantly to the unhyphenated forms: *a goodwill offering, the good will* (or *goodwill*) *of the community.*

go on a rampage. A cliché as applied to rivers that overflow.

go public. The expression has migrated from the world of finance, where it meant (and still means) to offer in the market shares of stock formerly held in a close corporation. Considering what the stock market has taken from the public, it seems only fair that the public should take *go public,* and whatever else it can get, from the market. Now the expression is gaining currency in the sense of disclosing some fact that was formerly kept private. "He decided to go public with the subject of his new play." *Go public* is to be found only in the 1971 Addenda Section of Webster, and there only in the financial sense. Its prospects for survival at least as an informal general term seem good. It has the irresistible appeal of the somewhat esoteric term that is nevertheless immediately intelligible.

got, gotten. *Have gotten* has passed out of use in England and has been supplanted by *have got. Have gotten* (for *have acquired, obtained*) is recognized as American idiom by six critics, though one considers *have gotten* and *have got* more appropriate to speech than to writing, and recommends a more precise verb. Another critic expresses a preference for *have got* over *have gotten,* but fails to point out the clear distinction noted by Marckwardt that *have got* conveys the idea of *being in possession of,* whereas *have gotten* means *have obtained* (e.g., "We have got [*possess*] the money" vs. "We have gotten [*obtained*] the money"). Random House gives *have got* as standard. Fowler explains that *have got* is colloquial in Britain for *possess;* this expression is not usual in America, where *have* alone is more likely. Bryant, however, cites examples from such sources as *Harper's* magazine, and calls the usage characteristic of speech or informal English. The consensus on *have got* for *possess* is that it is standard.

Two critics point out that *got married* may be necessary to distinguish the act from the state, since *were married* may be ambiguous. Bryant cites *got married* as frequent. *Have* (or *has*) *got to* for *must* (''I've got to go'') is regarded by Fowler as no better than "good colloquial," but another critic calls it thoroughly acceptable in the U.S. and Bernstein says it is likely to gain literary acceptance. Bryant cites it from *The American Scholar*. Webster calls it unliterary and more common in speech than in writing; to Random House it is standard, and this is the consensus.

Gotham. A once popular nickname for New York, now seldom seen. It came, according to Webster, from the name of a town in England noted for the folly of its inhabitants. Some might say that New York has lived up to the name to the extent that *New York* itself might now be applied in a similar way to some other place.

gourmand, gourmet. It has been aptly said that the first lives to eat, the second eats to live. *Gourmand* generally implies *glutton; gourmet, a connoisseur of food.* Random House unaccountably gives *gourmand* as a synonym of *gourmet:* Webster's *epicure* (for *gourmet*) is appropriate to the distinction recognized by the consensus.

graduate. The passive form (*was graduated,* declared requisite by purists) is described variously as old-fashioned, no longer standard, and inferior to *graduated* by six critics. American Heritage, Random House, and Webster give *graduated* as standard. They agree also that such forms as "He graduated college" are wrong, though Random House accepts *graduated college*.

graffiti. This newly popular term for writings on walls is a plural; the singular is *graffito,* dictionaries agree. Thus the newsmagazine picture caption, "Prague graffiti mocks Soviets" was wrong; it should have been *mock,* or *graffito.* It is regrettable that there should have been occasion for the term to come into general use at all, considering the barbaric defacement of buildings and other structures it reflects.

grammar. Often misspelled *grammer*, especially when advice on the subject is being given. This may only illustrate the natural perversity man must contend with, like the probability that a slice of bread will fall buttered side down. Fowler points out that grammar as a science includes inflection (changes in the form of words) and phonology (pronunciation), as well as syntax (the arrangement of words in sentences).

Perhaps the best book on grammar ever written is *Writer's Guide and Index to English,* by Perrin and Ebbitt, especially for use as a reference by writers of all ages, although it was once said to be the most widely used textbook for freshman composition courses in colleges. But that was when composition was still being taught in colleges, and even in high schools.

grammatical error. Objection to the expression on the ground that it is a contradiction in terms is pedantry. This is borne out by definitions in Random House and Webster, which define *grammatical* as *of or relating to grammar.* The criticism of the term has much in common with that of *climb down* and *head over heels.*

gratuitous. Has nothing to do with gratitude, though the words are related in origin. *Gratuitous* means *granted freely, uncalled for, unwarranted:* "a gratuitous insult."

gray, grey. The first is the American, the second the British, preference. Fowler adds the interesting note that *grey* has predominated in Britain despite the recommendation of Dr. Johnson and subsequent lexicographers. This is only one more bit of testimony to the inattention soothsayers on usage and grammar must endure.

Great Britain, British, English. *Great Britain* is an island comprising England, Scotland, and Wales. The *United Kingdom* is Great Britain plus Northern Ireland. *The British Isles* applies properly to the United Kingdom and the islands around it—Scilly to the southwest, the Isle of Man to the west, the Channel Islands to the east, and the Orkneys and the Shetlands to the north of Scotland. For all this, *Britain, United Kingdom,* and *England* (as well as *British* and *English*) are often used interchangeably. It is well to bear the distinctions in mind, however, for those occasions when they are useful. e.g., *British English.* Fowler concurs in general, and offers some special considerations limiting the terms from the viewpoint of the Englishman. See *Britisher.*

Grecian, Greek. The first now is usually limited to the ancient Greeks and their works and *Greek* is used in other connections.

grievous, -ly. Often misspelled *grievious -ly,* as a result, perhaps, of mispronunciation.

grill, grille. The cooking grate is *grill;* other gratings are *grill* or *grille,* though *grille* is somewhat pretentious. The verb for *interrogate* (always *grill*) is regarded by Evans as slang, but this is a severer judgment than is to be found in the current dictionaries. Webster considers it standard and American Heritage and Random House call it informal.

grind to a halt. A cliché.

grisly, grizzly. *Grisly,* which means *horrible, gruesome,* is often misspelled *grizzly,* which means *gray* or *grizzled.* Webster gives the terms as variants, but indicates that the distinction made here predominates. An advertisement by the Chicago Title Insurance Co. in the *Los Angeles Times* read: "Just try to sell your home without a Realtor. You'll have all kinds of people prowling everywhere.

Around the clock. Just ask anyone willing to remember the last time they tried to sell their own home. The stories are grizzly." Well, the bear facts often are.

groom. Two critics question *groom* for *bridegroom,* though it is common usage. Two others regard it as standard, and so do all current dictionaries. No usage has been more castigated in stylebooks, perhaps, than *groom* for *bridegroom;* not that this has discouraged it. Its critics scornfully hold that a groom is a man who tends a horse, which is true, but it shows also the age to which their thinking tends. Outside the horsy set, the term is uncommon as a noun and it may even be strange to the generations that have grown up since Henry Ford's great triumph.

ground, grounds. Interchangeable in the sense *basis:* ground(s) *for objection. Grounds* is usual in legal connections: *grounds for divorce.* Random House and Webster concur. Flesch recommends *because* in place of *on the grounds that,* a commendable criticism of wordiness.

group, bracket. Fowler derides the use of these terms in such contexts as *upper-income group, high-income bracket.* His objection was that the terms were popularized technicalities; that is, technical terms taken up enthusiastically and pretentiously by the layman, like *viable* and *ecology* in our own day, often without a clear idea what they mean. But he offers no satisfactory alternatives, and *bracket,* at least in connection with income and the taxes it incurs, is standard in the U.S. Often as not, the twisted meanings of technical terms, if they are used widely, force their way into dictionaries; this has happened to both *viable* and *ecology.*

Group Names, Words. See *Collective Nouns.*

guarantee, guaranty. Both are correct as noun and verb in the sense *ensure, warrant,* but *guarantee* is by far the more commonly used. Fowler says *guaranty* may be preferred in reference to the act rather than the security given, but this distinction is not observed in the U.S., where *guaranty* is mainly to be seen in the names of long-established firms dealing in insurance and finance.

guarded. The term has recently come to be used by doctors to describe the condition of patients, and apparently means *serious* or possibly *critical.* It has been taken up by the press, which always seems eager to jump overboard with new terminology. No dictionary yet gives any such definition of *guarded,* including Barnhart's work on new English since 1963. One would think the words already available for the sense in which *guarded* is used would be enough, and that a patient so described could only be in a prison hospital.

guerilla, guerrilla. Fowler prescribes the first spelling and Evans accepts either, but *guerrilla* is overwhelmingly predominant in the U.S.; this preference is indicated by dictionaries.

guest. Vain efforts have been made to restrict the term to recipients of hospitality, as distinguished from those who pay for their food, lodging, etc. It applies equally now to the paying and the nonpaying, although one often sees the qualified *paying guests*, when it is necessary to distinguish. Dictionaries recognize the application of the term to both those who pay and those who do not. An editor once forbade his reporters to describe people staying at hotels as guests, and was paid off when one reporter referred to them as inmates.

guest speaker. Usually redundant for *speaker* in announcements of meetings and the like. See also *feature*.

guilt (feelings, etc.). Although nouns steadily become adjectives, this is a matter of general acceptance and the consensus of usage. No dictionary yet recognizes *guilt* as anything but a noun, and consequently such expressions as *his guilt feelings*, which offend the fastidious ear, must be considered unacceptable in careful writing. Preferable: *his guilty feelings, his feelings of guilt*. See also *health reasons*.

guts. Described by Evans as coarse for *courage, fortitude,* or *impudence;* Flesch says its current wide use in these senses counteracts its designation in dictionaries as slang (Webster is the only exception). Flesch is right about its prevalence, although it cannot be denied that the word is always used with the deliberate intent to shock or to be rough-hewn.

gypsy, gipsy. Evans reports that the first is the American, the second the British preference in spelling; Fowler argues for *gypsy* on the basis of derivation (from *Egyptian*). Dictionaries give *gypsy* as predominant. Sometimes capitalized in reference to the people.

H

habitual. See *a, an.*

had. Criticisms of such sentences as "The motorist had his driver's license re-voked" on the grounds that it suggests the man instigated the revocation himself are dismissed by two critics as pedantry. Webster gives one meaning of *have* as "to experience, esp. by submitting to, undergoing, being affected by, enjoying, or suffering," and an older edition cited as an example "he had his back broken." A related idiom is illustrated by "The woman broke her arm in a bobsled accident." This is sometimes criticized on the same grounds as the foregoing. But anyone who objects to it would also have to object to *I broke my leg* or *He stubbed his toe* or *She cut her finger.* See also *break, broke; sustain.* Evans and Follett call such constructions as "I had my ankle broken" and "I had my house broken into" ambiguous, and recommend recasting. These constructions are similar to those cited earlier, but still not the same, and seem unlikely to be used.

had (have) reference to. Often wordy for *meant* or *mean:* "That was the property I had reference to." *meant.*

had better. See *better.*

hadn't ought. See *ought.*

had (would) rather. See *rather.*

hail, hale. *Hale,* in the sense concerned here, means *haul;* people are *haled* (not *hailed*) into court. *Hail* means *call, shout a greeting,* or *acclaim;* "We hailed a taxi"; "The new king was hailed by the crowd." Often confused, especially *hail* for *hale.* The accolade is *hale* (not *hail*) *fellow well met. Hail* is a headline stereotype for *approve, commend, praise.*

hairbrained. See *harebrained.*

half. See *cut in half.*

half-mast, half-staff. Some critics hold that a flag on a flagpole must be spoken of as flying at *half-staff* rather than *half-mast*. They reason that masts are found only on ships. But in fact *half-mast* is the predominant term on land and sea, and it is given as primary in both Webster and American Heritage. Masts, for that matter, are not necessarily confined to ships. Fowler called pride of knowledge a very unamiable characteristic, adding that its display is to be sedulously avoided. So much the worse when, as in this instance, the display is of ignorance.

hamstringed, hamstrung. Both forms are in use; one critic recommends the former, and two the latter, which predominates in the U.S. Dictionaries unanimously give the preference to *hamstrung*.

handfuls, handsful. See *-ful*.

handle in routine fashion. Overblown for *handle routinely*.

handsome. See *attractive*.

hang, hanged. See *hung*.

hang-up, hangup. In the sense *obstacle, inhibition, source of irritation* ("racial and sexual hangups have abated noticeably"), the expression graduated from slang in the 1960s (Webster's New World, Barnhart) to informal (American Heritage) in the early 1970s. By this time its utility and the contexts in which it is found have established it as standard. Harper considers it both slang and overworked. As is the way with hyphens in compounds, this one is disappearing.

happening. The use of the term as a noun for *event* or *occurrence* is denounced by Fowler as an affectation, defended as standard by Evans. Dictionaries recognize the usage without qualification. The term has gained a new vogue in the lexicon of youth for *public performance, demonstration, spectacle*.

harass. Sometimes misspelled *harrass*.

hara-kiri. The correct form for the Japanese ceremonial form of suicide, in the view of two critics; sometimes mistakenly given *hara-kari* and *hari-kari*. But Random House and Webster give the latter as a variant. Among the Japanese, the term *seppuku* is preferred, though it is virtually unknown in the U.S.

hard, hardly. The adverbial form of the adjective *hard* (in the sense *severely*) is preferably also *hard*, not *hardly*. *Hardly* in this sense may be ambiguous as well as unidiomatic: "The company was hardly hit by the Depression," when *hardly* may be understood to mean *scarcely*, though the intention was *severely*, which would have been conveyed unmistakably by *hard-hit*. *Hardly* for *severely* is labeled a Briticism by Random House; Webster gives several examples but they all seem to be from British writers.

hardly. A negative, and thus it should not be used with another negative as in *could not hardly, didn't hardly, can't hardly.* This also applies to *barely* and *scarcely.*

hardly . . . than, when. *Hardly than* ("Hardly had the pot begun to boil than the telephone rang") is regarded without dissent by authorities as an error for *hardly when.* This also applies to *barely . . . than, scarcely . . . than.*

hard put, hard put to it. The forms are equally acceptable, but Follett discourages the first as an unidiomatic clipped form. Both are considered standard by Random House and Webster; American Heritage gives *hard put.*

harebrained, hairbrained. Although the reference originally was to the brain of a hare, both Random House and Webster recognize *hairbrained* as a variant.

hark back, hearken. *Hark back* means to turn back to an earlier topic or circumstance; thus we speak of harking back to the Roaring Twenties, or to World War II. *Hark,* now quaint, means *listen: Hark, Hark, the Lark. Hark back* was originally a hunting phrase arising from the use of *hark* as a call to retrace one's course, according to the Oxford Dictionary of English Etymology. *Hearken* and *harken* (the latter chiefly U.S.) also mean *listen, heed: hearken to good advice.* Now and then the public prints come out with *hearken back:* "The performance hearkened back to his Dublin youth." *harked back.*

have. See *had.*

have got, have gotten. See *got, gotten.*

have sex. See *sex.*

Hawaii. Pronunciation is not the province of this book, but the determined practice of radio and television announcers making it Ha-VYE-ee in the face of the universal Ha-WYE-ee may deserve a comment. Ha-VYE-ee is thought by some to be based on the correct native version. This idea has been knocked down, however, by two authorities as wrong (*Introduction to the Hawaiian Language,* by Judd, Pukui, and Stokes; and the Rt. Rev. Harry S. Kennedy, Bishop of Hawaii). It is said that a mainlander once approached a native and inquired, "Sir, can you tell me whether it should be Ha-VYE-ee or Ha-WYE-ee?" "Ha-VYE-ee, of course," replied the native. "Thank you so much," said the mainlander. "You're velcome," was the response.

hearken See *hark back, hearken.*

he, she; his, her; him, her; himself, herself. 1. *He or she.* "The employee can appeal to the state if he or she feels that he or she is being exploited." *He or she* (and, in other circumstances, the other pairs) is not only clumsy but unnecessary.

It is a well-established convention that the masculine form alone is taken as applying to both sexes. The plural pronoun is commonly used in speech but is questionable in writing: "Every boy and girl had *their* own cup." *His* is preferable here, but Evans calls the plural form more natural English. See also *they* (*their, them*); *each; Femininism; Adolescent they.*

2. *He* (*Smith*), or whoever. "The county manager noted that the assessor's requests would add up to $4 million more than he (the manager) was willing to recommend." The writer has decided that *he* alone might be ambiguous, so he (the writer? yes) has placed *the manager* in parentheses beside it. Locutions like this constitute editing that has been obtruded on the reader. There is no more reason to write *he* (*the manager*) than to let any other lapse, together with its correction, stand in print. The example should have read *more than the manager was willing to recommend* (striking out *he*). This applies also to proper names following the pronoun: *he* (*Smith*); *she* (*Mrs. Jones*). If there is danger of ambiguity, let the name stand alone. Often the *he* (*Smith*) construction is the worse because there is no ambiguity to begin with. "The governor decided to resign in favor of the secretary of state, so that he (the governor) could be appointed to the Senate." *He* can logically be taken as referring only to the governor, but if the writer was doubtful he should simply have repeated *the governor.* "Lundberg asked which of his colleagues had told the mayor that he (Lundberg) had made the criticism." *He* can reasonably refer only to Lundberg, but if there is doubt, *Lundberg* alone will resolve it. The *he* (*Smith*) construction is called for only in a direct quotation when it is necessary to prevent ambiguity and at the same time preserve the exact form of the words quoted: "The observer reported, 'Some believe that he (Alexander) is only waiting for the right moment.' " Technically, the parentheses should be brackets, indicating an editorial insertion.

3. *His, her.* The pronouns should not be used if the antecedent does not exactly correspond: "It was the second time that tragedy struck the John Doe family. His two-year-old son suffocated two years ago." Whose son? Doe's, apparently, but the visible antecedent is *family.* *Doe's two-year-old son* would have been preferable. The society columns often refer to a couple (Mr. and Mrs. Roe) and then proceed with something like "He is a sanitary engineer. She first met him on a European trip." This irks the fastidious, who would prefer "Mr. Roe is a sanitary engineer; his wife (or *Mrs. Roe*) first met him on a European trip." "Things at first looked good for the Jones family. The Travelers Aid Society placed them in a hotel suite for the weekend, and he promptly got a job." *Jones,* not *he.*

4. Evans and Flesch consider the objective form acceptable in such sentences as "I thought it was him"; Fowler says such locutions have won standing as idiomatic spoken English but by implication disapproves of them in writing. See *it's me,* etc.; for *himself, herself,* see *myself.* See also *Pronouns.*

head over heels. Often criticized by the literal-minded as illogical since the usual place for the head is over (i.e., above) the heels. Webster reasonably gives one sense as suggesting the motion of a somersault. Alfred H. Holt, in *Phrase and Word Origins,* concedes to the critics that when one stops to think, it should be *heels over head,* and goes on to speculate that it may originally have been *over* *head and heels,* a translation of *per caputque pedesque* (Catullus). But it is no good trying to force language into the straitjacket of logic, least of all a sprightly idiom like this. Or is it now a cliché?

headquarter. As a verb ("The company is headquartered at Toledo"; "The expedition will headquarter in the valley"), rejected by Harper and American Heritage, but accepted as standard, in both transitive and intransitive use, by Random House and Webster. Desk dictionaries do not give it, which appears to indicate it is a neologism.

headquarters. May take either a singular or a plural verb, but the plural is usual: "The company's headquarters are (is) in New York."

head up. Frowned upon by three authorities for *head, direct, lead:* "A doctor was chosen to head up the study." *direct.*

health delivery services. Sometime since 1970, health services, especially those provided by the government, became *health delivery services,* especially in the press. This strange term was probably picked up from bureaucratic gobbledygook. How did *delivery* get in there? It is enough to make one wonder whether United Parcel has somehow gone into the business of providing health care. Let us hope the U.S. Postal Service is kept out of it, or the services will arrive late or not at all.

healthful, healthy. Three critics agree that although *healthful* means conducive to health and *healthy* means possessing it, *healthy* has established itself in both senses: "Eating apples is healthy." Dictionaries concur. One critic disapproves *healthy* as an intensive, as in "a healthy raise in pay," but Webster and American Heritage approve.

health reasons. This instance of making a noun (*health*) serve as an adjective is rejected by one critic and by the American Heritage panel as an "uncouth construction." See also *guilt feelings.*

heap, heaps. One critic describes the terms as not standard in the sense *large amount* (*heaps of self-confidence; a heap of living*); Webster recognizes them as standard and other current dictionaries designate them informal or colloquial. Fowler calls *heaps* colloquial and specifies that it takes a singular verb (heaps *is,* not *are*). The consensus is that the words are good colloquial usage.

hearken. See *hark back,* etc.

heart attack. The idea that the expression suggests an attack upon, or by, the heart, and thus cannot be used to describe a seizure, is absurd. The term is standard and is preferable to the newly prevalent *coronary* in reference to heart attacks. Technical language is best left to those equipped to use it precisely.

heart condition. Sometimes regarded as a euphemism or as an inexact term for *heart ailment,* on the ground that every heart has some condition, good or less so. Both unabridged dictionaries give *heart disease* but neither gives *heart condition,* nor does American Heritage. See also *Euphemisms.*

heartrending. Not *heartrendering.*

heave. *Heaved* and *hove* are both correct for the past tense, but *hove* is preferred in nautical connections: *hove into sight; hove to.*

Hebrew. In modern usage, the name of a language; not usually applicable to people except as the equivalent of *Israelite,* though sometimes it is resorted to as a genteelism in mistaken avoidance of *Jew, Jewish,* which see.

hectic. Fowler disapproves of the expression in the sense *excited, filled with activity* as a vogue word. The judgment on this point, implying that *feverish* is the only acceptable sense, was picked up almost verbatim from the original (1926) edition, and cites the Concise Oxford Dictionary's labeling of it as slang. The basis for this view is the Greek from which the word derives. In this instance, it appears, as in some others, Fowler neglected to take his own advice (given under the entry *True and False Etymology*) that "What concerns a writer is much less a word's history than its present meaning and idiomatic habits." Three American critics defend it as standard, a judgment concurred in by dictionaries.

hegira. Fowler asserts that the pronunciation with the accent on the long *i* is wrong, but this must represent British practice, since that version is given by all American dictionaries that list the word. Flesch frowns on casual use of the term as a synonym for *flight.*

height. Sometimes misspelled *heighth,* perhaps as a result of the frequent mispronunciation.

heir apparent, presumptive. Technically, the heir apparent will inherit if he survives; the heir presumptive will inherit unless someone else is born whose right takes precedence. For example, in the latter instance, a younger son will often displace a daughter. Both forms are used figuratively (*heir apparent to the presidency of the company*) but *heir apparent* is commoner.

heist. This slang term for *rob* or *hold up* is acceptable only for casual use; well-edited publications avoid it.

helicopter. Often mispronounced *helio-* and consequently sometimes misspelled.

help. The use of the word in such expressions as "Don't eat more than you can help" is described by one critic as idiomatic, but at the same time it is pointed out that recasting is available to anyone who considers this construction illogical.

Fowler's advice is much the same; the construction is designated a "sturdy indefensible," even though Winston Churchill is quoted as having used it. Random House and Webster give "refrain from, avoid" thus recognizing this usage as standard. The idiom is so well established that objections to it sound like pedantry. For *cannot help but,* see *can but, cannot but,* etc.

helpmate, helpmeet. Three critics agree that *helpmeet* is an erroneous form derived from a misinterpretation of Genesis 2:18, and that the correct form is *helpmate.* Both forms are considered standard by Random House and Webster.

hemorrhage. Pretentious in nontechnical contexts for *bleed.* "The victims were hemorrhaging profusely." *bleeding.*

hence. Bookish for *thus, therefore, consequently.* See also *from whence,* etc.

hep. See *hip.*

her. See *it's me; he, she,* etc.

here at, we at. These expressions, as they occur in "We at Nutzan Boltz, Inc." and "Here at Lefthand Monkeywrench," have come to be staple, slightly patronizing pomposities of the public-relations operators. Highly skilled practitioners sometimes manage to combine them: "We here at Lefthand Monkeywrench."

heroic. Takes *a,* not *an:* "A heroic deed." See *a, an.*

heroics. "Luck and heroics saved the 13,000 people of Gazli last spring when two powerful earthquakes destroyed or damaged every one of its buildings." But *heroics* does not mean *acts* of *heroism;* it means, in Webster's version, "vainglorious, unnaturally extravagant, or shamelessly flamboyant conduct, behavior, or expression." The adjective *heroic,* however, does mean "having to do with heroism," though it has other senses.

her's. There is no such form; *hers.*

herself. See *myself; Reflexives.*

hiccup, hiccough. *Hiccough* is declared erroneous by two critics but is given as a variant by both Random House and Webster; *hiccup,* however, predominates.

high, highly. *High* may be an adverb ("The plane circled high above the city"); the choice between the forms is governed by idiom. Usually *high* is preferred in the literal sense, indicating distance above something; *highly* in the figurative sense, as an intensive, means *to a high degree* ("We were highly amused by his chatter"). On this principle, *highly paid executive* is preferable to *high-paid,* though there are exceptions; *highly priced* is unacceptable for *high-priced. High-*

strung and *high-toned* are also idiomatic. The correct forms for most such combinations are to be found in dictionaries. American Heritage inexplicably omits to recognize *high* as an adverb.

high gear. In figurative use, a cliché: "The campaign is going into high gear."

highlight. Although some dictionaries make two words of *highlight* as a noun ("The song was the *high light* of the concert"), the fact that there is general agreement on one word as a verb ("The speech will *highlight* education"), and the consensus of usage of both forms, in addition to the way they are pronounced, indicate that *highlight* is to be preferred.

high-price, -priced. As a modifier, the participial form is preferable: "A *high-price* call-girl racket." *high-priced.*

high, wide, and handsome. The correct form of the expression, albeit a cliché. "The new satellite rode high, wide and handsomely around the earth this week." *Handsome. Handsomely* results from an undiscriminating overcorrectness.

hijack. One critic argues for the utility of the word in its newest sense, to seize, or commandeer, a vehicle illegally while in transit, and while describing this usage as casual, predicts that it will become standard. It is considered slang by the New Standard Dictionary, colloquial by Webster's New World, and standard by American Heritage, Random House and Webster. The usage is unhesitating and widespread in the press to describe the illegal seizure of airplanes, ocean liners, and other forms of transport. At the time such seizures began, *hijack* was known chiefly in the sense in which it had been used during the Prohibition era, to *steal while in transit,* relating to the theft of bootleg liquor being carried in trucks.

hike. Disapproved by one critic in the sense *increase.* American Heritage, Random House, and Webster regard it as standard, but two current desk dictionaries designate it colloquial.

hilarious. The word describes not merely amusement, but loud mirth. It is often used in a way that hopelessly exaggerates, especially in advertisements of plays and movies.

him. See *it's me,* etc.

himself. See *myself,* etc.

hip, hep. One critic and American Heritage recognize that *hep* is passé, having been displaced by *hip* (in the sense *au courant, up with the times, knowing*). Count Basie, the orchestra leader, was said to have been pestered by an insistent drummer who begged to be permitted to sit in with Basie's musicians. Basie politely explained that it wouldn't work, because the orchestra's music was scored, and his men labored through hours of rehearsal to produce the correct balance. The outsider remained insistent. "But, Count, man, I'm hep," he said. At this point Basie suavely responded, "I'm hip you're hep, man, and that's why you can't sit in."

Hip itself may now be passé, however, or at least obsolescent. Yet Barnhart quotes it as late as 1970, not only as a noun but as a verb (*to inform*) in *Harper's* magazine and *The New Yorker,* publications that may or may not be as hip as they might be. Passé or not, *hip* is slang.

hippie. The preferable form (rather than *hippy,* which had a previous meaning, *large-hipped*) for the nonconformist. The term now may have only historical interest, hippies having been superseded by other freaks.

hippopotamuses, hippopotami. Two critics express preference for the first form; Evans considers them equally acceptable. The form given as predominant by Random House and Webster is *-muses.* There is a good chance that the user of *hippopotami,* like the user of *stadia* for *stadiums,* is showing off.

his, her. See *he, she,* etc.

Hispanic. Newly popular as an evasion of or catchall for *Mexican, Puerto Rican,* etc. See *Mexican, Spanish.*

historic, historical. The first means *memorable, important,* or *figuring in history* (*a historic expedition*). *Historical* means merely *concerned with* or *relating to history.* A historical novel is one based on, or dealing with, history; a historic novel is a literary landmark, one that makes history. "The historical ranch changed hands recently" is wrong; *historic.* Random House and Webster generally recognize the distinction set forth here, while at the same time permitting interchange of the forms. *History, historian, historic, historical* take *a,* not *an* (see *a, an*); Fowler says the use of *an* with these terms lingers curiously.

hither. Described by two critics as archaic or obsolescent for *here;* Fowler adds, however, that the phrase *hither and thither* remains current. Random House and Webster consider *hither* current for *here, to this place,* but Fowler's view that the term tends to be literary or pretentious seems valid. It is sometimes used facetiously in the U.S.

hitherto. The word means *until now,* but sometimes displaces *previously,* as in "The economy then sank to a point hitherto not experienced." *until then.* Random House and Webster concur. One critic discourages use of the expression at all as old-fashioned.

hoard, horde. A hoard is a supply of something stored away (*a hoard of gold*); a horde is a swarm or crowd (*a horde of insects*).

Hobson's choice. This is no choice at all, not merely a choice, as in a dilemma, between things that are undesirable; Random House and Webster corroborate this. One critic calls it a cliché. The expression derives from an English hostler who compelled his customers to take the next horse in line.

hodgepodge, hotchpotch. Fowler reports that *hotchpotch* (in the sense *mixture, jumble*) prevails in Britain, and Evans that *hodgepodge* prevails in America, a sound judgment in which Random House and Webster concur, though *hotchpotch* is occasionally seen here.

hoi polloi. Two critics point out that *hoi* is *the* in Greek, so that English references to *the hoi polloi* contain an ignorant repetition. Random House and Webster, however, allow *the hoi polloi*. (The term means *the masses, the ordinary people,* and is usually used in a patronizing or derogatory way.) Criticism based on knowledge of a language many readers are unlikely to know, and challenging a term that has been solidly Englished, are pedantic, and analogous to the criticisms of *Sierra Nevada mountains* as redundant because *Sierra Nevada* means *snowy mountains* in Spanish; of *Sahara Desert* because *Sahara* means *desert* in Arabic; of *Rio Grande River* because *Rio Grande* means *big river* in Spanish. These objectors should consistently object to *City of Minneapolis* and *City of Indianapolis* because *-polis* means *city*.

hold. Widely though inexplicably aspersed, especially in journalism, in the sense *conduct* (*hold court, hold a meeting*). This is perhaps as good an example as can be found of what Fowler would call a superstition. No dictionary, new or old, British or American, gives any indication that the word is not thoroughly standard in this sense.

hold steady. An idiom; not *hold steadily*.

holdup. See *burglary*.

holocaust. One critic argues that by derivation, the term can properly relate only to destruction by fire (and loss of life). All current dictionaries, however, recognize it as denoting destruction in general, not necessarily by fire, and sometimes not necessarily entailing loss of life; another critic concurs in this but adds the distinction that a holocaust, unlike some other disasters, may be the result of human intention. No current dictionary suggests this.

home, house. Objections are often raised that an unoccupied dwelling cannot properly be referred to as a *home;* such a place, it is insisted, is a *house*. This is sentimental; no dictionary specifies occupancy as a requisite for applying the term *home*. Polly Adler, the ineffable madam, held that "a house is not a home," but then she was talking about a special kind of house, one that nobody would equate with a home. In general, the terms are interchangeable, except for some idiomatic phrases like *house and lot*.

No doubt Edgar Guest's well-known dictum that "It takes a heap o' livin' in a house t'make it home" figures in the prejudice against *home* for an empty house.

Real-estate agents knowingly choose *home* to describe their offerings, as having more warmth and thus more appeal for the prospective buyer than *house*. Robert Frost described *home* as "the place where, when you have to go there, they have to take you." *Home,* to be sure, has its own connotations, but *home* and *house* are so often used interchangeably in reference to dwellings as such, occupied or not, that any hard and fast distinction has been lost.

Three critics agree that *home* for *at home,* that is, using *home* as an adverb ("He was home all the time"), is good American usage, but not British. Fowler prescribes *homy* in preference to *homey,* but *homey* predominates in the United States.

Homeric. Obviously means having to do with Homer. Homeric laughter is inexpressible or inextinguishable laughter. But the senses *heroic* or *Herculean* are wrong, as in "The managers show no gratitude for the Homeric services done them."

home town, hometown. See *back yard.*

homosexual. Despite widespread misuse as applying only to men, the term denotes one who feels sexual attraction to the same sex, and thus may be applied to either a man or a woman. The opposite of *homosexual* is *heterosexual.* The misapprehension probably grows out of an assumption that *homo-* here is the Latin for *man;* it comes from the Greek *homo-,* meaning *same.* There is a strong tendency to use *lesbian* in contradistinction to *homosexual.*

honeymoon. Unexplainably proscribed in some newspaper stylebooks in favor of *wedding trip. Honeymoon* is the usual term, however, and it is considered standard by all dictionaries.

honor, honorable. To honor is to pay tribute to; the word is unsuitable in the sense *mark* or *observe,* as in "The community will honor Public Schools Week." *observe;* it is the schools that will be honored, not the week. *Honor* is not an adjective; therefore, not *honor guests* but *honored guests.*

Honour is British spelling, used in America mainly on invitations, where, as in other contexts, it is an affectation.

Honorable is a courtesy as a title in the United States; it has no official standing. It is never used with the last name alone unless followed by *Mr.;* either *the Honorable James Jones* or *the Honorable* (often abbreviated *Hon.*) *Mr. Jones.* This salute appears to be going out of use in our blunter age. Fifty years ago H. L. Mencken was using it derisively, and the appellation "his honor, the mayor" has been converted into the mocking *hizzoner.* The usage of *honorable* parallels that of *reverend,* which see.

Honorary Degrees. See *Dr.*

honored in the breach. See *Misquotation.*

hoof. The predominant plural is now *hoofs; hooves* has become literary.

hooky. The predominant spelling (*Play hooky from school*); not *hookey*.

hopefully. Until about 1960, the word was used only in the sense *in a hopeful way* or *feeling hope:* "The sailors looked hopefully at the sky for a break in the clouds." Since that time, however, it has been more and more widely used in the sense *it is hoped,* as in "A new session will meet late in the spring to vote new credits, hopefully at a reduced figure" and "The report will serve, hopefully, to keep Congress to the $4-billion mark." This misuse is protested by five critics and American Heritage. Considering how widespread it has become, however, the protests are undoubtedly in vain. The Standard College Dictionary, Random House, and Webster's New World have already admitted it as standard, in function like an adverbial clause modifying a whole sentence: "Hopefully, I'll finish next week."

Some theorists have ventured that the changed use followed the example of the German *hoffentlich,* which does mean *it is hoped.* But, like one widespread idea of the derivation of *tinker's dam,* it is probably "an ingenious but baseless conjecture," as the Oxford English Dictionary put it.

horn. As strictly used among musicians, the term refers to the French horn. Loosely, however, among both musicians and others, it may be applied to any brass instrument (especially the trumpet and trombone) and sometimes even to any wind instrument, including such woodwinds as the clarinet. This is especially true in the world of jazz.

host. As a verb ("The East Side Club will host the gathering"), considered objectionable by three critics and American Heritage. Both Random House and Webster accept the usage, which is endemic in the press.

hotel. Takes *a,* not *an.* See *a, an.*

hot-water heater. A redundancy for *water heater* but the term may be solidly enough established to have passed beyond criticism.

house. See *home, house.*

how. *How* for *that* ("He told us how he had watched the sun rise that morning") is aspersed by one critic as substandard. It is considered standard by another, however, and so given by Webster.

how come. In the sense *why* ("How come the pencils are missing?") regarded as idiom by Flesch but as unsuitable for writing by two critics. Random House considers it informal; Webster and American Heritage give it as standard.

however, how ever. *However,* as both an adverb meaning *in whatever manner* and as a connective meaning *nevertheless,* should be distinguished from the adverbial phrase *how ever,* an emphatic form of *how:* "It was a mystery, however he carried it off" (*in whatever manner*); "We noticed, however, that the money was not refunded" (*nevertheless*); "The neighbors wondered how they ever managed to pay off the mortgage"; "How ever did he get promoted?" (*how*). In this latter sense, *how* and *ever* are two words.

The main question about *however* as a connective concerns its placement. Its main function is to indicate a contrast, and it should not break a sentence except for that purpose. In "We noticed, however . . ." the stress of contrast is laid against *we noticed.* If the arrangement were, "We, however, noticed . . ." the stress would be against *we,* contrasted with others. If *however* comes first, it contrasts what follows with what has gone before. It modifies the whole sentence when placed at the end, but late placement is usually discouraged. The user must decide which element of his sentence is to be contrasted and place *however* accordingly.

When *however* begins a second clause, it is preceded by a semicolon: "Several topics of interest will be discussed; however, election of officers will be the main business of the evening." *However* as a connective is always set off by commas or otherwise. Flesch, however, reports a growing trend to dispense with the commas and says this speeds reading. It is questionable whether the examples he quotes represent deliberate omission of the commas or carelessness. *But however* is redundant; use one or the other.

huddle. A metaphor taken from football; overworked and generally inappropriate: "Government officials and labor leaders huddled this morning." *met, conferred.* See also *kick off.*

huge throng. Redundant; a throng, by definition, is huge.

huh-uh. See *uh-huh.*

human. The use of the word as a noun ("Humans are sentient beings") has been severely criticized. Three authorities, however, and American Heritage regard this usage as standard. It may sound quaint or technical in ordinary contexts, nevertheless; *person* or *people* are the usual words to distinguish, for example, between the human and the nonhuman ("The cast consists of nineteen humans and one goat"). *people.* This is essentially also the conclusion of Bryant, who finds *human* as a noun more frequent in speech than in writing. Follett says that while *human* as a noun can be defended, it is a stylistic fault. Dictionaries accept it, three of them as standard, one labeling it colloquial or humorous. The consensus is that while *human* is acceptable as a noun, there is still objection to it.

humanist, humanitarian. A humanist is a classical scholar whose subject is the humanities; a humanitarian is concerned about human welfare. The terms are sometimes confused; particularly, the scholar is called a humanitarian. *Humanity, humaneness,* and *humanitarianism* are approximate equivalents as nouns, not to be confused with *humanism* (the academic term).

humble. Takes *a*, not *an*.

humblebee. *Bumblebee* predominates; *humblebee* is described by Random House as chiefly British.

humble opinion. An obsequious expression. The truly humble, in any event, probably do not have opinions but instead humbly adopt the views of their betters. The expression unfortunately conjures up the image of Uriah Heep.

hung. Two critics say that *hung* is now standard in the sense *executed*, though at one time only *hanged* was considered proper. The distinction was usually illustrated by the dictum that pictures are hung, people are hanged. American Heritage and Harper accept only *hanged* for execution, but other current dictionaries do not asperse *hung*, though they indicate that *hanged* is the usual form. Bryant says *hung* is used but *hanged* is more common (this, incidentally, is the only sense in which *hanged* is now used). *Hung*, of course, has the rough-and-ready flavor of the Old West. Fowler insists on *hanged*. The consensus is that *hung* is standard, but more informal and less frequent.

hurl. Often an excited variant of *make* or *throw*, especially in *hurl a charge* (for *make an accusation*), a conspicuous concretion in the news columns. Epithets, too, are invariably hurled, together with insults and imprecations. The great advances in rocketry have given *hurl* another outlet; satellites, it seems, must always be *hurled into orbit*. *Hurl* is conspicuously journalese; its overuse and misuse grow out of straining for dramatic effect, a practice that defeats its own end. *Hurl* connotes great force, which makes "The people were hurling flowers and confetti at the distinguished visitor" inept.

hurricane, typhoon. See *typhoon, hurricane*.

hurt. One critic disapproves as "now only colloq." the use of *hurt* in such constructions as "The states are hurting from inadequate federal aid," Webster quotes *Newsweek* without qualification; "Atomic-energy programs are hurting from lack of enough scientific help." Random House gives "to cause injury, damage, or harm," which covers the same ground. American Heritage gives "The tax bill hurts." The consensus is that this sense (*cause or feel hardship or damage*) is standard.

hydro-. Solid as a prefix: *hydrocarbon, hydroelectric, hydrophobia*, etc.

hyper-. Solid as a prefix: *hyperacidity, hypercritical, hyperthyroid*, etc.

Hyphens. Perhaps a suitable introduction to this vexing subject is the warning by John Benbow in *Manuscript and Proof*, the stylebook of the Oxford University Press: "If you take hyphens seriously you will surely go mad."
   1. General use. Authorities generally agree that the use of hyphens tends to defy rules. Perhaps the best general advice that can be given is to consult the

dictionary, especially for the forms of compounds and nouns, and to determine whether a given prefix is joined solid or hyphenated. The tendency is for the hyphen to be used in a compound when it is new, but for it to be dropped after the expression becomes familiar. In the interval between Webster II and Webster III *pin-up* became *pinup, nimbo-stratus* became *nimbostratus,* and *saw-tooth* became *sawtooth.* It should be remembered, too, that the hyphen joins, in contrast to the dash, whose job is to separate.

2. Compound modifiers. These should be joined by a hyphen as necessary to assist understanding: *snow-covered hills, an odd-looking man, dark-brown cloth,* and *power-driven saw* do not require the hyphen, though its use is strictly correct. Such combinations as *strong-navy agitation, small-animal hospital,* and *old-time clock* require the hyphen for clarity. The desirability of the hyphen in such instances must be decided by the writer. Nevertheless, it is worse to leave out the hyphen where it is desirable than to use it where it is not essential. Judicious hyphening unquestionably aids comprehension and speeds the reader on his way. A dictionary will indicate the style for compound nouns as well as for some compound adjectives, but many compound adjectives are formed for the occasion and thus are at the mercy of the writer's judgment. One test of the desirability of the hyphen in such combinations is to apply the modifiers separately to the noun. If they are ambiguous unless taken together, they should be joined by a hyphen. Compound modifiers formed by several paired expressions, as in "a coalition of Southern white-big city-big labor-ethnic-minority elements" are confusing and should be avoided. This idea would be more clearly expressed in the form "a coalition representing Southern white, big-city, big-labor, and ethnic-minority elements." As a matter of prescribed stylistic practice, for unexplained reasons, *The Milwaukee Journal* does not use hyphens in compounds. This often leads to bafflement of readers, sometimes to absurdity. *The New Yorker* once cited a *Journal* headline reading, "Man eating / piranha sold / as pet fish," appending the comment, "Did he *look* like a fish?" An example of ambiguity caused by neglect of the hyphen: "They seem to enjoy the people watching as much as the shopping." *people-watching;* not, as might be understood without the hyphen, watching by people.

Consider "a total anti-air pollution system." A total pollution system that is anti-air? It may seem that this reading is wrongheaded, and that no reader would come to this conclusion. Probably so, but readers would not come to the *right* conclusion without stumbling. "A total anti-air-pollution system" would have made matters immediately clear.

Compound modifiers do not require the hyphen when they occur in the predicate position (that is, standing after the element modified). These often are combinations with *well: A well-educated man;* but *The man was well educated.* See *well.*

Flesch advocates imaginative compound modifiers, giving *early-business-letter English* as an example but protests against such clearer examples, common in journalism, as *Chinese-dominated town, Red-leaning Cambodia,* and *health-enforced retirement.* Fowler also deplores such constructions, which exemplify the compression characteristic of journalese, and result from avoiding prepositional phrases; *a town dominated by the Chinese, a retirement forced by ill health.*

3. Hyphens with numbers. The hyphen should be retained throughout compounds containing numbers; not *a 25-mile an hour speed* but *a 25-mile-an hour speed;* not *a 50-foot long relief map* but *a 50-foot-long relief map.* Numbers preceding nouns as simple modifiers, however, should not be hyphenated: *$400 million was raised,* not *$400-million;* the hyphen is required only when the number forms a compound with another modifier: a *$5-million building; a ten-foot pole.* Indications of quantity standing after the noun are not hyphenated: "The boy was 10 years old" (not *10-years-old,* as often appears in print). When the hyphen joins two figures, it means *through,* and it is generally used this way with dates: *July 15–19.* Otherwise, it is preferable to use *to* in indicating a span: "40 to 50 percent of the cost" (not "40–50 percent"). Hyphens are sometimes omitted from, but more commonly used in, compound numbers (like *sixty-eight*) and fractions (*three-fourths*).

4. Hyphens with phrasal verbs. Verbs that are formed by a combination of verb and adverb, such as *cash in, hole up, put out, pay off,* do not take the hyphen, but modifiers formed from them do, and nouns formed from them may. Examples: "The Communists *stepped up* infiltration" (phrasal verb, no hyphen); "A *stepped-up* campaign is planned for spring" (compound adjective modifying *campaign,* hyphen required); a *big flare-up* (noun, hyphen desirable, though such forms are often solid).

5. Prefixes and suffixes. In accordance with the principle stated earlier, hyphens are no longer used with many prefixes and suffixes that once were regarded as requiring them. Such prefixes as *mid-, non-, pre-,* and *super-,* and such suffixes as *-down, -fold, -less,* and *-wise* are usually joined solid. Such questions may most easily be settled by consulting the dictionary. For ready reference, here are the commonly used prefixes usually set sold: *a-, ante-, anti-, bi-, by-, circum-, co-, counter-, dis-, down-, electro-, extra-, fore-, hydro-, hyper-, hypo-, in-, infra-, inter-, mal-, micro-, mid-, multi-, non-, on-, out-, over-, pan-, post-, pre-, re-, semi-, sequi-, sub-, super-, supra-, trans-, tri-, ultra-, un-, under-, uni-, up-.*

Prefixes usually hyphenated: *all-, ex-, no-, self-, vice-, wide-.*

Suffixes usually set solid: *-down, -fold, -goer, -less, -like, -over, -wise.*

Suffixes usually hyphenated: *-designate, -elect, -odd, -off, -on, -to, -up, -wide.*

There are some inconsistent exceptions to these generalizations. A prefix or suffix otherwise set solid is usually but not always hyphenated to avoid doubling a vowel, and always to avoid tripling a consonant, or when joined to a word that is capitalized: *anti-intellectual, bill-like, non-Asiatic.*

Beyond this, common sense must be invoked to prevent strange combinations that may baffle the reader. *Antilabor* is one; preferably, *anti-labor. Nonnative,* as pointed out by Harper, is another: *non-native.*

6. Hyphens in titles. Hyphens are often used confusingly in corporate titles indicating combined positions; "He was chief engineer general manager." Not *engineer-general,* as might appear, but *chief engineer and general* manager. The dash would be better than the hyphen in such instances, if the use of *and* is too much to ask. The same objection holds for such forms as *vice president-sales* and *vice president—sales.* Fowler cites similar examples involving place names and

prescribes the same remedy. Sometimes the virgule, or slant (/), is used instead of the hyphen in such instances, and sometimes an odd beast known as the en dash, a hybrid of the hyphen and the dash. The en dash, however, is likely to be mistaken for the hyphen and it is often unavailable except in the typesetting equipment used for books.

7. Hyphen with adverbs. As Fowler points out, an adverb that is the first word of a compound should not be joined to the next unless it may be mistaken for an adjective: *little-used car* (vs. *little used car*). Words ending in *-ly* are almost invariably adverbs, and this is the signal that the hyphen is superfluous: *an easily grasped concept, a beautifully executed painting,* not *easily-grasped, beautifully-executed.* See also *almost.*

8. Hyphen in definitions. The dots used to separate syllables in entries in the dictionary should not be mistaken for hyphens, as they sometimes are. Hyphens are indicated in their usual form in such entries or sometimes by a double hyphen (=).

9. Hyphen vs. dash. The hyphen joins, the dash separates—a principle that, when fully grasped, will help prevent many errors in using these marks. The dash is formed on the typewriter by striking the hyphen twice; when this rule is observed, confusion is prevented when typescript is set in type. A stenographer at a Senate hearing, reading a transcript, noted that a dash occurred at a certain point. She was interrupted by a senator who had a copy before him. "Two dashes," he said. "Two hyphens—yes sir—a dash" was her flustered reply. See also *Dash.*

10. Superfluous hyphens. Hyphens are often used to join phrases when there is no reason for them: *profiles-in-depth, a pat-on-the back, once-a-week, point-of-view, minute-by-minute.* The hyphens are all unnecessary except when the phrases are used as modifiers (*a minute-by-minute account*).

To conclude: In *Harper's* of April, 1965, appeared an article by Charlton Ogburn entitled "Trials of a Word Watcher," which ended: "Do you know why Mariner I, the 'probe' aimed at Mars, went off course into oblivion? I ask you, do you know? Because, in all the complicated instructions fed into its guidance system, one hyphen was inadvertently omitted. One tiny hyphen that requires you only to extend your little finger to the upper right-hand corner of the keyboard. It cost the American people two million bucks. And, if you ask me, it served them damned well right."

hypo-. Solid as a prefix: *hypodermic, hypothyroid,* etc.

hypocrisy. Often misspelled *hypocracy.*

hysterical. Takes *a,* not *an.* See *a, an.*

I

I, we. Columnists and others using an informal style sometimes self-consciously avoid *I* by omitting it and starting sentences endlessly with verbs, leaving the subject to be supplied by the reader: "Appeared on a television program last week, and . . ."; "Was embarrassed by some criticism . . ." This avoidance is even more conspicuous than the use of *I*.

Fowler cites a number of literary precedents for *between you and I* and similar constructions in which *I* is the second of two objects ("criticized Charles and I" etc.). He concludes that despite its frequency, it is not approved, even colloquially, unlike *it's me* and *that's him*. American Heritage calls it nonstandard though common in speech.

There is a strong tendency to avoid the objective case in pronouns (*me, her, him, them*), perhaps resulting from criticisms in school of their incorrect use as subject: "Me and him are going." This leads sometimes to overcorrectness, resulting in "Don't wait for we girls." *us girls*. Prepositions, of course (in this case *for*) require the objective case.

A similar lapse is exemplified by "This is repugnant to we, the people." *We, the people* is a set phrase of some dignity, but when it is an object, *we must become us*. Of course, *us, the people* does not have the declamatory ring of *we, the people*. But if *we, the people* is considered essential, it must be placed first, in the position of subject. Reviewers are confronted with the question whether they should use *I* or offer their critiques impersonally. Arguments run both ways. Modest critics who avoid the personal pronoun say they have no business obtruding themselves on the reader by using it. On the other hand, the impersonal approach may make it sound as if the judgments are being handed down from on high and are unchallengeable, when after all they are only the opinions of the writer. Then there is the consideration that the use of personal pronouns help to create an intimate link between writer and reader. See also *Editorial* (*and Royal*) *we; it is I who* (*is, am*); *it's me*, etc.; *one*.

-ic, -ical. Authorities in general warn that some pairs of words having these endings (*politic, political*) have clearly differentiated meanings, while others (*electric, electrical*) are for practical purposes interchangeable. *Economic* and *economical* are fairly well differentiated, but not entirely so; the first is generally used to mean *pertaining to economics,* and the second *money-saving,* though occasionally the first is used in this latter sense. Fowler says that when the forms are synonymous

191

as adjectives, and the *-ic* form is also in use as a noun, it would be well to differentiate their use. Although *fanatic* and *fanatical* may both be adjectives meaning the same thing, he advocates that *fanatic* be reserved for the noun and that *fanatical* be used exclusively as the adjective form. *Musical critic* is not the idiomatic form in the U.S. since *musical* now suggests the production of music, rather than discord, which is often the critic's output. True, George Bernard Shaw wrote a book entitled *How to Become a Musical Critic*. This may mean either that *musical* where we now use *music* as an adjective is a Briticism or that it is old-fashioned. Similarly, *drama critic* is displacing *dramatic critic*, but here the difference is not so evident. Follett says both forms are in use but that the shorter is favored.

-ic, -ics. Confusion may arise in the use of certain words with these endings when the writer does not have clearly in mind whether he requires the noun form as a modifier (usually ending in *-ics*) or the adjective form. An example is *dramatic, -ics*. A *dramatic instructor* might be one who used histrionic techniques in putting his lessons (in whatever field) across; a *dramatics instructor* could only be a teacher of drama. The difference between an *athletic director* and an *athletics director* corresponds to that between a *musical critic* and a *music critic*. Nevertheless, *athletic director* is almost universally used for *director of athletics*. There is about as much chance of impressing the difference between *athletic director* and *athletics director* on the sporting fraternity as there is of getting it to pronounce *athletics* in three syllables instead of four.

Some other words with which the distinction should be observed are *narcotic(s)*, *cosmetic(s)*, and *economic(s)*. A *narcotics agent*, for example, is one concerned with narcotics; a *narcotic agent* would be a stupefying one.

Names of studies or activities ending in *-ics* are usually singular: *mathematics is, athletics is, politics is,* (not *are*). *Accoustics* may be either singular or plural; as a science it is singular, as an attribute, plural: "the acoustics are good."

icecap. Follett protests that the term is widely misapplied to the *polar pack* (the floes covering the North Pole). An icecap is a vast field of glacial ice, sloping from a high central point, over northern land areas. Dictionaries bear out the distinction.

identical. Two critics insist that *identical* takes *with;* Webster and Harper say usually *with*, sometimes *to*. Although *with* is favored, observable educated usage indicates that *to* is firmly established.

identify, -fied with. Pretentious for *belongs to, member of, works for, associated with, takes part in.* ("He is identified with the university.") Follett criticizes *identify* for *find, name,* or *define* (for example, problems), and adds that the drama critic should be careful to say he *identifies himself with* rather than *identifies with* the characters; from this, which surely ranks near the top of hairsplitting judgments, dictionaries dissent. See also *affiliated with*.

ideology. Three critics come to the defense of the word in its relatively new extension to politico-social systems from the original sense of a system of ideas; dictionaries concur. One critic cautions against applying it to lesser matters than communism, fascism, and the like. Another objects to it as a pretentious synonym for *idea* or *ideas*. Fowler warns that the spelling *idea-* is wrong on the basis of derivation, but Webster recognizes it as a variant.

Idiom. In this, as in any book on usage, there is frequent appeal to idiom as justifying some usage or other. Idiom, in the sense at hand, is defined by Webster as "an expression established in the usage of a language that is peculiar to itself either in grammatical construction (as *no, it wasn't me*) or in having a meaning that cannot be derived as a whole from the conjoined meanings of its elements (as Monday week for 'the Monday a week after next Monday'; *many a* for 'many taken distributively'; *how are you* for 'what is the state of your health or feelings?')." To this it may be added that idiomatic expressions are considered standard though they may defy grammatical analysis.

idiosyncrasy. Often misspelled *-cracy.*

idle. Approved in its new sense as a transitive verb ("The strike idled thousands of workmen") by one critic and dictionaries. Sports reporters have somewhat amusingly seized on the adjective *idle* to describe teams with no game scheduled. The term is usually pejorative and brings to mind the aphorism about the work that the devil finds for idle hands to do. No dictionary gives this application.

i.e. See *e.g.*

if, whether. Two principles, now generally regarded as superstitions, may raise doubts about the choice between *if* and *whether*. The first is that only *whether* may be used to introduce a noun clause (usually after *see, doubt, ask, learn, wonder, know*): "I do not know whether he will come." Four authorities agree, however, that *if* and *whether* are interchangeable in this construction, though Bernstein calls *whether* the "normal" word. Bryant finds usage divided. The second principle is that *whether* is required when an alternative is stated: "We shall go whether it rains or clears." This rule too is a superstition; Evans implies it is outmoded; Bryant says *whether* is commoner in such constructions in formal written English but that *if* occurs in conversation. Fowler says that *if* should be restricted to introducing a condition, and that *whether* should be used where an alternative is either stated or implied. The consensus is that *if* and *whether* are interchangeable where they make sense and are not ambiguous. *Whether* enjoys some preference where an alternative is stated or implied, but *if* is acceptable. Three critics object to *if* for *though:* "The fruit was delicious, if a trifle overripe." This is wrong-headed; dictionaries accept it.

if and when. Generally castigated as verbiage; one or the other is enough, as appropriate to the context. Sometimes the expression is given *if, as, and when,* which can only be more objectionable.

if I was (were). See *Subjunctive.*

if . . . then. The use of *then* to begin the conclusion that follows a conditional clause starting with *if* makes for unnecessary emphasis and perhaps indicates an immature style. Evans says that *then* usually detracts force: "If he can't be a bullfighter right away then he'd like to be a steeplejack"; "If one Democrat deserts to a united opposition, then the vice president can cast the deciding vote." Omit the *thens.*

ignoramus. The plural is *ignoramuses,* not *ignorami.*

ilk. The basic objection sometimes expressed is that *ilk* is a Scots term meaning *same name or place,* and thus may not properly be used to mean, as it incessantly is, *kind* or *breed* or *class* or *stripe.* Webster has two entries, one for the Scots denotation, which usually relates a personal name to a clan or place—"Scott of that ilk"—and the other giving the ordinary use. Bernstein and Fowler deplore the use of *ilk* in any but its pristine, Scots sense, though Fowler concedes that *ilk* for *kind* (*an educator of that ilk*) is often used facetiously. Two critics consider this sense well established. Bernstein says it is a mistake to consider *of that ilk* disparaging, but Flesch regards it as nothing else. The truth appears to be, as Webster points out, that it *is* often disparaging; the context shows the discerning reader whether it is or not. Dictionaries, except for Webster's New World (which designates it colloquial), recognize *ilk* for *kind* as standard; this is the consensus.

ill. See *sick.*

illegible, unreadable. Two critics point out that the first means *undecipherable* (for example, bad handwriting) and the second means *dull* or *badly constructed* (for example, poor composition). Dictionaries give *undecipherable* as one sense of *unreadable.* If *unreadable* were saved for *dull,* etc., a useful distinction would be preserved. It is generally observed among professionals in publishing and printing.

illiterate. There has been some criticism of the word in other than its primary sense of "unable to read and write": "Many college graduates these days are illiterate." But all dictionaries give as standard meanings indicating varying degrees of ignorance, or failure to meet an expected level of education. Careful writers rely on *functionally illiterate* to describe one who can make out what is on a printed page but not with any usefulness.

illuminate, illume, illumine. The second and third are discouraged by two critics as poetic, literary, or obsolescent.

illusion, illusive. See *allusion,* etc.; *delusion.*

illy. Although the word is in good odor, many have held their noses at it as an illiteracy. This may account for its being something of a rarity, or vice versa. The usual practice is to use *ill* as both adverb and adjective: *an ill-conceived plan; we do not think ill of it.*

image. In the sense *public impression* (*improving the image of the business world; the actor's image*), deplored as a fad by three critics. The newness of this sense is indicated by the fact that, among general dictionaries, only American Heritage explicitly recognizes it. Its popularity and usefulness are such, however, that it seems likely to be universally accepted as standard. Flesch says it seems to fill a need. Barnhart gives *image-builder, image-building.*

imaginary, imaginative. *Imaginary* relates to what exists in the imagination in contrast to what is real: "Pink elephants are likely to be imaginary." *Imaginative* means *characterized by,* or *showing use of, the imagination:* "The plans for the Civic Center are imaginative." Disregard of this distinction causes trouble: "A variety of imaginative space people have long thrived in the pages of science fiction." Did the writer intend to say that these people possess imagination, or that they are figments? He meant the latter, as the context showed, and thus the word should have been *imaginary* or *imagined.* Another possible interpretation of the example, but one not admitted by its context, is that the writers showed imagination in creating the space people; this would be correct but still ambiguous.

Immaculate Conception. The Catholic dogma refers to the conception of the Virgin Mary, not that of Jesus Christ, as is often erroneously assumed. The confusion is with *Virgin Birth,* which refers to the birth of Christ. This is corroborated by dictionaries.

immanent(ly), imminent(ly). See *eminent(ly),* etc.

immediately. Disapproved by Evans for *immediately after:* "Immediately the law was passed, a great howl was set up," *immediately after, as soon as.* The usage seems British rather than American.

immigrate. See *emigrate, immigrate.*

imminent(ly). See *eminent(ly),* etc.

immoral, amoral. Two critics point out that the first means contrary to moral standards, and the second means having no relevance to them; *unmoral* is synonymous with *amoral.* Dictionaries support this distinction.

immunity, impunity. Two critics profess that the terms are sometimes confused. *Immunity* means *exemption,* and is often used of diseases: *immunity from smallpox. Impunity* means *freedom from punishment.* Gilbert's pirates saw in the nieces of the Major General an opportunity to get married with impunity.

impact. *Impact* for *effect* or *influence* ("For years scientists have recognized the impact of the immense Greenland icecap on the North Atlantic climate") is criticized as a fad by four authorities. This view is contradicted by the fact that dictionaries recognize this sense as standard.

impeach. Despite widespread misinterpretation, the term means *bring charges,* not necessarily *remove from office,* though this may be the result of the impeachment process.

impeccable. A counter word of music-reviewing. Somehow considered preferable, in critical contexts, to *flawless* or *perfect.* See also *consummate.*

impecunious. Pretentious for *poor.*

impel. Sometimes misspelled *impell.*

impervious. Often used when *oblivious* or *regardless* would be a better choice. "The car lurched ahead a few yards at a time, impervious to the crowds in the way." *Impervious* means *impenetrable, immune to damage or harm;* or *not capable of being affected or disturbed* ("impervious to criticism"). *In spite of* would have been better in the sentence cited; *oblivious* would attribute human qualities to the car. "After a while, a worker in a glue factory becomes impervious to the smell." *oblivious.*

implement. Criticized by four authorities as a verb meaning *accomplish, fulfill, complete, carry out:* "The farm program will be implemented in the fall." It is standard but so characteristic of gobbledygook that the fastidious shun it; one critic recognizes the criticisms of it but defends it. The complaint that this usage is a novelty is demolished by the fact that it was aspersed by Fowler in the original (1926). All dictionaries now admit the usage as standard. Perhaps the only criticism that remains valid is that it is overworked.

imply, infer. To imply is to hint at, or suggest; to infer is to draw a conclusion. Only the speaker can imply, and only the hearer can infer. *Infer* is often used where *imply* is called for: "The remark inferred that he was not to be trusted." Only a person can infer, and he may do so without saying anything. The confusion is denounced by five critics and American Heritage, though a sixth is tolerant of it, saying *infer* has been used for *imply* for centuries. As distinguished a linguist as Kemp Malone has also called *infer* for *imply* long-established usage. The confusion is abetted by the fact that dictionaries tend to give *infer* as a synonym for *imply.* Random House is firm on the distinction; Webster quotes two examples of *infer* as standard that are actually misuses. The confusion does not occur except in writing that shows other evidences of unsureness. The distinction is a useful one, and worth preserving. What is written with care maintains the distinction. "He inferred that we were rascals." The writer meant he *implied* (hinted, suggested) that we were rascals" but what he put down is open to misconstruction as "He drew the conclusion that . . ."

important. See *more important(ly)*.

Impracticable, impractical. See *practicable, practical*.

impresario. Often misspelled *impressario*. The word has no relation to *impress*. *Impresario* comes from the Italian *impresa*, meaning *enterprise; impress* comes from the Latin for *press upon*.

in, into. Two critics insist that *in* may not be used with verbs of motion; that is to say, one may not jump *in*, but must jump *into*, the lake. This view is pedantry; American Heritage and Evans says *into* suggests motion more emphatically but that either may be used. Webster gives *broke in pieces, called in council, threw it in the fire, wouldn't let her in the house*. Random House gives as one sense of *in* "used to indicate motion or direction from outside to a point within," and cites as an example "Let's go in the house." All dictionaries except the Standard College equate *in* with *into*. The Concise Oxford Dictionary says *in* may be used with verbs of motion or change, and cites these examples: *put it in your pocket, throw it in the fire*. The consensus overwhelmingly approves *in* in the sense of *into*. See also *into, in to*.

in, at. See *at, in; in length*, etc.

in-. Solid as a prefix: *inaccessible, inalienable, inboard*, etc. See also *un-, in-*.

in addition to. Often roundabout for *besides*. See *together with*.

in advance of. Wordy for *before*. "The dinner was held in advance of the ceremony." *before*. See *prior to*.

in all probability. Excessive for *probably*.

in a manner similar to. See *like*, etc.

inapt, inept. See *unapt*, etc.

inasmuch (insofar) as. *Inasmuch as* is the correct form; not *in as much as* or *inasmuchas*. Even so, it is a clumsy expression whose meaning can usually be expressed more neatly by *because, since*, or *for*. "*Double sessions were instituted inasmuch as the school was overcrowded*." *because*. One critic also discourages the expression as formal and stilted; another calls it pompous for *since*. A third says *so far as* is preferable to *insofar as*. Yet another counsels avoidance of *in so far as* (*sic*), citing a variety of objectionable examples.

inaugurate. Pretentious for *open, begin, start*. See also *launch*.

in back of. See *back of, in back of*.

in behalf. See *behalf*.

incarnate. Repellent as the idea may be to Latinists, *incarnate* has long since departed from the sole meaning *embodied in flesh;* it now means also *embodying an ideal form:* "The rural setting was peace incarnate."

in charge of. Equally correct meaning *under the supervision of* (*the program is in charge of Smith*) and *responsible for* (*Jones is in charge of entertainment*). Sometimes it is protested that locutions like "the children are in charge of the nurse" are ambiguous but this is surely wrongheaded. Two critics suggest *in the charge of* when there is genuine danger of ambiguity.

inchoate. Fowler and American Heritage say the word means *just begun, undeveloped*. This is evidently a case of emergence of a new sense; Webster gives also *disordered, incoherent, unorganized;* the Standard College gives *lacking order, form, coherence*, etc., and Random House gives not *organized, lacking order*.

incident. Two critics note that the word has become a euphemism for *attack, violence, blow*, etc.: "The Negro pupils attempting to board the bus were surrounded and headed off by the police, but there were no incidents." The statement is contradictory in the light of the established meaning of *incident*, that is, an occurrence of no great importance, since what was described was itself at least an incident. No dictionary recognizes the extended meaning of *incident;* the consensus is that it is objectionable because it blurs the intended sense. *Incidents* (*occurrences*) and *incidence* (most often, *rate of occurrence: incidence of disease*) are sometimes confused.

incidentally, incidently. Evans calls *incidently* a once correct form that now is "simply an error"; Webster recognizes it though no other dictionary does. The consensus is that the form is likely to be considered wrong, though it is fairly common.

in close proximity. See *close proximity*.

include. Often inexactly used in the senses *belong to, comprise, consist of*, or *be composed of*. That which includes is not all-inclusive, careless use to the contrary. One should not say "The group includes . . ." unless the intention is to omit some members. *Are* or *comprises* is preferable to introduce the all-inclusive. ("Members of the group are . . ."; "The group comprises . . .").

incomparable. See *uncomparable*.

incompetence, -cy. The usual form is *-ce*, though both are standard.

in connection with. Generally regarded as verbiage when the phrase displaces prepositions like *by, from, about, at:* "He expressed his disapproval in connection with the exhibit." *of*.

incredible, incredulous. *Incredulous* applies only to people, and means *skeptical* or *disbelieving*. "The testimony was given with conviction, but the jury was obviously incredulous." *Incredible* may apply to people, but usually applies to statements and means *unbelievable:* "The alibi was incredible."

inculcate. May take *in, into, upon, with*. Some critics have insisted that an idea, for example, is inculcated *in* a person, and that he cannot be inculcated *with* it. These caveats, however, are pedantry, and not validated by either of the general dictionaries (Webster and Random House) that give examples of various contexts, nor by observable educated usage.

incumbent. See *present incumbent*.

independent. Sometimes misspelled *independant*. There is a choice, however, between *dependent* and *dependant* (which see) as either noun or adjective.

indexes, indices. The first is the Anglicized form, the second the Latin form. *Indexes* is recommended.

Indian. It seems incredible that confusion should have persisted for 500 years concerning the term *Indian* because of a misapprehension by Columbus concerning the destination he had reached. It is possible to distinguish, of course, by means of the forms *American Indian* and *East Indian* (referring to a native of India), but ambiguity often arises from the careless tendency to use *Indian* alone.

The patronizing attitude of Americans generally to the indigenous inhabitants here was eloquently deplored by Mrs. Joyce Brunette in a private communication to the author: "I find it hard to understand why newspapers often write about American Indians in such a condescending and, I feel, derogatory manner. A newspaper not long ago referred in a headline to a troupe of Indian dancers who were to appear at the White House as *White House braves,* and the story added that they would *whoop it up*.

"A few days later there was the same kind of ridiculous headline and the story also used the expression *whooped it up* and described the performance as 'exciting as a Technicolor wild 'n' wooly Western.' Why must these clichés always be used?

"Newspapers no longer refer to a Negro woman as *mammy* or to a Negro child as a *pickaninny,* so why should they continue to use demeaning words in referring to Indians?

"The writing about the Indian dances at the White House does not give the dances nor the dancers the kind of dignity and respect to which they are entitled. What it does is to maintain a public image of Indians which I am afraid many people have.

"A couple of years ago there was newspaper criticism of the annual Mummers Day Parade in Philadelphia, pointing out that it held the Negro up to ridicule. This is exactly what I am trying to point out about the way newspapers write about Indians—they only succeed in continuing to hold them up to ridicule.

"Under a picture of Ernest Borgnine, who is playing the part of an Indian in a television show, was a caption reading 'Him Versatile.' The writers of this kind of thing are anything but versatile to keep using these clichés. Silly captions like this would not be used if the role was that of a Jew, Negro, Chinese, or anything else.

"I wrote to a reporter once about his use of the term *Injun,* pointing out that it is as derogatory as the words *kike, wop, mick,* and all the others. His reply was that *Injun* was used in a humorous manner and was not intended to be derogatory.

"What is more derogatory than this kind of humor? As one who is half Indian, I'd rather be called a dirty, good-for-nothing Indian than an Injun. It shows ignorance or complete lack of understanding to use these words.

"Let me point out a couple of other examples of ignorant or condescending writing about Indians. A sterling silver necklace given by Mrs. Lyndon B. Johnson to a visiting dignitary was referred to as an Indian curio, and the wrong tribe was named as having made it.

"When Mrs. Annie Wauneka was one of the recipients of the Presidential Medal of Freedom she was referred to as a redskin and the cliché *Indian giver* was used in the news story. Marian Anderson got the medal at the same time, but the story about her was tastefully done, and it was not considered necessary to refer to her as a black or a mammy.

"Believe me, I am not interested in special treatment for Indians, and I hope I never reach the point where I cannot appreciate genuine humor about Indians. It's the condescending tone, the threadbare attempts at humor, and the never-ending, facetious use of such terms as *heap big chief, paleface, redskin, ugh, firewater, wampum, squaw, warpaint, Injun, brave, wigwam, papoose,* and others that infuriate me."

indicate. Criticized by two authorities as an overworked and imprecise variant of *say.* They also object to the medical sense of *indicate* (and *contraindicate*) in nonmedical contexts: "A large grant of money is indicated to keep the program going." *required.* Evans calls this usage a vogue. Fowler would probably have called it slovenly.

indict, indite. *Indict* is pronounced as if it were spelled *indite,* which is now quaint for *write* (a letter, for example).

Indirect Questions. See *Questions.*

indiscriminate. Not *un-,* though either *un-* or *indiscriminating* is correct. *Undiscriminating* is more usual. Fowler calls *indiscriminating* incorrect, but this may reflect British preference; most American dictionaries give it.

indispensable. Sometimes misspelled *indispensible.*

individual. While *individual* for *person* is recognized by dictionaries as standard ("Give the ticket to the individual in the green hat"), this usage is discouraged except when single identity is being contrasted: "Individuals and organizations have different rights." Use of the term in facetious or disparaging senses is now quaint.

indorse. See *endorse, indorse.*

in droves. See *droves.*

induction, deduction. The first is deriving a general principle from specific instances; the second is reasoning from a general principle to a specific instance.

inedible. See *uneatable, inedible.*

ineffable. One critic says the sense *indescribable* is a misuse, and another gives only *unutterable,* but every current dictionary gives *indescribable.*

in effect. Should not be set off by commas: "The former president of the Ford Motor Company, in effect, told his congressional critics to put up or shut up." Usually the commas are merely superfluous, but in this instance they may be misleading, suggesting that the person referred to was only in effect the former president of Ford.

inept. See *unapt,* etc.

inequity, iniquity. Sometimes ignorantly confused; inequity is inequality, iniquity is evil. "Punishment is visited upon the sons for the inequity of their fathers." Possible, but more likely *iniquity.*

inevitable. Fowler criticizes the term as overworked by critics of works of art, and as often inappropriately applied to what does not qualify as inevitable (that is, in perfect proportion or harmony, so that any change or omission would be damaging to the whole). He may be overlooking another sense of *inevitable,* however; *certain to come or occur,* which is what some critics may have in mind. All dictionaries give this sense, which may be regarded as predominant. For other overworked critics' terms, see *consummate; impeccable; adequate.*

in excess of. The long way around for *more than* or *over* (which see). "In excess of a thousand delegates will attend the convention." *more than, over.*

infer. See *imply, infer.*

inferno. See *flaming inferno.*

infinite(ly). Two critics caution, one somewhat equivocally, against careless use of the word for exaggeration when *great(ly)* or *far* will do.

Infinitives. 1. Split infinitives. Fowler, who first demolished the arbitrary rule against splitting infinitives as long ago as 1926, found the English-speaking world divided into five classes on the subject: (a) Those who neither know nor care what a split infinitive is (b) those who do not know, but care very much (c) those who know and condemn (d) those who know and approve; and (e) those who know and distinguish. Many writers still believe they will not go to heaven if they split the infinitive. The rule against it, like some others, grew out of the application of rules of Latin grammar to English; in Latin it is not possible to split infinitives, because they are single words. After the folly of this system of grammar was noted, English was analyzed on its own terms, and the rule against splitting infinitives went out the window. (An infinitive is said to be split when an adverb comes between *to* and the main verb: *to quickly go*.) The consensus of seven critics is that infinitives may be split when splitting makes the sentence read more smoothly and does not cause awkwardness. Some examples of awkwardness, in which the adverb would go more smoothly at the end of the sentence: "I want to consistently enforce discipline"; "His purpose was to effortlessly be promoted"; "Jones was ordered to immediately embark." On the other hand, there is good reason not to change the following: "Production of food fats is expected to moderately exceed domestic use and commercial imports" and "This will permit the nation to quietly drop her violent opposition to the treaty." See also *Compound Verbs*.

2. Infinitives of purpose. These indicate intention, as in "He went to the store to get some ice cream," but the construction is often awkwardly used when there is no reason to indicate intention, as in "He made the trek in four days to arrive here exhausted" and "Increased sales are announced by many companies to confound the pessimists." These examples would be better put with a participial phrase that would avoid ambiguity: "He made the trek in four days, arriving here exhausted"; "Increased sales are announced by many companies, confounding the pessimists." As the examples stood one might easily get the impression that the poor trekker had traveled with the intention of wearing himself out, and that the diabolical companies had announced increased sales just to confound the pesky pessimists.

3. Infinitive for the future. The infinitive is occasionally used to indicate the future: "He is to leave in the morning." Curme points out that this construction has some modal force, conveying the idea of necessity or compulsion, and Evans concurs. Very often, however, writers who use the infinitive in this way intend a simple future. They say "I am to meet the 5:15" when they mean simply "I will (or shall) meet the 5:15." The use of *am to, is to,* and *are to* for *shall* or *will* should be discouraged. This usage is possibly fostered by newspaper headlines, in which it is the convention to indicate the future with the infinitive: "Statesmen to Meet in London."

4. Misleading infinitives. Some other misuses of the infinitive create ambiguity: "It was the largest maneuver ever to be held in the South." The intended meaning was *that has ever been held,* but the reader might easily have understood *that will ever be held. Largest maneuver ever held* would have been unambiguous. "This is one of nineteen communities to have such a program." *That have,* or *that will have?* The intention was *that have,* and this form should have been used.

5. Infinitives with and without *to.* One critic cautions against omitting *to* where idiom calls for it, as in "An enriched instructional program is planned to assist pupils having deprived backgrounds qualify for college." *to qualify.* Evans offers a list of verbs and describes the circumstances under which *to* need not be used with them, but mastering them is a little like learning rules for English spelling it is easier to learn to spell than it is to learn the rules. The infinitive with *to* predominates in English, however, and *to* should be supplied if the construction sounds the least bit maladroit. There is little danger of using *to* where it is not required: "We were expected to help him [to] change the tire."

6. Infinitive displacing gerund. Two critics warn against unidiomatic infinitives: "She always enjoyed to look for an apartment." *enjoyed looking.* This is a matter primarily of having an ear for the preferable construction. Those who are impatient with grammatical definitions and distinctions can rely on the ear as a pretty good guide when questions about splitting infinitives come up. If a sentence doesn't sound good when read aloud, it is not well constructed, whether the infinitive is split, braided, or sawed in half.

infinitude. Described as an unnecessary variant of *infinity.*

inflammable. See *flammable.*

inflict, afflict. Two critics warn against confusion of these terms. *Afflict* takes *with, inflict* does not. "They were afflicted (not *inflicted*) with hives." The object of *afflict* must be or imply some living thing: "Sorrow afflicted (not *inflicted*) him"; "A crop failure afflicted the country" (in which *country* implies the people inhabiting it); *inflict* takes an inanimate object: "He inflicted (not *afflicted*) punishment."

informal, informally. Excessively used, especially in journalism, to describe what cannot be anything but informal: "perched informally on top of a desk"; "seen chatting informally"; "makes some of his most informal cracks while posing for pictures." The descriptives are foolishly superfluous under the circumstances, which could hardly be regarded as formal. See also *Colloquialisms* for *informal* as a status label.

informant, informer. Evans says that the first is neutral, and that the second strongly connotes the stoolpigeon. Both major dictionaries, however, as well as American Heritage, give *informant* as a synonym of *informer,* and it seems likely that the context will be decisive as to the sense intended.

infra-. Solid as a prefix: *infrahuman, inframundane, infrastructure,* etc.

infringe. Fowler holds that *trespass* or *encroach* is preferable to *infringe upon* (or *on*), and that *infringe* should be used only when it can stand alone, as in *infringe patents, infringe sovereignty.* Dictionaries, however, give examples with *on* or *upon.*

in future. A Briticism; American idiom calls for *in the future.* The same is true of *in hospital* vs. *in the hospital.*

-ing. See *Gerunds; Fused Participle* ("*him* vs. *his* seeing the light"); *Dangling Modifiers.*

ingenious, ingenuous. Two critics warn against confusing the terms. The first means *clever* (*an ingenious solution*) and the second either *frank and open* or, often, *naive: an ingenuous maiden.*

ingest. With the growing concern for the environment, there have been numerous incidents of oil spillages into the seas, and when writers report the harm done to living creatures by swallowing the oil, they seem unable to use such simple, everyday terms as *eat* or *swallow;* they must make it *ingest.* But the word seems to have too much of a laboratory smell about it to be suitable in writing aimed at a general audience; it is like calling a woman a female. *Ingest* is sometimes found in other inappropriate contexts: "But her mind, clouded by the first few pills, lost count and she ingested a lethal number." Inexcusable, in this context, for *swallowed.*

in (his, her) own right. The expression indicates individual possession of something that might otherwise be held in common. If a man is a poet, it is correct to refer to his wife as a poet in her own right. But if he is a religious leader, it is meaningless to refer to her as following some other endeavor in her own right: "Each morning, the mystic's fourth wife, a poet in her own right, massaged him with oil for two hours in accordance with Hindu practice." Since the mystic was not a poet, his wife should have been described simply as a *poet,* omitting *in her own right.*

inhuman. See *unhuman, inhuman.*

iniquity. See *inequity, iniquity.*

Initials. The use of a single initial (*R. Roe, J. Doe*) is considered inadequate identification by most publications, which insist on a full first name (*Richard Roe*), at least two initials (*R. W. Roe*), or a combination of given name(s) and initial. Preferably, the form should be that used by the owner of the name.

ink a contract. A hopeless mannerism, whose habitat is the sports pages. Someday a sportswriter will tell of a player *signing* a contract, and will be acclaimed as a phrasemaker.

in-law. The preferable plural form of such terms as *mother-in-law*, etc., is *mothers-in-law*, not *mother-in-laws*.

in length, in number, in size, etc. The phrases are often used redundantly, as in the following examples: *shorter in length; large (small, many, few) in number; rectangular (etc.) in shape; small, large (etc.) in size.*

in line. See *on line*.

innocent. See *plead innocent*.

innocent of. Fowler says the phrase in the sense *lacking* ("His head was innocent of hair") is wornout humor. But both Random House and Webster consider it standard; Webster cites examples from distinguished writers: American Heritage gives *devoid of* as one definition.

in nothing flat. The ultimate, perhaps, in clichés as well as speed.

innovation. See *new innovation*.

in number. See *in length*, etc.

inoculate, vaccinate. These terms for immunizing by vaccine are interchangeable. *Vaccinate*, however, has become firmly established by custom for immunization from smallpox. *Inoculate* is favored for immunization against diphtheria and other diseases. *Inoculate* is often misspelled *innoculate*, perhaps by the example of *innocuous*.

in order to, that. Three critics say *in order to* is usually excessive for the infinitive alone: "He bought the suit [in order] to impress his girl." Follett considers objections to the phrase pedantic, but he appears to strain for an example in which *in order* serves some purpose. *In order that* can usually be replaced, for the better, by *so, so that*.

in question. The phrase is superfluous except to designate one of two or more subjects that have been mentioned, one critic holds; another objects to it as "ugly."

inquire. See *enquire, inquire*.

in receipt of. Commercial jargon in such sentences as "We are in receipt of the shipment." *have received*.

in regard(s), relation to. See *regard*.

in respect to (of), with respect to. The idiomatic form of the phrase meaning *about* or *concerning* is *with respect to:* "Firm action was advised in respect to the Soviet Union." *with respect to; in respect to* may be understood to mean *having respect for,* and thus would make the statement misleading. "Requirements for lighting are stringent, particularly in respect of allowable brightness levels." Fusty; *particularly in allowable brightness levels;* or, perhaps preferably, *particularly in allowable levels of brightness.*

in routine fashion. An inflation of *routinely.*

insanitary. See *unsanitary, insanitary.*

in shape, in size. See *in length,* etc.

inside of. One critic says *inside of* is a standard variant of *inside.* Another and American Heritage say *of* is unnecessary, and no example by either of the major dictionaries uses *of.* The consensus is that *of,* if not wrong, is dispensable.

insigne, insignia. Technically, on the basis of the Latin derivation, *insigne* is the singular and *insignia* the plural. Evans cites literary examples of *insignia* as a singular ("The insignia was tarnished") and reports that in the U.S. Army, it is officially singular, with a plural *insignias* (a form Follett deplores as "manufactured"). Both major dictionaries, as well as American Heritage, recognize *insignia* as the singular and *insignias* as the plural; this may be regarded as the consensus.

insist. Often used in the press as a random displacement of *said* in *Attribution* (which see). *Insist* is appropriate only when there is insistence. *Contend* is similarly misused; it is called for only when there is disagreement or contention.

in size. See *in length,* etc.

insofar as. See *inasmuch as.*

insoluble. See *unsolvable, insoluble.*

inspirational. As applied to speeches and writings, particularly, this descriptive should be used with care, for the knowing tend to associate it, through experience, with pap.

in spite of (despite) the fact that. Usually excessive for *although.*

install. In such locutions as "He was installed president," idiom calls for *as* with *install:* "He was installed *as* president."

instance. Occurs in redundancies like *in the instance of; instance* is sometimes substituted for *case,* which see. "Obscenity was charged in the instance of this movie." Recasting is advised: "This movie was described as obscene." See also *Redundancy*.

instinctual. Two critics attribute the form to psychologists, and regard it as an unnecessary duplication of *instinctive*.

insufficient. Fowler regards *insufficient* where *not enough* is called for as worse than *sufficient* for *enough* (which see). Examples: "There was insufficient rainfall"; "We have had insufficient to eat" (*We have not had enough . . .*).

insure. See *ensure*.

integration, desegregation. See *desegregation, integration*.

intensive. Two critics complain that *intensive* tends to displace *intense* in such sentences as "He put in a period of intensive study." The implied principle: don't use the longer word when the shorter one will do. Another critic says *intensive* is overused for *steady, hard, strong, thorough*, a criticism that parallels the others. It is best to leave *intensive* to technical contexts where it has a precise and well-understood denotation.

inter-. Solid as a prefix: *interflow, interjoin, intermingle*, etc.

interesting. One critic comments that it is simpleminded of a writer to inform the reader that a fact being related is interesting, for interest is a subjective consideration and the reader will make his own judgment about it. The descriptive is often lazily substituted for something more specific and meaningful.

interfered. Often misspelled *interferred*, perhaps by the influence of *inferred*.

interment, internment. Interment, which oftenest appears in obituaries, means burial ("The good is oft interred with their bones"). *Internment* is a form of imprisonment; the term usually describes the confinement of aliens in an enemy country during wartime. Sometimes confused.

intermittent. See *continual*.

in terms of. The phrase is castigated by three critics as often an inflation of simple prepositions such as *at, in, for, by*. "The Chinese Army is well equipped in terms of infantry weapons." *with.* "One limitation of this method is that it is relatively slow in terms of production rates." *slow;* what comes after is surplus. Follett comments that *in terms of* supplies "a loose coupling of ideas whose exact connection had not been thought out by the author." Bernstein and Follett point out that, properly used, the phrase signifies translation from one kind of classification to another: *publishing activity in terms of textbooks; wealth in terms of gold*. Both describe its inexact use as pretentious.

internecine. The word has acquired a generally accepted meaning that departs from its original and derived sense. Basically, *internecine* means simply *destructive*. Fowler argues that the extended meaning of mutuality (that is, *destructive of one another*) "is what gives the word its only value, since there are plenty of substitutes for it in its true sense—*destructive, slaughterous, murderous, bloody, sanguinary, mortal,* and so forth." Dictionaries not only admit the idea of mutuality but recognize a further refinement, the idea of conflict within a group; this, in fact, is now the predominant meaning. World War II was certainly an internecine struggle in the original sense between the Allies and the Axis, but if the word were applied to it with that intention it would surely be misunderstood. We now think of internecine war as civil or intramural war. ("An internecine war over the corpse of Karl Marx has threatened to split the party for decades.") The tendency of popular usage is to broaden meanings; in this curious instance, the meaning has been narrowed. American Heritage approves the new sense, and regards the question of usage as hinging primarily on whether the conflict must be fatal or mutually destructive. Its panel's decision: not necessarily.

interpersonal. Excessively and meaninglessly used in academia. Professors seem unable to refer to any relation between people without calling it interpersonal; a glaring example is *interpersonal friendship.*

interpretative, interpretive. The words are exact synonyms; three critics prefer *-ative.* Fowler says this is a matter of the derivation from the Latin. But as between *preventative* and *preventive,* he curtly says the short form is better, and refers the reader to a lecture on the undesirability of long variants. Random House and Webster both give *interpretative* as predominant. American Heritage approves it. A critic concurring with Fowler says that *interpretive,* as the simpler form, is preferable, adding that usages based on knowledge of Latin have been steadily cast aside. Nevertheless, the consensus favors *-ative.*

in the altogether. The expression for *naked* ("We used to swim in the altogether"); *in the all together* is wrong.

in the amount of. See *amount.*

in the circumstances. See *circumstances.*

in the course of. See *course,* etc.

in the event that. The long way around for *if.* Fowler, usually critical of redundancy, describes the phrase merely as an Americanism, and gives as the British version *in the event of* followed by a present participle, such as *(something's) happening.*

in the final analysis. See *analysis.*

in the immediate vicinity of. Roundabout for *near*.

in the light of. The correct form for *taking into account, considering:* "The de cline in the gross national product was surprising in the light of the easing rate of inflation." There is a tendency to omit *the* (*in light of*) out of either ignorance or carelessness.

in the midst of. Often wordy for *amid*, Bernstein points out.

in the near (not too distant) future. See *future*.

in the neighborhood of. See *neighborhood*.

in the order. See *order*.

into, in to. The preposition *into* should be distinguished from *in to* (the adverb *in* followed by the preposition *to*): "We went into the city"; "We dropped in to coffee with the Smiths." An absurd confusion of these forms is illustrated by "A man wanted as an Army deserter for fifteen years turned himself into the police last night." For *in* vs. *into*, see *in, into*.

in toto. Often misspelled: "She said the story was ridiculous and denied it en toto." The phrase (for *totally, entirely*) is Latin, not French, and the preposition is *in*, not *en*. It is questionable whether any foreign phrase is suitable to most informal contexts; the consensus is to avoid them and use English. Fowler criticizes the misuse of *in toto* for *on the whole*.

intra-. Solid as a prefix: *intracollegiate, intramural, intrastate,* etc.

intrigue. Fowler in the original denounced *intrigue* for *arouse interest, desire, beguile, fascinate* or, as a noun, *curiosity* ("The handsome stranger intrigued her.") Another critic, following this lead, says the word is erroneously taken from the French, in which its meaning is *puzzle*. Long lists could be compiled of words taken into English from other languages and given changed meanings, however. In revising Fowler, Gowers gave up on the objection to the new senses, and contented himself with saying that sometimes *intrigue* displaces simpler words. The newer senses are standard and established; dictionaries have long recognized them; American Heritage accepts them narrowly, commenting, like Gowers, that they sometimes displace more precise expressions. Evans comments that *intrigue* is overworked.

introduction. See *foreword*.

intuit. Appears to be a pedagese back-formation from *intuition*, but the word is in fact standard and in dictionaries ("He was able to intuit the situation"); i.e., *sense by intuition*.

inure, enure. The words are simply variants, of which the first is preferred. The meaning, in the usual sense, is not just to become accustomed, but to become accustomed to something disagreeable: "For one inured to the singer's style, the transition is unsettling." *accustomed;* the context did not suggest the style was disagreeable. Bernstein warns that *immure (wall in)* is sometimes given for *inure;* Flesch regards *inured to* as bookish for *used to,* but that would be a misuse.

invective. Coupled with *hurl* (which see), a stock expression in the press.

invent. See *discover, invent.*

Inversion. The term refers to placing elements of a sentence in something other than their natural or ordinary sequence. Fowler deals with the subject exhaustively, describing some varieties as permissible, most of them as not. The treatment in this book deals mainly with the conspicuous, objectionable kinds of inversion, resorted to chiefly by journalists desperate to vary sentence structure. See *Attribution; as is, as are,* etc.; *Subject-Verb Agreement 5.*

Several authorities trace journalistic inversion to *Time* magazine, where it was a conspicuous mannerism in *Time*'s early years. Wolcott Gibbs' comment was: "Backward ran sentences until reeled the mind." Fowler quotes P. G. Wodehouse: "Where it will all end knows God, as *Time* magazine would say."

Like the atmospheric inversion that is blamed for smog, the inversion of sentences creates a kind of linguistic smog that puts the reader to work sorting out the disarranged elements, causes his eyes to smart, and perhaps makes him wish he were reading something else. As has been said, straining for variety in sentence structure is usually the cause. Tired of starting with the subject and adding the predicate, some writers make a mighty effort and jump out of the frying pan into the smog.

Sometimes they grab a hapless auxiliary verb by the ears, yank it out of the protective shadow of its principal, and plop it down at the beginning of the sentence: "Encouraging the United States were Britain and France." The natural way to say this is "Britain and France were encouraging the United States"; or, passively, "The United States was being encouraged by Britain and France." The usual word order has been varied by moving *encouraging* forward, but the variety has been gained at too high a price. Americans, unlike Germans and ancient Romans, are not used to holding some element of a sentence in suspension until the other pieces of the puzzle come along. Inversion, of course, is not grammatically wrong; it becomes an irritant and the mark of a faulty style when it is overdone, or misplaces emphasis. Versifiers have an excuse when they find it necessary to place the word with the rhyme at the end of the line. They can plead poetic license.

"Hiring the men will be ranchers in the vicinity" should be recast to "Ranchers in the vicinity will hire the men." Examples like "Damaged were the cars of two motorists"; "Suffering minor injuries in the crash was his wife, Viola"; and "Caught in the school during the explosion were twenty girls" are clumsy and inexcusable.

Sometimes writers start sentences with auxiliary verbs only because they think there is no other way out when introducing a series of names: "Passing their intermediate tests were George Sims, Ernest Worth, Allen Smith, Nelson Raddle, and Alex Jones." But there *is* another way out: "Those who passed their intermediate tests were . . ." ("Intermediate tests were passed by . . ." is possible but awkward.)

It should be kept in mind that emphasis is given a word that is taken out of its normal position. When a sentence is disarranged for no other reason than to give variety to its structure, the effect may be distracting. The reader gets an impression of emphasis where emphasis makes no sense. Better methods are available for structural variety, such as beginning with subordinate elements (e.g., clauses introduced by *when, although,* or *nevertheless*), prepositional phrases, infinitives, or participial phrases.

The uprooted word is sometimes an adjective: "Responsible for all cultural questions is a key member of the city administration." There is no good reason for standing this sentence on its head. Fowler calls the abuse of inversion one of the most repellent vices of modern writing, and adds that by betraying his anxiety over boring the reader, the writer only bores the worse. See also *Attribution 1*.

in view of the fact that. The long way around for *since, because,* or *considering that*.

invite. As a noun ("The invites went only to the contributors"), this barbarism is deprecated by three critics and labeled dialectal by Random House and Webster; American Heritage gives it the most reputable label, *informal*. Evans says that it has "remained impudently in use for 300 years" despite criticism, but warns that in some quarters it is condemned. The consensus is overwhelming that it is nonstandard.

invited guest. Often criticized as redundant on the ground that being invited is essential to guesthood.

involve. Too freely and imprecisely used for *cause, result in, mean, have to do with, use,* and other more appropriate verbs. "This involved a complete change of plans." *caused*. The meaning of *involve* is *enfold, envelop, engage:* "The realtor became deeply involved in the litigation."

inwardness. Described as literary and as often pretentiously used for *true meaning, reality,* or as superfluous.

in which. Often dispensable, and when it is then dispensed with, expression is improved: "Everybody is aware of the disorganized way [in which] the Senate and the House carry on their work." See also *Redundancy*.

Irish bulls. See *Goldwynisms*.

iron out. Two critics recognize this, in its figurative sense (*settle, remove difficulties*), as an Americanism in good standing, and Fowler welcomes its introduction to Britain. They warn, however, of its use in incongruous contexts (*iron out bottlenecks*). American Heritage and Webster consider it standard. Random House labels it informal.

irony, irony of fate. Irony denotes a double meaning and a double audience, one part of which gains a meaning that the other does not. Thus, in dramatic irony, the audience comprehends a part of the meaning of a statement uttered by an actor that the other actors do not. Or irony may be described as the contradiction between the literal and implied meanings of a statement. *Irony of fate* should be reserved for a contradiction of some kind; Follett cites as an example, you have a chance to cruise around the world—you should be happy, but you are ill and condemned to bed for six months. *Ironic, irony,* and *irony of fate* should not be applied to any oddity, disappointment, or defeat; Fowler regards the phrase, in any event, as a cliché.

irregardless. Criticized variously by five commentators as illiterate, a redundancy, and a barbarism, and by American Heritage, Random House, and Webster as nonstandard for *regardless*.

irrelevant. Often carelessly mispronounced *irrevelant* and consequently thus (or otherwise) misspelled. In the great student rebellion of the sixties, a great many things, particularly their studies, became "irrelevant" in their eyes. But the high unemployment rate of the middle seventies and the difficulty of getting jobs cured all that, and the word disappeared from campuses. *Irrelevant* indicates a relationship; the user of it should have stated or implied what his subject is irrelevant to, something users of the word did not always do.

irreligious. See *unreligious, irreligious*.

is, are. See *Subject-Verb Agreement*.

-ise, -ize. See *-ize, -ise*.

Israeli. See *Jew, Jewish*.

issue. See *noncontroversial issue*.

issue with. Described by Evans as redundant for *issue* but by Fowler as recognized and here to stay ("Every pupil was issued with a pencil and paper"). No current dictionary in this country gives an example containing *issue with,* and so it may be assumed that the form is not idiomatic in the U.S.

is to, am to, are to. See *Infinitives 3*.

it. Use of *it* as the anticipatory subject ("It was a raw, windy night") is not wrong, but can easily be overdone, and this makes for a muffled (Flesch says pompous) style. Sometimes, especially in official correspondence, such expressions as *it is believed* are used to avoid personal pronouns: "I believe." This is undesirable unless there is an overriding reason to keep the statement impersonal; personal pronouns have more interest and immediacy. See also *it is I who; it's me.*

Italics. Used generally in carefully edited material for the titles of books, musical compositions, paintings, and other works of art, for foreign words, and to convey emphasis or sharp contrast. On names of newspapers practice is divided in the U.S. Fowler warns against setting whole passages in italics to attract attention. Flesch advocates sparing use of italics for emphasis.

One should be certain that italics are available in the typesetting equipment to be used before indicating them (which is generally done in typescript and longhand by underlining). When italics are not available, titles are often enclosed instead in quotation marks, although the growing tendency is to set them without any distinctive mark beyond initial capitals. Boldface type is suitable in place of italics to emphasize single words, but not for foreign words or titles. When something that would ordinarily be set in italics occurs in what is already italicized, the desired differentiation is indicated by reverting to Roman. Some typographers consider any substantial amount of copy set in italics hard to read, and there is probably good reason for this because italics are not familiar to the eye.

it goes without saying. See *of course; needless to say.*

it is I who (is, am). In locutions like "It is I who am the nominee," strictly speaking the verb *am* agrees with *I.* But there is a strong tendency to use *is,* since *am* sounds artificial. Fowler cites a similar construction, *it . . . that,* and says the verb following *that* agrees with the word *that* represents: "It is trees like this that bear the best fruit." This is natural expression, since *that* refers to *trees.* See also *it's me.*

its, it's. *Its* means *belonging to it:* "The cat is washing its fur." *It's* is the contraction for *it is:* "It's one o'clock." None of the possessive pronouns takes an apostrophe: *its, hers, theirs, ours.*

itself. See *myself; Reflexives.*

It's me (her, him, us, them). One critic says the objective forms (as given here) are frequently found in conversation and in fiction, and calls them appropriate in speech; the nominative forms (*I, she, he, we, they*) are described as generally used in writing. Three critics regard the objective forms as standard usage, and make no distinction between speech and writing. Fowler and Harper find *it's me* colloquially acceptable, and so does Perrin, who comments: "All the large grammars of English regard *it's me* as acceptable colloquial usage—and since the expression is not likely to occur except in speech, that gives it full standing." Perrin approves of the objective forms generally "in their natural settings." Follett too finds *it's me* not only acceptable but preferable, though he prescribes *I* when it is followed by a relative clause: "It is I who am the nominee." (See *it is I who,* etc.) A construction like "It is I/me whom they nominated" would, by strict grammar, also require *I* on the principle that the case of a pronoun is determined by its function in its own clause. One critic and American Heritage approve *It is me* only in speech; this is the consensus.

-ize, -ise. With familiar exceptions (*advertise, advise, apprise, chastise,* and others), *-ise* is usually the British termination, *-ize* the American: *apologise, apologize.* This is so even though Fowler, quoting the Oxford English Dictionary, holds that *-ise* (on words other than the exceptions noted) is wrong. American use of *-ise* is likely to be considered affected or precious. See also *-or, -our.*

Tacking on *-ize* is a convenient way of making a needed verb from a noun, and sometimes from an adjective: *concertize, hospitalize, burglarize.* There are numerous such established verbs, but five critics discourage the formation of new ones, such as *accessorize, concretize, martyrize, secretize, decimalize, capsulize, comprehensiveize, therapize.* A surprising number of such verbs are accepted by Webster. The consensus is that such words tend to be ungainly and are often unnecessary. Nevertheless, what counts in the end is wide enough acceptance of a new verb in *-ize.* Some such words that have been the subject of wide criticism, like *finalize,* will be found in their alphabetical places.

J

Jap, Japanese. *Jap* was freely used during World War II, with malicious satisfaction in the fact that it was derogatory. Since then, *Japanese* is carefully chosen nearly everywhere as both noun and adjective: *four Japanese; Japanese ships.* The pejorative implication of *Jap* is so clear that it is avoided even in newspaper headlines, despite the pressure of small space. *Nip* (a clipped form of *Nipponese*) is equally offensive.

jargon. See *argot, jargon.*

jest growed. See *Misquotation.*

jetsam. See *flotsam, jetsam.*

Jew, Jewish. The terms are sometimes carelessly used in connection with Israel. Although that nation is closely identified with Jews and Judaism, the terms *Jew* and *Israeli* are not interchangeable. Israel, like other nations, is composed of peoples of many races and religions, including a substantial number of Arabs and Moslems, and Christians of various races too. *Jew* and *Jewish,* then, in reference to nationals of Israel, are called for only when those terms would be applied to the nationals of any other country. *Jewish* is not the name of a language; usually *Hebrew* or *Yiddish* is intended. *Jew* as an adjective is now derogatory, whatever it may have been when Frank Harris referred to "the handsome Jew journalist Catulle Mendes . . ." The inoffensive description today would be *Jewish journalist.* The *Los Angeles Times,* in a series on the Jews of Los Angeles, made an interesting comment: "Jew. The word has for so long been an epithet, a point of loyalty, a source of inspiration and mystification that it may never come to be used neutrally." For all that, there is no other neutral term. Jerry Lewis, the screen actor, once argued earnestly on television that *Jew* should be avoided in favor of circumlocutions using the adjective form: not *a Jew,* but *a Jewish person.* Still, Jews themselves, including Israelis, freely use the word and surely see no derogation in it.

jeweler, jeweller. The second is the British preference.

jewelry, jewels. There is a superstition to the effect that *jewelry* is properly applied

215

to what is in a jeweler's window, and that the same ornaments, when worn, become *jewels*. On this principle, the crown jewels, if on display, would have to be called the crown jewelry. *Costume jewelry,* it may be observed, is an invariable term, applied regardless whether the jewelry is worn or displayed. If there is a distinction, it is that *jewelry* is a collective likely to be applied to examples of the jeweler's art, and that *jewels* is a plural applied particularly to gems.

Jewess. Like *Negress,* often considered derogatory. Webster unaccountably does not label it.

jibe, gibe. See *gibe, jibe.*

job, position. Neither observable usage nor the definitions in Random House and Webster substantiate the idea sometimes advanced that *job* necessarily connotes manual labor or low rank. It is the homelier word, and *position* would probably not be applied to ditch-digging. *Job,* sometimes qualified by *big,* is applied casually to employment at all levels. *Position* is sometimes suspect because it may be used to confer a spurious dignity. See also *wage.*

job action. Rejected by Harper as a euphemism for *strike, slowdown.*

jobless. Once derided as an unnecessary invention, *jobless* has long since won its spurs; dictionaries recognize it. The inventor undoubtedly was a frustrated headline-writer confronted with fitting *unemployed* into two-fifths the space during the Great Depression.

join together, etc. Despite the example of the Bible, this redundancy might better be put asunder.

journalese, journalism, journalistic. Before 1954, when pressure was successfully brought against the G. & C. Merriam Co. by Sigma Delta Chi, the professional journalists' society, the definition of *journalistic* in the Merriam-Webster dictionaries was in effect the adjectival form of *journalese. Journalese* is what linguists describe as a pejorative; that is to say, a word that depreciates. It applies to all that is bad in journalistic writing. *Journalistic,* on the other hand, properly means *pertaining to journalism,* and ought not to have any derogatory connotation. Nor does it, ordinarily. The old Webster definition of *journalistic* was "Characteristic of journalism or journalists; hence, of style characterized by evidence of haste, superficiality of thought, inaccuracies of detail, colloquialisms, and sensationalism; journalese." In the revised definition, the derogatory aspects were replaced by "appropriate to the immediate present and phrased to stimulate and satisfy the interest and curiosity of a wide reading public—often in distinction from *literary.*" The definition of *journalistic* in the Third Edition of Webster has been further revised, but the effect is the same and it remains neutral.

The Third Edition defines *journalese* first as a style of writing held to be characteristic of newspapers, and goes on with "writing marked by simple, informal, and usu. loose sentence structure, the frequent use of clichés, sensationalism in the presentation of material, and superficiality of thought and reasoning."

Evans remarks that "As a term for all newspaper writing, *journalese* is a snob term. There is just as good and effective writing in the best newspapers as in the best books, and the faults that are commonly classed as journalese are to be found in all writing." This is a fair judgment, but something more may be said about snobbery. *Journalese* is seldom applied to all newspaper writing, and when it is, the tone is so bitter that there is little hope of bringing the critic to reason. The truly snobbish term is *journalism*, applied, as Webster put it, in distinction to *literature*.

Often, when used in this way, *journalism* is preceded by *mere; mere journalism*, says the reviewer, and thus consigns the subject of his comment to perdition. Such judgments are often stupid, and amount to depreciating folk music by comparing it with classical music. Journalism and literature nurture each other, like folk and classical music. Much that is unpretentiously journalism is superb, for example the writing often found in *The New Yorker;* much that pretends to be literary is atrocious.

Now and then *journalese* is mistaken for a neutral descriptive of newspaper style. The author of a book on English usage and the compiler of a college newspaper stylebook misapplied it as the term for the cant, or technical terminology, of journalism.

Most inferior writing is cliché-ridden, but journalese has developed its own clichés. In journalese, a thing is not *kept secret*, but *a lid of secrecy* is clamped on it; rain and snow do not *fall*, but *are dumped;* rivers do not *overflow* or *flood*, but *go on a rampage;* honors are not *won* or *earned*, but *captured;* divisions and trains are too often *crack;* a reverse does not *threaten*, but *looms;* an occurrence is not *unprecedented*, but *precedent-shattering*, as if precedents were glass, when everyone knows they are rubber; large buildings are not *extensive*, but *sprawling*.

All such expressions have something in common besides extreme fatigue. If the reader can shake off, for a moment, the anesthesia they produce, he will see that originally they were dramatic. Even if they were too dramatic to suit the occasion—another characteristic of journalism, not necessarily related to clichés—the first few times they were used they piqued the reader's attention. But that was long ago. How, then, do they continue to be used so much? The obvious explanation is laziness. These expressions and many equally tired ones have become fixed in the minds of the lethargic and unimaginative as the only ones that are suitably descriptive.

In a survey of the American press, *The Times* of London commented: "It is this fundamental striving to attract the attention of, as well as to inform, the normally indifferent citizen which gives modern American journalism some of its most striking characteristics. Notably, it is the cause of its tendency to oversimplify political and diplomatic situations and developments to the point of distortion; to heighten personalities and the part played; to describe complex events in vivid, breathless, exciting prose so that the regular reader must live with a perpetual state of crisis or develop a deliberate indifference as a protection against it."

Jacques Barzun has taken note of the overexcited tone of much journalism by referring to reporters as "writers whose professional neurosis is to despair of being attended to and in whom, therefore, a kind of solemn ritual clowning is inevitable."

When reporters are taxed with the stereotyped flavor of much newswriting, they sometimes offer as an excuse that most of their work must be done in haste, to meet a deadline. This does not happen to be a good excuse, however, for it would be easier and faster to use the plain language the clichés conceal.

Plain language—the words the cliché expert uses himself when he is talking instead of writing—often looks surprisingly fresh in print. It will never wear out, as the clichés have, because it is the natural and inevitable currency of expression. See also *Clichés; Elegant Variation; Variation.*

Jr., Sr. It is a growing practice to omit the comma once generally used before *Jr.* and *Sr.: Joseph Williams Jr.* Omission has grammar on its side, for such designations, like *II, III* in *William II, George III,* are after all close modifiers. The words are capitalized when spelled out and appended to a name: *Joseph Williams Junior.* A young woman should not be described as *junior* though her name is the same as her mother's or, for that matter, her father's. *Jr.* is considered unnecessary with the name of a man who has a title, such as *Dr.,* that is not possessed by the father.

Judaism. There are three branches of this faith: Orthodox (the most conservative); Conservative (in the middle); and Reform (the most liberal). (The common error is *Reformed.*) These terms should be used with some explanatory phrase such as *branch of Judaism,* for when standing alone they may be confusing to many readers. Few Orthodox congregations use *synagogue* as part of their name; Reform congregations use *temple,* and Conservative congregations use either. *Synagogue* may be loosely used in application to all. *Church* is generally inapplicable to Jewish edifices, but is acceptable as a casual term.

judgement, judgment. The first is the British preference, the second the American.

judicial, judicious. Three critics warn against confusing the terms; ordinarily the first relates to legal proceedings (judicial chambers), the second to wisdom or judgment (*a judicious choice*). In places where either term will fit it is well to use an unambiguous synonym or to recast to make the meaning inescapable.

juncture. Two critics say the phrase *at this juncture* should refer to a convergence of events, and should not merely displace *at this moment* or *now.* One calls the phrase pompous.

jungle gym. The correct form for the playground apparatus; not *jungle jim.*

junior, senior. See *Jr., Sr.*

junket. Not a neutral equivalent of *trip, journey,* or *excursion,* for the word has a derogatory meaning in that sense. One kind of junket is a trip taken by a politician at public expense, ostensibly on public business but really for his own enjoyment. Because of this connotation, the Foreign Press Association banned the use of the term in its bulletin and ordered the substitution of *facility trip* for travel provided to journalists. *Junket* is generally applied by newspapermen to joyrides provided not to facilitate news coverage, but to create goodwill. There is a hazy line between these and travel provided at someone else's expense, for example the military services or a corporation, to places that cannot otherwise be reached with legitimate news coverage in view. The Foreign Press Association apparently was not inventing a euphemism but attempting to discourage loose application of *junket* to trips for legitimate news coverage.

jurist. Two critics hold that, common newspaper use to the contrary, a jurist is merely one versed in the law; the word is not an exact synonym of *judge*. Another critic speculates that identity of meaning is becoming established; however, a third critic and Random House and Webster all give *judge* for *jurist*. Among four current desk dictionaries, only Webster's Collegiate recognizes the terms as synonyms. The consensus is against using the term *jurist* for *judge*.

just exactly. Criticized as a redundancy.

K

Kan., Kas., Kans. Confusion over the correct abbreviation for *Kansas* has raged for many years, especially within the state itself. The official version, however (disregarding the new system of postal designations for mail), is *Kan.* See also *State Abbreviations.*

keep pace with. The form of the idiom; not *keep in pace with.*

kerosene. Called coal oil in some parts of the U.S. and paraffin in Britain. Sometimes spelled *kerosine.*

ketchup. See *catchup,* etc.

kick off. Either as a verb (*kick off the campaign*) or as an adjective (*a kick-off dinner*), this is a frayed figure from the football field. Not given by American Heritage; labeled slang by Random House; given as standard in both literal and figurative uses by Webster.

kick over the traces. Nearly everyone is aware in a general way that this means *to defy* or *escape restraint,* but a generation has grown up that does not know what traces are in this sense. They are the straps or chains by which horses used to pull wagons.

kid, kids. A generation ago, teachers busily instructed their pupils that kids could only be young goats, but the real goats were the kids who swallowed this pedantry; *kids* for *children* is well established colloquially. Flesch calls *kid* on its way to acceptance as standard English. Random House calls it informal, the American College Dictionary slang, Webster's New World colloquial, and the Standard College and American Heritage dictionaries informal. Webster considers it standard. The consensus is that it is informal, which means well suited to most contexts.

kilt, kilts. Two critics hold that a kilt is a single garment, and thus "the man was wearing kilts" is an error for "a kilt." Random House gives *kilt* as a singular, but Webster cites an example like the one given. The consensus favors *kilt* as a singular. Thus the corrected example would be "The man was wearing a kilt."

220

American Heritage adds another distinction, that *kilts* is an acceptable singular in reference to a woman's skirt imitating the Scotch garment.

kin. The term has given rise to some interesting and contradictory comment. Two critics insist that it cannot be singular, but must refer to relatives collectively, a judgment that neither Random House nor Webster supports. Opinion thus is evenly divided. Flesch criticizes the term as found only in headlines and pompous literary prose, a view that is patently mistaken.

kind. Three constructions based on *kind* (and *sort*) cause trouble. The first is *these, those kind* ("Those kind of flowers"). Since *those* is plural and *kind* is singular, strictly speaking the correct forms are *that, this kind* or *these, those kinds*. Two critics disapprove of *those kind* followed by a singular (*of flower*), but a well-educated President is quoted as having said "Those kind of tests." Bryant calls *these kind* followed by a plural colloquial, but Fowler is receptive to it and quotes Shakespeare: "These kind of knaves." American Heritage and Harper roundly reject *those kind*. Evans calls this construction standard. The consensus is that while *kind* preceded and followed by a plural is irregular, it is easily forgivable.

The next difficulty arises with *kind of a, an* ("What kind of a notion is that?"). Four critics disapprove of the use of *a, an* (correctly, "What kind of notion is that?"); Bryant calls it colloquial; Evans defends it, citing Henry James; Fowler calls it the least excusable of faults with *kind*. The consensus is negative. (Similar constructions follow *sort, species, manner, type*.)

The third troublesome construction is *kind of* in the sense *somewhat* or *rather*: "It's kind of cold out." One critic discourages this usage; another, without making an explicit judgment, finds *kind of* standard in many parts of the country; a third describes it as widely heard at all levels, though universally condemned; another condones it; Random House considers it informal but Webster gives it as standard. The consensus is negative.

kindly. Two critics disapprove of *kindly* for *please; Kindly remit;* but Random House and Webster explicitly recognize this usage. One critic disapproves of such constructions as *you are kindly requested,* in which the requester seems to credit kindness to himself.

kith and kin. Called a cliché by Evans and an archaism by Fowler. Both explain that *kith* means acquaintances and *kin* means relations.

kneeled, knelt. Both forms are declared acceptable by Bryant, Evans, and Harper, though *knelt* is described as predominant for the past tense. Random House and Webster concur. Fowler admits only *knelt*, apparently a British restriction

knit, knitted. Three critics say the forms are equally acceptable, and that *knit* as a modifier (*a knit scarf*) is too. Webster recognizes this latter use but Random House does not. The consensus is that it is standard.

knock(ed) up. The difference in meaning of this slang expression in Britain and America has yielded much merriment. The British senses of *knock up* are *wake up* or *tire out;* the American sense is *make pregnant.* The latter is illustrated in Webster by "no girls get married around here till they're knocked up." There are other senses, but they are not confused.

knot. Often, incorrectly, *knots per hour;* a knot is a measure of speed, not distance, and it is a nautical mile per hour. *Knots* is also wrong as a measure of distance (*eighteen knots up the coast*) in place of *nautical miles* (a nautical mile is about one and one-seventh land miles). Fowler, however, while pointing out the misapprehension, condones *knots per hour,* and Random House, American Heritage, and Webster admit *knot* as a loose usage for *nautical mile,* which permits *knots per hour.* The consensus is against this usage.

know as. Rejected by Nicholson and American Heritage as a displacement of *know that* or *whether:* "I don't know as he's coming." *whether.* The absence of this point from other books on usage probably is explained by the strong dialectal flavor of the expression, leading to the conclusion that disapproval would be unnecessary.

know-how. Described as standard English by two American critics, Random House, Webster, and even by Fowler, who concedes it has made its way in England, after having originated in America. This is a considerable tribute; the mere fact of American origin or American popularity is usually enough by itself to damn an expression in the eyes of British critics. Bernstein, however, classifies it with fad words, by which he means it is overused.

kudos. Not a plural any more than *bathos* or *pathos;* thus one can no more speak of a *kudo* than of a *patho.* This confusion has led some stylebooks to specify that *kudos* takes a plural verb, an obvious error: "Kudos go to John Jones." *goes.* The term means *fame, glory,* and drives from the Greek by way of British university slang. Some sample misapprehensions: "The correspondent deserved a Congo kudo"; "Kudos are in order for this author." Sometimes *kudos* is misused as a verb: "Life Kudos Capitol's Cast Albums." Webster and the OED, however, both give *kudize* as a verb. This form is rarely encountered in the U.S. One critic adds that even used correctly, *kudos* is pseudo-literary, and calls it an academic affectation.

L

la, le. In proper names, see *de, du,* etc.

labor (a point). Idiom once called for this form, but *belabor* came into such wide use that it is now universally accepted as well.

labour. Should be thus spelled in reference to the British Labour Party; otherwise *labor* in American usage.

lacerations. A pomposity of the press, displacing *cuts.* See *Technical Terms.*

lack for. Where *lack* alone will do ("The program lacks for public interest"), rejected by American Heritage and Harper; Random House and Webster concur by implication, since none of their examples use *lack for.*

lady. See *woman, lady.*

Lafayette, we are . . . See *Misquotation.*

lama, llama. The first designates the priest in Tibet and Mongolia; the second is the South American beast of burden and source of fleece.

(a) large portion, number, of. Verbiage for *much of, most of, many.* "A large portion of his popularity is due to habit." *Much of.* "A large number of flamingos were crowding to the gate." *Many.*

largely. Two critics point out that after *loom* and *bulk,* idiom calls for *large,* not *largely;* examples in Webster bear this out. See also *writ large.*

larynx. Sometimes misspelled *larnyx.*

last, latest. *Last* and *latest* are often interchangeable, in spite of the occasional insistence that *last* can mean only *final.* Thus one may speak of an author's last book and be correctly understood as meaning his most recent, not his final, one. *Latest* is desirable in other references to mean *immediately preceding* where *last* could be misunderstood: "The *latest* issue is dated Dec. 15; the one to be published in January will be the *last.*" See also *past.*

late. Redundant in *widow of the late;* correctly, *widow of.*

latter. There is no occasion to displace pronouns with *latter:* ''No law can prevent a conflict of interest from affecting a government official. Though the latter [preferably *he*] may have . . .'' See also *former, latter.*

laudable, laudatory. Sometimes confused; what is *laudable* deserves praise, what is *laudatory* bestows it.

launch. Standard but overworked for *start, open, initiate, begin.* See also *inaugurate.*

law business, concern. One critic frowns on *law business* for *law profession* (though *legal* is usual in this phrase); *law concern* is unidiomatic for *law firm.*

lawman. One critic calls the term unnecessary in the popular sense *law enforcement officer. Lawman* should not be used for *lawyer.* Both Random House and Webster give *lawman* (for *law enforcement officer*) without deprecation, so the consensus is that the term is standard. Its growing popularity seems to be ascribable to Westerns on television, where the sheriff and his aides are often referred to as *lawmen.*

lawyer. See *attorney, lawyer.*

lay, laid. See *lie, lay.*

layman. The primary meaning is ''of or pertaining to the laity, as distinct from the clergy.'' It is well established, however, and recognized by dictionaries, as also designating one outside some other profession or field of endeavor. Thus *layman* may be used in contradistinction to *doctor, lawyer, engineer, teacher,* etc., as well as *clergyman,* despite some criticism of this practice.

lb., lbs. The use of these abbreviations (which derive from *libra,* the ancient Roman pound) for *pound(s) sterling* is wrong. The forms should be used only for the unit of weight. When the symbol for pound sterling, £, is not available, it is preferable to spell the designation out. A workable substitution for the symbol can be made on the typewriter by striking the hypen over the *L.* The plural form *lbs.* is unnecessary. This applies to any abbreviation: *in.* (not *ins.*); *sec.* (not *secs.*).

lead, led. The past tense and participle of the verb meaning *to head, direct* is *led:* ''They led us to the mouth of the tunnel.'' Sometimes given *lead,* perhaps from confusion with the name of the metal, whose pronunciation is *led.* In printing, *lead* is a verb (as well as a noun) pronounced *led,* meaning to add space between lines.

leading question. The term derives from the courts, and there it means a question that suggests or elicits (that is, leads to) its answer, not necessarily a significant or critical or unfair question. The legal definition is the only one given by Random House and Webster. The casual use in the sense *pointed, important,* or *embarrassing question* is, therefore, mistaken.

leak. In the sense *disclose information, become known* ("word of the appointment was leaked to the press") recognized as standard.

leap, leaped, leapt. *Leaped* is preferred in the U.S. for the past tense and participle; *leapt* (pronounced *lept*) is chiefly British.

Leapfrog. A problem of reference is exemplified by a practice we might call leapfrog. The leaping is done by the reader, whether he likes it or not. Here is an example: "A prominent businessman criticized the city's proposal for off-street parking today as too expensive and poorly planned. Rensselaer van Wart spoke at a meeting of the Chamber of Commerce Traffic Committee, of which he is a member." The link between *prominent businessman* and *Rensselaer van Wart* must be forged by the reader. Depending on a variety of factors, more or less hesitation ensues when he encounters such a gap. Neglecting to show relationships is an offense against clarity. Making the reader guess at or assume the connection is a slipshod practice. In the example, the second sentence should have been tied to the first by something like "The businessman, Rensselaer van Wart . . ." or "The criticism was expressed today by Rensselaer van Wart at . . ."

Another such obstacle course: "The judge discharged a juror, after learning that William Roark was related by marriage to the defendant's cousin." Roark was the juror, and this should have been clearly indicated.

leastways, leastwise. Two critics agree that *leastways* is nonstandard. Dictionaries call it dialectal. American Heritage and Random House designate *leastwise* informal; Evans and Webster consider it standard.

leave. See *furlough, leave.*

leave, let. Although *leave* (for *let*) *me alone* is widely used, a worthwhile distinction is lost by neglect of *let*. *Leave,* in its primary sense, means *go away from,* and *let* means *permit* or *allow. Leave me alone* strictly means *leave me by myself; let me alone,* which is usually intended, means *don't bother me. Leave* has become popular, with a whimsical tinge, in the imperative where *let* is called for: *Leave us go.* To corrupt George Washington: "Leave us raise a standard to which the wise and honest can repair." This is in fact a revival of an archaic usage. "This publisher leaves his editors alone, while he concentrates on business matters." Ambiguous as it stands; the editors are not left in solitude, but are spared interference. *lets.* These comments reflect the views of two critics; Random House, American Heritage, Bryant, and Evans defend *leave* with *alone* (for *let*) as standard, but call other uses of *leave* for *let* substandard. Webster accepts *leave alone* but calls such locutions as *leave him be* substandard. The consensus is that *leave* for *let* is acceptable only with *alone*. See also *let, let's.*

lectern. See *podium.*

legible, readable. See *illegible, unreadable.*

leisurely. Both an adjective and an adverb: "A leisurely trip"; "He walked leisurely along." This, incidentally, is one of the few exceptions to the rule of spelling that calls for *i* before *e*, etc. See *Spelling.*

lend, loan. See *loan, lend.*

lengthways, lengthwise. Both forms are standard.

lengthy. Seems to have displaced *long* in much writing. Fowler describes it as a jocular or stylish synonym for *long,* but says it also appears more usefully to suggest tedium, a judgment in which Evans concurs. The sense *tedious* is given by dictionaries. Bernstein says the word is often used vaguely, and recommends something more precise, such as *tedious* itself. The consensus is that *lengthy* is best used to suggest tedium and not merely as a variant of *long.*

-less. Solid as a suffix: *childless, conscienceless,* etc., except after *ll: bell-less.* Flesch discourages the fabrication of new words by appending *-less: sceneryless, moneyless.* Fowler, however, says there is no reason why any noun may not be compounded with *-less,* but objects to such compounds with verbs, except for those already established, like *tireless.*

less, fewer. See *fewer, less.* For *less* as an adverb wrongly joined to an adjective with a hyphen, see *almost.*

let, let's. Fowler and American Heritage warn against the wrong case in constructions like "Let you and me settle the matter," where the nominative is often erroneously used ("let you and *I*"). Evans considers the nominative wrong only when a third person is being addressed, as in "Let John and I settle the matter." Bryant considers *let us* formal, *let's* informal, and *let's us* colloquial. Evans considers *let's you and I, let's you and me,* and *let's us* all acceptable. Bryant describes *let's not* as standard and *let's don't* as colloquial. See also *leave, let.*

Letters to the Editor. No great judgment is shown by publications that print letters containing accusations against themselves or challenges of their factual accuracy, and neglect to reply. The readers of such letters may be left with any of a variety of impressions, none of them complimentary. One is that the publication, although it condescends to publish the criticism, is too Olympian to reply. Another is that the charge is true, but the editors cannot think of anything to say in answer to it, or hope no one will notice. Another is that the high command is not aware enough of the publication's contents to realize it is being criticized. An attack by a reader, when it impugns the publication's motives and does not merely express a divergent opinion, ought to bring forth a brief statement of justification. If a reader calls attention to an error of fact, the publication ought to be large-minded enough to make it clear he is right. Or, if he only thinks he is right, the publication owes it to all its readers to reaffirm the facts, rather than leave them wondering.

Even when the publication's own accuracy is not in question, an obvious misstatement of fact in a published letter might well be identified for what it is, especially when public questions are concerned.

A series of letters dealing with the same subject are best grouped under some inclusive heading, rather than scattered among letters dealing with other subjects.

let, leave. See *leave, let.*

let them eat cake. See *Misquotation.*

let the worst come. See *Misquotation.*

level. As a verb in such locutions as *level a charge,* excessive for *charge.* The popular use of *level* as a noun in such expressions as *on the local level* (for *locally*), at a *record low level* (for *at a record low*), at *the junior high school level* (for *in junior high schools*), and others where it is automatic, vague, and avoidable, is criticized by three authorities.

liable. See *apt, liable, likely.*

liaison. Evans holds that the term should be reserved for the military, cooking, and romantic senses, and not used indiscriminately for any kind of association. Random House and Webster allow extensions to other associations. The word is often misspelled; *liason,* among other ways.

libation. Disapproved as a humorous variant for *drink.*

libel, slander. In common parlance, the terms are used interchangeably for defamation, but in the eyes of the law, libel is defamation by graphic means, recording, or broadcast, and slander is defamation by other spoken utterance or by gesture. Fowler says in Britain the terms are interchangeable.

liberal. It may be misleading to capitalize the term in the general political sense; this should be done only in reference to a Liberal Party (as in New York or Britain). See also *conservative.*

lie, lay. The chief difficulty here is remembering that the past tense of *lie* is *lay,* not *laid*—"After dinner I lay down"; "The book lay on the table"—and that the participle is *lain,* not *laid:* "The tools have lain in the grass since Sunday." *Laid* is the past tense and participle of *lay* (meaning *place down*): "She has laid the silver in the closet." *Lay* and *lie* are often erroneously interchanged; "Let us lay down in the shade." *lie*. These principles, which represent strictly correct usage, are generally concurred in. Evans, however, regards "lay down for a nap," "the book is laying on the table," and "he has lain it down" as also correct; Bryant finds such uses common in well-educated speech, though not in writing; Follett calls the distinctions more trouble than they are worth; and Fowler, in an indulgent tone, says the confusions are common in talk. The consensus is that forms of *lay* for *lie* are verging into standard usage. Evans calls for *lay low* (not *laid*) as the past of *lie low*.

lift. Questionable in the sense *pick up, retain,* or *revoke,* just as it is in the sense of *steal*. It does not serve any purpose that is not met as well or better by standard expressions. "The new French premier has lifted most of his predecessor's program." *retained, adopted, kept.* Here *lift* has the unhappy (and unintended) suggestion of thievery. "The TVA has lifted the license of a luncheonette operator who refused to serve blacks." *revoked.* None of the three principal dictionaries give the sense *revoke*. See also *relieve*.

lighted, lit. *Lighted* and *lit* are both standard for the past tense and participle. "The lamps were lighted (lit)." Evans adds that this is true also of *light* in the sense *land* (*the ball lit in the water*) and *alight;* Random House and Webster concur except for *alight*.

lightening, lightning. The first is the act of making less dark or heavy, the second the flash in the heavens.

light opera. See *operetta,* etc.

lights burned . . . "Lights burned late in the offices of the government ministries" we are told repeatedly in times of crises. This is to assure us, apparently, that the officials were not working in the dark or by candlelight.

-like. Solid as a suffix: *childlike, lamblike,* etc. But hyphenated after *ll: bill-like*.

like, as, as if. 1. Four critics consider *like* standard as a conjunction; that is, introducing a clause: "He said the movies are not going to stand still *like* they have for twenty-five years." All warn, however, that there is widespread prejudice against *like* instead of *as* in such constructions. Bryant finds *like* for *as* common in informal expression, but says *as* is preferred in formal English; Bernstein concedes that the preference for *as* is not logical, but advises against the use of *like* as a conjunction; American Heritage, Harper, and Follett are adamantly against it. Random House recognizes *like* as a conjunction but warns that it is "universally condemned by teachers and editors, notwithstanding its wide currency"; Webster accepts it without qualification. The consensus is that while *like* as a conjunction is defensible, the user should be prepared for criticism.

A great furore was created by a slogan that was used for many years to advertise cigarettes: "Winston tastes good, like a cigarette should." The widespread protests against its "bad grammar" had no effect, of course; on the contrary the manufacturers no doubt rubbed their hands gleefully over the extra mileage their slogan was getting. Grammarians generally, Shakespeare, John Dos Passos, *The New York Times*, and H. L. Mencken are among those who have been cited as having approved *like* as a conjunction. Perrin commented, in an early edition of *Writer's Guide and Index to English*, that *like* "is obviously on its way to becoming generally accepted and is a good instance of a change in usage, one that we can observe as it takes place." In her revision, Wilma R. Ebbitt advised uncertain writers to use *the way* in place of *like:* "We live the way the pioneers did."

The disapproval of *like* for *as* has generated in some writers an undiscriminating fear of *like* in any context. Thus they shun it even when it is required in its legitimate role as a preposition, and out of overcorrectness commit error. They write things like "He ate as a beast," "She trembled as a leaf," and "Editors, as inventors, are creative people." In all three instances, *like* is not only right but inescapable, and *as* is wrong. Of one such error, Bernstein commented, "It sounds as hell."

2. *Like* for *as if, as though. Like* is often used in place of *as if, as though,* as in "The Kremlin has been making noises like it wants such a meeting." The acceptance of this usage by the authorities parallels that of *like* for *as,* and the same consensus applies. For those who want to avoid all criticism of these usages, a rule propounded by Frank O. Colby (*Practical Handbook of Better English*) is useful: "If *as, as if, as though,* make sense in a sentence, *like* is incorrect. If they do not make sense, *like* is the right word." But this rule will not help anyone whose ear is so bad he is capable of writing "He ate as a beast."

3. *As with* for *like.* Some who strain to avoid *like* use *as with* or go the long way around with *in a manner similar to:* "The offense was relatively trivial, as with going barefoot to a black-tie affair"; "The unique plane stands on the ground in a manner similar to a camera tripod." In both instances, *like* is called for. *As with* is suitable when neither *like* nor *as* will do: "The best course, as with so many things, lies somewhere in between." Such expressions as "He ran like mad" and "They cheered like crazy" are considered acceptable by three critics.

For the error illustrated by "Like many patient folk, Russian violence can be brutal," in which *like that of* is required, see *False Comparison.* For *should, would like,* see *shall, will, should, would.* See also *such as; as is, as are,* etc.

like for. As in "We would like for it to rain," a Southern locution considered acceptable at least in speech. American Heritage rejects it.

likely. As used for *probably* ("The concert will likely be a benefit"), approved by two critics, oddly regarded as acceptable but quaint by Evans, and approved as an American usage by Fowler. Two critics and American Heritage hold that it must be preceded by *very, quite,* or *most* to be correct in this sense; Evans regards this as the standard usage. Both Random House and Webster consider *likely* for *probably* standard. The consensus is that it is correct. To people unaccustomed to it, however, it sounds objectionable. See also *apt, liable, likely.*

likes of. One critic and American Heritage disapprove of *likes of* for *like of* (*the likes of Scott Fitzgerald*), but both Random House and Webster regard *like of* and *likes of* as standard.

limited. Four authorities criticize the use of the word for *small, inadequate, few, rare* (*limited funds, limited interests, limited ideas,* etc.) in contrast to applying it where a limit has actually been set. The definitions in Random House and Webster appear to confirm this judgment.

limp into port. A grand old cliché as applied to disabled vessels. More recently it has been applied to partly disabled airplanes—in one instance to a four-engine jet with one engine out, even though the difference is not noticeable in flight.

linage, lineage. Four critics advocate restricting *linage* to printed lines (as most often used concerning advertising) and *lineage* to considerations of descent. Dictionaries give the forms as synonymous for *printed lines*.

line. Regarded as slangy for *occupation* by two critics as in the title of the television show, *What's My Line?* Evans concedes, however, that it is now all but standard. Fowler gives *what's my line* without aspersion (as a near-synonym of *field*) and American Heritage, Random House and Webster also recognize this sense as standard. See also *on line*.

linguist. Ordinarily, the term would have been used a few years ago to mean only one fluent in languages. This remains one sense, but another is becoming more and more common: a student of or expert in linguistics; that is, the science of language.

lion's share. In one of two fables from which the expression derives, the lion's share was not the greater part, but all or nearly all. One critic insists on this sense. The currently predominant *greater part* is accepted by two critics, American Heritage, Random House, and Webster. However used, it is a cliché.

Lisp. The rendering of a lisp, like the handling of such archaisms as *thee* and *thou* together with the verb-forms they take, is the downfall of many a writer. Look at this hapless example: "Thirty days hath Theptember, and tho have all the othersth, I guessth." If this kind of thing is necessary, it should at least be consistent and pronounceable.

lit. See *light*.

litany, liturgy. One critic objects to *litany* in such contexts as "The lecture was a litany of complaints about the high cost of living," arguing that the term is misused except in reference to a religious ceremony. Random House, however, gives "a prolonged or monotonous account," and Webster gives "a recital or chant having the resonant or repetitive qualities associated with a litany (the author recites his litany of the great mysteries)." American Heritage also approves this usage. Two critics are concerned about the confusion of *litany* (a form of responsive prayer) with *liturgy* (a form of public worship or a particular arrangement of services).

literally. Unliterally used to mean (1) *figuratively,* (2) *almost* or *virtually,* or (3) nothing much at all. Seldom is the word employed in its exact sense, which is *to the letter, precisely as stated.* Some examples: "The actor was literally floating on applause." The word wanted was *figuratively,* unless levitation occurred. "Flowing through the buttes and deep washes of South Dakota, the Missouri River literally cuts the state in half." *Literally* here is excess baggage, for the sentence is more forceful without it. So also is "A marble bust of Tom Paine may soon leave Philadelphia, where it literally has been a controversial object for years." It has become a habit of heedless writers to use *literally* for a usually unnecessary emphasis, without reference to its meaning. Webster, however, gives as one sense *in effect,* which would legitimize the misuses cited. The consensus, however, is heavily against this sense; Random House and American Heritage do not recognize it, and five authorities criticize it.

Literary Allusion. Fowler holds that the writer should temper the use of this device to the comprehension of the audience, and that, like foreign terms, allusions must be accurate. Bernstein concurs. See also *allusion; Misquotation.*

literature. One critic defends application of the term to the body of writing on a subject ("the literature on taxation") but regards its use for sales brochures and other promotional material as not standard. This, however, is an established and useful sense; Fowler considers it colloquial and adds it is on the verge of becoming standard. Random House and Webster recognize the application to handbills, etc.; American Heritage accepts "printed material of any kind."

little man, people. In an author's note in *McSorley's Wonderful Saloon,* Joseph Mitchell wrote: "The people in a number of these stories are of the kind that many writers have recently got into the habit of referring to as 'the little people.' I regard this phrase as patronizing and repulsive. There are no little people in this book. They are as big as you are, whoever you are." *The little man* has incurred the distaste of the Canadian Press, whose stylebook enjoins: "Do not use the term *little man* in referring to the population generally or any segment of it. The term has no precise or defensible meaning in that connection and has long since become objectionable."

littler, littlest. One critic objects to the forms as dialectal or juvenile and recommends *smaller, smallest, less, least.* Evans, however, holds that they fill needs that the other words do not. Dictionaries give *littler, littlest* without aspersion. The consensus is that they are standard.

littoral. Considered pretentious in ordinary (that is, nontechnical) contexts where *coast* will do.

liturgy. See *litany, liturgy.*

live. Often enclosed in quotation marks when used in reference to broadcasts ("The show was televised 'live' "), presumably to warn the reader that this is the term that rhymes with *hive* and not the one that rhymes with *give.* But the chance of confusion seems remote, since the association of *live* with television is abundantly familiar. Two critics and dictionaries regard the usage as standard. Bernstein warns that *live* and *alive* are not interchangeable: "Frank Buck brought them back alive" (not *live*).

lives with his wife at . . . The phrase, often found in biographical sketches, has an unhappy ring, because it seems to suggest the alternative of separate maintenance. Something like "He and his wife live at . . ." or ". . . make their home at . . ." sounds more suitable.

livid. One critic holds that the term means either black and blue or the color of lead (grayish). These hues are included in Webster's definition, which adds that *livid* can qualify several colors (*livid pink*), and that it can also mean *pallid, ghastly, gray,* or *lurid;* Random House also gives *bluish, deathly pale, ashen;* the judgment of American Heritage is similar. Oftenest used of one who is angry, and then probably means pink or red (faced).

llama, lama. See *lama, llama.*

Lloyd's. The correct form in reference to the place in London where underwriting is done; not *Lloyds* or *Lloyds'.*

loan, lend. The idea that *loan* is not good form as a verb is a superstition ("Loan me your pencil"; "The bank was ready to loan the money"). It is recognized as standard by dictionaries; one critic recognizes its legitimacy but recommends *lend;* another calls it a needless variant; a third describes it as thoroughly respectable, especially in reference to money; a fourth regards it as standard. The consensus is overwhelmingly that it is beyond reproach, though still the object of occasional criticism. *Loan* perhaps is encouraged by the curious avoidance of the past tense of *lend,* that is, *lent,* in favor of *loaned.*

loath, loathe. *Loath* is the adjective meaning *reluctant* ("I am loath to criticize him"); *loathe* is the verb meaning *detest* ("I loathe spinach"). "Officers have been loathe to make arrests in such cases." *loath.* It's *loathsome* (*repulsive*) not *loathesome. Loth* is an obsolescent spelling of *loath.*

locate. Properly, the word is not a synonym for *find,* but means *discover, fix the position of,* four critics hold. Thus one would *find,* not *locate,* a lost child but *locate* a lighthouse. Two critics allow *located* for *situated* ("the barn is located near the creek"). They also approve *locate* for *settle, become situated,* etc., ("They located in Boston") but Flesch recommends *settle.* Three critics point out that *located* is often superfluous: "The house is [*located*] on the wrong side of the tracks." Dictionaries corroborate all these views except for Flesch's dissent.

lone. See *Poesy.*

Long *s.* Writers are sometimes fascinated by the fact that a character resembling *f* was used in colonial times for what we uniformly render as *s.* In attempting to reproduce it, they use *f:* "For thif you have every inducement of fympathy and intereft." Further, the character is often *called f.* The colonial letter was not *f* but what was known as the long *s;* the horizontal stroke was not a crossbar, as in *f*, but rather a projection to the left. The long *s*, still used in modern times in the black letter or German Gothic alphabet, was used only within a word; the modern form was placed at the beginning and the end.

loom. A journalistic stereotype for *threaten, be expected.* See also *largely.*

loose, lose. *Loose* is often misused (or mistaken) for *lose:* "Don't loose your money." *Loose*, though principally an adverb (*the gown hung loose*) or an adjective (*loose change*) is occasionally a verb, but then it is the equivalent of *let go*, or sometimes of *loosen: loose the animals.*

loot. The slang use of the term to mean a large sum of money or valuables in general is unsettling because of the conflict with the standard denotation of ill-gotten gains. Thus the result may be ambiguity, as in "He will pay roughly a million and a quarter for the mansion, which contains that much loot in the form of tapestries and paintings." The writer meant simply *value;* the owner of the place would be justified in taking offense at the implication, though unintended, that the tapestries and paintings were stolen goods. The use of *loot* for objects of value, with no suggestion of being ill-gotten, is considered informal by Random House and standard by Webster.

lot, lots. The sense *a great deal* is informal but suitable to nearly any context. Fowler points out that Winston Churchill did not hesitate to use it, nor did an unnamed author on style whom he quotes. Random House calls the usage informal; Webster gives it as standard. The consensus is that if it is not now standard it is so nearly so that to call it into question is quibbling. Bryant and Random House approve *a lot, lots* as informal adverbs ("He sees her a lot"; he eats here lots"). Evans and Webster consider them standard; Evans says *a lot* is oftener used. American Heritage gives *very much* for *a lot.*

loud. Defended as an adverb by Evans ("They sang too loud"); Bryant says *loudly* is more frequent in formal writing and *loud* commoner in speech. *Loud* as an adverb is recognized by dictionaries.

lulled into a false sense of security. A cliché.

lunch, luncheon. The second is more formal.

luxuriant, luxurious. The first means *lush, thick, flourishing;* the second means *rich, lavish, choice, costly.* A head of hair or tropical vegetation can be luxuriant but not luxurious; a dwelling or a meal can be luxurious but not luxuriant.

-ly. Fowler and Flesch caution against the disagreeable effect caused by an adverb ending in *-ly* modifying another: "It was nearly certainly a failure." *almost certainly.* Two critics say there is no need to add *-ly* to ordinals (*firstly, secondly,* etc.) but add that if it is done it should be done consistently in a sequence. Fowler says insistence on *first,* etc., is pedantry.

The hyphen is wrong after adverbs ending in *-ly;* an adverb can only modify the adjective following: *an equally-good choice.* Omit the hyphen.

lyrics. Evans describes the term as slang in reference to the words of a song ("The tune is good but the lyrics are poor") but Fowler and dictionaries recognize this usage as standard.

M

mad. The idea that *mad* should not be used to mean *angry* is now a nearly forgotten pedantry; Evans says this sense has been long and universally in use, but warns that it may bring on criticism, and describes *angry* as the formal word. Flesch, Random House and Webster agree that *mad* is standard, and this is the consensus. American Heritage labels it informal. (Perhaps it should be explained that the purist traditionally insisted *mad* can mean only *insane*, a sense that remains in use; it is somewhat literary.)

madam, madame. *Madam* is the term for the keeper of a whorehouse, not *madame*. The polite term of address, now obsolescent, is also *madam; Madame* (often *Mme.*, plural *Mesdames, Mmes.*) is the form for a title prefixed to a name: *Mme. Lafond.*

made possible. The phrase has grown tiresome, and is often probably an over-statement, in acknowledgments of assistance in literary and other endeavors. All hail, then, the author who said such assistance had made his book less impossible than it might have been. See also *possible*.

Magna Charta, Magna Carta. Although *Charta* is neither Latin nor English, Evans points out that it has become well established in America, a judgment borne out by the fact that dictionaries give it as the predominant form. Fowler asserts there is unimpeachable authority for *Carta*. The consensus favors *Charta*, at least in the United States. The OED gives "Magna Charta, Magna Carta," indicating both forms are in current use. Most of its citations give *Magna Charta*.

magnitude. One critic discourages the figurative use of the astronomical term *of the first magnitude* as a cliché; another objects to *magnitude* as pretentious when *size* will do. See also *order*.

Mahomet. See *Mohammed, Mohammedan*.

maintain. Often questionably used in attribution in newspapers; what is maintained should have been previously asserted. See also *Attribution*.

major. Four critics agree that *major* as an adjective is correctly used only in the

235

sense *greater*, with comparison in mind, and that it is misused for *important, chief, principal, weighty, fundamental,* etc. Thus a major work would be one that stands out by comparison with others, not a great one in absolute terms. Webster's New World Dictionary concurs. The authorities also agree that whether correctly used or not, *major* is overworked as a modifier. Random House, however, gives "great, as in rank or importance; *a major question; a major artist*"; Webster gives "notable or conspicuous in effect or scope"; the Standard College Dictionary gives "having a primary or greater importance, excellence, rank, etc." American Heritage concurs. The consensus is that the comparative sense is preferable, but that the positive sense (*important*, etc.) is well on the way to becoming standard. *Major portion* is excessive for *most;* Evans says it is pretentious and vague for *greater part.*

majority, plurality. A majority is more than half, and the term is best reserved for elections and other circumstances involving numbers. *Majority* should be distinguished from *plurality*, which refers to the largest number of votes received by any of three or more candidates. Five authorities disapprove *majority* where *most, the greater part, many* will serve, and where numbers are not concerned: "The majority of the land was sold." *most.* Fowler approves *great majority*, but calls *greater* and *greatest majority* illiterate as forms of intensification; American Heritage concurs.

major portion of. Excessive for *most of.*

mal-. Solid as a prefix: *maladjusted, malapropos, malfeasance,* etc.

male. The term (like *female*, which see) is too technical or clinical for ordinary contexts where *man* will do.

man-, -man. See *Feminism.*

mania, phobia. Why *mania* should be confused with *phobia* is inexplicable, but it often happens. A *mania* is a craze, as a *mania for cards;* a *phobia* is an exaggerated or irrational fear, as a *phobia of snakes.* Fowler considers *phobia* a popularized technicality (borrowed from the writings of Freud).

manner. Circumlocutions are often formed on the word in place of using an adverb: *in a patient manner (patiently), in a laughable manner (laughably).*

(to the) manner born. See *Misquotation.*

manner, shape, or form. "He would not accept the honor in any manner, shape, or form." A pomposity.

mantel, mantle. In their usual senses, a mantel is a shelf above a fireplace and a mantle is a cloak or covering. Although the distinction is usually observed, some dictionaries allow *mantle* as a variant of *mantel.*

Manufactured Verbs. Although language is in a constant state of flux, so that some parts of speech take on the functions of others (nouns becoming verbs, etc.), deliberate wrenching of a word into a new role is to be discouraged as making for an artificial style. An example of this is: " 'My wife is upstairs pressing my suit,' jovialed Roy, a generous host," in which *jovial*, an adjective, has been uncomfortably miscast as a verb. See also *Utterance by Proxy* under *Attribution; -ize, -ise.*

marginal. Two critics object to the loose use of the word in the sense *small* or *narrow* or *slight*, and recommend that it be saved to describe what may easily fall on either side of a borderline, or for its use in economics. By this reasoning, one might speak of a marginal return on an investment (barely over the line from loss), but not of a marginal effort to accomplish something. This corresponds with the definitions in Random House and Webster; American Heritage, however, approves "marginal writing abilities." For the smallest possible amount, Fowler prescribes *minimal* when *small* is unsatisfactory.

mariage de convenance. If the French must be used, it had better be spelled thus, instead of the frequent mélange of French and English. But the English *marriage of convenience* is to be preferred.

marine. Capitalization of *marine* in reference to a member of the Marine Corps, with all due respect to that force, seems unduly deferential. If *marine* is capitalized *soldier, sailor, airman* should be too. And if *Marine Corps* is capitalized, as it undoubtedly should be, consistency dictates capitalizing *Army, Navy, Air Force,* and *Coast Guard* as well.

marital, martial. The easy transposition of letters that makes the one the other is the bane of proofreaders and editors, and the source of some unintentional humor, especially when what is intended to be *marital* comes out *martial. Marital* relates to marriage, *martial* to arms and war.

marry, married. There is a delicate and fairly widespread conviction that the man *marries*, but the woman *is married to*, or, rarely, *by*. The idea behind it is that the man is, or is supposed to be, the aggressor in marriage. In these days of equality of the sexes, however, there seems no warrant for preserving this polite fiction, and it appears to be disappearing, except perhaps from society pages. It attracts no notice now, usually, to say a woman *married* a man, instead of saying she *was married to* him. Random House gives an example in which the woman marries the man. The phrases *married his wife, married her husband* are open to the objection that the wife and husband acquire their status by the act of marriage; the expressions cited suggest they already had it. Sometimes there is regrettable clumsiness: "Chaplin married four times, first to Mildred Harris," *was married;* or *four times; his first wife was . . ."*

marshal. The spelling *marshall*, as either noun or verb (*parade marshal; marshal the forces*), is likely to be considered a misspelling; only Webster gives it.

massive. Fowler complains with justice that the word has become a fad in the senses *large, sweeping, vigorous,* etc.: *a massive program to combat illiteracy.*

masterful, masterly. Five authorities agree that *masterful* means *domineering* ("she wanted a masterful husband") and that *masterly* means *skillful, expert: a masterly work of art. Masterful* is often misused in the latter sense, and, as three critics concede, the error is probably encouraged by the lack of an adverbial form of *masterly,* leading to the use of *masterfully* ("He played the violin masterfully"). When the adverbial form is required, they prescribe recasting the sentence to preserve the distinction. Both Random House and Webster equate *masterful* and *masterly* without aspersion, however, and Flesch adds in an afterthought that perhaps the fight to keep the distinction is lost. The consensus still favors it.

masthead. Strictly, the masthead of a newspaper is the listing, usually on the editorial page, of the staff and other information; American Heritage gives only this sense. The term is widely applied, however, to the name of the paper as displayed on the front page (the nameplate), and both Random House and Webster recognize this sense.

material, matériel. The second is a military term for supplies and equipment as distinguished from personnel; the terms are not interchangeable.

materialize. Five authorities and American Heritage criticize use of the term for *develop, occur, happen, appear,* etc., instead of *take material form.* Thus "The clear skies predicted for the weekend failed to materialize" would be objectionable, but "Mephistopheles materialized for Faust" would be correct. Random House and Webster, however, both recognize the senses *appear, become fact* as standard. The consensus is against this usage, but it unquestionably is on the way to becoming standard.

mathematics. See *-ic, -ics.*

matriculate. Despite widespread impression to the contrary, the word does not mean *graduate from* but rather *enrol.* Many are matriculated, few (but perhaps still too many) graduate.

mature, maturity. Euphemisms for *middle-aged, old* or for the period of life thus described. A magazine published by the American Association of Retired Persons, whose members must be at least 55, is entitled *Modern Maturity.* Such usages, like referring to mentally retarded children as *exceptional,* spring from the delusion that by changing the name of something one can change its nature. *Mature* means fully grown or developed. Those who are middle-aged or beyond have long since reached that stage.

matutinal. Objected to as pretentious for *morning:* "The matutinal song of the birds."

maunder, meander. Two critics warn against confusing these terms. The first means to whine, grumble, or complain; the second, to follow a winding course (*the stream meandering through the valley*).

may. See *can, may.*

may, might. *May* is sometimes misused for *might* to describe hypothetical conditions, or when the past tense is required: "The Bible ought to be banned; then it may be read instead of gathering dust on shelves" *might;* "If property owners had not seen the new sign erected during the night they may not know they are officially in the county" *might;* "If the committee had had all the facts, it may have changed its mind" *might.*

maybe. The term was questioned in the original Fowler as literary for *perhaps;* Evans accurately spots this as a British view, and the revised Fowler not only concedes that it is the ordinary word in America but finds it is making headway in Britain. *Maybe* is not good usage as an adjective: *a maybe erroneous decision; a maybe enjoyable occasion (possibly).*

may God bless. See *God bless.*

may or may not. This expression overstresses the uncertainty: "The matter *may or may not* be presented to the City Council tonight." *May* alone fully poses the alternatives.

M.D. See *Dr.*

M.C. See *M.P., M.C.*

me. See *it's me*, etc.

mean. See *average, median, mean.*

Meaning. It is a delusion that any but the primary or basic meaning of a word is suspect if not actually erroneous. The significations of some of the simplest and commonest words run on for columns in unabridged dictionaries. The most that can be said with any validity is that some meanings are older than others; in many instances, the form from which a word developed is traced back in the dictionary to an original in another or a predecessor language (Latin, Greek, Middle English, French, etc.). Those who hold the primary-meaning delusion would likely say that the most reputable sense is that which most closely approximates that of the root. But in many instances that meaning is obsolete. Usage and acceptance are what establish meaning, and any sense given in a dictionary without a qualifier such as *dialectal, substandard,* or *slang* is regarded as standard. Perrin points out that no one can tell whether *check,* by itself, is noun or verb or adjective, much less which of its forty senses is intended. Fowler in the original (under *Spiritism*) derided an "extravagant theory that no word should have two meanings—a theory that would require us . . . to manufacture thousands of new words." Fowler also points out (under *True and False Etymology*) the obvious fact, of which authorities on usage sometimes seem to be oblivious, that the derivation of a word is not a reliable guide to its current meaning. See also *Colloquialisms*.

The word *set* has been shown to have 286 different meanings. Ninety percent of all words have one meaning; the average is three meanings each. This means that the relatively small number of common words have large numbers of meanings. It is also sometimes wrongly assumed that the order in which definitions are entered in a dictionary indicates rank. There is no basis for this idea. See also *Dictionaries*. If more than one spelling of a word is given, the first is usually predominant, but not any more correct.

means. In reference to money, the term is always plural ("His means were inadequate for his tastes"); otherwise, in the sense of an agency, it may be either singular or plural: "The means (is, are) justified by the ends." Follett does not except money, though this may be an oversight.

meantime, meanwhile. Harper's holds that *meantime* is a noun and *meanwhile* an adverb: "In the meantime . . ."; "Meanwhile, we rested." But dictionaries, including American Heritage, all say *meantime* may also be an adverb: "Meantime, we had something to eat."

Mecca. Figurative use of the term (literally, the holy city of Islam) should be reserved, Evans says, to describe a place to which people are attracted by some deep purpose, not merely a place to which people go for lesser reasons; Bernstein objects to its figurative use as a cliché, a view that seems better based. Both caution against using the term in connection with other religions, such as Judaism or Christianity, which may result in a ludicrous inconsistency and possibly give offense.

Medal of Honor. The correct form; not Congressional Medal of Honor, though it is awarded by Congress.

media, medium. *Media* is the plural of *medium:* "The media used were newspapers, magazines, and television." Thus *medias* is incorrect, and so is *media* used as a singular: "In the debate over toll TV the mathematics peculiar to a mass media have tended to run away with common sense." This is the view of four critics and American Heritage. Evans, however, finds *medias* acceptable. Flesch and Webster recognize *media* as a singular but Random House does not; none recognizes *medias*. The consensus is that *media* is the standard plural, and that *medias* as a plural and *media* as a singular are incorrect. *Mediums* is a standard alternative plural form though usually applied in connection with spiritualism. *Media* is preferred for agencies of communication.

median. See *average, median, mean.*

mediate. See *arbitrate, mediate*.

medic, medico. Two critics deprecate the terms as not standard; Random House calls them slang, though Webster considers them standard and American Heritage informal (for doctor). The consensus is that they are not standard.

mediocre. Most dictionary definitions are *of average quality, medium, commonplace, neither very good nor very bad.* The word is commonly used, however, to mean not *average* but *poor* or *inferior;* this is so common that the writer who uses the word in the dictionary sense may be misunderstood. Evans recognizes this, and speculates that the pejorative use of *mediocre* may become standard. That time appears to have arrived; Random House gives *rather poor* or *inferior,* and American Heritage acknowledges, "Usually used disparagingly." Webster gives *poor worth* or *inferiority* for *mediocrity.*

medium. See *media, medium*.

meet. There is an unreasoning prejudice, especially by newspapers, against the term as a noun in the sense *meeting* (of which, no doubt, it is a clipped form). *Track meet* and *swimming meet* are of course established, even in the press. *Meet* as a noun in the general sense is unqualifiedly recognized by dictionaries, and no authority on usage has anything to say against it.

meet, pass. Though the terms are carelessly interchanged with respect, for example, to trains on parallel tracks or to automobiles on the same highway, a distinction is worth encouraging, especially to make accounts of accidents clearer. *Pass,* in these connections, at least, might be abandoned in favor of *overtake.*

memento. Sometimes misspelled *momento;* the plural is *mementos* or *mementoes.*

memorandum, memorandums, memoranda. The plural is either the Latin form *memoranda* or the Englished *memorandums.* Evans accepts *memorandas,* but dictionaries do not recognize it. The consensus is that it is nonstandard.

menial. Though the term was once neutral, designating a class of servant, it is now derogatory and should not be used unless aspersion is intended.

mental attitude. Although an attitude may be mental or physical, the context always makes clear which is intended, and so the phrase may be set down as a redundancy.

mentality. Three critics object to the term as overused in the sense *mental attitude* ("The mentality of the prisoners"); Fowler adds that it is also often disparaging, which adds to its appeal.

mental telepathy. Since telepathy is thought transference, *mental* is redundant.

Mercedes. Sometimes causes a problem for those who clip the name of the automobile Mercedes-Benz. "Twelve Mercedes' were parked outside," we read, but alas, the plural cannot be formed with the apostrophe. It would have to be *Mercedeses*, admittedly a clumsy form. In this construction it might be well to revert to the full name: Mercedes-Benzes.

merchandise, merchandize. The second is a correct but uncommon variant.

meretricious. The word has something to do with *merit,* but in an adverse way; it means *appearing to possess merit but lacking it.* Not to be confused, though it is, with *meritorious,* which means *possessing merit.*

message. Recognized as a verb ("They messaged headquarters") by Webster but not by American Heritage or Random House.

Metaphors. The usual difficulty is mixing metaphors, the figures of speech in which a comparison or identity is implied for rhetorical effect ("The sun cut a flaming swath across the sky"). The writer who loses sight of the images he is creating, or is carried away by his eagerness for effect, is likely to mix metaphors, that is, to pair them incongruously, as in an example cited by Flesch: "A clash of wills between the White House and the Southerners jelled after Rep. Smith postponed the hearings." A clash, of course, cannot jell.

methodology. Two critics object to the form as a pretentious displacement of *method:* "The methodology of early-day logging operations was extremely wasteful." Evans gives as the proper sense of *methodology* a branch of logic seeking to show how abstract principles of a science may be used to gain knowledge. There are other technical senses, none of which is synonymous with *method,* as indicated by dictionaries. The conclusion is that *methodology* should not be used when *method* will serve.

meticulous. One critic insists that the word may not be used to mean *careful* or very *careful,* but must be restricted to its derived sense, which is that of care prompted by timidity or fear. This was the view of Fowler in the original, but the revised edition recognizes the new and universally accepted sense of *careful, exact, punctilious, precise,* etc., adding that "it would be idle to try to put it back into an etymological straitjacket." Meticulous may mean *overcareful* or *fussy,* but it also has a positive sense: *commendably thorough* or *precise.* Webster designates the connotation of timidity obsolete, and Random House omits this sense. Evans and Harper recognize the shift in sense from the original. Follett says the term has lost its overtone of fear and has come to seem just the right word for *exceedingly careful.* The consensus is overwhelming that the word now means *painstaking, fussy,* and may have a positive as well as a faintly disparaging sense.

Mexican, Spanish. *Spanish* (or *of Spanish extraction, Spanish-speaking*) has become an evasion for *Puerto Rican* in the East and for *Mexican* in the Southwestern U.S. Technically, any citizen of Mexico, regardless of ancestry, is a Mexican. Most Mexicans, however, are *mestizos,* in this case of mixed European and American Indian blood, possessing dark skin, black hair, and high cheekbones, and thus easily recognizable. See also *Hispanic.*

The large numbers of Mexicans who have settled in the Southwest have been the object of active discrimination, which, however, has noticeably diminished, especially with respect to the second generation. *Mexican* continues, nevertheless, to have a derogatory connotation. In efforts to avoid any slighting implication, *Spanish* and the other terms cited are resorted to, but this is misleading. It confuses Mexicans with Spaniards.

A member of a panel discussing integration in schools of a Western community, for example, delicately referred to students of Negro, Oriental, and Spanish descent. The number of Spanish descendants in the West is negligible; she meant *Mexican* but feared to say so.

In dealing with racial problems it seems best to face the facts head-on, and consequently it is desirable to use *Mexican* rather than avoid the term in favor of anything as misleading as *Spanish* or related evasions. The evasions are insulting in their own way because they suggest there is something wrong with being Mexican.

It must be conceded that *Mexican* is sometimes objected to by Mexicans themselves, but generally this is true only of the uneducated. *Mexican-American* is a more exact term than *Mexican* for citizens of the U.S.; *American of Mexican descent* is better yet. More recently journalists have discovered *Hispanic* as an evasion of *Mexican* or *Puerto Rican.*

mickey finn. Harper's holds that this slang term means only a drink that induces diarrhea, not one, as popularly supposed, that knocks the drinker out. This is wrongheaded; dictionaries also give *stupefy, render helpless* as its effects.

micro-. Solid as a prefix: *microbiology, microcosm, microfilm,* etc.

mid-. Solid as a prefix: *midday, midiron, midriff,* etc.

Mideast, Middle East. The areas designated by these terms (especially *Middle East; Mideast* appears to be a recent compression), as well as *Near East,* have gone through a series of modifications, and there were also differences in British and American views of what they meant. Present American usage, which prefers Middle East, is not a matter of unanimous agreement, but generally, it designates the area from Libya on the west to Iran or even Pakistan on the east. *Near East* appears to have fallen into disuse; it once designated, roughly, the areas now usually referred to as the Middle East.

Midlands, Middle West, Midwest. *Midlands,* originally applied to the middle counties of England, may be an affectation as applied to the central United States. *Midwest,* because of its concision and prevalence, is preferable to *Middle West.*

might, may. See *may, might.*

might perhaps. Like *possibly may,* redundant; either *might* or *perhaps* will do.

mighty. As an adverb (*a mighty fine day*) considered informal by Bryant, quaint by Evans, colloquial by Fowler, objectionable by Harper, informal by Random House, and standard by Webster. American Heritage rejects it in writing, accepts it in speech. The consensus is that it is informal.

militate, mitigate. See *mitigate, militate.*

minimal. The adjective comes from *minimum.* Fowler says it may mean only *least possible,* but Random House and Webster give also *very small, extremely minute.* Flesch considers it pretentious in these senses.

minimize. Four critics are corroborated by Random House and Webster in insisting that the word means only *reduce to the smallest possible amount* or *estimate in the least possible terms,* and cannot properly be used to mean *diminish, belittle, brush off, underrate,* etc. American Heritage, however, gives *depreciate.* Nor, American Heritage agrees, since it denotes an absolute idea, can it rightly be qualified by *greatly, as far as possible, somewhat,* or any other adverb. It is often unintentionally used in a way that reverses the intended sense: "Its influence on modern American architecture cannot be minimized." The writer meant that the influence cannot be overstated or overestimated, not that it is so small nothing can diminish it.

minister. See *reverend.*

minority. *Minority,* in reference primarily to race, is commonly used to refer to a group smaller than one of which it is a part. In this sense it is a collective noun. There is a strong tendency to apply the term to an individual who is a member of a minority group: "He was the only minority who signed the petition." Similarly, *minorities* is being used to mean not only groups but also individuals (i.e., members of minority groups): "Twelve minorities attended the meeting." These senses are too new to be in any dictionary, but the odds are that they will establish themselves.

minus. Criticized as facetious by two critics in the sense of *lacking* or *having lost* (*minus a tire; minus three teeth*). Both unabridged dictionaries recognize this sense as standard, however; American Heritage calls it informal.

minuscule. Often misspelled *miniscule.*

mis-. Solid as a prefix: *misadventure, misinform, mispronounce,* etc.

mishap. See *accident, mishap.*

mislead, misled. Confusion about the form of the past tense is often evident, as in "The voters were mislead on this issue." The problem is analogous to that of *lead, led,* which see.

Misquotation. Many familiar quotations have acquired versions that not only differ from the originals, but are better known. Usually the changes do not affect the meaning. Occasionally, the popular interpretation of a quotation, for one reason or another, is far afield from the original. Some famous remarks were never made by those to whom they are credited.

Bernstein and Fowler differ on whether well-established misquotations are open to criticism, e.g., "In the sweat of thy brow" (correctly, *face*) and "even tenor of their way" (correctly, *noiseless*). Bernstein insists on the exact form; Fowler is inclined to be lenient about variations, which seems a more sensible attitude, as long as the meaning is not changed. It can also be argued that some misquotations are improvements on the originals. There are, of course, a number of dictionaries of quotations in which exactness can be checked. The best known of these are Bartlett's *Familiar Quotations, The Oxford Dictionary of Quotations,* and Stevenson's *Home Book of Quotations* (by far the most comprehensive). Some of the most frequent misquotations, or misapprehensions of quotations, follow, arranged in alphabetical order by their key words.

Alas, poor Yorick. "Alas, poor Yorick," we hear it declaimed, "I knew him well." But the line from *Hamlet* runs "I knew him, Horatio; a fellow of infinite jest, of most excellent fancy."

All that glisters. "All that glisters (not *glistens*) is not gold." *Merchant of Venice.*

A poor thing. Touchstone, in *As You Like It,* said of his chosen virgin, "An *ill-favoured* thing, sir, but mine own."

Baldness. "Baldness may not be pretty, but it's neat." This was credited on at least one occasion to Anon. For one thing, the wording is not quite right, and Anon did not say it. The original version is "There's one thing about baldness— it's neat," and the author was that wit and baldhead, Don Herold. Other versions of this witticism turn up from time to time, but usually without a mention of Herold, even in most dictionaries of quotations. These words are unquestionably destined for the ages, and they are properly credited in at least one book, Evan Esar's *Dictionary of Humorous Quotations.*

Battle of Waterloo. The Duke of Wellington, an indifferent athlete at Eton, denied having said the Battle of Waterloo was won on the playing fields of Eton, according to Will and Ariel Durant (*The Age of Napoleon*).

Blood, sweat, and tears. Rudolf Flesch points out in *The Art of Plain Talk* that Churchill's famous wartime offer to the British nation, which is generally remembered as "blood, sweat, and tears" was in fact "blood, toil, tears and sweat." Flesch notes that Churchill's intention was to encourage people in the war effort, and that the popular distortion of what he said not only damages the rhythm but also ends on a defeatist note, *tears.*

Brevity the soul. The comment by Polonius in *Hamlet* that "Brevity is the soul of wit" is usually taken to mean that brevity is the soul of humor, but as pointed out by F. L. Lucas in *Style,* Polonius had in mind intelligent discussion, which was the meaning of *wit* in Shakespeare's day.

Cinderella. This is not a misquotation, but is included here as a bit of curious lore. The slippers in which Cinderella danced the evening away were not made of glass, which seems to be an incredibly unsuitable material. The English version of the tale comes from the French story, *Cendrillon,* by Perrault. Perrault wrote of *pantoufle en vair* (a slipper of fur), but the translator confused *en vair* with *en verre* (*of glass*).

Cloud no bigger. The cloud "no bigger than a man's hand" that has become the standard reference to a small but menacing omen was pristinely, "There ariseth a little cloud out of the sea, like a man's hand" (I Kings 18:44).

Consistency the hobgoblin. Consistency is often flatly called the hobgoblin of little minds, but Emerson qualified the original: "A foolish consistency . . ."

Cry havoc. Usually given "Cry havoc, and unleash the dogs of war." But in *Julius Caesar* the lines run "Cry, 'Havoc!' and *let slip* the dogs of war."

Devil can. "The devil can *cite* Scripture for his own purpose" (not *quote*). (*The Merchant of Venice* I, iii.)

Disapprove of what you say. Most of us were brought up believing that Voltaire wrote, "I disapprove of what you say, but I will defend to the death your right to say it." The chances are that he would not only disapprove of our attributing the remark to him, but also decline to defend it. For these words are merely what S. G. Tallentyre (the *nom de plume* of E. Beatrice Hall, a British writer), thought Voltaire should, or might, have said. She put them in quotation marks, however, and defended them as a paraphrase. The remark does reflect Voltaire's philosophy. What great thinkers neglect to express, industrious biographers will put in their mouths.

Entangling alliances. George Washington is often misquoted as having warned against them in his Farewell Address. The phrase comes, however, from Jefferson's First Inaugural Address: "Peace, commerce, and honest friendship with all nations—entangling alliances with none." Washington did say toward the end of his Farewell Address: "Taking care always to keep ourselves on a respectable defensive posture, we may safely trust to temporary alliances for extraordinary emergencies." He also said: "The great rule of conduct for us in regard to foreign nations is, in extending our commercial relations, to have with them as little political connection as possible."

Far from the madding. Thomas Hardy used care in borrowing *Far From the Madding Crowd* as the title of a novel, though Thomas Gray is often supposed to have made it (in his *Elegy Written in a Country Churchyard*) "Far from the maddening crowd." The sense intended by Gray evidently was *frenzied, raving.* Still, Webster gives *maddening* (in the sense of *driving mad*) as a synonym of *madding,* a word seldom heard any longer except when Gray is exactly quoted.

Fiddle while Rome. The idea that Nero not only played his lyre and sang while Rome burned, presumably so that he could rebuild it nearer to his heart's desire, is evidently at odds with the facts, which are that he did everything possible to check the fire. He did indeed rebuild after the fire and thereby improved the city (Evans). Though a cliché, and factually incorrect, the statement conveys so graphic a picture that it will neither be corrected nor abandoned.

For whom the bell. Ernest Hemingway carefully preserved the original in entitling his novel *For Whom the Bell Tolls,* but John Donne's line is often pluralized to *for whom the bells . . .*

Gild the lily. Salisbury, in *King John,* said not *gild the lily,* but "To gild refined gold, to paint the lily."

God rest ye. "God rest ye, merry gentlemen" is the way we often see it, but perhaps not without remembering we have also seen it "God rest ye merry, gentlemen." Still, the latter version does not quite seem to make sense, and Bartlett's puts the comma after *ye.* Charles D. Rice explained in *This Week,* "The comma should be placed after *merry; God rest ye merry* was a common greeting in early England." *The Oxford Dictionary of Quotations* concurs in the late comma.

Hoist with his. Hamlet thought it sport "to have the enginer Hoist with his own petar" (not *by*). Often given *petard* (an explosive device used to break down a door); *petar,* the original, is an obsolete form.

Honored in the breach. The quotation from Hamlet, "more honor'd in the breach than the observance" is generally used to refer to some desirable thing that is not enough observed; in the play, it referred to a custom that is best not observed at all.

How dear to my heart. Emily Kimbrough, in entitling a book thus, did nothing to curb the misquotation of "How dear to *this* heart are the scenes of my childhood" (Samuel Woodworth).

Jest growed. Topsy, the character in *Uncle Tom's Cabin,* is often invoked in comparison with something or someone that "jest growed." Her remark, however, was void of jest: "I 'spect I grow'd."

Lafayette, we are. Popular fancy has General John J. Pershing striding down the gangplank at the head of the American Expeditionary Force, striking a pose, and declaiming to a throng of bug-eyed Frenchmen, "Lafayette, we are here!" But the declaimer was Charles E. Stanton, chief disbursing officer of the AEF, whom Pershing deputed to speak for him at the tomb of Lafayette in Paris on July 4, 1917. Pershing never offered a satisfactory excuse for having failed to think up this immortal announcement himself. The public assumption that he was its author, however, may well have taken the edge off the winning of World War I for him, and may have poisoned the life of Stanton.

Let them eat cake. Marie Antoinette never made such a remark, historians agree; on the contrary, during the bread riots of 1788 "she contributed abundantly from her own purse to public relief." (*Rousseau and Revolution,* by Will and Ariel Durant.)

Let the worst. Cervantes said, "Let the worst come to the worst," not (more logically, perhaps) "If worse comes to worst."

Mills of God. The quotation correctly is "Though the mills of God grind slowly, yet they grind exceeding small" (a translation from the German of Friedrich von Logau by Henry Wadsworth Longfellow). Often given *mills of the gods, exceedingly small, exceedingly fine.*

Money, the root. Money is unduly berated as the root of all evil, but it is the *love of money* that the Bible denounces. (I Timothy 6:10) This at least gives the rich more comfort than the pronouncement that it is easier for a camel to go through the eye of a needle than for a rich man to enter into the kingdom of God.

Music hath charms. It was a savage *breast*, not *beast*, that Congreve said music hath charms to soothe.

Power corrupts. Lord Acton is usually quoted as having said, "All power corrupts" but the uncorrupted version was not quite so flat: "Power *tends to* corrupt, and absolute power corrupts absolutely."

Pride goeth. It is not a fall that pride goeth before, but "Pride goeth before destruction, and an haughty spirit before a fall." (Proverbs 16:18)

Prophet without honor. The "prophet without honor in his own country" is, more precisely, "not without honor save in his own country." (Matthew 13:57)

Screw your courage. "Screw your courage to the *sticking-place*" (not *sticking-point*). (*Macbeth*)

Skin of teeth. "I am escaped with (not *by*) the skin of my teeth." (Job 14:1)

Such stuff as dreams. Puck (in *The Tempest*) saw us as "such stuff as dreams are made *on*," not *of*, though of course *of* comes naturally to the modern tongue.

Survival of the fittest. Not originated by Charles Darwin, as he himself acknowledged: "The expression used by Mr. Herbert Spencer of the Survival of the Fittest is more accurate and sometimes more convenient."

Tilting at windmills. The popular metaphor is often erroneously given "tilting *with* windmills." The reference is to an episode in which Don Quixote charges a windmill with his lance, thinking it a giant. *Tilt* in this sense always takes *at.*

To the manner born. The correct version, as it appears in *Hamlet;* not *to the manor born.* The phrase refers to familiarity with local customs, not breeding or inheritance.

Touch of nature. "One touch of nature makes the whole world kin" (*Troilus and Cressida*). Nature then meant *inborn characteristic*, not *the physical world*, as often misapprehended.

Voice crying. "The voice crying in the wilderness" is, accurately, "the voice of one." (Matthew 3:3)

Water, water everywhere. This concludes "nor any drop to drink," not "and not a drop to drink." (Coleridge's *Rime of the Ancient Mariner*)

Weather. "Everybody talks about the weather, but nobody does anything about it." This is a case of questionable attribution; the beneficiary is Mark Twain. Charles Dudley Warner, however, when he was editor of the *Hartford Courant,* wrote in an editorial: "A well-known American writer once said that while everyone talked about the weather, nobody seemed to do anything about it." Warner may have been ascribing the remark to Twain, a close friend. Bartlett's says that although it is often attributed to Twain, it is not found in his published works. Burton Stevenson was persuaded to change the attribution from Twain to Warner in *The Home Book of Quotations.* Some other dictionaries also credit Warner.

Misrelated Modifiers. See *Dangling Modifiers.*

Miss. See *Mr., Mrs., Miss; Ms.*

missile. Often misspelled *missle.* And, curiously, *missive* (message) and *missile* (projectile) are sometimes confused.

misspell. Often, with ultimate perversity, misspelled *mispell.*

mitigate, militate. To mitigate is to soften ("His apology mitigated the insult"); to militate (with *against*) is to have an adverse effect on ("The rumor militated against her success"). *Mitigate* is sometimes used where *militate* is required.

Mixed Metaphors. See *Metaphors.*

modernistic. The word is often misused for *modern* in reference to painting and design. *Modernistic* in this connection refers to Cubism or, in general, to a school of angular, jagged design that lived and died in the twenties and thirties. Random House, however, gives a derogatory sense, *falsely modern.* Other dictionaries do not recognize a distinction, and it may be that only people versed in art and design are sensitive to it.

Modifiers. 1. Participial modifiers. One-word participial modifiers beginning a sentence are a peculiarity of journalese: "Shortlived, the committee was a thorn in the growers' flesh"; "Married, he is the father of a young son." Better, because less clipped and telegraphic: "Although the committee was shortlived, it was a thorn in the growers' flesh"; "He is married and the father of a young son."

Fowler objects to opening a sentence with a participle modifying the subject as a device that is overworked in newspapers. This is patently so in the United States as well as Britain.

Appositives are used similarly, but perhaps are less objectionable: "A salesman, he spent a lot of time away from home." But the pattern is overdone in newswriting.

The participial modifier should form a logical sequence with the rest of the sentence. This principle is often disregarded in biographical sketches: "Born in Illinois, he was admitted to a partnership in the firm at the age of 24." Better: "Mr. Smith, who was born in Illinois, was admitted . . ."

2. Position of modifiers. It is preferable that modifying phrases and clauses should stand next to what they modify: "He has been executive vice president since 1952, an office that will not be filled immediately." But the clause after the comma does not modify *1952.* "Since 1952, he has been vice president, an office that . . ."

3. Elision of modifiers. "This self-effacing, dedicated woman in her mid-40s bears one of the most delicate yet little-known responsibilities of anyone around the president." Adverbs that modify adjectives in parallel constructions should not be carelessly elided; the reader does not readily apply *most* to *little-known,* as the writer intended, because *most little-known* is not idiomatic. *most delicate and yet least known.*

4. Piled-up adjectives. This is a mannerism primarily of the news columns; it reflects the urge to condense, and hasty work. Some examples: "He was arrested on conspiracy and concealing stolen property charges" (*on charges of conspiracy and receiving stolen property*); "A 15-cent per $100 assessed valuation road tax increase was proposed." (*A road tax increase of 15 cents per $100 assessed valuation . . .*) The cure is to limit the number of adjectives before the noun and to use prepositional phrases for the sake of readability.

5. Limiting adjectives. These are often used in a way that has an ambiguous effect: "His labor turnover is nominal, and he is proud of the loyalty of his nonunion employees." This sounds as if the subject may have had two kinds of employees, union and nonunion, and as if only the nonunion ones were loyal. In fact, however, all the employees were nonunion, and this might have been expressed by "He is proud of the loyalty of his employees, who are nonunion." "The speaker cited Professor A. M. Low, Britain's inventive version of Thomas A. Edison." The effect is to suggest that Edison was not inventive. Unambiguous: "Professor A. M. Low, Britain's counterpart of Thomas A. Edison."

6. Misplaced modifiers. "Details are slipping out of plans for the first Soviet-bloc beauty contest." Emended, the example should read "Details of plans for the first Soviet-bloc beauty contest are slipping out." Another example, whose correction requires a different approach: "The Israelis were accused of firing on the Egyptian post of Deir el Balat for ten minutes without causing casualties." This may sound like a reproach for poor marksmanship. *for ten minutes; there were no casualties.*

7. Present vs. past participle. Modifying phrases that contain present participles sometimes become structural atrocities in the hands of inexpert writers. Such phrases must indicate either a connected sequence of events, or simultaneous occurrence: "Going to the door, he turned the key" (connected sequence). "Laughing gaily, she turned to go" (simultaneous occurrence). If there is an appreciable interval between what is conveyed by the modifying phrase and the main clause, a past (rather than present) participle is called for. "Joseph Doakes is a graduate of Columbia University, receiving his degree in 1978." *having received.* "The mother said her daughter fell out of the car, apparently opening the door when no one was looking." *having opened.*

8. Nouns as adjectives. Any flat ban on pressing nouns into service as adjectives would be foolish. One part of speech easily assumes the role of another; this is one of the most distinctive and useful characteristics of English. Sometimes, however, nouns forced into the role of adjectives leave a bad taste. These are undesirable examples: "The officer expressed reluctance to discuss the case for security reasons"; "The general was retired for health reasons"; "The situation may soon reach disaster proportions"; "The service will be discontinued for economy reasons"; "She admitted her guilt feelings."

The difficulty cannot be with the words used as modifiers, for *health, security, disaster, economy,* and *guilt* all sound acceptable as adjectives in other combinations: *health insurance, security measures, disaster preparations, economy drive, guilt complex.* Whatever the explanation, *reasons of security, reasons of health, proportions of disaster, reasons of economy,* and *feelings of guilt* all sound undeniably better than the versions first cited. It may be a matter of idiom. Recasting in these instances may mean more words, but there is no all-redeeming virtue in brevity.

9. Repetition of defining modifiers. Redundancy is evident in the useless repetition of defining modifiers. Once a man has been identified as a hotel porter he should be referred to as *the porter* rather than *the hotel porter.* (This is not to be interpreted as discouraging the use of *he* or *him.*) The examples that follow illustrate other instances of excessive identification. The descriptives that should be omitted are in parentheses:

"George Jones was found guilty of second-degree murder today. A jury composed of seven men and five women returned the (second-degree) verdict after five hours. The (second-degree-murder) conviction carries a penalty of five years to life."

"A dinner will be held Sunday at 7 p.m. Reservations (for the dinner) may be made by telephone."

See also *Adjectives; Adverbs; Dangling Modifiers; False Titles.*

modus vivendi. Flesch agrees with Fowler that the phrase (from the Latin) means a temporary arrangement that enables people to carry on pending settlement of a dispute, but both Random House and Webster recognize *manner of living, way of life,* and it is hardly arguable that this sense is by far more usual.

Mohammed, Mohammedan. John Gunther said that there are at least a dozen ways to spell *Mohammed,* the form American usage calls for. Random House gives *Mohammed* as the primary form, but Webster surprisingly gives *Muhammed.* Fowler grudgingly concedes that *Mohammed* has established itself, displacing *Mahomet.* The consensus is that *Mohammed(an)* is the prevalent form, and that *Mahomet(an)* and *Muhammed(an)* are unusual variants. Fowler calls *Muhammed(an)* pedantic.

Moslems are said to object to the term *Mohammed(an)* and its variants as implying that Mohammed is the object of worship, that is to say, a deity, but the term is firmly established without any such intention. *Moslem* means "those who submit to the will of God." Although Random House and Webster regard *Muslim* as the predominant form, this is plainly wrongheaded as far as America is concerned; as American Heritage points out, *Moslem* is the preferred form in journalism and popular usage. *Muslim* is gaining on *Moslem* in Britain, Fowler reports. It is curious that the American Black Muslims should have adopted the spelling they did. *Mussulman* is a variant of *Moslem*.

moisturize. Used to mean *impart moisture to, moisten;* apparently invented by the writers of cosmetics ads, since it is seldom seen elsewhere. Recognized only by Random House among current dictionaries. This may mean only that it is a new word.

molten. Two critics point out that usually *molten* (rather than *melted*) is used for what requires great heat to liquefy (metals, lava), and this distinction appears to be borne out by usage. Webster cites *molten Parmesan cheese*, but there may be some question whether this is not figurative.

momentarily, momently. Two critics hold that *momentarily* means *for a moment* (*momentarily out of breath*) and *momently* means *from one moment to the next* (*momently expecting a telegram*). But dictionaries give them as synonyms.

moment of truth. Flesch refuses to recognize any application of the term except the original, that is, the point in a bullfight at which the matador is about to make the kill. It is hardly arguable, however, that the other sense given by Random House, the moment of an extreme test or a critical moment, is the one in widest use and thus is unexceptionable.

Money. See *Sums of Money*.

mongolian idiot, mongolism. G. W. Strong, in a letter to the *Pasadena Star-News,* questioned whether the term *mongolian idiot* (a widely used term for a kind of congenital idiocy) should not be displaced as "illogical, unscientific, and especially impolitic. It seems strange that a word which designates the world's largest race of human beings should be used by another race to specify a certain class of its abnormal births. Whether there is slight or close resemblance between the features of a child so tragically afflicted and those of the race indicated is hardly justification for the Caucasian ethnocentrism reflected in the expression *mongolian idiot*." The medical term for this condition is Down's syndrome.

moot. As an adjective in ordinary contexts, the term means *debatable, open to doubt,* as in "It is a moot question whether the issue has been settled." Sometimes misused in the sense *hypothetical* or *academic*. This is a technical sense and out of place except in legal contexts (*a moot court*), as the examples in Webster show. Both senses are correct in their proper habitats.

more, most vs. -er, -est. For comparison of adjectives (e.g., *more beautiful* vs. *beautifuler*, etc.), see *Comparison 4*. For comparison of absolutes see *Comparison 3*.

more important(ly). The American Heritage panel divided evenly on the acceptability of these forms; Harper rejects *more importantly,* Bernstein defends it. *More importantly* appears to be a contraction of *what is more important:* "More importantly, he said the accusation was mistaken." No one would write "what is more importantly." As a contraction *more important* seems preferable; nothing is accomplished by making an adverb of *important*. Sometimes *importantly* alone is used ambiguously: "Importantly, the Pravda article did not criticize the senator for holding a press conference." Although this was not likely to be misread, *significantly* would have been more appropriate. *Importantly* means *in an important manner:* "He strutted importantly into the room."

more preferable. Redundant for *preferable,* which alone is a comparative.

more than one. Takes a singular verb ("More than one of the legislators was embarrassed by the disclosure").

more well-known. See *most well-known.*

mortician. Mencken described the term as "a lovely euphemism" invented by undertakers to give their macabre trade respectability. Fowler calls it an American genteelism. Random House and Webster both give the term straightfacedly, however, and it is likely that it is now so common that it has lost the derisory or pretentious overtones it once had.

Moslem. See *Mohammed, Mohammedan,* etc.

most, almost. The schoolgirlish *most* for *almost* is called colloquial by Bryant and Fowler, folksy by Bernstein, and dialectal by Follett ("Most anyone can participate"). Flesch, however, calls it idiomatic usage, and Evans sees no objection to it. Random House considers it informal, and Webster gives *most* as a standard shortened form of *almost*. American Heritage rejects it. Webster's New World and the Standard College Dictionary consider the usage informal or colloquial. The consensus is that it is good informal usage. See also *almost* for misuse of the hyphen with *most*. *Most times* is a gaucherie for *usually, generally:* "Sterility is most times due to physical causes."

most well-known. An inexcusable gaucherie for *best-known:* "He is the most well-known banker in the city." *Most* cannot modify *well*. The same principle applies to *more well-known*.

motif, motive. Interchangeable in reference to a recurrent theme, for example in music, but *motif* greatly predominates in that sense.

motivate, motivation. Criticized as pretentious when *cause* (as verb or noun) or *reason* will do: "His motivations for declining the part were obscure." *reasons*.

motor. See *engine, motor*.

M.P., M.C.   M.P., for *Member of Parliament*, has been solidly established for a long time, and its solidity is probably assisted by the fact that the letters are the usual form of reference ("He was an M.P."). But the attempt to establish M.C. for *Member of Congress* has not caught on, although some congressmen use it in signing letters. M.C. is more familiar for *master of ceremonies* (also given *emcee*).

Mr., Mrs., Miss.   Flesch and Fowler agree that it is improper for a woman or man to use the title in referring to their spouses. There is a growing tendency in the press to dispense with the honorifics *Mr., Mrs., Miss* after having once given the full name, and to refer to men and women alike by their last names alone. Most newspapers that ordinarily dispense with *Mr.* use it as a mark of respect in obituaries, and in subsequent references (after the first full identification with *Reverend*, which see) to Protestant ministers. *Mrs.*, strictly speaking, should not ordinarily be used with a woman's given name (*Mrs. Ethel Adams*) but only with her husband's given name (*Mrs. Anthony Adams*). This rule may now be passé, however, and in any event is little observed. *Miss* is properly applied to women, married or not, when they are named in connection with their careers, and whether or not, as is often true of actresses, they have professional names that differ from their legal ones. *Miss* or *Mrs.* should not be used with other titles, such as *Dr.* (*Mrs. Dr. Smith*), whether the title is the woman's own or her husband's, nor with the indication of an academic degree (*Mrs. John Smith, Ph.D.*).

Mr. should never be self-applied, as by some men in identifying themselves when they answer the telephone, for example. An exception is generally considered allowable for teachers addressing their pupils in elementary and secondary schools. *Mr.* is a proper designation for any member of the Protestant clergy, and has the advantage of sidestepping the difficulties in the use of *Reverend* (which see). *Mr.* is sometimes affixed to titles to create a formal term of address: *Mr. President, Mr. Secretary*.

Ms.   This designation, intended to conceal a woman's marital status, broke upon the scene in the early 1970s with the resurgence of feminism known as the women's movement. The argument for it ran that whether a woman is married is a private matter, and that there is no more occasion to advertise her marital status by the way she is addressed than there is to advertise a man's, and of course *Mr.* is noncommittal. The argument is irrefutable, and numerous publications, particularly newspapers, seized upon *Ms.*, in part perhaps to prevent charges of male chauvinism and in part to placate the strident feminists among their readers. The usual follies and excesses that accompany fads soon made their appearance in the form of such things as *Mr. and Ms. Smith, Ms. Henry Jones* and the use of *Ms.* with mention of the full name (*Ms. Marjorie Jones*) to indicate, the writer said, "my status—female"—which was already unmistakably indicated by her first name.

An unexpected development occurred when a number of newspapers, having noticed that the designation was not being received with universal enthusiasm, conducted polls among their women readers and discovered that by sizeable majorities they did not like *Ms.* but instead preferred the traditional *Mrs.* and *Miss.* Those who preferred *Ms.* were usually activists in the women's movement, divorcees, and widows, classifications that were not mutually exclusive, nor did they constitute any substantial part of the papers' readerships. Many newspapers thereupon restricted the use of *Ms.* to women who specifically requested it. Then began a trend to refer to women, on second and subsequent mentions in news accounts, by their last names alone, as had been the practice of most papers for years in referring to men. (From time immemorial, *The New York Times* continues to use *Mr.* in second and subsequent references in the absence of any other title, and it also prescribes *Mrs.* and *Miss. Ms.* is outlawed except in quoted matter, letters to the editor, and discussions of the term itself. The *Times* may well be the only newspaper in the country that continues to use the ceremonious *Mr.*) Objections to *Ms.* came from subjects of stories on the society pages. No young woman whose betrothal or marriage is being announced cares to have doubt raised whether she has been previously married, which is what the use of *Ms.* inescapably does.

There was also a certain amount of lint-picking. Some critics said *Ms.* should not be followed by a period because it was not an abbreviation. To questions about how the designation should be pronounced, the answer was "Miz." Critics responded that this had long been a dialectal pronunciation of *Mrs.* in certain backwoods areas, and so the spoken version of *Ms.* did not solve the problem it was aimed at.

Incidentally, the origin of *Ms.* apparently had nothing to do with feminism. It appears to have first been used in salutations in correspondence when the marital status of the woman addressed was unknown or in doubt; its use was advised in Lois Hutchinson's *Standard Handbook for Secretaries* (1956) in these circumstances. It is still useful in this way, though *Miss* has always been correct in addressing a woman in a business letter or in connection with her occupation.

The founding of a feminist magazine entitled *Ms.* apparently did nothing to rescue the term from the difficulties that beset it and its consequent loss of popularity.

News stories in which everyone is referred to by his last name alone create a certain confusion; the use of *Miss* and *Mrs.* help the reader to keep the cast of characters straight. If two of them are man and wife, or possess the same last name, *Mrs., Miss* (or *Ms.*) seems unavoidable. See also *he, she,* etc.; *Feminism; Mr., Mrs., Miss.*

much. For *much* as an adverb wrongly joined to an adjective with a hyphen, see *almost. Much* cannot properly modify plurals: "The chairman said he agreed with much of Burns' remarks''; ''Much, if not all, of these developments were meaningless.'' *many* or *most*.

muchly. The form is superfluous; *much*. The judgment is more or less substantiated by the fact that American Heritage and Random House do not include the term and Webster describes it as now not often in formal use, indicating that, as Fowler says, it is usually facetious. Harper rejects it.

mucous, mucus. The first is the adjective, the second the noun: *a secretion of mucus; the mucous membranes.*

multi-. Solid as a prefix: *multipolar, multimotor, multimillionaire,* etc.

munch. A journalistic stereotype that regularly displaces *eat, chew,* etc. *Munch,* the dictionaries agree, means to eat with a crunching sound, and its overuse in news publications can be traced to the journalistic straining for effect, regardless of appropriateness. The ultimate may have been reached by the newsmagazine that described someone as munching soup.

music, musical. See *-ic, -ical.*

music critic. See *-ic, -ical.*

musical, musical comedy. See *operetta,* etc.

music hath charms . . . See *Misquotation.*

Muslim. See *Mohammed, Mohammedan,* etc.

must. Two critics describe *must* as standard as both noun and adjective: ''Aid to education is a must on the administration's legislative program''; ''The lawmakers have their own idea of must legislation.'' Fowler regards the term as colloquial, and says that it sometimes should still be enclosed in apologetic quotation marks; two critics consider this unnecessary. Random House does not give this sense. Webster considers it standard; this is the consensus. American Heritage considers the noun standard, the adjective informal.

must needs. See *needs must.*

mutual. The term has occasioned much hairsplitting. Precisians insist (or used to) that it must be restricted to the idea of reciprocity; that is, to the relation of two or more persons to *each other.* Thus they may have a mutual admiration, but not a mutual friend. *Mutual friend* is considered correct; no doubt the title of Dickens' novel had much to do with encouraging its acceptance. The reason given is that *common,* which ordinarily would be the precise word here, is capable of being misunderstood in the sense *commonplace, ordinary.* Three critics and American

Heritage insist, however, that in describing such things as a shared interest, the expression should be *common*, not *mutual*. Three others accept *mutual* where *common* would be regarded as strictly correct. Random House says *mutual* is open to criticism though commonly used to describe what does not involve an exchange but rather a relation to a third person or thing; Webster recognizes *a mutual hobby* and similar uses. The consensus thinly accepts *mutual* where *common* (*mutual interest*) would formerly have been insisted on.

Mutual is often used redundantly with words like *cooperation, each other, both, friendship.*

my dear. In salutations, see *dear.*

my, mine. Evans and Fowler contradict each other about the correct form in such constructions as "my and her cars"; Evans says it should be *mine*, Fowler that it should be *my*. Since this construction is now quaint and little used, the point is more or less academic. Logic and consistency favor Fowler's opinion, however.

myself. The disagreements over the use of this form revolve around whether it is acceptable when *I* or *me* will serve. (The same reasoning applies to other reflexives, *himself, herself, yourself, yourselves, itself, ourselves, themselves.*) There is no argument about the strictly reflexive use, when *myself* is an intensive referring to *I* as subject: "I did it myself"; "I hurt myself"; "I myself take the responsibility." In general, three critics and American Heritage object to *myself* in a compound subject in place of *I* ("Myself and my wife will be present"); two others and Webster approve (Evans calls this usage old-fashioned and describes it as criticized; Random House does not specifically deal with it). There is no consensus here but rather a 4–3 split. As part of a compound object of a verb or as the object of a preposition ("My income supports my wife and myself"; "The honor was accorded to the mayor and myself"), three critics and Webster approve, but two others, American Heritage, and Random House disapprove. Random House disapproves of *myself* where *me* is normally called for, as when *myself* occurs as a single object: "He gave it to myself." Evans also criticizes this by implication. Evans and Webster specifically approve of *myself* in comparisons after *than* or *as:* "He is as tall as myself." The conclusion is that, in general, opinion is evenly divided on what have formerly been regarded as wrong uses of *myself*. In instances like this it is safe to assume that the criticized uses are standard or will soon be so. Meanwhile, perhaps the best advice is: don't use *myself* where *me* or *I* will fit, and follow the corresponding practice with other pronouns. See *Reflexives*.

N

naïf, naïve, naïveté, naivety. Three critics favor *naive* over the French original *naif,* with the difference that one prefers *naïve,* though recognizing that the word is often printed without the dieresis. Random House and Webster both indicate that the form with the dieresis predominates. But American Heritage gives *naive* as predominant; this is observably correct. All three critics agree that *naïvete* (retaining both dieresis and acute accent) predominates over the Anglicized *naivety,* a conclusion in which dictionaries concur except for American Heritage, which gives *naiveté* (accent, but no dieresis).

naked. See *nude, naked.*

Names of People. Flesch objects to the use of commonplace names like Smith and Jones when it is desired to conceal identity; more interest is aroused, he says, by using "natural-sounding fictitious names" like *Agnes Gentry,* or first names with the initials of the last names, or first names alone, while explaining that they are fictitious.

Names of people should be given in the form they use themselves: Richard Harding Davis (not *Richard H. Davis*); John D. Rockefeller (not *John Davison Rockefeller*), Norman Vincent Peale (not *N. V. Peale*). Departing from the familiar form is inexcusable and only causes confusion. See also *Abbreviations; he, she, 2; Initials; Reference.*

nameplate. See *masthead.*

naphtha. Often misspelled *naptha.*

narcotic, -ics. See *-ic, -ics.*

national. A national is a person belonging to a country or nation and the word should no more be capitalized than *citizen* or *countryman.*

nature. Widely criticized as roundabound and superfluous as used in locutions like *comment of an adverse nature (adverse comment), a mixture of a cloudy nature (a cloudy mixture), the neighborhood is of a restricted nature (is restricted).* See also *case; character.*

258

naught. Regarded as quaint or bookish for *nothing* or *zero*.

nauseated, nauseous. Three critics and American Heritage hold that the original difference in meaning should be maintained; that *nauseated* means *suffering from nausea*, and that *nauseous* means *causing nausea*. Thus sufferers from seasickness are *nauseated;* the illness itself is *nauseous*. Random House, however, allows *nauseous* in the sense *nauseated* as informal, and Webster gives *affected with* or *inclined to nausea* for *nauseous*. The consensus favors the distinction. Confusion of these terms is a conspicuous mark of a shaky grasp of language. Another reason for preserving the distinction is that neglect of it often results in unconscious humor: "I am nauscous" means, to the discerning, "I cause nausea."

naval, navel. Often confused; *naval* pertains to *navy; navel* is the depression in the belly where the umbilical cord was attached. The orange is *navel*, owing to its having a similar depression.

near. An adjective as well as an adverb, as illustrated by the familiar though fuzzy expression *near future*, and others like *near relative, near thing*, and even the now happily evaporated *near beer*. Expressions like *near-riot, near-holocaust, near-disaster* were probably encouraged by the practice in World War II of referring to a *near-miss* in a bombing attack. There is no consistency among authorities in hyphening these expressions, and it seems useless to discuss this point, though Fowler attempts a distinction that leads him to the opposite of what is the general practice in America (hyphening). For the form in a specific case, the reader is referred to a dictionary. Such expressions are standard.

near future. See *future*.

nearly. See *almost; -ly*.

nee. Most authorities insist on the sense corresponding to the derivation: *born*, and applicable only to a married woman to indicate her maiden name: *Susan Warfield, nee Smith*. (There is a masculine form, *ne*, but it is rarely used.) Webster, however, gives four examples of *nee* followed by a given name instead of a surname alone, which is regarded as the strictly correct traditional use, including a curious instance, "nee Miss Carol Milford," quoted from Sinclair Lewis. It goes farther, giving *formerly* as an extended meaning and describing *nee* as applicable to "a group (the Milwaukee Braves, nee the Boston Braves), a place (Kernville, nee Whiskey Flat—Roy Milholland), or thing (sonata for flute, oboe, and basso continuo nee sonata for violin and harpsichord—P. H. Lang)." Some may feel these extensions to be facetious, but Webster attaches no label to them, which means they are considered standard. And there can be no doubt that *nee* is often used in these ways. Nonetheless, the consensus overwhelmingly favors the narrow application given at the beginning of this entry.

needless to say. The phrase should usually be omitted, but like *goes without say-ing* and *of course* (which see), it is a conventional device for conceding that the reader may have drawn the conclusion or acquired the information that follows, and it is an escape hatch from giving an impression of pomposity or didacticism. There is no consensus here, but the writer would do well to think twice before using the phrase.

need must, must needs. Regarded as archaic constructions by Evans and Flesch (''He must needs find himself''). Fowler says they are now restricted to ironical or contemptuous expression.

negative, affirmative. See *affirmative, negative.*

Negatives. Reversal of sense often occurs as the result of inattention by the writer. Two examples once appeared in a single issue of *The New Yorker* in the quotations of lapses from newspapers that it uses to fill out columns: ''And quite suddenly this young pianist of tired mien is immersed in the business of producing sounds of such high-voltage individuality as to quickly dispel any notions that the evening would be anything but routine.'' The writer apparently was carried away by his determination to produce an effect. Perhaps haste prevented a critical second reading before the words were committed to print. Obviously, he meant ''dispel any notions that the evening would be routine.'' The other example: ''Not even a blizzard prevented friends of the former ambassador and his wife from missing their cocktail party yesterday in honor of a former Washingtonian here from London on a holiday visit.'' *prevented . . . from attending* or *was enough to make friends . . . miss.* Involved construction probably helped to lead the writers astray in both instances. See also *Double Negative.*

negotiate. Narrowly rejected by American Heritage in the sense *get over* or *through* (*negotiated the heavy traffic*); considered standard by Random House and Webster.

Negress. Unquestionably derogatory; seldom seen any longer.

Negro. *Black* is now considered preferable, and predominates, in references to the Negro race, among whom it is generally favored. Some black objectors to *Negro* consider it disparaging. *Negro* is generally capitalized, but *black* (like other colors designating race, *white, red, yellow*) is not.

(in the) neighborhood of. *In the neighborhood of* for *about* is considered ob-jectionable (as pretentious and redundant). Evans considers it standard but ''awkward, vague, and unnecessary.''

neither. One critic and Webster agree that as a pronoun, *neither* may take a plural verb if a prepositional phrase intervenes, as in ''Neither of them (come, comes) regularly.'' Fowler calls the plural here an error, though he acknowledges that it is often seen, and Random House gives only an example with a singular verb. Two critics and American Heritage also consider the plural wrong. Opinion on this usage thus favors the singular.

Two critics hold that *neither* as a pronoun may refer to more than one: "Hope, faith, charity, neither were evident," and thus, as here, may take a plural verb. Two critics and American Heritage say that *neither* may refer only to one of two alternatives. Webster cites *neither of three,* and thus opinion is divided.

One critic, Random House, and Webster say that *neither* may be followed by *or* and not necessarily by *nor;* three critics and American Heritage consider *or* wrong; Evans curiously regards *neither . . . or* as archaic. The consensus narrowly favors *neither . . . nor* over *neither . . . or.* See also *either.* For *neither* with *they, their, them,* see *anybody, anyone; everybody, everyone.*

neither . . . nor. See *neither; either 3.*

neophyte. Discouraged where *beginner* (or, as an adjective, *new* or *novice*) will do.

nerve-racking (wracking). See *rack, wrack.*

new innovation. Redundant for *innovation.*

new record. See *record.*

news. Despite occasional perverse criticisms, the word is singular: "The news *is* good."

newsman. Though sometimes criticized as illegitimate, the term is standard.

Newspaper Names. Often given inaccurately, because some newspapers incorporate the names of their cities in their own names and some do not. Forms like the New York *Times* and the Washington *Post* are wrong. (Whether quotation marks or italics are used depends on the style of the publication in which the reference appears.) The correct forms are *The New York Times* and *The Washington Post.* On the other hand, it's the Baltimore *Sun;* the name of the paper is *The Sun.* The same principle applies to the name of any newspaper.

nice. The puristic injunction, now less heard than a generation ago, is that *nice* should be reserved for the senses *exacting, precise* (*a nice sense of balance*) or *decorous* (*a nice girl*) and should be avoided in the greatly predominant sense *agreeable* (*a nice day; a nice compliment*). The Concise Oxford Dictionary labels the sense *agreeable* colloquial, and Fowler, in a complaint reproduced from the original edition of 1926, counsels avoidance of it. The indications are, however, that these are British scruples, which have no meaning in America. Most American authorities omit any mention of *nice,* which may be taken as indicating they consider the issue settled; two critics acknowledge that the term is used overwhelmingly in the sense *agreeable,* which they recognize as standard; the context indicates whether some other sense is intended. Both Random House and Webster also give the sense *agreeable* as standard; this is the unanimous view of American authorities.

nicely. For *satisfactorily* (*the suit fits nicely*), approved by American Heritage and considered standard by Webster; Random House does not give a specific definition.

nicety. Preserves a specialized sense of *nice,* and does not mean something pleasant or agreeable. In general, a nicety is a detail or a minute distinction, as in "The niceties of formal etiquette are seldom observed today."

nickel. The form *nickle,* which originated as a misspelling and became common, is recognized by Webster for the coin but not for the metal (for which the coin was named). American Heritage and Random House do not recognize it; the consensus is that *nickle* is a misspelling.

Nicknames. The prevalent practice today is to introduce a nickname in parentheses, rather than enclose it in quotation marks: *Meyer* (*Mike*) *Berger.* The use of nicknames in print to refer to people who are not widely and publicly known by them may be regarded as patronizing or unduly familiar; it is avoided by carefully edited publications.

nigger. Contemptuous and seldom seen in print except in direct quotations and fiction intended to reproduce the speech of people who use the term.

Nip. See *Jap, Japanese.*

nobody, no one. For the agreement of verbs with these and other pronouns, see *anybody, anyone; everybody, every one.*

nod. Probably the two most familiar gestures by which verbal meaning is conveyed are the nod and shaking the head. Yet there are writers who evidently do not know the difference and write things like "He would nod his head 'no.' " Nodding is moving the head up and down, and always means "yes," unless the nodder is nodding as a prelude to falling asleep, in which event it means nothing. *Shake his head* is what the writer of the example meant: rotating the head from side to side, a gesture whose meaning is *no.*

   Nod, in addition, has taken on a meaning that seems to be peculiar to journalism and one that the dictionaries have overlooked, perhaps on purpose. Its particular habitat is *Newsweek,* where readers find sentences like "With a nod to the chairman, he suggested another meeting." This is not the nod that indicates assent, but one that denotes recognition, acknowledgment, or deference. It is hard to tell exactly what, because the meaning must be deduced from the context. No such definition is to be found in dictionaries.

no exception. To particularize by describing something as no exception to a stated generality is to be trite: "The employees were underpaid, and he was no exception."

nohow. The word has a standard sense, *not, in no way; could nohow start the car.* Evans warns against its use in a double negative as ungrammatical (*couldn't nohow*) and Random House calls the term dialectal but gives only a sentence with a double negative as an example of use. The consensus is that *nohow* has a standard use. But it so often occurs in a double negative that it is likely to be regarded as substandard by most readers in any context.

noisome. Sometimes confused with *noisy; noisome* means *disgusting, foul-smelling,* etc.

non-. Solid as a prefix: *nonadhesive, noncommittal, nondefining,* etc. Fowler objects to the random creation of negative forms by affixing *non-* to positives, as in *nonessential,* when *inessential* is already available; and Flesch objects to *non-* forms on principle as "ugly" a judgment that seems quixotic.

noncontroversial issue. A pertinent observation for this age of controversy was made by Robert M. Hutchins in *Look:* "An issue is a point on which the parties take different positions. A noncontroversial issue, therefore, is as impossible as a round square. All issues are controversial; if they were not, they would not be issues." By the same token, the frequent *controversial issue* is redundant. See also *controversial.*

noncooperative. See *cooperate,* etc.

no-no. The slang expression for something forbidden (evidently adopted from babytalk) is properly given in this form, not "a no, no."

Nonrestrictive Modifiers. See *Restrictive and Nonrestrictive Clauses.*

Nonstandard. See *Standard.*

no one. With *they, their, them,* see *anybody, anyone.*

noon luncheon. Redundant to the extent that luncheons are usually held at midday.

noplace. Considered standard for *nowhere* by Evans and Webster and colloquial by Bryant; Random House labels it informal (*We argued but got noplace*). Follett gives only *no place,* and calls it a barbarism. The consensus is that it is standard.

nor. See *neither 2; or, nor.*

Nordic. See *Scandinavia.*

normalcy. Authorities agree that President Warren G. Harding has been unjustly derided as having invented this expression. *Normalcy* is (and was, long before Harding) a standard equivalent of *normality,* i.e., *the state of being normal.* Though Fowler looks down his nose at the word and the Concise Oxford Dictionary calls it irregularly formed, both Random House and Webster consider it standard, making for a solid consensus. The American Heritage panel rejects it, however, by 59 percent, although the editors describe it as widely employed in standard usage.

no sooner. Followed by *than,* not *when:* "*No sooner* had the whistle blown *than* the workmen thronged out of the factory."

nostalgia, nostalgic. While *nostalgia* originally meant *severe homesickness,* two critics are willing to accept the popular and extended senses of longing or yearning for the past or for a return to some place. Evans is suspicious of those newer meanings. They are extremely popular, however—much more so than the original sense—and Random House, American Heritage, and Webster accept them without question. The consensus thus solidly favors them.

no such. See *such.*

not. *Not* is sometimes inadvertently introduced into sentences whose meaning is then reversed: "Current discussions cannot be oversimplified merely by referring to the administration as anti-business." The intended meaning was *can be oversimplified.* Contrasts beginning with *not* should be set off by a comma: "The agent of belligerency was the regime not the people"; "He emphasized that his subject was tax avoidance not evasion." *regime, not; avoidance, not.* For similar errors, see *underestimate; minimize; Double Negative; Negatives; not un-.*

not about to. An odd colloquialism with the sense *not going to.* It should be avoided in writing, for it also has the literal sense *not on the verge of:* "The secretary said he isn't about to make another trip to press for an agreement." Ambiguous, as Harper comments; the desired meaning was *does not intend to,* but the statement might have been understood as saying the secretary would not make a trip soon. The American Heritage panel was reported in an introductory essay as rejecting the expression, but this judgment was not included in the lexicon.

not all, all . . . not. The problem of placement is similar to that of *only* (see *only, not only*). Fowler, who usually insists on exactitude and no nonsense, takes a liberal view in both instances, which may only illustrate that even oracles have their foibles. Perhaps this was his way of paying off some early teacher for what he considered pedantry. Those who wince at the misplacement of *only* wince oftenest, probably, at "All is not gold that glitters" (correctly, *glisters,* as Fowler quoted it, but no one says that any more). We all know, of course, what is meant; not, as might be perversely construed, that everything which glitters is not gold, but *"Not all* that glitters is gold."

A more modern example, outside the precincts of Shakespeare: "Every story with an unusual feature does not call for a humorous headline." We all know here, too, what is meant: *"Not every* story with an unusual feature . . ." Fowler held it not worthwhile to make any great point of this misplacement. Four authorities agree with him, while leaving the door open for more precision in word-order. Fowler predicted that *all . . . not* for *not . . . all* would pass away in time. But the time is not yet. Careful writers put *not* where it belongs, as Follett and American Heritage recommend.

not all that. See *all that.*

not . . . but. This construction, meaning *only* and followed by a number, as in "I did not notice but three umbrellas," is described by Bryant as standard but occurring mainly in speech, and by Webster as often considered substandard. It is, after all, a double negative.

note. Such expressions as *strike a happy* (or *sour*) *note* pass for humor or cleverness among many when they are writing about a subject that has some connection with music, no matter how remote or inappropriate. Obvious straining for effect kills the effect. See also *Attribution* for use of *note* as a verb.

not . . . not. See *not un-.*

not only . . . but also. See *only.*

not, repeat not. "Getting to the ballet on a rainy Wednesday night was not, repeat not, half the fun." This mannerism, evidently picked up from the practice to emphasize the negative in military radio communications, is foolish in ordinary contexts.

not so . . . as. See *as . . . as,* etc.

not (so, as) much . . . as. The correct form; incorrectly, *not* (so, as) *much . . . but:* "Not so much sinning *as* sinned against."

not that. Se *all that.*

not too. In the popular and literal sense *not very* ("She testified that her husband was restless and did not like to stay put too long"), generally disapproved because it is imprecise and open to misconstruction as meaning *not more than enough.* For example, the statement "Elsewhere, there was not too much resistance to the price-support program'' may be understood as meaning that the resistance was inconsiderable (as intended) or that it was not excessive. Fowler calls this construction illogical but is nevertheless indulgent of it, an attitude perhaps explained by the reasonable suspicion that *not too*, like *not that*, originated in Britain. Fowler and Harper are its only defenders. *Not too* is a new turn of phrase, having displaced *not very*, which had the advantage of being unambiguous. For that matter, neither *too* nor *very* is necessary to convey the intended meaning. Somehow, the tendency to water down direct, explicit statement has triumphed again.

notorious. Means *well known for unfavorable reasons* (*a notorious prostitute; a notorious deadbeat*). Not to be confused, as it sometimes is, with *famous, noted,* or *notable.* Similarly, *notoriety* should not displace *notability, celebrity,* or *notice.* A publication for professors once described one of their number as a modest fellow who did not seek notoriety. The adverse implication of *notorious,* it should be remembered, applies only to people; Webster gives *well* or *commonly known* as one sense, but the examples are impersonal: *Iron is a notorious conductor of heat; a notorious fact.* Other dictionaries concur in this distinction.

not un-. The deliberate creation of a positive, albeit a weak one, by a double negative on this pattern ("We were not unaccustomed to doing this"; "The pleasure was not unexpected") is grudgingly accepted by two critics only in what they consider appropriate contexts, i.e., those in which understatement is called for. Both regard it as overworked and recommend avoiding it in general; one critic calls it pompous. To this it might be added that it creates a momentary puzzle for the reader, who is then put to the task of deducing the intended meaning. A similar effect is created by a sentence like "I would not be annoyed if they did not agree with me," which must be untangled to "I would not be annoyed if they disagreed with me." American Heritage considers the construction generally accepted. See also *Double Negative; Negatives.*

Nouns of Address. See *Comma 7.*

Novelty Hunting. See *Fad Words.*

now. The word has become popular as an adjective in teenage argot (*the now generation, a now fashion*). Neither Random House nor American Heritage recognizes this usage but Webster does; its examples, however, seem to come from an earlier time: *the now judge; the now king.* It appears from this that the current vogue for *now* is a revival and modification of an older usage. The older *now* meant *present;* the new one means fashionable, up-to-date. The new sense is not found in careful writing. In conventional usage, the hyphen is superfluous in "the now-bankrupt financier" and *now* is no longer set off by commas: "Once there were ten applicants; now(,) there are eight."

nowheres. Considered standard by Random House, peculiar to speech by Evans, and dialectal by another critic and Webster. The consensus is that it is not standard in writing.

nth. Fowler is very positive in asserting that the term, as used in such expressions as *to the nth degree,* indicates only an unknown quantity of any size, and he denounces its use in the sense *to the utmost* or *infinitely.* Dictionaries, however, recognize these senses without qualification.

nubile. Originally the term meant only *suitable for marriage,* but the sense that now predominates is that given by Webster as "physically suited for or desirous of sexual relationship." Random House does not recognize this meaning, but American Heritage says the word has a suggestion of sexuality.

nude, naked. As applied to people, *nude* is at the same time something of a euphemism and, paradoxically, more suggestive than *naked.* This connotation may arise from the reader's sensing that *nude* has been chosen to sidestep the honest starkness of *naked.* In a poem entitled "The Naked and the Nude," which appeared Feb. 27, 1957, in *The New Yorker,* Robert Graves wrote: "For me, the naked and the nude stand as wide apart / As love from lies, or truth from art."

number. Evans regards the term as applied to a song (*She performed a couple of numbers*) as substandard, but it is recognized as standard by Random House and Webster.

With rare exceptions, when preceded by *a, number* is plural: *a number were waiting.* Preceded by *the,* it is singular: *the number of voters was diminishing.*

For *number* in the grammatical sense see *Collective Nouns; Subject-Verb Agreement; Plural and Singular.*

Number in Addition. Singular and plural verbs are equally frequent in such constructions as "Two and two is (are) four."

Numbers. 1. Figures vs. words. Whether numbers should be spelled out or given in figures is a matter primarily of style, that is to say, of arbitrary choice between practices that are both correct. Newspapers generally follow the rule of ten, under which the numbers one through nine are spelled out and those larger are given in figures. Exceptions are usually specified, however, such as time of day, ages, vote totals, and most units of measurement, among others. Evans, following a style used in editing books, recommends that figures be used for any number that cannot be expressed in two words (*sixty-eight;* but *101*); Flesch considers it pompous to spell out any number. The avoidance of figures in printed matter leads one to suspect that they are somehow considered indecent. Repetition of numbers and words—"He gave six (6) reasons"—is absurd except in legal documents, where this practice may be necessary.

2. Figure at beginning of a sentence. It is not the usual practice to begin a sentence with a figure ("2,000 troops were surrounded") although the question

"why not?" is raised from time to time without calling forth any answer. See also *there*.

3. Consistency. Even though strict observance of the rules may require it, both a figure and a spelled-out number should not appear in the same sentence: "Six of the statues were damaged, but the other 12 were intact." *other twelve*. This principle is generally followed by newspapers, which also usually call for handling large figures in such forms as *22 million, $9 billion* to enhance readability.

4. Separation. Figures standing next to each other should be separated: "The students totaled 2,456, 900 of whom were freshmen." *2,456, of whom 900* (to improve readability and prevent confusion).

5. Hyphenation. Hyphens are uniformly used for compound numbers (*sixty-eight*) and for fractions (*nine-tenths*).

6. Useless counting. Writers often seem obsessed with giving the reader small totals that he can perceive unaided: "They were joined by their *three* children, John, Ruth, and Mary"; "He was referring to Egypt and Saudi Arabia, *two* nations that control much of the strategic Red Sea coast line"; "Sports and music are his two hobbies." Delete the numbers.

7. Cardinals and ordinals. Cardinal numbers are the figures themselves: 2, 6, 12. Ordinals are the adjectival forms: *second (2nd), sixth (6th), twelfth (12th)*. Once again, the choice between the forms of ordinals, like the choice between figures and words, is a matter of individual preference, usually specified in the stylebooks of publications. The use of words is considered more formal and is probably prevalent.

See also *Collective Nouns; Prepositions 1; a, an* (with *hundred, thousand*, etc.); *Roman Numerals; Figures; Variation.*

numerous. The word is an adjective and may not be used as a pronoun: "Numerous errors defaced the typescript" but not "Numerous of the errors were misspellings." This judgment is borne out by dictionaries. In the second example the word should be *many*.

O

O, oh. Several authorities make the distinction that *O* is used in invocations: "O Lord, we beg thy forgiveness" and *oh* otherwise, as in ordinary exclamations: "Oh, you forgot the dessert!" Neither Random House nor Webster recognizes this distinction; American Heritage does, but allows *oh* for exclamations and describes it as more independent, so that it can stand alone. Fowler cites a volume in which *O* is used uniformly. The distinction is not consistently observed; indications are that the forms are becoming interchangeable.

objective. The displacement of *object* by *objective* is called pretentious by three critics, one of whom prefers *aim*. In general, the object is the purpose, the objective (as in military connections) is the goal. "The objective was to tell the people about the record of Congress" *object*. The simplest advice is to use *object* when possible.

objet d'art. Often erroneously given *object d'art*.

obligate, oblige. *Obligate* should not be used to acknowledge a favor; the term should be *oblige* ("I am obliged to him for his help"). Not *obligated*, which is a narrower term, often found in legal contexts, and indicating the imposition of a duty: "The decision obligated him to remove the fence." On these points three critics and American Heritage agree. Random House and Webster, however, regard the terms as synonyms; the consensus narrowly favors the distinction.

obliqueness, obliquity. Two critics hold that the first usually applies to the physical ("the obliqueness of the angle") and the second to the abstract ("We were surprised by the obliquity of his viewpoint") or divergence from moral conduct, etc. In general, Random House and Webster corroborate this view, though it seems to be contradicted by the expression *obliquity of the ecliptic,* in which the sense is clearly physical.

oblivious. Two critics insist that the term should be restricted to its original sense, *forgetful;* two others and American Heritage are willing to accept the meanings *unaware, heedless, unconscious,* or whatever. Bernstein and Fowler agree, however, that it is best to use the word precisely suited to the occasion: *forgetful, unaware, unconscious,* etc. Dictionaries accept the extended senses, which means the consensus heavily favors them. In the sense *forgetful, oblivious* takes *of;* in other senses, it may take either *of* or *to.*

Obscenity. See *Vulgarity.*

observance, observation. The first is the word for following, conforming to, or marking a religious rite, holiday, etc.: "The bank was closed for observance (not *observation*) of Veterans Day." *Observation* is *looking, watching, noticing:* "The candidates were under observation." Random House follows this principle; Webster allows *observation* for *observance.* American Heritage gives the converse. The consensus favors the distinction.

obsolete. As a verb ("Technology will obsolete equipment at an ever-increasing rate") admitted by both Webster and Random House, but still seems objectionable. American Heritage does not list it, giving only the adjective. The usage seems to have a military origin, which will set many against it, just as origins in bureaucratic prose prompt widespread prejudice against many expressions.

obtain. Considered pretentious when *get* will do. See also *get.*

obtrusive, -ly. Sometimes misspelled *obstrusive, -ly.*

obviate. The word means *make unnecessary* ("His resignation obviated his dismissal"), but it is often misused in the sense *remove* ("The difficulties were obviated"). Dictionaries support this distinction.

occasion. Often misspelled *occassion.*

Occupational Titles. See *False Titles.*

occur, take place. Two critics and American Heritage agree, though other dictionaries do not make the distinction, that what occurs is accidental and unforeseen ("The accident occurred in the rain") and that what takes place is planned or arranged ("The coronation will take place May 12"). *Occurrence* is sometimes misspelled *occurrance.*

octopus, octopi. Fowler, whose decisions are often based on Latin or Greek derivations, flatly considers *octopi* a wrong form for the plural: two other critics, however, say it is nevertheless established and standard. Dictionaries recognize it, together with *octopuses,* which seems less affected.

oculist, etc. Although the word is technically equivalent to *ophthalmologist* as designating an M.D. whose specialty is the eye, a shadow, apparently acquired through misuse at one time, hangs over it, and it is avoided by the medical profession. Attention is called to the distinctions between these terms and *optometrist,* for one who is licensed to prescribe glasses but is not an M.D., and *optician,* the term for the technician who makes glasses. An optometrist possesses the degree O.D. (doctor of optometry), and while optometrists are qualified to use the title *doctor,* not all of them do. In some states they must specify, if they use the title, that they are O.D.s.

-odd. Hyphenated as a suffix: *thirty-odd,* etc. Redundant with *some:* "Some thirty-odd soldiers." Use one or the other. See also *some, -odd.*

oe, e. See *ae, e.*

of. The phrase designating a person's town of residence (*George Smith, of Poughkeepsie, said*) should ordinarily be set off by commas because it is a nonrestrictive or free modifier. An exception to this would be the rare occasion when it would be necessary to distinguish between two persons of the same name but having different places of residence, in which event the comma would not be used: *George Smith of Poughkeepsie* as distinguished from *George Smith of New York.* See *Prepositions; Comma; all of; off of; Possessives 3.*

of a. Often erroneous for *a:* "This is as insulting of a proposition as I have ever heard." *a*

of any, of anyone. See *than any, than anyone; Comparison 1.*

of between, of from, etc. Prepositions are often doubled with numbers indicating a range: "An appropriation of from six to eight million dollars." *of six to eight.* "A rise in temperature of between three and five degrees." *of three to five.*

of course. It is sometimes advisable to concede that the reader may already know what he is being told, lest the writer sound didactic; at the same time, the writer may not be able to risk omitting what he qualifies by *of course,* if it is essential to comprehension by those who do not know. Overly cautious writers tend to slip in *of course* by reflex action, as a kind of running apology. Sometimes it is attached to curious facts that only the rare reader could be expected to have at his fingertips; this is obsequious. Every *of course* should be weighed critically with a view to striking it out. This applies also to *as is well known, needless to say, as everyone knows,* and *it goes without saying;* the critic may object that if it goes without saying, why not let it go unsaid?

off. See *off of.*

off-, -off. Oftener solid than hyphenated as a prefix: *offhand, offset, offshoot, offshore,* etc. But *off-color, off-white, off-peak.* Solid as a suffix: *cutoff, sendoff, blastoff, writeoff.*

offense, offence. *Offence* is the British preference.

offhand, offhanded, offhandedly. The first, as both adjective and adverb, will do neatly for the other two, which are cumbersome forms, though correct.

office. As a verb, recognized only by Webster ("We were officed in an old barracks"); disapproved by Harper. The usage has the odor of gobbledygook about it.

officer. One critic objects to the application of this term to ordinary policemen (as distinguished from those holding a rank above patrolman): however, any policeman is an officer of the law. Evans adds that there is a tendency to reserve the term for those holding higher rank. American Heritage, Random House, and Webster do not recognize the distinction.

official, -ly. Overused in contexts where there is no occasion to think the action described could be unofficial, as for example the conduct of business by public bodies.

Officialese. See *Gobbledygook*.

offload. The word has gained currency in recent years as a synonym for *unload,* especially in the press, whose writers are all too eager to snap up something new and strange. Recent dictionaries recognize this usage. But *offload* has technical senses apart from *unload* that have to do with shipping, aircraft, and rocketry. They will not be gone into here on the assumption that the people who need them know how to use them. *Offload* seems unnecessary for *unload.*

off of. *Of* is superfluous with *off:* "He jumped off of the bridge." *off the bridge.* Bryant considers the usage informal.

of from. See *of between,* etc.

offspring. The word has been recognized as both singular and plural as long ago as the turn of the century, as evidenced by the Century Dictionary. Forming the plural by adding *s* is often considered a misuse, but *offsprings* is accepted as standard by both Random House and Webster.

often. An adverb, and thus erroneously joined to adjectives with a hyphen; *often-warring elements.*

oftener. Complaints are occasionally heard that *more often* is preferable. There is nothing to this. The choice should be governed by the rhythm of the sentence.

of the order of. See *order.*

of which. See *whose* vs. *of which.*

oh. See *O, oh.*

oh-oh. As the equivalent of the exclamation *oops!,* takes the form given; not *oh, oh.*

O.K. Much space has been given by various commentators to speculation on the origin of the expression, to which no attention will be given here. There are various forms: *O.K., okay, oke, okeh, okey,* among others. Although only one commentator expresses an opinion, it is easy to deduce from both books on usage and dictionaries that the form O.K. greatly predominates, though there is no basis for considering the others wrong. The consensus is that the expression is informal or colloquial, though Webster regards it as standard. The American Heritage panel accepts *O.K.* only as a noun ("His O.K. was necessary") and rejects it as a verb, adjective, or adverb.

This seems an indefensible inconsistency, and accords with neither Random House, Webster, nor general usage.

old. See *elderly; Ad Lingo*

old adage. Redundant for *adage.*

old cliché. "We cannot escape that old cliché, where there is love, there is hate." *Old cliché* is usually an unconscious redundancy, like *false illusion.* Clichés obviously get to be clichés by being old, or at least well-worn. It is arguable that there are old, less old, and perhaps even relatively new clichés, if the occasion arises to classify them in this way, which seldom happens. Then the qualifier would be allowable.

older. See *Comparison 2; Ad Lingo*

older, elder. See *elder,* etc.

old-fashioned. The form of the modifier (*an old-fashioned girl*); not, as sometime given, *old-fashion.* Webster gives *old-fashion* as archaic; the current use of it appears to be merely careless.

old friend. The delusion is widespread that *old* may mean only *aged* or *elderly;* thus the expression *old friend* is often given *"old" friend* to assure the reader that *of long standing* is meant and not *aged.* But the quotation marks are foolish; the expression would never be misread.

Old Guard. (The) Old Guard is a collective that cannot properly be pluralized as *Old Guards* in reference to individuals. *Members of the Old Guard.*

oldster. The term, which looks as if it might have been invented by *Time* magazine, is considered objectionable or derogatory by Evans and Flesch, but there is no hint of this in either Random House or Webster, which give it as standard; American Heritage considers it informal. Nor is it new; it appears (labeled *colloquial*) in the Century Dictionary, published in 1897.

-ology, -ologies. Two critics discourage the loose use (and coining) of terms with these endings. Follett explains that they are often erroneous, since the endings indicate a theory or system or science, and not the thing itself. Thus, for example, *methodology* is used when *method* is meant.

Olympian, Olympic. Evans and Fowler hold that the first relates to Olympus, including the sense *majestic* (or sometimes *pompous*), and the second relates to the games. The definitions in Random House accord with this, but Webster and American Heritage give both *Olympic* and *Olympian Games*. The latter form must be considered a rarity, however. Opinion is unanimous that only *olympian* is used in the senses *majestic, lofty,* etc.

Omission. See *Ellipsis*.

on. More precise prepositions are increasingly displaced by *on,* as in these examples: "He can be reassured on one thing" (*about* or *of*); "The mayor was dismayed on the denial of the permit" (*at* or *by*); "We were waiting on him" (*for*); "Developments on Middle East problems dominated the session" (*in*); "Apathy marks the public's attitude on government" (*toward*); "The aim is to educate the public on the proper use of English" (*in*). Let's start now, if it's not too late. Bernstein traces such misuses to the all-purpose use of *on* in newspaper headlines, but it seems likely that other causes are also at work here, considering their prevalence.

on-. Solid as a prefix: *oncoming, onlooker, onrush,* etc.

on behalf. See *behalf*.

on, in. See *in, on*.

on, upon. The consensus on the choice between these words, which have no clearly defined difference in meaning, is to use *on* whenever possible. American Heritage says they are often interchangeable. Idiom, however, sometimes demands *upon: put upon* (in the sense *imposed on*).

on account of. For *because,* a regional spoken colloquialism, not found in writing except what represents speech.

once. Often mistakenly joined to adjectives with a hyphen: *a once-quaint area.* For an explanation, see *-ly*.

one. A coy displacement of forms of *I,* as used by a music critic: "This program brought conviction that Mozart is one's favorite composer." Which one's? Anyone's, the reader might hastily deduce, for he is generally on the run, and likely to seize upon the first sense that suggests itself. But he would soon decide it is unlikely that the critic was suggesting Mozart is the favorite composer of everyone. And so he would decide that the critic really meant "*my* favorite composer," but strained to avoid the personal pronoun. Such excessive and confusing modesty is unlikely to win the reader's regard; a forthright *I, my, me* is surely preferable in the expression of personal opinions. "This artist is, one suspects, headed for international recognition." The suspicion was the critic's, but by saying *one* instead of *I* he misleadingly, if unintentionally, suggested it was more widely held. If there were grounds for expressing a consensus, it should have been done unmistakably: "It is generally agreed that this artist is headed for international recognition." The use of *one* for *I*, then, has three strikes against it: false modesty, quaintness, and ambiguity. *One* should be used, if at all, as an indefinite pronoun meaning *someone* or *anyone* or *a person: One does one's duty*. Fowler logically enough points out that the impersonal *one* takes *one's* and the *one* used in place of *I* takes *his:* "One saw his hat on the table." This usage is uncommon in America. *One* as a noun takes *a,* not *an:* "Such a (not *an*) one is readily available." *An* is archaic. See also *Editorial We; you.*

-one. A distinction should be made between the pronouns *anyone, everyone, someone,* and the adjective-pronoun phrases *any one, every one, some one:* "Anyone can do that"; "Take any one of the pieces"; "Everyone knew the story"; "They walked off with every one of the awards"; "Someone is on the phone"; "Some one of the books will have the answer." Usually the indefinite pronouns refer to people, the phrases to things, but not invariably.

one and the same. The phrase is losing its emphasis through overuse.

one another. See *each other.*

one of the (few, etc.) . . . if not. The sentence "California is one of the few, if not the only, states subsidizing its college students" illustrates a common snare; *states* does not go with *only.* Rearrangement in the pattern "California is one of the few states subsidizing its college students, if not the only one" (moving *if not* to the end) is recommended.

one of those who, etc. Doubt about the correct number of the verb often arises with such sentences as "I am one of those who hope (*hopes?*) for a peaceful settlement." Four critics and the American Heritage panel hold that the verb should be plural (*hope*) to agree with *those.* Four others say that although the plural is strictly correct, the singular is often used and is unexceptionable. Opinion is thus divided.

oneself, one's self. Both forms are standard, but the second seems clumsy.

one that is. Generally excessive: "The situation is one that is ripe for controversy." *The situation is ripe.*

on line. When *The New York Times* said, "The reporter got on line and grabbed the premier's hand" some readers were ready to decide they had been wrong all their lives in thinking the expression is *in line,* because they were brought up to believe that if you see it in *The Times* it's right. They probably had seen *on line* here and there, especially in *Newsweek,* but dismissed it as a typographical error. But Bryant tells us that *on line* is almost universal in all types of speech in New York City and the Hudson Valley. *In line* is found, she continues, in all other areas and generally in formal written English. New Yorkers have a way of attempting to foist their provincialisms on the rest of us. Will we resist in this case? *On line* calls to mind Christopher Robin in A. A. Milne's *When We Were Very Young.* Christopher, it will be remembered, carefully refrained from stepping on the lines in the sidewalk lest he become the quarry of bears whose natural prey standers-on-lines are. Perhaps some retribution awaits those who stand and write *on line.* American Heritage gives it as standard; neither Random House nor Webster includes it.

only. The problem here is placement, and it may be illustrated by the sentence "He only arrived a week ago." This arrangement is often criticized on the ground that *only* belongs before *a week ago* to convey the meaning intended, and that as it stands the sentence will be interpreted "None but he arrived . . ." or "He did nothing but arrive . . ." Two critics vehemently insist that the supposed misplacement of *only* represents the usual form of expression, and that it is fussy to insist that it be placed before the element it modifies. A sentence from the publication *Word Study,* "I hit him in the eye yesterday," illustrates that eight different meanings result from placing *only* in the eight possible positions. *Only* is allowable in some position other than before the element it modifies when misunderstanding is unlikely; in general precise placement is encouraged. Bryant reports that a study of magazines shows *only* to be precisely placed 86 percent of the time, and regards inexact placement as characteristic of speech rather than writing. Evans devotes much space to justifying the loose placement of *only* except when there is good reason to place it elsewhere, which seems somewhat ambiguous advice. American Heritage favors precise placement. About the most that can be said is that opinion is divided. There is general agreement, however, that *only* should be precisely placed if there is good reason for it (that is, avoidance of ambiguity), and there is no reason why anyone who chooses to be precise about it should not do so.

George Orwell, a highly self-critical writer, permitted himself to say, "Mr. Auden's brand of moralism is only possible if you are the kind of person who is always somewhere else when the trigger is pulled." Precisians would insist upon *possible only.*

Ambiguity seems more likely with loose placement of *not only . . . but also:* "The strike has not only created problems for the company in maintaining the goodwill of its customers but also of the public." *Customers* should be counterpoised to *public,* and the only way to do it is by writing "not only of its customers but also of the public." See *not all . . . all not*, which presents a similar problem.

Only for *except that* ("He would have bought the suit, only it cost too much") is rejected by American Heritage but considered standard by Random House and Webster.

only too. Discouraged as imprecise and overworked in such expressions as "only too glad," "only too willing," etc. See also *not too*.

on the basis of. Criticized by two authorities as a cumbersome and overused expression that can often be replaced by *on, by, after, because of.* "The change was made on the basis of expediency." *for. Based on* is often similarly open to criticism. Fowler points out that such expressions as *on a permanent basis* are overblown for *permanently*.

on the grounds that. See *ground, grounds*.

on the order of. See *order*.

on the part of. Usually excessive for *by, among:* "There is less studying on the part of high school students these days."

on to, onto. Four authorities call attention to the distinction between *onto* in the sense *to a position on* ("He climbed onto the table") and *on to* in such constructions as "We traveled on to San Francisco," in which *on* becomes part of a phrasal verb (*traveled on*).

onward, onwards. Only *onward* can serve as an adjective: *the onward thrust* (never *onwards* in this construction). *Onward* may also be an adverb (we pressed *onward*), but where there is a choice between the forms *onward* is preferred by two critics; Random House mistakenly gives *onwards* as an adjective, but Webster observes the distinction, which is also favored by the consensus.

operation. The fad of giving projects names like "Operation Breakthrough," which had its origin in World War II, is criticized by two authorities. At that time, military operations were so designated but with code names carefully chosen to give no inkling of what they referred to. "Operation Overlord," for example, was the designation for the Allied invasion of France. Since the war, military and other undertakings have been widely designated "Operation This" and "Operation That," usually with names intended to indicate their nature. The practice has grown tiresome, especially when writers resort to it casually: "The Legislature began Operation Adjournment this week."

operetta, light opera, musical, musical comedy. *Operetta* is now an old-fashioned word applied to an old-fashioned genre, for example, the works of Gilbert and Sullivan, and in America, those of Victor Herbert (*Sweethearts, The Red Mill, Babes in Toyland*), Rudolf Friml (*Robin Hood*), and others of that era. *Musical* *comedy* is applied to more modern works of the same kind (light music, spoken dialogue), such as Rodgers and Hammerstein's *South Pacific* and *Oklahoma!* and Lerner and Loewe's *My Fair Lady. Musical* is the clipped form of *musical comedy. Light opera* is a term sometimes applied to what has been identified here as operetta, but never to musical comedy.

ophthalmologist, optician, optometrist. See *oculist,* etc.

opine. Considered quaint or facetious. This is the consensus; although the two unabridged dictionaries regard it as standard, three of four current desk dictionaries designate it humorous.

opposite. See *reverse,* etc.

optician. See *oculist,* etc.

optimism, optimistic. Four authorities agree that the terms denote a hopeful outlook and that *optimism* or *optimistic* should not displace *hope* or *hopeful* in reference to specific instances, as in "She was optimistic about being admitted to college"; nor should *optimistic* displace *favorable* or *encouraging,* as in "He cited several optimistic factors." Random House, Webster, and American Heritage in general appear to support these views, though the first gives *an optimistic plan* and the second gives *an optimistic view.* The consensus favors the distinction. See also *pessimism,* etc.

optimum. Three critics protest against the loose use of the term as a synonym for *best;* it properly means *most favorable,* or *best under the circumstances.* Definitions in both unabridged dictionaries support this distinction. Thus "The optimum readability of a line of type depends upon the size of the type and the length of the line."

optometrist. See *oculist,* etc.

or, nor. Either *or* or *nor* may be used after a negative in such sentences as "They will not fish (or, nor) cut bait." But *nor* must be used if the negative in the introductory statement does not affect what follows the conjunction: "They refused to fish, nor would they cut bait." The difference here is that the negative (*refused*) does not affect the part of the sentence following *nor.* See also *neither 2; either; between; Subject-Verb Agreement.*

Or (like *and, but, nor*) may be used to begin a sentence. When this is done, it should not be set off by a comma: "Or (,) the tables may be turned." See also *and.*

-or, -our. When there is a choice between these endings, *-or* is American practice and *-our* British: *honor, honour.* Fowler points out that even in British usage there is no consistency since it calls for *horror, pallor, tremor,* not *horrour, pallour, tremour,* and concludes in general that there is no real basis for the British *-our.*

"Our first notification," Fowler wrote, "that the book we are reading is not English but American is often, nowadays, the sight of an *-or*. 'Yankee,' we say, and congratulate ourselves on spelling like gentlemen; we wisely decline to regard it as a matter for argument. The English way cannot but be better than the American way; that is enough." He went on to say that Britons do not approach the question of *-our* vs. *-or* with an open mind, and concluded by predicting (in 1926) that *-our* endings would gradually give way to *-or* in Britain. But if this is so, the process is not exactly rapid; revising Fowler in 1965, Gowers retained these comments unchanged.

oral, verbal. Five authorities and American Heritage encourage observance of the distinction that *oral* means *by mouth* and *verbal* means simply *in words,* either spoken or written. *Verbal* is often used ambiguously: "He verbally assaulted the committee." This does not specify whether the assault was spoken or written. *Verbal,* however, is often used to mean *oral,* particularly in *verbal contract, verbal agreement.* Both Random House and Webster give *oral, spoken* as synonyms for *verbal,* however, and Flesch concurs. The consensus favors *verbal* to mean *in words* and not specifically *oral* or *written.* If exactness is important, the writer should choose between *oral* and *written,* and not take a chance on *verbal.*

orate. The word (a back-formation from *oration*) usually has a derisory or humorous connotation.

orchestra, band. The basic distinction, as applied to groups playing classical or light classical music, is that an orchestra contains stringed instruments and a band does not, being made up entirely of woodwinds and brasses, with the possible exception of a bass viol or two. Thus the term *wind orchestra,* as applied by a university to its concert band, was a misnomer. As applied to jazz ensembles, however, *band* does not necessarily imply the absence of strings. These distinctions are supported by Random House and Webster, though American Heritage makes no distinction.

order (on the order, of the order). *On* (sometimes *in*) *the order* and *of the order,* followed by quantities, are inflations of the technical writer. They sound to the uninitiated as if they have some deep and precise meaning, but they are merely ostentatious displacements of *about* or *approximately.* Apparently *on the order* and *of the order* are offshoots of *order of magnitude,* which does have a precise technical meaning: "A range of magnitude extending from some value to ten times that value (two quantities are of the same order of magnitude if one is no larger than ten times the other, but if one is one hundred times the other it is larger by two orders of magnitude)."—Webster. Some examples of the pretentious use of *order:* "The number of troops is estimated to have increased sharply, to something on the order of 10,000." *something like (approximately, about) 10,000.* "The budgetary deficit is still on the order of $150 million." *about.* See also *in order to, that.*

ordinance, ordnance. Often confused; an ordinance is a law, usually local (*a curfew ordinance was adopted*); ordnance is military weaponry, usually cannon or other artillery.

orient, orientate. The shorter form is preferable in all senses; Fowler regards the longer as likely to predominate in figurative use, which apparently reflects British practice. Dictionaries indicate that *orient* is the primary form: "The compass needle would not orient itself."

orphan. Though Random House and American Heritage allow the word for a child who has lost one parent, the term is likely to be understood as meaning one who has lost both, and thus Webster's *half-orphan* is recommended to make the distinction.

oscillate, osculate. Absurdly though not uncommonly confused. *Oscillate* means *flutter* or *move to and fro;* a pendulum oscillates. *Osculate* means *kiss,* and the word is now heavy humor. Readers are amused by occasional references to osculating fans.

ostensible, -bly; ostentatious, -ly. Two critics consider it necessary to distinguish these terms, the first of which means *apparent(ly)*, and the second *showy, demonstrative*. The confusion is rare, if it is not in fact a nonce-error that happened to catch the eye of the commentators.

other, any other. For comment on such constructions as "He has more readers than any other financial writer on a New York newspaper" see *Comparison 1*.

other than. In general, without going into hairsplitting distinctions, it may be said that critics discourage the use of this construction when *otherwise, otherwise than,* or *except* will fit. "The door was kept locked other than when the neighbors were at home." *except.*

otherwise. *Otherwise* used as an adjective in such sentences as "She did not like any of the hats, fashionable or otherwise" and "The museum contains a miscellany of oriental vases, authentic and otherwise" is roundly denounced by Follett and Fowler, although both admit that this construction is widely prevalent and all but idiomatic. The objections to it are based on the reasoning that one could not say *otherwise hats* or *otherwise vases* (placing *otherwise* in the attributive position). Evans defends the construction; Random House and Webster both list *otherwise* as an adjective. Both give examples placing it in the attributive position: *their otherwise friends*. American Heritage not only recognizes *otherwise* as an adjective but gives an example using it in the predicate position: "The evidence is otherwise." The objections to *otherwise* as an adjective appear to be pedantry.

Fowler protests against *otherwise* as a noun: "His competence or otherwise was not in question." This complaint seems better based, since dictionaries do not recognize *otherwise* as a noun. Yet the usage is well established.

ought. Bryant describes *hadn't ought* as not used in present-day writing, and American Heritage calls it and *had ought* wrong; Fowler deprecates the similar form *didn't ought*, apparently common in Britain but seldom heard in the U.S., as a colloquial vulgarism. The consensus is that *ought* with auxiliaries (in this case, *had* and *did*) is not standard in writing; this includes *had ought*, which should be simply *ought*. Follett deplores the omission of *to* after *ought*, as in "He thought he ought not go" and "We ought not think of it." Evans regards the retention of *to* as preferable. The unabridged dictionaries bear this out by implication, since none of their examples omits *to*.

-our, -or. See *-or, -our*.

ours. The form *our's* is wrong.

ourself, ourselves. See *Editorial* (*and Royal*) *We* for the first, and *myself* and *Reflexives* for the second.

out. *Of* is superfluous in the sense *from inside: out the window*.

out-. Solid as a prefix: *outargue, outdo, outfox*, etc.

outside. *Of* is superfluous with *outside* as a preposition ("They stood outside of the door") two critics and American Heritage say, though another considers *of* acceptable, as does Webster. Thus opinion is divided, and the writer may exercise his preference. One critic disapproves *outside of* for *except for* ("Outside of the climate, the place has no advantages"). Another critic and Webster consider this usage standard; Random House and Harper label it informal, and Bryant considers it colloquial. The reasonable deduction is that it lies somewhere between colloquial and formal. American Heritage accepts *outside of* in both uses, but its panel preferred *outside*.

over. It is a superstition endemic to newspapers that there is something wrong with *over* in the sense *more than*. Curiously enough, in view of how widely this idea is held, until recently only one dictionary of usage took up the point, and then to ridicule the notion. The prejudice against *over* for *more than* apparently stemmed from Ambrose Bierce's *Write It Right*, an extremely idiosyncratic guide published in 1909, many of whose opinions now fly in the face of standard usage, if in fact they ever represented anything but the author's crotchets. At any rate, *over* for *more than* is recognized without cavil by all dictionaries.

Bierce also aspersed *over* for *down upon from above*, as "He was hit over the head," but this expression is given to illustrate one sense of *over* as a preposition in both Random House and Webster. American Heritage unaccountably overlooked it. *Over* for *more than* was approved by 63 percent of the American Heritage panel, and rejected by 63 percent of the Harper panel. So much for panels.

Over is often misused in such constructions as "Considerable reductions over single-performance prices are again being offered," when *from* or *under* is called for.

over-. Solid as a prefix: *overdress, overcorrect, overdrive,* etc.

overall. Three critics object to the loose and sometimes superfluous use of the word in the senses *absolute, complete, comprehensive, general, inclusive, total, whole,* etc. Often it appears to be simply an intensive ("The overall result of the discussion was confusion") when it might as well be omitted. In the sense under discussion, Random House gives the definition *covering or including everything* and Webster gives *of or relating to something as a whole,* with *viewed as a whole, general, comprehensive* as synonyms. Perhaps the best advice in this case is to make certain that the word is used in those senses, and that it cannot be dispensed with.

overestimate. See *underestimate.*

overlay, overlie. The same principle governs the forms of these verbs as governs *lay* and *lie,* which see.

overlook, oversee. Although two authorities criticize the use of *overlook* in the sense *supervise* ("The foreman overlooks the construction"), holding that *oversee* should be reserved for this use, American Heritage, Random House, and Webster all give *supervise* or its equivalent as one sense of *overlook,* and so do desk dictionaries. The context must be depended on to prevent ambiguity caused by understanding *overlook* in its sense of *ignore, fail to notice.*

overly. Two authorities severely criticize the use of this word, holding that *over-* as a solid prefix is preferable; *overgenerous* rather than *overly generous, overenthusiastic* rather than *overly enthusiastic.* But Evans defends it as acceptable in the U.S., and both major dictionaries give it without qualification. The American Heritage panel accepts it. The fact that a word duplicates one already available seems like a thin reason to object to it, since English is full of such examples.

oversee. See *overlook, oversee.*

Overwriting. See *Journalese.*

owing to. See *due to.*

owing (or due to) the fact that. Redundant for *because, since.* See also *due to.*

P

pachyderm, pachydermatous. Criticized as synonyms for *elephant, elephantine.* *Pachyderm* was at one time the fond variant for *elephant* among newspaper writers, and elsewhere was often intended to be humorous. It is not so specific a synonym as its fanciers may think, however. Meaning *thick-skinned,* the word is equally applicable to the rhinoceros, the hippopotamus, the tapir, the pig, and perhaps even the politician.

package. The fondness for *package* in such expressions as *a package deal* and *package fares* is deplored by three critics; American Heritage, Random House, and Webster, however, give *package deal* as a separate entry, and Webster offers so many examples of *package* in these senses that the usage seems to be established beyond quibble. Obviously, though it once was a fad, it serves too useful a purpose to be aspersed. Two critics concede that it serves a purpose, though it is overused. Two others examine the new uses of *package* as a verb and adjective (*package a TV show; a package plan*), and not only refrain from disparaging them but concede their utility. The consensus favors these extended meanings, overused or not.

packing. Journalese as used in weather stories: "A hurricane packing 90-mile-an-hour winds."

painful. As descriptive of a beating or injuries, sometimes criticized as superfluous on the ground that there is no such thing as a painless beating or injury. This objection seems captious, since *painful injury* conveys a graphic meaning.

pair, pairs. Either form may be used as a plural (*six pair of trousers; six pairs of scissors*), though *pairs* is the newer form and is predominant. *Pair* in relation to people should take a plural verb (like *couple*): "The pair of comedians were next on the program." See also *couple.*

pajamas, pyjamas. The first is the American spelling, the second the British.

palpable. Two critics point out that the word means *capable of being touched* or *perceptible by any means;* Evans criticizes *palpable lie* as a cliché; to Flesch the word sounds bookish and is to be avoided. The consensus seems to be that this is a term whose misuse or overuse has raised the hackles of the commentators, and thus it should be handled with care.

pan-. Solid as a prefix: *panatrophy, pangenesis, pansophism*. But most combinations with *pan-* are proper names, with the result that the hyphen is used and both elements are capitalized: *Pan-Arabic, Pan-American, Pan-Pacific*. Exception: *Panhellenic, -ism*.

panacea. A panacea is a cure-all, and whether the term is used literally, in reference to ailments, or figuratively (*a panacea for economic woes*) it is not properly applied to a single affliction. Thus one could not well speak of *a panacea for debt*. The definitions in Webster and Random House support this conclusion.

pander, panderer. Although *panderer* seems to be favored by the press, headline writers, who are always up against it for space, will be glad to hear that *pander* is equally correct as the noun and in fact is the basic version.

para-. Solid as a prefix: *paratroop, paramilitary, paramarine*, etc.

paradise, etc. The preferred adjective form among the several available (*paradisaic, paradisaical, paradisal, paradisiacal, paradisial, paradisian, paradisic, paradisean, paradisiac, paradisical*) is, two critics agree, *paradisal*. But Random House gives *paradisiacal* as primary, and Webster accords that form and *paradisal* equal standing.

paraffin. See *kerosene*.

Paragraphs. Bernstein, Evans, Flesch and Fowler agree on warning against excessive length. The reason is that long paragraphs create an oppressive effect. To avoid it, newspapers have abandoned the rhetorical rules for paragraph structure and arbitrarily keep paragraphs very short.

Parallelism. The name for following the same pattern with constructions that naturally fall into it. It makes for ease in reading and therefore is to be encouraged. Most offenses against parallelism consist in switching verb forms: "It is a matter of letting tavern owners know their rights and to avoid confusion." *Of letting* should be matched by *of avoiding*. Some other examples, with corrections: "Vladimir Petrov was reported as having asked for and was granted asylum in Australia." *having asked for and having obtained*, or *having been granted*. "The state suspended sixteen driver permits, and one was revoked for vehicle violations" is not incorrect, but it does violate the principle of parallelism by changing from active to passive: *suspended sixteen . . . and revoked one*.

parameter. A technical term that is being pressed into general use and, as usually happens in such instances, is being corrupted. For *parameter*, American Heritage gives "a variable or an arbitrary constant in a mathematical expression, each value of which restricts or determines the specific form of the expression." An example might be *radius*, a concept whose value would vary with the size of the circle. There are other definitions, and the chance that the term as described by any of them would occur in ordinary discourse is far from fat. Some people confuse *parameter* with *perimeter* (a more common term, meaning the distance around a plane figure, or something analogous). This, of course, is plain ignorance: "Society puts a parameter around marriage, but what does age have to do with it?" Others evidently think *parameter* is a synonym for *limit*. A displaced and resentful government functionary was quoted in a news dispatch as saying, "We don't have to be lectured and scolded by the president and told that we can only talk about this parameter of activities . . ." Meaningless; what she had in mind was *scope, range,* or something of the kind. Bureaucrats love esoteric words, and if they do not know what they mean they love them all the more. Senator Patrick Moynihan, an erstwhile Harvard don, was not above invoking the old fallacy to the effect that *tinker's damn* should be *tinker's dam* in a public scolding of someone he thought had misused the term. Sometimes *parameter* is thought to mean *requirement*, as in a document put out by a university detailing the qualifications for its president. Parameters for this, that, and the other thing were listed but they were not parameters at all. There is no help for it; *parameter* is being bastardized as surely as *ecology, viable,* and *state of the art.*

paramount. Two critics warn against loosely using the term for *first, important;* it means *preeminent, chief in rank.* Random House and Webster corroborate this view.

Parentheses. The problem here is the relative position of the period and the closing parenthesis. If an entire sentence is enclosed, the period comes first. If the enclosed matter is the last part of the sentence, the parenthesis comes first. (This and the following sentence will illustrate.) Such problems, however, are usually left to the compositor or proofreader (sometimes inadvisedly).

parenting. For "acting as a parent," a neologism straight from the mildewed halls of sociology, and repugnant for that reason alone. Sentences containing it should be recast to substitute *parenthood, being a parent.* "Parenting grows more difficult every day." *bringing up children.*

parliamentarian. One critic objects to the use of this term to mean *a member of parliament* (as distinct from *an expert in rules of procedure*) but this sense is recognized by both Webster and Random House; the latter, however, designates it as British. American Heritage does not give it.

parlous. Two critics discourage this term as affected or heavily humorous. (It is a variant of *perilous*.)

parson. Two critics describe the term as somewhat rustic, or as used humorously for the most part in the United States. This judgment is obviously correct, though neither Webster nor Random House gives any indication of this shade of meaning.

partake of. Criticized variously as a cliché or as stilted.

part and parcel. The phrase is discouraged as a cliché.

partially, partly. Where there is a choice, as in "The words were partly unintelligible" and "The grass was partly mowed," *partly* is recommended over *partially*. Although the words are recognized as synonyms in this sense by dictionaries, *partially* also has the meaning *showing favoritism* (i.e., *being partial*) and thus there is danger of ambiguity in some contexts when *partially* is used in the sense of *partly*. American Heritage gives a distinction no other book does; that *partly* applies in physical connections and lays stress on the part, *partially* refers to conditions or states and stresses the whole.

Participles. See *Dangling Modifiers; Fused Participle; Gerunds; Modifiers*.

particular. Described by two critics as often used for an unnecessary emphasis when there is no need to particularize. The test of its usefulness is to strike *particular* out and decide whether anything has been lost, or whether it has just been put in by reflex action. Those addicted to the word say "this particular book," "this particular moment" when they mean simply *this book* and *now*.

parting of the ways. Regarded as a cliché by two critics.

party. *Party* when *person* is called for is inappropriate or humorous. "Firemen helped remove the injured parties from the car." *people*. The term comes from the jargon of telephone service ("Your party does not answer") and is also legalese ("party of the first part").

pass, past. *Passed* is the past tense of *pass* ("We passed a tree on the hill"); *past* may be an adverb, adjective, noun, or preposition, but not a verb. "My era has past" is wrong; *passed*. Evans curiously approves of such usages as "They past the crossroad" but dictionaries do not recognize *past* as a verb; this is the consensus. See also *meet, pass; past*.

pass away, pass on. Objectionable euphemisms for *die*.

passion flower, fruit. It may show something of the preoccupations of our age that these are often assumed to be aphrodisiacs. But here *passion* is used in reference to the passion of Christ. The name was given because portions of the flower resemble the cross. Figurative use (*my little passion flower*) perversely always has a sexual connotation.

Passive Voice. The use of the passive, in which the subject is acted on by the verb

("The ball was thrown by the boy" vs. "The boy threw the ball") has a long history of discouragement as a weak form of expression. Two critics content themselves with repeating the general discouragement; the others present more discriminating analyses, including concessions that the passive has its uses. Two critics find that the passive is on the increase, discouragement or no, and they agree that its use is much commoner among the well educated and sophisticated than among those less favored. There is general agreement that the passive is permissible, and perhaps desirable, when the performer of an act is unknown or of no importance, so that he may be omitted ("The door was opened quietly") and that the active voice is preferable to the passive in narration and description. Two authorities criticize the use of the passive to evade responsibility, as is sometimes done in bureaucratic correspondence ("It is felt that your request must be denied" vs. "We [or *I*] must deny your request"). The active voice remains far more common because of its naturalness and vigor. The writer who wants his prose to be direct and lively will be aware when he is using the passive and will do so only when he has a good reason for it. Use of the passive simply to vary structure, in such sentences as "Further education was gained in Europe" (in a biographical sketch) and "France and Germany were visited next" (in a travel account) is objectionable. See also *Double Passive*.

past. Redundant with *history*, since history is inevitably of the past. This is true also of *experience, records, precedent, achievements, accomplishments* except when there is reason to differentiate those that are past from others. See also *last, latest, past*.

patron. Four authorities criticize the term in the sense *customer* as pretentious. Dictionaries, however, give this usage as standard. The Concise Oxford Dictionary does not recognize it, which, together with Fowler's disapproval, may indicate that *patron* for *customer* is an Americanism. This is unquestionably true of *patronize*, as is corroborated by Fowler's disapproval of it in the sense *trade at*. But American standard usage differs.

peacenik. *Tips and Slips*, the critique of its own content put out by the *Cleveland Press*, commented that this is "a manufactured word with a built-in sneer. Forget it. There is nothing wrong with being in favor of peace." The expression is too new to be in any dictionary. It is the successor to *peacemonger*, and apparently was generated by the hawks-doves division on the Vietnam War. It may have sunk into oblivion since the issue that generated it no longer exists.

peacock. The use of this form instead of *peahen* in reference to laying eggs and other female functions is regularly criticized, often scornfully. Strictly speaking, the peacock is the male of the peafowl. But *peacock* as a general term of reference to members of this species is sanctioned as standard by both Random House and Webster, as well as most desk dictionaries.

peculiarly. One critic says the word cannot properly be used in the senses *espe-*

cially or *particularly*, but may mean only *highly individually*. This judgment, like most that are based on derivation (in this case, from Latin), is erroneous; it is supported by neither Webster nor the Concise Oxford Dictionary (Random House does not give a separate definition.)

Pedagese. One of various terms, none of them complimentary, that are applied to the academic counterpart of *Gobbledygook* (which see). Others are *academese, educationese, sociologese*. This does not refer to the use of technical terminology in technical contexts; it refers to the disease that infects much of the academic world, causing its victims to believe they must couch their writing in as unintelligible, polysyllabic, euphemistic, circumlocutory language as possible, or it will not have the desired effect of profundity. Many an academic treatise, when stripped of its obfuscation, has been found to be barren of ideas. Some academicians avoid plain English on principle; others are incapable of expressing themselves plainly. Both varieties tend, by example, to infect students with the noxious idea that what is difficult to understand is necessarily deep, and that if an idea is simple to begin with it should be expressed in as complicated language as possible.

pedal, peddle. To pedal is to operate something worked by pedals, such as a bicycle; to peddle is to hawk or distribute some item or idea. "The government back-peddled fast when it looked as if pressure groups were beginning to frown." *back-pedaled.*

Pedantry. See *Pomposity*.

pedigreed. See *thoroughbred*.

peer, peer group. *Peer* is often mistakenly thought to mean *superior;* in fact, it means *equal*. The misuse is illustrated by "He regarded all men as his equals, but none as his peers." *Peerless* thus means *without an equal*, not *without a superior*. The confused usage in this respect probably arises from another sense of *peer: nobleman*. *Peer group* is sociological and educational jargon that is often used in inappropriate (i.e., nontechnical) contexts.

Peking, Peiping. The name of the capital of China was Peiping ("Northern Peace") from 1928 to 1949; in 1949 it was renamed Peking ("Northern Capital") by the Communists. There is much confusion on this subject, though it is explained by both Random House and Webster. But all this is now of only historical interest, for the masters of China have decided that they prefer *Beijing* as conforming more closely with the pronunciation, in accordance with the Pinyin system of transliteration (as against the old Wade-Giles system). The press associations and many large newspapers have adopted the new version.

penny. The term is sometimes criticized as used in reference to the U.S. cent, but two critics describe it as standard, a judgment borne out by dictionary definitions.

people, persons. One critic holds to the traditional view that the terms are not interchangeable, and that *people* correctly designates a large and indefinite group, as *the British people* or *We, the people.* The corollary, observed in newspaper offices, particularly, is that a figure must always be followed by *persons,* never by *people: Sixteen persons.* Three critics, however, opt for *people* in preference to *persons,* which now often sounds stiff. Two critics warn against following the traditional rule out the window, as is often done in newspaper writing, on the assumption *people* is to be avoided, leading to such absurdities as "The job of the comedian is to make persons laugh." Two critics, nevertheless, favor *persons* with an exact number, and the definitions in both Random House and Webster follow the traditional rule of using *people* only in the indefinite sense. American Heritage considers the forms interchangeable for small numbers. Opinion thus is divided on this usage, with a slight edge favoring the traditional rule. See *Feminism.*

per. Three critics frown on the indiscriminate use of *per* for *a* (*the mailman used to come twice per day*); three critics object to *per* for *by* (*he traveled per automobile*) and to *as per* for *in accordance with,* as used in business correspondence. Two critics prefer *a year* to *per annum.* The consensus is heavily against *per* where *a* or some other native expression will do.

peradventure. Described by Fowler (who calls it archaic) and Flesch (who considers it pompous) as often inappropriately used: the usual phrase is *beyond the peradventure of a doubt,* which is probably unintelligible to many a modern reader. The word means (as a noun) *chance* or *uncertainty.*

per capita. One critic protests that this is a legal term, incorrectly used in the sense of *per person, per head,* but he is outnumbered by American Heritage, Random House, Webster, the Standard College, and the New World dictionaries, which give this sense as standard.

percent, per cent. Either form is correct. Technically an abbreviation for *per centum,* which prompts some to write it *per cent.,* but the period is so long gone in general usage that its use must be set down to fussiness.

It is easy to be ambiguous in constructions like "The measure would lower the rate from 3 to 2 percent." Here the reader must decide whether 3 and 2 percent are the present and proposed rates, or the proportions by which the rate would go down. The intention here would have been unequivocally expressed by "The measure would lower the rate from 3 percent to 2 percent."

percentage. Not necessarily a small part; a percentage may be any fraction of the whole. *A large percentage* in place of *most* or *many* and *a small percentage* in place of *few* are woolly. See also *fraction.*

perfect. The idea, approved by two critics, that *perfect* as an adjective is an absolute and thus incapable of being qualified (*more perfect, most perfect*) is said to be without substance by four others, and the same conclusion is indicated by examples in Webster, which quotes, among other things, the Constitution: "We, the people of the United States, in order to form a more perfect union . . ." Random House cites *nearly perfect;* American Heritage allows comparison. Curme, the distinguished grammarian (*Syntax*, p. 504) says ". . . we do not feel such forms as *more perfect, most perfect, deader, deadest, more unique,* etc., as pleonastic since we have in mind degrees of approach to something perfect, dead, or unique." Thus the consensus is that *perfect* may be freely compared. See also *Comparison 3.*

(a) period of. Usually verbiage, as in *a period of years; for years.*

period of time. A redundancy for *period* or *time: a short period* (*of time*); *a long time* (not *period of time*).

permit of. *Of* with *permit* in the sense *admit* or *allow* ("The document permits of two interpretations") is unnecessary, but this form is regarded as standard by dictionaries.

pernickety, persnickety. The consensus of the dictionaries is that the first is the original form, but most of them give both versions, and so they must be considered equally correct.

perpetrate, perpetuate. Misuse of the first for the second sometimes occurs. *Perpetrate* means *commit, perform, do* (usually something objectionable); *perpetuate* means *continue, make endure.* Examples of misuse: "He is the worthy perpetrator of an illustrious tradition." *perpetuator.* "This outmoded theory is still perpetrated in many schools." *perpetuated.*

perquisite, prerequisite. A perquisite is an advantage or special privilege, often in addition to pay: "The perquisites of the office include the use of an automobile and a place to live." A prerequisite is something required as a condition. In schooling, basic courses are prerequisites to advanced ones. Hard work, it is said, is a prerequisite to success (though success does not necessarily follow, and some succeed without really trying).

per se. "Some of them feel that college students per se live in a vacuum for four years because they are engrossed in study." *Per se* itself is not often the occasion for error; this sentence is quoted to illustrate the point that foreign expressions are sometimes resorted to in the hope that they will sound impressive and without awareness of their meaning. The overriding principle is that the skillful writer puts down nothing about whose meaning he has the smallest doubt. It is easy to pick up mistaken ideas of the meanings of unusual words if one relies on the notions created by occasional encounters with them. *Per se* means "of, by, or in itself or oneself or themselves." Applying the definition to the example cited at the outset, it is impossible to imagine what the writer had in mind; "college students *as such*," perhaps, but this is pointless.

persecute, prosecute. Sometimes confused. To persecute is to *afflict, harass,* or *annoy;* "The Nazis persecuted the Jews." To prosecute is to carry out the legal procedure against one accused of a crime: "Trespassers will be prosecuted."

persistence, -cy. The words are equivalents, and the only reasonable basis for a choice between them is the rhythm of the sentence.

persnickety. See *pernickety.*

persona. It has become a fad to use *persona* where *person* will do, just as *simplistic* erroneously displaces *simple. Persona* is a technical term of psychology, referring to the facade or image that a person presents to the world in contrast to his private character.

personal, personally. *Personal* is often obtrusively used to qualify what can be nothing else: *friend, charm, opinion* are the leading examples. *Great personal charm* has become a tiresome set phrase. An employer was described as "personally popular with his workers." There is something distasteful about the idea these examples suggest, that friendship, charm, and popularity have been so devalued as qualities inseparably associated with the person that they must be specifically identified with it.

Personally is often used for a meaningless emphasis: "It has never been possible for him to attend a board meeting personally." *attend a board meeting.* Attendance is not possible other than personally. Opinions are often stated in some such way as "Personally, I believe . . ." This is unnecessary except in the rare cases when one may have differing personal and official or public opinions.

personnel. Two critics think the term, introduced into English from French, still needs defending against criticisms that it is an objectionable neologism. Two others and American Heritage disapprove of its use with a figure (*three personnel were fired*), but a third considers this usage standard, and so does Webster, which gives *34,000 personnel.* Random House, however, favors use of the term only to indicate a large or indefinite group: *the personnel of the factory; military personnel.* The term is stiff and official when it displaces *people.*

persons. See *people, persons.*

persuade. See *convince.*

persuasion. Phrases on the model "of the Republican persuasion" are discouraged as outmoded.

peruse. Two authorities criticize the loose substitution of the word (which means *read with great care or attention*) where *read* is called for.

pessimism, pessimistic. See *optimism;* the views on use of the term are analogous, except that there is no dissent in the dictionaries from the principle that *pessimistic* relates to an outlook and properly is applicable to a person, as distinguished from a factor, etc. "At this pessimistic juncture in East-West relations" would better be "At this discouraging juncture."

petite. Overworked in connection with blondes; are there no petite brunettes?

phantasy. See *fantasy, phantasy.*

phase, faze. See *faze, phase.*

Ph.D. See *Dr.*

phenomenal. Two critics agree that the sense *prodigious, extraordinary, remarkable,* although originally a corruption, can no longer be argued against. The original meaning applied to that which was apprehended by the senses, as contrasted with that which was not. Dictionaries give the newer meaning as standard, and most people will be surprised to learn it was ever under a shadow.

phenomenon, phenomena. Three critics hold that the first is the proper form for the singular (*this phenomenon*) and the second for the plural (*these phenomena*); one critic recognizes *phenomenons;* another considers *phenomenons* or *phenomenas* acceptable plurals; Random House and Webster also accept *phenomenons* but do not give *phenomenas,* and so the consensus is that it is nonstandard, and that *phenomenons* (as well as *phenomena*) is correct.

Phileas; Phineas. Confusion often arises in reference to these given names. Phineas was the name of P. T. Barnum; Phileas that of the hero of Jules Verne's *Around the World in Eighty Days* (Phileas Fogg).

Philippines. Often misspelled *Phillipines, Phillippines.* (Named for King Philip III of Spain.)

Philology. The term and its analogues, once having to do with the science of language, are being displaced by *linguistics* and *its* analogues.

phobia. See *mania, phobia.*

phony. Considered slang by two critics, informal by Random House and Harper, and standard by Webster. Fowler discusses theories of its origin but does not indicate any disparagement. Its progress to standard seems to be beyond doubt. The dictionaries and Fowler recognize the variant spelling *phoney,* but it is not usual.

Phrasal Verbs. See *Hyphen 4.*

phrenetic. See *frenetic, phrenetic*.

pick, choice. *Pick* is loosely interchangeable with *choice* or *selection*, but its use in this sense is avoided in careful writing, except in such set phrases as *take your pick, the pick of the crop*. "We are studying American authors, and he is my pick" is a disagreeable construction. Sportswriters, when they gaze into their crystal balls, like to speak of their *picks* as the victors in forthcoming contests, but the word sounds no better here either.

piece. Sometimes criticized in reference to a literary composition, but the term is given as standard in dictionaries.

pier. See *dock*.

pinch hitter. The original meaning, which comes from baseball, is a replacement sent to bat with the expectation he will do better than the player he is substituting for; the expression is often misused in other connections simply to describe a substitute, with no suggestion of superior performance. The sense *substitute* is recognized by dictionaries, however, and is in such wide use that there is no use in insisting on the original meaning in figurative applications.

place. Its adverbial use, as in *a place [in which] to live* and *going [to] places* is considered questionable by one critic but approved as idiomatic by two others. Dictionaries are not explicit on this point, though Random House calls *go places*, in the sense *succeed*, slang.

plan. The fulcrum for a number of redundancies. Planning must relate to the future unless otherwise qualified; thus *plan ahead, advance plans*, and *future plans* are redundant, though they occur often in educated prose.

planned withdrawal. See *Euphemisms*.

plane, plain. A plain is a flat stretch of ground; a plane, in the sense sometimes confused, is a level of development. "A high ethical plain." *plane*.

plans and specifications. The distinction may be clear to an architect, but in ordinary contexts this is just a pompous redundancy.

play (wreak) havoc. Clichés.

plead innocent. There is no such plea in jurisprudence; the correct form is *plead not guilty*. The term *plead innocent* is often prescribed in newspaper journalism to avoid the danger of inadvertent omission of *not* from *not guilty*; American Heritage considers the form well established in unofficial contexts.

pleasantry. Now means not something pleasant, or amiable conversation, but a joke or banter. "They exchanged pleasantries about the rigors of campaigning."

please be advised. A Victorian pomposity of business correspondence that is better discarded, like "Yours of the 18th inst. received and contents noted." Don't ask correspondents to be advised; simply tell them what's on your mind.

pled. Recognized as a standard form of the past tense of *plead,* as acceptable as *pleaded,* by four critics; to another, it is "unsavory." Recognition of *pled* as standard by dictionaries makes the approval nearly unanimous, however.

plenty. Five critics disapprove of *plenty* as an attributive adjective in such expressions as *plenty brains, plenty money* (correctly, *plenty of*); American Heritage calls it informal. Random House, however, gives *plenty helpers,* and Webster gives *plenty men.* The consensus is against the usage.

plow, plough. *Plough* is the British preference.

Plural and Singular. **1.** Proper names. The plurals of proper names ending in *s* are formed by adding *es: Jones, the Joneses; Adams, the Adamses.* Such plurals are often erroneously formed by adding an apostrophe, which indicates possession: *the Adams'.* Proper names ending in a sibilant (*sh* or *ch*), *x,* and *z* also form their plurals by adding *es: Bush, Bushes; Wilcox, Wilcoxes, Broz, Brozes.*
    2. Figures, letters. The plurals of figures and letters may be formed by adding *s: the 1920s, GIs, MPs,* unless this forms a word: *As, Us.* (This is a relatively new practice that appears well established: older practice called for adding *'s:* the 1920's).
    3. Compounds. The singular, rather than the plural, is used in such locutions as *six-mile race, three-month investigation* (not *miles, months*). *Right-of-way* becomes *rights-of-way, passer-by* becomes *passers-by, son-in-law* becomes *sons-in-law.* Such questions are best answered by consulting a dictionary for the specific term.
    4. Plural forms are sometimes used pretentiously or meaninglessly. "Charges of vagrancy were lodged against the transient." *a charge.* "The dedication ceremonies were canceled." *ceremony was.* "He has ambitions to be a bank president." *an ambition.*
    See also *Collective Nouns; court-martial; general; -ic, -ics; it is I,* etc.; *Subject-Verb Agreement; anybody, anyone; each, everybody, everyone; lb., lbs.; Number in Addition; with.*

plurality. See *majority, plurality.*

plus. Not the equivalent of *and,* one critic and American Heritage agree, pointing out that consequently it takes a singular verb: "Three plus two is (not *are*) five." Two other critics say the verb may be either singular or plural. American Heritage adds that a plural verb is required, however, when the subject is plural: "His talents plus his ambition were irresistible." *Plus* for *besides* ("The liquor was expensive, plus it was of poor quality") is a disagreeable vogue.

p.m. See *a.m., p.m.*

podium. There is widespread confusion of this term for the platform a speaker or orchestra conductor stands on with *lectern,* the rack on which a speaker places his manuscript. One critic, after reading in a newspaper that a speaker had pressed both hands down hard on the edges of the podium to emphasize his words, concluded that he must have been on his hands and knees. The confusion has been dignified by the recognition of *podium* in the sense *lectern* by Webster, but other dictionaries do not accept this. The distinction should be maintained.

Poesy. The gentlemen of the press are sometimes eager to show that the often humdrum task of reporting the news has not entirely numbed them to the finer things in life. They do this with random poetical touches, like *'twas, 'tis, 'twere* and *'twill. Lone* is a commoner example; it has all but supplanted the homely *only* or *sole:* "He cast the lone dissenting vote." Fowler cited *save* (in the sense *except*) and *ere* as examples of words abandoned to the journalists, who, he said, had not yet ceased to find them beautiful. The fault lies in using words inappropriate to the context.

poetess. See *Feminine Forms.*

poetry, verse. *Poetry* and *poem* are loosely applied to anything in verse form. The discerning, however, use the terms only for what has some literary merit. The general and neutral form for what has meter, rhyme, or both is *verse.* It is well to make the distinction for what obviously has no artistic pretensions, for example limericks and other humorous verse. Lack of judgment may be indicated by calling verse (a neutral, technical term) poetry, but not by calling poetry verse. In brief, all poetry is verse, but not all verse is poetry.

pointed out. See *Attribution 2.*

point of view. Use of the phrase in pompous constructions like the examples is criticized by two authorities. "His point of view was that the program was unnecessary." *view, opinion.* "From the point of view of legibility, typing is preferable to handwriting." *Typing is more legible than handwriting.* See also *viewpoint.*

point with pride. Political bombast that has long been the object of ridicule, but this has not entirely banished it. Often counterpoised to *view with alarm,* which is equally objectionable.

Polack. Derogatory and offensive; *Pole.*

politic, political. See *-ic, -ical.*

political pot. As elections approach, it begins to simmer or boil; thus it ever was since the advent of the first political writer.

polyglot. Things are seldom, as Captain Corcoran observed, what they seem; *polyglot,* for example, is not what it seems to some who use it. But no one who has a feeling for derivation will go astray here, for the word literally means *many-tongued.* A man who speaks a number of languages may properly be described as a *polyglot,* and there are related senses. But how now: "Most of the valley is a verdant and prosperous polyglot of cities." Perhaps the writer was reaching for *complex.* A city can be described as polyglot, if many languages are spoken there. But how cities could *constitute* a polyglot is unaccountable. Sometimes *polyglot* is misused in the sense of *mixture.*

pompom, pompon. Both terms have various meanings, relating among other things to weaponry and fish. But the differentiation that caused confusion and perhaps pain was that a pompom girl was a prostitute and a pompon girl one who flourished ornamental tufts at athletic contests as part of the ritual of cheerleading. But *pompom* in relation to prostitution has died out. Some dictionaries give both *pompom* and *pompon* in connection with cheerleading; the terms may now safely be interchanged in this sense.

Pomposity. All agree that the use of unnecessarily long words, complicated constructions, or technical language is a serious fault. This is not the curse it once was, the apostles of clarity and simplicity having got their message across in many quarters. Nonetheless, eternal vigilance is required to preserve those qualities. The examples given here are intended merely to illustrate the vice of using more or longer or harder words than necessary; they hardly scratch its surface. But for anyone who develops a critical awareness of pomposity, the battle is half won.

"One thousand dollars was voted *to help defray* [toward] expenses *in connection with* [of] the celebration." (The bracketed expressions might have been used in place of the italicized ones they follow.)

"About 200 youngsters were turned over to probation authorities last year. This year the number will be *far in excess of that figure* [much larger]."

"Authorities awaited the results of *toxicological tests on tissue samples* [tests to discover any sign of poisoning]."

"The lower tax rate is *attributed to elimination of* [results from dropping] the special high-school tuition charge."

"This equipment *was received in a nonoperative condition* [would not work when it arrived]."

"The group was organized to *render assistance in the placement of veterans in employment* [help veterans find jobs]."

"The woman who had shot herself refused to *divulge her reason* [say why]."

"Gradually the boy learned to *function more adequately* [behave better] both at home and at school." (*Behave better* was precisely the meaning, as the context showed.)

"The defendant was placed on probation on condition he *refrains from consuming alcoholic beverages* [does not drink]."

Some common phrases are mushmouthed: *voice* as a verb inspires some of them. *Voice objections* usually would better be *object; voice approval* would better be *approve. Is employed by* is more dignified, perhaps, but longer than *works for; resides* is ostentatious for *lives; position* is highfalutin for *job* and often applied to routine employment. *Adequate in size* has dignity, but *big enough* is better.

But what can we expect of an age when garbage men are sanitation specialists and janitors are maintenance engineers? See also *Gobbledygook; Pedagese; Scientific English.*

Popularized Technicalities. The term was invented by Fowler in the original to describe expressions that have been objectionably popularized. Judgments on this matter, of course, are even more idiosyncratic than judgments on usage in general, since technical terms are constantly being placed in general use, often with more or less distorted meanings. Among recent examples are *viable* and *ecology.*

pore, pour. The second is often given when the first is intended, e.g., *pour over a book. Pore* means *read studiously; pour* means *tip out of a container.* A newspaper account said, "This kind of conduct was considered beyond the pail." That must have been the pail that is used for pouring over books.

portland. In relation to cement, not a proprietary designation but a generic term growing out of the fact that this type of hydraulic cement was regarded by its inventor, Joseph Aspdin of Leeds, England, as resembling stone quarried on the Isle of Portland. Nearly all cement used today is portland cement, and the term is not capitalized.

posh. A widely repeated story holds that the word is an acronym for "port out, starboard home," dating from the era when Great Britain was truly a seat of empire and her colonial emissaries were making regular trips from London by steamer to India, Australia, and other far-flung territories. Preferred accommodations aboard were "away from the weather"—port side outward-bound and starboard side homeward-bound. Engaging as the explanation is, no evidence has ever been produced to support it, although it has been examined by several authorities.

position. See *job, position.*

Possessive Pronouns. The possessive pronouns ending in *s* (*yours, his, hers, its, ours, theirs*) do not take apostrophes: *Its fur was mangy; The purse was hers.* The commonest error here is confusing the contraction *it's* (*it is*) with *its* (*belonging to it*). (This represents modern usage. Two centuries ago, the forms *their's, our's, her's* were considered correct.) See also *Possessives.*

Possessives. 1. Such possessive forms as *the water's temperature, the sky's color* (rather than *the temperature of the water, the color of the sky*) are described as standard by one critic and criticized as sometimes infelicitous by two, and two others disapprove of them altogether. (The question here is whether the possessive form may be used for inanimate things; no such question ordinarily arises concerning such expressions as *the dog's collar* and *the cat's pajamas,* and even some referring to inanimate things, such as *today's newspaper*.) The consensus disapproves such possessives.

2. Apostrophe vs. Apostrophe-s. There is no disagreement with the universal principle that the possessive of words ending in any letter but *s* or *z* is formed by adding *'s: boy, boy's; men, men's; George, George's; paper, paper's*. Uncertainty arises, however, over forming the possessive of singulars that end with *s* or *z* (or an *s* or *z* sound): *Jesus, Jones, Keats*. These are mainly proper names, but some common expressions, like *conscience's sake, innocence' evidence,* come under this heading. The apostrophe alone is used to avoid a triple sibilant in pronouncing the possessive form: *Moses'* rather than *Moses's* (which would be pronounced *Moseses*), *Jesus'* rather than *Jesus's*. Fowler seems ambiguous on this point. Three critics prescribe *'s* to form the possessives of proper nouns ending in *s: Keats's, Charles's;* two critics say *Keats'* and *Charles'* are equally acceptable. One widely followed principle is that pronunciation should be allowed to govern the choice in forming all possessives on *s* or *z* sounds, and one critic allows exceptions when physical possession is not indicated, as in *Holmes' London*. Two critics favor *conscience' sake;* another approves both that form and *conscience sake*.

3. Double genitive (possessive). The term refers to constructions like *a property of Smith's, a friend of my uncle's, an opinion of the teacher's*. Technically, the possessive forms *Smith's, uncle's* and *teacher's* are redundant because possession has already been indicated by *of*. Two points are worth noting: the object of the phrase is always animate (usually a person or an animal), and identical constructions in which the object is a pronoun are inescapable: *a friend of mine, some books of yours*. Double genitives, though avoided by some writers as excessive, are idiomatic. Fowler does not discuss the subject, but appears to give tacit approval by citing an example in another connection that contains a double genitive. The construction often appears in sentences like "Their idea is the same as that of the tariff commission's"; "The footprint is fully as long as that of a large gorilla's." These (with *that of*) are sometimes considered more objectionable than other double genitives. They may be avoided by dispensing with either *that of* or the possessive form of the noun that follows: "as long as a gorilla's." Users of the double genitive, several authorities point out, must be on guard against ambiguity, especially in speaking. Thus, *an opinion of the teacher's,* spoken, might be taken to mean either *an opinion held by the teacher* or *an opinion concerning the teachers*.

4. False possessive. Modifiers ending in *s* are often wrongly construed as possessives and given apostrophes they should not have: *a General Motors scholarship* (not *Motors'*); *United States* (not *States'*) *citizen*. The use of the appositive in such phrases as *five months' probation, six weeks' vacation* is considered necessary by one critic but considered optional by two others.

For a discussion of locutions like *him going* vs. *his going*, see *Fused Participle;* for the use of the apostrophe in forming plurals (*1920's*) see *Plural and Singular.* See also *sake.*

possible, possibly. The expression *possibly may* is redundant, since *possible* includes the contingency expressed by *may.* In such constructions as "I will charge you no more than possible," *possible* illogically displaces *necessary.* The construction, common in newspapers, on the model *a possible fractured jaw* is open to criticism; *possibly* is required here. Bernstein argues for limiting *possible* to its strict sense of *capable of being done,* and criticizes the common tribute to those who are said to have made something possible, when in fact they brought it about. Fowler is more lenient.

One author grew so tired of acknowledgments in the front of books paying tribute to those who had made them possible that he directed his own appreciation to those "who made this book less impossible than it might have been."

post-. Solid as a prefix: *postglacial, posthumous, postwar,* etc. But *post-Aztec, post-Renaissance* (followed by a capital).

postmaster general. See *general.*

postmistress. See *Feminine Forms.*

postprandial. Objected to as polysyllabic humor.

pother. Considered a literary word (for *fuss*).

pound(s) sterling. See *lb., lbs.*

pour. See *pore, pour.*

power corrupts. See *Misquotation.*

powerful. The attachment of this adjective to the names of legislative committees, particularly the House Ways and Means, has become automatic in the press, and something of a joke. A cartoon in the Feb. 26, 1977 issue of *The New Yorker* showed the door to the committee room with the words "The Powerful" on a placard that had been taped above the sign "Ways and Means."

practicable, practical. Sometimes confused. What is practicable is capable of being done or accomplished: "Construction of cities under the seas is now considered practicable." What is practical is useful or adapted to use or to actual conditions: "Practical solutions are better than theoretical ones." Two critics give the negative forms as *impractical* and *unpractical,* respectively; two others say that *impractical* (as the negative of *practical*) is wrong. Yet *impractical* is given as standard by dictionaries; *unpractical* is seldom seen. The standard negative of *practicable* is *impracticable;* Webster does nothing to settle matters by equating *impracticable* and *impractical.*

practically. In the sense *almost, virtually, in effect (it is practically worn out),* considered objectionable by three critics; two conclude that the words have become all but, or practically, interchangeable. Dictionaries recognize *practically* as standard for *nearly, almost;* these terms are recommended as preferable, however, by three critics. The American Heritage panel narrowly (51 percent) accepted *practically* for *in effect* and rejected it (64 percent) for *nearly, almost,* though these expressions are often interchangeable, as in one of the examples cited to illustrate the supposed difference. Opinion is thus divided on the acceptability of *practically* in these senses.

practice, practise. The first is the American form of the verb and the second is the British.

pre-. *Pre-* has become the darling of the adwriters' overheated prose (*precooked, preheated*), and true to the overheated tradition it becomes attached to words where it is redundant: "The secretary of state denied that the president had made a foreign ministers' meeting a precondition of a treaty"; "They bought a house in the area after having pretested it on several summer vacations." *condition, tested.* Preplanning is an asininity; planning cannot be anything but *pre-.*
  Pre- is solid as a prefix: *preempt, preprint, prewar.*

precede, proceed. Subject to a variety of confusions, including being mistaken for one another. To start with, *precede* means *go before; proceed* means *go* or *move forward.* The commonest error is spelling *preceding preceeding.* Sometimes *proceed* is given *procede. Precede* may appear as *preceed.*

precipitate, precipitous. Sometimes confused. The first means *hasty, rash,* the second *steep: a precipitate decision, a precipitous roof.*

precondition. See *pre-.*

predate. See *antedate.*

predicate. One critic objects to *predicate on* in the sense *base on:* "Several senators predicated their misgivings on what effect it would have on European security." This sense is otherwise universally regarded as standard, however. The use of *predict* for *predicate,* which some authorities warn about, is evidently a British error. *Based on* is simpler than *predicated on.*

predominate. Not recognized as an adjective by Random House or American Heritage: *the predominate characteristic (predominant)* but considered standard by Webster. *Predominant* makes *predominantly, predominate* makes *predominately,* but the distinction is rather fine, and perhaps not really useful.

preempt. Now one word after an uneasy transition through a siege of dieresis (*preëmpt*) and hyphenation (*pre-empt*).

preface. See *foreword,* etc.

prefer. The usual idiomatic forms with *prefer* in comparing two things are illustrated by *prefer* (*to do*) *this rather than* (*to do*) *that* (to avoid the awkwardness of *prefer to do this to to do that*); *prefer this to that; prefer doing this to doing that. Prefer than,* as in "They prefer going to the show than dancing" is not acceptable.

Prefixes and Suffixes. See *Hyphens 5.*

premier. Aspersed as pretentious for *first, foremost: a premier musician.*

premiere. Rejected as a verb (*premiered a new film*) by American Heritage and Harper; considered standard by Random House and Webster.

premise, premises. The singular form means *a basis for reasoning or argument;* its plural is *premises.* Only *premises,* which is always a plural, may be used in the sense of *property:* "Trespassers were warned off the premises."

preoccupy. One word; not *pre-occupy.*

preparatory to. A pretentious displacement of *before:* "He put out the cat preparatory to going to bed." What is preparatory to should be in preparation for.

prepared. Criticized when it displaces more direct expression as in "The senator was not prepared to admit his part in the affair." *not willing, would not.*

preplan. See *pre-.*

Prepositions. 1. Piled-up prepositions. Two critics agree that prepositions are often unnecessarily doubled, and sometimes tripled, when a range is being specified, especially in newspaper writing: "The weatherman predicted a low temperature of between 75 and 80 degrees" (omit *of*). "The airlift is expected to speed up the delivery of mail by from twenty-four to forty-eight hours" (omit *from*); "Investments of from two to four million dollars were reported" (omit *from*). Sometimes a single preposition is superfluous: "A low temperature (of) near 45 degrees is expected"; "The Sierra received (from) two to four inches of slushy snow"; "(At) about nine o'clock last night."

    2. Prepositions and idiom. Information on the idiomatic prepositions that go with various verbs, e.g., that *acquiesce* takes *in, grate* takes *on* is perhaps most conveniently and exhaustively available in examples appearing after definitions in the unabridged dictionaries, especially Webster.

    3. Preposition at end. A couple of professors of English were mountain-

climbing on vacation, when all at once they saw an avalanche bearing down on them.

"Heaven help us," cried one. "We're done for." "For God's sake, Henry," returned the other, "don't end your last sentence with a preposition."

This may be funny enough on the surface, but it is a joke that could not have been made up by a grammarian. The *for* in *done for* is not really a preposition but an adverb that has merged with the verbal modifier *done* to form a new expression, whose meaning depends on both words taken together. Anyway, who could imagine an English professor, even on vacation, using a colloquialism like *done for?*

The notion that it is wrong, or undesirable, to end a sentence with a preposition has been derided by Fowler and many another authority on language. The most telling blow was struck by Sir Winston Churchill, who, when accused of ending a sentence with a preposition, is said to have replied: "This is the type of arrant pedantry up with which I shall not put."

You can show that sentences with the preposition at the end are more forceful than those that have been recast to avoid it; you can cite masters of English prose from Chaucer to Churchill who employ end prepositions freely and consciously; and you can prove that such usage is established literary English, but the superstitious will still wince at it.

In writing, as distinguished from rule-reciting, the avoidance of the end preposition is more evident, perhaps, in structural detours that start with a preposition followed by *which*. Few care about making the world a better place *to live in,* but nearly everyone wants to make it a better place *in which to live.* "The car she was riding in," after editing with zeal and ignorance, becomes "The car in which she was riding."

The use of circumlocution to find another place than the end for the preposition not only weakens the sentence but gives it a stilted sound. "What are we coming to?"; "There was nothing to talk about"; "It was something he had always dreamed of"; and "The situation was too much to contend with" are perfectly good English in any context. The alternatives are clumsy: "To what are we coming?"; "There was nothing about which to talk"; "It was something of which he had always dreamed"; and "The situation was too much with which to contend."

Avoidance of the preposition at the end came from applying Latin rules of grammar to English. In Latin, it is all but impossible to place a preposition after its object. Linguists now, however, have decided that the rules of one language make a Procrustean bed for another.

Sometimes jesters cite the little boy's complaint, "What did you bring that book to be read to out of up for?" as the ultimate in putting the preposition at the end. Maybe it is a shame to spoil their fun, but only the final *for* functions as a preposition here (its object is *what*). *Out of,* together with *to be read,* form a phrasal verb, and the *up* that precedes it is an adverb.

4. Misplacement. Prepositions are often unexplainably placed after modifiers like *both* and *either:* "The Soviet bloc and most of the Arab states refused to pay either for the Middle East or the Congo operations" *pay for either;* "The speech had been reviewed both by the President and the Secretary of Defense." *by both* *the President. Both* and *either* modify the objects of the prepositions (*for, by*) and their proper position is behind them.

5. Prepositions repeated. Prepositions are often repeated needlessly before a series of objects: "If you're the average American motorist, every 9.2 years you're going to get a ticket for running a red light, for speeding, or for reckless driving." The force of the first *for* will carry over to *speeding* and *reckless driving: for running a red light, speeding, or reckless driving.* There are places, however, where a preposition must be repeated to prevent ambiguity: "He was fined for lack of character and of reliability." Without the second *of* the fine would appear to be for reliability rather than its lack. "The paper's independence from pressure groups, lack of opportunism, and timidity were not sufficiently emphasized." A Freudian lapse, possibly; *and of timidity* was intended.

prerequisite, perquisite. See *perquisite.*

prescribe, proscribe. Sometimes confused; to prescribe is to lay down a direction or instruction; to proscribe is to forbid, denounce, or outlaw. A doctor prescribes medicine; he may proscribe tobacco.

present incumbent. Redundant; delete *present.*

presently. In the sense *at present, now, currently,* the word is grudgingly accepted by four critics, all of whom think it would best be reserved for *by and by, before long.* Another critic complains that it has displaced *now,* and American Heritage and Harper reject it in that sense. *Presently* for *now* is a revival of a long abandoned usage. Both unabridged dictionaries give the sense *now* as standard; this is the consensus. *Presently, at present,* and *currently* are often redundant, however, with a verb in the present tense unless the desire is to express contrast or give emphasis: "He is (presently) living in Topeka."

present (-ed) with. Frowned on in some stylebooks as excessive in the sense *give; present* alone is recommended instead: "He was presented a token of esteem." This is faulty advice, however. *Presented with* is good idiom; *present* alone grates on the ear. The real case against *present with* is that it is slightly pretentious. Those who are prejudiced against it would do well to use *give* instead. This, of course, will lead to *was given* (which see), afflicted with a prejudice of its own.

present writer. See *Editorial (and Royal) We.*

pressure. As a verb in the sense *exert influence, pressure* is newly arrived in the dictionaries: "The mayor was pressured to fire the chief of police." Acceptable but not often used: "A muffled concussion pressured the eardrums."

prestige, prestigious. The archaic sense (as designated by Webster) of *prestigious* is "of, relating to, or marked by illusion, conjuring, or trickery." This is likely to come as a surprise to most Americans, to whom the word means *possessing* *prestige. Prestige* itself has a corresponding history. Of the authorities being compared, only Follett regards *prestigious* as continuing to carry its old connotation; three critics, American Heritage, Random House, and Webster consider it standard and unexceptionable in the current sense, which is the only one given by Random House. There is reason to conclude that *prestigious,* in the sense *possessing prestige,* is new and an Americanism. Fowler approves *prestige* in the modern sense, but neither he nor the Oxford dictionaries give *prestigious* in the sense *possessing prestige.* No authority asperses *prestige* for *status.*

presumptive, presumptuous. *Presumptive,* a technical term having to do usually with heirs (an heir presumptive being one whose right might be lost by the birth of another heir), sometimes is misused for *presumptuous,* which means *presuming:* "It was presumptive of him to sit down at the head table." *presumptuous* (two critics; interchange of these terms is designated archaic or obsolete by Random House and Webster). *Presumptuous* is sometimes misspelled *presumptious.*

pretense, pretence. The second is the British preference.

Pretentiousness. See *Pomposity.*

pretty. Considered acceptable as an adverb in the senses *somewhat, moderately; a pretty good bargain, a pretty reasonable explanation.*

prevent. Constructions on the pattern of *prevent me leaving* (instead of *prevent me from leaving* or *prevent my leaving*) are criticized by three authorities and American Heritage but considered acceptable by a fourth. See also *avert, avoid; Fused Participle.*

preventative, preventive. The second (and shorter) form is considered preferable as both adjective and noun: "He took preventive measures"; "This medicine is a preventive." See also *interpretative,* etc.

previous to. Pretentious where *before* will do.

prewar. The use of the word as an adverb (*the conditions prevailing prewar*) instead of exclusively as an adjective (*prewar conditions*) is criticized by Fowler but considered standard by Webster; Random House and American Heritage give only the adjectival use.

pride goeth before . . . See *Misquotation.*

principal, principle. Often confused. *Principal* is an adjective meaning *chief* or *leading,* as in *the principal reason;* it is also a noun meaning *chief* or *leader,* as in *the principal of the school. Principle* is a noun only, meaning *a rule,* as in *a principle of conduct.*

prior to. Considered pompous in the sense *before:* "Prior to attending the theater, we all had dinner." *before.*

prise, prize. Two critics prefer the first spelling to differentiate the act of forcing by leverage ("The brick was prised out of the wall") from that of valuing highly ("He prized the view from his living room"). However desirable the distinction may be, it is not generally observed in America: *prize* is given by both unabridged dictionaries as the primary spelling in both senses.

private industry. A redundancy. People who leave government employment are often described as going into *private industry* (or business). Since *industry* or *business* alone has no connotation of government ownership, however, either should suffice alone.

privilege. Often misspelled *priviledge, privelege,* but a *privilege* by derivation is a private *law* (*lex, legis*) not a private ledge.

pro-. Hyphenated as a prefix meaning *favoring: pro-slavery, pro-abortion;* otherwise, in the senses *before, forward, substituting, projecting,* usually solid: *pronucleus, prognathous, procathedral.*

probate. Only Webster recognizes the sense *place on probation;* the primary and generally accepted sense is in connection with wills. There it means *prove, establish as valid.* In either sense, *probate* is chiefly an Americanism.

probe. Use of the term as a noun or a verb to mean *an investigation* or *to investigate* undoubtedly comes from newspaper headlines, where space is at a premium. Three critics discourage its general use in this sense; a fourth considers the use acceptable, and it is regarded as standard by both unabridged dictionaries. Opinion is thus divided.

proceed. The word is pretentious when it displaces *go, come, travel, walk, move.* It is suitable only to express the idea *go forward. Proceed to* is often superfluous; e.g., *proceeded to open the meeting* for *opened the meeting.* See also *precede, proceed.*

procure. Pretentious where *get* will serve. "They interrupted their house-hunting long enough to procure a marriage license."

Profanity. See *Vulgarity.*

profession. The professions once were more or less agreed to be medicine, law, the clergy, and teaching. *Profession* now is often loosely used as a synonym for *calling* or *vocation,* and this extension of the term is recognized by dictionaries. "People of many professions were summoned to the meeting." This is harmless enough, but since the word suggests learning and distinction, strenuous efforts are made to apply it to occupations of no great standing.

Whether *profession* suitably applies to a given vocation the reader will have to decide for himself. The American Newspaper Publishers' Association once argued that newspaper reporters qualify as professionals; the object was not to enhance their status but to keep from having to pay them more money under a federal law that exempted professionals. Those who hope to acquire dignity by labeling their work a profession might consider the requirements Webster sets forth: "A calling requiring specialized knowledge and often long and intensive preparation including instruction in skills and methods as well as in the scientific, historical, or scholarly principles underlying such skills and methods, maintaining by force of organization or concerted opinion high standards of achievement and conduct, and committing its members to continued study and to a kind of work which has for its prime purpose the rendering of a public service."

Although architecture was not one of the original professions no one is likely to argue that it does not qualify. Engineering, science in all its branches, and other learned occupations surely do too.

By profession is often used redundantly, as in "He is an architect by profession." A descriptive of this kind is called for only when a distinction is made, as in "He is an architect by profession and an artist by avocation."

professor. The title is properly reserved for one who holds the rank; it is not to be indiscriminately applied to college teachers. Some colleges do not have professorships. For much the same reasons that apply in the use of the title *Dr.* (which see) in the academic world, professors often prefer to be called *Mr.* In general, the more distinguished or qualified they are, the more likely this is. As usual, those whose entitlement to rank is questionable are the most insistent upon the recognition it confers. Use of the title *professor* at random for teachers of music is an old-fashioned, small-town quirk that has all but disappeared, and usually now is humorous.

programed, -ing. Music, computers, and much else are programed these days, and the predominant spelling calls for one *m*.

progression. See *arithmetical, geometrical.*

prohibit. Takes *from,* not *to:* "The audience was prohibited to smoke." *prohibited from smoking.*

prone. Two critics would confine the meaning to *lying face downward* (in distinction to *supine, face upward*), but three others say it may also mean lying flat in any position. So do the two unabridged dictionaries, Webster's New World, the Standard College, and the American College dictionaries. The same is true of *prostrate,* though the original sense was (like that of *prone*) *face downward.* Three critics and dictionaries agree, however, that *supine* means lying face upward.

Pronouns. In general, the antecedent (the noun to which a pronoun refers) must be stated, and there should be no doubt over which of two preceding nouns a pronoun refers to. An example in which the antecedent is absent: "He was operated on immediately, and it was susscessful in spite of haste." Here *it* refers to the *operation*, which should have been stated. An example in which the antecedent is uncertain: "If the dog does not thrive on raw meat, it should be cooked, *The meat* should replace *it*. The antecedent should usually precede the pronoun: "The senator was the true heir, if indeed he had an heir, of Lyndon Johnson." *He* refers to *Lyndon Johnson*, but the reader may momentarily take it as referring to *the senator*. Preferable: "The senator was the true heir of Lyndon Johnson, if indeed he had an heir" (placing *Lyndon Johnson*, the antecedent, before *he*).

On the other hand, young writers especially tend to shun pronouns in favor of naming the subject again, though the antecedent is inescapable. It makes for clumsiness to forego the terseness, naturalness, and ease of expression that come from writing simply *he* instead of *the official, she* instead of *the housewife*, and *it* instead of *the proposal under discussion*. Let us look at some examples:

"Three governors planning to attend the conference have stated their intention of turning public schools over to private hands. The three are . . ." Why not *They are . . . ?*

"A mechanic's helper shot and killed his estranged wife with a shotgun while she slept with one of the couple's three children." When the writer set down *the couple's* instead of *their*, he fled from the smoother construction to the more awkward one. "A spokesman said the group gave a vote of confidence to the negotiation committee and endorsed the latter's stand in refusing a wage increase." Why not *its* instead of the clumsy *the latter's?*

In this book other difficulties having to do with pronouns are dealt with under more specific headings, such as *I, we; he, she; anybody, anyone*, etc. See also *Possessive Pronouns; Ellipsis 1; Variation; it's me; they*, etc., *-one*.

-proof. Solid as a suffix: *waterproof, acidproof, fireproof*, etc.

propellant, propellent. One critic and Random House say *propellant* is a noun only (*a solid propellant*) and that *propellent* may be used as both an adjective (*a propellent force*) and a noun. Another critic and Webster consider the forms interchangeable as both noun and adjective. Opinion is thus divided on the use of *propellant* but there is full agreement that *propellent* may be used both ways. *Propellant* predominates as the noun, especially in technical contexts.

prophecy, prophesy. Often confused. *Prophecy* is the noun ("He uttered a prophecy") and *prophesy* is the verb that describes what the prophet does ("He prophesied rain"). "It takes no gift of prophesy to see the outcome." *prophecy*. Webster, however, considers the forms interchangeable; Random House and American Heritage do not, nor is there any observable tendency to merge them in general usage.

prophet without honor . . . See *Misquotation*.

proportion, proportions. The first figures in a number of pretentious redundancies, where it would be better replaced by *most, more, a large part: the greater proportion, the larger proportion, in greater proportion.*

Proportions is commonly used in the sense *dimensions, size, extent:* "A storm of cloudburst proportions." Bernstein objects to this on the ground that a proportion indicates a relationship and has nothing to do with size. This use is considered standard, however, by all other authorities.

proportional, proportionate. Fowler threw up his hands at any effort to differentiate these words, and since the tendency is almost always in the direction of less discrimination rather than more, any such attempt at this late date would be futile. *Proportional* is in more common use than *proportionate,* especially in set phrases like *proportional representation.* But in general the terms must be considered equally acceptable, and this is true also of the adverbs *proportionally* and *proportionately.*

proposition. As loosely used for *proposal, task, job, project, enterprise* ("The contract was a questionable proposition"; "a paying proposition"; "a tough proposition"), the expression is deplored by three critics. Random House regards this usage as informal, Webster as standard. As a noun or verb meaning to suggest sexual relations, *proposition* is considered slang by two critics, standard by a third, all but standard by a fourth, and standard by Random House and Webster, and informal by American Heritage. The consensus is that this sense is now standard.

proscribe. See *prescribe, proscribe.*

prosecute. See *persecute, prosecute.*

proselyte, proselytize. Both forms are standard as verbs; Follett's dictum that only the second is acceptable as a verb represents British practice. But even this apparently is no longer true, to judge by the Concise Oxford Dictionary.

prostrate. See *prone.*

protagonist. The sense *proponent, champion of* is, etymologically speaking, a corruption, since by derivation from the Greek the meaning is *principal actor;* the term had to do primarily with drama. Two critics insist on the original sense, and so did Fowler. American Heritage accepts *leader* but vaguely disapproves *champion.* But as Gowers, Fowler's reviser, points out, the misuse has become far commoner than the original sense and he concedes that the fight against it is lost. The senses *spokesman, leader, champion* are considered standard by both Random House and Webster. The consensus favors full acceptance of the new sense.

As Fowler commented concerning barbarisms, his term for words wrongly formed on their foreign roots, "it can hardly be expected that the susceptibilities of so small a minority [those versed in Latin and Greek] should be preferred to the comfort of millions . . ."

The natural assumption is that *protagonist* is the opposite of *antagonist*, and that since *antagonist* means *fighter against*, *protagonist* means (or ought to) *fighter for*. *Agonistes*, the root of both words, has two meanings. One is *fighter* and the other is *actor*. *Antagonist* developed from the first sense, and *protagonist* from the other. *Pro* in this instance does not mean *favoring*, but comes from *protos*, meaning *first*.

It is likely that even when *protagonist* is used in its originally correct sense of *leading actor*, it will be understood in the sense *fighter for*, so prevalent has this usage become. Further, there are many more occasions for this use. Perhaps the most irretrievable of lost causes are those based on the knowledge of a language that has become the property of a handful of pale classicists, and is no longer the mark of an educated person.

pro tem. Though the expression is a clipped form of *pro tempore*, Latin for *temporarily*, it is seldom written with a period any longer, and the full form is not often used ("He served as chairman pro tem").

protest. As a noun preceded by *in*, takes *against* or *to* rather than *of*: "The group was organized in protest against racial discrimination." (not *of*).

Protestant. The religious connotation of the word is so strong that it may be best avoided or at least used with great care in the generic sense *objector*. True, *Protestant* in the religious sense is capitalized, but proofreading is not always all it might be, and the reader often feels called upon to supply his own capitals. *Protester, objector* are recommended in nonreligious connections.

proud of. Properly used concerning only that which the person expressing pride can take some credit for. A person may be proud of having succeeded, and a parent may be proud of his children, but one can only admire, not be proud of, the achievements of one with whom he has no connection. The misuse suggests an unwarranted identification with the object, and perhaps a desire to share in the credit.

proved, proven. Four critics and American Heritage object to *proven* as the past participle of *prove:* "The mine has proven worthless." Three others consider *proved* and *proven* equally acceptable, and both Random House and Webster regard *proven* as standard. Opinion is thus divided.

There is reason to suspect that those who declare for *proved* are taking their cue from Britain. Fowler defends *proved* as regularly formed, and traces it to a Scots expression (though even the Scots, as he notes, had an exception). Haggling over the propriety of *proven* vs. *proved* in a language like English, which is nothing if not irregular, is surely unreasonable.

provided, providing. As a conjunction meaning *on condition that* ("Water will be supplied free of charge providing the rent is paid promptly''), *providing* and *provided* are considered equally acceptable by four critics; American Heritage and Fowler prefer and Follett insists on *provided*. *Providing* is considered standard by both Random House and Webster; thus the consensus overwhelmingly approves of it. Five critics discourage either *provided* or *providing* as pretentious, however, when *if* will serve: "We shall have a picnic provided it does not rain." *if.* The words imply something desirable, and are sometimes misused concerning what is unwanted: "A few of the sightseeing guests provided problems." *presented, created.*

psychological moment. Criticized as pretentious and trite in the popular senses *at the critical moment* or *in the nick of time*. The displacement shows how strongly we are attracted by the pompous and apparently technical.

pulling my leg. See *putting me on.*

Puns. Bernstein and Fowler spiritedly (and properly) challenge the widespread assumption that puns are the lowest form of wit. Puns, on the contrary, often reflect a keen wit, and the criticism of them is likely to come from those who are incapable of such flights of fancy. Many puns depend upon gross distortion of a word, and automatically call forth groans. Perhaps the only general test of a pun is that it should be amusing, but this does not carry us very far, because ideas of what constitutes humor vary so much. Perrin warns against unconscious puns, which can produce ludicrous effects not unlike mixed metaphors. A good pun makes sense both ways, like the comment of the drama critic (Eugene Field?) that an actor in *Richard III* "played the King as if in constant fear that someone else was about to play the ace." The puns that cause pain and give them all a bad name are those that depend upon twisted pronunciations and work only one way.

pupil, student. In general, *pupil* is applied to those attending elementary school and *student* to those attending high school or college. While Random House and Webster recognize this distinction, they also give the terms as synonyms. *Scholar,* the ten o'clock scholar to the contrary, is no longer applied to young learners, but rather to researchers.

Purist. The purist generally is an authoritarian in his attitude toward language; he wants someone else to make decisions for him, preferably a long time ago. When the dictionary does it on the only reasonable basis possible—the consensus of literate usage—he is unlikely to accept decisions he recognizes as representing change.

A purist, further, is anyone whose ideas of grammar and usage stand to the right of those held by the user of the term. It is, of course, a deprecatory epithet, much like *Puritan* on the lips of a libertine. In this book, *purist* and *purism* are used for the most part concerning rules and distinctions that have no standing in usage and no effect on meaning.

Purple Passage. Purple passages are characterized by (1) brilliance or (2) ornate, highly rhetorical writing; *purple* does not mean risqué, as in "The novel had difficulty finding a publisher because of some *purple* passages." This was a case of confused colors, for *blue* has the meaning, in a literary sense, that was intended. Recent literary trends in the use of vulgar and obscene language, however, may well have made *blue* obsolete in reference to writing.

purport, purported. Three critics agree that the verb is improperly used in the passive: "The vase is purported to date from the Ming Dynasty." *purports.* They hold also that the subject of *purport* may not be a person considered as such: "The minister purported to set a good example for his parishioners." *pretended, attempted,* or whatever is suitable. The first restriction conforms with dictionary definitions of *purport* as a verb. Webster gives the adjective *purported* as applying to either persons or things: *purported spies; purported original oils.*

purpose. Such expressions as "*With* (or *for*) *the purpose of* advancing," or whatever, are redundant; *to advance.* "He is studying with the purpose of bettering himself." *to better.*

put it all together. A catch-phrase that had a dismaying vogue in reference to any kind of achievement, no matter how trifling or ill-defined. Fortunately it seems to be dying out, like "tell it like it is."

putting (me) on. The popularity of this expression in the sense *kidding, fooling, making fun of,* is another example of the new admiration for British slang and other mannerisms of speech. The noun *put-on* ("I thought it was a put-on"—i.e., *sham, pretense*) is recorded in the Smaller Slang Dictionary by Eric Partridge, an Englishman, in a slightly different sense. The verb appears in the revised (1967) edition of Wentworth and Flexner's *Dictionary of American Slang,* which traces it to jazz, student, and swinger origins. *Pulling my leg,* which carries the same sense as *putting me on,* is another import from Britain. Still others, which will be found in this book: *early on, not too, not all that.* The theatrical world seems particularly fond of such expressions. They may sound affected.

Q

qua. The use of the Latin term where *as* will do is discouraged ("A woman *qua* mother").

qualified expert. Redundant for *expert;* an unqualified expert is hardly an expert.

quandary. Often misspelled *quandry.*

quartet. See *trio.*

quasi. Usually two words with a noun: *a quasi contract; a quasi difference.* Hyphenated with an adjective: *a quasi-historical play; a quasi-humorous speech.*

query. Two critics disapprove of using the word for *investigation,* or for *inquiry* in the sense of *investigation* (but not in the sense *question*). This accords with dictionary definitions.

question as to (of) whether. The words between *question* and *whether* should be omitted when they can be done without, which is nearly always.

Questions. The indirect restatement of a question does not make the restatement itself a question: "He asked the director of the museum whether the paintings on display were originals?" The question mark is wrong. The error occurs also with speculative statements, as "I wonder whether my application has been considered?" The statement is declarative, not interrogative, though it describes a state of indecision. Another error: "What he would like to know is how the police found out about this?" "Guess what I did today?" is an imperative, not a question.

Two critics disparage the use of the question mark in parentheses to indicate sarcasm: "He received his education (?) in the South."

quick. Rejected as an adverb ("They move quick in this place") by American Heritage; Random House and Webster equate it with *quickly.*

quiet, unassuming. A cliché of character sketches.

quieten. An American critic regards this verb as a Briticism, and as a conspicuous affectation when used in America, but Fowler rejects it for Britain, too, in favor of *quiet.* Both unabridged dictionaries corroborate that the form is chiefly British.

quip, quipped. "The actress gave her age as thirty-seven, but later quipped to newsmen, 'Confidentially, I'm fifty-seven.' " The use of *quipped* amounts to nudging the reader in the ribs and saying, "It's a joke—get it?" *Quipped* with any direct quotation is a fit candidate for outlawry. Perhaps there is a place for it in those rare instances when the reader has no way of knowing the speaker is joking. Otherwise, if a quip is too weak to stand on its own legs and be recognized, why trouble to quote it?

Quip is overgenerously applied to nonquips: "This street has gone to pot," the mayor quipped. A respectable pun, but why hit the reader over the head with it?

Cracked, as a truncated form of *wisecracked,* is in the same league with *quipped,* like *wisecracked* itself, *joked, jested,* and *gagged.* "Questioned whether Italy's long siestas have anything to do with its overpopulation and housing problem, Scelba cracked, 'In Italy, a siesta is a time for rest, not work.' " There is no surer way to insult the reader's intelligence than to make him feel he has to have a joke explained to him. And as all should know, explaining a joke generally kills it. Let us take the advice of the *Chicago Tribune's* Line o'Type column: "Hew to the line, and let the quips fall where they may."

quite. May mean either *entirely, wholly, altogether;* or *somewhat, to a considerable degree.* Both senses are considered standard by dictionaries; two critics regard the second as colloquial. But this sense now seems predominant, one of the critics and American Heritage agree, and its Usage Panel approved. "I was quite happy with the editorial," said a legislator who had received an accolade. Although a purist might accuse him of ambiguity, everyone else would immediately understand that the speaker was pleased though not carried away. Thus also: "The franc is quite stable"; "Christian Dior has done something to the female bosom that might prove quite startling." Yet careful writers tend to use *quite* only in the sense *entirely.*

Quite, like *rather* (which see) is sometimes ineptly used to diminish the force of a strong modifier: "He managed to get past this quite huge stumbling block." Was it really huge, or only moderately large? When *huge* is knocked down by *quite,* we cannot tell.

Quite all right is criticized by one authority but defended uncertainly, on differing grounds, by two others. American Heritage approves of it. *Quite a,* as in *quite a few, quite a little,* is found to be well established informally by two critics, and is defended as good English by Fowler; both American Heritage and Random House regard it as standard.

quiz. Two critics object to the use of the term, which occurs principally in headlines, to describe a formal interrogation of some kind, as in legal proceedings; Random House gives *a questioning,* but Webster does not recognize *quiz* as a noun in this sense. Both Random House and Webster give *to quiz suspects* (by the police). The American Heritage panel accepts the noun and rejects the verb, both by narrow margins.

Quotation. 1. Meaningless. Three critics protest the excessive and meaningless use of quotation marks, which is most conspicuous in newspaper writing, to set off informal expressions or slang. Just as often they are ignorantly placed around words used in standard senses. Examples: *Some "swapping" may be necessary; Winston Churchill once gave Basic English a "plug" over the radio; The professor is likely to "hedge" his answers on this subject.* The consensus is that if the writer finds it to his purpose to use slang or colloquialisms, he should do so forthrightly, without the apology indicated by quotation marks. And in any event it would be well to ascertain whether what the writer suspects is slang is not really a standard term, like *hedge* in the last example.

2. Fragmentary quotation. The annoying and usually meaningless practice known as fragmentary quotation is also endemic in newspapers. This consists in breaking back and forth between indirect and direct quotation in the same sentence, for no perceptible reason. Example: The secretary of the treasury told Congress today that the nation "will get into serious difficulty" if the present tax burden "is continued over a long period." Either the whole sentence should have formed a direct quotation, or the quotation marks should have been removed altogether to make one continuous indirect quotation. This criticism is not aimed at fragmentary quotation that is skillfully employed to give the sense of a long passage by combining a portion of it with indirect quotation for the sake of brevity.

3. Wrong person. An example: "In point of fact," the historian remarked, "he couldn't bear to go—he was too immersed in the production of his fourteenth book." Since, as the context made clear, the historian was referring to himself, *he* should have been *I;* the writer was hopelessly mired between direct and indirect quotation. Another example, with the mixture of direct and indirect quotation that is more likely to show this fault: Stevens said he "feels in his heart that the responsibility was entirely his." Either dispense with the quotation marks, making the sentence an indirect quotation, or use first-person forms within the quotation marks.

4. Quotation marks. The comma and the period go inside quotation marks, and the colon and semicolon go outside. This is a matter of a difference between American and British printing practice: in Britain, the reverse is true. Another difference is that the British use single quotation marks to enclose the primary quotation and double marks for quotations within quotations. Americans start with double marks and then go to single marks.

If a quotation runs to more than one paragraph, the quotation marks are left off the ends of paragraphs except the last, where the quotation ends. Each continuing paragraph of the quotation *starts* with quotation marks.

5. Use for emphasis. Quotation marks may not be used for emphasis: "The world can feed itself for some time 'if' it mobilizes its resources." *If* should be in italics, or failing that, in capitals or boldface.

6. Changing indirect to direct. A common misdeed of inexperienced copy editors is converting indirect quotations to direct quotations, possibly with the idea of brightening things up. But only the writer knows what the exact words of the speaker were; in composing indirect quotations he probably was paraphrasing. Thus converting indirect quotations to direct quotations amounts to putting words in the speaker's mouth, and can be dangerous.

7. Figurative sense. Quotation marks are justified around a word or phrase to indicate that it is to be taken in some other than its literal sense. "Management officials said yesterday they won't budge from their 'last offer.' " Many a purported "last offer" is succeeded by another in labor negotiations. "For many years, Kansas was a 'dry' state." An ironical use of *dry*, as made clear by the context, which explained that at the time when Kansas was legally and technically dry, it was in fact illegally and sopping wet. When a word is used in some other than its expected sense, *so-called* is excessive in addition to quotation marks: *the so-called "blacklist."* Either *so-called* or the quotation marks suffice. See also *Attribution 5; Comma 15; Misquotation.*

quote, quotes. *Quote* for *quotation* ("He interpolated a quote from Shakespeare") is deplored by three critics and American Heritage, but considered standard by Harper and both unabridged dictionaries.

Quotes for *quotation marks* is regarded by two critics as acceptable only as a technical term in the printing and publishing field but the convenience of the clipped form is probably irresistible; Random House accepts *quote mark* and Webster accepts both *quote* and *quote mark* in this sense.

Quoted for *quoted as saying*, as in " 'There was no connection between that charge and my administration,' the President was quoted," is denounced by some critics.

quoth Regarded by two critics as archaic (a judgment in which Random House and Webster concur) and thus unsuitable to a modern context.

R

rabbit, rarebit. See *Welsh rabbit, rarebit.*

rack, wrack. Two critics regard either *rack and ruin* or *wrack and ruin* as correct; one chooses *rack and ruin.* The versions are considered interchangeable by dictionaries. In general it is agreed that *wrack* means *wreck* and *rack* means *stretch* or *strain.* By this reasoning the phrase is *nerve-racking* (not *-wracking*). Dictionaries give both forms but regard *-racking* as predominant. Since a rack is a frame, clothes hangers and the instrument of torture are *rack.*

racket, racquet. The first is considered preferable for the bat used in tennis and other games. *Racquet,* however, is not wrong: Random House and Webster consider the terms interchangeable in this sense. Two critics warn against the jocular use of *racket* to describe legitimate occupations or businesses, since the usual meaning in this connection is *an illegal activity.*

radio-. *Radio* as a prefix is doggedly hyphenated by many, but it is not given thus in any dictionary, and carefully edited publications observably set it solid. The commonest combination, perhaps, is *radioactive* (one word). Other examples are *radiotherapy, radiotelephone, radiotelegram, radiothermy.* It's different, of course, when *radio* is an adjective: *radio tube, radio station, radio spectrum.* When in doubt, use the dictionary.

railroad, railway. The first is seldom used in Britain; the terms are more or less interchangeable in the U.S. Random House and Webster indicate that *railway* is applied to the tracks, but *railroad* is not, and that as applied to the system *railway* designates a shorter line and lighter equipment. American Heritage applies both terms to the track. The fact is that these niggling distinctions are meaningless as applied to rail systems, since the forms are obviously used interchangeably.

raise, rear, rise. At one time it was earnestly argued that children are *reared,* animals *raised. Raise* in reference to children is now standard, a judgment concurred in by five critics, American Heritage, Random House, and Webster.

For an increase in pay, the word is *raise* in America and *rise* (though *raise* is winning acceptance) in Britain, though Bryant surprisingly reports a considerable incidence of *rise* in this sense in the U.S.

raison d'être. Since this French phrase translates *reason for existence,* it is pretentious and wrong where only *reason* is called for.

rambunctious. Accepted as standard by American Heritage, Random House, and Webster.

rampage. A stereotype of journalism in reference to flooding; rivers are almost invariably said to *go on a rampage,* just as forest fires *blacken acres,* storms *pack winds,* and snow and rain are *dumped.* See also *Journalese.*

rap. A fairly recent slang term for *talk discursively, discuss;* it is too new to have found its way into any but the American Heritage dictionary. One theory is that it derives from the French *en rapport* or the English *rapport* (harmonious relation) but this seems as fanciful as the idea that the criticized use of *hopefully* (which see) comes from the German *hoffentlich.* Slangsters seem unlikely, on the whole, to be conversant with foreign languages.

rara avis. Two critics disapprove of the phrase (Latin for *rare bird*) for *rarity.*

rarebit. See *Welsh rabbit, rarebit.*

rarefy. *Rarify* is likely to be regarded as a misspelling; only Webster gives it as a variant.

rarely ever. Considered established colloquial idiom by one critic; rejected by another and American Heritage. Preferable: *rarely; rarely if ever.*

rassle. *Wrastle, wrassle, rassel, rastle* are regarded as dialectal or colloquial forms of *wrestle,* growing out of the vernacular mispronunciation. An attempt was made in a California lawsuit, however, to establish *rassling* as the designation for professional wrestling. The proponents described rassling as a combination of vaudeville and tumbling, with a prearranged conclusion, and added that professional wrestling is now a form of satire, having deteriorated as a sport.

rate. As a verb in the sense *deserve* ("This letter rates a reply") rejected by American Heritage, not recognized by Random House, but considered standard by Webster, which quotes *Harper's* magazine in the sense *have rank, influence, position* ("She really rates around here"). Rejected in this sense too by American Heritage but considered standard by Random House.

rather. Often called upon to do too big a task. In the sense considered here, it is the equivalent of *somewhat; a rather cold day* we understand to be chilly but not unendurable. The word is a mild qualifier, and is often coupled with too strong an adjective. The impression is left that a milder adjective would have been more suitable in the first place.

"The revelation was rather astonishing"; "The contradiction was illustrated in rather amazing fashion''; ''He suffered a rather staggering loss'' exemplify this. *Astonishing, amazing,* and *staggering* are all too wild to be tamed by *rather,* and the attempt leaves the reader in a fog as to the force intended.

Rather, somewhat, slightly, pretty, etc., and a strong descriptive tend to cancel each other. What is rather astonishing obviously is not astonishing at all but something more nearly approaching surprising. *Rather amazing* comes down to much the same thing. Losses that are rather staggering appear to have been severe but no more.

Those who use *rather* in expressions like these want to have it both ways; they yearn for effect, and very likely *amazing, astonishing,* and *staggering* by themselves would convey the true state of affairs. But then they are so frightened by the verbal power they have unleashed that they timidly invoke *rather* as a counterbalance. What they end with stops pretty much on dead center, and they would have been better advised to stick with their first choice, undiminished.

Slightly is often misused in much the same way, though sometimes a humorous effect is intended. *Slightly amazing,* however, and similar expressions are often set down seriously. It may be deposed that *slightly amazing* comes under the same heading as *slightly pregnant.* ''The official hailed the year as 'a rather spectacular one for the union.' '' See *very; quite.*

Had rather and *would rather* are defended as idiomatic by four critics and American Heritage.

rattle. For *unnerve* (''The accusation rattled him''), considered standard.

ravage, ravish. Sometimes confused. To ravage is to damage or destroy; to ravish is to rape, abduct, or enchant. A building may be ravaged by fire; a woman may be ravished, ravishing, or ravaged (ordinarily by age).

rave. As an adjective applying to enthusiastic reviews of entertainments, a dismal cliché. Or, one might say, a shoutword. See also *adequate; consummate.*

re. This Latin term for *concerning, in reference to* is inappropriate in ordinary contexts and best left to legal documents, five critics agree. This applies also to *in re (in the matter of). Re* is not an abbreviation and thus does not take a period.

re-. The prefix is generally solid, even when followed by *e; redo, retell, reelect.* Care should be exercised in distinguishing, by use of the hyphen, such pairs as *recreation (amusement)* and *re-creation (creation again), recollect (remember)* and *re-collect (collect again).*

reaction. Five critics object to *reaction* in place of *opinion, reply, response, feeling,* and the like: ''What was the reaction to the change?'' *response.* In general, their view is that *reaction* is primarily a technical term belonging to science, and is not properly applicable to people. Nevertheless, Random House gives *the nation's reaction to the President's speech* and Webster gives *her reaction to the news.* American Heritage appears to concur with the critics.

readjust, -ment. "For the time being, certainly, it had been found necessary to make a readjustment of rations (Squeaker always spoke of it as a 'readjustment,' never as a 'reduction')."—*Animal Farm*, George Orwell. "Speaking of taxes, the secretary recalled that in the past year he had frequently stated that the central element in the reform measure would be a proposal to readjust the rate structure. I had not thought it necessary to spell out the fact that readjustment necessarily meant readjustment downward."—The Associated Press. Thus do the dealers in gobbledygook lose all idea of precision.

Readjustment, it is obvious, is a favorite euphemism for *reduction* among Big Brotherly and bureaucratic types, when they are not using *downward revision*. Preferable in these contexts: *cut, reduction*. See also *Gobbledygook; Euphemisms*.

real. *Real* for *really* ("I was real tired") is considered colloquial and unsuitable in writing by five critics. Dictionaries label this usage informal. *Real* for *serious*, to provide emphasis, is considered objectionable by two critics (*real trouble, real danger*). It is questionable, however, whether *real* in such contexts is not intended to mean *actual* as contrasted with *supposed* or *imagined*, in which event the usage is not open to criticism. See *sure*.

real facts. See *fact, facts*.

realise, realize. The first is the British preference.

realistic. This descriptive and its opposite, *unrealistic*, are often misused, three critics agree, not in reference to realism, but to mean *true, correct, sensible, acceptable*, etc., indicating approval or disapproval, for example in collective bargaining, when one side describes its own proposals as realistic and those of the other side as unrealistic. Random House, however, gives *practical* as one definition and Webster gives *not impractical*.

realtor. The term was invented and registered as a trademark by the National Association of Real Estate Boards in 1916. In observance of this proprietorship, it should properly be capitalized and applied only to members of the organization. Its convenience in place of *real estate agent*, however, has caused it to be widely and indiscriminately used. Random House recognizes only the proprietary sense; Webster and American Heritage also recognize the general sense *real estate agent*. Owners of trademarks can protect their proprietary interest by exertions to inform the public about them (usually by means of advertisements aimed at the editors of newspapers and magazines, and also by writing remonstrative letters to those who have misused the trademarks). But the owner has no other recourse against a publication that has misused a trademark, though his exertions will prevent its use by competitors. The proprietary interest in some trademarks has been lost for want of effort to preserve it. Among these are *zipper, aspirin, milk of magnesia*, and *shredded wheat*.

rear. See *raise, rear, rise.*

reason is because. This common expression, in place of *reason is that,* is denounced as redundant by five critics and American Heritage, and defended as standard and idiomatic, despite frequent criticism, by three. *Reason is that* has the edge. See also *simple reason.*

reason why. Rejected as redundant by American Heritage, but defended by Evans as having been standard English idiom for centuries. Evans adds, "As a rule, it is better to be natural than to be correct according to theories that other people have never heard of." This principle, if universally observed, would wipe out thousands of rules of grammar and usage, perhaps for the better.

rebut. See *refute.*

receipt, recipe. Usage has differentiated them to the extent that it now attracts slightly surprised attention to use *receipt* to mean a formula for cooking, although this sense is technically correct. The word for the formula is now almost invariably *recipe; receipt* is all but exclusively used to mean a written acknowledgement, as *a receipt for a payment.*

receive. See *suffer, sustain, receive.*

recipient. Disapproved as pretentious in such constructions as "He was the recipient of an award" for "He received an award."

reckon. Regarded now as dialectal or rustic in the senses *guess, suppose, consider* (as distinguished from *calculate*), though it has respectable literary precedent. The unabridged dictionaries concur in this judgment.

reconvert. Threatens, as a redundancy, to drive out *convert,* especially in connection with the adaptation of buildings to new uses. Homes, for example, are erroneously spoken of as being *reconverted* to apartments. What is *re*converted must already have been converted. *Reconvert* gained currency after the war, when industrial plants that had been converted to war production were reconverted to their original uses.

recollect, re-collect. *Re-collect* (*collect again*) should be distinguished by the hyphen from *recollect* (*recall, remember*). See also *re-; remember.*

record. *All-time, new high,* or even *new* is usually redundant with *record* in reference to an unprecedented level of achievement; therefore, *set a record,* not *new, new high,* etc., *record.*

recorder. As the name of a musical instrument, confusing to many who think it refers to a recording device. The instrument, popular in the baroque era and revived in recent years, is an ancestor of the flute.

recourse, resource. The usual confusion is using *resource* for *recourse* in the set phrase *have recourse:* "When he needed encouragement, he had recourse (not *resource*) to liquor."

recreate, re-create. The hyphen is necessary to distinguish *recreate* (*amuse, divert*) from *re-create* (*create again*), and especially *recreation* from *re-creation*.

recrudescence. Fowler holds that the term should be used only concerning the renewed breaking out of something that is objectionable, such as disease; Evans argues that in the U.S. *recrudescence* is neutral, and means simply *a renewed breaking out*. Thus it may be applied to what is desirable. Random House defines the term neutrally, while Webster holds to Fowler's view, and opinion is divided. It is likely that some connotation of undesirability attaches to the term in the popular mind.

recur, reoccur. One critic sees a distinction between these forms to the effect that *reoccur* suggests a single repetition. Neither unabridged dictionary recognizes this difference, however. Two critics regard the forms *reoccur, reoccurrence* as superfluous, and the Concise Oxford Dictionary does not even list them. Nor does any American desk dictionary. The consensus is that *recur, recurrence* are preferred, and that in any event the two forms mean the same thing.

red-faced. The expression may have some virtue as the invariable substitute it has become for *embarrassed* in the press, but if so, the virtue is not apparent. Account might be taken of the fact that most people may be embarrassed without blushing.

redhead, redheaded. Some newspaper stylebooks forbid the use of these terms to describe people having red hair. The prohibition is ignorant and quixotic, since all dictionaries recognize this application as standard.

Redundancy. The sportsman does not use a shotgun when a rifle will do. When it comes to writing, the rifle can't be beat. He who closes his eyes, pulls the trigger, and lets fly with a barrage of words ought to be told that somehow they lose their force in bunches. A single, well-chosen shot will bring the quarry down. In general, the fewer the words the better the writing.

The soporific habit of using several words where one will serve may be illustrated by *a sufficient number of* vs. *enough, at the present time* vs. *now,* and *in the immediate vicinity of* vs. *near.* These woolly expressions, which occur so often they pop unbidden into the mind, are readily used by the uncritical writer. Hunting them down and nailing them to the wall is a salutary exercise.

An excellent dictum on redundancy was set forth by William Strunk, Jr. in *The Elements of Style:* "A sentence should contain no unnecessary words, a paragraph no unnecessary sentences, for the same reason that a drawing should have no unnecessary lines and a machine no unnecessary parts.''

A repulsive pair of expressions has grown onto *future: in the near future* and *in the not-too-distant future.* Translated, *in the near future* means *soon,* and *in the not-too-distant future* can mean *before long, eventually, finally, next year, sometime,* or *sooner or later.* The reader, poor fellow, must decide.

Case is the progenitor of a hardy breed of villains that seem impervious to attack: *in case* (*if*), *in most cases* (*usually*), *if that were the case* (*if so*), *not the case* (*not so*), *in the case of* (which often may be omitted entirely, and if not, replaced by *concerning*), and *as in the case of* (*like*).

"It is possible that this material may become mixed with clouds in some cases and induce rain sooner than otherwise would have been the case." Stripping this down to what counts, we get: "This material may become mixed with clouds and induce [cause?] rain sooner."

"This station will be able to track more satellites over longer distances and do more observations than is the case with most other tracking stations in the world." Omit *is the case with.*

Instance sometimes appears in place of *case: in most instances,* etc.

Some redundancies have become classic targets of critics: "*at the intersection of* Market and Main" (*at*); "*consensus of opinion*" (*consensus*); "*entirely* destroyed" (*destroyed*). Also undeservedly popular are *despite the fact that* (*although*), *due to the fact that* (*because* or *since*), *during the period from* (*from*), and *for the purpose of* (*for*).

Redundancy is a vast and overfertilized field. Among its varieties, as classified by scholars, are pleonasm (using more words than necessary), tautology (repeating an idea in different words), and circumlocution or periphrasis (talking around the subject). The point of this preachment is not so much to urge the outlawing of the particular expressions cited as to encourage the critical sense. Nevertheless, the examples have been chosen for their prevalence, and anyone who does forgo them will certainly not harm his writing.

Ignorance of what common words mean, or unwillingness to trust them to do their job unaided, is responsible for some specimens of redundancy. *Experience, records, custom,* and *history* come only from the *past;* thus there is no occasion for *past experience, past records, past custom,* and *past history. Gifts* and *passes* are by definition *free,* even if the advertising gentry cannot be made to see it. An *innovation* is by its nature *new,* as are a *beginner* and a *tyro;* and an *incumbent* is inescapably of the *present. Plans* are willy-nilly of the *future,* as must be *prospects* and *developments. Planning* can be nothing but *advance.*

What is *friendship* if it is not *personal?* And what is *business* if not *official?* Both *agreed* offends the thin-skinned, for *both* is two taken together and *agreement* is a coming together. *Equally as* is a horse of the same color. *On account of* is distasteful for *because of,* and *in excess of* is even worse for *more than,* because it is not only redundant but pompous.

"*In order to* balance the budget," or what have you, might better be simply *to* balance. *In back of* is a gaucherie for *behind,* though *in front of* (a building, for example) serves a purpose that *before* does not. *Advance reservations* seem to be getting ahead of themselves. *In which* is often superfluous, as in "Each candidate will be given fifteen minutes [in which] to express his views." An accident victim is taken to a hospital *for treatment*, inevitably; why labor it?

New construction is Navyese for a ship abuilding; why apply it to structures, when nothing is more self-evident than the newness of what is under construction? These random examples show, if nothing else, that the pen is mightier than the pitchfork.

reenforce, reinforce. The second predominates in the sense *strengthen: reinforce the troops, reinforced concrete.*

refer: See *allude, refer.*

refer back. Redundant for *refer.*

Reference. It was once considered enough to identify a person by his full name and then to use the last name for subsequent references. Something of a fad, however, has sprung up in recent years to see how many different ways the subject can be styled.

Richard Nixon, for example, was thus identified in an article about him. In the middle of things, however, he suddenly became "Dick Nixon." A page later, unaccountably he emerged fullblown as "Richard Milhous Nixon." Sometimes the subject, for no apparent reason, will be referred to here and there by his nickname alone. This skipping around from one form to another can become as confusing as a Russian novel, where the characters all seem to have twelve polysyllabic names and are referred to indiscriminately by any of them. No wonder many never make it through *War and Peace*.

Some of this trickiness is traceable to *Time* magazine, which once went out of its way to dig up little-known middle names of well-known people and startle its readers with them. Middle names may be interesting, but they can be presented unobtrusively: "John D. (for Davison) Rockefeller." There is no excuse for flaunting such small facts or leaving the reader in doubt what the usual form of the name is. Random reference to public figures by their nicknames is objectionable because it may sound patronizing or unduly familiar, but there are exceptions, when people are better known to the public by their nicknames than otherwise or when the tone of the writing calls for familiarity, as is often true of sports stories. Usually, however, once identification has been established, it seems sensible to stay thereafter with a standard form—usually the last name, but sometimes the nickname or first name. Switching forms of reference when there is no apparent reason for it annoys the reader. See *Names of People*.

referenda, referendums. The English plural is now in such wide use as to make the Latin (*referenda*) sound affected.

refined. See *cultured, cultivated.*

Reflexives. It is a common error to set off reflexive pronouns with commas: "I, myself, am in complete charge." *I myself am in . . .* See also *myself; Comma 4; self.*

reform, re-form. The hyphen is necessary to distinguish between *reform* (*improve*) and *re-form* (*form again*).

Reform Judaism. See *Judaism.*

refuse. See *decline* (*or refuse*) *comment.*

refute. To refute is to destroy by argument, or prove to be false or mistaken. The word is often misused for *deny, contradict, reject, rebut, dispute.* A statement, for example, is not refuted simply by saying it is not so; evidence must be presented that effectively demolishes it for refutation to take place. To test whether *refute* is called for, substitute *disprove.* One writer on usage has the muddled impression that *refute* means *rebut,* and offers *confute* for *disprove.* The fact is that *refute* and *confute* both mean *disprove,* not merely *rebut* or *contradict. Confute,* however, is a bookish word, not in common use.

regard. *Regard* leads to two barbarisms: *irregardless* and *in regards to. Irregardless* is beyond the pale, and no more need be said, except perhaps that it comes from heedless analogy with *irrespective. In regards to* is an illiterate variant of *in regard to. In regard to, with regard to,* and *as regards* are not actually crimes, but the writer who is neat will eschew all three for *regarding, concerning,* or *about.*

"National politics are different in some regards from state politics" will offend the discriminating, who would prefer *respects.* American Heritage rejects *in some regards* in favor of *in some respects:* it approves *as regards* (for *about, concerning*).

Regard in the general sense *consider* takes *as.* Fowler expressed concern over the omission of *as* ("He was regarded a bum") but this fault appears to be rare, having been succeeded by the unwanted pairing of *as* with *consider* (which see).

regrettable, regretful. What is regrettable causes regret; *regretful,* applied to people, means *feeling regret.* Thus the thunderstorm that spoils the picnic is *regrettable,* not *regretful.* The distinction applies also to the adverbial forms *regrettably* and *regretfully.*

regular. Redundant with any word that indicates periodic recurrence: *a regular weekly meeting, a regular monthly review, a weekly meeting, a monthly review.*

rehabilitate. One critic insists that the word applies properly only to people (e.g., criminals), and not to things, but this view is not taken by either Random House or Webster. The criticism appears to be supported by the definitions in American

Heritage, but it seems untenable in view of the widespread application of the word to urban redevelopment.

rein, reign. See *free rein.*

reinforce, reenforce. *Reinforce* predominates in the sense *strengthen.*

relating to. See *regard.*

relation, relative. Interchangeable in the sense *kinsman,* though there is an edge of preference for *relative.* The unabridged dictionaries give the terms as equivalents.

Relative Clauses. See *Restrictive and Nonrestrictive Clauses; Ellipsis 4.*

relatively. See *comparatively, relatively.*

relevant. During the widespread campus disturbances of the 1960s, one of the chief complaints of students was that their studies were "not relevant." No one explained, however, what they were not relevant to. Relevance apparently was rediscovered as economic conditions worsened and jobs became harder to find, giving a college education at least a theoretical value.

Relative Pronouns. See *Restrictive and Nonrestrictive Clauses: Ellipsis 4.*

relict. Two critics say that the word (meaning *widow*) is not now in common use except in legal papers. This is corroborated by Random House, which calls it archaic; Webster does not label it.

relieve. *Relieve* in the sense *deprive of* or *take away from* sounds facetious, but its users are not always aware of this. "The city initiated action to *relieve* the bus line of its franchise" and "The pickpocket *relieved* several tourists of their wallets" are examples. *Relieve* in the first example is so inappropriate it must have been used unwittingly. See also *lift.*

religion editor, center. The religion editor handles religious matters; he may not himself be religious and consequently *religious editor* is ambiguous as a job description. Campus buildings where religious activities are concentrated are *religion,* not *religious,* centers.

religious. As a noun ("Two religious were kneeling in prayer" and "The pilgrimage was made by a party of religious and laymen"), the word is churchly cant, so seldom seen in ordinary contexts as to cause a moment of puzzlement.

remainder. See *balance.*

remains. Probably regarded by its users as a euphemism for *corpse,* but the term is distasteful to many, and beyond that has grown quaint. *Body* generally is preferable.

remediable, remedial. Sometimes confused. What is remediable is open to remedy: "A weedy lawn is remediable." What is remedial does the remedying: "Weedkillers are remedial."

remember, recollect. Two critics, Random House, and Webster hold that *recollect* implies an effort to bring to mind, and that *remember* denotes what is effortless or spontaneous. Both unabridged dictionaries, however, also give *remember* as a synonym of *recollect*.

remind. The verb is transitive, which means it must take an object. Thus such uses as "Taxes will be due April 1, the collector reminds" are wrong, because the example leaves the reader up in the air, groping vainly for the missing object. "Taxes will be due April 1, the collector reminds taxpayers." Both unabridged dictionaries give *remind* as transitive, and so does American Heritage.

remittance. Considered pretentious where *money, payment* will do. "The remittance for the books may be sent later." *payment.*

remunerate. Pretentious where *pay* will do. Sometimes misspelled *renumerate.*

renaissance, renascence. Although they are synonyms and generally interchangeable, usage has pretty well settled on *renaissance* for the great revival of learning and things associated with it, and on *renascence* for rebirth in general. Webster concurs with this; Random House gives the forms as interchangeable, though it regards *renaissance* as predominant.

render. Pretentious and quaint for *sing* or *play* (*render a selection*). Cub reporters used to be warned off the word by being told only lard could be rendered (i.e., extracted by melting) but this obviously was only a journalistic delusion.

rendezvous. Sometimes aspersed as a verb ("The searchers *rendezvoused* at Horner's Corner"), but it is standard. It gained popularity from frequent use in naval operations during World War II.

rendition. Approved by American Heritage for *performance* (*her rendition of the song*), as distinguished from or not necessarily including *interpretation,* and considered standard by Webster; Random House does not give this sense.

renege. *Renege on,* in the sense *go back on* ("She reneged on her promise"), is standard.

renowned. The correct form of the adjective; often erroneously given as *renown,* which is the noun: "By 1926, he had become a renown pianist." *renowned.* Not even Webster, which is hospitable to many usages widely considered erroneous, recognizes this one. *Renown* and *renowned* are sometimes misspelled *reknown*, *reknowned*.

reoccur, reoccurrence. Needless and cumbersome variants of *recur, recurrence*.

repast. Quaint or pretentious for *meal, dinner*, etc.

repeat again. Redundant for *repeat*.

repel, repulse. To repel is to cause aversion, drive or force back, keep at arm's length; *repulse* also means *drive back*, and is the stronger term. The usual error is to associate *repulse* with *repulsive*, but there is no relation. One may be *repelled* (not *repulsed*) by an idea; a suitor may be *repulsed*, two critics say; Random House and Webster give the terms as synonyms.

repellent, repulsive. Both mean *causing aversion*, but the second is much stronger. It is difficult to deduce this from dictionary definitions, however, which appear to make the terms equivalents. Random House and Webster give the variant spelling *repellant;* American Heritage does not.

repertoire, repertory. More or less interchangeable in the sense of compositions, plays, etc., available for performance, though the first is usually used for this meaning, especially in reference to music: "Her threadbare repertoire included only a few arias." *Repertory*, as both noun and adjective, is favored in connection with the theater in other senses than that described above, as *a small repertory house*. Random House and Webster appear to concur in general, though they give the terms as synonyms.

Repetition. Bald repetition of phrases and sentences seems to imply a lack of confidence that they have sunk in. This is no tribute to the reader's intelligence, nor does it reflect any credit on the writer's. Footless iteration like the following is often encountered:

"The president, smiling broadly, said today that ever since he was five years old his brother has been criticizing him." But two paragraphs later, we get this warmed-over dish: "Smiling broadly, the chief executive replied that his brother had been criticizing him since he was five years old."

As garnish, perhaps, the broad smile has now been moved forward; the president is interestingly referred to as the chief executive; and *has been* is changed to *had been* for some mysterious reason.

"The lumber strike is over, and the president of the union calls it 'a draw.' " Passing by the unnecessary quotes around *a draw*, let us proceed to the second paragraph: " 'We neither won nor lost the strike. It was a draw,' said George Willard . . ." All right, it was a draw, as the union president saw it. But after having established this, why not let it go at that?

And again: "She's tall, she's tanned, and she says the new Dior 'flat' look 'came just in time to save me.' " Four paragraphs later: " 'I think Dior came just in time to save me,' she said."

"He said last night that never before in the history of astronomy have the scientists been able to study a satellite which has traveled as fast as the Russian earth moons.

" 'We've never had this in astronomy before,' said Dr. Whipple."

Here's not just duplication, but triplication:

"The White House said today it does not know whether reports of a Russian manned-rocket flight are true or not." (There were quotes around *true or not*, compounding the felony.)

" 'We have no knowledge of the truth of these stories,' the press secretary told reporters.

"Hagerty persisted in his refusal to comment on the reports 'because I don't know whether the story is true or not.' "

And so to bed, to bed, to bed.

Unconscious repetition of closely related words or sounds in the same sentence is generally to be avoided, but Fowler says that a dozen sentences are spoiled by ill-advised avoidance of repetition for every one that is spoiled by ill-advised repetition. Fowler's exhaustive treatment of this subject (under *repetition of words or sounds*) is commended to the reader.

It is a mark of an undeveloped style to purposelessly review, sum up, or restate what has just been said. Summaries should be made deliberately, with a view to assisting the reader, and should not simply betray fuzzy-mindedness in the writer, as in these instances:

"He became pastor of the church when it was completed two years ago. Prior to accepting the pastorate, he was a student." *Before that,* he was . . .

"They tried to break a safe out of a 500-pound block of concrete. Failing to free the safe from the concrete, they fled." *Failing, they fled.*

"Sixteen people were killed in a tragic crush on New Year's Day. Those victims were killed when a tremendous crowd surged across a narrow bridge." *on New Year's Day when a tremendous crowd surged . . .*

See also *Ellipsis; Repetition of Defining Modifiers* under *Modifiers; Variation.*

replace. The word has two common senses, which must be carefully differentiated: *put back into place* and *succeed or substitute for.* Thus the word may be ambiguous; unless the context makes the meaning clear, "The king was replaced on the throne" may be taken to mean he was put back or someone else was substituted. See also *substitute, replace.*

replete. Two critics say the word does not mean *complete* or *filled with,* but only *abundantly supplied with.* American Heritage concurs, but both unabridged dictionaries give both senses.

replica. To begin with, the term has a technical meaning in the fine arts: an exact copy by the maker of the original. This is so specialized, however, that the layman is unlikely to be aware of it, though two critics will admit no other use. The commonest misuse is in the sense *model* or *miniature*. Evans regards *replica* for *copy* as loose. Both unabridged dictionaries give *copy* or *reproduction* as one meaning of *replica*, however, and the American Heritage panel also accepts it. This is the consensus. *Exact replica* is redundant.

reportedly. *Reportedly* has been sneered at and even proscribed on the ground it was not to be found in dictionaries. Now, the fact that a word is not in the dictionary is no reason it should not be used. If everyone took this attitude there would be (1) no words, and (2) no dictionaries, for, of course, words come first and dictionaries later. Until 1960 or so, *reportedly* was indeed hard to find in dictionaries, though Webster II did include it in small type at the bottom of the page. The word is now given as standard in all current dictionaries. Some newspaper editors asperse *reportedly* on the ground that only verifiable fact should be reported, arguing that this leaves no place for it. Such views are matters of policy and have nothing to do with the virtue of the word. They would also rule out *allegedly, supposedly,* and other speculative expressions. The important thing is to distinguish between fact and speculation, which is what *reportedly* handily does. Follett deplores it on grounds that are difficult to credit.

represent. Two critics object to the displacement of *is, are,* by *represent:* "The figure represents half his income." *is.*

repulse. See *repel, repulse.*

repulsive. See *repellent, repulsive.*

republican, Republican. The capitalized form should be reserved for references to the political party, the other for references to the form of government. See also *democrat; conservative; liberal.*

require. Objected to where *want* or *need* will do.

reside. Regarded as pretentious where *live* will do.

resin, rosin. *Rosin* is not, as is sometimes supposed, an error for *resin; rosin* is a distilled solid form of resin used to make the bows of string instruments tacky, among other purposes.

resistance. Sometimes misspelled *resistence.*

respect. See *in respect to.*

respective, respectively. Often used unnecessarily: "They returned to their respective homes." The reader will not otherwise assume that they returned to each other's homes. The words should not be called into play unless there is a need for sorting out: "Mrs. Jones and Mrs. Smith selected carnations and snapdragons, respectively,'' which matches the women with the flowers in the order given. Words like *former, latter* (which see), as well as *respective, -ly,* which oblige the reader to match things up, are to be avoided. Sometimes used unnecessarily: "Shavers big and small will thus get a chance to compare the respective blades." No need for *respective.* The test is to leave out *respective, -ly* and observe whether the sense is affected.

(the) rest. See *balance.*

restaurateur, restauranteur. The awareness that this word does not contain an *n* was once regarded in newspaper offices as distinguishing the seasoned reporter from the cub. Webster now admits *restauranteur* as a variant but no other dictionary does.

rest easy. The form of the idiom; not *easily,* which is overcorrect.

restive. Three critics hold that the word can only mean *resistant to control* (a dog on a leash or a horse in a corral thus might be restive) and that the sense *restless* is wrong. Nevertheless, Random House and American Heritage give *restless;* Webster gives *fidgety.* It is obvious that popular misuse has added another sense.

Restrictive and Nonrestrictive Clauses. Failure to distinguish these by proper punctuation may mislead the reader as to the meaning intended or may result in ambiguity. Restrictive and nonrestrictive clauses are relative clauses, which means that ordinarily they begin with *which, that, when, where, who, whose,* or *whom.* A restrictive clause is one whose meaning is essential to the sentence; that is, it defines the word it modifies. "I waved at the girl who was standing on the corner." The same clause may be made nonrestrictive by being set off by commas: "I waved at the girl, who was standing on the corner." The girl in this example must have been previously mentioned; the clause merely modifies, and does not define. The example illustrates, too, that whether a clause is restrictive or nonrestrictive depends on the writer's intention. Relative clauses depending on proper names ("He next performed in Chicago, where he was well received") are invariably nonrestrictive, except in the rare case where the purpose is to distinguish between two places or persons having the same name. Very frequently the comma in such sentences, when there is no question whether the clause is nonrestrictive, is omitted, even in generally well-edited publications. It is impossible to say whether this reflects ignorance of what is considered correct punctuation, or a feeling by the writer that the clause could not be understood as restrictive and thus the comma is superfluous. In the most carefully edited material, however, the comma is used to set off nonrestrictive modifiers.

Restrictive clauses are essential to the meaning and are never set off; nonrestrictive clauses are not essential, but merely descriptive or additive, and are always set off. The *whose*-clause in "No woman whose clothes make her conspicuous is well dressed" is inescapably restrictive, since the sentence no longer makes sense if it is dropped. An example of ambiguity caused by failure to punctuate correctly:

"The rule excepts commercial lots where there is no restriction on all-night parking." The writer intended that commercial lots are unaffected, but by omitting the comma before *where* gave the impression that the rule affects only certain commercial lots where there is no restriction on all-night parking. See also *that 4; Appositives*.

result. Takes *in*, not *with:* "The program is likely to result with a collapse of confidence in the City Council." *result in.*

reticent. Sometimes displaces *reluctant* ("He said so many actors come to Hollywood that he was a little reticent to do so"). The word usually means *disposed to keep silent;* it may also mean restrained in general, as in speaking of a reticent piece of writing, or a reticent musical performance. No definition justifies the use of the word in the sense *reluctant,* as in the sentence quoted.

retire. Pretentious for *go to bed.*

retro-. Solid as a prefix: *retroactive, retrocession, retrofit,* etc.

reveal. See *Attribution 2.*

Revelations. Two critics consider this form acceptable in casual reference to *The Revelation of St. John.* Random House also sanctions this usage, but Webster and American Heritage do not give it. The consensus favors it.

reverend. Strictly speaking, an adjective meaning *deserving of reverence.* Four critics prescribe the forms *the Reverend John Jones* (*the* plus the first name) and *the Reverend Mr. Smith* (*the* plus *Mr.* with the last name alone). Two critics and American Heritage also accept *Reverend John Jones* (omitting *the* with the first name). The same critics accept *Reverend* with the last name alone (*Reverend Jones*) and they accept *reverend* as a noun: "The reverend was standing on the porch." Random House and Webster also admit this usage as standard; American Heritage calls *reverend* as a term of address "impolite."
 It is obvious, however, that usage, even among the clergy themselves, is shifting away from the strict formality described at the outset. It is questionable that offense is either intended or felt by use of *reverend* as a noun of address. The layman cannot understand why, if you can call a senator *Senator* and a doctor *Doctor,* you cannot call a clergyman *Reverend.* But *Reverend,* as a term of deference and respect, is no more to be applied by a person to himself than *Mr.* These comments have to do with the Protestant clergy; a Catholic priest is referred to as *the Reverend Father* (or simply *Father*) *Jones,* and a rabbi as *Rabbi.*

Reversal of Sense. See *Negatives; Double Negative; not un-; minimize; underestimate; not.*

reverse, converse, opposite, vice versa. These terms are sometimes applied to what is not logically or unequivocally capable of reversal: "There's no need to be a blackguard to be successful. In fact, the reverse is true." Here are three possible reversals of this statement: there's a need to be a blackguard to be successful; there's a need to be a blackguard to be unsuccessful; there's no need to be a blackguard to be unsuccessful. But, the reader will object, we know what was meant: It is necessary not to be a blackguard, etc. Yet confusion is possible, and at any rate the statement is unclear.

Consider also: "This is Voltaire in reverse: I agree with everything you say but reject your right to say it." This is a logical reversal, for Voltaire (in the popular notion) disagreed, but would defend the right to say. The effect of devices like *the reverse* and *vice versa* should be instantly evident, as in an example cited by Webster: "It was with vast relief that we came upon a man pretending to be a machine, rather than *vice versa*."

Herbert Depew in *Tortured Words* cites "We thought the law would punish him, but the reverse took place." He punished the law? Of course not; it would have been both more concise and more explicit to have said "but it did not."

"A fare increase will cause loss of bus patronage; the reverse would also be true—a fare reduction would increase the use of buses." Reversal is placing things in an opposite relation, and that is what happens in this case: fares up, patronage down; fares down, patronage up. *Reverse* is more often used in physical rather than abstract connections (the reverse of a coin, reverse a motor). *Converse* would be equally acceptable here, perhaps more so, because it always goes with abstract relations. *Opposite* would also do, if homelier English is acceptable. See also *minimize; Double Negative; Negatives; not un-; minimize; underestimate.*

revert back. Redundant for *revert.*

review, revue. *Revue* is preferred for the stage performance, *review* in other senses, including reports on books, concerts, etc.

revise, revision. *Revise* is often loosely and improperly used for *rearrange, reorganize.* Revision has to do with changing or amending something that is written or otherwise expressed; printers' proofs, laws, and opinions may be revised. "The lower courts were revised in California in 1953." *reorganized.*

revision (upward, downward). See *Euphemisms.*

rhetoric. Became what Fowler would have called a vogue word (like *relevant*) in the turbulent 1960s in one of its several senses: artificial elegance of language, discourse without conviction or earnest feeling; inflated language (verbosity, bombast) ("That passion, sir, is not empty rhetoric"—Virginia Woolf).—Webster. The term is not new in this sense; the Century Dictionary (1897) gives "display in language; ostentatious or meretricious declamation."

Rhyme. As a fault in prose. See *rime, rhyme.*

rid. The preferred form for the past tense and present participle is *rid* rather than *ridded,* though both are correct: "He rid the lawn of crabgrass last week"; "We rid the closet of moths."

right. In the sense *very much,* or *greatly,* or *much, right* is not now standard: "We were right surprised." Neither Random House nor Webster even gives the sense. See also *in (his, her) own right.*

right-of-way. The plural is usually *rights-of-way;* Webster accepts *right-of-ways.*

right on. A sixties slang term of enthusiastic approval, already apparently fading. Perhaps an abridgment of "right on target."

right-to-work laws. It is generally realized that this is a political euphemism, concocted to make a kind of law that labor considers repugnant palatable to the voter. As a result, carefully edited publications now designate such legislation as *so-called right-to-work laws.* The purpose of such laws is not to preserve any right to work but to outlaw the union shop. See also *fair-trade laws.*

rile. For *anger, annoy* ("The inattention in the classroom riled him") approved by American Heritage and considered standard by Random House and Webster; called informal by Harper.

rime, rhyme. *Rhyme* is preferred in the sense *identity of sound.* Rime is best reserved to mean *hoarfrost* or *frozen mist.*

ring, rung. The past form *rung* ("He rung the bell") is standard, but *rang* is preferred, five critics agree. American Heritage considers *rung* nonstandard.

Rio Grande River. See *Sahara.*

rip off. Fairly new slang for *steal, cheat;* it seems to have some staying power.

rise. See *raise, rear, rise.*

rob. What is robbed is the person or place from which something is taken, not the thing itself; thus a bank is robbed, but not the money that is stolen. This is the view of three critics, but Webster quotes Dryden "rob the honey." This, however, may be archaic, since Webster's treatment otherwise conforms with the limitation set by the others.

robber, robbery. See *burglary.*

rock, stone. *Rock* generally connotes large size and *stone* small size, but *rock* is often used of what may be thrown; "They threw rocks at the squirrels." Random

House gives for *rock* "a stone of any size" and Webster gives "ranging in size from a boulder to a pebble." American Heritage equates the terms. Literary usage more or less observes the distinction (*Rock of Ages*), especially in England. But *stone* has been reputably used for objects of considerable size, for example in reference to the stone that was rolled away from the sepulcher of Christ.

role. Two critics recommend dispensing with the circumflex and italics (*rôle*) and accepting the term as fully naturalized English. Dictionaries also indicate this preference. *Role* is sometimes used when *roll* is meant (*relief roles*); though as Fowler notes, the words have the same origin, differentiation is now fully established.

Roman Catholic. See *Catholic.*

Roman Numerals. The ability to read—or even decipher—Roman numbers larger than, say, X (*for ten*) is now possessed by so few that their use may be considered a deliberate attempt to obscure. There was a time when the year of copyright of books was often given in this manner, but that practice has now happily been abandoned in favor of the Arabic numbers everyone can read.

Roman numerals continue to be used ceremoniously, however, for cornerstones and often to indicate the volume number of periodicals. (The number is changed annually, by some publications at the beginning of the year, by others on the anniversary date of their establishment.)

The *New Haven Journal-Courier,* confronted by its 191st year of publication, had to consult a classical scholar at Yale before it could decide whether to give the volume number in the classical style (CXCI) or the early Roman style (CLXXXXI). An office boy who asked why not just use 191 and forget the whole thing was told, according to an account in *Publisher's Auxiliary,* to shut up. That may have been an example, of which many more significant ones could be cited, of hidebound tradition speaking to a public that wants to understand what it is reading. Habit and the reluctance to change play an astonishingly large role in writing.

If Roman numerals must be used, *one* is represented by I, not by the Arabic 1. Such mixtures as X11 are seen in both typescript and printed material.

romance. With the meaning *exaggerate, invent,* the use of the word goes back to 1671. "The clergyman's wife had nearly been romanced out of a $203,000 inheritance," while aspersed by one critic, represented clear and standard usage. In the sense *make love* ("They were romancing in the moonlight") *romance* has been censured as nonstandard by two critics, but there can be little doubt that this is now the predominant meaning. Webster and Random House accept it as standard; American Heritage gives the sense *woo* as informal.

root of all evil . . . See *Misquotation.*

rosin. See *resin, rosin.*

rough. Once criticized in the sense *difficult* (*a rough time*), but now accepted as standard by Webster and Random House and as informal by American Heritage.

round, around. "The reporter who turned round a well-known cliché and characterized somebody as a man who kills one bird with two stones likewise showed inventiveness." The editor of the publication where this sentence appeared received a sharp criticism from a reader—sharper than it might have been, perhaps, because the publication was one that gave instruction in the correct use of English. "A glaring use of the wrong word," the complainant said. *"Round* should have been *around."* *Turned around* is more usual in America; *turned round* is characteristically British. The use of *round* in Britain where we would say *around* is very noticeable, as citations from the OED show: "I had a fit of giddiness; the room turned round"; "She turned round to where her brother stood." *Round* for *around* does occur in expressions familiar in America, however: *the year round; all-round* and *all-around* are about equally frequent and both correct to express the idea of versatility.

rout, route. *Rout* means *drive out.* "The troops prepared to rout the invaders"; *route* means *select,* or *send along, a path:* "Hannibal planned to route his army through the Alps." The past tense (*routed*) is the same for both words.

routine training flight, exercise, etc. Usually redundant; omit *routine.*

row. The use of the word for *dispute,* especially in headlines, to describe serious differences, for example in international relations, is criticized by two authorities. It is accepted as standard by dictionaries, however, for *noisy dispute* or *quarrel.*

rules and regulations. A wornout stereotype that cannot bear examination: how do rules differ from regulations?

rung. See *ring.*

S

s, 's, s'. See *Possessives; Long s.*

s (long). See *Long s.*

Sabbath. Not necessarily Sunday; to Jews and Seventh-day Adventists it is Saturday, and to Moslems it is Friday.

sabotage. Two critics insist that the word should be used figuratively (*sabotage the legislation*) only when it is intended to imply malice, not simply obstruction, destruction, etc. Random House, however, gives "any undermining of a cause" and Webster gives "any act or process tending to hamper or hurt"; American Heritage has a similar definition.

sacrilegious. Often misspelled *sacreligious,* logically enough, since its usual meaning is *profane, disrespectful of what is sacred.*

Sahara Desert. Those versed in Arabic and some others are aware that *Sahara Desert* is redundant, for *Sahara* means *desert.* Two critics agree that there is no point in proscribing it. American Heritage concedes it is widely used but calls *the Sahara* preferable. Similarly, Sierra Nevada, the name of the great rocky spine of California, means *Snowy Range* in Spanish, and Rio Grande means Big River. Some are distressed by the illegitimate but common plural *the Sierras,* rather than *the Sierra.* But those who protest against the widely used forms of these names are engaging in pedantry, and they should logically also object to *City of Minneapolis* and *City of Indianapolis,* since the suffix *-polis* means *city* in Greek.

said. Described by three critics as legalese in the sense *aforesaid, aforementioned: the said editor; said contractor.* American Heritage and Random House concur that it is used chiefly in legal connections. Thus the term is to be avoided in ordinary writing. Almost always the definite article (*the*) suffices in reference to what has already been specified. "The editor of the local newspaper, together with members of the clergy, refused to take a position in the controversy. Said editor would not give his reasons, however." *The editor.* See also *say, said; Attribution 9.*

336

said in a statement. Redundant in attribution, unless it is essential to indicate that a quotation came from a formal statement rather than a speech or otherwise. See also *Attribution*.

sake. Two critics agree that in such expressions as *for goodness sake, for conscience sake*, and others where the word preceding *sake* ends in a sibilant it may be written without an apostrophe and should be written without *'s*. Webster, however, gives *goodness' sake*.

salad days. Criticized by two authorities as a cliché. It may now be necessary to explain, however, that the expression means days of youth and enthusiasm and inexperience, since it seems to be growing quaint and disused.

salary, wage. It is sometimes said that a job pays a wage and a position pays a salary. The distinction between *job* and *position* is not, however, what it is often thought to be. In general, *wage* is applied to compensation for work at the lower end of the scale in prestige. A teacher may get less than a truck driver, but the teacher's pay is not likely to be referred to as a wage, though that of either may be referred to as a salary. Employers often pay salaries by the week or month, wages by the day. See *job, position*.

saloon. See *bar, saloon*.

same, the same. *Same* as a pronoun ("He collected the money and deposited same") is not the best English; it bears an unwholesome odor of the world of commerce. The usage achieved a species of immortality and perhaps even an appearance of sanction from "Sighted sub, sank same," the laconic and famous report of an aviator in World War II. Kipling, too, had Tommy Atkins say, "We 'ave bought 'er the same with the sword and the flame." But Tommy Atkins would hardly be accepted as an arbiter of these matters. In good usage, *the same* becomes *it*. "The publication will be mailed regularly and costs for same will be chargeable to member organizations." Omit *for same*.

    Two critics agree that either *as* or *that* may be used after *same* as an adjective: *the same thing as (that) I heard*. See also *such*.

Samson. The name of the Biblical strong man is often misspelled *Sampson*.

sanatorium, sanitarium, sanitorium. Three critics agree that the first two are generally interchangeable forms today, though at one time the distinction was made that the first was more of a health resort and the second more of a hospital. *Sanitorium* is regarded by two critics as an error, though Webster recognizes it, together with *sanatarium*, as a variant spelling. Random House gives the original distinction but also gives *sanatorium* and *sanitarium* as synonyms. It does not recognize *sanitorium* or *sanatarium*. *Sanatorium* is the general all-purpose form, and it would be well if the variants were discarded.

sanction. Attention is called by three critics to the fact that in ordinary connections, *sanction* means *permission, approval* ("The administration gave its sanction to the wage increase") but that in international relations, sanctions are penalties or deterrents ("Sanctions were voted against the aggressor").

sanctum, sanctum sanctorum. Criticized as clichés in ordinary use in the sense *private place.*

sank. See *sink.*

sans. Objected to by two critics as a pretentious displacement of *without.*

Santa Ana, santana. *Santa Ana* is the correct name for the strong, hot, dry foehn winds from the north, northeast, or east in Southern California, Random House and Webster agree; the designation comes from the mountain range and canyon through which they are channeled. *Santa Ana* is also the form sanctioned by the federal government. It is sometimes said that the term should be *santana,* from a supposed Indian word for *devil wind,* but anthropologists say no such word existed.

sartorial. Objected to by two critics as pretentious.

satisfied. Although the word can mean *convinced,* two critics warn against using it in contexts where the meaning *contented* may be ambiguously understood: "The police were satisfied that no one could have survived the crash." It seems unlikely, however, that any such misapprehension would occur.

savant. Two critics object to it as a random variant for *professor, scholar,* or *scientist* (or anyone who knows more than the user, which may not be much).

save. *Save* for *except* ("All save the fisherman had departed") is regarded as affected by five critics; all but Evans comment that this usage is commonly an attempt to pretty up newspaper writing. See also *Poesy.*

saving, savings. As a modifier in such connections as *savings bank, savings bond,* the plural form is required. *Savings* as a noun takes a plural verb: "His savings were disappearing." The corollary, as pointed out by American Heritage, is that one may not properly speak of *a savings of five dollars* (*a saving*). The correct form is *daylight-saving* (not *savings*) *time.*

say, said. Four authorities criticize the mannerism, oftenest seen in newspapers, of seeking variety by displacing *said* in favor of conspicuous and often inexact variants. Some of them are *affirm, assert, declare, asseverate, state, contend, insist, emphasize, avow, aver, claim.* See *Attribution; Quotation.*

scan. For *look through hastily* (*scan the newspapers*), approved as standard by dictionaries. American Heritage makes the useful point that the context should show that another sense of the word, *examine minutely,* is not meant.

Scandinavia. The term formerly applied only to Norway, Sweden, Denmark, Iceland, and the Faroe Islands. All are linked by racial heritage and by languages similar enough so that the speakers of them can understand each other. In recent years, however, Finland has increasingly come to be regarded as a part of Scandinavia, logically enough on a geographical basis. But Finns have a different racial origin, apparently linked to the Mongolians, and speak a totally different (and very difficult) language that belongs to the Finno-Ugric family and is related, among the languages of Europe, only to Magyar, the language of Hungary, and to Estonian. American Heritage is the only dictionary that admits Finland under the Scandinavian umbrella, in one broad definition. Because of common interests, Finland has entered into certain cooperative agreements with Norway, Sweden, and Denmark, and thus geography and economic interest have created a linkage between Finland and the rest of the original Scandinavia in the absence of linguistic and racial ties. Finnair, the Finnish national airline, has carried this so far as to attribute the origin of smorgasbord, a Swedish and Norse national collation, to a prehistoric Finn in a series of facetious advertisements. A touch of nurture may make the whole world kin. What has been said here applies also to *Nordic.*

scarce, scarcely. *Scarce* as an adverb for *scarcely* ("She was scarce out of her teens") is considered affected by two critics. *Scarcely . . . than* (displacing *scarcely . . . when* or *before*) is criticized by four authorities and American Heritage: "Scarcely were the words out of his mouth when (not *than*) the music began." Bryant considered *scarcely than* informal. *Scarcely* is a negative and should not be used with another negative: *scarcely enough* rather than *not scarcely enough.* Sometimes the fault is not so obvious: "It was impossible to see scarcely anything through the fog." *Impossible* is another negative. See also *Double Negative; hardly; Negatives.*

scattered in all directions. Redundant for *scattered.*

scent, sense trouble. According to one stylebook, a person does not *sense* trouble, he *scents* it. But what about the kind of trouble that has no odor?

sceptic. See *skeptic, sceptic.*

scholar. The term is no longer applied to schoolboys like the ten o'clock scholar, but rather is reserved for specialists at universities and the like who are deep in their subjects, four critics agree. Dictionaries, however, also give *student, pupil.*

Scientific English. See *Technical Terms.*

scientist. See *engineer, scientist.*

Scot, Scotchman, Scotsman, Scotch, Scottish. Much as the inhabitants of San Francisco object to having their city called Frisco, inhabitants of Scotland object to being called Scotchmen. *Scotchmen,* however, is a reputable term, and the only reason for avoiding it is to keep from giving umbrage to Scotsmen (the term they prefer). *Scot* is the original name for an inhabitant of Scotland. For practical purposes, *Scot, Scotchman,* and *Scotsman* are synonyms. Scotsmen generally reserve *Scotch* for things (*whisky, plaid*) and *Scottish* for people. This conforms with general usage, for *Scottish whisky* is unheard-of.

In the sense *extirpate, kill, destroy* and the like ("He scotched the rumor that the farm was for sale") *scotch* has nothing to do with Scots and thus should not be capitalized: *scotched.* See also *welsh.*

scrip, script. Certificates used in place of money and certain other fiscal documents are known as *scrip,* not *script:* "The workers are paid in scrip." *Script* has a number of senses, none of which give difficulty.

sculp, sculpt, sculpture. The first two are derogated by one critic as back-formations from *sculpture,* an allegation denied by Random House, which says *sculp* comes from the Latin verb *sculpere* and *sculpt* from the French *sculpter.* *Sculpt* is the more frequent term today. Follett approves only *sculpture* as the verb. All three forms are recognized by dictionaries.

scut. An old term having other meanings, but revived by the new feminists in the expression *scut work.* The *Dictionary of American Slang* gives *scut* as the secondary form of *scud,* defined as a noun meaning "Hard, boring, or tedious tasks; minor details that are unrewarding and time-consuming." The term as used by feminists, to be found in no general dictionary, refers to menial tasks assigned to women.

seasonable, seasonal. What is seasonable comes at the right time or is appropriate to a season; what is seasonal depends on or is connected with a season. Snow in winter is seasonable; some jobs are seasonal. "The unemployment rate is always seasonably adjusted." *seasonally.* "A couple of seasonably unemployed pickpockets who could not work with frosty fingers . . ." *seasonally.*

second, secondly. See *first, firstly.*

secular, sectarian. *Secular* means *worldly* or *temporal,* in distinction from *religious* or *spiritual; sectarian* means *pertaining to a religious sect or sects.*

secure, obtain. *Secure* in the sense of *obtain* is an old and reputable use, though often denounced. But *get* is often preferable, as simpler, to *secure, obtain,* or *procure,* as Evans points out. "The reporters secured complete details from the police." Pretentious for *got.* See also *get.*

seeing as how. See *as how.*

seem. See *can't seem.*

see where. This common locution ("I see where the Mets won") is rejected by two critics and American Heritage in favor of *see that.* Nevertheless, it is so firmly established in speech, particularly, that it is unlikely to be dislodged by the more formal *see that.* Partridge also rejects it, though describing it as "astonishingly common."

seldom ever. Rejected by two critics as contradictory. Preferable: *seldom, seldom if ever.* This common lapse puts one in mind of the supercautious small-town character who expressed uncertainty with "You never can always sometimes tell."

self. Not good usage for *I* or *me:* "Please reserve tickets for self and family," two critics hold. Dictionaries, however, consider it standard. See also *myself.*

self-. Three critics warn against compounds with *self-* (*self-confessed, self-deprecating, self-conceited,* etc.) when *self-* adds nothing to the meaning. The test is to delete *self-* and decide whether anything has been lost.

-self, -selves. For the usage of words with these terminations (that is, reflexive pronouns) see *myself; Reflexives.*

semi-. Solid as a prefix; *semiarid, semireligious, semitropical,* etc. Usually hyphenated when followed by *i: semi-idle, semi-intoxicated.*

Semicolon. The form *semi-colon* is endemic in the writings of professors, journalists, and others who can be expected to know better. Although hyphenated versions tend to be succeeded by solid ones, no precedent can be found for *semi-colon* in any dictionary, British or American.

senior, junior. See *Jr., Sr.*

senior citizen. A distasteful euphemism to many, including some seniors (that is to say, old people) themselves. Sometimes ineffectual attempts to avoid it are worse: "a nine-story apartment designed for senior persons." *elderly* (or perhaps *retired*) *people.* Decried by four critics and American Heritage. See also *elderly.*

sensational. Criticized by Bernstein, Evans, and Fowler as overworked.

sensual, sensuous. When a distinction is made, *sensual* connotes something gross, *sensuous* something refined or intellectual. This view is borne out by Random House and Webster.

sentient, sententious. Although *sententious* has the sense of "terse and energetic in expression: pithy," it is used almost entirely in the derogatory sense of "marked by pompous formality." It may be said that only this latter meaning effectively survives; we can hardly expect a word to bear two nearly opposite senses. *Sententious* is sometimes unhappily confused with *sentient* (*capable of sensation*). Neither word means *wise,* as is sometimes assumed.

sentiment, sentimentality. In general, as denoting feeling or emotion, *sentiment* indicates sincerity, *sentimentality* excessive sentiment or mawkishness. American Heritage tends to blur the distinction by giving "emotion that borders on mawkishness" as one definition of *sentiment.* The distinction is usually observed, however, and it is surely useful enough to be preserved.

separate, separation. Often misspelled *seperate, seperation.*

Sequence of Tenses. Many an absurdity is committed in the name of a widely misapplied rule of grammar, the one governing sequence of tenses. The general idea is that the tense of the verb in the main clause of a sentence governs the tense in a subordinate clause. Sometimes this is called attracted sequence; that is, the tense of the verb in the clause that follows is attracted to the tense of the verb in the main clause.

Let us look at an example: "He *said* he *was* tired of everything." The verb in the main clause, *said,* is in the past tense so the verb in the dependent clause, *was,* naturally falls into the past tense. Most of the time, this is not the kind of rule it is necessary to stop and think about. Here are some other examples of the normal sequence of tenses:

"The man *wore* a pained expression as the officer *forced* his car to the curb."

"The motorist *explained* that he *tried* to buy a replacement for his defective headlamp."

"She *promised* that she *would be* there."

Some writers seize upon the rule of sequence and follow it out the window—or, just as bad, into the next sentence. The rule has an important exception, which can be relied on to forestall a good deal of nonsense: The *present* tense, rather than the past, is used in the subordinate clause to express a continuing or timeless state of affairs. Consider: "He *said* the world *is* round." Applying the basic rule of sequence, *is* here would be *was* because the main verb, *said,* is in the past tense. But that would make it sound as if the world no longer were round. (A sentence concerning the shape of the earth is invariably cited in discussions of sequence of tenses, and it may even be illegal not to do so.)

In the name of common sense, exceptions to the rule are properly made to describe any condition that continues in effect at the time of writing, four authorities agree. Here are some examples:

"The surveyor *reported* that the terrain is [not *was*] rugged."

The president *pointed* out that there *are* [not *were*] seventy-five to eighty independent government agencies, each of which *consumes* [not *consumed*] his time."

"The girl said yesterday she was a virgin." Was then, or said then?

Although the rule applies properly to one sentence at a time, succeeding sentences are often attracted into the past tense, sometimes with preposterous results. Here is an example:

"The chances of Richard Roe, candidate for Congress, *were considered* good. Roe *was* a Catholic from a predominantly Catholic district."

Since Roe's candidacy continued at the time of writing, this gave the unintended impression that he might have changed his religion. Lapses like this, which can be prevented by knowing when to make an exception to the rule, have drawn indignant protests to editors, to say nothing of having confused readers.

"Nehru *said* he *would go* before the U.N. tomorrow to seek a vote on Hungarian intervention." A dispute arose among editors over whether it should have been "Nehru said he *will go*."

Considerable spleen, righteous indignation, sarcasm, and the like were vented, but when the smoke had cleared the situation was left, if anything, more confused than before. Now, which is correct—"Nehru said he *would go*" or "Nehru said he *will go*"? Both versions are. But the use of *will* is a modern trend. The rule of sequence, as we have noted, requires the tense in a subordinate clause to correspond with the tense in the main clause. Consequently, the past-tense *said* requires a past-tense *would go*. But several participants in the discussion held that "Nehru said he *will go*" is more direct and thus preferable. They could find some support in a pronouncement by George O. Curme, a grammarian's grammarian. In his *Syntax*, regarded by scholars as a classic, he took note of "a tendency in indirect discourse to break through the old sequence when a more accurate expression suggests itself."

One of the more interesting aspects of the debate was the confusion over the function of *would* in *Nehru said he would*. Several of the disputants mistook it for a subjunctive form indicating uncertainty. They seized on this as affording an excuse in the event Nehru did not carry out his intention.

Would in this instance, however, is not a subjunctive form, but the past tense of *will*. "I *would* if I could" illustrates the subjunctive, indicating a conditional state, but "I said I *would*" illustrates the past indicative, indicating simple intention.

sergeant. Sometimes misspelled *sargeant* and otherwise by the attraction of pronunciation.

Serial Comma. See *Comma 6*.

service. The use of *service* as a verb where *serve* will do is derogated by three critics and American Heritage: "The bus line services the northern suburbs." *serves*. Evans, however, is indulgent toward this use. The critics agree that *service* is useful, if not indispensable, in the sense of providing maintenance: *service an automobile, a TV set*, etc. This view corresponds in general with the definitions given in Random House and Webster.

Service also has an agricultural meaning (as a synonym for *breed*), a fact the city-bred are not always aware of, and one that should discourage its indiscriminate use. Readers of John Steinbeck's *The Grapes of Wrath* are not likely to forget this:

"See that sign 'longside the road there? Service Club. Luncheon Tuesday, Colmado Hotel? Welcome, brother. That's a Service Club. Fella had a story. Went to one of them meetings and told the story to all them businessmen. Says, when I was a kid my ol' man gave me a haltered heifer and says take her down an' git her serviced. An' the fella says, I done it, an' ever' time since then when I hear a business man talkin' about service, I wonder who's gettin' screwed."

sesqui-. Solid as a prefix: *sesquicentennial, sesquipedalian,* etc.

set, sit. In general, *set* is transitive (takes an object): "Set the package down"; *sit* is usually intransitive (takes no object): "They sit and rock on the porch." *Set* for *sit,* as in "They set on the porch," is not considered standard. There are numerous idiomatic exceptions to these principles, however; a hen *sets,* the sun *sets,* an object may *sit* on another (a book, for example, on a shelf); by the same token, *sit* is sometimes transitive; a rider *sits* a horse, one may *sit* oneself.

settlement. Takes *of,* not *to:* "Look for a fast, easy settlement to the steel wage talks." *of.*

Seventh-day Adventist. The denomination prescribes this form; not *Day.*

sewage, sewerage. *Sewage* is the waste material, *sewerage* the system used to carry it off or the process of carrying it off, three critics agree. Evans concurs, but with Random House and Webster accepts *sewerage* as a synonym for *sewage,* and this usage is observably common. As a practical matter, however, *sewage* is predominant as both noun and adjective ("The sewage is treated in four plants"; "A sewage system has been installed"). *Sewerage* is seldom seen as a noun (The sewerage was faultily designed"); the choice in this context is generally *sewage system. Sewerage* is falling into disuse, but no harm is being done, for the distinction between it and *sewage* serves no useful purpose. American Heritage recognizes the true state of affairs by giving *sewage* as a synonym for *sewerage.*

sex. Follett disapproves of *sex* in the sense *sexual organs,* used by Frank Harris in his autobiography, as a French term that is inappropriate in English. The word has also been used this way in the writings of James Baldwin. Neither unabridged dictionary nor American Heritage recognizes this sense. *Sex* for *sexual intercourse (having sex)* is standard.

sexist, sexism. The terms grew out of the new feminism, and are too new to be in dictionaries, but they are surely standard. Anyone who can read must know that they pertain to discrimination practiced on the basis of sex, particularly to the disadvantage of women. See *Feminism.*

shake one's head. See *nod.*

shake down, shakedown. In the sense *extort, extortion (a shakedown of custom-*

ers) approved by American Heritage and considered standard as verb and noun by Random House and Webster.

Shakespeare, Shakspere, etc. *Shakespeare* has indisputably established itself against all its rivals; Random House and Webster consider it predominant. There is no appeal to an original version, for the poet spelled his own name in different ways at various times, in accordance with the lighthearted approach to orthography that prevailed.

shall, will; should, would. If you paid attention in school, you learned a little formula for the use of these verbs. It went like this: To express the simple future, or let us say to indicate a simple intention, use *shall* with the first person and *will* with the second and third persons.

This gives us "I shall grow old one day" and "You [he, she, it] *will* grow old one day." Plurals follow the same pattern: "We *shall* . . ." but "You [they] *will* . . ."

Then, to express determination, or insistence, the pattern is reversed: "I *will* demand my share, no matter what they say" and "You *shall* obey the law like everyone else."

The mass mind that decides on questions of usage appears to have rejected this method of making the distinction between simple future and determination, however. Even textbooks, although they carefully recite the formula to stay within the law, are conceding that usage now largely ignores it.

For better or worse, *shall* and *should* have taken on a distinctly flossy overtone, at least in the United States, and few can use them without a twinge of self-consciousness, except in certain circumstances. We mentally note down the person who says, "I shall take the 5.15 home as usual" as somewhat affected, or perhaps precious. Those who insist that they use *shall* not as an affectation but as the unconscious result of careful training can only be insensitive or uncommonly resistant to what they hear all around them.

Six authorities and American Heritage agree that the distinction between *shall* and *will* is almost universally ignored in the U.S., and that *will* is indiscriminately used with all persons to express both the simple future and determination; only Follett insists on the traditional usage, which is still observed, more or less, in Britain, though Fowler concedes that American practice has made enormous inroads there and that insistence on the traditional pattern may soon be considered pedantry.

The purists among the English lump Scots, Irishmen, and Americans together when they fix the blame for the downfall of *shall*.

"The story is a very old one," writes Sir Ernest Gowers, "of the drowning Scot who was misunderstood by English onlookers and left to his fate because he cried, 'I will drown and nobody shall save me!'" Fowler mentioned the same story, calling it much too good to be true. The time may now have arrived when it is necessary to explain that the Englishmen, construing their grammar strictly, understood the Scot as insisting that he was determined to drown and would allow no one to save him.

Shall, then, seems well on the way to extinction, much like the hapless Scot, except in certain constructions where it is used idiomatically by instinct; e.g., questions, like, "Shall I answer the telephone?" and "Shall we dance?" *Shall* also remains firmly entrenched as a means of expressing compulsion or obligation, especially in legal contexts: "The sum shall be repaid in monthly installments."

To the ignorant, *shall* has a tonier sound than *will,* and this causes them to put it in impossible contexts: "I look forward to the time when delegates like yourselves shall meet in every country of the world." *will.*

Should has fallen under much the same shadow as *shall.* "I should like to attend the premiere" and "If the price fell, I should buy the property" grate on the ears of most Americans as high-toned. *Should* is generally used now only in the sense of *ought to:* "We should put the car in the garage before it rains."

The nice distinctions of determination vs. simple future that once hung on the choice between *shall* and *will* are now made in speaking by the tone of voice and in writing by a choice of words that cannot be misunderstood ("you *must*" rather than "you *shall*").

A curious misquotation of, or perhaps attempt to improve on, Winston Churchill turned up in a television panel discussion in which an Englishman was criticizing American usage. According to this critic, Churchill said, "Give us the tools and we shall finish the job." But what Churchill really said was "Give us the tools and we *will* finish the job."

In announcing the British nation's intention to finish the job of defeating the Nazis, Churchill was giving expression to the determination that carried Britain so far, if not quite so far as he expected at the time. Thus, in strict correctness, he said *will.*

Should is often used in weather forecasts in a way that seems inappropriate: "Rain should fall before morning." This seems absurdly to suggest an obligation; perhaps the weatherman feels that the elements are obliged not to embarrass him by failing to carry out his prediction. *Is expected to* seems preferable in such contexts.

shambles. The word originally designated benches or stalls where meat was sold, and later a place of carnage. The argument today is whether *shambles* can properly be used to mean a scene of wreckage, or even simply a mess, disregarding any idea of bloodshed. Two critics, one British, say no; American Heritage, Random House and Webster say yes, while one critic gives qualified acceptance. The valid criticism is that newspaper writers and others are too fond of the word.

shan't. Correct as a contraction for *shall not* but uncommon in the U.S.

sharp, sharply. In reference to time idiom calls for *sharp* as the adverb, not *sharply: At 7 o'clock sharp.*

shatter. Journalese at its most histrionic, as *shatter a precedent, shatter a production record.*

she. Reference to nations as *she* and *her* ("Britain must guard her traditions") is approved by two critics with certain qualifications excluding incongruities and inconsistencies; American Heritage calls the usage traditional and Random House vaguely accepts impersonal applications. *It* is preferred by two critics. The same reasoning applies to use of the word for ships and cities.

shear, sheer. Sometimes confused. *Shear* means *cut off:* "The runaway car *sheared* [not *sheered*] a power pole." *Sheer* as a verb is most commonly used in the sense *veer away:* "The wheels hit a rock, and the car sheered away from the cliff."

shekels. Wooden whimsy in reference to money in general, but at least it should not be misspelled *shekles,* as so often happens.

shepherd. Don't ask why, but in the sheep-raising areas of the West the man who tends the flocks is not a *shepherd,* but the comparatively clumsy variant, *sheepherder. Shepherd,* for some mysterious reason, seems on the way to becoming literary.

shibboleth. Originally, a test or password; by extension, a peculiarity distinguishing a sect or group. Two critics and Webster permit the senses *catchword* or *slogan;* a third and Random House do not.

shipshape. "Cities like Chicago and Milwaukee plan to spend millions to get their docks in shipshape" may give an old salt a touch of seasickness, for *shipshape* is an adjective, not a noun. *Make their docks shipshape* would be better. Any analogy with *in shape* is false.

shop. Widely used as a transitive verb; that is to say, one does not shop at, or in, the stores, as of yore; one shops the store itself, or the merchandise. He who is really *au courant* shops the better stores. Those who live far from the madding admen can shop the mail-order catalogs. Yet this use is unlikely in careful prose.

should, would. See *shall, will.*

show. Bernstein considers the term unacceptable in the sense *show up* or *appear:* "Several holders of reserved seats failed to show." Random House and American Heritage call this usage informal; Webster regards it as standard.

showed. Not incorrect, but rarely used as a past participle: "We left after they had showed the movies." More commonly, *shown.*

shrink. *Shrank* predominates for the past tense ("The sweater shrank in the laundry") but *shrunk* is acceptable. This is American usage; *shrunk* is now archaic in Britain.

shrouded. *Shrouded in fog* (or *secrecy*) is a cliché.

sibling. This expression, meaning a brother or sister not a twin, is a technical term of anthropology and sociology, unsuitable for ordinary contexts. Its use is pretentious when *brother* or *sister* will do.

sic. The term (Latin for *so, thus*) should be restricted to assuring the reader that what has immediately preceded is correctly quoted when there is reason to think he might question its accuracy, and not to jeer at grammatical errors, to call attention to jokes (see also *quip, quipped*), nor (in place of quotation marks) to indicate an ironical use of a word. *Sic* is often used (correctly) to indicate that a misspelling in quoted material appears in the original. *Sic* and *sick* are interchangeable in ordering a dog to attack, but obviously *sicked* and *sicking* are necessary for the past and participle.

sick, ill. In British usage, *sick* means *nauseated, sick at one's stomach;* in America, *sick* and *ill* are interchangeable. It is therefore an affectation in the U.S. to restrict *sick* to the sense *nauseated,* three critics agree; Random House and Webster give the general as well as the other senses. American Heritage slightly prefers *sick at* to *sick to* (one's stomach). *Sick* for *morbid* (*sick humor*) is considered standard by dictionaries. See *black humor*.

sideswipe, sidewipe. The second form is an artificiality to be found in some newspaper stylebooks but not in dictionaries.

Sierra Nevada. See *Sahara*.

sight, site, cite. Sight is vision, or something seen; a site is a location (*a five-acre building site*); *cite* is a verb meaning to give as an example or charge with an offense. The commonest confusion is *sight* for *site;* it is so unexplainable that taking note of it may sound like the invention of a horrible example. But here is an example, and it was not invented: "We have no assurance an on-sight inspection would succeed." *on-site*.

simian. The journalese variant for *monkey, ape*. See *Variation*.

similar. Often used where *same* or *identical* is called for: "Rice exports through the first seven months of this year were 20 million pounds greater than during a similar (actually, *the same*) period last year." "The cottages are occupied by children of similar age and sex." *the same. Similar* means *resembling*. It should not be used as an adverb: "The oboe sounds similar to the English horn." *like*. See also *like, as*.

similar(ly) to. *Like* is preferable in such constructions as "The oboe has a double reed, similar to the bassoon." See also *like, as*.

simple reason. *For the simple reason* is verbose for *because*. There is usually no occasion to point out the simplicity of a reason when this phrase is used; its effect is often to make the reader feel patronized.

simplistic. Taken by pretentious writers to be an impressive form of *simple*. *Simple*, as all must know, means, in general, uncomplicated, though definitions of its various senses fill nearly a column in Webster. *Simplistic,* however, has one meaning and one only: *oversimplified.* What is simplistic, then, is not merely simple, which would ordinarily be a virtue; it is oversimplified, which is a fault.

simultaneous. The only point among several hundred taken up that the American Heritage panel agreed on unanimously was that *simultaneous* may not be used as an adverb: "The concert was broadcast simultaneous over radio and television." *simultaneously.* The dictionary calls this misuse common, though no other critic has noticed it, and both Random House and Webster give *simultaneous* only as an adjective.

since. It is a delusion that *since* may be used only as an adverb in a temporal sense ("We have been here since ten o'clock"). It is also a causal conjunction meaning *for* or *because:* "Since it is raining, we had better take an umbrella." The perfect tense is called for with *since* in the temporal sense: "He has not returned since he resigned" (not *did not return*), because *since* brings the time referred to up to the moment. See also *as* vs. *because, since; ago.*

sine qua non. Ordinary English (e.g., *essential*) is preferable to the Latin phrase (for *without which nothing*).

-sion. See *-tion,* etc.

sing. *Sang* is now preferable to *sung* for the past tense: "She *sang* a lullaby."

sing up a storm. A cliché.

Singular and Plural. See *Plural and Singular.*

sink. The past tense is either *sank* or *sunk:* "The boat sank (sunk) in three fathoms." Dictionaries give *sank* as predominant. *Sunk* is the correct past participle: "They have sunk (not *sank*) the pilings."

sip. The journalese preference for *drink,* as *munch* is for *eat.*

sir. The British title for a knight or baronet is used correctly only with the full name or the first name, never with the last name alone: *Sir Winston Churchill* or *Sir Winston;* never *Sir Churchill.* The wife of a knight or baronet enjoys the title *lady* with the surname: *Lady Churchill.* See also *dame.*

sit. See *set, sit*.

site. See *sight, site, cite*.

situate. See *locate*.

skeptic, sceptic. The first is the preferred American spelling and the second the British. Fowler recommends that the British adopt *sk-*.

skid road, row. *Skid road* comes from lumbering operations in the Northwest, where logs are slid down a kind of channel made of other logs that have been peeled and sunk into the ground. The connection between such a slide and a gathering place for derelicts is none too clear. It seems, rather, that the gathering place should be *skid row* instead of *road*, the *skid* drived from *on the skids* and the *row* from the sense of a street and its buildings, as in *Rotten Row*. Regardless, *skid row* is more prevalent than *skid road*.

The Webster files show *skid row* to be commoner in the East and *skid road* in the West, especially in Los Angeles and Seattle. But in Los Angeles an official city commission on slum clearance even incorporated *skid row* in its name. In Seattle, however, or for that matter the whole states of Washington and Oregon, the use of *skid road* seems to be practically a religion. Its high priest was the author Stewart Holbrook, who, if he had not gained fame otherwise, might have won it by his incessant and impassioned public endorsements of *skid road*.

Webster cross-references the terms as synonyms, but relates *skid road* to loggers and defines *skid row* in the general sense of a rundown district and resort for derelicts; American Heritage's treatment is much the same. Webster and Random House give *skid row* as standard; American Heritage calls it slang.

skills. Follett calls *skills* a false plural, but it is recognized as standard by Fowler and dictionaries. Follett evidently objects to *skill* as a noun meaning a special ability as distinguished from a general proficiency, but this is surely pedantry.

slander. See *libel, slander*.

slash. Journalese, particularly in reference to prices or reductions in general.

slate. Often criticized in journalism (where it is oftenest used, especially in headlines) in the sense *schedule: Conference Slated*. The argument is usually that the word can only mean *berate*. This meaning, in fact, is British usage, and so the criticism is inapplicable in the U.S. Random House and Webster give the sense *schedule* as standard; all Webster's examples, however, come from news publications, indicating that the word has a distinctly journalistic flavor. Though American Heritage asked its panelists for their opinion on *slate* in the criticized sense, no judgment was included in the dictionary.

slay. Criticized by three authorities as overused in newspapers, especially in headlines.

sleep the sleep of the just. Derogated by two critics as a cliché.

slightly. See *rather*.

sloe-eyed. Means either "having soft dark bluish or purplish black eyes" (from comparison with the fruit named *sloe*) or "having slanted eyes" (Webster); or "having soft, slanted, dark eyes" (American Heritage). What is unmistakable is that the expression connotes exotic beauty, despite wrongheaded efforts to link the descriptive with the taste of the fruit (sour).

slough, slew. The body of water is *slough* (pronounced *slew*); the verb meaning *shed* or *cast off* is *slough* or infrequently *sluff* (both pronounced *sluff*). The verb meaning to skid sideways is *slew* (or *slue*).

slow, slowly. *Slow* is equally an adverb and an adjective, so that *go slow* is just as correct as *go slowly*. An Englishman was outraged by a road sign that read DRIVE SLOW. Reacting violently and misguidedly, as people often do when their linguistic prejudices are crossed, he knocked it over. When he was haled before a magistrate for damaging public property, he pleaded that the sign was ungrammatical—that it should have read DRIVE SLOWLY. As it happened, the magistrate was enough of a scholar to be able to show him he was all wrong and had the additional pleasure of fining him. Four critics and dictionaries concur in this view, though Bryant finds *slowly* predominant in writing. The Harper panel, however, overwhelmingly endorsed *go slowly* over *go slow*. So much for panels.

small in size (number, etc.). Redundant; omit *in size, in number*. Similar lapses: *few, large, many in number; rectangular* (etc.) *in shape,* etc.

smell. Fowler says that *smell* as a verb meaning *give off an odor* should be followed by an adjective, not an adverb: *smell bad, sweet, sour, good;* American Heritage concurs but inconsistently cites *smells disgustingly.* Evans allows *smell sweetly,* which American Heritage disapproves. The adjectives seem more in accord with good usage.

smog. In its pristine sense, smog was a mixture of smoke and fog. The term originated in the East. What has plagued Los Angeles and other cities is not smog in this sense, but a substance generated by the action of sunlight on pollutants in the atmosphere. St. Louis and Pittsburgh had smog in the original sense. This is offered only as curious linguistic lore, for everyone knows only too well what smog is, and if Los Angeles did not have the original title to the word, it has certainly earned one.

smoky, smokey. The first is widely preferred.

smut, smutty. The presence of these words in a criticism of the decency of a literary or dramatic production often indicates Comstockery at work. Those of prudish bent have taken these expressions for their own. Others are more likely to say *risqué, obscene,* or *pornographic,* as the spirit moves them and the occasion requires.

snack. Recognized by dictionaries as standard as a verb ("They snacked on sandwiches and milk"). Overused in the press.

so. The use of *so* as an intensive meaning *very* ("It's so cold today") is considered informal and more suitable to talk than to writing by three critics. It is often feminine; Fowler regards it as silly. Yet Random House considers it all but standard. Opinion is divided on whether *so* as a conjunction must be followed by *that:* "He got an education so (that) he could succeed. *So that* is at least more formal. *So* beginning a sentence should not be followed by a comma: "So, we took the train." *So we took* . . .

soar. Journalese as a synonym or variant of *rise,* as in "The budget soared," "The temperature soared."

so . . . as. See *as . . . as,* etc.

so as (to). Redundant: "We took the train (so as) to save time." See also *in order to; for the purpose of.*

so-called. Excessive with an expression that has been placed in quotation marks to indicate ironical use: *the so-called "blacklist."* Either *so-called* or the quotation marks suffice.

social disease. A euphemism for *venereal disease.* The phrase is growing quaint.

Socialist, Communist. See *Communist, Socialist.*

Sociologese. See *Pedagese.*

so far as. See *as (so) far as.*

so far from. Defended by Fowler as an idiom, though illogical, for *far from:* "So far from dominating the field, he finished in last place," but he leaves to the writer a preference for *far from.*

solicitor general. See *general.*

solon. This term, which comes from the name of the Athenian lawgiver, is journalese in the sense of *legislator*. It may be inescapable, and thus grudgingly admissible, in headlines, but in text it is to be avoided.

so long as. See *as long as, so long as.*

some, -odd. With numbers, the words indicate an approximation. They are inept, therefore, with anything but a round number: "Some sixty-nine horsemen" and "Waco is 94-odd miles south of Dallas." Omit *some* and *-odd;* the numbers are, or appear to be, exact.

some, somewhat. *Somewhat* is preferable in such examples as "He is some better today"; "The weather warmed up some." Random House considers this usage informal; Webster gives it as standard. See also *rather.*

somebody, someone. It is a superstition that one is preferable; rhythm, however, may control the choice. The same is true of *nobody, no one.* See also *anybody, anyone; -one.*

some day, someday. See *some time, sometime.*

some few. Sometimes criticized as a needless and possibly dialectal displacement of *a few:* "Some few of the travelers were left behind." It may be an obsolescent expression; Charles Darwin used it in *The Voyage of the Beagle.* It apparently is a Briticism.

some of us. Which possessive pronoun is used with *some of us* depends on whether the speaker regards himself as part of the group designated: "Some of us lost *our* heads" is correct if the speaker lost his head and is willing to admit it, but if not, he would properly say "Some of us lost *their* heads."

someplace. Considered standard in the U.S., despite some criticism that the preferable form is *somewhere,* by three critics, Random House, and Webster; Bryant calls it colloquial; American Heritage rejects it for writing.

something, somewhat (of a). Although sometimes sanctioned as interchangeable in such expressions as *somewhat of a coward,* it is noticeable that *something* is preferred in careful writing. The reason may be that *somewhat* as a pronoun is obsolete and sounds out of place.

some time, sometime, sometimes. *Some time* is an adverbial phrase meaning *an interval or period:* "He stayed some time" (not *sometime*). *Sometime* is an adverb indicating an indefinite occasion: "He will come sometime, I am sure." The same distinction applies to *some day, someday. Sometimes* means *occasionally* or *at one time or another:* "Sometimes it rains in the summer in the desert."

Sometimes is often wrongly joined with another modifier; *a sometimes-fatal disease.* It is unnecessary to indicate, by means of the hyphen, that *sometimes* and *fatal* form a unit modifier; *sometimes,* as an adverb, cannot modify anything but the adjective *fatal.* See also *almost.*

Sometime and *sometimes* are archaic as adjectives: "It was his sometime preoccupation"; "the sometimes waste of foreign aid." *occasional.*

someway. Considered standard by Random House and Webster but rejected by American Heritage.

somewhat. See *rather.*

somewhat (of a). See *something, somewhat (of a).*

somewheres. Substandard, three critics agree; Webster calls it dialectal.

son-in-law. See *in-law.*

son of a gun. It is said that in the days when ladies of easy virtue were brought aboard warships for the diversion of the crews, they were always entertained on the gun deck, and consequent offspring, officially fatherless, came to be referred to as sons of guns. In those days *son of a gun* were fighting words.

sonic wall. The Style Guide of the Aerojet-General Corporation says:
"An example of a misused word that contributed to confusion among both technical men and laymen in recent years was 'the sonic wall.' When pilots first approached the speed of sound, they found that aircraft control was difficult and uncertain. The difficulties were first referred to as 'obstacles' to supersonic flight, then as a 'barrier,' and finally as a 'wall.' This last term became so popular with journalists that, after the speed of sound had been exceeded repeatedly, they felt called upon to announce the 'discovery' that there was no 'sonic wall.' "

sooner. See *no sooner.*

sophisticated. Once upon a time—and not so long ago, either—*sophisticated* was applied only to people. In recent years it has been unsettling to some to see devices and methods frequently characterized by this word: "These are sophisticated chemical reactions"; "Our technology is more sophisticated than theirs." This is not an innovation but merely the introduction of an old and respectable technical sense into everyday contexts.

sort. See *kind.*

sort of. See discussion of *kind of* under *kind.*

so . . . that. No comma should be used before *that:* "The car was so badly damaged that it had to be towed away."

sound barrier. See *sonic wall*.

sound out. Approved by American Heritage for *test opinion* (*sound out the electorate*). Neither Random House nor Webster gives it, which may indicate it is newer than it seems to be.

Source Attribution. See *Attribution*.

South. As a part of the U.S., by common consent (like North, East, West) usually capitalized.

Southland. *Southland,* in California, means *Southern California,* which is practically a separate state, if not an empire. Used in California as a synonym for *the South* (the Ole South, that is), *Southland* will cause either confusion or indignation.

sovereignty. *Sovereignty* is supreme political power, and is enjoyed only by autonomous states; that is to say, nations. The term has been misused by some states in efforts to assert their authority against the federal government. No state of the American republic enjoys sovereignty or anything approaching it, despite such presumptuous designations as "the sovereign state of Maryland." "This is an example of how each of the 50 states can be deprived of its sovereignty." Nonsense; they have none to be deprived of. It was long a mannerism at national political conventions for delegates to announce, when casting votes, that they came from "the sovereign state of . . ." but this pompous practice seems to be dying out.

Soviet, Soviets. The use of *Soviet* to mean *Russia,* and of *Soviets* to mean *Russians,* is sometimes criticized in stylebooks. Only the Concise Oxford Dictionary gives the former; Random House and Webster give the latter.

A Russian defector who jumped ship in Texas was described as carrying a Soviet-American dictionary. But there is no such language as Soviet, and some would say there is no such language as American, either, but that is at least arguable.

sox. Called not standard by Evans, but recognized as such nevertheless by American Heritage, Random House, Webster, and the Standard College Dictionary.

Spanish. See *Mexican, Spanish*.

spark. In the sense *cause, prompt* (*sparked a revolt*), approved by American Heritage. Neither Random House nor Webster gives it, which indicates that it must be new; both, however, give a near sense, *kindle enthusiasm; sparked the players to a comeback.* There is little question that *spark* for *cause* is predominantly journalistic usage.

spat. A trivial, usually brief, quarrel; the term is generally applied to skirmishes in the war between the sexes. Often inappropriately applied to differences of larger dimensions, as for example an incident in which a man was assaulted to the extent that his attacker was fined $100 and sentenced to 30 days in jail. See also *tiff*.

spate. Regarded by three critics as a bookish or vogue word for *sudden flood, rush,* or *outpouring.*

spayed, spaded. *Spaded* is an error for *spayed* (said of a female animal that has been neutered).

speak to. In the sense *speak about, on,* parliamentary jargon that is creeping into general use. *Speak to* means *address* ("I'll speak to Master Rackstraw in the morning") except in the technical sense of commenting on a motion in parliamentary procedure. There seems no warrant, and none is given in any current dictionary, for "Resource leaders at the conference will speak to the theme, 'Waging Peace in Southeast Asia.' " *speak on.*

spearhead. Journalese for *lead, head, direct:* "Dr. Russ will spearhead the studies of alcoholism." Excessive use has blunted its point.

special, especial, etc. See *especial,* etc.

specie, species. Often confused. *Specie* is coin: "The payment was made with a combination of specie and paper money." A *species* is a distinct scientific category of animal or plant: "Monkeys of this species are found only near the equator." *Specie* is sometimes given when *species* is meant, but *species* is both singular and plural.

Speech Tag. See *Attribution.*

Spelling. 1. Simplified spelling. That absolute tyrant of the language, the public, is remarkably conservative in its resistance to variant spellings. Brevity and convenience seem to count for nothing; witness the hard sledding of such simplified forms as *tho, thru, altho, nite.* Most publications, including newspapers, ban them. Yet *hi-fi* (high fidelity) has become standard, and there seems every reason to think that *hi-rise* has too, though it is a newer term and not to be found in dictionaries except for Barnhart. Americans, though they are likely to look up to the English as mentors when it comes to language, reject their handily telescoped forms like *spoilt* and *connexion* and *learnt.*

It is apparent that any attempt to influence spelling appreciably in the direction of simplicity is doomed. Periodicals that attempt this are likely to accomplish nothing more than to inconvenience their staffs and make their readers smile. The fact that not one of the *Chicago Tribune's* millions of readers commented on its virtual abandonment of fonetic (oops) phonetic spelling in 1955, after years of persistence in such oddities as *frate* for *freight* and *sofomore* for *sophomore,* seems to indicate the subscribers thought they were seeing typographical errors all that time.

But large-scale, consistent efforts to simplify spelling are more logical, at any rate, than the random, freakish deviations found in some stylebooks. An example of this is the insistence by one newspaper for many years on *hight* for *height*. *Hight* is in the dictionary as a dialectal variant, but its presence there at all stunned every new staff member. Copy editors delighted in working *hight* into big headlines, where readers took it for glaring typographical error. The press generally for many years used *cigaret* and *employe* for *cigarette* and *employee* but has lately adopted the forms everyone else uses. Such spellings, like leaving *the* off the beginnings of sentences, together with a number of other curious practices, were thought to impart breeziness to the writing.

2. Troublesome words. Here are some words that seem to give the most trouble: *accommodate* (not *accomodate*) *anoint* (not *annoint*), *accordion* (not *accordian*), *exorbitant* (not *exhorbitant*), *exuberant* (not *exhuberant*), *existence* (not *existance*), *fictitious* (not *ficticious*), *fluorescent* (not *flourescent*), *inoculate* (not *innoculate*), *liquefy* (not *liquify*), *marshal* (not *marshall*), *nickel* (not *nickle*), *objet d'art* (not *object d'art*), *Philippines* (not *Phillipines*), *rarefy* (not *rarify*), *resistance* (not *resistence*), *violoncello* (not *violincello*, though the long form is disappearing in favor of *cello*).

Rules for spelling English are so complicated and beset by exceptions that it is easier to learn to spell than to learn the rules. There is, however, one familiar and useful rule:

> *i* before *e*
> Except after *c*
> Or when sounded like *a*
> As in *neighbor* or *weigh*.

Some exceptions: *either, neither, inveigle, seize, leisure.*

3. British preferences. British preferences are conspicuous when used in America, and the writer who favors them may be suspected of affectation. Indeed, there is a tendency on the part of some young writers to consider them more elegant. But they are not likely to get past the editor's pencil. British preference is for *ou* in certain words where American usage calls for *o: behaviour, labour,* for *behavior, labor.* Other such words: *ardour, clamour, colour, dolour, favour, honour, mould, moult, odour, splendour, valour, vapour, vigour.* Note, however, that *glamour* is preferred to *glamor* in both Britain and America. Other British preferences:

> *ce* for *se: defence, offence, pretence.*
> *ss* for *s: biassed.*
> a terminal *e: axe.*
> *que* for *ck: cheque.*
> *xion* for *ction: connexion, inflexion.*
> *oe* for *e: homoeopathy, oecumenical.*

> *s* for *c: practise.*
> *e* for *a: grey.*
> *y* for *a: pyjamas.*
> *ise* for *ize: apologise, visualise* (see *-ize, -ise*).
> *dge* for *dg: abridgement, acknowledgement.*
> *re* for *er: accoutrements, centre, fibre, theatre.*
> *ae* for *e: aeon, aesthetic.*
> *ll* for *l: apparelled, councillor.*
> *l* for *ll: dulness, enrol.*

These are merely examples, and it should be noted that in some instances what were originally British forms have established themselves in America without driving out the American versions. See also *-ize, ise; -or, -our.*

4. Spelling as humor. In his preface to *A Subtreasury of American Humor,* E. B. White transfixed a foible that he noted particularly, he said, in the humorous writing of fifty to one hundred years ago. It is still to be seen in print today, however, particularly in comic strips and stuff of the folksy, rural, or old-home-town persuasion. Mr. White wrote, "It occurred to me that a certain basic confusion often exists in the use of tricky or quaint or illiterate spelling to achieve a humorous effect. For instance, here are some spellings from the works of Petroleum V. Nasby: he spells 'would' *wood,* 'of' *uv,* 'you' *yoo,* 'hence' *hentz,* 'office' *offis.* Now, it happens that I pronounce 'office' *offis.* And I pronounce 'hence' *hentz,* and I even pronounce 'of' *uv* . . . the queer spelling is unnecessary, since the pronunciation is impossible to distinguish from the natural or ordinary pronunciation . . ."

5. Variant spellings. Until recently, the first entry in most dictionaries (if the versions appeared side by side), or the one under which the definition was given (if they were separated), was considered the preferred version. Webster, however, departs from the practice of indicating a preference. Variants are generally given in alphabetical order; all versions given without a qualifying label are regarded as standard. If the variants are not in alphabetical order, the first is "slightly more common." All dictionaries explain their practice in this respect in the front-matter of the book.

The choice among variant spellings, then, is a matter of taste, not correctness. Publications often govern the choice by rule, so that their content will be consistent. Many commonly misspelled words will be found at their alphabetical places in this book. Thorstein Veblen fairly described English spelling and at the same time offered the reason for overcoming its difficulties: "It is archaic, cumbrous, and ineffective; its acquisition consumes much time and effort; failure to acquire it is easy of detection."

spell out. Approved by American Heritage but derogated by Bernstein as overworked. Both, however, asperse *spell out details* as redundant. Random House considers *spell out* informal; Webster gives it as standard. Both its examples, however, are from newsmagazines.

spiral. In the sense *move up* (*prices spiraled all week*), as distinguished from *spiral up*, or *upward*, rejected by one critic but approved as standard by American Heritage and Webster.

spite. See *in spite of.*

spitting image. Authorities mostly agree that this is a corruption of *spit* and *image*, but *spitting image* is now recognized by dictionaries as predominant.

splendid romp. A stereotype of reviews describing a lighthearted performance.

Split Infinitive. See *Infinitives 1.*

Split-Verb Constructions. See *Adverbs; Infinitives 1.*

spokesman. A spokesman is one who speaks on behalf of others. The writer who referred to "a fluent spokesman of idiomatic English" meant "a fluent *speaker.*"

spoof. Approved by dictionaries as standard as both noun (*a spoof of Broadway*) and verb (*spoofing Congress*) in the sense *parody.*

spoonfuls, spoonsful. See *-ful.*

sport. As a verb, *sport* is appropriate concerning only something that would be displayed or flaunted; a man might sport a moustache, or a red necktie, but hardly thick-lensed glasses, as a newsmagazine reported. *Sport*, in any event, is overused in newswriting. "The vast majority of Jews were, of course, law-abiding and sported a much lower crime rate." No definition of *sport* validates this.

sporting. As an adjective in the sense *pertaining to sports, sporting* is now quaint. *Sporting editor* is redolent of a generation that is gone; the sporting editor's successor is the sports editor. *Sporting* in the sense of *sports* may prompt a snicker because it suggests the sense *sporting house* (*whorehouse; bordello*). That term, however, is also an anachronism. Yet all this does not impugn such expressions as *a sporting proposition*. And *sporting goods* survives without a shadow.

Sportswriting. Is there anything to the assumptions that sportswriting is more creative than other kinds of newswriting and that the sports page has been the launching pad for numerous literary rockets? One cynic said nothing more is needed to demolish this idea than to lay a number of sports stories beside other kinds of news stories, all selected at random, and compare them for evidences of creativity. It is true that sportswriters generally enjoy more latitude in choice of language, and in exhibiting individuality, if any, in their work. What use do they make of this latitude? We have two opinions, separated by more than thirty years.

One of them was expressed by H. W. Fowler in *Modern English Usage* in 1926 under the heading *sobriquets:*

". . . games and contests are exciting to take part in, interesting or even exciting also to watch, but essentially (i.e., as bare facts) dull to read about, insomuch that most intelligent people abandon such reading; the reporter, conscious that his matter & his audience are both dull enough to require enlivening, thinks that the needful fillip may be given if he calls fishing the gentle craft, a ball the pill or the leather, a captain the skipper, or a saddle the pigskin, & so makes his description a series of momentary puzzles that shall pleasantly titillate inactive minds."

The following comments were made by Bergen and Cornelia Evans in *A Dictionary of Contemporary American Usage,* under the heading *sports English*:

"Because it deals with struggle, sports writing is required to be vigorous, and because it scorns formality it must be slangy and colloquial. But slang is particularly unfitted for frequent repetition and sports writing is, above any other type of contemporary writing, repetitious, laden with clichés. The wretched sports writer, with slight material and often (one suspects) even slighter interest, is compelled to assume concern he does not feel and to conceal his yawns under forced shouts of excitement . . . No one, apparently, using only the normal resources of the richest language known, can make sports interesting . . ."

A legend has grown up that the sports pages have produced many writers who have gone on to literary triumphs. But as Nunnally Johnson asked, after Lardner, Broun, Kieran, Pegler, Gallico, Reynolds, and Considine, who is there? "Bad writing, grammar-school humor, foolish styles, threadbare phrases, spurious enthusiasm and heavy-footed comedy . . . nauseating sentimentality and agonizing slang . . . [and] above all, breeziness, breeziness, breeziness!"

In a letter to the editor of the *Long Beach Press-Telegram,* John P. Odell wrote: "In sports everything is either *tough* or *beautiful*. A tough game, a tough opponent, a tough win, a tough loss, a tough coach. To a sportscaster all plays are *beautiful*. And, of course, golfers must always *fire* their scores. But let's have an occasional ugly forward pass. And give us a respite from clean-cut athletes. Surely there must be a few dirty-cut athletes lurking somewhere. Obviously, those are the ones who are thrown in the hoosegow for various infractions of the law, not to mention those who violate standards of common decency."

In a defense of sorts, Paul Roberts wrote in *Understanding English:* "In fairness we should realize that sports writers and announcers deserve sympathy as much as criticism. They have to report, day after day and year after year, activities in which the same features are endlessly repeated. Moreover, they must always report these activities feverishly. The announcer is scarcely at liberty to say that today's football game is a pretty routine affair and the performers of no more than average competence. He must, every Saturday, bubble about how this is the most exciting grid spectacle that he and his colleagues have been privileged to see in a long time and how he wished all us fans could be out there in the stadium with him to see these two great teams fighting their hearts out."

spouse. Regarded by four critics as bookish, legal, or jocular.

sprawling. The greatest love affair of all time is not that between Romeo and Juliet, nor that between Abelard and Heloise, but between reporters and this word, as used to describe an extensive building. See also *Journalese*.

sprightly, spritely. *Spritely* appears in the dictionary as an archaic variant of *sprightly;* it is thus out of place in a modern context. "A collection of spritely verse." *sprightly.* The adverb is *sprightlily;* a clumsy word, to be sure, and seldom . used.

square. Should be carefully placed in dealing with dimensions or areas. *Twelve miles square* means a square twelve miles on a side, or 144 square miles; *twelve square miles* is what it says.

Sr., Jr. See *Jr., Sr.*

stabilize. Often a euphemism as applied to prices; stabilization in this connection is not necessarily aimed at keeping prices steady (the true meaning), nor at preventing them from rising, but at keeping them from going down.

stage. The use of the word as a verb in the senses *present, exhibit, offer, put on, perform, accomplish,* etc., is discouraged as loose or journalese by two critics, who agree that *stage a comeback* is a cliché. There is a tendency to discourage *stage* except in reference to performances that are actually given on a stage, and this appears to be the most acceptable sense. The criticized senses are given as standard in Random House, American Heritage, and Webster, however.

stake out, stakeout. These terms, referring to surveillance of a place or area, continue to be police argot to the extent that their use is discouraged in well-edited publications intended for a general audience.

Stalin, Joseph. The name is transliterated thus in Random House, Webster, and American Heritage; not *Iosef,* a form sometimes seen.

stalk. Outworn in connection with death personified, as "Death stalked the highways," which is warmed over and served up after every holiday.

stalling for time. Technically redundant, though in common use. Stalling is inevitably for time. *Stall* in this sense, as well as *stall off* (*stall off bill collectors*), is considered standard by American Heritage and Webster, informal by Random House.

Standard. The term is often used in this book to describe usages that are, in Webster's definition, "substantially uniform and well-established . . . in the speech and writing of the educated and widely recognized as acceptable and authoritative." Random House has a similar definition. The descriptive has come into fairly wide use in this connection. General dictionaries ordinarily do not use *standard* as a status label; the implication is that unless otherwise labeled, e.g., *dialect, slang, informal, colloquial,* etc., a term is standard. Webster does use *substandard* to describe a usage differing from that of "the prestige group"; *nonstandard* describes similar usages that are more widespread than those designated *substandard.* See also *Colloquialisms.*

state. Often inappropriately used, simply for variation, where *say* would be preferable. *State* means to set forth in detail or to make a formal declaration. See also *Attribution.*

State Descriptives and Abbreviations. Following is a list of the official forms of reference to residents of states, together with the traditional abbreviations for the names of the states. Although the Postal Service has adopted a set of two-letter capitalized abbreviations, probably to speed mechanical sorting of mail, they have not found wide favor for use in printed matter. For example, neither of the principal press associations nor *The New York Times* uses them. Alabamian (Ala.), Alaskan, Arizonian (Ariz.), Arkansan (Ark.), Californian (Calif.), Coloradan (Colo.), Connecticuter (Conn.), Delawarean (Del.), Floridian (Fla.), Georgian (Ga.), Hawaiian, Idahoan, Illinoisan (Ill.), Indianian (Ind.), Iowan, Kansan (Kan.; not *Kas., Kans.*), Kentuckian (Ky.), Louisianian (La.), Mainer, Marylander (Md.), Massachusettsan (Mass.), Michiganite (Mich.), Minnesotan (Minn.), Mississippian (Miss.), Missourian (Mo.), Montanan (Mont.), Nebraskan (Neb.; not *Nebr.*), Nevadan (Nev.), New Hampshirite (N.H.), New Jerseyite (N.J.), New Mexican (N.M.), New Yorker (N.Y.), North Carolinian (N.C.), North Dakotan (N.D.; not *N. Dak.*), Ohioan, Oklahoman (Okla.), Oregonian (Ore.; not *Oreg.*), Pennsylvanian (Pa.), Rhode Islander (R.I.), South Carolinian (S.C.), South Dakotan (S.D.; not *S. Dak.*), Tennesseean (Tenn.), Vermonter (Vt.), Virginian (Va.), Washingtonian (Wash.; not *Wn.*), West Virginian (W. Va.), Wisconsinite (Wis., not *Wisc.*), Wyomingite (Wyo.). Note that there are no official abbreviations for eight states: Alaska, Hawaii, Idaho, Iowa, Maine, Ohio, Texas, and Utah. (In addition to the descriptive forms listed, Webster recognizes the following: Alabaman, Arizonan, Arkansian, Floridan, Louisianan.)

state of the art. The expression comes from the terminology associated with granting patents, and has to do with the level of development of technology in a given field. Lately the pompous have taken it for their own and, undoubtedly to the bafflement of many readers, have used it to refer to the extent of development in any field, not necessarily associated with invention. It had best be left to its native habitat.

stationary, stationery. Often confused. The first is the adjective that means *standing still* or *in a fixed position;* the second is the noun that means *writing paper.*

statistic. One critic disapproves of the word as a false singular derived from *statistics.* Another, however, recognizes it as now standard, and so do dictionaries.

statuesque. Overused to describe beauties of larger than average size.

Status Labels. See *Colloquialisms; Standard.*

statutory charge, offense. Euphemisms now less used than at one time for charges or offenses relating to sex, such as rape, sodomy, and incest. The expressions are carefully nondistinctive in themselves, for all crimes are defined in statutes of one kind or another. The result of using *statutory* only in connection with sex crimes is that the expression came to be taken as applicable only to such crimes. *Statutory rape,* however, is the name of a specific offense: sexual intercourse, even with consent, with a girl who has not reached whatever the law sets as the age of consent.

stave. In nautical connections ("The hull of the tug was stove in") the preferable form for the present participle and the past tense is *stove.* In other connections, either *staved* or *stove* is acceptable, though *staved* is usual. *Staved off* (defeat, etc.) is invariable.

stayed away in droves. See *droves.*

stem from. Two critics say that *spring from* is preferred in Britain; another regards *stem from* as literary and overused, but dictionaries give it as standard.

sterling. As applied to silver, sometimes regarded as meaning pure, but in fact it means 92.5 percent pure (silver).

stewardi. A facetious invention for the plural of *stewardess;* thought by some to be erudite, but it is nonsense. The plural of *stewardess* is *stewardesses.* The future of *stewardess* itself does not look bright, however, for the new feminism has pressed for *flight attendant* with some success.

still. As an adverb, should not be joined to a succeeding adjective with a hyphen: *the still-effervescent stock market. still effervescent.*

still and all. Objected to by two critics as dialectal and redundant (for *nevertheless, even so*), but recognized as standard by Random House and Webster.

still continues (persists, remains). Though *still* may sometimes add a desired emphasis, such phrases are often thoughtlessly redundant, except when *still* is used in the sense *nevertheless.*

stink. Three critics consider *stank* (rather than *stunk*) the usual form for the past tense; dictionaries give it as predominant. One critic favors *stunk* and considers *stank* bookish. Both forms are standard.

stoic, stoical. Two critics agree that the first is more appropriate in reference to the Stoic philosophy, the second to impassivity in general.

stomach. See *belly*.

stomp. In the sense *stamp on*, considered standard by two critics, Webster, and American Heritage, and informal by Random House ("The thief was beaten and stomped"). Rejected by American Heritage in the sense *strike the ground with the foot*.

stone. See *rock, stone*.

stormy petrel. This, once a numerous species, appears to be extinct as a metaphor. Too bad. One could imagine them dipping and screaming in the troughs of the waves that bring the tempest. Is it possible General Billy Mitchell was the last of the stormy petrels? Latter-day petrels seem less stormy than petulant.

stove. See *stave*.

straddle. For *equivocate* (*straddle the issue*) approved as standard by American Heritage and Webster; labeled informal by Random House.

straightforward. One word.

strait-, straight-. The circumstances that are constricting are *straitened*, not *straightened*. The confining garment is *straitjacket*, not *straight-*, in the view of three critics, though dictionaries recognize both forms as standard.

strata. See *stratum, strata*.

strategy, tactics. Technically, as applied to military operations, strategy is the overall plan, and tactics the specific means by which it is carried out. But the terms are often loosely interchanged with no loss, especially when there are not two levels of activity.

stratum, strata. Two critics hold that *strata* is the plural of *stratum;* this follows the Latin (for *layer*) from which the words come. One critic allows *strata* as a singular, with the plural *stratas*, but no other authority recognizes this obvious misuse. Two critics as well as dictionaries accept both *stratums* and *strata*.

streamline, streamlined. Interchangeable as adjectives: *a streamlined* (*streamline*) *train. Streamlined*, however, seems predominant.

stress. Often loosely used in attribution, simply for variation, when there is no occasion to indicate emphasis. See *Attribution*.

strew. *Strewed* and *strewn* are both standard as the past participle.

stricken. As the past participle of *strike, stricken* is standard in the sense *afflicted* in such phrases as *stricken with disease, poverty-stricken, the stricken population*. Two critics allow *stricken* or *stricken out* for *deleted* ("The remark was stricken from the record"). Dictionaries recognize the first use but not the second, indicating that *struck, struck out* predominate for *delete*.

stricture. In the physical sense, a stricture is a contraction or narrowing, as in a tube; in the nonmaterial sense, it is censure or adverse criticism.

strived. As the past and past participle of *strive, strived* is being driven out by *strove* and *striven*. One critic says *strived* is still heard and acceptable; dictionaries concur.

structure. As a verb in place of *build, form, organize, set up*, etc., particularly in the writings of academia, the word is criticized as pretentious and as jargon.

student. See *pupil, student*.

stunning. A counterword of reviewers, used to express high approval. Overused to the point of being worn out.

style. There are two fairly distinct though often confused applications of the word in literary connections. The commonest relates to a manner of expression, as would be described by *an informal style, an elegant style, a polished style, etc*. This is the style of which Buffon said it is the man. The other sense is quite different, relating to a code of mechanical practice governing such details as capitalization, abbreviation, and spelling (insofar as there are reputable choices). Many publications compile stylebooks to ensure consistency in such matters. This book deals with both concepts at one time or another.

sub-. Solid as a prefix: *subaudible, subarid, subhuman*, etc.

subfreezing. See *freezing*.

Subject-Verb Agreement. Only general cases are dealt with here; cases dealing with specific expressions are in their alphabetical places.
   1. Subject disagreeing with complement. Ordinarily, the subject rather than the complement governs the number of the verb. Thus "Potatoes are a vegetable" (not *is*); "Letters to the merged corporations are (not *is*) the next topic"; "The cargo was watermelons" (not *were*). Apparent plurals designating periods of time take singular verbs ("A few months was spent," not *were*); also sums of money ("The delinquency was $56 million, of which $44 million was owed by the Communist bloc," not *were owed*). See also *Number in Addition*.
   2. Compound subjects with *and*. Fowler declares it a mistaken idea that when one part of a compound subject is plural and the other singular, the verb follows the nearest. All compound subjects with *and* are plural and take plural verbs: "The bonds, the stocks, and the money are in the safe-deposit box" (not *is*). Four

critics agree, however, that if the sense of the subject is such as to form a single idea (*food and drink; toast and jam*), a singular verb is preferable.

3. Compound subjects with *or*. With subjects of different number either recast the sentence or use the number of the subject nearest the verb. "Father or children *were* present"; but "Children or father was present."

4. Attraction of an intervening phrase. Four critics warn against the common error caused by losing sight of the subject and giving the verb the number of a phrase that intervenes: "The height of the buildings was (not *were*) limited by city ordinance."

5. Inversion. The problem here resembles that of para. 4, in that some element other than the true subject leads the writer astray, and he is the more easily distracted when the verb precedes the subject. Four critics warn against the error of such constructions as "After the reception comes dancing and refreshments." *come.* See also *one of those who; Collective Nouns; there; with.*

Subjunctive. The subjunctive mood is used most commonly to describe conditions contrary to fact, but the subjunctive is sharply on the decline in English, a fact easily observable. The points taken up here are those considered by two or more commentators.

1. In sentences expressing a condition contrary to fact and calling for a choice between *was* and *were* ("If I were king"; "If she were you," two critics and American Heritage insist on *were;* one considers *was* preferable, except in *If I were.* Another does not admit any usage but *were* in such circumstances, and a fourth regards it as the mark of education. One restricts the use of *were* to what is not merely contrary to fact but impossible or out of the question, a distinction that seems difficult to apply in any practical way. The consensus, then, overwhelmingly favors *If I were* over *If I was* for conditions contrary to fact. But, as four critics warn, the writer must distinguish between a statement of a timeless condition contrary to fact and the statement of a simple condition relating to the past: "If he was (not *were*) present at the meeting he did not vote." Clauses beginning with *if,* then, do not necessarily take a subjunctive verb (*were, be*).

2. Mixing subjunctive and indicative verbs in the statement of a condition and the result of its fulfillment is described as an error by two critics. An example: "If he *went* to college, he *will have* an advantage over the others." Either "If he *went* . . . he *would have*" (both subjunctives) or "If he *goes* . . . he *will have*" (both indicatives, expressing a simple condition). The second form is considered preferable; the use of subjunctive forms where the indicative will serve is considered unnecessarily formal and even pretentious.

subliminal. This word, as used to describe advertising flashed on a screen so quickly the watchers don't consciously perceive it, often is printed *sublimal.* This is going from the subliminal to the pediculous as far as spelling is concerned.

subpoena. Although *subpena* is also correct, *subpoena* predominates, defying the tendency to abandon digraphs like *ae, oe* (which see).

subsequent, subsequently, subsequent to. The first two are described by two critics as pretentious for *later*, and the last is described by three as pretentious for *after*. American Heritage lists these uses without aspersing them.

Substandard. As a status label, see *Standard*.

substitute, replace. *Substitute*, which means *put in the place of*, is followed idiomatically by *for; replace*, which means *take the place of*, is followed by *by*. Careful attention to the choice of the appropriate prepositions will prevent the usual misuse, which is that of *substitute* for *replace*. "Natural rubber has been largely replaced (not *substituted*) by synthetic rubber"; or "Synthetic rubber has been largely substituted for natural rubber."

succeed. May not be followed by an infinitive: "He succeeded to keep the place to himself." *succeeded in keeping*.

such. Possible as a pronoun, but some such uses jar the ear. The Bible says "the father of such as dwell in tents" and "Suffer little children to come unto me, and forbid them not, for of such is the kingdom of God." This usage is still current, though it has an archaic flavor. It is difficult to say why some uses of *such* are acceptable while others stick in the craw. Fowler highhandedly solved the problem by citing objectionable ones and terming them illiteracies.

Such is objectionable when used as a personal pronoun (for example, in place of *it* or *them*) or in place of such indefinite pronouns as *any, all, one,* or in place of demonstrative pronouns like *this, these.* "Dues are used for political purposes, but a dissenting member or minority group is without protection against such," *this,* or *this practice.* "As long as stores sell toys that encourage violence, and parents place such in children's hands . . ." *place them.* "The government will grant asylum to members of the crew who request such." *request it.* In spite of disapproval by commentators on usage, both Random House and Webster give examples indicating they regard this use of *such* as standard, as does Bryant.

Such as an intensive ("We had such a good time"; "It was such a nice day") is considered feminine by one critic, regarded as standard by four others. One of them, however, recommends substituting *so* when this is possible without artificiality, e.g., *so trifling an objection* vs. *such a trifling objection*. This usage of *such* is considered standard by dictionaries.

The correct form is *no such*, not *no such a:* "There is no such beast as the Loch Ness monster."

such as. *Like* is often preferable to *such as:* "Sudden and totally unexpected upheavals such as that in Guatemala . . ." *like. Such as* for *those who* (*such as frequent these places*) is considered colloquial by one critic, standard by another. This construction occurs frequently and seems likely to establish itself as standard if it has not already done so. *Such as* should not be followed by a comma:

"Musical instruments, such as, French horns, flutes, and clarinets." Omit the comma.

Two critics point out that in locutions like "The banks refuse to make such loans that are not backed by sufficient collateral" *such* must be followed by *as*, not *that: such loans as are not.* However, *make loans that are not* would be better. When *that* introduces a clause of result, *such that* is correct: "His surprise was such that he refused to believe the letter."

such is the case. See *case*.

such stuff as dreams . . . See *Misquotation*.

such that. See *such as*.

sudden death. Often criticized on the curious ground that death is always sudden. Not so; it often approaches by obvious degrees. The meaning of *suddenly* in this context is *unexpectedly*, a definition given by all dictionaries. Webster and American Heritage both have separate entries for *sudden death*, which should be enough to establish its legitimacy.

suddenly collapsed. Redundant. Suddenness is the essence of collapse, unless the word is otherwise qualified (*collapsed by degrees*).

suffer from, with. American Heritage rejects *suffer with* in relation to ailments: "He suffered with dandruff." *from*. Webster and Random House concur.

suffer, sustain, receive. Properly speaking, people suffer *injuries*, and such wording as "The driver suffered a broken leg" is frowned on by some critics because they think it says, in effect, that the driver suffered a leg. Such criticism has dubious foundation, for the writer said *broken leg*, i.e., the breaking of a leg, and that is how all but the captious will read it. "The driver received a broken leg" offers no refuge from these critics, who have been known to respond to such intelligence with "How? By parcel post?" In any event, such sentences seem open to improvement: "The driver's leg was broken." There is no reason why one should not write "The driver suffered [or *received*] a fracture of the leg," however. See also *break, broke;* and *had. Sustain* is often used in these contexts; *suffer* and *receive* are considered preferable by four critics, though *sustain* is standard.

sufficient. Fowler deprecates the displacement of *enough* as a noun by *sufficient:* "We have had sufficient." Webster recognizes *sufficient* as a noun but Random House and American Heritage do not. The use of *sufficient(ly)* where *enough* will do (*sufficient money; punished sufficiently*) is considered pretentious by four critics. *Enough* is also preferable to *a sufficient amount*.

Suffixes. See *Hyphens 5*.

suggest. It is a common affectation, especially among those who shy away from direct statement, to use *suggest* instead of *say*. " 'The dam would not have enough capacity,' he suggested." A suggestion is tentative; *suggest* is not suitable for a positive statement like the example. "He suggested that the supposed difficulties will be nonexistent in actual practice." *predicted.* "I would like to suggest my views on the tax proposal." *offer, present, give.*

suggestive(ly). So preponderantly used in the sense *risqué* or *indecent(ly)* that the writer who wants merely the simple meaning of *suggesting* should beware of ambiguity or unconscious humor. "Why doesn't someone write a book suggestively entitled *The Greatest Photographs?*" What, the reader might wonder, would be suggestive about this title?

suicide. Considered standard as a verb by Webster and Random House ("He had suicided"); American Heritage labels it informal. Avoided in careful writing.

suit, suite. Three critics hold the correct form is *suite* in such connections as *a musical suite, a suite of rooms, a suite of furniture,* though the terms are actually the same. Dictionaries also observe the distinction; it is so well established that *suit* for *suite* is considered a glaring error, though broadcast advertisements sometimes use it either deliberately or ignorantly. *Suite* is pronounced *sweet,* which the advertisers may consider affected.

Sums of Money. Logically considered singular, not plural: "The deliquency was $56 million, of which $44 million were owed by the Communist bloc." *was owed.* Redundancy often results from the use of *cents* and *dollars* in such expressions as *$.22 cents, $5 million dollars.* The form *22 cents* is preferable to $.22 because it is simpler and unambiguous. See also *Numbers.*

sung. See *sing.*

sunk. See *sink.*

super-. Solid as a prefix: *superhuman, superhighway,* etc.

Superlatives. See *Comparison 2, 4.*

supersede. Often misspelled *supercede.*

supine. Means *lying face upward,* authorities agree. This is of interest in connection with the broadened sense of *prone,* which see.

supplement, augment. See *augment, supplement.*

suppose to, supposed to. The second is the correct form: "We were suppose to fall in half an hour before the signal sounded." *supposed to.*

supra. Solid as a prefix: *supraliminal, supraorbital, supramolecular,* etc.

surcease. Three critics and Random House agree that the noun is archaic, and the implication is that its use is affected. Webster, however, labels only the verb obsolete, thus strengthening the suspicion that the noun, though it may have fallen into disuse for a time, is now experiencing a revival ("There followed a surcease of political accusations").

sure. *Sure* as an adverb ("That sure was a good dinner") in place of *surely* is considered substandard by two critics, colloquial by another and Random House, informal by American Heritage, and standard by Webster. The consensus is that this usage is questionable. *Sure enough,* however, is regarded as standard by two critics. Compare *real.*

surprize. A variant listed by Webster, but so seldom seen it is likely to be considered a misspelling. American Heritage calls it rare.

survival of the fittest. See *Misquotation.*

suspected. See *accused.*

Suspensive Modifiers. See *Comma 9.*

suspicion. As a verb ("Police suspicioned the vagrant"), considered substandard.

sustain. See *suffer, sustain, receive.*

swap. One critic deprecates the use of the word in serious contexts, but both Random House and Webster consider it standard. American Heritage labels it informal.

swing into high gear. A threadbare metaphor.

swum. *Swam* is the preferred from for the past tense, not *swum,* and *swum* is correct for the participle: "She swam (*has swum*) the English Channel."

synagogue. See *Judaism.*

Synonyms. For the use of synonyms as a stylistic fault, see *Variation; Elegant Variation.*

synonymous. Sometimes misspelled *synonomous.*

T

tablespoonfuls, tablespoonsful. See *-ful*.

tactics. See *strategy*.

tailored. A cliché as used figuratively: "The job was tailored to his abilities."

take. See *bring, take*.

take a fling. "After studying speech at Wesleyan, she spent a brief but futile fling at the footlights in New York." Idiom calls for *took a fling*.

take delivery on. A mercantile pomposity for *receive, be delivered*.

take it easy. An idiom; not *take it easily*, which results from overcorrectness.

take off. There can be no reasonable objection to extending this term beyond its primary sense relating to aircraft, but it is overworked in place of *leave, depart*, and in addition has a slangy flavor ("He took off for the suburbs"). That, however, may be what its users want. Considered slang by one critic and American Heritage, informal by Random House, and standard by Webster.

take place. See *occur, take place*.

taps. The bugle call is said by one critic to be plural and thus to require a plural verb ("*Taps* were sounded"); Webster says it is usually singular in construction and American Heritage says flatly "used with a singular verb," a conclusion that appears to be supported by general usage.

tar. Some sailors on liberty once got into trouble with the police, and the headline on the resulting news story referred to them as *tars*. As it happened, they were blacks, and a delegation from the local black community shortly appeared in the editor's office, demanding an apology for what they considered an unnecessary racial slur. They got it, too. But although *tar* and *tarbrush* sometimes have a racist connotation, it does not figure in the use of *tar* for *sailor*. The expression is

371

variously explained as a shortened form of *tarpaulin* and as a reference to the tar sailors once smeared on their pigtails.

target. The use of the word in the sense *quota, goal, deadline, objective,* which became popular in World War II, is discouraged as tiresome and often inaccurate by three critics. An example: "Contributions have exceeded the target," in which *goal* or *quota* would have been a better choice; at any rate, a target would be *missed,* to pursue the metaphor consistently, not *exceeded.* As a verb ("The oilfields were targeted for bombing") given as standard by Random House and Webster; not listed by American Heritage.

taunt, taut. *Taunt* means *jeer at* or *tease:* "The losing team was *taunted* by the students." *Taut* means *stretched tight:* "The clothesline was not *taut* enough." *Taunt* is often misused for *taut.* A strange confusion is possible in references to ships. In the Navy and otherwise, the common expression *a taut ship* refers to one that is well disciplined, in good order. Sometimes the phrase *a taunt ship* is regarded as an error, but it has a different sense, i.e., tall-masted. The origin is unknown.

taxpayer. One word.

Tchaikovsky, Tschaikovsky, Tschaikowsky. The differences are matters of opinion on transliteration from the Cyrillic alphabet used for Russian. In modern practice, however, there is a nearly unanimous tendency to settle on the first version. The other two are likely to be found in older writings.

teaspoonfuls, teaspoonsful. See *-ful.*

technic, technique. Though these forms are interchangeable, *technique* has a long running start. In any event, the word is always pronounced tek*neek.* *Technic* may as well be abandoned.

Technical Terms. The use of technical language, or of the cant belonging to a specialized field, in what is aimed at a general audience is a temptation to those who think it will make their writing sound learned and impressive.

The use of technical terms is hard to avoid in writing that deals with advances in physics, medicine, and the other sciences, and often no satisfactory synonyms are available in plain language. The writer who keeps his audience in mind, however, will be careful to follow the unfamiliar technical terms he must use with definitions in as simple language as possible.

Science writing, a special case, is usually handled by writers who make it a specialty and have no need to be warned of such pitfalls. But what about writing that deals with such everyday subjects as automobile accidents? These accounts often abound with *contusions, abrasions, lacerations, fractures,* and other terms redolent of the hospital. Everybody knows, of course, that a fracture is a break. Lacerations are cuts, for practical purposes, although the doctor may mean something more complex by this expression. It is doubtful that *contusions* presents any clear picture to the layman. What's wrong with *bruises* instead of *contusions*, *scrapes* instead of *abrasions*, *cuts* instead of *lacerations*, and *sewing* instead of *suturing?* This much is certain: although many readers may know what some medical terms mean, there are many more who do not.

Hemorrhage is certainly undesirable for *bleed* in anything but a medical journal. *Coronary occlusion, carcinoma, thrombosis,* and *first-, second-,* and *third-degree burns* may all require translation for the ordinary reader. It is a good principle not to send the reader to the dictionary, but to send the writer there instead.

In one city, an outbreak of sleeping sickness (encephalitis) was attributed to the *culex tarsalis* mosquito. Newspaper stories on the subject, which caused considerable public alarm, ran for weeks before anyone thought of describing *culex tarsalis* and its habits, and giving some idea how common this variety was among the dozen or so in the area.

In another instance, the term *low low water line* was used again and again in connection with an important waterfront project. Yet no one but seafarers knew what that line was, and the press failed to give any help to the others. See also *Overwriting*.

teen-age, -ager, -aged. The consensus is that the terms are hyphenated.

telecast, televise. Technically the first means to broadcast by television and the second to record and then to broadcast. But the distinction has no meaning to laymen, *televise* being used interchangeably with *telecast* in the sense *broadcast*, a conclusion supported by the definitions in both unabridged dictionaries, neither of which recognizes the restricted sense of *televise*.

temblor. This term for *earthquake* is often wrongly given *trembler, tremblor*. Chiefly used by newswriters as a variant. For either or both of these reasons, the Canadian Press bans it.

temperature. Two critics asperse *temperature* for *fever*, as in "The patient has no temperature." Two others speculate that this is a euphemism. A third regards the expression as firmly established colloquially and beyond cavil. This sense is also recognized as standard by dictionaries.

tempo. Has to do with rate of speed or rhythm; its commonest application is to music. Often used ineptly: "The Berlin crisis will mount in tempo." Obviously the writer did not mean that the crisis would become faster. A rule of thumb is that *tempo* suitably applies to what is in motion.

tend to. Rejected by one critic and American Heritage in the sense *apply attention:* "The lawyer said he would tend to the matter." *attend.* Considered dialectal by another critic, standard by Random House and Webster.

tenet, tenable, untenable. A tenet is something one holds to—a principle, doctrine, or belief. What is tenable, then, is something that can be held—abstractly, such as a doctrine, or physically, such as a battle line. What is untenable cannot be held. "Under such circumstances, living as a hermit is untenable." Unacceptable, undesirable, impossible, perhaps, but not untenable. (*Tenable* also has the sense *habitable*, but that does not figure in the confusion dealt with here.) *Tenet* is often mispronounced and sometimes misspelled *tenent*, perhaps by confusion with *tenant*.

Tenses. See *Sequence of Tenses*.

tenterhooks. These are hooks on which curtains are stretched, and the term was once applied to hooks from which poultry was hung in a shop. The word is now usually used figuratively in the phrase *on tenterhooks*, meaning *in suspense*, and sometimes ludicrously given *on tender hooks*.

term. See *consider*.

terminate. Considered pretentious by three critics where *end* will do (*terminate the marriage*).

terrible, terribly. See *awful(ly)*.

than. The question is whether *than* shall be considered a conjunction or a preposition in sentences like "He is taller than me." If it is a conjunction, the sentence should read *than I*. Fowler concedes that *than me* is very common in speech, and both he and Evans recommend sidestepping the question in writing by recasting in some such form as *than I am*. Flesch considers the objective case (*me*) idiomatic with *than;* this, however, is an oversimplification. The analysis of this problem is tortuous, and more confusing than helpful. In general, the tendency is to regard *than* as a conjunction and thus to put the pronoun following it in the subjective case ("He is better informed than I") unless the pronoun has an antecedent or a word closely linked with it in the objective case ("We have hired less honest men than him"). All the commentators point out that ambiguous statements are likely with *than* and a preposition: "He likes the teacher better than her" (better than he likes her, or better than she likes the teacher?). Obviously, *she* is called for here, but it sounds pedantic. In such cases, recasting is recommended ("better than she does").

   Than whom in such constructions as "An architect than whom none is more reputable" is correct, instead of *than who*, but three critics consider the expression clumsy and recommend avoiding it. For other hazards involving *than*, see *Comparison; hardly; scarce, scarcely;* for *than is, than are*, see *as is, as are*.

than any, than anyone. "He has more readers than any financial writer on a New York newspaper"; "He is more interested in the capture of his wife's murderer than any person on earth." In both instances, logic requires *any other*. As pointed out by Perrin, the rule is that *other* is required in the comparison of things in the same class. Fowler calls sentences like "She is the best-dressed woman of anyone in town" idiomatic but adds that those who object to the construction as illogical may recast.

than is, than are. See *as is, as are.*

thankfully. Increasingly misused (like *hopefully,* which see) to indicate thankfulness by the writer: "The decision, thankfully, was in our favor." To put it another way, the word is used to mean *we* (or *I*) *feel thankful,* rather than *in a thankful manner:* "They raised their voices thankfully in song."

thanking you in advance. Oddly, more than one critic of language considers this rude or inconsiderate, on the ground that the writer is attempting to escape expressing appreciation at the proper time; that is, after the favor is done. They miss the point; those who thank in advance are, if anything, overcourteous. They hope that the expression will pave the way. It could be interpreted as presumptuous, but nobody does so. The phrase is, however, overeager and perhaps sophomoric.

thanks to. Considered standard in the sense *due to, because of* by three critics, Random House, and Webster ("Thanks to early registration, all classes began on schedule"). The phrase is sometimes also used ironically: "Thanks to your help, I failed the course." See also *credit.*

than whom. See *than.*

that. 1. As a conjunction. All the authorities surveyed agree that *that* may be omitted as a conjunction, and most of them agree that this is stylistically preferable when there is no reason for its inclusion: "He said (that) he was starving." The tendency to omit *that* is too strong, however; it is agreed equally that the conjunction is often omitted when it should have been used. This is mainly a matter of having a sensitive feeling for correct construction. Usually, *that* is best omitted in short sentences, and when the relation of the elements it would otherwise connect is immediately clear. Some examples of undesirably omitted *thats* will be given here.

"Metzman said on Jan. 1 the fleet stood at 1,776,000 cars." *That* is required after *said* to indicate that Jan. 1 was the date on which the fleet stood at the figure given; as it is, *Jan. 1* may be taken as the date on which Metzman made the statement. "The speaker said last November the outlook improved." "Said *that* last November . . ." for the same reason.

"He added the proposed freeway could follow the existing route." "Added *that* the proposed freeway . . ."; *that* is necessary to keep the reader from going off on a false scent and assuming that *freeway* and not the entire clause is the object of *added.*

"The deputy foreign minister said last night that Panama does not receive its fair share of Panama Canal revenues, and sentiment for a 50 percent increase is likely to grow." "And *that* sentiment . . ."; parallel construction and unambiguous expression require *that* with both of a pair of coordinate clauses. In this instance, doubt is raised whether both clauses are attributable to the speaker.

"The board was told the point is really one of economics, and that if the ordinance were repealed, meat markets would be driven out of business." "Was told *that* . . ." for the sake of parallel construction.

2. Before direct quotation. *That* is excessive before a direct quotation: "The Point Four director in Iran reported that 'More than half the population of the village have been killed under the falling walls of their homes.' " *"reported, 'More than . . .' "*

3. Doubled. *That* is sometimes unnecessarily doubled: "It is hard to realize that as he lives in quiet retirement at the age of 88 *that* a generation is coming up that knows him only by reputation." The italicized *that* is superfluous; its work has already been done by the first *that*.

4. As a relative pronoun: *that* vs. *which*. All the authorities surveyed deal with this question, and except for Evans they agree that *that* is preferable to begin a restrictive clause ("The rule exempts commercial lots that place no restriction on all-night parking") and that *which* is preferable to begin a nonrestrictive clause ("Los Angeles, which dates back to Spanish days in California, is an exception"). (More information on the distinction between restrictive and nonrestrictive clauses—sometimes called limiting and nonlimiting, or defining and nondefining—may be found under *Restrictive and Nonrestrictive Clauses*.)

It is generally conceded, however, that *which* is often used to introduce restrictive clauses ("We attended the reception which followed the concert") and that this cannot be considered an error. It may be a useful reminder at this point that nonrestrictive clauses are set off by commas, and restrictive clauses are not. A rule of thumb may also be useful. If *that* will fit comfortably, it is correct, and furthermore the clause is restrictive. *That* introducing a nonrestrictive clause is a blunder: "The sun, that had a murky orange color, soon burned off the fog." Evans unaccountably says *that* may introduce nonrestrictive clauses in current usage, but cites examples dating from times long past, when this practice was acceptable.

In "It was easy to find the house which was on fire," *that* can be substituted for *which*, and in accordance with our rule of thumb it thus is preferable. The chief use of the distinction given here between *that* and *which* is that it helps in distinguishing between restrictive and nonrestrictive clauses, a far more important matter than any arbitrary preference of pronoun. The punctuation, however, remains decisive in indicating the distinction. American Heritage offers the helpful comment that a nonrestrictive clause theoretically is capable of being enclosed in parentheses. Or it can be dropped without changing the meaning of the main clause.

5. As a relative pronoun: *that* vs. *who*. Two critics consider *that* freely interchangeable with *who* in restrictive clauses where it fits smoothly, "The man that was walking in the park yesterday." Fowler prefers *who* for particular persons (*you who*) and *that* in generic references (*a man that*), but concedes there is a strong tendency to use *who* out of politeness in generic references (*ladies who*). *That* for *who* is sometimes objected to, but the objection has no basis. Random

House says *that* may refer to a person, and so do American Heritage and Webster.

6. As a pronoun: omission. The tendency is strong to omit *that* as a relative pronoun when it is the object in a restrictive clause: "The apple (that) I was eating . . ." This usage is standard. See also *Ellipsis 4.*

7. *That* for *so* ("He was that rich he didn't know how much money he had") is considered colloquial by Bryant and dialectal by Evans. See also *all that; same; such as.*

8. But that. *But that* sometimes sticks in the craw of the critical, in such sentences as "I do not doubt but that society feels threatened by the homosexual." Technically, *but* is excessive here. Yet its use by good writers has gained it a respectable place. See also *all that.*

that of. Often useless: "One of the most popular hobbies is that of building boats." What of? The hobby of, obviously; so we get "One of the most popular hobbies is the hobby of building boats." Omit *that of.* The lyricist of *Home on the Range,* observing the stars, wonders "if their glory exceeds that of ours." What of? But *exceeds ours* would not fill out the meter, a better excuse for *that of* than the prose writer who uses it can muster. See *False Comparison; Possessives 3.*

that vs. which. See *that 4.*

the. Four critics deplore the journalistic mannerism of omitting *the* when idiom or grammar requires it, in the mistaken idea that by doing so the writing is made brighter or breezier. Necessary *the's* are oftenest omitted in newspaper writing at the beginning of a story, or at the beginning of any sentence. The reader is not sped on his way, as the writers hope, by the omission; rather, he is made to stumble, and to choose between the possible shades of meaning that the writer has neglected to specify. An example: "Crux of the situation is belief expressed by board members that legislation should govern the use of the reservoir by the public." If the object is to be telegraphic, why not go all the way: "Crux of situation is belief expressed by board members that legislation should govern use of reservoir by public"?

The rationalization of newswriters for omitting *the* is that the article conveys little or nothing and only stands in the way of the reader, who is panting to get at meatier words. This is nonsense.

It is not true that articles convey nothing. If this were so, they would be dropped from conversational speech, especially at the least literate level, which hews to essentials. *The* particularizes what it precedes; *a* and *an* designate one of a class. Meaning of a sort *can* be put across without these subtleties, but not the sort of meaning that is the most readable and lucid.

Does it really speed the reader on his way to leave an article off the beginning of a sentence? Surely not if he pauses, as he will, to wonder what happened to it, and finds himself obliged to choose between possible shades of meaning. The writer's job has been foisted on the reader, and he has every right to feel irked.

It is a conspicuous mannerism in some newspapers to say "City Council last night" instead of "The City Council . . ."

In a critique of *The New York Times,* Theodore M. Bernstein cautioned: "Remember what the Bible says: 'If I forget *the,* O Jerusalem, let my right hand forget its cunning.' "

As a sidelight, we may note that *the* has been dropped in popular use of the name *Congress.* Who can say why? Certainly it never occurs to anyone to drop the article from *the Supreme Court, the Cabinet,* or *the Senate.* It is noticeable that recent Presidents have meticulously referred to "the Congress."

An interesting commentary appears in the introduction to *The President, Office and Powers,* fourth edition, by Edward S. Corwin (New York: New York University Press, 1957).

Professor Corwin noted that the Constitution says *the Congress* twenty-six times and *Congress* only five times. Although the Congress established by the Constitution was the last of a succession of congresses, "no sooner did the Constitution go into effect than the term *the Congress* was scrapped by all and sundry." Washington, Jefferson, and Chief Justice Marshall, among others, all said *Congress.*

Professor Corwin attributed the recent reversion to the archaic form "to which Presidents Truman and Eisenhower and Chief Justice Warren have all succumbed," to Franklin D. Roosevelt, "who was never disinclined to resort to the bizarre when it was calculated to focus attention on himself; besides, FDR may have reckoned that his pious revival of the original expression ought to stop the mouths of the critics of his Court-Packing plan."

Three critics agree that it is preferable not to capitalize *the* even though it may form part of the title in constructions like "I read it in the *New York Times.*"

Two critics warn about carelessly using *the* where *a* or *an* is required. This may suggest a distinction that is either inaccurate, unintended, or both. Referring to John Jones as *the vice-president of the Smith Corporation* implies that the corporation has only one vice-president. *Laurence Olivier, the actor* is acceptable on the assumption that he is well enough known so that his name will be recognized. On the other hand, referring to a movie starlet, Hazel Gooch, lately of Broken Bottle, Iowa, as *the* (rather than *an*) *actress* leaves the reader with a rattled feeling that he has not recognized a name he should know, though the fault is in fact the writer's.

It is a tortuous business to generalize about the places where *the* is or is not normally required. The matter is governed by idiom, which does not yield to rules anyway. Let's admit this: We all know very well when we are leaving out a desirable *the;* it is never done by accident.

theater, theatre. *Theatre* is the British preference; in America, it is an affection of theatrical folk.

Theatrical Cant. It has shouldered its way into everyday discourse. The use of showbiz expressions, casually and out of their element, may suggest that the user is showing off his familiarity with the world of the theater. Their popularity at least proves Jimmy Durante's thesis that "everybody wants to get inta da act," and also that Shakespeare was right when he said "all the world's a stage." We have, for example, *catch* (for *see* or *attend*) in reference to a performance ("Did you catch the show?"), as used, not by actors, but by ordinary showgoers. There is also *break up,* as used to describe the situation in which one performer causes another to laugh out of character. This is all right in its technical sense, but it is often used as a casual synonym for *cause to laugh* ("His jokes after dinner broke the guests up"). *Sing* (or whatever) *up a storm* may not be actually theatrical lingo but merely a promotional description that is applied *ad nauseam* to performers. Perhaps the most distasteful of all is the expression *bit,* used as an extension of the showbiz term for a small role (*bit part*). One night a television watcher saw a girl being interviewed in a newscast about a field of pumpkins her father had grown. Asked whether she had helped him, she replied, "Sure, I watered, hoed, and the whole bit." Whereupon the television watcher turned off his set and opened the newspaper. The comments in this article reflect a personal opinion that may at best be idiosyncratic.

thee, thou. *Thou* is the nominative and *thee* the objective form of these archaic pronouns; the difference is the same as between *I* and *me,* or *he* and *him.* (The modern equivalent of both *thou* and *thee* is *you,* which has the same form for the nominative and the objective cases, and for that matter for the singular and the plural.) The usual error is to use *thee* where *thou* is ordinarily called for: "Thee art my ideal." Quaker usage, however, is specialized, and calls uniformly for *thee.* For related problems, see *-eth.*

Some foreign languages have two forms for *you;* the familiar, used for intimates and subordinates, and the polite, used for others, especially those toward whom respect is intended. In German, for example, these forms are *du* and *Sie.* Sometimes the familiar form is translated into English as *thou.* This is technically correct, since in Middle English and later *thou* was the familiar form. But the more modern translation of *du* (and its equivalent in other languages) into *thou* is wholly misleading, for the connotation of the term to us is now Biblical, poetic, or reverential. *Life* magazine, for example, translated the title of a German periodical publication, *Du,* as *Thou,* but it would have come closer with *Hey You.* Moral: translate *du, tu,* etc., as *you,* and explain if necessary that the familiar form was used.

theft. See *burglary.*

their. See *they (their, them); Collective Nouns; Adolescent they.*

their's. No such form; *theirs.* Also *ours, hers, its* (the possessive forms).

them. See *it's me,* etc.; *they (their, them).*

themselves. See *myself; Reflexives.*

then. Follett disapproves of *then* as an adjective (*the then mayor*) but this usage is given as standard in dictionaries.

there. Two critics recommend care in choosing the number of the verb in a clause having *there* as a false subject. Attention should be fixed on the true subject, which governs the verb: "There are (not *is*) six flowers in the vase"; "There were (not *was*) an outing and a dance after the golf tournament." One critic says a plural verb is preferable in "There were a sausage, an orange, and a piece of cheese on the table" (rather than *was*). But another finds that the singular verb predominates overwhelmingly in standard usage when the first part of a compound subject following *there* is singular, as in this example, and a third critic and American Heritage concur. Thus opinion is divided on this point.

Max J. Herzberg, as the editor of the periodical *Word Study*, found that three subjects got his readers' dander up higher than anything else: the split infinitive, proposals to dispense with the apostrophe, and the use of *there is* or *there are* to begin a sentence (or clause). This construction is often criticized as objectionably indefinite and the product of lazy thinking. Nonetheless, it is frequent in good literature, particularly the Bible: "There were giants in the earth in those days"; "Now there arose up a new king"; "The fool hath said in his heart, 'There is no God' "; and "There were in the same country shepherds . . ." Other examples have been cited: "There is a pleasure in the pathless woods" (Byron); "There is the smack of ambrosia about it" (Lowell).

It seems apparent that the construction was used thoughtfully, rather than lazily, in these examples, to avoid an undesirable emphasis on the true subject that would come of placing it first. "Giants were in the earth in those days" would lay an undesirable stress on *giants,* weaken the sentence, and destroy the rhythm. If "Now there arose up a new king" became "Now a new king arose up" *a new king* would take emphasis from *arose up.* Considerations of rhythm also enter here.

The *there* construction may be clumsy and objectionably indirect with a passive auxiliary: "As in the previous ruling, there was no jail sentence imposed." Surely "no jail sentence was imposed" would be better. "Yesterday there were four more cases reported." Better: "Yesterday four more cases were reported." The clumsiness is aggravated when *has* or *have,* as auxiliaries in passive constructions, follow *there:* "There have been thousands of people killed"; "There have been two surveys taken." These are weak and indirect.

It is generally not considered good practice to begin a sentence with a figure, and this causes some writers to shy away even from starting a sentence with a number that has been spelled out. They resort to the *there* construction: "There are eleven organizations representing health, welfare, and youth groups in the county"; (*Eleven organizations represent . . .*) "There were nineteen military experiments connected with the explosion;" (*Nineteen military experiments were . . .*).

This timidity with numbers unnecessarily carries over to those beginning clauses: "At present, it is said, there are 102 of the county's 167 dairies shipping milk into the area." *There are* only defeats the prominence that *102* deserves, and gives the sentence a woolly effect. *It is said 102 . . . are shipping . . .* Besides, the verb *are shipping* is unidiomatically divided by the submerged subject. Unidiomatic division of verb forms also figures in the unhappy sound of the passive constructions cited earlier. These points may be made, at any rate: The *there* construction is not to be condemned out of hand; it is both idiomatic and common in the best literature; it is clumsy and to be avoided with a passive verb; and in view of the prejudice against it, the writer who uses it discriminatingly should take heart and be prepared to defend himself, for defense is indeed possible. See also *Numbers*.

thereafter, etc. The use of such words as *thereafter* (instead of *after that* or *then*), *thereby, therefrom, therein,* etc., instead of modern alternatives is discouraged by two critics as stiff.

therefore, therefor. Sometimes confused. *Therefor* means *for that* or *for it:* "He explained the cause of action and the basis therefor" (that is, the basis for it). *Therefore* means *consequently, as a result:* "The conclusion, therefore, is that we have no case." Two critics, Random House, and American Heritage agree on this view; Webster gives *therefore* as a synonym of *therefor*. American Heritage labels *therefor* archaic, and it is obviously passing out of use.

these. See *this, these*.

these kind, sort. See *kind*.

they (their, them). In reference to singular pronouns, see *Adolescent they; anybody, anyone; each; everybody, everyone; Collective Nouns*.
   They as an indefinite subject ("They say the climate is getting colder") is beyond reproach.

thief. See *burglary*.

think. See *feel*.

thinking man. This expression, as used in such sentences as "Every thinking man must agree that . . ." is criticized as insidious and as offensive to the reader.

this, and this. Use of *this, and this* to introduce a subordinate clause is quaint: "It certainly is gratifying to see a group of property owners joined in civic interest and pride, this despite all the talk we hear of overburdened taxpayers." *interest and pride despite the talk.* "Talk among the pickets themselves was that the strike would be short-lived—*and this* because of the strategic nature of the plant's production." *short-lived, because of . . .*

this, these. There are two misuses of *this* as a pronoun. One is placing it at the beginning of a sentence or clause in reference to a noun or pronoun, rather than to the general idea preceding. "The Senussis established what has been called a theocratic empire, spilling over political frontiers. This [better *It* or *The empire*] was then broken up." An example of correct use: "Because of inherited venereal disease, their population remains static. This worries the elders of the tribe."

Otherwise, the demonstrative *this* should not be used in place of personal pronouns. "We were much impressed by the chief. This [better *He* or *This man*] is an able and progressive citizen." "Since 1927 he has lived in his studio, and it has long been his wish that this [better *it*] be kept as a museum after his death."

These as a demonstrative pronoun tends, like *this,* to be used in the place of personal pronouns. "Her heartbeat tripled and her rate of breathing was three or four times normal, but as the rocket reached its orbit, these [better *they*] returned to normal." "She digs up whole pages of evidence and serves these [*them*] hot." A correct example: "I get all the oysters I want at home, but these taste like brass doorknobs." The oysters being eaten were contrasted with those at home.

Follett curiously protests at length about the use of *this* to summarize a preceding clause or sentence, but this usage is considered correct by three other critics and American Heritage. Webster says *this* is "often used with a general reference to something stated or implied in the previous context but without particular reference to a noun or noun equivalent in that context." Perrin too says *this* is regularly used to refer to the idea of a preceding clause or sentence. One critic prefers *that* in reference to what has been stated; another finds *this* more frequent, adding that the summarizing *this* has been common since the time of Shakespeare, and quotes, "This above all: to thine own self be true."

this reporter, this writer, etc. See *Editorial We.*

tho. A generally rejected curtailment of *though.*

thoroughbred, pedigreed, purebred. The tendency is to restrict the first to horses and to apply the second and third terms to other animals. *Pedigreed* is applied particularly to dogs.

thoroughgoing. One word; not *thorough-going.*

those. Sometimes used redundantly. "Those persons going to the airport . . ." Either *Those* or *Persons.*

those kind. See *kind.*

thou. See *thee, thou.*

though, although. *Although* once was considered more emphatic, and preferred by many writers "to introduce a fact as distinguished from a supposition, and in formal style." (Webster II). But the words are now synonymous and interchangeable where either will fit. Some commentators cite examples of constructions where only *though* will do, such as *as though, even though,* and "The sky was still cloudy, though," but it is inconceivable that anyone would use *although* in such instances. American Heritage objects to *though* for *however* as used in the preceding example, usually at the end or in the middle of a sentence; Random House and Webster consider this usage standard. Usually idiom, sometimes rhythm, sometimes the tone of the writing will dictate the choice.

Two critics say that *though* or *although* should be used only to indicate concession: "Though some students did not meet the standards for admission to the college, the requirements have been changed." These ideas are not opposed, and should be stated as a sequence: *Because some students did not . . .* "Earthquakes are infrequent, although little damage has been done by them." *. . . and little damage . . .* Another critic objects to the comma preceding *though* in the sense *however:* "The audience did not respond, though." This is in accord with the modern tendency toward open punctuation. It is observable that the comma is still a fixture in this construction, however. See *Comma 1.* For *as though* see *as if, as though.*

thrifty. In careful writing, applied to people, occasionally to plants: *a thrifty housewife.* Adwriters, however, loosely and liberally apply it to products: *a thrifty shortening, a thrifty toothpaste,* a usage that is distasteful to the discriminating, who would use *economical* in such contexts. Whether this distinction will be done in by the brevity and breeziness of *thrifty* vs. *economical* remains to be seen.

through. Accepted as standard for *finished* (*through with the book*) by American Heritage, Random House, and Webster. In the senses *having no further relationship, done for* (We're through"; "He's through in politics") considered informal by American Heritage, standard by Webster, and not given by Random House.

throwaway. See *free, freely.*

thru. Though there is much to be said for simplified spelling, forms like *thru* have gained no real acceptance.

thundrous, thunderous. The first is an error.

thus. See *for.*

thusly. Regarded by five critics as a superfluous variant of *thus;* rejected almost unanimously by the American Heritage panel. Aspersed by Random House; given as standard by Webster.

tidelands. In the original sense, this was the area exposed by low tide, but the term has been extended to the location of offshore, underwater oil deposits.

tiff. A tiff, like a spat (which see) is a petty quarrel. The term has been known to be misapplied—for example, to a race riot in which 16 persons were injured and 40 were jailed.

till, 'til, until. There is no difference between *till* and *until; till* is said by Fowler to be the usual form. This seems British. The forms *'til* and *'till* are wrong. One critic and American Heritage object to *till* or *until* for *before:* "It was not five minutes until the rain stopped." But this is a British quibble, and such constructions, which are always negative, are sanctioned by Random House and Webster.

Time Elements. The misplacement of time elements too early in the sentence is a conspicuous gaucherie of much newspaper writing, despite continual criticism. The usual version that appears in print is something like "The City Council last night voted a street improvement program" (instead of *voted a street improvement program last night*) or "John Jones Thursday shot his mother-in-law" (instead of *shot his mother-in-law Thursday*). The natural place for the time element is generally after, rather than before, the verb, and sometimes at the end of the sentence. The journalistic idiosyncrasy of placing it immediately after the subject perhaps has two causes: eagerness to put it in a prominent position, and a disinclination to pause and consider where it would fit most smoothly, for this is a matter that does sometimes require a moment's consideration. The reflex action of placing the time element after the subject obviates any such consideration, and the damage this placement does to the flow of the sentence apparently is not regarded as counting for anything. Sentences on the model of the "John Jones Thursday" example given earlier have been endlessly ridiculed as suggesting that *Thursday* is the subject's last name.

Placement of the time element immediately after the verb and before an object can also be awkward: "An American novelist was awarded today the Nobel Prize for Literature" (*was awarded the Nobel Prize for Literature today*). Sometimes the element will go as well first as last: "World War II veterans next year will collect $220 million in dividends on their government life insurance." Either *Next year veterans will* or *on their government life insurance next year;* as it stands, the sentence is clumsy.

Sometimes the time element, which is usually crowded into the first paragraph of news accounts, would be better deferred until the second. And sometimes it would better be omitted altogether because it misleads or confuses. "The Soviet Communist chief is in trouble today. He is fighting valiantly to hold together the empire left him by his predecessors." *Today* is not only obtrusive but ludicrous, because it suggests that a long-continued situation is of only a day's duration, or developed only today. "An eighty-year-old nun stood firm today [*is standing firm*] against plans to turn her little nation into a Communist state."

time frame. A great favorite as a displacement of *period* among the practitioners of gobbledygook, who cannot bear to use the simple word. See also *at this point,* etc., as it displaces *now*.

times less, times more. "This procedure is 100 times less effective." The sentence does not convey a clear meaning, since *times* implies multiplication, not division or diminution. Better: *one one-hundredth* (if that is what it was) *as effective.* "The new star is probably 25,000 times fainter than the sun." Baffling. *One twenty-five thousandth as bright;* or "The sun is 25,000 times as bright as the new star." *Times more* is ambiguous; "His income is four times more than it was last year." This may be taken to mean quadrupled or quintupled; *four times as much as.* See also *almost more, less.*

tinker's dam, damn. Authorities differ on or decline to state a preference as to which is correct. The Oxford English Dictionary, however, says that the theory that the expression refers to a small dam of putty erected by tinkers to contain solder is "an ingenious but baseless conjecture." If this conclusion is correct, it appears that *tinker's dam* is nothing more than a bowdlerization of *tinker's damn*, deriving from tinkers' purported habits of idle cursing.

-tion, -ion. Warnings against writing sentences that contain a series of words ending in this sound are given by five critics. An example: "The educa*tion* of the popula*tion* of the na*tion* is substandard." The repetition is irksome, and such sentences should be recast. Such writing exemplifies the style that tends toward abstractions rather than the concrete; the concrete is always to be preferred as more vigorous and effective. The sentence quoted could be improved to "Education in this country is substandard."

'tis. See *Poesy*.

Titles. It is objectionable to double titles. This is good practice in German (*Herr Dr. Kurt Weiss*, the equivalent of *Mr. Dr. Kurt Weiss*) and in England (*General Sir Hugh Borrow*), but not in America. Doubling usually occurs in such instances as *Superintendent of Schools Dr. Gerald Whitcomb, City Librarian Miss Tillie McDonald, Councilwoman Mrs. Edna Gleason*. If it is desirable to give both designations, clumsiness may be avoided by writing *Dr. Gerald Whitcomb, superintendent of schools; Miss Tillie McDonald, city librarian;* otherwise, simply *Superintendent of Schools Gerald Whitcomb; Librarian Tillie McDonald*. Doubled titles are doubly objectionable when there is more than one mention of the name; in such examples the office can be specified on first mention and subsequent mentions will take care of *Dr., Mrs., Miss* or whatever.

The world record for piled-up titles may have been set by "The speaker was former Assistant Secretary of Commerce for International Affairs and Occidental College graduate H. C. McClellan."

It is generally considered good form to dispense with titles in designating the author of a book (especially in the book itself) and in identifying public performers, such as singers and actors. See also *False Titles; Capitalization; Rev.; Dr.; Mr., Mrs., Miss; Ms.*

-to. Hyphenated as a prefix: *lean-to, set-to,* etc.

to all intents and purposes. A windy way of saying *practically, in effect*. Derives from a legalism, *to all intents, constructions, and purposes*.

to be. See *Infinitives 4*.

together with. See *with*.

token. The expression *by the same token* is derogated by three critics as pompous and archaic.

Tomb of the Unknowns. This form of reference to the Tomb of the Unknown Soldier gained a certain fleeting popularity after the Army used it on guide signs in Arlington National Cemetery. It was dropped after protests, however, and the Army verifies that the correct term is *Tomb of the Unknown Soldier* although other unknown service men are buried there.

tome. A conspicuous journalese variant of *book*, as *white stuff* is of *snow, yellow metal* of *gold*, and *pachyderm* of *elephant*. *Tome* is strictly applicable to a volume forming part of a larger work, or to any book, but it has been found in bad company too often.

too. *Too*, like *not too* (which see), is sometimes used illogically. In his book *The Press* A. J. Liebling quoted a statement from the New York *World Telegram* in 1953 denying "charges by some followers of Adlai E. Stevenson, the Democratic candidate [for President in 1952] that the press was too lopsided in its support of President Eisenhower." Liebling's comment was "Just lopsided enough, he must have meant."

Setting off *too* with commas is old-fashioned: "They, too, depend on cash flow to finance their activities." *They too depend.* See *not too; Comma 1.*

top. One critic objects that the word is overused as an adjective (*top singer, top administrator, top prices*) in the senses *foremost, principal, highest*, etc., especially in journalism. Another critic takes notice of this use without expressing any disapproval except such as may be implied in the comment that it appears mostly in journalism and advertising. Recognized as standard by dictionaries.

tortuous, torturous. Sometimes confused. *Tortuous* means *twisting, winding* (*a tortuous road up the mountain*); *torturous* means *causing torture* (*a torturous stiff collar*). All authorities observe the distinction.

toss. Often preferred to *throw* in newswriting. See *Journalese.*

tot, tote. Often confused in their past tenses, *totted* and *toted*. *Tote* is a dialectal expression meaning *carry:* "We toted our own wood for the fire." *Tot* (with *up*) means *add up:* "The accountant totted up the column of figures."

totally (completely) destroyed (demolished). Redundant for *destroyed* or *demolished*. It is true, of course, that something may be partly destroyed, but the sense of the words is absolute without a qualifier.

to the manner born. See *Misquotation.*

touch. See *finishing touch.*

touch of nature. See *Misquotation.*

tour of duty. Military lingo that may best be left to military connections. A policeman going off duty has been known to be described as "ending his tour of duty." In the military, a tour of duty is an assignment to a post or locality for a considerable period, and the expression is not applied to a watch or shift or day's work.

toward, towards. The second form is generally considered preferable in Britain, the first in the U.S., though the second is gaining favor in this country. Both, of course, are standard. There is a notion that *towards* goes with tangible objects (*towards a table*) and *toward* with intangibles (*toward an understanding*) but this is fanciful.

to we. "We, the people . . ." has a fine historical ring, and thus to many the phrase seems hallowed and immutable. They are therefore led to write things like "The issue should have been referred to we, the people." Ungrammatical, of course, since the preposition *to* calls for *us, the people.* Admittedly, the noble declamatory effect has now evaporated. "This is no joke to we bus drivers." *us.* Here the fault probably lies in an ignorant overcorrectness that makes for avoidance of objective pronouns (*me, him, her, them, us*).

track, tract. A confusion that sometimes turns up in reputable surroundings. A track is what a train runs on, among other things; a tract is a pamphlet, usually religious and admonitory, or a piece of land.

trademark. One word; not *trade mark* or *trade-mark.* Most combinations with *trade,* however, are two words: *trade name, trade practice, trade wind;* but *tradesfolk, tradesmen.*

Trade Names. An initial wire-service story about a woman left injured in an isolated area by a plane crash told how she gained her only nourishment by sucking Lifesavers. But this was only until some overzealous copy-editor wielded his pencil on it; later versions read "candy mints."

As was brought out in protests from subscribing editors, the substitution was decidedly unhappy, and more than overbalanced the drawback of any free advertising the makers of Lifesavers might have received. Lifesavers are a product known to everyone; the name creates a specific image that *candy mints* cannot match. *Candy mints* succeeds only in swaddling in wool the precise fact the fuzzy-minded are so frightened of.

Often the identification of the make of an automobile can send a shaft of light into a sentence. It conveys something, for example, if the Sultan of Swat, who is worth his weight in rubies, is described as driving a battered old Volkswagen. Or if a relief client is described as pulling up to the welfare office in a new Cadillac.

A group of Russians on a tour of the United States visited a Chevrolet plant, but numerous editors who could not see the news for the superstitions changed it to *automobile plant.* An American visiting in Russia smuggled a copy of *Time* to an eager student there, but this became *an American newsmagazine.* Newspapers sometimes refer mysteriously to "a national magazine": *The Atlantic* or *Mad?*

Does the casual appearance of trade names really constitute free advertising? And if so, what of it? Newspapers often pretend they do not know the names of papers in neighboring places. The *Dogtown Yelp* (circ. 2,964), for example, will refer to the *Metropolitan Uproar* (circ. 289,436), which is published in a city 25 miles away and relied upon by most *Yelp* readers for everything except tidings of Dogtown potluck suppers, as "an upstate big-city daily." Readers are amused at such transparent efforts to conceal, and marvel anew how it is possible to publish successful newspapers without invoking common sense.

For that matter, rival metropolitan dailies in the same town (if such still exist) will often act as if they have never been introduced. One will refer to the other, when such reference is unavoidable, as "a Bigtown evening paper."

Television possibly has taken its cue from this, or perhaps out of its own inspired chintzyness has evolved the prissy "another network" evasion instead of coming right out and acknowledging what the other network is. Listeners who want to know can easily find out. What usually interests the program-seeker, however, is the channel number. But if the networks concluded a pact of mutual recognition, look at all the free advertising they would get from each other. See also *realtor*.

tragedy, tragic. What is termed a tragedy should have impressive or at least respectable dimensions: "The tragedy is that there is seldom complete agreement as to which direction change should take in yielding to progress." An inconvenience, no doubt, perhaps a stumbling block, but hardly a tragedy. Devaluation of *tragedy* to describe ordinary misfortunes is one of the marks of the overwriting common in journalism. The definitions in Random House bear out this distinction; Webster, however, gives as synonyms *bad luck, misfortune,* though the examples nearly all conform with the distinction. Sometimes misspelled *tradgedy,* etc.

tragicomedy. Thus; not *tragic comedy*.

trained expert. Redundant, like *qualified expert;* an expert without training is no expert.

trans-. Solid as a prefix: *transarctic, transoceanic, translocate,* etc.; but *trans-American, trans-Mississippi* (followed by a capital). *Transatlantic* and *trans-pacific* are solidly established, however.

transcendent, transcendental. Two critics agree that *transcendent* is the word for *surpassing, supreme* (*of transcendent importance*); *transcendental* means *visionary, outside experience,* etc. (*transcendental idealism*). *Transcendental* is oftenest used in its strict sense in religious or philosophical contexts. Random House and Webster, however, both accept *transcendental* as a synonym for *transcendent.* Opinion is thus divided, but the view of the dictionaries indicates at least that the words are well on the way to becoming interchangeable in the sense of *surpassing*.

transpire. Formerly the only meaning was *leak out* or *become known;* commonly the word is now used in the sense *happen, occur, go on:* "No one would say what transpired at the meeting." *Transpire* in the new sense is considered established as standard by two critics, one of whom, however, warns that its use may prompt criticism. *Transpire* for *happen* is considered unacceptable by four critics and American Heritage. Webster's Second Edition said *transpire* for *occur* or *happen* is (or was—the book was published in 1934) "disapproved by most authorities but found in the writings of authors of good standing." Webster's Third Edition omits the caveat and quotes several authors as using the word for *occur. Occur, happen, take place* is the first sense given in Random House. Thus opinion is almost evenly divided, which in itself is a strong indication that the new sense is well on the way to acceptance as standard, especially since two new dictionaries recognize it. Writers who are unsure of themselves, however, or fearful of being taken to task, may limit their use of *transpire* to mean *become known.* In the strictly correct sense it is regarded by three critics as somewhat pretentious for *become known.* Webster's New World says *transpire* for *happen* is "still regarded by some as loose."

transverse, traverse. *Transverse* is an adjective meaning *crosswise:* "Transverse stripes were painted on the paving"; *traverse* is a verb meaning *travel across:* "The signal transversed the vast reaches of space"; unlikely unless the signal was more erratic than we could expect. More likely *traversed.*

tread, trod. Ordinarily, *trod* is the past tense of *tread* ("They trod the straight and narrow") and *treading,* not *trodding,* is the participle. There are occasional instances of the use of *trod* for *tread* ("She will trod the boards tomorrow") and of *trodding* for *treading* ("He's trodding softly, meanwhile, on that borrowed oriental rug"). It seems safe to regard this as a misuse, though Webster does give for *trod, trodding* "to follow as a chosen course or path." This, however, is not the same as *step* or *walk on,* and at *tread* Webster does not give *trod* as an alternate form for the present tense, nor *trodding* for the participle. Evans and Random House do not recognize *trod* except as the past of *tread.*

Next thing we know we'll be seeing:

> "Will you walk a little faster?" said a whiting to a snail,
> "There's a porpoise just behind us, and he's trodding on my tail."

No doubt, too, fools will rush in where angels fear to trod.

trek. Two critics object to the term to describe other than mass migration (like those of the Boers in South Africa, where the expression comes from), and to its loose extension to mean simply *go* or *travel.* The definitions in Random House and Webster in effect concur with this, allowing *trek* for *journey* only when difficulty or hardship is present. This is also the view of the American Heritage panel.

tri-. Solid as a prefix; *tricentennial, tricolor, triennial,* etc.

tribute to. In the sense *illustrative of* (*a tribute to his perception*), approved as an idiom by American Heritage and considered standard by Webster; Random House does not give this sense, and Fowler disapproves.

trigger. Three critics object that the word is overused as a verb displacing *cause, start, begin, produce, signal, precipitate, initiate,* and others that the reader may easily think of. The American Heritage panel sanction this usage but considers it informal. Its popularity is traced to the advent of the atomic bomb and its triggering mechanisms. Perhaps its vogue was inevitable in an age of armament races, wars, and rumors of wars.

trio. Journalese as a collective reference to three of anything whether they have any relationship or not. See also *Useless Counting* under *Numbers.*

triple, treble. Interchangeable as both verb and adjective in the sense *three times* (*triple, treble one's savings; triple, treble damages*) though *triple* is perhaps more used in the U.S.; British usage prefers *treble* as the verb.

triumphal, triumphant. *Triumphal* means expressing or celebrating triumph; *triumphant,* feeling or experiencing triumph. *Triumphal* often applies, for example, to *procession;* a procession could be described as triumphant, however, if its participants were exultant. Usually *triumphant* applies to people, *triumphal* to things; *the triumphant victors; a triumphal arch.* Random House gives *triumphant* as a synonym for *triumphal* in the sense *exultant* and Webster gives it as a general synonym. American Heritage says *triumphal* is obsolete in the sense *triumphant.*

trod. See *tread, trod.*

trooper, trouper. Sometimes confused. A *trooper,* in its commonest senses, is a *cavalryman* or *a mounted policeman; a trouper* is an *actor,* or *member of a troupe.*

troubled. The word has undergone a curious shift in application recently. It is used these days, especially in the press, to describe anything that is in some kind of difficulty—a corporation, program, or airplane. Time was when *troubled* would have been applied almost invariably to people, which accords with most of the definitions of *trouble* as both noun and verb. True, *troubled waters* has a long history, but it is more or less a set phrase, if not a cliché. Almost without exception the entries in dictionaries of quotations apply the adjective to people or their faculties (*a troubled heart, troubled mind*), though Shakespeare did write "A woman mov'd is like a fountain troubled" (*The Taming of the Shrew*). The random application of *troubled* to inanimate things seems a fad, in any event.

troublous. Two critics agree that the word is now archaic for *troublesome.* Random House labels it thus, but Webster considers it standard.

truculent. Bernstein holds that the word, which dictionaries define as *savage, cruel, ferocious,* is rarely used in that sense today, but that instead it is intended to mean *challenging, sulky, disagreeably pugnacious,* or *aggressively defiant.* No observant reader can deny this. American Heritage became the first dictionary to recognize the new sense, and its Usage Panel explicitly approved it.

true fact. See *fact, facts.*

Truman, Harry S. President Truman has pretty much passed into history, where he has a respectable place. His name is given here to point out that newspaper editors made much, while he was living, of giving his name *Harry* S (look, Ma, no period!) because Truman had simply adopted the initial, which stood for nothing. Now this pedantry is being ignored. Few things better illustrate the penchant of newspaper editors for straining at gnats while swallowing camels.

trustee, trusty. Both are people in whom trust has been reposed; confusion oftenest arises in the plural forms: *trustees, trusties.* A trusty is an inmate of a prison who enjoys special privileges because of his trustworthiness. A trustee is a member of a controlling board, as of a college or foundation. Irresponsible trustees, however, sometimes end as trusties.

try. As a noun for *attempt, effort* (*give it a good try*), narrowly approved by American Heritage; considered standard by Random House and Webster.

try and. As severe a critic as Fowler in the original described *try and* (displacing *try to*) as an idiom that should not be disapproved when it comes naturally; he regarded it as meeting the standard of literary dignity. Bryant finds the phrase informal standard English; it is considered standard by four other critics. A fifth grudgingly allows that it has its uses in certain contexts, but remains suspicious of it on the whole. American Heritage rejects it. Three critics discern shades of difference in meaning between *try and* and *try to;* their examples show that the writer is likely to make the right choice by instinct. "The candidate will try and carry the South" was criticized elsewhere as misleading on the ground that it says the candidate will not only try but also carry. This proves nothing but the lengths to which the wrongheaded will go to make nonexistent points. The consensus overwhelmingly validates *try and.*

tuber. The journalese variant for *potato.* See *Variation.*

tubercular, tuberculous. Fowler insists that the terms should be differentiated, the first having to do with tubercules and the second with tuberculosis. Evans recognizes them as interchangeable in reference to the disease, and so do Random House and Webster; Webster, in addition, recognizes them as interchangeable in reference to tubercules. The distinction prescribed by Fowler may represent

British usage, but it is not recognized in ordinary American expression as distinguished from technical usage.

tummy. See *belly*.

turbid, turgid. Sometimes confused. *Turbid* means *muddy* (*turbid water*); *turgid* means *swollen, inflated,* and is oftener used figuratively, perhaps, than literally (*turgid prose*).

turn in to, into. See *into, in to*.

'twas, 'twill, 'twere. See *Poesy*.

twelve noon, midnight. Redundant for *noon, midnight*.

twit. A transitive verb; twitting is done to someone, and is not ordinarily reciprocal. "When he courted Jane Hadley, Kentucky twitted with him; when he finally won and married her, Kentucky rejoiced with him, too." *Twitted with* is unidiomatic; *twitted him*. "They couldn't help twitting about the relationship between the city council and the city manager's office." *Joking,* perhaps, but not *twitting,* which requires an object.

tycoon. Considered standard by dictionaries, informal by Evans, and colloquial by Fowler, who notes that it is taking hold in Britain after having been first applied in the popular sense in the U.S., where, Partridge comments, it is overdone.

type. There are several things to be said about the misuse of this noun as an adjective (*the intellectual type employee, athletic type persons, a new type antenna*). The first is that no one with any sensitivity to the nuances of expression uses the word in the way illustrated, in either speech or writing. Such locutions are characteristic of the untutored speech of New York's lower East Side or the Bronx, as reproduced so amusingly in the fiction of Arthur Kober. A hyphen between *type* and the modifier preceding it at least brings this construction within the pale: *the intellectual-type employee, athletic-type persons.* But those who fancy *type* as an adjective are not the type who can be depended on to appreciate the role of hyphens. *Type* with a hyphen is most acceptable in technical connections, as in *V-type engine, O-type blood, cantilever-type bridge.* Three critics consider *type of* necessary, as does American Heritage; a fourth says *type of* is preferred in formal written English although *type* is frequent in speech and business prose. Neither Random House nor Webster recognizes *type* as an adjective; the consensus is heavily against it.

Typewriter Tricks. First, the number 1 is formed on the typewriter by striking the lower-case l (ell, that is), not the I.

The dash is formed by striking the hyphen twice, and it is standard practice to leave no space between the strokes or at either side of the dash—nor, for that matter, at either side of the hyphen. A hyphen with a space at either side may be mistaken for a dash. Convention requires that the period and the colon be followed by two spaces, the comma and semicolon by one.

A number of useful marks may be made by using the characters on the ordinary typewriter. The exclamation point may be formed by striking the apostrophe and then the period while holding the space bar down.

Reasonably satisfactory brackets ([ ], used to enclose interpolated matter) can be made by use of the underline (__) and the virgule, or slant (/). To form the upper horizontal lines, the underline must be struck on the line above that on which the brackets are being formed. A box may be made by joining a pair of brackets.

Acceptable facsimiles of diacritical marks are also possible with the typewriter. The double quotation mark, if struck over a letter, will serve as an acceptable umlaut, and the single quote will serve at least as a gesture toward the *grave* or *acute* accent, although it will not be possible to tell one from the other. Perhaps these marks are best made with a pen. A cedilla may be made by striking the comma under a *c*.

typhoon, hurricane. Both are tropical cyclones but *typhoon* is applied only to those occurring in the area of the Philippines, the China Sea, or India.

U

uh-huh. This interjection, common in speech and sometimes reproduced in writing, is defined by Webster as used to indicate affirmation, agreement, or gratification. Paul Trench, writing in the magazine *Editor & Publisher* (June 14, 1969), protested that the spelling should be *mm-hm,* or something of the sort. He pointed out also that the negative version, which by analogy with the positive form would be written *huh-uh,* is not recorded in Webster (nor is either form to be found in Random House or American Heritage).

ultra-. Solid as a prefix: *ultraconfident, ultramontane, ultrafashionable,* etc. But *ultra-ambitious* (followed by *a*).

Umlaut. See *Diacritical Marks; Typewriter Tricks.*

un-. Solid as a prefix: *unadaptable, unbreakable, unnamed,* etc. See also *un-, in-.*

unapt, inapt, inept. *Unapt* and *inapt* are generally interchangeable in the senses *inappropriate, not suitable, not apt; inept* is sometimes used in those senses, but generally is reserved for the meaning *foolish, incompetent.*

unaware, unawares. Fowler holds that *unaware* is the adjective (*they were unaware of the joke*), *unawares* the adverb (*observed unawares*). American Heritage explains and thus apparently endorses the distinction. But the majority view (Evans, Random House, and Webster) is that *unaware* may be either adjective or adverb (*taken unaware, an unaware sentry*). Evans considers *unawares* the preferred form for the adverb, a view that appears to be corroborated by observation of usage.

unbeknown, unbeknownst. Two critics regard these expressions as rare, but neither Random House nor Webster gives any indication of this, and there is reason to believe that though they may have fallen into disuse for a time, they are now fairly common.

unbend, unbending. Two critics are concerned over possible confusion as the terms are applied to people. One who unbends relaxes, loses his stiffness of manner; one who is unbending remains stiff and inflexible in his attitude.

uncomparable, incomparable. Evans says the first means *incapable of being compared,* the second either that or *matchless,* and adds that *incomparable* is most likely to be used in both senses. *Uncomparable* is in fact rarely seen; Random House merely includes it in a list of *un-* compounds without definition; Webster does not give it at all. Both dictionaries give both senses for *incomparable.*

uncooperative. See *cooperate,* etc.

under-. Solid as a prefix: *underdevelop, underrate, undercapitalize.*

underestimate. "It would be a mistake to underestimate the Russian leadership," commented a newsmagazine. Well, yes; a mistake is indeed a mistake. "The role that his wife played in the importance of the office cannot be underestimated" should read *overestimated.* Such reversals of sense result from inattention. See also *Double Negative; Negatives.* A similar error: "The effect of such factors on the U.S. economy should not be exaggerated." *can easily be exaggerated.*

underhand, underhanded. *Underhand* predominates for the style of pitching a ball and *underhanded* in the sense *crafty, deceitful,* though the forms are interchangeable.

underprivileged. This term was disparaged some years ago by Lord Conesford, a captious and often wrongheaded critic of American usage who unfortunately had a faulty grasp of American idiom, as a leading example of "American pretentious illiteracy." This harsh judgment was based on the Latin meaning of *privilege—* that is, *a private law.* It is stupid, he said, to pretend favoring equality before the law and at the same time use a word like *underprivileged,* which complains, in his view, that there is not enough inequality. The fundamental error here is the reliance on the original meaning of the word in another language from which it was derived to determine what its meaning should be in correct English. Many English words that have been adopted from other languages have departed considerably from their original senses, and it is well recognized that etymology, or derivation, is a poor guide to present usage. Fowler, for example, has remarked on this subject (under *True and False Etymology*) that a writer should be less concerned with a word's history than with its present meaning and idiomatic habits; yet he comments on *underprivileged* in a way that implies disdain for the term. Flesch criticizes it from another direction, as being a euphemism for *poor,* an objection that has some merit. The word is recognized as standard, however, by all current dictionaries; Webster defines it as "deprived through social or economic oppression . . ." The British scorn for *underprivileged* apparently arises, as is often true in such instances, from the fact that the term was fabricated in America. This appears to be an instance in which an American expression has not been widely taken up in Britain; it is not given in the 1964 Concise Oxford Dictionary. But apparently it is making headway there, or Fowler would not have commented on it at all. H. L. Mencken traced its origin to the New Deal of Franklin Delano Roosevelt. Raven I. McDavid, Jr., as editor of the abridged edition of Mencken's

American Language, which appeared in 1963, quotes *The New York Times* as having protested in an editorial (Oct. 6, 1961) that *underprivileged* and *culturally deprived* are euphemisms for *slum dwellers.*

Underprivileged is in such wide use now, however, that it may no longer be a euphemism, but rather may have become a literal term, since of course euphemisms cease to be euphemisms when awareness of them as such is lost. There is no question that *underprivileged* is standard in America. It may be significant that no American writer on usage but Flesch has even raised a question about its acceptability. Sometimes misspelled *underpriviledged.* As a euphemism, *underprivileged* may be giving way to *disadvantaged.*

undertaker. See *mortician.*

under the circumstances. See *circumstances.*

under way. The correct form; not *under weigh.* The confusion perhaps arises from another nautical term, *weigh* (meaning *raise* or *lift*) *anchor.* Though the adverb (*let's get under way*) is often given as one word (*underway*), American Heritage, Random House, and Webster give it as two words. Webster gives the adjective (*underway refueling*) as one word.

underwhelm. A heading in *The New York Times Magazine* a few years ago read "Premier Andreotti Underwhelms the Italians" and a press-association story reported "an underwhelming lack of interest" in a contest to select a campus queen. *Overwhelm* is familiar enough, but *underwhelm* is something new; at first glance it looks like a facetious play on *overwhelm.* But it is included in Barnhart, and also in the 1971 Addenda Section to Webster III. The definition is what might be expected: "to fail to impress or stimulate." *Overwhelm* is, in fact, something of a redundancy, since *whelm* suits any context where *overwhelm* might be used. *Whelm* is seldom to be found in print, though Webster cites examples from Mary Heaton Vorse, G. M. Trevelyan, William Faulkner, and Kenneth Rexroth, among others. The Harper panel was underwhelmed by *underwhelm,* which is the usual reaction of panels of this kind to neologisms. Yet there is no reason why it should not be accepted as standard, as was done by both Webster and Barnhart, which cites *The Times* of London.

The fact that a new word has appeared in few or no dictionaries does not constitute a valid reason to reject it. If everyone took this attitude there would be (1) no words and (2) no dictionaries, since of course words come first and dictionaries later.

undue, unwarranted, unduly. Often used redundantly and, indeed, absurdly, as in "The situation does not warrant undue concern." This says that the situation does not warrant unwarranted concern. More logically, "The situation does not warrant concern"; or, if this is not strong enough, "The situation does not warrant great (or any of a number of other adjectives) concern." See also *Double Negative; Negatives.*

uneatable, inedible. Fowler makes the distinction that the first applies to what cannot be eaten because of its condition (e.g., spoiled meat) and the second to what is unsuitable for food (e.g., grass). This is borne out to some extent by the definition in Webster, but *inedible* is given as a synonym for *uneatable*. In general, it appears that *inedible* is likely to be used in both senses in the U.S. *Uneatable* does not appear in desk dictionaries, and Random House lists but does not define it; the implication is that it is the opposite of *eatable*.

unequivocally. Sometimes misspelled *unequivocably;* there is no such word.

unexceptionable, unexceptional. See *exceptionable, exceptional*.

unhealthful, unhealthy. See *healthful, healthy*.

unhuman, inhuman. The first is simply the negative of *human*, meaning *not possessing human qualities;* the second goes beyond this, meaning *cruel, barbarous, savage*, etc., according to Fowler. But *inhuman* is used in both senses in the U.S., Evans points out, a view that is corroborated by dictionaries. American Heritage makes a general distinction of words beginning with *un-* and *in-*, corresponding with Fowler's dictum; that is, that the prefix *un-* is neutral, the equivalent of *non-*, while *in-* implies an adverse judgment. *Unhuman* is rare.

uni-. Solid as a prefix; *uniaxial, unicycle, unisexual*.

uninterested. See *disinterested, uninterested*.

unique. The doctrine that *unique* is an absolute modifier that cannot be qualified may be a noble one, but it has no connection with the facts of usage. When used without a qualifier, as in "His outlook on the world was *unique*," it means *without a like or equal*. There are so few unique things under the sun that generally the word is used with a qualifier. This simply extends its usefulness without diminishing its force as an absolute when used alone. "So unique then was a ship carrying only tourists that port officials greeted them with alarm" and "The college shares with other private schools several points of uniqueness" are not open to reasonable criticism. *More unique, most unique, quite unique,* and the like are equally acceptable. Yet the fastidious reserve *unique* for the absolute sense. *Unique* takes *a*, not *an*. For the views of critics, see *Comparison 3*.

United Kingdom. See *Great Britain*, etc.

unless and until. Disparaged as redundant; one or the other is considered enough. See also *if* and *when*.

unlike. "Unlike in France, the telephone company does not make one wait months for a phone." A gaucherie; the prepositional phrase *in France* cannot be the object of *unlike:* "Unlike the practice (or whatever) in France . . ." See also *False Comparison*.

unmoral. See *immoral,* etc.

unpleasantry. See *pleasantry, unpleasantry.*

unpractical. See *practicable, practical.*

unprecedented. If, as the Bible says, there is no new thing under the sun, there is no occasion for *unprecedented.* At any rate, the word is often loosely used for *uncommon, unusual;* what is unprecedented has never happened before. The word is often loosely used, especially in newspaper writing, where *uncommon, unusual* would be more appropriate. This view is borne out by Random House and Webster. See also *Journalese.*

unravel, ravel. Since we have *ravel, unravel* seems both unnecessary and supererogatory. But it is so well established in the writings of the reputable we can hardly spurn it.

unreadable. See *illegible, unreadable.*

unrealistic. See *realistic.*

unreligious, irreligious. The distinction that the first means merely having no connection with religion and the second lacking in religion, sinful, is observed primarily in Britain. In the U.S., the primary sense of *unreligious* is *irreligious,* and its secondary sense is *nonreligious, lacking in religion.* The distinction may be made clearer by saying that *irreligious* is disapproving, if not derogatory, and that *unreligious* in its primary sense is equated with *irreligious. Unreligious* in its secondary sense is neutral. Examples: "Public schools are supposed to be unreligious" (secondary sense). "The irreligious (unreligious) scoffed at the bishop's interpretation." Thus the context must be relied on to indicate the sense wanted.

unsanitary, insanitary. *Unsanitary* is the customary form in the U.S., and the words are considered synonyms, a view substantiated by Random House and Webster. The distinction, set forth by Fowler, that *insanitary* implies danger to health while *unsanitary* means merely *lacking in sanitation* is not observed in the United States.

unsolvable, insoluble. The usual term in the U.S. is *insoluble* for both *incapable of being dissolved* ("It was insoluble in water") and *incapable of being solved* ("The problem was insoluble"), and the words are considered synonyms. This view is corroborated by Random House and Webster. But *unsolvable* would not be used to mean *incapable of being dissolved.*

unthinkable. Three critics consider it necessary to explain that in ordinary (i.e., nontechnical) use the word does not mean that which cannot be thought, since anything that can be named can be thought. It now ordinarily means *unaccepta-*

ble, preposterous, improbable, out of the question, etc. Random House and Webster, however, both give *unimaginable* as the first sense. American Heritage gives *inconceivable*.

until. See *till,* etc.

until and unless. See *unless* and *until.*

untimely end. Objected to as hackneyed and illogical. Whether an end is untimely is, of course, a matter of opinion, but there is such a thing as a reasonable consensus in such matters, which perhaps justifies the phrase from the standpoint of logic.

unveil. Journalese for *announce, display, reveal, exhibit.*

unwarranted. See *undue,* etc.

up. As a verb ("Prices have been upped again"), considered standard by Webster and American Heritage, informal by Random House.

up-, -up. Solid as a prefix; *upbear, upend, upstate,* etc.; solid as a suffix except after a vowel: *buildup, holdup, windup,* but *close-up, shake-up.*

upcoming. Considered objectionable for *forthcoming, coming, approaching,* etc., by two critics. It is considered standard, however, by both Random House and Webster. It says nothing, however, that *coming* alone does not, and its usual habitat is the press.

upon, on. *Upon* is often used where idiom or simplicity calls for *on,* perhaps because of some ill-defined idea it is more elegant. "As chief speech writer, he provided many of the phrases upon which the candidate campaigned." *on.* "He's cashing in upon the publicity." A clear case of defiance of idiom; *on.* "This is an opportunity to cut down the drain upon our shrinking gold supply." *on.*

There is no clearcut difference in sense between *on* and *upon,* although *upon* more distinctly connotes *on top of. Upon,* once favored as more formal, is falling into disuse where *on* will do, and in those places tends to sound stilted. Earl Wilson, the columnist, has seen humor in some occurrences of *upon:* "He kissed her passionately upon her reappearance"; "She walked in upon his invitation"; "She fainted upon his departure." See *on, upon.*

Up Style. See *Capitalization.*

uptight, up-tight, up tight. This expression, which originated in hippie and teen-age argot, seems to be hovering on the brink of acceptance as standard. Only Webster (Addenda Section, 1971) gives it as standard, however; Webster's New World, Barnhart, and American Heritage all label it slang, Harper denounces it.

The usual meanings are *tense, nervous, conforming rigidly to convention;* Webster also gives *angry,* and American Heritage also gives *on intimate terms.* Both Webster and American Heritage give also *destitute,* an unusual sense.

American Heritage's designation of the two-word form as predominant is open to question; most well-edited publications now use the one-word form, though *up-tight* is sometimes seen.

upward, upwards. The first form is generally preferred in the U.S. *Upwards* may not be used as an adjective; *an upwards slope. upward.* American Heritage disapproves *upward(s) of* for *less than, about,* or *almost;* this seems an imaginary misuse. *Upwards of* is a favorite journalese variant of *more than,* which seems plainer English and preferable. It calls to mind *in back of* for *behind* and *close to* for *nearly.*

upward revision (adjustment). See *Euphemisms.*

us. See *it's me,* etc.

usable, useable. Both forms are correct, but the first predominates and is to be encouraged on the principle that simplicity is desirable.

usage, use. *Usage* relates to a customary practice or manner of use: *usages of the church, rough usage.* In reference to language, for example in this book, it relates to a standard of use. Follett makes a curious and obvious error, as any dictionary will show, in saying that *usage* has no use outside the subject of language. *Use* relates to the act of employing something. Four critics and American Heritage protest against *usage* where *use* is called for: "He didn't like the word *no* and wouldn't permit its usage by others"; "This custom is no longer in usage"; "Year-round usage of the schools is recommended." In each instance *usage* should be *use.* In general, the misuse of *usage* is laid to pretentiousness. *Useage* is a misspelling.

use. In the sense *exploit, turn to one's own end* ("Some analysts wondered whether Carter was 'using' religion as a political tool"), considered standard by Webster, informal by American Heritage, and not given by Random House. Webster's New World, one of the newest of the desk dictionaries, however, also gives it as standard. The apologetic quotation marks as used in the example are necessary to distinguish the sense at hand from the usual one: *employ.*

use to, used to. The phrase is now used only in the past tense: "We used to go skating every Saturday." Negative statements and questions with *did,* however, take the form *use to:* "We didn't use to build a fire unless it was bitterly cold"; "Did there use to be trees along here?" These latter constructions are considered clumsy by two critics. Fowler describes *didn't use to* as an archaism in England, but recognizes it as accepted usage in the U.S. American Heritage accepts this as well as the negative and interrogative constructions illustrated here.

utilize. Criticized by three authorities as a long and usually unnecessary substitution for *use*. Evans says *utilize* means *make practical or profitable use;* Fowler concedes this distinction of senses once existed but says it has now disappeared. Random House and Webster both give *use* as a synonym, but also give Evans' version as one sense. American Heritage gives simply *put to use,* and it must be admitted that this is the overwhelmingly predominant sense and the one likely to be understood no matter what is intended.

utopia. Takes *a*, not *an*.

V

vaccinate. See *inoculate, vaccinate.*

van, von. See *de, du,* etc.

variance. Takes *with,* not *from; at variance with previous ideas.*

Variation. Conspicuous variation to avoid repeating a term is not only worse than repetition, as Fowler said, but may suggest a distinction that is not intended and thus mislead or confuse the reader. The problem is often neatly solved by ellipsis: "He played with Charlie Barnet's Orchestra and worked with Red Norvo's Sextet." By changing from *played* to *worked* the writer was merely straining to avoid repeating the same word. Yet he might have said "played with Charlie Barnet's Orchestra and with Red Norvo's Sextet." "Russia's army newspaper *Red Star* claims there are now 33 million Communist Party members in seventy-five nations. The breakdown gave Indonesia one million. France was said to have five million Red voters; Italy, 1.8 million card-carriers." Are Communist Party members, Red voters, and card-carriers all the same?

The writer assumed this to be so, but of course it is not. The changes are rung obtrusively and unnecessarily. Once it had been established that *Communist Party members* is the subject of the discussion, the writer might have trusted the reader's memory beyond Indonesia to "France was said to have five million; Italy, 1.8 million." "About 76 percent of Russia's doctors are women, while in the United States only 6 percent are female." *Women* would have sounded better repeated; or *but the proportion in the United States is only 6 percent.* "Cigarette smokers puffed a record 205 billion cigarettes in the first six months of this year, 4.4 percent more than they lit up in the same time last year." Lighting up and puffing are different things, and the variation is absurd: *4.4 percent more than in the same period last year.* "In cases where both parents are obese, 72 percent of the offspring also are fat. When one parent is fat, 41 percent of the children are overweight. When neither parent is obese, only 4 percent of the offspring are fat." The writer danced an ungainly dance between *obese, fat,* and *overweight* on one hand, and between *children* and *offspring* on the other. He might have put it, "When both parents are fat, 72 percent of the children are. When one parent is fat, 41 percent of the children are. When neither parent is fat, only 4 percent of the children are."

402

One aspect of variation might be called the geographical fetish, since it requires that the second reference to a place be in the form of a geographical description. In Southern California, under these ground rules, it is permissible to name San Francisco once, but the second time it is mentioned it must become *the northern city*. Other samples of this aberration: "The caravan plans a dinner in Podunk and an overnight stop in the Razorback County city" and "A three-day international convention opened today in Nagasaki on the anniversary of the atom bombing of the southern Japanese city." Desirable information about locale should be offered for its own sake and not made a device to avoid naming a place again. In the first instance *there* should have been used place of *the Razorback County city* and in the second simply *the city* would have been preferable to *the southern Japanese city*.

"Children who want to enter a frog in the event may pick up an amphibian at the Chamber of Commerce office." *may pick one up*. "A search for a mountain lion was abandoned when no sign of such a carnivore was found." *Such a carnivore* is a pompous substitute for *such an animal* or even *one*. Sometimes the writer evidently sets out to astound the reader with the number of different names he can think up for the same thing. But the reader may be more repelled than astounded by such a shallow trick. Thus a game becomes successively a *contest*, an *event*, a *match*, a *set-to*, a *tilt*, an *encounter*, and a *tussle* in the references of as many paragraphs.

Some synonyms that are popular with journalists in their quest for variation: *simian* for *monkey*, *jurist* for *judge*, *bovine* for *cow*, *feline* for *cat*, *quadruped* for any four-legged animal, *equine* for *horse*, *optic* for *eye*, *tome* for *book*, *white stuff* for *snow*, *bivalve* for *oyster*, *pachyderm* for *elephant*, *yellow metal* for *gold*, *solon* for *legislator*, and *savant* for *professor*.

"To use a vulgar expression, they were spitting with the wind, whereas in Italy, which has enjoyed a persistently favorable balance of payments, they were expectorating against the wind." It is surely inexcusable to use an expression one considers it necessary to apologize for and then obtrusively sidestep it in the same sentence.

See also *Elegant Variation; Pronouns; Journalese.*

various. Two critics and American Heritage object to the word as a pronoun, as in "Various of the specimens were imperfect," though Fowler concedes that it may become established. Webster recognizes this use but American Heritage denounces it, and Random House gives only the adjective (*various books on the subject*). See also *different*.

vastly. Fowler objects to the use of the term where measurement or comparison is not at issue, as in "We were vastly amused." Evans regards this as standard American usage, and so do Random House (by extension from a definition of *vast*) and Webster.

vault. Bernstein holds that *vault,* in the sense of *a place of safekeeping,* is a permanent part of a building and generally large enough to walk into. American

Heritage appears to concur; both Random House and Webster also apply the term to a compartment, cabinet, or strongbox.

venal, venial. Sometimes confused. *Venal* means *mercenary, corruptible, open to bribery* (*a venal official*); *venial* means *excusable* (*a venial transgression*).

verbal, oral. See *oral, verbal.*

Verbiage. See *Redundancy. Excess verbiage* is itself redundant; verbiage is excess.

Verbs. See *Adverbs; Infinitives; who,* etc.; *Parallelism; Passive Voice; Time Elements; Sequence of Tenses; Hyphens 4; Attribution 4; Ellipsis 4; shall, will.*

veritable. Three critics complain that the word is often used for excessive emphasis: "It was a veritable cloudburst."

verse. Evans complains that the word is misused for *stanza,* but dictionaries give *stanza* as a synonym; this is widespread standard usage. The sense that a verse is a line is not general usage but a technical usage of prosody.

very. The main point is whether *very* (rather than *much,* or *very much*) may be used before a past participle, as in "We were very inconvenienced by the strike" and "Jones was very pleased to be invited." Fowler and American Heritage hold that only participles that have come into common use as adjectives may be preceded by *very;* this means that *very pleased* is acceptable, and *very inconvenienced* is not. The test of whether a participle is commonly used as an adjective is to place it in the attributive position, that is, directly before a noun; *a pleased expression* sounds unexceptionable, but *an inconvenienced public* sounds less so. The difficulty is that even grammarians are likely to disagree on whether a given participle has become an adjective. Three critics favor the distinction, though one of them admits it is not always easy to apply; four others take a more liberal view and allow *very* wherever it will not affront the ear. Random House, perhaps sidestepping the question, gives no example of *very* used as described here; Webster gives *very pleased, very separated.* Opinion is thus divided on this usage. *Very much* (*inconvenienced,* or whatever) solves all such problems.

   Very is often used in attempts to strengthen that in fact have the effect of weakening. *Very wonderful* is an example; the writer has overstrained, and would have done better to have said *wonderful. A very lovely singing star, a very splendid performance, a very excellent dinner*—all are diminished by *very.* The writer leaves the impression that he is trying to convince himself, that he is reaching for an effect he does not quite believe in. *A very great man* sounds to the reader less great than *a great man.* William Allen White is said to have discouraged excessive *verys* by adjuring his reporters to write *damn* instead, and then cross out the *damn.* See also *rather; quite.*

via. The word, which comes from Latin, meant in that language *by way of*. If derivation is strictly observed, then, it would be correct to say "We traveled to San Francisco from Chicago via Los Angeles" but not "We traveled via train" nor "They talk to their friends via ham radio." That is, *via* is often used in the sense *by means of*, and sometimes it displaces *by* or *through*. The use of *via* in any but its original sense is more or less severely·criticized by four authorities; Evans condones it. The extended meaning is also sanctioned by Random House, which gives *a solution via scientific investigation*, and by Webster, which gives several similar examples as standard usage. American Heritage gives only *by way of*. The consensus slightly favors restricting *via* to its original sense.

viable. The term is criticized as overworked and misused. In its original sense, it meant *able to live and grow*, but it need not be restricted to what is alive; it could as well be applied to a city or a country. The critics tend to limit *viable* to this meaning, but dictionaries now give *real, workable, vivid, practicable, important*, newer definitions that seem only to confirm the critics' complaints that the word has had the edge hopelessly ground off it. The criticism that *viable* is overworked is hardly open to question. What is intended by the word in the following is anybody's guess: "It's not that the present system can't work. It's just that it's not very viable." There is reason to suspect that *viable* sometimes displaces *valid*, which may have been intended here.

vice-. Usually hyphenated as a prefix with nouns denoting offices: *vice-admiral, vice-governor, vice-consul*. But *viceroy, viceregal*. And *vice president* is often given thus.

vice, vise. A vice is an evil ("He knew all the vices before he was 18"); a vise is a clamp, usually mounted on a workbench ("The subassembly is held in a vise while braces are welded on it"). The occasional confusion is aggravated by the fact that *vice* is an alternate spelling of *vise*, but *vice* is rarely used in this sense.

vice versa. See *reverse*, etc.; *Reversal of Sense*.

vicinity. See *in the (immediate) vicinity of*.

vicious, viscous. Sometimes confused. *Vicious* means *depraved, immoral; viscous* means *oily* or *sirupy in consistency*, and is said usually of liquids.

victuals. Discouraged by two critics as quaint.

view. Two critics agree that *with a view to* is preferable to *with a (the) view of*. One of them and a third agree that a participle rather than an infinitive should follow *with a view to*, e.g., *with a view to succeeding* rather than *with a view to succeed*.

viewpoint. American Heritage reports that some writers and grammarians consider *viewpoint* inferior to *point of view,* but no such opinion is expressed by any of the other authorities consulted. The American Heritage panel itself sanctions *viewpoint.* See also *point of view.*

vilify, vilification. Sometimes misspelled *villify, villification.*

villain. Often misspelled *villian.*

violoncello. Sometimes incorrectly given *violincello.* The fact is, however, that the long form has been all but forgotten in favor of *cello,* and the form *'cello* is considered fussy.

Virgin Birth. See *Immaculate Conception.*

virile. The word comes from *vir,* Latin for *man,* and retains its association with maleness as such. Three critics agree that *virile* is inappropriate where *male, masculine* cannot be substituted, and the dictionaries bear this view out. Above all it should not be applied to women in the senses *forceful, vigorous,* etc. Partridge curiously warns against using the term to describe sexual power in women.

virtual, virtually. Virtual means *in effect though not in fact;* often misused in the sense of *bordering on* or *near* or sometimes *veritable:* "It was a virtual cloudburst." A correct use: *a virtual rejection.*

virus. *Virus* for *disease* or *illness* ("He is in bed with a virus") is incorrect because the virus is the organism causing the disease; neither Random House, American Heritage, nor Webster allows *virus* in this sense.

visa, visé. Evans says the British use *visé* for what in America is called a *visa,* but Fowler says *visa* is now established in Britain.

vis-à-vis. The expression (from the French) means *face to face,* and is sometimes misused in English, two critics say, to mean *concerning, regarding,* and in other ways. Dictionaries, however, give also *in relation to, in comparison with, toward,* definitions that seem to indicate that the phrase has been Anglicized and thus protests based on its original meaning are irrelevant.

vise, vice. See *vice, vise.*

visionary. Means *existing in imagination only,* hence chimerical or impractical. It usually has a derogatory connotation, and should not be used in place of *farsighted, prophetic,* or *imaginative.* "The speaker closed with an appeal to city officials in the audience to do some visionary planning." *farsighted, imaginative.*

visitation. A formal or official visit, as of an inspector; thus not interchangeable with *visit.* Dictionary definitions bear out this distinction, though Random House gives as one sense *the act of visiting*. Despite this, there seems no excuse for displacing the simpler word with the longer one, with its official connotations.

visit with. The expression refers primarily to conversation, not necessarily to physical presence, and so it is possible to *visit with* by telephone. Thus, too, it is not a displacement of *visit;* American Heritage calls it informal. For that matter, however, both Random House and Webster give *converse* (as by telephone) as one sense of *visit* alone. Probably no question concerning the standing of *visit with* would have arisen except that it was one of numerous expressions denounced by Lord Conesford, on a visit to the United States, in the course of which he exhibited a lamentable ignorance of the American idiom he made bold to criticize. In this instance, Lord Conesford mistook *visit with* for a useless elaboration of *visit* in its primary sense. Thus it may be in Britain, for Fowler asperses *visit with* on the same grounds.

vocal cords. See *chord, cord.*

vocalize. Although dictionaries give the meanings *express, voice,* the word is so predominantly used for *sing* that those senses may sound ludicrous. "He vocalized his objections." Sang them, the reader may wonder?

Vogue Words. See *Fad Words.*

Voice. See *Passive Voice.*

voice. For *express, state* (*voiced objections*), considered objectionable by two critics. This sense is given as standard by Random House and Webster, however. Evans explains that in Britain *voice* is considered impermissible for *express* except for what is spoken, as contrasted with what is written. This view apparently is outmoded, however, for the Concise Oxford Dictionary specifically recognizes *voice* as applied to what is printed. There is no question that *voiced objections, voiced praise* are wordy and indirect for *objected, praised.*

volume. See *de, du,* etc.

von. See *de, du,* etc.

vow. A journalese variant of *say* or *promise,* and as often used in newspapers it implies an inappropriate solemnity. Definitions in American Heritage, Random House and Webster agree that the term has this connotation.

Vulgarity. Profanity and vulgarisms have gained considerable access to the printed page during the last quarter-century or so. Few newspapers, for example, now hesitate to print *hell* as a quoted expletive, or even as a casual comparison (*a hell of a time; hot as hell*) to say nothing of using the term as a true place-name.
Similar freedom is evident with respect to *damn*. The name of the Lord is

facilely taken in vain: "God knows." Irreverent allusions to Christ are less common, but fairly frequent in quoted matter: "For Christ's sake, shut up."

The vulgarism *son of a bitch* (and its abbreviation S.O.B.) has been admitted to the columns of some of our most august journals, which might have felt like resisting until these expressions turned up in utterances by two presidents of the United States, Harry S. Truman and John F. Kennedy.

Other vulgarisms have gained a surprising currency in the news pages; *bull,* for example (as in "That's a lot of bull," he said). This, obviously, is a variety of synecdoche, the figure of speech in which the whole takes the name of a part. *Bitch* as a verb (*Soldiers always bitch*) is not unusual in the press, nor as a noun applied to a woman.

This latitude palely mirrors what has been happening in the world of literature, where the four-letter words descriptive of defecation, breaking wind, urination, and copulation have become relatively common. It may be well to bear in mind, however, that some of these words occur in Shakespeare, Chaucer, and the Bible.

Webster's Unabridged offers an interesting commentary on how far opinion has progressed, or retrogressed, as the case may be, in this department. The Second Edition, published in 1933, omitted numbers one, two, and four in the preceding list. The public temper, at least among that segment likely to consult a dictionary, was such that nobody missed them. The editors of the Third Edition, which appeared in 1961, almost entirely overcame the squeamishness of their predecessors except, as one reviewer put it, for the most important of the four-letter words, referring to (but not citing) *fuck.* American Heritage frankly includes both its literal and figurative senses. At least two dictionaries of slang (although four-letter vulgarisms are not really slang) do too.

The be-all and end-all of English dictionaries is, of course, the great Oxford. It is for the most part considerably older than Webster's Second Edition, but unexpectedly enough, in view of the era that produced it (1888-1933), it contains all the four-letter vulgarisms except the one that has consistently stuck in Webster's craw. There is something ingratiating about Oxford's starchy and yet indulgent descriptions of the vulgarisms it does include: "Not now in decent use." These words invest the soiled terms with a certain retroactive dignity, which certainly is not spurious, for there were times when they were freely employed in polite society, just as *ain't* once was used freely and considered correct by the cultivated.

Some years ago the Associated Press was curious enough about modern receptivity to profanity to run a little survey on one of its stories. Of 30 papers checked, two deleted *damn,* one changed it to d---, and 27 used the word as sent.

In 1964 the epithet *son of a bitch* was used in a trial that had nationwide interest, and the Associated Press again ran a survey. Of 111 papers checked, 52 used the phrase, 30 substituted dots or dashes, 19 abbreviated it, and 10 deleted it.

Not so long ago (at least if you are middle-aged, it does not seem so long) the closest any newspaper would come to printing *hell* in any context was h—. What appeared after the *h,* as well as in such renderings as G— d—, was an elongated solid dash.

Refinements were gradually introduced, to the extent that some of the letters were replaced by hyphens: h---, G-d d--n. The theory behind the hyphens was possibly that the susceptibilities of the young were being spared. But the expressions might as well have been spelled out frankly and in full, because no one old enough to read could miss the import of such easily decoded evasions.

Some publications continued to quail at vulgarity and refused even to give the strong hint of the initial letters: "She called me a --- -- - -----." But readers are bound to work out such little puzzles, often with assiduity. Sometimes, however, this device did tax the reader's ingenuity: "We had someone say to her, 'You rotten -----,' to test her reaction." Bitch? Whore?

This field has other peculiarities. Some apparently feel that *damn* is less profane if the *n* is omitted, in this fashion: "America's done *dam'* well." Or perhaps the idea is to indicate the pronunciation. But who pronounces the *n* in *damn,* and how? On the other hand, *dam'* may be a contraction of *damned. Damnedest* is sometimes telescoped to *damndest.* Why not *damndst?* Likewise, *darnedest* becomes *darndest* (*Kids Say the Darndest Things*). Webster and Random House give both *damndest* and *darndest;* American Heritage gives *damndest.*

Haphazard researches have yielded some diverting sidelights on this subject. Profanity may be against the law, particularly when directed at a policeman. A Cranston, R.I., man was charged with disorderly conduct for, as the Associated Press delicately put it, questioning the parentage of the officer who had stopped him for speeding.

The judge dismissed the charge, commenting that the epithet resorted to by the defendant had become "something of a presidential expression." No doubt the disposition of the case was in accord with public opinion. But what seemed particularly interesting was the judge's assumption that presidents necessarily set an example in linguistic matters. Vulgarity aside, they have not all shown the adeptness and discrimination in expressing themselves that would warrant imitation.

In April, 1958, *Editor & Publisher* reported that the advertising executives of the four (at that time) San Francisco dailies felt called upon to rule on the propriety of using the movie title, "The Respectful Prostitute," in advertising. This work became something of a contemporary classic in drama. The *Examiner* and the *News* decided to remove the word *prostitute* from the title, perhaps to protect the sensibilities of readers not sufficiently hardened by free use of *rape* and circumstantial accounts of sex crimes in the news columns. The *Chronicle,* which had a reputation as a sophisticated and civilized newspaper, stood fast, together with the *Call-Bulletin.* The odd thing about all this was that *prostitute* and *prostitution* were already widely accepted as genteelisms for what the Bible calls *whore* and *whoring.* See also *Euphemisms.*

The so-called underground press took the lead, in the middle 1960s, in the use of vulgar language in print, and the college press quickly followed suit. But as outraged administrators got used to it and either ceased to express outrage or found themselves helpless against editors who increasingly asserted their independence, invoking the First Amendment with the support of the courts, college editors no longer found any fun in the practice and it died down, though not out. Many papers, college and general, confined such language to direct quotations in circumstances when they judged it necessary to give the true flavor of what was said.

Profanity and vulgarisms have now become so common in print, even in much of the metropolitan press, that they have lost their shock value. This raises the question whether a whole lexicon of new indecent terms will be invented, or whether the concept of indecency in language will disappear, eroded by familiarity.

The suitability or unsuitability of certain terms is an arbitrary matter. There is no logical reason why the four-letter versions of *copulate, defecate,* or any other vulgarity should be less acceptable than the decent ones except that custom has made them so. It is doubtful that anyone, male or female, no matter how sheltered his surroundings, has reached the age of eight without knowing what they all mean. But under the mores that prevailed until recently, most men would not use them in mixed company and most women and some men would not use them at all.

There is a difference between profanity and obscenity; vulgarity, as that which offends good taste, embraces them both. Profanity primarily is irreverent or blasphemous, such as taking the name of the Deity in vain (or swearing). Obscenity is offensive to decency, and usually relates to sexual matters or excretion; the so-called four-letter words are obscene by usual standards.

W

wacky. The slang term for *mentally unbalanced* or *eccentric* is preferably thus spelled, not *whacky*.

wage. See *salary, wage*.

wait on. Substandard for *wait for:* "I'm waiting on the bus." A waiter *waits on* (diners).

waive, wave. Sometimes confused; the first is used in the sense belonging to the second. *Waive* means to relinquish or forgo (*he waived the privilege*); *wave* denotes a motion (*we waved goodbye; the flag waved above*). *Waive* for *wave* is obsolete.

wane. Evans says that what wanes, except as the word is applied to the moon, declines or decreases permanently, but there is no sign in dictionaries that this is necessarily the meaning.

want, want for. In the sense *lack*, *want* is falling into disuse, and consequently sounds a trifle old-fashioned: *This shirt wants a button*. In the sense *should, ought to* ("You want to listen carefully") *want* is considered conversational by Bryant and standard by Evans. Dictionaries do not give this sense; the consensus is that it is questionable in writing. American Heritage rejects *want for* to express *wish, desire:* "We want for them to leave." It accepts *want for* for *lack* as standard: "We do not want for leisure."

want in, out, off. These expressions, which telescope *want to come (go) in, out,* or *want to get off,* are considered regional by three critics. American Heritage and Random House label this usage informal; Webster considers it standard. The consensus is that it is not fully approved.

War Between the States. The term favored in the South for what generally is known as the Civil War.

warm (cold) temperatures. Strictly speaking, a temperature, as a reading, can only be higher or lower, not warmer or cooler.

warn. There is a notion in journalism that *warn* cannot be used intransitively: "The Better Business Bureau warns of unscrupulous magazine sellers"; "Taxes will go up, the legislator warned." There is no basis for this; *warn* is given as both transitive and intransitive in American Heritage, Random House, and Webster. This, however, may be a relatively new usage; Fowler calls it "now common in journalism," and the Century Dictionary and Cyclopedia, an American work published in 1897, gave *warn* only as transitive. The criticism that *warned* is often a random displacement of *said,* in reference to a statement that could not be considered a warning, may have more validity. *Warn* takes *of, about, concerning, against,* not *on.*

was, were. See *Subjunctive.*

was a former. The phrase is illogical in reference to a living person: "Like Hull and Padrutt, Johnson was a former Progressive." Once a former, always a former. *Was a former* (and *was a onetime*) can be sensibly used only of a dead person to describe a condition that ceased to exist before he died. Even then, the meaning is more clearly expressed with different wording: "The late governor was at one time a Farmer-Laborite."

was given. The frequent criticisms of this construction appear to have originated in the strictures of Ambrose Bierce, who argued that a sentence like "The soldier was given a rifle" is inadmissible because "What was given is the rifle, not the soldier . . . Nothing can be 'given' anything." "The soldier was given a rifle" is a variant arrangement of "A rifle was given to the soldier." Curme writes that sentences in which the accusative becomes nominative "are often preferred in choice expression" and cites as an example "They were given ample warning." Simeon Potter, in *Our Language,* says, ". . . in spite of loud protests from prescriptive grammarians, 'Me was given the book' has become 'I was given the book' by the most natural process in the world." The Oxford English Dictionary quotes as an example of the uses of *give* "He was given the contract." Random House and Webster have similar examples. The criticism of *was given* thus is obviously superstition.

was graduated. See *graduate.*

wave. See *waive, wave.*

wax. As a verb in the sense *become,* sometimes erroneously modified: "His speeches belittled glamorous TV commentators who waxed authoritatively in the studio but seldom went out and actually covered a story." Well, no wonder they seldom went out; they were too busy waxing (the furniture, perhaps?). *waxed authoritative,* not *authoritatively; authoritative* modifies *commentators,* not *waxed.*

way, away. *Way* as an adverb, for *away, far, as far as,* was found by Bryant to be common in ordinary and educated speech and in informal writing: "Way back in the good old days"; "We went way to Chicago"; "That's way too much." Three critics and Fowler describe it as an Americanism that is becoming established in Britain. American Heritage calls it regional. Both Random House and Webster give the sense as standard; this is the consensus.

way, ways. *Ways* as a noun in place of *way* (*a long ways*) is considered unacceptable by two critics and American Heritage and loose by a third, but given as standard by Random House and Webster.

way, shape, or form. A tiresome redundancy ("We would not consent to change in any way, shape, or form"). Sometimes "manner, shape, or form."

way, weigh. See *under way*.

we. See *I, we; Editorial (and Royal) we.*

wean. One critic points out that the word is sometimes misused in the sense *bring up* or *raise on:* "He was weaned on the old rules," rather than in its proper meaning of *deprive* or *end dependence on,* as derived from the primary sense of *accustom to loss of mother's milk.* This objection is borne out by dictionary definitions.

weaponize. Governmentese of such uncertain meaning the Merriam-Webster editors, who were widely criticized for excessive indulgence in putting together their Third Unabridged Edition, did not see fit to include it. The statement "Army personnel are completing weaponization of the Redstone ballistic missile system," which appeared in a news service dispatch, drew an agonized protest from a subscribing editor. "Do you mean," he demanded, "that the missiles are being warheadized? Or that the system is undergoing agonizing reappraisalization? Or is it that the writer didn't know just what was going on and so called it weaponized?" The wire service, having no definition to offer, apologized.

we at. See *here at, we at.*

Weather Reports. Whether nothing can be done about the weather has become a questionable proposition since the development of cloud-seeding. There is no question, however, that something can be done about weather stories in the newspapers. First, let's sacrifice all that impressive but unintelligible mumbo jumbo about high- and low-pressure areas, well-defined frontal systems, and other technicalities of the forecasting business. That stuff may be all right for the detailed report in the back pages, for it undoubtedly is interesting to some, like every other specialty. But such complexities seem out of place in the general weather story, because the average reader does not understand them. There may be some question whether even the forecasters understand them, when you compare the forecasts with the weather.

Temperatures are commonly spoken of as *cooler* or *warmer,* although a temperature, being a reading, can only be *higher* or *lower.* An *increase* (rather than a *rise*) or a *decrease* (rather than a *drop*) is no better.

Weather writing, like all newsdom, has its clichés. One might expect that anything as changeable as the weather would inspire some variety in the terms used to describe it, but this seems a vain hope. Newspaper readers, especially in a wet season, must be unnecessarily depressed to read without variation day after day that the rainfall has been *boosted;* that rivers are *on a rampage;* and that rain and snow are being *dumped*—like garbage, presumably. Rain is also often spoken of delicately as dampening (never *wetting*), but a rain that merely dampens hardly qualifies as a rain. Typhoons usually *pack* winds of such-and-such velocity. Twenty-five-mile-an-hour winds could be more neatly disposed of as *twenty-five-mile winds.*

The temperature, when high, gets where it is in only one way; it *soars.* On the other hand, when it drops quickly, it must *plummet.* The fog always seems to *roll in.* This sounds as if it's on wheels, instead of cat feet, as Carl Sandburg had it. The weather writers' gods, of course, are Jupiter Pluvius and Old Sol.

A faithful standby in stories related to wet weather is the comment that the rain *failed to dampen the spirits* of some person, group, or occasion. Maybe so, but where the rain fails, banalities like this are likely to succeed.

For the saying "Everybody talks about the weather . . ." see *Misquotation.*

wed. Except for newspaper headlines, *wed* is considered obsolescent for *marry* by three critics. Neither Random House nor Webster gives any such indication.

weigh, weight. The confusion of *weigh* with *weight* in such contexts as "I weight only 129 pounds" is too frequent to be set down as a typographical error. *Weight* can be verb or noun, which probably gives rise to the confusion. See also *under way.*

weird. Two critics complain that the word has been devalued by inappropriate and trivial use. Dictionary definitions give *supernatural, unearthly, fantastic, bizarre,* etc.; the usage referred to by the critics substitutes *weird* for *unusual, strange, out of the ordinary.* Sometimes misspelled *wierd.*

welch. See *welsh, welch.*

well. Fowler says flatly that the combination of *well* with a participle (*well-read, well-tuned,* etc.) is hyphened only when used attributively and not when used predicatively. That is, it may be hyphened, but not necessarily, when it stands before the noun modified (*A well-tuned* piano) but not after (*The piano was well tuned*). American usage, however, as is indicated by Random House and Webster, is inconsistent in the use of the hyphen in the predicate construction; American Heritage omits it.

The best advice perhaps is to follow the dictionary for such *well-* terms as may be found there. Fowler is right, however, when he says that the hyphen grammatically serves no purpose in the predicate construction, and so it may well be omitted; in such instances, *well* can modify nothing but the verb form following it. See also *good*.

well and good. The two most inane expressions of recent years are *well and good* and *still and all*. *Well and good* apparently reflects the influence of radio and TV announcers, who seem unwilling to trust any word to convey an idea by itself, especially when they are ad-libbing, but must bolster it with a synonym. *Still and all* (sometimes rendered *still in all*, which surely means no less) has even found its way into the ordinarily well-culled pages of *The New Yorker*.

well breeding. Apparently the misshapen descendant of *well bred*: "The apology showed well breeding." *Well* cannot be used as an adjective in place of *good*: "The apology showed *good breeding*." *Well breeding* will have to be reserved for breeders of wells, presumably well-drillers.

well-known. There is a widespread idea in journalism that *widely known* is preferable to *well-known*. Like many other journalistic assumptions about language, it has no basis. This usage is specifically sanctioned by American Heritage, Random House, and Webster, and is criticized by no authority.

well-nigh. Considered objectionable, primarily because it is archaic and thus affected, by three critics.

welsh, welch. Fowler says *-sh* predominates for the form meaning *pertaining to Wales*, but cites established exceptions; Webster and Random House also give *-sh* as the primary form. *Welsh* is also preferred for the verb meaning *to swindle someone in a bet*, or *to go back on a commitment*, though *welch* is acceptable. Welshmen have been known to object to the term as unjustly aspersing them. It is unlikely that anyone has Welshmen in mind when using it, however, and the Oxford English Dictionary diplomatically describes its origin as obscure. In any event, *welsh* in this sense is never capitalized. See also *Scotch*, etc.

Welsh rabbit, rarebit. The original form was *Welsh rabbit*, and is said to have been a joke at the expense of Welsh hunters. (The dish is melted cheese poured over toast or crackers.) *Rarebit* represents an attempt to dignify that caught on; the form is now commoner than *rabbit*. Two critics disapprove *rarebit* as a corruption, which indeed it is; two critics regard it as established; Random House and Webster consider *rabbit* the basic form. The consensus favors *rabbit*, though as Follett points out, *rarebit* predominates in cookbooks and on menus.

were, was. See *Subjunctive*.

West. As a part of the United States, by common consent (like *North, South,*

East) usually capitalized. This is true also of references to the Western Hemi-sphere or to the Free World as a political entity.

we, the people. See *I, we.*

wharf. See *dock.*

what. Long discussions of the number of the verb to be used with *what* when it is followed by a plural predicate—"Let me point out what seem(s) to be some misplacements of emphasis"—are presented by two critics. It is difficult to com-pare these discussions, since they approach the question from different directions. On this much there is agreement by six critics and American Heritage: *what,* despite the assumptions of some writers, is not necessarily singular, but may be plural. Two critics say that *what* may be followed by either a singular or plural verb, so that in the example given at the outset, either *what seems to be* or *what seem to be* is correct. In constructions like "What remains are a few trees" Fowler favors *is* or *what remain,* but Bryant finds that *are* is commoner. Two critics say that with a linking verb (chiefly forms of *to be—is, was,* etc.), *what* is considered singular: "What I saw *was* eight white horses." Beyond this, the reader can only be referred to the authorities themselves for explanations of what they consider good usage in various constructions involving *what.*

whatever, what ever. In questions, the second form is proper, three critics agree: "What ever (not *whatever*) can he be thinking about?" Follett concedes, how-ever, that the distinction is often ignored; Random House and Follett both admit *whatever* as an interrogative without qualification. The consensus slightly favors *what ever* in questions. The distinction is clear enough to anyone who stops to analyze the forms, but it seems well on the way to being forgotten. Follett disputes Fowler's further insistence that the interrogative *whatever* is colloquial, and in this has the support of the two big dictionaries, neither of which gives any such indication. Two critics point out that *whatever* should not be followed by *that:* "Whatever is decided that should be final." Omit *that.* This error seems rare.

when. See *when, where; no sooner.*

when and if. See *if and when.*

whence. See *from hence, whence.*

whenever, when ever. As with *whatever, what ever* (which see), three critics hold that the interrogative form should be two words ("When ever will you be ready?"); Evans and Fowler consider the form colloquial, and Follett says it must now be regarded as standard. Random House accepts the one-word form in ques-tions, but Webster considers two words preferable. The consensus, then, is that two words are preferable in questions and that the expression is standard. Other-wise, as a conjunction ("We saw him whenever we chose") or as an adverb

("Whenever shown, the painting attracted crowds"), the one-word form is standard.

when . . . then. See *if . . . then*; the same comments apply.

when, where. Used in definitions ("Music is when there is a concordance of pleasing sound"), the words mark an immature style, four critics agree: American Heritage calls this usage unacceptable. Bryant finds the construction defensible but says many educated people avoid it.

When *where* begins a clause, a decision must always be made whether a comma should be placed before it. "It is equally true of Italy [,] where the elections next spring will have great significance." See *Restrictive and Nonrestrictive Clauses*.

where. As used for *when* or *if*, criticized by two authorities. "Employees of the company are given compensatory time off, or where this is not possible, they get extra pay." *when, if.* See also *when, where; from whence; see where.*

whereabouts. Though it looks like a plural it is a singular, two critics hold, but Random House, American Heritage, and Webster say it may be construed as either singular or plural. Thus opinion is evenly divided: "His whereabouts was (or *were*) unknown."

whereas. Flesch objects that the word is stuffy and prescribes *while* instead, but Follett points out that *while* is stretched when it is used in the sense of *whereas* (*but by contrast*). Flesch's opinion seems captious and is perhaps based on the fact that some *where-* combinations, as Fowler points out, have been displaced in modern use. But *whereas* is not one of them.

where . . . at, etc. Warnings against this redundancy ("Where is the ball at?") were assiduously pounded into the heads of schoolchildren a generation or two ago, when English was still being taught, but now it is often heard from supposedly educated adults. This makes it no more acceptable. Evans says that *at* requires an object, and *where*, as an adverb, cannot serve. This overlooks the fact that *where* may also be a pronoun or a noun (not to mention a conjunction). Avoidance of this expression, on which three authorities agree, must be based on the fact that *at* is superfluous with *where*. On the same grounds, American Heritage accepts *where . . . from* but balks at *where . . . at* and *where . . . to*. The reasoning is sound.

whereby. The word is being displaced in modern use by *by which* or other constructions.

where . . . from. See *where . . . at*, etc.

wherein. The term is becoming archaic and thus sounds pompous. *In which, where, when* are displacing it.

where . . . to. See *where . . . at,* etc.

wherever, where ever. The form should be two words in stating questions. See the similar cases of *whatever* and *whenever.*

wherewithal. Quaint for *means:* "We wanted to make a trip but we lacked the wherewithal."

whether. See *as to; doubt(ful); if, whether.*

whether or not. Four critics say *or not* should be omitted when this is possible, a matter easily determined. When an alternative is clearly posed, as in "The program will be placed in effect whether the council decides or not," *or not* is clearly indispensable. Random House and Webster both give examples omitting *or not.* Fowler does not discuss omission, but his examples in other connections include *or not.* The consensus favors omission.

which. Two critics and American Heritage warn that *which* may be ambiguous in reference to the whole clause preceding, rather than to just the nearest noun or pronoun: "Styles of the 1920s did nothing to set off the female figure, which frustrated girlwatchers." *figure; this frustrated.* Flesch concedes that the *which* construction is generally frowned on, but approves it anyway as idiomatic. Follett objects to it. Webster says that it is widely used by speakers on all educational levels and by many reputable writers, though disapproved by some grammarians. The consensus is that it should be used with care. See also *this.*

Fowler inveighs against *which* for *who* or *that* ("the finest poet which the nation has produced"). Webster calls this usage archaic but adds it is still occasionally seen in current writing; Random House says *which* may never be applied to people. *That* is freely interchangeable with *who;* see *that 3.* For *which* vs. *that* see *that 4;* see also *and (but) which,* etc.; *in which; Ellipsis 4; Restrictive and Nonrestrictive Clauses.*

while. The word is best reserved to mean *at the same time* or *during the time that,* and is often objectionable in the sense of *and, but, although* or *whereas,* three critics and American Heritage agree. ("One brother was born June 9, 1898, at Oakland, while [*and*] the other was born July 19, 1893, at San Jose"; "The cannon will be based on Okinawa while [*and; but*] the rockets are being sent to Japan"; the examples are ambiguous.) Bryant says that *while* is standard in the senses *whereas* and *although,* but concedes the possibility of ambiguous construction. Evans approves *while* for *although* or *but,* but not for *and.* The consensus favors restricting the use of *while* to its temporal sense, particularly when there is danger of ambiguity or looseness. See also *awhile, a while.*

whimsy, whimsey. Standard variants, but *whimsy* predominates.

whiskey, whisky. Although the forms are often used interchangeably in reference to Scotch (and sometimes Canadian) whisky, the preferred form for these varieties, as distinguished from bourbon, is *whisky,* a fact expounded at some length in *The New Yorker* of Nov. 14, 1964. The distinction is corroborated by American Heritage, Random House, and Webster.

white. Not capitalized in reference to race (nor are the names of other colors used in this way: brown, yellow, red, black). This is the consensus of dictionaries; Webster says sometimes capitalized.

white stuff. The journalese variant for *snow.* See *Variation.*

whither. Flesch calls the word pompous, and Fowler regretfully concedes that it is obsolescent; Random House's classification is "archaic." The consensus is that the word is questionable in ordinary contexts.

who, whom; whoever, whomever. "If a boy ignores his arithmetic teacher and states that 8 times 7 are 63, he will be laughed at by his friends; but if he *obeys* his English teacher and says, '*With whom* are you going to the party?' instead of '*Who* are you going to the party *with?*' *he will also be laughed at.* Grammar, at least as taught by many old-fashioned teachers, is almost purely directive and bears little relation to the way English is actually spoken and written." *Language in Thought and Action,* S. I. Hayakawa.

In a survey by Norman Lewis, "How Correct Must Correct English Be?" (*Harper's,* March, 1949), "Who did you meet?" was given 43 percent acceptance in an opinion poll of 468 high school and college teachers of English, authors, editors, journalists, radio commentators, lexicographers, and a random sampling of subscribers to *Harper's.* Kyle Crichton, associate editor of *Collier's,* commented:

"The most loathsome word (to me at least) in the English language is *whom.* You can always tell a half-educated buffoon by the care he takes in working the word in. When he starts it, I know I am faced with a pompous illiterate who is not going to have me long as company."

The Oxford English Dictionary calls *whom* "no longer current in unstudied colloquial speech." *Whom* is regularly nominated for oblivion. Yet there remain a good many people to whom its strictly correct use, whatever that may be, is the touchstone of education. The chief among these once were the editors of *The New Yorker,* who steadily noted misuses under the snide caption, "The Omnipotent Whom." But more recently they desisted after discovering most readers did not know what the point was.

It appears that critics of the supposed misuse of *who* or *whom* are on shaky ground. *Whom,* of course, is the objective (or accusative) form. Most of the trouble with *whom* comes in relatively complex constructions that must be taken apart to determine what is subject and what is object. Most of us, especially in view of the ambiguous standing of *whom,* pay little attention to which form is used.

"He summoned the officer, whom he said had just been commissioned." *Whom* is not the object of *summoned,* as may appear, but rather the subject of had been *commissioned,* and should be *who.*

"She explained her presence to the Hungarian hussar, whom she hoped would fall in love with her." *Whom* is not the object of *hoped,* but the subject of *would fall,* and should be *who.*

These sentences illustrate the commonest "misuse" of *whom.* Yet when the critics of such errors must indict the translators of the Bible, together with Keats and Shakespeare, as having known no better, their preachments take on a hollow ring:

"Young Ferdinand *whom* they suppose is drown'd"; "Arthur, *whom* they say is killed tonight." Shakespeare.

"*Whom* say ye that I am?" Matthew 14:15.

"I have met with women *whom* I really think would like to be married to a poem." Keats.

The consensus is that either *whom* or *who* is acceptable in these constructions.

There is general agreement among grammarians that a preposition or verb following *who* does not make it *whom* even if it is the object. Thus *"Who* are you going with?" and *"Who* did you invite?" are not only correct, but preferable to *whom. Than whom* is an idiom: "An architect *than whom* there was none more clever."

In Boston, according to Ernest Weekley, the owls say "To-whit, to-*whom*." And George Ade wrote, " 'Whom are you?' he asked, for he had been to night school."

As long ago as the early 19th century Noah Webster called *whom* useless, and H. L. Mencken anticipated Hayakawa's verdict, cited above, in *The American Language.* Among the authorities current in 1970, three prescribed continuing to follow the strict traditional rules of grammar in the choice of *who* and *whom.* So did Random House and American Heritage, which, however, permits *who* for *whom* in speech. Since then one of the authorities has reversed himself and, in fact, launched a campaign to dispense with *whom* except after a preposition (*to whom, for whom*). No general change in usage has ever been known to come about as the result of a campaign, however; acceptance in educated expression is what turns the tide. In any event, in this instance the barn is being locked after the horse is gone. In 1978, six authorities and Webster advocated accepting as standard the usage that actually predominates, as described in this entry.

Rather than attempt to outlaw *whom,* it seems more sensible, in view of the examples cited earlier in this entry, to ignore the problem and allow the *who's* and *whom's* to fall where they may, which is what is happening anyway.

"Who are you going with?" Strictly, *whom. Whom* sounds precious when spoken, and even strict constructionists allow *who* in speech, while insisting on *whom* in writing. Webster quotes Raymond Paton: "Of who I know nothing," with the preposition standing before *who;* even the libertarians generally agree that in this position the word should be *whom.*

Webster's comment on this problem perhaps best sums up the consensus: "[*Who* is] used by speakers on all educational levels and by many reputable writers, though disapproved by some grammarians, as the object of a verb in the clause that it introduces (old peasants who, if isolated from their surroundings, one would expect to see in a village church—John Berger) or less frequently as the object of a preposition in the clause that it introduces.'' Of *whom* Webster says, ''Sometimes used as the subject of the clause that it introduces esp. in the vicinity of a verb of which it might be mistakenly considered the object (a recruit whom he hoped would prove to be a crack salesman—Bennett Cerf) (people whom you never thought would sympathize—Shea Murphy).''

The verb following *who* should agree with its antecedent in number, three critics point out: ''It is perfectly clear to me, who has given much study to the matter.'' *have*, to agree with *me: I have*.

A letter from C. S. Corey, published in the *Arizona Star*, reads: ''On page 5 of the *Star* of Jan. 30, 1975, there is the headline: WHOM SHOULD BE LAID OFF FIRST? The answer is obvious. Whom wrote the headline? Him should be laid off first. Him doesn't know enough about English grammar for the job him has.''

See *and (but) which*, etc.; *Restrictive and Nonrestrictive Clauses;* for *who* vs. *that* see *that 5;* for *who* vs. *which* see *which;* for *than whom* see *than; Ellipsis 4.*

whodunit. Considered informal by Random House, American Heritage, and the desk dictionaries, and slang by Fowler. There is no uncertainty about the form or spelling, however, and thus no excuse for *whodunnit, who dun it,* etc. Webster gives it as standard; this is the consensus, on the basis that what is informal is standard.

whoever, who ever. Evans distinguishes between the interrogatory *whoever* (''Whoever did he choose?'') and the combination of *who* with the adverb *ever*, as in ''Who ever would think of such a thing?'' and prescribes the one-word and two-word forms accordingly. Follett apparently does not make quite the same distinction but requires two words in any question, and Fowler concurs. Compare *whatever* and *wherever*. But both unabridged dictionaries give the one-word form for what other authorities would regard as the interrogative, or as the pronoun with the separate adverb. Such distinctions seem hairsplitting and a waste of effort.

wholehearted. One word; not *whole-hearted*.

whole new. A tiresome intensive (''a whole new purchasing plan'').

whom. See *who, whom*.

whopping. A journalese stereotype (''a whopping inheritance''). *Whacking* and *thumping* fit the same description.

whose vs. of which. It is a superstition that *whose* may refer only to people (*the tree whose leaves were falling*). The *of which* that is sometimes prescribed instead is to be avoided as clumsy. The mistaken idea concerning the application of *whose* apparently grew out of the fact that the nominative, *who*, does ordinarily apply only to people, though it is sometimes applied to animals, especially those having names, and occasionally to organizations.

who's, whose. *Who's* means *who is* or *who has; whose* means *belonging to whom.*

why. See *reason why.*

wide-, -wide. Usually hyphenated as a prefix: *wide-angle, wide-awake, wide-open,* etc. (as part of a compound adjective standing before the noun modified). But *widespread.* Solid as a suffix: *citywide, countywide, nationwide.* Evans dissents from this, but dictionaries give the solid form.

widow of the late. A redundancy; *widow of.*

widow woman. A rustic expression.

wife, widow. Whether a man should be described as survived by his wife or his widow is a subject of disagreement in journalism. The definition of *survive* ("to remain alive or in existence") argues for *wife.*

will. See *shall, should, would.*

win. Aspersed by one critic as a needless noun ("a win over great odds"). Considered standard in this sense by Random House and Webster; American Heritage would restrict it to sports events and Webster's New World labels it colloquial.

-wise. The practice of forming adverbial modifiers by tacking *-wise* onto nouns ("Dollarwise, sales are up") is deprecated by five critics and American Heritage; all, that is, except one of those who comment on this mannerism. The exception is Fowler, surprisingly enough, since his criticism of such devices is usually scathing. Fowler (or, to be more specific, Gowers, his reviser) merely notes that such compounds "made for the occasion from nouns" exist. Occasionally such terms may be convenient: "This scheme is clumsy productionwise" is surely easier than *with respect to production* or *when it comes to production,* though perhaps *for production* is possible. Usually, as the critics point out, the *-wise* compound displaces direct language: "Solano is the largest county populationwise and assessed valuationwise." *in population and assessed valuation.*

The *-wise* used to make an adverbial modifier is not to be confused with the suffix *-wise* meaning *possessing wisdom* (*weather-wise, worldly-wise*) nor the one that is joined to a noun to produce an adjective meaning *in the manner of* (*clockwise, crabwise*); *lengthwise,* too, is beyond criticism. Such terms are solidly established. *Wise*-words like *dollarwise, saleswise, productionwise* have been widely jeered as samples of Madison Avenue prose at its worst. It was only to be expected, then, that the writer of "Budget-wise housewives are looking for economical buys" should have been taken to task, as indeed he was. But the critic was barking up the wrong avenue that time. If the sentence had read "Budget-wise, housewives are confused," the writer would have been guilty as charged. Madison Avenuers have denied inventing, using, or even hearing used among their associates the expressions blamed on their kind. Observation shows that *wise*-words, at least, were being manufactured long before Madison Avenue existed as a mythical institution, or as a fount of supposedly defiled language.

wisecrack. See *quip, quipped.*

wish. *Wish* for *want* ("Do you wish some more potatoes?" "What do you wish?") is considered objectionable by three critics and American Heritage; Random House and Webster, however, give it as standard.

wishful thinking. Disparaged by Evans as a cliché and admired by Fowler as a useful neologism. Another illustration of how the soothsayers disagree. Accepted by dictionaries as standard.

wit and wisdom. A tiresome pair, often unjustifiably applied.

with. Two critics and American Heritage hold the traditional view that parenthetical phrases beginning *along with, together with,* or *with* do not make an otherwise singular subject plural: "The apple, together with the orange, was (not *were*) shrunken." Two other critics say such constructions may take either singular or plural verbs, just as the number of the verb with collective nouns depends on what the writer intends to stress. Partridge (*Usage and Abusage*) also expresses this view, and cites Onions' *An Advanced English Syntax.* Curme says in *Syntax* that a plural verb may be used if the idea of number is prominent. The same reasoning applies to such connectives as *as well as, besides, in addition to, and not alone, like.* See also *Subject-Verb Agreement; Collectives; as with.*

Four critics and American Heritage deplore the habit, most conspicuous in journalism, of using *with* to tack elements of sentences together with no clear indication of their relationship. Some examples, with suggested emendations: "Smith was struck in the chest and right hip with the third shot going wild (*hip; the third shot went wild*); "The United States ranks ninth in infant mortality with Sweden having the best record" (*mortality; Sweden has . . .* or *and Sweden has . . .*).

with a view to. See *view.*

within. Unpracticed writers often use *within* when *in* will do: "He remained within the building." *in.* The simpler form, when it will serve, is generally preferable.

within the framework. Deplored by two critics as pretentious.

without. *Without* for *unless* ("I won't go without he does") is disparaged as substandard by four critics and as dialectal by Random House and Webster;

American Heritage calls it regional. Bryant reports it is occasionally heard in cultivated speech. This usage is actually a revival.

with regard to. See *regard.*

with respect to. See *in respect to,* etc.

with that. See *at that.*

with the exception of. Often redundant for *except, except for.*

with the purpose of. Verbiage in place of an infinitive construction. *With the purpose of circumventing* equals *to circumvent.*

witness. Misused, three critics agree, when it displaces *see, watch, observe* (*witness a ball game, witness a school play*). *Witness* has a legal or official connotation that is out of place in ordinary contexts.

woke. See *awoke, etc.*

woman, lady. Rudyard Kipling's cavalier verdict was that "A woman is only a woman, but a good cigar is a smoke." But women now are reasserting themselves, and cigars are frowned upon for more reasons than one. The conflict between *woman* and *lady* in American usage is curious. In one widely accepted view, *woman* suggests commonness, if not vulgarity, while *lady* suggests breeding and refinement. It is this idea, no doubt, that has led to the rejection of *women's* in such designations as *Ladies' Aid* and *Ladies' Auxiliary.* A few notches up the social scale will be found organizations with names like *Woman's Club* and *Women's Alliance* and *League of Women Voters.* This choice is usual among the country-club, study-group, and college-alumnae sets.

Newspapers commonly forbid the use of *lady* in their columns as a synonym for *woman,* holding that *lady* belongs only in titles (*Lady Astor*). Even so, no newspaper has been known to insist that ladies' aids be referred to as women's aids. At the same time, *neighbor woman, widow woman,* and *the Smith woman* are discouraged as disparaging.

Lady is in general use as a courtesy, as in the salutation *ladies and gentlemen.* Most people, addressing a group of women, would say *you ladies* rather than *you women. Lady* remains useful when a touch of courtliness is desired, but *woman* is the workaday word, and the idea that it contains a hint of disparagement is mistaken and generally held by the uneducated.

These comments represent in general the views of four critics. Fowler frowns on such designations as *lady doctor,* preferring *woman doctor.* This is unquestionably in accord with educated American usage, which prefers *woman* in the absence of any overriding reason to use *lady.* But the new feminists are incensed over any unnecessary description of an occupation by sex. See also *female; Feminine Forms; Feminism.*

wonder. The expression of wonder is a declarative statement, not a question, and does not take a question mark: "I wonder what people expect of bus drivers?" *drivers*. See also *Questions*.

Word as a Word. To call attention to a word as such, use italics or quotation marks, not commas. "Magnuson suggested that he had used the word, bottle, a little perversely." The writer of this used commas a little perversely: "the word *bottle*" or *the word "bottle."*

Word Division. There is nothing esoteric about this, but it is apparently becoming a lost art. The loss has been aggravated by the displacement of traditional methods of typesetting by photocomposition, in which computers make many errors in dividing words. Of course, the errors are really those of programmers who do not foresee exceptions to the instructions they give the computers. Sometimes computer decisions, while correct, produce amusement. One newspaper found the division *fig-urine* distasteful, and barred it.

The basis rule is that words are properly divided only on syllables. The way to resolve questions about this, and they are many, is to consult a dictionary. The dots used in dictionary entries to divide syllables are often mistaken for hyphens (gob·ble·dy·gook). Hyphens intended as such are printed in their usual form in dictionary entries or sometimes as double hyphens (=).

Division of words in typescript is generally discouraged, especially in material intended to be set in type. Hyphens at the ends of lines in manuscript can raise unnecessary questions for the compositor. The lines as set in type will not correspond to the way they break in the manuscript, and thus he cannot always be sure whether the hyphen in a compound modifier, for example, that happens to fall at the end of the line in the manuscript is intended if the word falls elsewhere in type.

Single-syllable words, no matter how long, cannot be divided: *through, though, would, smooth.* Divisions on one letter, like *a-round*, are improper. *English for Printers*, the instruction manual of the International Typographical Union, says: "Singular nouns of one syllable, pronounced as if they were words of two syllables when pluralized, cannot be divided: as, 'horse,' *horses;* 'inch,' *inches;* 'fox,' *foxes;* 'dish,' *dishes.*" Divisions of words ending in *-es* and *-ed* are not uncommon, however, when they are separate syllables.

Divisions of figures and of names of people are to be discouraged, but are unavoidable in printing set in narrow measure.

Word Order. See *Adverbs; Modifiers 6; Dangling Modifiers; Infinitives 1; Inversion; Time Elements.*

worsen. A suspicion is abroad that *worsen* is not all it should be, even in the sense *get worse*, to say nothing of *make worse.* But the Oxford English Dictionary describes it as having been reintroduced to literature about 1800 to 1830 by writers like Southey and DeQuincey. No critic finds fault with it.

worst to worst. See *Misquotation: let the worst.*

worth. In expressions like *money's worth, eight dollars' worth,* the possessive form is required.

worthwhile. Three critics, Random House, Webster, and three of five current desk dictionaries give the one-word form as preferred; British preference, however, as pointed out by Fowler and some of the dictionaries, is *worth-while.* Three critics complain that the word is overused and misused, and there can be no doubt that, as Fowler says, it has become a fad for the description of any kind of merit.

would, should. See *shall, will; Subjunctive.*

would appear, would think, would seem. This way of expressing oneself, in place of more direct statement ("It would seem that someone is at fault" vs. *it seems* or even flatly *someone is*), is deplored by Flesch as timid and described by Evans as extremely cautious or very modest. The conclusion to be drawn is that framing statements in this way is to be avoided and should not be allowed to become a habit, because of the weakening and mealymouthed effect it produces.

would have. *Would have* is erroneous for *had* in a conditional statement ("If a doctor would have been on the premises, a death certificate would have been signed"). *If a doctor had been . . . Would of* for *would have* is an occasionally encountered illiteracy. But those who think they are hearing it in speech are usually hearing *would've.*

would like, should like. See *shall, will,* etc.

would rather. See *rather.*

wrack. See *rack, wrack.*

wraps. In reply to a reader who wrote in asking about the sentence, "Will they really put the wraps on the senator?" *Newsweek* explained: "*Wraps* is a sports term meaning: 'A turn of the reins around the jockey's hands to restrain a horse, hence, restraint.' " All very interesting, but the expression is constantly used and interpreted in a less esoteric fashion, to wit, in the sense of *wrappings.* Most readers probably visualized the senator as restrained, muffled, or gagged, rather than drawn up short. *Newsweek* itself uses *wraps* in this way: "The army demonstrated its latest antitank weapon and removed some of the secrecy wraps that have surrounded the project for several years." Dictionaries do not give the horsey definition.

wrassle, wrastle. See *rassle.*

wrath, wrathful, wroth. Evans and Fowler agree that *wrath* is the noun ("His wrath was awe-inspiring''), *wrathful* the attributive adjective (*a wrathful reply*), and *wroth* the predicate adjective ("The king was wroth"). Both Random House and Webster, however, allow *wrathful* and *wroth* as adjectives in both positions (that is, before and after the noun modified). American Heritage calls *wroth* archaic, which is surely correct.

wreathed in smiles. The expression itself is ready to be wreathed—and interred.

writ large. The correct form of the phrase. "Ireland's contribution to peace and the noble aspirations of the human effort are written largely on the pages of history, Johnson said." This sentence, from a news dispatch, illustrates a not uncommon error. *Writ large*, the usual form of the archaic expression, means *written in larger form, more clearly. Writ largely*, on the other hand, means *written for the most part, chiefly*, a different matter altogether. *Writ large* is oftenest used figuratively.

write. Sometimes used clumsily: "The Daily Spectator wrote in its Feb. 3 issue that . . ."; "The newspaper wrote an article describing the qualifications of its staff." Observed usage tells us that writers write, publications publish. *Wrote* is a gaucherie in the first example; *said* would have been natural and unexceptionable. The second example calls for *published* or possibly *ran. Write* denotes the act of setting down words on paper, and it can hardly be attributed to anything but people. Such constructions as "Writing in the February *Atlantic*, he explained . . ." are not open to criticism, however.

writer, present. See *Editorial We*.

wrong, wrongly. The preferred usage of *wrongly* is before the word modified: "The wrongly identified man stood up." Otherwise, *wrong:* "the word was spelled wrong."

wroth. See *wrath*, etc.

X

xerox. Recognized as a verb by Random House and American Heritage but not by Webster, probably because the term is so new ("They xeroxed several copies of the letter"). It means, of course, to reproduce by xerography, and comes from the invented trade name *Xerox*. See also *Trade Names; realtor*.

Xmas. The use of this form (which derives from a reverent form used in the early Greek church, on the basis that *X* represents the first letter of Christ's name in Greek) is discouraged; it is considered demeaning or irreverent by many.

Y

Yankee. Fowler says the British err in applying the term to other than New Englanders or Northerners in the Civil War. The fact is, however (as reported by Random House and Webster), that the expression is widely used to denote any inhabitant of the U.S. This usage was firmly established during the World Wars; often clipped to *Yank.*

yclept. The use of this expression (an obsolete word for *called, named*) is discouraged as worn-out humor.

ye. Two critics hold that *ye* as an article meaning *the* (*Ye Olde Tobacco Shoppe*) should have its original pronunciation, *the.* (*Ye* in fact results from an error, in which a now disused printing character for *th,* known as *thorn,* was mistaken for *y.*) This, however, is information possessed usually only by scholars; Random House and Webster approve the pronunciation that is heard everywhere: *ye,* American Heritage gives *the.*

year round. The preferable form, rather than *year around.*

yellow metal. The journalese variant for *gold.* See *Variation.*

yet. *Yet* as a conjunction beginning a sentence, meaning *but* ("Yet he continued to hope"), is disparaged as pompous by Flesch. This judgment seems quixotic in the light of widespread use in this way in all contexts, and considering also that in detailed discussions of various uses of *yet* neither Evans nor Fowler makes any such objection. Both recognize *yet* as a conjunction, as do Random House and Webster, and in general there is no reason why conjunctions may not begin sentences, as Flesch himself recognizes.

Yiddish. The name of a language, really a variety of German with admixtures from other tongues, spoken by many European Jews and often written with Hebrew characters, and not to be confused with Hebrew, a totally different language.

you. Two critics agree that the use of *you* to address the reader ("If you want to have a good time, try to be agreeable") conduces to informality and directness.

Flesch, in his *Art of Plain Talk,* argued persuasively that the use of *you* creates a link between writer and reader, and thus enhances interest and readability. Obviously, this usage is not suitable for all contexts.

Follett and Fowler warn against mixing the indefinite *you* with *one:* "If one wants to succeed, it helps if you know the right people." Either *one* and *one* or *you* and *you.* See also *one.*

you-all. Southerners often become indignant when it is suggested that they use the expression *you-all,* which is indigenous to their region, as a singular, that is, to address or refer to a single person. Bryant says that though *you-all* may be addressed to one person, it implies others; Evans says merely that it is a respectable plural of *you,* and does not take up the possibility of its use in the singular. Random House gives only the plural use, and Webster's definition concurs with Bryant's.

Defenders of *you-all* as used in the South are prone to assertions that are not borne out by observation. One such assertion is that *you-all* is always used as a plural, never as a singular.

"All the South has one word in common and that is the *you-all* [y'all or yawl] that Yankees usually mess up. It is used only in a collective sense and takes a plural verb," wrote James Street in *James Street's South.* Arthur Gordon is cited to similar effect in Webster, which says *you-all* may be used in addressing one person as representing another or others.

Southerners have been known to cite such examples as "Tell your family I want you all to come" and the Biblical "The grace of our Lord Jesus Christ be with you all" in justification of the Southern *you-all.* They also regard the hyphen connecting *you* and *all* as a damyankee intrusion.

But such examples are unexceptionable in any context; *you all* in these instances is used to emphasize inclusiveness. The Southern *you-all* is used where *you* alone suffices. Originally, perhaps, *all* was tacked on to give an emphatic plural feeling to *you,* just as *you* sometimes becomes *youse.*

you know. This inane expression is relied upon by many young people and athletes (as interviewed on television) as a kind of mindless punctuation, interjected every few words. It seems to be a pathetic though perhaps unconscious appeal for concurrence or acceptance by the listeners, from someone who lacks confidence that he has anything to say. The expression has something in common with the meaningless *like* that was the trademark of the beat generation and was taken up by their successor hippies.

John F. Odell wrote in a letter to the editor of the *Long Beach* (Calif.) *Press-Telegram:* "I hesitate to attend church services these days for fear the minister might have a case of the *you-knows* and recite the Lord's Prayer like this; "Our you-know Father who art in you-know heaven, hallowed be thy you-know name. Thy you-know kingdom come, thy you-know will be done on you-know earth as it is in you-know heaven."

your. Evans, Random House, and Webster approve of *your* in place of *a, an,* or *the*, or when no article at all is necessary, as in "Your water is a sore decayer of your whoreson dead body" (*Hamlet*). It must be remembered that the gravedigger in *Hamlet* was a clown. American Heritage calls this usage informal, and one critic objects to it.

your's. No such form; *yours*.

yourself, yourselves. See *myself; Reflexives*.

youth. Attempts have been made to set an age limit for this term, as a discouragement against applying it to those who are no longer young. Such limits are difficult to enforce, however, since it is evident that youth, like beauty, is in the eye of the beholder, and perhaps even more so in the mind of the possessor. We all know elderly men and women who refer to each other as *boys* and *girls*. *Youth* as applied to individuals means only males (*four youths were sauntering down the walk*); as a general term (*the youth of the nation*) it includes both sexes. See also *elderly*.

Yugoslavia, Jugoslavia. *Jugoslavia* was commonly seen a few years ago, and both forms are correct. There is now overwhelming preference for *Yugoslavia*.

Z

Zeros. Usually dispensed with as superfluous, except in technical writing, in designations of even hours (*9 o'clock,* not *9:00 o'clock*) and even sums of money (*$10,* not *$10.00*).

zoom. The original meaning (and one still in use) was to make an aircraft climb briefly at an angle sharper than it would be capable of in sustained flight. On this is based the insistence in some quarters that applications of *zoom* must always imply an upward direction. The word also has an imitative sense, however, that all dictionaries now recognize, and used thus has no relation to direction: "The car zoomed down the incline"; "The jet zoomed across the Atlantic."

Bibliography

The following list contains books that were consulted in addition to the dictionaries of usage and general dictionaries named in the preface as having been compared to determine the consensus:

Barnhart, Clarence L., Steinmetz, Sol, and Barnhart, Robert K., *The Barnhart Dictionary of New English Since 1963*. New York: Harper & Row, 1973.

The Century Dictionary and Cyclopedia. New York: The Century Co., 1897.

Curme, George O., *Syntax*. New York: D. C. Heath and Company, 1931.

Davies, Hugh Sykes, *Grammar Without Tears*. New York: John Day Company, 1953.

Flesch, Rudolph, *The Art of Plain Talk*. New York: Harper & Brothers, 1946; and *The Art of Readable Writing*. New York: Harper & Brothers, 1949.

Fowler, H. W., and F. G., *The King's English*. London: Oxford University Press, 1906.

Gowers, Sir Ernest, *The Complete Plain Words*. Baltimore: Penguin Books, 1962.

Graves, Robert, and Hodge, Alan, *The Reader Over Your Shoulder*. New York: The Macmillan Company, 1961.

Hayakawa, S. I., *Language in Thought and Action*. New York: Harcourt, Brace and Company, 1949.

Jordan, Lewis (editor), *The New York Times Manual of Style and Usage*. New York: The New York Times Company, 1946.

Mencken, H. L., *The American Language,* as abridged and updated by Raven I. McDavid. New York: Alfred A. Knopf, 1963.

Partridge, Eric, *Usage and Abusage,* second edition. New York: Harper & Row, 1942.

Perrin, Porter G. and Ebbitt, Wilma K., *Writer's Guide and Index to English,* fifth edition. Glenview, Ill.: Scott, Foresman and Company, 1972.

Quiller-Couch, Sir Arthur, *On the Art of Writing*. New York: G. P. Putnam's Sons, 1961.

Strunk, William Jr., and White, E. B., *The Elements of Style,* third edition. New York: The Macmillan Company, 1979.

Summey, George Jr., *American Punctuation*. New York: The Ronald Press Company, 1949.

Wentworth, Harold, and Flexner, Stuart Berg, *Dictionary of American Slang*. New York: Thomas Y. Crowell Company, 1960.